BRANSON AND THE OZARK MOUNTAINS

by
Fred Pfister
and
Jennifer Marsh

The Insiders' Guide®
An imprint of Falcon® Publishing, Inc.
A Landmark Communications company
P.O. Box 1718
Helena, MT 59624
(800) 582-2665
www.insiders.com

•

Sales and Marketing: Falcon Publishing, Inc.
P.O. Box 1718
Helena, MT 59624
(800) 582-2665
www.falcon.com

•

THIRD EDITION
1st printing

•

•

Printed in the United States of America

•

Front cover and bar photo of lake: A.C. Haralson/Arkansas Dept. of Parks and Tourism. Back cover, spine, and bar photos of dance ensemble and parasailing: Branson/Lakes Area Chamber of Commerce. Bar photos of girl dancers and Marvel Cave: Silver Dollar City.

Publications from *The Insiders' Guide*® series are available at special discounts for bulk purchases for sales promotions, premiums, or fundraisings. Special editions, including personalized covers, can be created in large quantities for special needs.
For more information, please contact Falcon Publishing.

ISBN 1-57380-085-6

Preface

Chances are that if you've picked up this book you have one of two questions. If you've never heard of Branson, you're probably wondering where it is. If you have heard of it, but never been here, you probably want to know what it is. Then again, if you have been here before or already live here, congratulations! You can skip the formalities and get right to the meat of the book.

LOOK FOR:
- **Location**
- **Big Stars**
- **Visitor Statistics**
- **Theme Parks**
- **Outlet Shopping Mecca**

The answer to the first question is easy. Branson is within a day's drive of half the country's population. More specifically Branson is in south central Missouri about 12 miles north of the Arkansas state line and 39 miles south of the state's third largest city, Springfield. Now, the answer to the second question is a little more complicated. Some call Branson the "live music capital of the world" and others think of it as a small rural town. Ironically, both descriptions apply to Branson and Ozark Mountain Country. We have 35 live performance theaters and an annual visitor count of more than 6.5 million, yet our city population is just around 5,000. Nationally known performers like Andy Williams, Bobby Vinton, Mickey Gilley, the Lennon Sisters, Sons of the Pioneers, and Mel Tillis all call this place home. In 1999 and 2000 Branson hosted the Miss USA pageant which was broadcast live on CBS to a worldwide audience. And yet when you pick up a copy of our local newspapers, the *Branson Tri-Lakes Daily News*, or the *Taney County Times* you'll find out real fast that the small town mentality is alive and well in Branson. With front-page headlines like "Flowers are planted for city," "Man receives grocer award for his service," and "Operation Shoebox comes to Branson," it's easy to see that Branson is nothing like other major tourist destinations around the country. It truly is a place where music stars, hillbillies, and everyone in between sit down at the same dinner table.

In the pages that follow we attempt to provide you with the answers to the question "what is Branson?" We'll tell you about the music stars and their constant game of musical chairs. We'll tell you how to land a trout on Lake Taneycomo, one of the premiere trout fishing spots in the country. We'll explore the history of the Bald Knobbers and share some not-so-flattering stories about the area's notorious outlaws. If we've stumped you with the word *hillbilly*, we'll clear that up in the History chapter. We've got information on how to maneuver your way through traffic on The Strip, the Red Route, the Blue Route, and the Yellow Route. We'll introduce you to the nearby towns of Reeds Spring, Forsyth, Hollister, and Springfield, Mo. and Eureka Springs, and Mountain View in Arkansas.

If you're thinking about moving to Branson, we have information on the current real estate climate. We've got listings for many of the area's schools and childcare centers. Retirees will find information on housing, health care, and social organizations. You'll find out everything from which hotels let kids stay free to how Table Rock Lake was formed to which of our championship golf courses the locals like best.

We will tell you about the people, both past and present, who have become icons for the Ozarks. You'll get to know Harold Bell Wright, author of *The Shepherd of the Hills*, artist Rose O'Neill, creator of the famous Kewpie doll, entrepreneur Mary Herschend, who opened Silver

The Branson/Lakes Area Chamber of Commerce is located on the north end of Branson at Mo. Hwy. 248 and U.S. Hwy. 65. Make it one of your first stops!

Photo: Branson/Lakes Area Chamber of Commerce

Dollar City some 40 years ago, raku guru Brent Skinner, and storyteller Judy Dockery Young just to name a few.

When you visit Branson you'll come face to face with the people who keep the wheels turning every day. It's the front desk clerks, restaurant servers, theater ushers, fishing guides, and Duck captains who embody the true spirit of Ozark Mountain hospitality. One of the things visitors comment on is the friendly attitude of the folks who live and work here. We even have a hospitality training program for area employees, sponsored by a company called Branson Hospitality, Inc., that provides incentives for employees who go out of their way to make guests feel welcome and appreciated. Don't think that the big music stars are above this kind of service either. Most of them sign autographs and pose for pictures after the shows. They even board motor coaches to chat with visitors and routinely host charity events.

If you get lost in our maze of side streets or break down on U.S. Highway 65, a local will come along soon enough or another visitor will most likely lend a hand. It seems as if Branson attracts the kind of person who knows a little about the golden rule. People who come to hear the smooth sounds of the Glenn Miller Orchestra at the Bobby Vinton Theatre or the sweet gospel music of Barbara Fairchild are hardly the kind of people to pass by someone in need.

The "powers that be" have done everything possible to ensure that Branson remains the kind of place where veterans are honored, where kids can play in the parks without having to be fingerprinted first, and where crimes are so rare that you seldom hear about burglaries or other violent acts. Local businesspeople, church leaders, and politicians have opposed the introduction of gambling at every turn and have been successful, for the most part, in keeping out adult-oriented book and video stores. It's highly unlikely that you'll hear a single off-color remark on any stage in Branson. Many of the theaters host free Sunday morning gospel services where local singers and musicians provide the entertainment while a touring minister or speaker leads the program.

Branson is not just a place for golden girls and guys. While we do have our share of entertainers who know the better side of 60 and who primarily appeal to folks of the same age, we have plenty of attractions for young adults and children. Silver Dollar City's National Children's Festival is a real draw in the summertime as is White Water theme park and Branson USA

Amusement Park. In the chapter on Kidstuff you'll find everything from go-cart tracks to wild animal parks to museums. We'll also tell you which of our more than 80 music shows appeal to young audiences.

Water sports are a perennial favorite for the young and young at heart. With three area lakes you can do everything from snorkel, to water ski, to parasail. Rent a houseboat and spend your entire vacation on the water if you're so inclined. Dozens of resorts line the shores of Table Rock Lake and Lake Taneycomo. We've got everything from your basic cabin with little more than four walls and a roof, to deluxe condos with Jacuzzis and cable TV, to quiet bed and breakfast inns that will cater to your every whim. Camping and hiking are very popular in the Ozarks as well.

Now that Branson has become one of the top outlet shopping destinations in the United States, families on a budget can find great bargains on brand name clothing, housewares, books, electronics, music, and more. We've got a huge selection of souvenir shops with super cheap T-shirts and such, but for a one-of-a-kind souvenir there are places like Engler Block and Silver Dollar City, where you can take home the work of more than 100 resident craftspeople who make everything from pottery to furniture. The students at College of the Ozarks will weave a rug or make a fruitcake while you watch. There are a number of extremely talented craftspeople in the Branson area whose works are on display in boutiques and galleries.

We've tried to leave no stone unturned and no appetite unsatisfied. Speaking of appetites, if you've got one, our restaurants feature everything from Mexican to Chinese to Cajun to Greek. Our specialty, of course, is old-fashioned traditional American. And yes, it's mostly fried. You can get a salad here, but we like to put fried chicken on top. It's so much better that way. Branson is not totally oblivious to the perils of those with special dietary needs. You can get sugar-free candy and fudge, and low-cal salad dressing. Okay, so we still have a way to go in this department.

All in all, there's something for everyone to see and do in Branson all year long. We have even added a fifth season to the year to provide more variety for visitors. We call them Spring, Summer, Fall, Ozark Mountain Christmas, and Hot Winter Fun. During each season there are dozens of special events and festivals like Branson Fest, Veterans Homecoming, Cruisin' Branson Lights Automotive Festival, Plumb Nellie Days, Kewpiesta, and the list goes on.

Keep in mind that Branson is a dynamic town and things change often. The entertainers like to hop from theater to theater during the off-season and new restaurants and retail shops are opening all the time. Hotels change names and businesses come and go. The maps of Branson today don't look anything like they did a few years ago and the hills between Branson and Springfield are being blasted away to make room for straighter and wider highways. The Branson/Lakes Area Chamber of Commerce, (417) 334-4136 is a great source of information on what's new in town. Give them a call and they'll be happy to mail you a package containing brochures, coupons, and lots of other useful information.

We hope your journey through the pages of this book will lead you to Branson and Ozark Mountain Country. If you've made it this far, then you're well on your way to arriving at a truly unforgettable destination. Welcome to Branson!

About the Authors

Fred Pfister

Fred Pfister is a native Ozarker (read: real "hillbilly") who was born and raised on the old Emmett Kelly farm (Weary Willie of circus clown fame) in Houston in Texas County. He brags that it's the biggest town (population: 2000) in the biggest county (in area) in Missouri. He was delivered by a neighbor because the doctor got there late, who took only a piece of apple pie in payment for "checking things out" after the fact, one of the cheapest deliveries on record.

He is a retired English professor who edits *The Ozarks Mountaineer,* a bi-monthly regional magazine that covers the Ozarks. He spends time writing, teaching special classes, and giving lectures throughout the state for the Missouri Humanities Council on Missouri folklore and other language and literature topics. He also portrays poet Walt Whitman in a Chautauqua presentation, the reason for the "gray beard look" he wears.

He has a degree from The School of the Ozarks (where he was in the college's first graduating class and where he taught for 26 years). He worked his way through college as a radio announcer and as an actor in the college's local Beacon Hill summer stock theater. He has an M.A. from the University of Arkansas and a doctorate from the University of Mississippi. He's the author of various scholarly articles and poetry. Other writings have been published in *Newsday, The Ozarks Mountaineer, Reader's Digest,* and various regional papers. He is the author of *The Littlest Baby: A Handbook for Parents of Premature Children,* published by Prentice-Hall.

Fred is active in Branson's community life. He is a member and past president of the Branson Arts Council. He is membership chair of the Ozark Writer's League, and a past president, and he has served on the Missouri Ethics Commission. He is actively involved with funded community book discussion programs in Branson, Kimberling City, and other Ozarks towns. Hobbies include reading, writing poetry, cutting the winter's wood, gardening, canoeing Ozark streams, and beekeeping.

He lives only a block off Branson's Strip, and almost in spittin' distance of Lake Taneycomo with his wife, Faye, a retired art teacher from the Hollister Public Schools and his teenage daughter, Falecia, the former pound and a half preemie who is now a student at Southwest Missouri State University. Sharing the wooded acreage with the family are household cats Pflip and J. R. Mewing, Ignatius the iguana, and over half a million honey bees.

Jennifer Marsh

Even though Jennifer Marsh grew up in north central Arkansas, only a few hours away from Branson, and made regular shopping excursions to Springfield, Missouri, she didn't make her first trip to Branson until she was 21. After graduating from Arkansas State University in Jonesboro, in 1993, with a degree in journalism/public relations, her parents urged her to check out the booming entertainment industry in Branson. Her first job in town was with the *Branson Tri-Lakes Daily News* as an entertainment reporter and copy editor. During her time with the paper she interviewed stars like BoxCar Willie, Andy Williams, Moe Bandy, T.G. Sheppard, Ricky Van Shelton, Wayne Newton, and many others. She made her first trip to New York City as a reporter for the paper covering the world famous Radio City Rockettes, who have been bringing their show to Branson each Christmas since 1994.

A little less than a year after taking the job with the newspaper, Jennifer was assigned to interview Branson theater developer, Andrew Marsh, an attorney from Muncie, Indiana, whose family had written the musical drama, *Gettysburg* and was planning to produce it in Branson. A few months after Jennifer broke the news on *Gettysburg,* she and Andrew were married.

Jennifer left the paper to become Mrs. Marsh and marketing director for the Gettysburg Theatre. When *Gettysburg* closed in 1995, Jennifer moved on to head up the marketing department for Jennifer's Americana Theatre, home of Jennifer Wilson, previously known to some as Jennifer in the Morning.

Today, Jennifer works as an independent marketing consultant with clients ranging from theaters to tour companies to performers as well as special events.

No stranger to the stage herself, Jennifer has appeared in a Branson Tri-Lakes Community Theatre production and while still in college she performed at the Sam Walton Center for the Performing Arts in Clarksville, Ark.

Jennifer has written numerous articles for local and regional publications such as, *Ozark Mountain Visitor, On The Lake, All Roads Lead to Branson, Travel Host, Lifeworks* magazine, and many others.

When you get to town you may run into Jennifer and Andrew strolling through Dogwood Canyon or catching a few rays on Table Rock Lake. In May of each year you'll find them at Rocky's Italian Restaurant, which is located behind the old newspaper building in downtown Branson, celebrating the anniversary of their first date there.

Acknowledgments

Fred Pfister

In writing a book of this scope and under such short deadlines, I feel the Beatles' "I get by with a little help from my friends" describes precisely the situation I found myself in. There are many close friends who gave advice, recommendations, and reviews of shows, attractions, accommodations, and restaurants. Their two cents worth totaled up to a large amount of help and a big debt of gratitude! Add to them the tourists I pumped for insights, recognizing that being an insider is not always conducive to accurate observations or fresh insights, and I have a sizable crowd to thank.

Specifically, I'd like to thank Milton Rafferty for his geographical and historical information and former teacher, writer, and photographer Townsend Godsey for helping me appreciate my hillbilly heritage. Viola Hartman and Kathy Van Buskirk need recognition for their research into the area's past that always proved helpful; Harry Styron, for his insights and observations on the area; Camille Howell and Jeanelle Duzenberry of College of the Ozarks for information and pictures; Lynn Nitzschke, Mark Weisz, and Anne Symington for gathering materials and teaching me the ins, outs, and trends in the local real estate markets. Randy Warner of Branson's Parks and Recreation Department deserves a thanks for informational help and for serving as a sympathetic reader. Susan Marcussen and Bil Godsey of the Branson Arts Council are to be thanked for materials and insights as well as their enthusiasm and support. The Taneyhills Library and Lisa Boushehri and Allen Brackin are to be thanked for helping run down old articles and books and odd facts.

All the writers who have written about the Ozarks over the years for *The Ozarks Mountaineer* and who provided insights, observations, and information are to be thanked, as well as its publisher, Barbara Wehrman.

Others who need to be thanked are Myrna Carlson of the Taney County Health Department and Linnea Smith of the Branson City Health Department and Scotty Penner and other members of the Branson Police Department. Bob Corbin needs recognition for his insane phone calls that kept me sane during the entire project. There are certainly others in and around Branson who need to be thanked, and omission of them is because of their request, lack of room, or pure and simple oversight.

Thanks to Insiders' editor Sarah Clark for all the help, and for being so flexible during the project. A big thanks goes to co-author Jennifer Marsh who helped make the project fun and who always seems to have a clipping or article that was of help.

Certainly a big thanks goes to daughter Falecia who planned homework and computer use around my schedule and introduced Stinky, the gray squirrel who grew from a baby fed with an eye-dropper to a busy and curious adult during the project, to the household menagerie, and my wife Faye who put up with the clutter of books and clippings and brochures in the study and around the house.

Jennifer Marsh

Shortly after I moved to Branson, I remarked to my parents that someday I'd like to write a book about Branson. I just couldn't imagine why someone hadn't already come out with an everything-you-could-ever-want-to-know-about-Branson guide. Back then I hardly knew enough to fill the first page much less 300, but over the past seven years I have learned a few things and met many of the people who work hard to make the town worthy of its very own Insiders' Guide.

Thanks go first to all the people who have been instrumental in making Branson the kind of place you read about in books.

Without the encouragement of my parents Charles and Jo-Carroll McCullough, I would never have ventured to Branson in the first place and certainly would not have taken on this project. A thanks also goes to Martha Hoy Bohner, who gave me my first job here. Martha also supplied information for this book via her position as publicist for Silver Dollar City, Inc. Branson Tri-Lakes Daily News Entertainment Editor, Jimmy Lancaster has contributed more than he knows to this book for as his copy editor I learned the real "scoop" on the entertainment scene back when new theater announcements came in on what seemed like a daily basis. And a big thanks also goes to Jimmy for his superb matchmaking skills.

Thanks also goes to my co-author Fred Pfister, who knows this area and its history like the back of his hand. His consistent support and helpful critiques were greatly appreciated. Our debates on the difference between a hillbilly and a redneck were a lot of fun.

To thank the dozens of people who provided specific information for this book would take again this many pages. I didn't encounter a single uncooperative soul. When I claim that the people who live and work in Branson and Ozark Mountain Country are a friendly lot, it's because I have experienced it first-hand on more than one occasion.

A very special thanks goes to the folks at Insiders' Publishing, Inc., for making this project possible and for allowing me to be a part of it.

Thanks to Bill Dailey for allowing me to spread my wings and take on this project and for teaching me the ins and outs of marketing.

Most of all I want to thank my husband, Andrew. As his business partner I have had the opportunity to be involved in countless projects and learning experiences that have enriched my life and contributed immeasurably to this book. He supported me every step of the way through-out the writing process with kind words and even kinder deeds. I am truly convinced he is the greatest husband, friend, and partner anyone could ever have.

And to all the people who have awaited the printing of this book, thank you for your patience and encouragement.

Night falls on a peaceful scene in the Ozarks.

Photo: Branson/Lakes Area Chamber of Commerce

Table of Contents

Directory of Maps

BRANSON

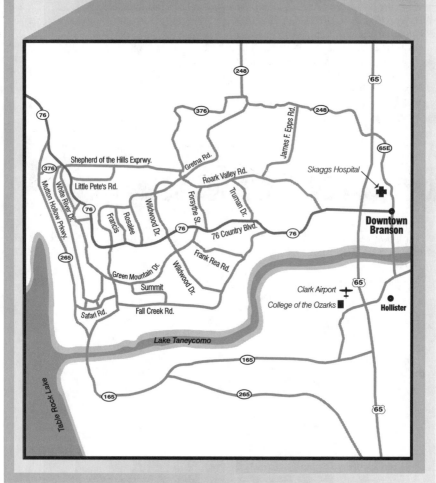

SOUTHWEST MISSOURI

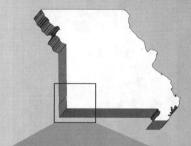

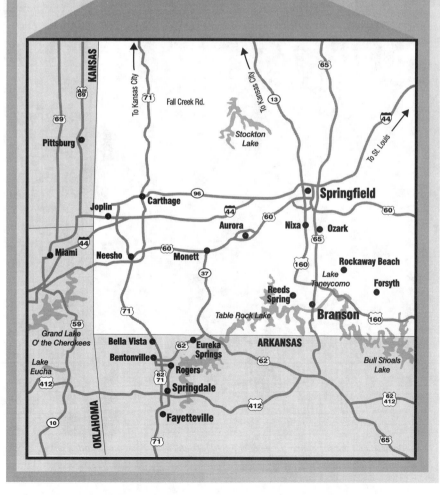

Branson and the surrounding area offer fun for granddaughter and grandmother alike.

Photo: Branson/Lakes Area Chamber of Commerce

How to Use This Book

We Ozarkers are practical people, and this book reflects that practicality. It gives you quick and easy access to useful information whether you are a visitor and tourist, a "come here" (someone who plans to move here and join our community) or even a current resident or native. It's a book designed to be used—not displayed on your coffee table. If you're visiting the area, don't leave it in your hotel room. Keep it in your car or backpack or carry it with you. Dog-ear a page to mark a favorite restaurant or attraction. Forget the schoolmarm admonition about never ever writing in a book. Make your own notes and observations. Write in the margins: you'll be making the book more useful for you.

The book also reflects the Ozarks in another way: like our meandering streams and roads, you can meander in this book. The chapters are independent of each other and can be read in any order. Meandering doesn't mean disorganized. Far from it! We've organized our information to make it easy for you to explore areas that interest you and breeze through those that don't. However, we encourage you to explore those chapters that may not immediately interest you. You may not be buying a home here, but the assessment of the area real estate situation will help you understand the Branson phenomenon. And you don't have to be a history buff to appreciate the story of the Ozarks or how the geology of the area affects development. You may have come to Branson just for a couple of the shows, but you might want to check out the Recreation and the Great Outdoors chapter and Lakes and Rivers chapter to see what else the area has to offer. If you need lots of information about the area fast, the Branson/Lakes Area Chamber of Commerce, (417) 334-4136, is a great source of information on what's new in town. It's at 269 Mo. Highway 248, north of town.

The Insiders' Guide to Branson and the Ozark Mountains covers a rather small town in detail but a fairly large area in general. Branson, that small town on the old White River that has become the No.2 vacation destination in the United States, has a population of over 5,000. But the book is also about the greater Ozarks, a 55,000-square-mile area of steep and rugged terrain in southwestern Missouri and northern Arkansas, even reaching into southeastern Oklahoma.

The title explains the book. We figure Branson is your primary reason for coming to the Ozarks. After all, over 7 million people a year visit our town. There must be something that attracts them, and we explain what those attractions are. Therefore the focus is on our town. But we also want to introduce what you can explore in the Ozarks using Branson as your base. We've included a general history of the Ozarks, major annual events in area towns and suggested daytrips. Information about fishing, canoeing, and water activities can be found in the Lakes and Rivers chapter. Hunting, hiking, and all land-based outdoor activities can be found in our Recreation and the Outdoors chapter. We even have an

entire chapter devoted to shopping in the area. When you get here, we suggest places to stay. We have an entire chapter devoted to Bed and Breakfast Inns, and the lakeside resorts and hotels and motels are covered in the Accommodations chapter. Camping and RV Accommodations have a chapter to themselves. The Table of Contents is a good place for you to start with this book. It should give you an idea of what you want to look at first. The very end of the book is also handy, so don't ignore the Index. To find information quickly, scan the Index. Shows, attractions, and activities are also indexed.

Our Close-ups are short features scattered throughout the book. They give interesting history and background or focus on a local artist, craftsperson, personality, or phenomenon, providing depth and insight on our area. They are great magazine-type articles that can be read when you have some quiet moments in your busy vacation schedule and give you background information, and insight or clues for some new activities you may want to investigate. We've also scattered tips and tidbits throughout the book. Insiders' tips are those special little details only the locals are likely to know and are found in boxes on various pages. They can be of great help. Ozark-speak might give you an insight to the local mind and help you with the local lingo—or at least give you an appreciation of it. It won't make you a bona fide hillbilly, but it can help you talk like one, if you can get the accent right.

We've tried to keep everything simple but complete. We've given you the area codes for all phone numbers. (Though we cover a fairly large area, you'll only be dealing with four different area codes.) Everything in Missouri in the immediate Branson area is in the 417 area code. Only well east of Branson in the Big Springs area of the state will you be getting into the 573 area code. Arkansas, less than a dozen miles away, will have area codes of 501 or 870. (We're unlucky enough to live close to the dividing line between the state's only two area codes, but if that's the biggest problem to complicate our lives, we're thankful!)

Branson is in Taney County and every person and business has been recently assigned an official 911 address, and we've provided those official street addresses, though some could hardly be classified as streets. Since we have only recently gone to street and road names with numbered addresses, we are just getting used to it ourselves. Don't expect all businesses to have official addresses prominently displayed—or displayed at all. We're used to giving directions in relationship to landmarks: "where the old Wal-Mart used to be" or "just a jag down the road from Mr. Thornton's white, two-story frame house that burned down last year" or "just after that patch of sassafras that was so colorful last fall." Well, you get the drift. Nearby Stone County, which has been part of the Branson Boom area, is in the process of assigning official 911 street addresses, but signs and numbers may not be up, and folks are in the process of getting used to them. We've given you the best we can; and we've provided directions. If you get lost looking for something, stop and ask. A friendly Ozarker will be glad to set your feet or your wheels on the right path. Be aware that not all names are on maps—some are too small or insignificant to map makers, but not to those who live there! Also, be aware that some places or communities have official names and the more common name that we all use. (One of our favorites is Mount Pleasant, officially, which everyone knows locally as Seedtick.) Mo. Highway 76 W. in the city limits of Branson is known officially as "76 Country Boulevard," but the highway signs refer to it as Country Boulevard and everyone calls that section "The Strip." All the names are the same place, so don't get confused! Another point of possible confusion could be old U.S Highway 65, which goes through Branson and Hollister and is referred to as U.S. Business Highway 65. It was recently renamed Veterans Boulevard, but not everyone knows it yet and those that do haven't all changed their addresses, nor are all the signs up.

Since we in the Ozarks abhor a straight line, the twisting and turning of the roads can get flatlanders right confused so that they don't know which direction they're going! We suggest you read our Getting Here and Getting Around chapter carefully, provide yourself with a good local map, have an official Missouri highway map when you venture out on daytrips and never be reluctant to stop and ask for directions. If you get lost, that can be part of the fun!

Getting Here, Getting Around

LOOK FOR:
• Highways
• Flight Service
• Rental Cars
• Beat the Showtime Rush
• Road Condition Information
• The Strip

The maps of Branson today don't look anything like the maps of a few years ago. As the number of residents and visitors continues to climb, so do the miles of roads. The main arteries leading to town are being widened and improved to ease the flow of traffic into Branson. Visitors who came to town as little as two years ago endured major traffic jams on Mo. Highway 76, the main east-west route through town. Now, with all of the side streets and major improvements in the roads, traffic jams are becoming a thing of the past. By 2001 the Missouri Department of Transportation expects to have completed the expansion of U.S. Highway 65 to four lanes leading from Springfield to Branson.

One of the major roadway improvements currently under construction is Mo. Highway 465, which will provide a bypass leading west of Branson from Mo. Highway F through Stone County near Silver Dollar City to the junction of Mo. Highway 265 just south of Hollister. The overpass at Mo. F, which is just a few miles north of Branson, is now complete, but access to Mo. 465 is still closed. By 2002, the section of Mo. 465 from Mo. F to Mo. 76, about one-third of the loop, should be done. Once finished, this road will provide easy access to The Strip for visitors entering Branson from both the north and south.

One service Branson lacks is a commercial airport. The nearest facility is in Springfield, a good hour's drive away. Many area politicians and business leaders have explored the possibility of building an airport in Stone County, just west of Branson, but to date nothing has materialized.

Until about three years ago, Branson was serviced by Greyhound Bus Lines, which brought passengers to and from Springfield, but that service has been discontinued. A number of trolley operators have tried their hand at providing public transportation in town, but none has lasted very long.

Your best bet when it comes to getting here is to drive your own vehicle or purchase a package from a motor coach operator. After you finally make it to town, stop by one of the many area visitor information centers or the Branson/Lakes Area Chamber of Commerce at the corner of U.S. 65 and Mo. Highway 248. They will give you a city map, or you can have them send you one by calling (417) 334-4136.

Before you leave home, choose a lodging facility near the particular theater or attraction you plan to visit. This can save you a lot of time in trying to get from one end of town to the other. Two of the most impor-

INSIDERS' TIP

As you wind through the Ozark Mountains, you may be a little confused about which direction you are going. North-south roads are always odd numbered and east-west roads are always even numbered.

The Ozarks offer scenic splendor even off the updated highways.

Photo: Branson/Lakes Area Chamber of Commerce

tant factors to consider when you figure out how much time to allow for driving through town is the time of day you will be traveling and the location of your destination. The biggest traffic snarl in town usually occurs in the eastbound lane of Mo. 76 between 6 and 7 PM, when many people leave Silver Dollar City for the day. If you are traveling to a 7 PM show, be sure to allow at least an hour if you have to go more than a few miles. Although you may be interested in seeing the famous Strip, be sure to check out Shepherd of the Hills Expressway and Mo. Highway 165. These two roads will lead you to numerous restaurants, theaters, shopping centers, and attractions. Traffic usually flows much faster on these two roads.

One thing we'd like to warn you about is asking for directions. Because the roads have sprung up so fast around here, it's hard for locals to keep up with the best routes. Our advice is to rely on a map, a new one that is.

Getting To Branson By Car

If you come to Branson by car (unless you go out of your way to take the back roads) chances are you'll travel a portion of U.S. 65, the north-south thoroughfare connecting Springfield on the north to Harrison, Arkansas, on the south. Depending on where you're from, you may consider U.S. 65 more of a back road than a major highway. Nonetheless, it's the best we can do for now. Much of the route from Ozark to Branson is three lanes, but work is well underway just north of Branson and south of Ozark to widen the road to four lanes. By 2001 all four-laning in Taney and Christian County is scheduled to be complete. The Missouri Department of Transportation projects that to widen the stretch from Branson to the Arkansas state line to four lanes will take until 2004. As you wind through the majestic Ozark Mountains on your trip to Branson, you'll understand the amazing amount of rock blasting that has to be done to complete such a project. What took Mother Nature millions of years to build up and carve out, road crews can blast away in a matter of months. When you look at it like that, a few years doesn't seem like much of a wait.

If you're coming from St. Louis or other points east, or

INSIDERS' TIP

For road conditions call the Missouri State Highway Patrol at 1-800-222-6400.

GETTING HERE,
GETTING AROUND

INSIDERS' TIP

To keep up with the latest construction areas on the roads in and leading to Branson, log on the Missouri Department of Transportation's website at www.modot.state.mo.us.html.

from Tulsa, Oklahoma, northeast Texas, or other points west, you'll take Interstate 44 to Springfield where it connects to U.S. 65 just 35 miles north of Branson. If you're coming from Kansas City or other points north, you have your choice. Either take the four-lane U.S. Highway 71, which takes you through Carthage and on to I-44 just east of Joplin, or you can take the quicker, but busier, mostly two-lane Mo. Highway 13 to I-44 just a few miles north of Springfield. The Mo. 13 route will save you the hour's drive from Carthage to Springfield, if you don't mind the two-way traffic and road construction.

U.S. Highway 60 runs parallel to I-44 through southern Missouri and connects to U.S. 65 just south of Springfield's city limits. From the east, U.S. 60 connects to U.S. Highway 63 at Cabool and continues on to Interstate 55 just west of Memphis. If you're traveling from the south or east of Memphis, you can take the mostly two-lane U.S. 63 or you can hop on Interstate 40, head west to Little Rock, Arkansas, and then enter Branson from the south on U.S. 65.

If you're coming from Texas via Oklahoma City and want a more scenic route than the I-44 path, take I-40 east to U.S. 71 North. You'll travel alongside the Arkansas River on I-40, then on U.S. 71 you'll pass through the Arkansas cities of Fayetteville and Springdale. U.S. 71 winds through the hills to meet U.S. Highway 62 just west of Beaver Lake and Eureka Springs, Arkansas. (Check out exciting sight-seeing opportunities in Eureka Springs in our Daytrips chapter.) Continue east on U.S. 62 to U.S. 65 and from there you're just 30 miles south of Branson.

Now that we've covered the major arteries leading to Branson, it's time to tell you about the back roads. For the truly adventurous driver, try U.S. Highway 160 South, which leads you out of Springfield through Nixa and Highlandville. The passage takes well over an hour and can be quite treacherous in wet or snowy weather. Once you come to the Reeds Spring Junction, you can continue on Hwy. 160 to Mo. 248 or you can go west to Mo. 13 until you come to Branson West, formerly called Lakeview. From there you can turn east on Mo. 76 and travel to Silver Dollar City, Inspiration Tower, and the Shepherd of the Hills Homestead. (See our chapter on Attractions for more information about these sites.)

If you continue south on Mo. 13 at Branson West, you'll come to Kimberling City, known for its many marinas and resorts on Table Rock Lake. If you decide to stay on Hwy. 160 at the Reeds Spring Junction, this route will take you back across U.S. 65 East to the Taney County seat of Forsyth. Mo. 248 leads south past the Mel Tillis Theater to the Shepherd of the Hills Expressway, known as The Other Strip. Shepherd of the Hills Expressway runs from Mo. 248 to the western end of Mo. 76, or what locals call The Strip, where it runs into Mo. Highway 376 at the Country Tonite Theatre. The Shoji Tabuchi Theatre, IMAX Entertainment Complex, and dozens of motels and restaurants line Shepherd of the Hills Expressway. The entire portion of Shepherd of the Hills Expressway from Mo. 248 to Mo. 76 is 3 and 4 lane. The expressway was built to connect traffic from Mo. 248 to the western end of Mo. 76 so visitors to the Shepherd of the Hills Homestead could avoid congestion on The Strip.

The Many Aliases of Mo. Hwy. 76

The stretch of Mo. Highway 76 between downtown Branson and the Country Tonite Theatre is known locally as The Strip. The City of Branson renamed the famous section 76 Country Boulevard. You won't hear locals refer to it as 76 Country Music Boulevard very often though. We prefer to say The Strip or just 76. When we refer to points west of the Country Tonite Theatre or east of downtown Branson, we say west 76 or east 76. Even though the official name includes the word country, many locals have dropped the word in an attempt to broaden the public's perception that Branson is more than just a country music town. Road signs leading to Branson, however, have the word music dropped and read 76 Country Blvd. Many of the businesses located on The Strip list their addresses as 76 Country Boulevard. While this name game may be a little confusing, remember that The Strip, 76 Country Music Boulevard, and 76 Country Boulevard are all the same stretch of black top.

Getting Around Branson

In Town

In Branson, Mo. 76 or The Strip runs from the intersection of Mo. Hwy. 376 east into downtown Branson where it intersects U.S. Business 65, which was recently renamed Veteran's Boulevard. Many businesses along U.S. Bus. Hwy. 65 continue to use that name as their address. We will note the exceptions. Branson developer Jim Thomas, owner of the Lodge of the Ozarks and the Celebrity Theatre was one of the first to build commercial property on The Strip. When he originally purchased the land where his Lodge of the Ozarks resort and theater complex now sits, it was being used as a dirt airstrip since it was the only level spot in Taney County. Today, you can't come to Branson without taking at least one pass down the famous road. Few building sites are left on the five-mile stretch.

A few years ago locals did everything they could to avoid The Strip because of the tremendous traffic jams, especially before the shows. But traffic moves along much faster now that a number of side roads carry cars on and off The Strip every few hundred yards or so. The rush before and after shows can still be a little nerve wracking, especially in late fall when visitor numbers are highest. If you're taking The Strip just to see the sights, try it before 10 AM or between 7 PM and 9:30 PM. Most people either haven't gotten around by 10 AM or are parked for a show after 7 PM.

INSIDERS' TIP

The center lane on The Strip is a turn lane, and travel lane for emergency vehicles. If the police catch you driving down the turn lane without your signal light on, or driving too far without turning off, they'll pull you over to explain the concept.

Red Route, Blue Route, Yellow Route

Have you wondered what the red, blue, and yellow road signs that look like a capital B standing on a guitar neck are for? They are road markers for time saving routes. The red route is Shepherd of the Hills Expressway. The blue route is Gretna Road and Roark Valley Road, and the yellow route is Fall Creek Road, Green Mountain Drive, and Wildwood Drive (but only the portion of Wildwood south of The Strip). These roads also contain red, blue, and yellow diamonds painted on the pavement every few hundred yards or so. The Branson Roads Scholar map, printed by the Branson/Lakes Area Chamber of Commerce, has these passages color-coded and suggests using them as alternates to The Strip. It you really want an education on these routes, tune in to The Vacation Channel. (For more information on The Vacation Channel see the Media chapter.) They devote an entire program to decoding the color codes.

If you need to get from one end of town to the other and want to avoid The Strip, we suggest trying Gretna Road. Gretna Road runs parallel to The Strip on the north, beginning at Mo. 248 just south of where Shepherd of the Hills Expressway meets Mo. 248. Gretna Road winds through the Branson Meadows development past Factory Shoppes of America outlet mall to the intersection of Roark Valley Road and then on past the Promise Theatre. From Gretna Road you can see the backs of numerous buildings facing The Strip. A number of short roads connect Gretna Road to The Strip including Wildwood Drive, Rosalee Street, and Frances Street. Gretna Road stops at The Strip next to the Osmond Family Theater. On the south side of The Strip, Gretna Road becomes Mo. 165.

Roark Valley Road, which breaks off the north side of The Strip just east of the U.S. 65 exit, runs parallel between The Strip and Mo. 248 and intersects Gretna Road a half-mile from Shepherd of the Hills Expressway. James F. Epps Road connects Roark Valley Road to the eastern half of Mo. 248. Forsythe Street and Truman Drive connect Roark Valley Road to The Strip. With a little creative maneuvering you can get from Mo. 248 to The Strip to Mo. 165 in no time flat. Now, if you want to travel the side streets south of The Strip, start with Fall Creek Road, where it breaks off from The Strip between Engler Block, an arts and crafts mall, and

Inspiration Tower at Shepherd of the Hills Homestead is 230 feet tall.

Photo: Branson/Lakes Area Chamber of Commerce

the Dixie Stampede. Fall Creek Road takes you to Wildwood Drive where you can jump off and head on over to Green Mountain Drive, the road that runs behind the Grand Palace and past numerous hotels and restaurants. Green Mountain Drive eventually connects with Mo. 165 near the Ain't Misbehavin' Supper Club. If you continue on Fall Creek Road, you will eventually wind through to Mo. 165. A turn north will take you back to The Strip and a turn south will lead you to the Welk Champagne Theatre and Resort, as well as the Shepherd of the Hills Fish Hatchery. Green Mountain Drive continues on across Mo. 165 to White River Drive, which runs behind many theaters and hotels on the west end of The Strip.

Also on the west end of The Strip is Mo. 376 linking Shepherd of the Hills Expressway with Mo. 265. Mo. 265 takes you south to Mo. 165, across Table Rock Dam and then to U.S. 65 just south of Hollister.

INSIDERS' TIP

An estimated 17,000 to 19,000 cars travel U.S. 65 between Springfield and Branson each day during the summer months, according to the Missouri Department of Transportation.

Downtown Branson

You won't find too many maps of downtown Branson since most area map printers tend to focus on The Strip. The old part of town, as it is called, is home to dozens of mom and pop ice cream parlors, restaurants, and gift shops covering four or five blocks. Parking is limited downtown, but you may find a space in the lot between Commercial Street and Mo. Bus. 65 (Veterans Blvd.) or in the parking garage just off Sycamore Street east of Commercial Street. The city dedicated a new Park 'N Lot in 1999 that has helped ease the congestion even more. When locals refer to the lakefront, they are usually talking about the area east of BoxCar Willie Drive, where the Sammy Lane Boat Dock, Dimitri's Restaurant, and the Branson City Campgrounds can be found. If you follow The Strip east from U.S. 65, it turns into Main Street and takes you right down to the banks of Lake Taneycomo.

Getting to Branson By Air

Boone County Airport
2424 Airport Rd., Harrison, Ar.
• (870) 741-6954

A mere 30 minutes from Branson, the Boone County Airport has a 6,150-foot paved and lighted runway open 24 hours a day. There is no landing fee. Crown Aviation, (870) 741-4510, (800) 558-8359 provides self-serve avionic gasoline 24 hours a day, and its staff is on call around the clock for maintenance and other needs. They will also help you make transportation arrangements to Branson, or you can check out the Avis counter at the terminal, (870) 741-2237. Crown Aviation does not charge a daily tie-down fee if you purchase gasoline. The airport's

When the Taney County 911 emergency service system was installed, many of the area's roads were renumbered or renamed. Throughout this book we have done our best to provide the most logical road name in the address of each business listing. Since many businesses do not as of yet use their 911 addresses, we have chosen to list the address the way the business prefers. Stone County is in the process of getting 911 addresses. We have listed the 911 address when available.

only commercial carrier, Lone Star Airlines 1-800-877-3932 provides service to Dallas and St. Louis. Visit its website at www.ruidoso.net/reservations/lonestar.html.

M. Graham Clark Airport
College of the Ozarks, Hangar One,
Point Lookout • (417) 332-1849
• www.cofo.edu

Located just two miles south of Branson on Mo. Hwy. V, the M. Graham Clark Airport accommodates private aircraft and charter planes with a 3,600-foot lighted runway at an elevation of 940 feet, a parallel taxiway, a rotating beacon, and two approved instrument approaches. The airport provides aviation gasoline, jet fuel, major and minor airframe and powerplant maintenance, and avionics. The airport is open from 7 AM to 7 PM August through May and from 7 AM to 9 PM during the summer. Tie-downs and hangar space is available along with airplane rentals. The 16,000-square foot terminal has restrooms, phones, and vending machines. Avis-Rent-A-Car, (417) 334-4945, is located on the premises for car rentals.

INSIDERS' TIP

Many of the parking spaces in downtown Branson have a two-hour limit. Each space is clearly marked with a sign.

Springfield/Branson Regional Airport
5000 W. Kearney, Springfield
- **(417) 869-0300**
- **www.sgf-branson-airport.com**

A 40-to 50-minute drive from downtown Branson, the Springfield/Branson Regional Airport is the closest commercial airport in the area. Servicing 70 flights each day, the airport is owned by the city of Springfield and features one-stop service to 360 domestic and 16 international cities. The 100,000-square foot terminal has 10 gates, a full service travel agency, complete airline ticketing facilities, sky cap service, automated baggage handling, an on-site restaurant, a chapel, gift shop, lounge, and visitor information center.

Five carriers provide flights to major cities. American Eagle, (800) 433-7300, flies to Dallas Ft.-Worth and Chicago. Northwest Airlink/KLM, (800) 225-2525, provides service to Memphis. TWA/TWExpress, (417) 865-1232, (800) 221-1900, flies into St. Louis. United Express, (800) 241-6522 takes passengers to Denver. USAir Express, (800) 428-4322, flies to Kansas City. The airport also offers hangar and tie-down space for private aircraft and 24-hour fueling. Tie-down fees for single engine planes are $3 a day or $30 per month. Twin-engine rates are $4 a day and $40 per month. Small jet rates are $5 a day and $60 per month.

The airport provides a full range of aircraft repair and maintenance services along with aircraft sales, flight school, and air taxi and charter services of all types, including jet. Four rental car companies are located in the main terminal of the airport next to the baggage claim area. They are: Avis, (417) 865-6226; Budget, (417) 831-2662; Hertz, (417) 865-1681 and National, (417) 865-5311. A few hundred yards from the main terminal are Dollar, (417) 862-6090; Practical, (417) 863-7368; and Thrifty, (417) 866-8777.

All three offer shuttle service to and from the terminal. There are 209 short-term parking spaces and 724 spaces in the long-term lot at the airport. All parking is open air. Short term parking is $8 per day. Long-term parking is $5 a day, $25 a week and $60 a month.

INSIDERS' TIP

If you want to avoid the rush for 7 PM and 8 PM shows, take in a morning or afternoon show instead. You'll miss the traffic jams and you'll probably get better seats, too.

If You Need Transportation

Many hotels and motels provide transportation for their guests in Branson for a fee. A few of them will pick you up at the airport in Springfield. If you need transportation from the airport to Branson, and plan to use one of the shuttle services listed in this section, be sure to make your reservations well in advance.

If you want your own set of wheels, you can contact one of the rental car companies in Springfield or the following companies in Branson: A-1 Auto Rental, (417) 335-3932; Avis, (417) 334-4945; Dollar, (417) 335-8588; or Enterprise, (417) 338-2280. Depending on where you are staying, and what activities you have planned, you might be able to see much of The Strip on foot. Just remember that you're in hill country.

A-1 Airport Shuttle, (417) 335-6001, has two cars, and one van available to take individuals and families from Springfield to Branson and motor coaches for groups of 15 or more. One-way trips start at $50 per person but drop to $15 per person for groups of 10 or more. For an extra charge they will take you to Kimberling City. Call at least three days in advance. While they do not provide transportation for individuals or families in Branson, they will chauffeur groups of 15 or more around town. Airport Shuttle, (417) 336-8244, will take you and one guest to Branson for $45. Each additional person up to a total of 15 is $10. If you need a larger group picked up, call for a quote. Call at least two days in advance. All Occasion Limousine, (417) 272-3427, based in Reeds Spring provides service from the Springfield airport and around Branson. Trips from the airport range from $87.50 for up to two people depending on the type of car you choose. Their six-passenger limo is $125 and their eight-passenger limo is $162.50. In Branson their rates range from $50 per hour for a sedan to $80 per hour for an eight-passenger limo. Allow a five-day notice. Branson City

INSIDERS' TIP

When you're traveling down The Strip and see someone trying to pull on from a side street, let the person in. Motorists in Branson are some of the most courteous around.

U.S. Highway 65 is being widened to four lanes all the way from Springfield, north of Branson, to Harrison, Arkansas, south of Branson.

Photo: Branson/Lakes Area Chamber of Commerce

Cab, (417) 334-5678, charges the first person $2.15 to get in the cab plus $1 for each additional person. Their rate is $1.50 per mile. They operate 24 hours a day, seven days a week, year round. You must call for service. Hillbilly Shuttle, (417) 334-5678, offers transportation from the Springfield airport for $60 for up to two people and $20 per person for groups of 15 or more. In Branson their rates range from $3 per person to $5 per person for groups of three or more.

J. Howard Fisk Limousines, (417) 862-2900, one of the area's oldest and biggest limo services, provides transportation to Branson from Springfield for up to three people for $105, and $150 for up to eight people. Groups of 14 or more pay $150 for a shuttle bus. Individuals in Branson pay $35 per hour for transportation and groups can call for package quotes. Many of the J. Howard Fisk Limousines vehicles are equipped with TVs, VCRs, phones, beverages, and other amenities.

Joey Riley Limousine Service, (417) 725-6004, (800) 218-4490, provides one way trips from Springfield for $65 and round-trips for $80. Their standard rate is $50 per hour with a 2-hour minimum.

Yellow Cab, (417) 862-5511, is the Springfield-based cab company to call if you need a ride to Branson. You can expect to pay $55 for up to five people and they will take you to any location in Branson. You can usually find a Yellow Cab waiting at the airport if you land during the day, but if you arrive after dark you should call as soon as you land.

Motor Coach Tours

One of the best ways to get to Branson and get around while you are here is via a chartered motor coach. Many tour companies in Branson provide complete travel package planning for groups of 20 or more. They will make your transportation arrangements from your home city to Branson and then see to it that you get to all the shows, restaurants, gift shops, and other neat attractions you so desire without having to look for a parking place. Most of the time you'll be dropped off at the front door. As with any destination, there are advantages to seeing Branson with a group. If you don't come on a motor coach, but still want to get the royal tour by an experienced guide, hop aboard Ride the Ducks, (417) 334-3825, for a trip down The Strip and into Table Rock Lake. Not only is the ride a blast, but the driver will point out all the sights along the way and throw in some Ozark humor as well. Taking a trip on a duck will help familiarize you with The Strip. (For more information about Ride the Ducks, see our Attractions chapter.)

INSIDERS' TIP

Roads often have names reflective of their place: Fall Creek Road, Skyline Church Road. But how would you like to have an address on Ho-Hum Road or at Poverty Point?

GETTING HERE, GETTING AROUND

Ozark-speak

That road has more twists and turns than a bushel of snakes.

History

Branson and the Ozarks:
Ozark Meandering

As Ozark novelist Donald Harrington pointed out, everything in the Ozarks meanders. Perhaps that is a statement of the obvious, but it bears examination, for like the obvious, it is frequently missed for being under our very noses.

Rivers meander in their babbling journey to either the Missouri or the Mississippi. Roads meander as they follow ridge lines or make their sinuous S curves around hillsides. Snakes meander in their crawling toward where ever it is their serpentine mind and method is taking them. Grapevines meander snake-like among sycamore limbs which in turn meander, making shade over Ozark streams. Butterflies meander from flower to flower like a hillbilly meanders from still to home after tasting its nectar. Good stories meander in their telling, and any devotee of Mark Twain knows they are the better for it.

Though this book is largely the story of Branson, that small town on the old White River that has become the No. 2 vacation destination in the United States (according to the American Tour Association) it is also about the greater Ozarks, too.

The name for this 55,000 square mile area of steep and rugged terrain between the nation's two great mountain ranges, the Rockies and Appalachians, is fairly recent, though the area is old. An explorer in 1815, S. H. Long, is credited as being the first to use the term "Ozark Mountains." The 19th-century explorer Henry Rowe Schoolcraft ventured into the area in 1818 and 1819, three years before statehood, to explore part of Thomas Jefferson's bargain land purchase of the Louisiana Territory in 1803. Though he explored much of the Ozarks, including the Branson area, Schoolcraft never used the term "Ozarks" for the area in his voluminous journals. Another explorer some 75 years later, the legendary one-armed explorer of the Grand Canyon, John Wesley Powell, who was a noted geologist and the second director of the U.S. Geological Survey, called the region "the Ozark Mountains" in his writings. Somewhere in a period of 75 years the term Ozarks became the accepted name for the region. Most etymologists believe the word is an abbreviation of the French phrase "aux Arcs" (pronounced like the Ozarks of today) meaning "to the Arkansas," referring to the French territory on the outposts of that river named after the American Indian tribe, or meaning "to the arcs"—the bows (arcs) of the area's meandering rivers and creeks in general. This meandering makes possible a 20-mile float on the Gasconade River, with the takeout point being only a mile's walk from put-in point, and floaters often marvel at the meandering miles of Ozarks streams. Missouri's new tourism slogan "Where the rivers run" (1998) doesn't take into account their roundabout method of doing so.

Today Branson and the Ozarks are almost a unit. You can't say one without thinking of the other. And so we meander in our History chapter amongst other nearby areas of the Ozarks the way the great White

River meanders amongst the Ozark hills. Branson's history is intertwined with the story of the Ozarks. Enjoy the meandering. The shortest point between "A" and "B" may be a straight line, but it's not usually the most interesting.

The Land

You can't know and understand the Ozarks today unless you know something about its yesterdays. Development issues, environmental concerns—every problem or situation we face—actually have roots that go down as deep as the 500 million year old limestone beneath us.

So how do we tell so long a story? We follow Alice's (of Wonderland fame) advice: "We start at the beginning, proceed to the middle, and continue until we come to the end." And our beginning is 500 million years ago when the Ozark Mountains weren't mountains at all, but a shallow sea. During that period, large quantities of shelled creatures, often only microscopic in size, died, and the accumulation of their calcium exoskeletons became the thick layers of limestone and dolomite we see today, so neatly exposed for reading in recent road cuts. Several thick areas of sandstone indicate that the area was also desert in climate after the seas retreated, and later layers of limestone indicate other undersea development. Gradually, there was a general uplift of that area we now call the Ozarks highlands, roughly south of the Missouri River and north of the Arkansas River, with Oklahoma and Kansas on the western border and the Mississippi River on the eastern border. It takes in a region that is the largest area of steep relief between the Appalachians on the east and the Rockies on the west. It encompasses more than 50,000 square miles, and were the Ozarks a state, it would rank 23rd in size. Milton D. Rafferty in *The Ozarks: Land and Life* remarked that "the Ozarks is one of America's great regions, set apart physically by rugged terrain and sociologically by inhabitants who profess political conservatism, religious fundamentalism and sectarianism, and a strong belief in the values of rural living."

The Ozark upland varies in altitude from 400 to 2,500 feet above sea level, and the plains area of Springfield running east toward Cabool and Willow Springs forms a major dividing ridge. Many of our major local rivers start within miles of each other in that area and flow their different directions: the Jacks Fork and the Eleven Point flow east; the Big Piney flows northeast; the Gasconade flows north; and the North Fork of the White River and Bryant Creek flow southwest. All the oldest rivers of the Ozarks show a peculiar meandering trait, characteristic of rivers in lowlands and plains area. They began their life probably before the uplift, laying down a basic channel that became more entrenched during the slow uprising of the area and over time, an uplift so slow and gradual and widespread that seldom were the layers of rock buckled and broken. Gradually, these rivers cut their path deeper and deeper into the layers of limestone and sandstone laid down during the Paleozoic era. It doesn't take a trained geologist to see that most of the peaks in the Ozarks are about the same height. One can see an exposed layer of rock on one side of a river and find the same layer at the same altitude, sometimes miles away, on the other hillside across the river.

Outsiders coming into Branson from the north on U.S. Highway 65 often think they are driving "into the mountains"—mountain is rather a grandiose term for them; hills would be more accurate—when actually they are coming down from the Springfield plateau. Highlandville, between Springfield and Branson, is actually the line of demarcation, as its name suggests. Coming from Branson and going north, it is the "high land" before the general leveling of the plateau. Though it may not feel like or look like you are going down when you drive south toward Branson, your reason confirms it when you look at the map and see that the James River, which starts north of Springfield, flows southwest into the White River (now Table Rock Lake). Springfield has an altitude of 1267 feet while Branson is 330 feet lower at 937. The highest point in the Missouri Ozarks,

INSIDERS' TIP

The Missouri state insect is the honey bee, an oddity of choice because like many people now living in Ozark Mountain Country, it is not a native but a "comehere," having been introduced to North America by the early colonists. In 1839 Missouri had to expend $30,000, the cost of calling out the state militia for the Honey War, fought with the Territory of Iowa over a boundary dispute resulting when a Missouri resident cut a bee tree in territory claimed by Iowa.

Taum Sauk Mountain, is only 1,772 feet, and the highest point in the Arkansas Ozarks, in the Boston Mountains, rises to 2,578 feet.

The Quachita Mountains, south of the Arkansas River, are generally higher in elevation than the Ozarks and are considered part of the ancient highlands development. The two regions are similar: steep hillsides carved by water with modern economies dependent on tourism, and before that, mining and timbering, grazing, and subsistence agriculture. Westerners may sneer at the "peaks" in the Quachitas, the Boston, and the Ozark chains as hardly being mountains at all compared to those of the Rockies. If the Ozarks are less than mountains, they are certainly more than hills. However, at 500 million years compared to the Rockies' babyish 200 million, the Ozarks region has been uplifted and weathered longer than any area of the country. When we use the metaphor, "as old as the hills" in the Ozarks, it has real meaning! Like the furrows on the brow of an old man, the furrows of the hollows and valleys on the face of the Ozarks are indicative of age.

The Ozarks' surface landscape of rugged bluffs and hillsides, clear rivers and streams that are still cutting into the solid rock, and gushing springs early attracted nature lovers, hunters, floaters, and anglers. Hunters came for the game in the forests, and the White River and its tributaries attracted floaters and anglers from the time that outsiders were first able to venture easily into the Ozarks. Caves, such as Marvel Cave (earlier called Marble Cave) beneath today's Silver Dollar City and Talking Rocks (once known as Fairy Cave) attracted their share of early adventurous tourists. Missouri could be known as the cave state, for it has more caves than any state in the Union. Caves give a glimpse through a glass of an equally important landscape of the Ozarks, that beneath the feet of the tourists who are admiring the surface landscape.

The entire Ozarks can be compared to a landscape of guacamole dip spread on the surface of a giant Swiss cheese. The green guacamole is the shallow soil supporting the grass and trees. The Swiss cheese is the limestone base. Geologists call such subsurface karst, land characterized by fissures and caving, formed as limestone dissolves over time because of contact with slightly acidic water. That which doesn't run off into streams and creeks flows into the "Swiss cheese" and becomes part of the water table or emerges at lower altitudes as springs. The surface of the land is characterized by wet weather streams, disappearing streams (with water going underground), springs (at which an underground conduit surfaces) and sinkholes, which appear when the roof of a cave falls in. The underground conduits become caves when the surface rivers cut deep enough to intersect the underground streams and drain them. This is why you see cave entrances in the bluffs as you float Missouri streams. Some are rather small, but others, such as Jam Up Cave on the Jacks Fork River have entrances so large that you would be able to stack a dozen buses in the opening. Sinkholes are part of the natural drainage system and should not be filled or have garbage and rubbish thrown in them, for it will pollute the water table and springs. Some sinkholes are modest, but others are quite large. Marvel Cave at Silver Dollar City was discovered by someone investigating a sink hole. Beneath it was a room, dissolved out of the solid rock over eons, that is large enough to float a hot air balloon. (Ask the cave guide there about the world's underground balloon altitude record!) Grand Gulf, near Thayer, is part of the Missouri State Park System. The spectacular gorges, a miniature Missouri "Grand Canyon" was formed when the roof of a gigantic cave gave way. The remaining portions are natural bridges over the huge furrow in the stone. After a heavy rain, the gorges fill with water 75 to 90 feet deep—which rapidly drains away into a system further underground. Bales of straw thrown in the gorge have emerged seven miles away at Mammoth Springs, Arkansas, a spring so large that it is the source of Spring River.

Some springs are "wet weather springs" and run only after a rain or when the ground is saturated. Others are "all weather springs" that flow all year. Some are small and have a tiny flow, but others, like Mammoth Springs or Big Springs, are veritable behemoths, springs the size

INSIDERS' TIP

With a population of 5,000 Branson had to design a water system that could provide water to an equivalent city of 50,000. Most of the city's water (80 percent) is drawn from Lake Taneycomo. A record water use of 5.8 million gallons was recorded August 1, 1999. Usage peaks at "the 5 o'clock flush," when thousands of visitors return to their rooms after a day of activity, cool off with a shower and get ready for dinner and a show.

Downtown Branson before Table Rock Dam. See the Shopping chapter for the same scene today.

Photo: White River Valley Historical Society

of rivers, with enough dissolved mineral content in the water that entire trainloads of dissolved limestone are being removed each year. The cave forming process is always at work.

Like a cave, the temperature of the water of springs is constant, and early settlers relied on springs for family water sources. Even during the dog days of August, you will feel a blast of air-conditioned air as you near a spring. The air is often misty, as the cool waters meet hot summer air, and cool and wet weather plants abound around springs: ferns, columbines, and mosses. Spring water is often characterized by a plant called watercress growing in the water, whose pungent, radish-like taste and greenery add zest to salads and which can even be picked in the dead of winter, growing in the constant-temperature water. On cold days in winter, springs often exhale "steam" as the warmer water of the spring meets the frigid winter air.

Springs were a source of cool, pure water for early settlers and allowed them to avoid the laborious job of digging a well. Some built below a spring and took advantage of the force of gravity and actually had running water by piping it into their cabins. Some pioneers took advantage of nearby caves for "natural air conditioning." Larger springs were often used by early settlers to power mills for grinding grain or even sawing lumber, and mills still remain at nearby Zanoni, Sycamore, and Dawt, much like the recreated Edward's Mill and Museum at the College of the Ozarks.

Many of the big springs in the White River are now under the lakes, but east of Branson on the North Fork of the White, Current, and Eleven Point Rivers are a number of impressive springs, and though the 100 to 150 miles from Branson make for a long daytrip, it is worth it. The area can serve as an interesting stopping-off point if you are coming to Branson from the east (See our Recreation and Lakes and Rivers chapters). Branson visitors who choose to do so can stop and rubberneck at some of the most spectacular springs in the world.

Big Spring is aptly named. Once a state park, it is now part of the Ozark National Scenic Riverways. Located in Carter County near Van Buren, it is the largest spring in the Ozarks and one of the largest in the world. From under a bluff, a turbulent river issues, flowing around mossy boulders. A popular picture point in the springtime, the bluff with its dogwood, redbud, and serviceberry trees makes an interesting mixture of colors amongst the blue and black of the water and the green of the mosses, watercress, and ferns. The spring gushes forth an average flow of 276 million gallons a day, and a maximum of 840 million gallons. Even during the extended drought years of the 1950s, the minimum flow measured with 152 million gallons per day. These figures can be put in perspective when one considers that Springfield's population of 150,000 may use 30 million gallons on a "big water day."

The springs of the Ozarks are its cave factories. According to studies by hydrologists, Big Spring removes about 175 tons of dissolved limestone a day, based on its average flow. Thus, in a year's time, enough limestone bedrock is removed to form a cave passage 30 feet high by 50 feet wide and a mile long. This erosion is, of course, spread out over the entire solution channels of the many square miles of its drainage system, but the spring's cavern system grows bigger each day. Divers who have entered the spring via a small pit cave from above the bluff were not able to penetrate the system because of the turbulent current but report a tantalizing glimpse of "an immense cavern." Someday, when the spring is undercut and the water table drops, it too, like so many of Missouri's cave marvels, will be exposed to human sight.

Alley Spring, in Shannon County, with its red pioneer mill, is one of the most photographed points in Missouri. The mill was used to grind meal and flour, cattle feed, operate a saw mill, and furnish electrical power for nearby houses. The powder blue water issues forth at an average flow of 81 million gallons per day, forming a large stream that meets the Jacks Fork a half mile away. Alley Spring was once a state park, but is now part of the Ozark National Scenic Riverways.

Also part of the Ozark National Scenic Riverways is the former state park at Round Spring. The spring's average flow of 26 million gallons a day rises quietly in a circular basin formed when an ancient cavern roof collapsed. Part of the roof remains intact as a natural bridge beneath which the waters of the spring flow toward the nearby Current River.

Less accessible, except to floaters, are Cave Spring and Blue Spring on the Current River. There are many Blue Springs in Missouri (there's one on the Jacks Fork at Jam Up Cave), but the one near Owls Bend is the deepest blue, so blue it was known by Native Americans as "the spring of the Summer Sky." It is also the deepest known spring in Missouri at 256 feet. It ranks sixth in size in the state with an average daily flow of 90 million gallons.

Cave Spring issues forth from a cave and is big enough for canoeists to paddle back into it, and most floating the Current River can't resist the quick cave excursion without leaving their canoe. In the winter when the river water is cold, bass and sculpins by the hundreds take shelter in the warmer spring waters. During the spring mating season, the cave is shelter to many hellbenders (large river salamanders). The spring has a drainage connection to the nearby Devils Well, a large sink which can be entered only by a 100-foot descent in a bosun's chair and winch. The 400-foot long underground lake, impounding more than 20-million gallons of water, is one of the largest in the nation.

Greer Spring, the second largest spring in Missouri, is on the Eleven Point River and retains much of its wilderness character. One can see little change today from photographs taken over a hundred years ago. It is not as easily accessible as Big Spring. Visitors must travel a steep path which begins next to the 1899 mill that made use of the spring's constant flow by a turbine far below. You can feel the air temperature change as you descend to the spring, and the mosses and ferns in the micro environment are green all year because the spring keeps the air cool in summer and warm in winter. A portion of the spring issues from a cave in a bluff, but most of the spring issues from a large pool that bubbles up like a huge boiling kettle. The spring's average daily flow is 187 million gallons, enough to double the flow of the Eleven Point River where it meets the river. Because the spring is now part of the Eleven Point National Scenic Riverway and within the Mark Twain National Forest, its pristine, wilderness character is likely to be preserved, and signs posting rules remind visitors to make minimum impact when visiting.

If you are coming to Branson from the east, you may want to check out the area on your drive across the state. If you are already in Branson, to reach our "big spring region," head north on U.S. Hwy. 65, then east on U.S. Hwy. 60 to the Mark Twain National Forest. The locations of the springs are marked by highway signs.

The People

The Ozarks has greeted many visitors over the past 10,000 years, and the area, like all of Missouri, shows the influence in its place names and culture of the peoples that controlled the area: Native Americans, the Spanish, the French—and after the Louisiana Purchase in 1803, the Americans. The area has a long tradition with Native Americans, though not many Native American place names. The first evidence of inhabitation was the Paleo-Indian bluff dwellers, who have left bone and stone tools, clothing, corn cobs, and even dog collars in well-preserved cave finds. It is a regrettable price of progress that many of the best sites of the early bluff-dwelling inhabitants had their ancient archeological record buried beneath the waters behind the dams built on the White River.

Following these first inhabitants, early Hopewell-Mississippian people were active as traders, often trading obsidian, sea shells, and other commodities. They were the people Hernando DeSoto found when he plundered villages in southeast Missouri and northeast Arkansas in 1540, but in just over a century, when the French explorers Marquette and Joliet arrived in 1673, these peoples were gone, replaced by the powerful local tribe known as the Osages. They expanded their domain quickly over much of Missouri, and by 1690 there were 17 Osage villages in the Ozarks. American Indians valued the Ozarks for the game, and later, as a place of refuge. Because the Ozarks did not have rich farming land, the area was less desirable to the advancing white settlers, and the westward migration for a time went around the Ozarks. As a result, the Ozarks was an area much more slowly settled and developed than the rest of the state. Though the Osages ceded the Ozarks area to the federal government in 1808, they continued to use the area as a hunting ground, claiming they had only given up the land, not the game on it. As eastern tribes were pushed westward, the area had contact with the Cherokee, Shawnee, Peoria, Kickapoo, Delaware, and the infamous "Trail of Tears" went through the Ozarks when the Eastern Cherokee nation was shattered in 1838. The removal by Presidents Jackson and Van Buren of all Native Americans east of the Mississippi resulted in the mass migration, and roughly a third of the 20,000 Cherokees died over the "Trail of Tears." These displaced tribes traveled through the Ozarks to the new Indian Territory or sought shelter in the remote hills and hollows, and were viewed as outsiders by the Osage tribe. The Osages were a tall, well-built people, heavily armed because of trade contacts with both the French and the Americans, and superb horsemen, and the displaced Eastern tribes were often at their mercy. The Osage tribe dominated the Ozarks until they too were relocated in Indian Territory. A good many of the Cherokee and other members of displaced eastern tribes stayed in the Ozark hills or intermarried with the white settlers, and today many Ozarkians have "Indian blood." After all, Taney County is only 90 miles from Oklahoma, which used to be known as "Indian Territory" until statehood in 1907, and the Ozark Mountain area extends into southeastern Oklahoma.

The occupation of the immigrant tribes and the Osage posed no real friction in the early waves of pioneer settlers. There were clashes, but full-fledged warfare was not part of the history of settlement of the Ozarks. The French, and later the Americans who lived in the Ozarks, dressed much like the Native Americans, in buckskin and, when they could get it, calico. They ate the same foods, hunted and trapped the same game. Both groups liked tobacco and whiskey and used them as trading commodities. The local tribes loved to gamble, betting deerhides and beaver pelts, moccasins, robes, and other valuables, and early settlers visited villages to play the native game called "chuckaluck." The similarity of the two groups frequently saw the settlers and the natives forming joint enterprises in hunting and trapping. Area towns with names like Osceola, Wappapello, Tecumseh, Sarcoxie, and Ginger Blue show the respect Missourians had for Native American leaders, and a few place names like the Missouri and Niangua rivers and Neosho are of American Indian origin. Largely, the Native American influence on place names is not great, for those people had been pushed into Indian Territory when the great wave of settlers flowed into Missouri. The Ozarks today was a silent witness to a history and culture that lingers with a few place names and the occasional arrowhead or other relic turned up during spring plowing or the developer's bulldozer.

Missouri was under Spanish political control from 1763 to 1800, but Spain did not take much interest in the area, and certainly not the Ozarks. Place name influence is largely on the Mississippi River side of the state. Three of the state's original counties were organized and named by

INSIDERS' TIP

The gunplay on the square in Springfield July 20, 1865 in which James Butler "Wild Bill" Hickok shot and killed Dave Tutt for wearing Hickok's watch in public—which Tutt had won at poker—became the prototype of the "Main Street show-down meeting" found so often in westerns. According to the transcript of the trial, each shot one time, with Tutt firing first. Wild Bill's revolver shot struck Tutt in the heart from a distance of 75 yards, a feat which caused the encounter to be written up afterwards in *Harper's Weekly* and the fare of dime novels.

A Look at the Ozarks Hillbilly

Hillbilly is a fightin' word for some hill folks in the Ozarks. Nobody enjoys being called slovenly, ignorant, and uncouth. Hillbilly is taken by a lot of people to mean those very things. For some, it is a politically incorrect word. On the other hand, hillbilly to others is simply a term for a person who lives in the hills. It has no derogatory meaning at all, no more than flatlander does when used by people who are lucky enough to live in hill country.

What the term conjures up in the mind for some is the cartoon stereotype of a shiftless, barefoot, single-gallused, rifle-totin', corn cob pipe smokin', moonshine drinkin', long-bearded man who is slow in mind and speech. The women, if they're past middle-age, are characterized much the same, but without the beard. If they're young, they're portrayed as curvaceous Daisy Maes. They're all stereotypes that you still find in some of the shows on The Strip in Branson and right out of "Snuffy Smith" in the Sunday comics or the older "Li'l Abner" by Al Capp of a previous generation.

A factor in helping define the stereo-type is the dialect and accent we use here in the Ozarks. There is something about the language of the Ozarks that is different from standard English that marks us: dead-on, bull's-eye metaphors, but also convoluted euphemisms, a grammar and diction that are more Elizabethan than modern, and a sound that has the softness of the old South and the twang of Texas but with a pushingtogetherofwords or a contraction of them found nowhere else (oropry for opera and "C'mere. Letsqueet" for "Come here. Let's go eat.")

Mike O'Brien, columnist for the *Springfield News-Leader,* made note of our Ozark-speak when he coined the word Ozonics. Dale Freeman, former city editor of the same Springfield paper, was aware of our area's peculiar dialect when he served as a lexicographer of sorts for the Ozarks and wrote his *How to Talk Pure Ozark in One Easy Lesson.* However, though essentially accurate, he was playing up the stereotype for the tourists and also poking a bit of fun at us in this somewhat exaggerated dictionary of Ozark lingo. Though there were (and still are) people who speak that way, the ability to use standard English when they want to is a characteristic of more and more of us hillbillies, the result of the influence of radio and network TV—and tourists—on our peculiar hillbilly dialect.

Hillbilly is a word that isn't as old as the Ozark Mountains. The earliest reference in print, according to the Dictionary of American English, is 1902. As for its etymology, it's simply labeled as "unknown." May Kennedy McCord, longtime columnist for the Springfield paper and pioneer radio columnist with her *Hillbilly Heartbeats* on Springfield's KWTO years ago as well as an indefatigable collector of Ozarks folklore, said that the term was "sort of a smart-alec nickname that got attached to the hill men of any hilly country" in the early years of this century. She figured that its source was the billy goat "because he roams the hills."

For some it is a term of contempt and derision applied to people of rural origin in general—not just hill people. It is a term whose dim meaning has been gleaned from old Ma and Pa Kettle movies, the *Green Acres*, and *Beverly Hillbillies* TV series, and James Dickey's novel *Deliverance*, with much of it drawn from the movie version of the novel. Folklorist Vance Randolph in *Down in the Holler* quotes Rose O'Neill who said she first heard the word in her community after 1900 but that it wasn't common until 1915. Randolph mentions a John O'Neill who shot and killed a St. Louis man in 1934 for calling him a hillbilly, but by the time streets were named in Hollister, Hillbilly Lane was a perfectly acceptable name.

For those hill people who recognize that many use it as a term of disparagement, there are feelings of anger, resentment, and shame. Others terms from the Ozarks, like Shakers, Quakers, Baptists, and Methodists were all coined by opponents of the respective movements and took a term of derision and turned it into a perfectly

"The Arkansas Traveller," a painting that established the Ozark hillbilly hangs in Little Rock's Old State House.

Photo: Arkansas Territorial Restoration

acceptable-in-polite-company noun. Take what other people consider as a badge of contempt and wear it with honor.

The change came, according to Otto Rayburn, author of the *Ozark Encyclopedia*, after the Ozarks began developing as a playground and tourist area; "the term was cleaned up and accepted in the best of society." Some of the older businesses of that period of deveopment in the Ozarks used the term hillbilly in their name and the hillbilly stereotype in their advertising. A May 1943 article in *National Geographic* by Ozarker Frederick Simpich freely and without disparagement used the term hillbilly and praised the marksmanship of "gun-loving hillbilly boys" who "were among the first to enlist."

Congressman Dewey Short referred to himself in public speeches as a hillbilly, but R. P. Weeks who represented Douglas County in the Missouri Legislature, avoided the word hillbilly but admitted that he was a flint-buster. (Other names used for hill people include acorn-crackers, briar-hoppers, bush busters, brush-apes, ellum-peelers, fruit-jar suckers, haw-eaters, hay-shakers, hog-rangers, pumpkin-rollers, ridge-runners, sorghum-lappers, hogmolly-eaters, sprout-straddlers, and squirrel-turners.) Layne Morril, president of the National Association of Realtors from nearby Reeds Spring wears the label hillbilly "with pride." Bob Corbin says a hillbilly is someone who is practical and down to earth—"a person who can repair anything with baling wire and duct tape, a person who can eke out an existence on hardscrabble land where others would starve to death." One sixth-generation hillbilly, with tongue planted firmly in his cheek, says that he "dislikes the term" and "prefers the more formal hill-william." The term of derision has gradually changed to a term of acceptance, sometimes with a feeling akin to pride.

The stereotype of the hillbilly existed before the word. No work of art had greater influence in picturing the typical hillbilly in the American mind than did a painting *The Arkansas Traveler*. Painted in 1858 by Vermonter Edward Payson Washburn, an artist then in his 20s, the work was reproduced by the lithographic process in New York and widely distributed. The painting, combined with the story and the

(Continued on next page)

HISTORY

Three generations of Baldknobbers—four musicians and two hillbilly comedians.

Photo: Baldknobbers

famous fiddle tune both attributed to Col. "Sandy" Faulkner, did much to establish the stereotype of the Ozark hillbilly. Of course most of the hill folks' ancestors from Scotland, Wales, and the Irish west country had endured jokes and jibes in their native lands about "Kerry Men" and fightin' and drinkin' Irish, tall tale-tellin' Welsh and skin-flint Scots, who loved only to play the pipes, hunt, and drink the national brew. (It seems as though hill folk have always been the brunt of flatlanders' jokes!) Washburn's painting and the accompanying story probably were meant only to be funny and not a put down, but in any event *The Arkansas Traveler* of Faulkner and Washburn is still with us, whether for good or bad. You can near the fiddle tune sometimes in shows on The Strip and at the Ozark Folk Center in Mountain View, Arkansas (see our Daytrips chapter). The painting has survived—badly restored— and can be seen at the Old State House in Little Rock, Arkansas.

The stereotype lingers on and is frequently played upon for the tourists. They make postcards of hillbilly scenes, carefully posed and costumed with the appropriate props: rickety outhouses, bonneted women, and lazy, whiskey drinking, corncob-pipe-puffing, sleepy men wearing floppy straw hats. The hillbilly industry was found as early as the 1930s when Pearl "Sparky" Spurlock moved to the Ozarks and became the area's taxi driver and tour guide over the county's rough roads. She proudly promoted the hillbilly. She was as much of a sit-down comedian and travelogue lecturer as driver as she pointed out sights from seat of her Ford taxi. She proudly claimed the rank of hillbilly and would describe the degrees she had to obtain before becoming a full H.B., remarking, "I am really proud to be classed as one, among these real mountain people."

The music shows in Branson get a lot of comedic mileage out of the hillbilly stereotype. Hargis in the Moe Bandy Show, Gary Presley's Herkimer in the Presleys' Jubilee Theatre, and Droopy Drawers in the Baldknobbers Hillbilly Jamboree Show (see our Shows chapter) are characters that draw on the Ozark hillbilly stereotype, but their creators (some are real hill folk) would be the first to admit that they are characters not so much to be laughed at but laughed with. Other folks, however, put such comedy in the same class as that of the blackface minstrel shows at the turn of the century. The Presleys and the Baldknobbers, the oldest shows in Branson, must be doing something right to have survived the competition when country-and-western big names came in, and yuckin' it up by their comic artists has been a factor in the groups' popularity. Russian comedian and comehere (the local term for a tourist who becomes a resident) Yakov Smirnoff has looked at the hillbilly to give us a fresh perspective of ourselves as he jokes about making the transition from Red to redneck.

Many of the folk artists and craftspersons in the area and the theme parks are taken by tourists to be real hillbillies but are actually comeheres. They were attracted to the more laid-back lifestyle they found in the Ozarks, learned a craft from others and delight in teaching and demonstrating it. They have taken to heart the words of a Stone County lawyer who defended his client in a divorce case after his wife had called him a hillbilly. "An 'Ozark hillbilly' is an individual who has learned the real luxury of doing without the entangling complications of things which the dependent and over-pressured city dweller is required to consider as necessity, and who forgoes the hard grandeur of high buildings and canyon streets in exchange for wooded hills and verdant valleys" (Moore v. Moore Mo. Ap., 337 S.W. 2d 781, 789).

The observation is probably true, and there even may be some truth to what early tour operator Pearl Spurlock used to tell tourists: "God has to keep people chained up in heaven for fear they'll come to the Ozarks and become hillbillies."

the Spanish: St. Charles, Nuevo Madrid (1788) which became translated and corrupted to New Madrid (with the accent on the Mad) and Cape Girardeau—which obtained the name of a French ensign stationed at Kaskasia. The land picked up a De Soto (1893) after the discoverer of the Mississippi, and Stone County has Ponce de Leon, a spa town that wanted the Fountain of Youth connection the name gave. The Spanish also named a river, Rio Corriente, which was simply translated the Current River.

The French were more adventurous than the Spanish and traveled up the rivers, hunting and trapping game and exploring, trading with the Native Americans, and frequently intermarrying with them. They named rivers and streams and other geographical features and made a larger linguistic impression with place names. When the area came under American influence with Jefferson's purchase of the Louisiana Territory, the French gradually became assimilated in the expanding American culture. The French influence can be seen in the faces and features of early pioneers in the paintings of George Caleb Bingham, and French names linger over the landscape, though the early French might not recognize the pronunciation today. Bois D'Arc is pronounced Bow Dark; Versailles is pronounced like it looks, not like the French city and palace; Pomme de Terre (the river and lake, French for "potato") comes out of our mouths something like "Pom le Tar"; and Tour de Loup (wolf track) was corrupted to Toad a Loop. Names which didn't change pronunciation were translated, and "la Riviere Blanche," named by the French for its white water shoals and rapids, became the White River.

Branson is becoming more of an international tourist destination, now that Europe is discovering the USA has a Midwest and does not just consist merely of an East and West coast and now that Missouri and Arkansas actively court foreign tourists. Missouri's tourism industry generated more than $18 billion in 1999, and an increasing number of those spending money are not from the United States. The Spanish and French visitors who come can smile at the changes in the names their

INSIDERS' TIP

The nearby town of Protem (Latin "for the time being") chose its name when several name requests were rejected by the U.S. Postal Department because the names were in use already. They received instructions to "use any name pro tem." They did, and it has had that temporary name since 1888!

Old-fashioned fun at Springfield's Frisco Days.

Photo: Collette

countrymen placed on the land, but there can be no doubt of their influence on the language and culture of those who live in Missouri and the Ozarks.

Ozark Hillfolk

Henry Rowe Schoolcraft described the lifestyle and character of early pioneers in the Ozarks in his journals of his travels, remarking that "Corn and wild meats, chiefly bear's meat, are the staple of food. In manners, morals, customs, dress, contempt of labor and hospitality, the state of society is not essentially different from that which exists among the savages. Schools, religion, and learning are alike unknown. Hunting is the principal, the most honourable, and the most profitable employment....They are consequently, a hardy, brave, independent people, rude in appearance, frank and generous, travel without baggage, and can subsist anywhere in the woods..."

He thus first records an account that was to become a type. The stereotypical, cartoon-version of the Ozarker, the hillbilly, with bare feet, long beard, flop hat, and single-gallused trousers and the accoutrements of a stone jug of moonshine and a rifle perhaps owes something to Schoolcraft. Certainly such stereotypes are abundant in Branson—in the motifs of restaurants, in yard ornaments, postcards, and the myriads of crafts and tasteless t-shirts and gewgaws found in gift shops that sprawl alongside the highways and byways of Branson—and in the humor of some of the music shows.

As with any stereotype, there is some truth behind the cartoon cutout. The Ozarks was the moonshine capital of the nation, if one is to base that title on the number of stills per capita, because whiskey was value added to corn and was cheaper and easier to store than the grain. It was an easy way to make "cash money," and after Prohibition it was an easy operation to hide in the maze of hollows and caves and forests. The Ozarks produced its share of sharpshooters because hunting was necessary to put meat on the table, and it was a rare family that didn't possess at least several guns. Having a sharp "shooter's eye" was something to be proud of and thankful for. The hardscrabble hill existence led to a poor lifestyle that put low emphasis on clothes and style and a high priority of getting the true value out of long wear. Furthermore, the ancestry of the hillfolk was often of the eyebrow-raising type according to Susan Klopfer's *How Branson Got Started*.

"It was not uncommon for early settlers to be criminals and black sheep of their families. People with something to hide often stopped off here. A lot of the natives, as a result, don't have the backgrounds of their families because relatives have kept the information a secret," says fourth-generation native Jerry Coffelt, a former cast member and public relations director of the Shepherd of the Hills play. It was easy for a person with a past to hide it, or find a future, in the Ozark hills. Wright's novel, *The Shepherd of the Hills*, has that idea as a major motif.

Most Ozarkers are of a Scotch-Irish ancestry, the descendants of Scottish Presbyterians who settled in Northern Ireland during the 17th century under the plantation system instituted earlier by Elizabeth I to "pacify the wild Irish." Though both the Scots and the Irish are of Celtic ancestry, the plantation scheme involved giving to the Protestant Scots large areas of land that had been inhabited for centuries by the Catholic Irish. The present religious and political problems in Ireland today stem from this 400-year-old endeavor.

Continual fighting with the Catholic Irish and new, higher taxation by the English produced a Scotch-Irish exodus to the new world. Even before the American Revolution, some 250,000 of them had crossed the Atlantic for a better life in the wilderness of America. They were a breed of people who were an equal match to the hardships of a new land. They became the quintessential frontiersmen and the sharpshooters in Washington's army; they were the scouts who led the settlers further westward. Most of these immigrants landed in Boston and Philadelphia, and they sought out landscapes that reminded them of their only hilly home country, frequently settling in the Appalachian Mountains area. Some moved south to the frontier opportunities in the Great Smoky Mountains of the Carolinas or west through the Cumberland Gap, settling in Kentucky and Tennessee. Later, they or their children, moved further west into Missouri and Arkansas. They frequently married Native Americans or other immigrants of Welsh, Irish, English, and German background. Perhaps the best exponents of these people were the Boone family, who had already settled on Missouri's frontiers when Lewis and Clark began their famous voyage of exploration up the Missouri in 1806.

In the isolation of the Ozarks, aspects of the older Scotch-Irish culture persisted and continued, long after it was abandoned by others who settled in other areas. Characteristic of that culture was a deep sense of independence and a suspicion of government and outsiders. They preferred simple but lively music performed on the familiar instruments they brought with them: fiddles and dulcimers. They created crafts from materials at hand, weaving baskets or building homes and furniture from the wood and stone they found in their immediate environment. The crafts and the folk music of the Ozark Folk Center in Mountain View, Arkansas (See our Daytrips chapter) and the more modern versions heard on The Strip are based on the older models, older traditions. Anyone who has traveled in Ireland will notice their connections to the Ozarks, and perhaps those connections account for the pleasant surprise that Irish and Scots tourists have when confronting the familiar as they visit the Ozarks, and why country artists like the late BoxCar Willie have a large following in Ireland, Scotland, and Wales. Similarities can be found in subtle connections of grammar and metaphor in the language of Ozark hillfolk with that of an older, archaic English language. The Scotch-Irish settlers were interested in storytelling and storytelling music such as ballads, than in books and abstract music. Thus the inherent suspicion of "book larnin'" by the Ozarker, the belief that everyone must be able to tell a good story, and the existence of ballad variations that have been traced to similar versions in Scotland and Ireland. These people, like their Celtic ancestors, preferred herding to dirt farming and

INSIDERS' TIP

Newspaper columnist and poet Mary Elizabeth Mahnkey won a trip to New York City in 1935 where she saw Broadway's hit dancing and singing Cole Porter musical *Anything Goes*. She remarked to a reporter: "I'm an old-fashioned woman and I'll never get used to naked women." When corrected that they weren't naked, she retorted, "Those on the stage didn't have enough clothes to wad a shotgun."

favored hunting and fishing to any agricultural endeavor. They were less interested than most in the trappings of material wealth, seeing it as a snare that took away independence. Often clannish and more concerned with family and the nearby community than the far-off government of the state and nation, they were proud of their isolation and independence. They could be passionate about love, politics, and religion, and they could be deeply stirred by the natural beauty of the hills or be emotionally responsive to music and the spoken word.

Today's country music and crafts and culture draw on this history, and they have evolved and adapted to the American experience of the early Scotch-Irish settlers. As another great wave of migration has come into the Ozarks with the advent of the modern tourist industry and the modernization as the result of roads and dams, the Ozarker retains many of those early traits and again adapts to a changing time—but is always proud to be a hillbilly.

The Civil War in the Ozarks

Missouri was a border state in two ways, north and south, the most obvious, but also east and west, with the Mississippi River being the dividing line. Looking back at the perspective after the war, battles fought in Missouri as part of the Transmississippi War had little influence concerning the outcome, and because of the sparse population of the area, battles in this border state pale to mere skirmishes compared to the large scale slaughter in eastern battles. In spite of having little impact on the Civil War's outcome, the Civil War had a tremendous impact on the Ozarks, and Missouri had a higher percentage of participants in the War than any other state—109,000 Union solders and 30,000 Confederate soldiers, 60 percent of all men old enough to be mustered.

At the outbreak of the war, the Ozarks was still sparsely populated, and in that sense was of little importance. It did not contain strategic materials needed by either the Confederacy or Union, but events in Missouri were harbingers of what was to happen back east later. Carthage, in Jasper County, was the site of the first land battle of the Civil War, July 5, 1861, preceding the first Battle of Bull Run by 16 days and Missouri's biggest battle at Wilson's Creek by more than a month.

The Ozarks area was marked by two large-scale battles. The first, Missouri's biggest, was the Battle of Wilson's Creek, southwest of Springfield on August 10, 1861. Lasting for six hours, this brief but savage encounter of Gen. Sterling Price's Confederate forces with those of the Union's Gen. Nathaniel Lyon produced 2,330 casualties. One of the battle's dead was Gen. Lyon himself, the first Union general to be killed in the Civil War. Wilson's Creek was a Confederate victory, but the Union regained control of southwest Missouri by the winter of 1862 (see "Wilson's Creek Battlefield" in our Daytrips chapter).

The second major battle in the Ozarks was about 50 miles southwest of Branson at Pea Ridge, Arkansas, March 6-8, 1862. It was the turning point of the war in the Ozarks. After the victory at Wilson's Creek, the Confederate forces expected a victory, especially since they outnumbered their Union foes 2 to 1. Included in the Confederacy's forces were a thousand Native Americans from the Five Civilized Tribes who had been moved to the Indian Territory some 30 years before. This band of Cherokees, Seminoles, Chicasaws, Choctaws, and Creeks was under the leadership of Cherokee Stand Watie, the only Native American to achieve the rank of general, and the last Confederate general to surrender after the war. The tribes were divided on Civil War issues, but it was politically expedient to back the Confederacy, especially after the Union defeat at Wilson's Creek. But the outnumbered Union forces prevailed at Pea Ridge; as a result, the Ozarks area was ostensibly under Union control and many Native Americans reversed their loyalty.

The compelling issue of the Civil War, slavery, was not a burning issue in the Ozarks. It did not develop a slave economy. The hilly, rocky Ozarks did not support the kinds of crops, largely cotton and tobacco, grown on the Southern plantations which demanded a large labor force. Land use in the Ozarks consisted of small farms, worked by the landowner and his family within large areas of wilderness forest. The only farmers who had large holdings of slaves were those in the "Little Dixie" area along the fertile Missouri River, north of the Ozarks, and those in the bottom lands of the rivers south of the Ozarks, the Arkansas, and the lower end of the White. Some Ozark families had slaves, but not many. The 1860 census in Taney County showed a holding of 84 slaves spread over 24 families, with the largest owner having ten. There were five free blacks. Compare that to the better farmland area of Greene County, which had nine free blacks and 1,668 slaves. Douglas County (named after Stephen B. Douglas) recorded no African Americans, slave or free. In fact, many Ozarkers, even into this century, lived a life during which they never laid eyes on an African American. Most Ozarkers in Taney County were indifferent to the slavery issue or were generally supporters of the Confederacy. As one resident said, "Our sympathies are with the South but our interests are with the Union." This pro-Southern leaning is evidenced by the name of the county seat (after John Forsyth of Georgia) and the names of the county and the nearby village of Taneyville, after Roger Brooke Taney, the U.S. Supreme Court Chief Justice in the Dred Scott Decision of 1857. Though the county has been named for him 20 years earlier, there was no outcry to change the county name.

In a region that today is staunchly conservative and in which most residents are registered with "the party of Lincoln" as voters, one finds it difficult to conceive that 150 years ago, voters looked with disfavor on Abraham Lincoln, his policies and the new Republican Party. In fact, residents of Greene County were shocked when Lincoln polled 42 votes in the 1860 election. In the counties of Taney, Stone, Christian, Ozark, and Douglas, not a single vote was cast for Lincoln. The next election produced equally lopsided results for Lincoln, largely because the Federals controlled the area, many Southern sympathizers were in the army or had been driven away, and because Union soldiers voted in local elections.

The hostilities that resulted with the election of Lincoln produced, as pointed out, not large-scale battles; instead, hostilities were in the form of innumerable and interminable raids, forays, and skirmishes by roaming bands of bushwhackers. The use of small, mobile bands of marauding irregulars was introduced by the Confederacy. Such raiders could harass the stronger Union enemy and tie up resources and men that could be more effectively used in the more important and bigger battles east of the Mississippi.

The Missouri Ozarks, with few slaves, an indifference to the issue of slavery, and an independent people who just wanted to be left alone to hunt, trap, and till their garden and farm, was caught between two radical and passionate elements. Not far from Taney and Stone counties is Kansas, where radical abolitionist feelings predominated. Arkansas to the south just a few miles was a strong pro-Confederacy state, dominated by the numerous plantation owners of the big river valleys. The geography and the independent temperament of the Scotch-Irish who settled here had both served to isolate the Ozarks. Now, as the result of politics, these people and their region were caught squarely in the middle of the conflict. The Ozarks was at the mercy of roving marauders from both sides—and to those who believed in neither faction but used the excuse of war to raid, rape, rob, and pillage. To compound the bad situation of being caught between two forces, Indian Territory just west in what is now Oklahoma, was just an easy ride's distance. It was a refuge for outlaws, vagabonds, and desperadoes of every ilk, and the no-man's-land law that prevailed there allowed gangs to make hit-and-run attacks on helpless Ozark homesteads whose men had enlisted and were off to war for one side or the other. Bands of guerrillas and bushwhackers terrorized the surrounding countryside. Those who weren't killed fled in terror. As an example of the decimation of the area's population, consider that the 1860 census counted 6,883 residents in Jasper County, but by the end of the war only 30 were left.

Names of desperadoes whose careers may have begun during the war but frequently continued after it are legion and some became well-known beyond the region of local history: Frank Dalton and gang, Cole Younger, Jesse and Frank James, "Bloody Bill" Anderson. A name less known is John R. Kelso, one of many leaders who were respected citizens in peacetime but when exposed to the rigors of war became psychopathic fanatics. Kelso was known as a scholar of languages and philosophy who became a school teacher at Ozark, but one who became an ardent Unionist and held all Confederates to be traitors, guilty of treason, and deserving death. It was said of Kelso that he could lie at the side of a road in ambush, with a Latin grammar in one hand and a cocked pistol in the other waiting for his intended Confederate sympathizer victim. One of his reported exploits was creeping alone one night into a camp of three Confederate bushwhackers who were asleep and dispatching them silently with his knife. He was said to be a man of

Ozark-speak

A devil's lane is the space between two fences built separately by landowners who cannot agree on their mutual property line.

HISTORY

exceptional self-control; he believed in a Spartan diet and did not smoke or drink, and he believed in the benefits of exercise, physical and mental. He was considered modern and liberal and forced his wife and daughter to adopt the freedom-giving dress advocated by Amelia Bloomer. After the war, he was elected to Congress as a radical Republican and did all he could to thwart the president's efforts toward a rational plan of reunification and reconstruction.

Alfred Cook might be considered a pacifist bushwhacker. At the beginning of the war, Cook and his wife Rebecca and their seven children were living on a farm north of Taneyville. Both Alfred and Rebecca were descendants of slave-holding families, and their parents with the family slaves, had come to Taney County in the 1830s and settled along Beaver and Swan creeks. Though probably sympathetic to the Southern cause, Cook tried to remain neutral, but foraging parties from both sides raided area farms, taking what they pleased and displeasing those from whom it was taken. Men who stayed at home might be called to the door and shot down by some fanatic of one side or another. Confederate sympathizers, or those whose loyalties were unknown, were plagued by the "Mountain Feds" scattered through the area who served as informants for the Unionists. Cook and his family, caught in the vortex of the Rebellion, faced starvation. Driven by desperation and criminal acts committed against them and their families, Cook and 13 or more others banded together for mutual protection. They adopted the tactics of their despoilers, and Cook and his followers made retaliatory raids against those persons who had robbed them. Cook and his band may have saved themselves from starvation, but their vindictive and deadly activities came to the attention of the Federals who began scouring the middle border from Ozark to the lower North Fork River for them.

Cook and his band took refuge in a cave high on a bluff which had a natural stone wall at its entrance so it could be easily defended and a spring which provided fresh water. It did not, however, have any other opening. In January, of 1865, Lt. Willis Kissee and 25 men on a scouting trip with orders to capture or exterminate Cook's band learned from an informer of the hideout. Kissee located Cook's small son and forced him to act as a guide to the gang's cave, where he surrounded the entrance. Kissee demanded that the raiders surrender. It was a demand which if complied with, would have meant death. No one emerged. Kissee called out that the raider would be treated as prisoners of war and not harmed if they surrendered and gave them four hours to decide. When the time expired, 11 of the men emerged from the cave. Cook and two others refused to surrender. Not wishing to risk lives in an effort to take the remaining raiders, Kissee built a huge fire on the ledge above the entrance and pushed it over the cliff into the mouth of the cave where wind blew smoke inside. Blinded and nearly suffocated by the smoke, Cook and his companions emerged from their lair. They were gunned down and left where they fell. The bodies were later retrieved by two neighborhood girls, a 13-year-old boy, and an old man then buried in a common grave overlooking the stream that flowed from the spring at Cook's cave.

Another home-grown variety of bushwhacker was Stone County's Alf Bolin, who instituted a reign of terror during the war that is almost unequaled. Bolin, a large, wiry man with a long, chest-length red beard, was a bushwhacker with no allegiance to either North or South, bragged of having killed more than 40 men. One of those 40 was Calvin Cloud, his surrogate father. Bolin and his gang, at the height of his career, sought refuge one day at the home of Calvin and Mary Jane Cloud near McCall Bridge in Stone County. Alf, wearing a mask, demanded that Calvin supply him with food and guns. Calvin denied the request, and Bolin drew his gun and shot him in the head. He then threatened to kill Mary Jane, who was pregnant, and her four children. Mrs. Cloud, who recognized the voice behind the mask, would later play another role in Bolin's career.

Bolin and his band of renegades, numbering several dozen at times, preyed on defenseless homesteaders, though Bolin was bold enough to bushwhack small units of Union soldiers. His motives behind his various crimes were seldom clear. One of his victims, 16-year-old Dave Tittsworth, was killed by his home near Walnut Shade, north of Branson. Some nearby women took Bolin to task for killing such a young boy. He is said to have replied, "Get in the house and shut your mouths if you want to save your scalps. That makes 19 I've killed."

Another victim was Bill Willis, who lived along Roark Creek just north of the White River. Bolin shot the 12-year-old boy off a rail fence. Other known victims of Bolin's gun were James Johnson, killed on Camp Creek in Christian County, and Bob Edwards, slain near the community of Bluff on Bull Creek, nine miles north of Branson. Once Bolin forced an 80-year-old man from his wagon just after he had crossed the White River on Hensley's ferry, made him wade into the river, shot him, and left his body to float down river.

Bolin raped, robbed, and murdered persons from Union families over a wide area between Ozark, Missouri and Crooked Creek, Arkansas. Many of his crimes occurred at Murder Rocks, sometimes referred to as Bolin Rocks, a castle-like geological formation on the Carrollton-Forsyth road just south of present-day Kirbyville on Mo. Hwy. JJ. The fortified position which wagons had to pass by allowed Bolin to ambush his victims with ease.

So numerous and monstrous were Bolin's crimes that a $5,000 reward was offered by the Federal government for his capture, dead or alive, as the Union militia fruitlessly pursued him and his band. One man who attempted to gain the reward pretended to join up with Bolin's gang and got the drop on the sleeping renegade by putting his Bowie knife to the sleeping Bolin's throat. A kick by Bolin disabled the bounty hunter, and he was stripped and branded with a hot poker: "I found Alf Bolin" on his chest and sent packing. Others trying to cash in on the reward were found dead, brazenly displayed on trees, hanging by their own belts.

The outlaw's bloody reign was finally ended by Robert Foster and his wife, who were, ironically, Confederate sympathizers. Foster was a Rebel prisoner being held in the stockade at Springfield. Foster, who lived close by Murder Rocks, was uneasy at the thought of his wife alone in their cabin, though the Fosters had never done anything to antagonize Bolin and his band. So Foster struck a deal: he would betray Bolin if the Union would parole him. He then convinced his wife to cooperate with a 22-year-old corporal from the Iowa Volunteer Cavalry, Zachariah E. Thomas. Zach Thomas was sent to the Foster farm, while Robert Foster remained in the stockade.

Thomas, dressed in a Rebel uniform, hid in the loft of the Foster cabin, his Colt revolver under his jacket. Bolin had been invited to the cabin by Mrs. Foster on the pretext of having Bolin buy their household goods, as her husband was to be released and they were going to leave the area. On the morning of February 2, 1863, Bolin came to the log cabin. He was not suspicious, as he had regular dealings with the Fosters, but the hidden Thomas accidentally made a noise in the loft. Improvising, Mrs. Foster told Bolin she was hiding a lone Rebel soldier, and Corp. Thomas was asked to come down from the loft. Thomas and Bolin talked and even shared a meal, and the suspicious Bolin gradually relaxed. They both examined and discussed a coulter from a plow that was lying by the fireplace. Bolin turned his back when he bent down to the fireplace for a coal to light his pipe, and Thomas dealt him a blow to his head with the heavy coulter. Why he didn't use his revolver, no one knows—perhaps just to save ammunition. Foster bashed Bolin's head three more times for good measure.

He and Mrs. Foster dragged the body outside to a log barn, but Bolin revived as she was cleaning up the blood on the hearthstone in the cabin. Thomas, who was saddling his horse, used the Army Colt that he had never drawn in the cabin to finish off Bolin before leaving. When he returned at dawn the next day, Foster was with 25 Cavalry troops, led by a major and two mule-drawn wagons. Bolin was placed in one wagon and all of the Fosters' meager belongings in the other, and the troop headed toward Forsyth.

In the county seat, news of Bolin's death attracted hundreds of locals who came to view the corpse. An Iowa soldier wrote of seeing the dead Bolin: "He was a long, sinewy man and must have been of great strength and endurance. His hair was matted with blood and it was clotted over his face, rendering him an object of disgust and horror." When the caravan headed north toward Ozark, a bitter local, Colbert Hays, whose relatives had suffered during Bolin's reign of terror, stopped the procession just north of Forsyth and asked to identify the bushwhacker. He did so, but before the amazed group could stop him, he beheaded the dead Bolin with an ax. The headless body was unceremoniously buried, and with Bolin's bloody head in a gunny sack, the troops continued toward Ozark, the county seat of Christian County. It was Mary Jane Cloud, widow of Calvin Cloud and surrogate mother of Alf Bolin who was ordered to Ozark to make a positive identification of Bolin's head. According to the story, she rode the thirty miles on horseback through a February snowstorm to confirm the identification. At Ozark the head was impaled on a

INSIDERS' TIP

Be a rockwatcher. The geology of the Ozarks can be read especially well in some of the recent road cuts. It gives a "clean page" and you can see the layers that were put down when seas covered the area. They may be inviting to climb, especially for kids, but a word of caution is in order: some layers are shale and crumble easily.

pole and displayed. It is said that children threw rocks at it and that people cut locks of his hair and long red beard off for souvenirs. The grim trophy finally reached Springfield, was reduced to a skull and sent to Jefferson City, where it disappeared. To this day, no one knows what happened to Alf Bolin's head.

In a recent footnote to history, Mary Jane Cloud's grave was discovered in the spring of 1998. She had died in 1906 and was buried beside her husband in the family cemetery near her cabin, but the graves had become forgotten and overgrown. Their discovery in the gloomy, dark hollow in Stone County sparked renewed interest in Bolin's bloody history.

And what of the $5,000 bounty on Bolin's head? The full bounty, a tremendous sum of money in those days, was awarded to Corp. Zachariah Thomas, who was further rewarded by being commissioned a second lieutenant March 24, 1863. Robert Foster was released from the stockade as agreed and reunited with his wife, and Thomas, remembering the bravery and the quick thinking of Mrs. Foster that had saved his life, gave the Fosters $3,000 of the bounty in a generous gesture.

Though the Civil War ended two years later, peace did not come easily to the Ozarks. Today, few people know of the gruesome Ozark bushwhacker episode of Alf Bolin, and certainly not many of the 7 million visitors to the area. At Silver Dollar City during the mock train robbery when the scruffy bushwhacker bandit announces, "I'm Alf Bolin and I'm takin' yer valuables," be aware that the mock robbery has historical roots in the Ozark past, and for the robbed, a much happier ending than the victims of the real Alf Bolin.

The Bald Knobbers

The guerrilla warfare carried on by the borderland Rebels against the Union forces during the last two years of the war was difficult to "shut off" when surrender was ordered and the war was over. During the war Ozarks towns had been decimated. Of the 51 structures that comprised Berryville, Arkansas in 1860, only Hubbert's Hotel and two small residences remained when peace was declared. The hotel was spared the torch, it is said, because Masonic records and regalia were stored in the upper story. Yellville, Arkansas was destroyed by Union forces and bush-whackers, and before the fighting ceased 32 buildings had been burned. Dubuque, Arkansas on the White River had been a busy steamboat landing with a thriving community, but the community and landing were totally destroyed by Union forces because the area had a lead smelter that furnished shot for Confederate forces. It was never rebuilt.

In Missouri, six of the border counties with Arkansas had their county seats destroyed by fire. Rockbridge, the first county seat of Ozark County was burned and never rebuilt on the old townsite. Today only foundations remain, a post-war mill, the spring, which offers excellent trout fishing, and a newly rebuilt restaurant that is justly famous for its trout dinners. Vera Cruz, the pre-Civil War county seat of Douglas County, met a similar fate. After the war the county government was reestablished at Arno on Beaver Creek, and later moved to Ava. On April 22, 1863, Union troops burned Forsyth, county seat of Taney County. All that remained of the town when settlers returned to rebuild were the scorched walls of the three-story brick courthouse. The county seat towns of Galena in Stone County, and Ozark in Christian County had incendi-ary fires but escaped total destruction. The courthouse in Ozark, however, burned soon after hostilities ceased. Farms and homesteads suffered even more, and few remained standing at the end of the war, the inhabitants having fled.

The end of the war did not see the end of the factional hatred. Each survivor, each returning refugee, had cause to hate someone. This animosity was nurtured and kept alive in the hearts and minds of many as they began the arduous task of rebuilding homes and lives. It destroyed rational thought. It poisoned the souls of those who were afflicted by it. The lawless period of the war encouraged a general lawlessness, and hatred often flared up in acts of revenge. In the period

Ozark-speak

A heavy rain in the Ozarks is a gully-washer, frog-strangler, fence-lifter, or goose-drowner.

Treenware artist Roger B. Sandstrom demonstrates the craft of making wooden utensils.

Photo: Silver Dollar City

from 1832 to 1860 only three murders had been reported in Taney County. In the post war period of 1865-1885, there were 40 murders—and not a single conviction.

To combat the lawlessness, vigilance committee organizations were formed. There was the Anti-Horse Thief Association; another was simply called the Citizens' Committee. Greene County had its "Honest Men's League"—which soon became a part of the problem it attempted to resolve. In Taney County, the "Law-and-Order League" came into existence April 5, 1885 in an outdoor organizational meeting on Snapp Bald. Because its members met on the treeless top of a mountain, known locally as a bald, enemies dubbed the organization "the Bald Knobbers." The vantage point of the bald offered a wide view of the surrounding countryside. Its barren top prevented spies from sneaking up and spying on the secret organization, who discussed the crimes of lawless neighbors and decided what kind of vigilante justice should be dispensed. Their story and the organization's impact on the area is the interesting study of Bald Knobbers: *Vigilantes on the Ozarks Frontier* by Mary Hartman and Elmo Ingenthron, found in many local book stores.

The Bald Knobbers' desire to promote peace and prosperity was the stated motive for the organization's existence. Improved roads and the return of steamboat traffic on the White River after the war were now bringing more people into the Ozarks and allowing those who lived here a way to transport goods and produce to outside markets. Crossroads stores and post offices were coming into existence to service drovers and freighters along new roads, and the new settlers moving into the Ozarks. The budding community of Branson was one such new town. Reuben Branson had given his name to the post office of his country store in 1882. However, darker reasons also existed—motives of revenge on the part of some who still harbored grudges from the past.

One of the newcomers to the area was Nathaniel "Nat" Kinney. He bought 267 acres of White River bottom land in 1883, just down river from Branson along what is now Lakeshore Drive. His money came from the operation of a successful Springfield saloon. Kinney was a big man—6 feet, 6 inches and weighed 300 pounds. He was a bare-knuckles prize fighter and a veteran of the

Union army. Known as Capt. Kinney (more for alliteration than accuracy, for army records show him only as a private) in a photograph by the backbar in his saloon, a huge man with huge, folded arms and a large handlebar mustache. With a grim, unsmiling countenance and a close-cropped head, he looks like he could easily serve as his own bouncer—and delight in the job.

Kinney was also a religious man and founded a Sunday school at Oak Grove School near Snapp Bald (out on the current Missouri Highway T). He was disgusted with the lawlessness he found in Taney County. As a successful businessman, he wanted order so that his farmland venture would prosper. When he assembled the group of nearly 200 on Snapp Bald that April night, Kinney saw the ordered elements of society: lawyers, mill and store owners, county officials. Seven were preachers—two Baptist, three Methodist, and two Disciples of God—and a great many were Masons. All would have been considered solid citizens of the community, taxpayers and churchgoers, but that did not mask darker motives. There was also a political twist to the situation. The Bald Knobbers were strongly Union and Republican. Their opposition were largely ex-Confederates and Democratic in politics.

The night after that April organizational meeting, a hundred armed and masked Bald Knobbers rode into Forsyth and placed a hangman's noose on the jail door of Newton Herrell who was awaiting trial for the killing of Amus Ring, his mother's lover. They also left a noose draped over the judge's bench as a symbolic reminder that should the court not punish Herrell, the Bald Knobbers would.

Within a week the Bald Knobbers actions moved from the symbolic to the active. It stemmed from the troublesome Taylor brothers, Frank and Tubal, two hellions who had gotten into a ruckus with J. T. Dickenson. Dickenson was an outsider and an Englishman who had come to Taney County and started a Socialist commune. When it failed, he became a capitalist and operated a general store. The two Taylors, angry that Dickenson would not give them credit for a pair of boots, shot him in the mouth with a .32 caliber revolver. The bullet knocked out four of his teeth, but its energy was spent and deflected. The bullet exited his neck. After shooting him again, they fired five times at his wife. She was hit in the neck, and a finger had been shot off. Thinking them dead, the Taylors left, but both survived.

It was such lawlessness that had spawned the Bald Knobbers. They now combed the rugged hills in search of the Taylors. A $1,000 reward was offered, and it was the reward that introduced a bizarre twist to events. The two brothers concocted a scheme with friends to turn them in. The friends would collect the reward, use part of it to bail them out, and then they would split the remaining reward money. So Frank and Tubal and their buddies rode into Forsyth, April 14, 1885 and surrendered, joking with locals and the arresting lawmen. For the boys it was an adventure and a joke, a profitable one: they'd reap the money for their own reward, and they would be acquitted. They were, after all, longtime residents and the English storekeeper an outsider. Such had been the pattern of justice in the past.

That pattern changed that night when Kinney and his band of Bald Knobbers broke down the jail, dragging the two pleading boys to a large black oak by the Chadwick Road, and lynched them. Was the hanging preplanned, or did an attempt to shock the two Taylor brothers just get out of hand? No one knows. Ozark poet Mary Elizabeth Mahnkey, who was 8 years old when the event took place, later wrote about the lynching tree in "The Tree Accurst":

"Whene'er I pass that grim old oak I felt a sense of dread. It spread its arms so wildly—It tossed its blighted head. The shade it cast was black and still, The earth was bleak and bare; No flowers, no birds, no nestlings, No sweet winds lingered there. Then someone told the story Of this piteous cursed tree And then I went another way For fear that I might see The helpless wretches dying, Swinging from that oak, Victims of the savage mob In sable hood and cloak."

The double lynching was an event that made news even beyond the Ozarks. *The New York Sun* carried the story of 100 masked men breaking down a jail in order to provide a

INSIDERS' TIP

The sassafras tree was valued by Ozarkers for the tea made from the roots dug in the spring, said to "thin the blood" and serve as a spring tonic. Tender green branches and leaves, used to beat a chicken roost, were said to kill lice with its pungent aroma. Green wood was used with hickory to smoke meats. The wood, half as light as the next lightest wood, was often used for feather weight but strong boat paddles.

necktie party for two people who were not African-Americans. It also made some members of the Bald Knobbers ashamed, disgusted, and revolted by their own lawlessness, and a number refused to participate further in revenge justice.

The Bald Knobbers became a vortex of activity. For every one who had quit, there were a dozen to take his place, and were often people less high-minded than the original organizers. Soon the membership was at 1,000 in the vigilante force. Infractions that could bring a warning or a flogging were expanded. No longer only horse thieves and murderers received midnight, masked visitors. Gamblers, drunkards, "loose women," those "living in sin" or accused of marital infidelity merited a flogging. Debtors, especially those who owed money to Bald Knobbers, might expect a midnight visit. Before the vigilante justice ran its course, 30 men and 4 women died at the hands of the Bald Knobbers. Many others were forced to flee their homes, and the Taney County nightriders made national news.

The Bald Knobbers were in control, and many believed they were corrupt. A planned audit of the county's books by an impartial, outside auditor never took place because on the night of December 19, 1885, someone broke into the brick, three-story Taney County courthouse, rebuilt within the walls of the structure gutted during the Civil War, and saturated its floors and stairways with kerosene and started a fire under the stairs. Many people blamed the Bald Knobbers.

Several events caused a reaction against the Bald Knobbers. One was Kinney's murder of Andrew Coggburn (which Kinney declared to be self-defense) just after the Bald Knobber leader had preached a sermon at the Oak Grove church. Another was the later murder of Sam Snapp, the only witness (but one who refused to testify) to Coggburn's shooting. The Anti-Bald Knobbers organized and formed a local militia. Some of their more neutral neighbors finally appealed to John S. Marmaduke, the Missouri governor. Marmaduke, fearful that warfare like that during the Rebellion would break out in southwest Missouri, sent his adjutant general in April 1886 to the area. J C. Jamison was ordered to make the Bald Knobbers, and the local militia that opposed them, disband; if they didn't, they'd face the consequences. The Missouri adjutant general had been a gold miner in California during the 1849 rush, had been a captain in William Walker's attempt to gain control of Nicaragua in 1855, and had served under Gen. Sterling Price in the Civil War. (Jamison's Confederate background was viewed with suspicion by the Bald Knobbers.) He was a seasoned soldier, and his demands could be backed up with state militia if need be.

On April 10, 1886, Jamison met with both sides of the conflict in Forsyth and informed each that they and their organizations were illegal. Jamison gave Nat Kinney 24 hours to disband, or he'd bring in the state militia to restore peace and order. Kinney asked for 48 hours, and Jamison agreed. A resolution was drawn up, signed, and forwarded to the governor. With the Bald Knobbers disbanded (though only on paper) the ill feelings by many toward Kinney did not disappear. Of course he'd been a target for killing from the beginning, but he was a formidable foe. Now, he never went anywhere without several armed bodyguards. When he preached now, Kinney would lay two Colt 45s—"Short Tom," a snub-barreled pistol, and "Long Tom," a long-barreled pistol—on the pulpit before he began his sermon. Anti-Bald Knobbers were known to offer prayers to God to strike Kinney dead; more practical ones offered to buy out his land holdings at a good price on the condition he leave Taney County forever. Kinney, however, had other ideas for his future. Since the Bald Knobbers controlled local elections, Kinney had his sights on becoming the area's next state representative.

The energy that had fueled the Bald Knobbers spawned similar enclaves in nearby counties. Christian County had its own version of the Bald Knobbers, though the territory toward the highland north lacked the balds of the White River country and forced the vigilantes to meet in caves. Dave "Bull Creek" Walker was the touchy fellow who was the driving force for that Bald Knobber franchise. The group was more inclined than the Taney County version to punish neighbors for smaller indiscretions, slights, and even jokes. The Christian County group used the "bull from Hell" mask now associated with the Bald Knobbers from murals by Steve Miller and by its use in the Shepherd of the Hills outdoor play (see our Attractions chapter.) The mask was a cotton corn sack whose corners were tied up with corks inside to form horns and whose eyeholes were stitched or painted with red or black. Some even spent the two bits that could buy a custom designed mask.

It was the Christian County Bald Knobbers who became involved in the episode that effectively ended the reign of the vigilante group. Bill Edens had compared a Bald Knobber to a sheep-killing dog. He had already been previously flogged once for his Anti-Bald Knobber comments.

The new insult was reported on the eve of the Bald Knobbers' disbanding, and it was decided by the hot-tempered, hard-drinking young son of Dave Walker, Bill, and his impressionable cronies to obtain revenge, in spite of Gen. J. C. Jamison's threat.

At 10:30 at night, the band surprised the sleeping Edens and his wife in their cabin. With them were his elderly parents, James and Elizabeth Edens, and another couple, Charles and Melvina Green, and the Greens' two small children. Threats were made, and gunfire erupted, leaving Edens and Charles Green dead. James Edens had been shot and his head bashed with an ax, but he was alive. The two young widows were left screaming as the children, unhurt in the spray of bullets, crawled through the blood toward the fireplace.

By now, there was an anti-vigilante feeling and local law enforcement authorities were not intimidated. Those responsible for the murders were hunted down, but some escaped. Those who were caught cooperated under pressure to bring their former cronies to justice. The four Bald Knobbers deemed most responsible for the outrage were sentenced to hang, including Dave Walker and his 16-year old son, Billy—dubbed "the Baby Bald Knobber" by the press. Others, including a Baptist minister (who conducted the funeral service for Edens and Green after the murders), were sentenced to prison terms. Before the hanging, the two Matthews brothers, put their woodcarving skills to use and escaped by whittling a key, but James was recaptured. The successful escapee, his brother Wiley, it is said, made his way to the frontier of Indian Territory in Oklahoma and lived out his life as a wood cutter, dying in 1937. His brother and other two compatriots weren't so lucky.

They were executed on the Ozark courthouse square, May 10, 1889 at 9:55 AM behind a stockade fence designed to provide some privacy and to keep at a respectable distance the thousands who had gathered—and to prevent a possible Bald Knobber rescue attempt. The trio had refused to have the hangings done by a professional hangman from Kansas City, and left the duty to the sheriff who had been a friend. Sheriff Johnson, it would be hoped, was a better sheriff than a hangman. He did not know how to calculate the proscribed drop based on the weight and build of the victims. Matthews was lucky and his neck was broken when the trap door was sprung. Dave Walker, his feet barely dragging the ground, was allowed to slowly strangle. The third, young Billy, escaped hanging during the first attempt when his head slipped out of the noose during the fall, only to be dragged back up the stairs of the scaffold and quickly rehanged. The professional hangman, a Mr. Daniel Binkley, commented to the *Kansas City Star* about the Ozark effort by a rank amateur, calling it "a horrible botch, crude and inartistic."

Meanwhile in Taney County between the sentencing and hangings in Ozark County, Nat Kinney was gunned down in a store. As the story goes, five Anti-Bald Knobbers rode to Springfield to consult Almus "Babe" Harrington, a prominent lawyer who lived on the James River. Asked what constituted a valid defense against first-degree murder, Harrington replied, "self-defense." The visitors paid the lawyer a $500 retainer in case one of them might be charged with murder, then retired to Harrington's barn and played a bizarre game of poker. The "loser" would have to kill Nat Kinney. A young farmer from Taney City (now Taneyville), Billy Miles, threw away enough good cards to lose the game.

INSIDERS' TIP

Artist and historian Scottie Snider has painted the Bald Knobber past in a mural on the wall of the Ozark City Hall.

The opportunity came soon enough. An Anti-Bald Knobber businessman, J. S. B. Berry, had to declare bankruptcy. Kinney was named as the receiver in Berry's bankruptcy filing. Berry had hired Billy Miles and his brother Jim as bodyguards because of a feud with a business friend of Kinney that had taken a nasty turn. Kinney was in the store, taking stock of the inventory for the bankruptcy sale when the two brothers entered. Kinney threatened them and reached for his revolver, but Billy drew his own .44 double-action Smith & Wesson. His first shot entered Kinney's left arm, breaking both bones and traveled up into his body. A second shot hit his heart. A total of five shots were fired, but none by Kinney. He dropped dead behind the store's counter. Reloading his gun, Billy stepped outside. "I have just killed Cap'n Kinney in self-defense," he told the gathering crowd of townspeople.

Billy and Jim Miles later shot it out with a Bald Knobber sheriff, Galba Branson (brother of Reuben, who named Branson) and his deputized gunfighter at an Independence Day picnic at Kirbyville, killing both. The fact that Billy and Jim Miles were acquitted of all three killings was evidence that the people and the judicial system were fed up with the Bald Knobbers. Years later, in 1912, Jim Miles—described as "always trigger happy"—shot and killed a Branson merchant in his store and was convicted of second degree murder and sentenced to 10 years.

It was years before things settled down, and gunfire was not an unusual sound in the Ozark hills. Old scores were often settled violently, and Taney County had gained an international reputation with its flirtation with vigilante justice, with accounts appearing in papers from coast to coast, as well as Paris, London, and Berlin. The coming of the railroad in 1906 and Harold Bell Wright's novel about the Ozarks the next year, *The Shepherd of the Hills,* in which the Bald Knobbers have a role, brought tourists to the area and opened a market for timbering and fruit crops. When the *Ozark Weekly News* remarked in an editorial that "Bald Knobberism is buried in oblivion, never to be resurrected again," the editorial writer was only half-right. Today on The Strip music lovers are attracted to the first music show to open in Branson, the Baldknobbers (one word for the music group), and they witness the vigilante group's terrorism in the outdoor dramatization of Wright's novel. The Mabe family, which makes up the Baldknobbers (see our Shows chapter) is an old Ozark family who have no nightriders in their ancestry, but those visitors who see the entertainment resurrection of the Bald Knobbers should be aware that what now passes for amusement has roots in the not-too-distant Ozark past.

Rivers, Railroads, and Roads

The Ozarks, liked a rugged butte sticking up in a flat landscape, saw most of the great wave of western migration pass around it, much the way a stampeding herd of buffalo parts and goes around an object, or the way the water of a river separates and flows around a boulder. The growth and development of the Ozarks can only be understood in context of the development of transportation that could take people in (and products out) of the Ozarks. In a sense, the story of the Ozarks is a story of the evolution and development of transportation, a story of rivers, railroads, and roads.

Travel had always been a challenge in the area, and the earliest settlers followed old Indian trails along the James and White rivers, or they used the rivers themselves, the area's first "roads." These early Native American trails either followed rivers or ridge lines; either way, it always made for meandering routes, and the roads developed from them were equally winding, and travel was not easy. River travel was no easier and always a tricky proposition because of danger of upset in shoals and rapids, and travel was largely limited to going downstream. As the population in the Ozarks grew and commerce increased, wagon roads became necessary. By the mid-1830s a road was developed between Springfield, then the seat of most of southwest Missouri and the junction of Swan Creek at the White River, the eventual townsite of Forsyth, so that Springfield could have access to the White River. Reflecting the confidence placed in the promise offered by steamboat navigation, the official seal of Taney County (formed in 1837) bore a steamboat in its center, and steamboat traffic became a major topic of conversation among those living in southwest Missouri and northwest Arkansas. There were high hopes that farmers would be able to send products to markets down river as well as take advantage of cheaper prices of products being brought in. The problem was two large shoals: Buffalo Shoals and Elbow Shoals. The *Eureka* finally conquered Buffalo Shoals in June, 1851, but was turned back at Elbow. In June the next year, the *Yohogony* finally conquered Elbow Shoals, but only after laboring a full day and unloading 300 sacks of salt below the shoals. It was the first steamer to make it to Forsyth, and designers of the Taney County seal had proved prophetic. Steamboat design and technology were improving, and with the development of high pressure boilers, these small, light paddle wheelers could make it up sometimes as far the mouth of the James but only during high water in the spring, and only by using both paddle wheel and a steam winch, hooking a cable to large trees above the shoal and pulling themselves over the rapid water and rock ledges. After the

HISTORY

Ozark-speak

A genuine hillbilly is a person who is shrewd enough and lazy enough to do it right the first time.

first steamboat made it as far as Forsyth, steamboat traffic on the upper White increased dramatically, but the Civil War brought river commerce to a halt. (An interesting and dramatic account of the White River steamer era can be found in *Steamboats and Ferries on the White River* by Duane Huddleston, Sammie Rose, and Pat Wood and can be found in many Branson book stores.)

In 1858 the Butterfield Overland Mail began operation as a result of an authorization bill introduced by Senator William Gwinn of California and Congressman John S. Phelps of Missouri and passed the year before. It started at Tipton in central Missouri and ran southwest through Stone County, into Arkansas, and then westward to California. By the time of the Civil War, the segment of this route in the Ozarks was called the Wire Road because of the telegraph wire strung along its route from Jefferson Barracks at St. Louis to Ft. Smith, Arkansas. The road was used by both sides in the Civil War, but little used for commercial purposes during the war because of danger of guerrillas and bushwhackers. Today's Interstate 44 which bisects the Ozarks incorporates lengthy portions of the Wire Road.

When commerce began to grow again, the 1870s north-south roads were cleared and widened for use by large freight wagons. The major freighting route in Stone County followed a well-established Native American trail called the Wilderness Road. From Springfield it more or less followed today's U.S. Hwy. 160 and Mo. 13 south through Spokane, Reeds Spring, and through Blue Eye to Berryville, Arkansas. In Taney County three freight roads connected outlying communities as far south of the White River as Harrison and Berryville to the Springfield railhead (Springfield had rail service by 1869) and the Chadwick railhead—as far south as a railroad could easily be built. Ponderous freight wagons traveled to market loaded with tobacco, cotton, animal pelts, and railroad ties and returned with merchandise to be sold in small stores along the route. The round trip could take as long as two weeks, with nights spent in campgrounds along the way or boarding houses in small towns. Roads wound back and forth, climbing steep hills and meandering along ridge tops; today's paved highways frequently follow these same routes, widened, upgraded, and paved. By the 1880s this road network required constant maintenance, and counties were divided into road districts. Men over 21 were scheduled to work 2 to 4 days in lieu of certain taxes. Those who did not work had to pay the tax. The roadwork involved keeping trees and brush out of the roadways, pulling out and sometimes blasting out rocks, filling mud holes, and establishing safe fords across creeks. Work was done with axes, shovels, crow bars, and mule-drawn scrapers called slips. To slice through roots that clogged drain ditches or humped roads, a "rooter" was used, a plow with two guide handles and single, sharp vertical cutting blade pulled by a team of four mules.

While roads were being developed, efforts continued to expand the railroad into the hilly Ozarks. By 1858, a railroad had been built from St. Louis to Sullivan, Missouri, and by 1861 tracks had been laid to Rolla. The outbreak of the war delayed further extension, but on April 21, 1870 citizens of Springfield greeted the *Cuba*, the first locomotive to steam into town on track laid only hours earlier. A line was extended to Chadwick in 1883, but the major problems of the hills to the south were still to be conquered. Plans and various routes had long been considered and debated, but had been opposed by steamboat interests. In addition the building of the necessary trestles and tunnels was considered too expensive. But the gradual increase in commerce made the second argument less plausible. Debate continued, but actual work did not begin until spring 1903 by the White River, Iron Mountain Railway Company to extend the line up the White River valley. But it was not until January 21, 1906 that the first puffing, noisy locomotive hauled a few cars down the Turkey Creek valley into the town of Hollister, a town whose population had grown to 250. The trains' steam whistles could be heard as far as 9 miles north of Branson, and so disturbed a relative of artist Rose O'Neill at Bonniebrook that he packed up and moved down to Hemmed-in Holler, a box canyon off the Buffalo River so he could have "some peace and quiet." The shrill whistles of the new locomotives had finally replaced the dying echoes of the steamboats' whistles on the river. With the coming of the railroad, steamboat traffic dwindled, and a new era dawned. Depots in Branson, Hollister, and Reeds Spring were soon stacked high

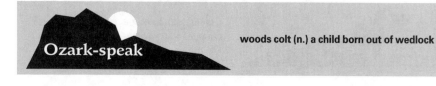

Ozark-speak

woods colt (n.) a child born out of wedlock

with departing goods: tons of mussel shells from the White River to be made into buttons; railroad ties, lumber and cordwood; cotton from gins at Kirbyville, Mincy, and Kissee Mills; tobacco; fruit, and livestock. Coming in the area were cheaper staples, new luxuries—and tourists.

The coming of the railroad in 1906 actually spurred growth in road building. In 1914 citizens of Reeds Spring and Branson formed two cooperative road districts to build a road between the two towns. The road crossed the slope of Dewey Bald and ran past the Shepherd of the Hills farm and Marble Cave. Sometimes the roadbed eroded into steep, rocky stairsteps, but the tree-lined road was often like a country lane. Certainly it made travel much easier between the two towns. In 1936 that route was reconstructed and later paved, becoming Highway 76. In days before the Table Rock Dam, the rocky goat pastures filled with trees and sprouts that sloped down to the creeks on each side of 76 could be had for less than a hundred dollars an acre—the price depending on whether the land came with or without the goats. Now that it has developed as the famous Strip in Branson, those prices are dream deals of the past. The road made the scrub land valuable (See our Real Estate chapter).

In building roads, the many creeks and rivers posed problems. Most creeks could be forded except during high water, but to cross the bigger White River, ferries were used, and there were more than two dozen ferry crossings on the White and the James rivers. Today only the Peel Ferry, which take cars across Bull Shoals Lake at Missouri Highway 125 south of Protem, is still operating. Ferries began disappearing in 1914 after four bridges were built across the White River. Arriving motorists voiced complaints about the general lack of bridges and the unpaved streets and roads, and in the mid-1920s when local businessmen and residents began buying cars, funds for road improvement became available, and in 1929 from local property taxes and state and federal sources. Bridges (often low water bridges) were built over the many creeks, and all streets and secondary roads were "paved" with gravel.

Upgrading of U.S. Hwy. 65 to concrete or asphalt from Springfield to the Arkansas border began in 1929, but work faltered during the Depression. It was completed eight years later as a WPA project to provide jobs for the unemployed. Rather than a two-day trip by wagon from Branson to Springfield, the journey over the new asphalt road could be completed by automobile in just under two hours. In the process of upgrading U.S. 65, both Branson's and Hollister's downtown areas were bypassed, with the highway (now U.S. Business 65) going a block west of Commercial Street and Main Street and east of Hollister's Downing Street. Merchants howled and predicted the death of both towns. The old steel bridge at the foot of Branson's Main Street was bypassed, and a new bridge was built across Taneycomo. New concrete bridges were also constructed over Roark and Turkey Creeks and over the railroad in Hollister.

Recognizing that adequate roads would be necessary for the area to develop Jack and Peter Herschend, developers of Silver Dollar City, lobbied hard for improvements to U.S. 65. In a continuing series of engineering feats begun in the mid 1960s and finished in the mid 1970s, a new U.S. 65 was cut through the mountains from Springfield to the Arkansas border, with new bridges being built over Roark Creek and Lake Taneycomo. The new, straighter U.S. 65 bypassed downtown Branson, again with the prediction that the town would die, but more tourist traffic allowed Branson to grow west along The Strip. The new Hwy. 65 made the area more accessible and increased the numbers of people who annually discover the Ozarks, and it allowed many Ozarkers to discover the rest of the country. Driving time to Branson from Springfield was cut to 30 minutes, and as those coming in today know, construction continues to make the entire drive four lanes. Branson will again be bypassed with the completion of the Ozark Mountain Highroad. Again, extensive lobbying by the Herschends for the project, especially Peter, caused local wags to dub the proposed bypass "Pete's Pike" because the loop west around Branson would have exits near Silver Dollar City, along with exits at Mo. Hwy. 248 (the old U.S. 65), Shepherd of the Hills, and The Strip.

Better roads brought more tourists. More tourists brought more development. More development made necessary more roads, and since 1992 the city of Branson has spent $37.5 million developing 16 miles of parallel and improved routes to provide shortcuts and alternatives to the often crowded Hwy. 76. One of the alternative routes was the Shepherd of the Hills Expressway, developed not by the government but by developer and owner of the Shepherd of the Hills Homestead, Gary Snadon.

In a film *The Visionaries*, Snadon remarked: "Back in the late 70s, the State Highway Department laid out this road and the gas shortage ruined funding for it. I happened to see the plans and started acquiring the land in '82 or '83 and started construction in '85. Missouri Hwy. 76 was carrying 27 or 28 thousand cars a day in 1985. The capacity of the highway was reached. Traffic would back up and simply stop. I had just purchased the Shepherd of the Hills Homestead, and we couldn't get people out to the farm to get their tickets." The Expressway has since been taken over and rebuilt by the state, and development along it almost equal to that of The Strip.

Visitors buy postcards that say, "All Roads Lead to Branson." That's not true, but the ones that do are less meandering and are much wider and straighter than they were just several decades ago. Many people resent roads so straight that people can drive like Hell through God's country, that something has been lost with the meandering. New and better roads have brought more people to see what the Ozarks and Branson has to offer, but it also has set off another round of development and improvement. It's been that way since the first settlements; only the pace has quickened. Though many decry the changes, plans for an airport to handle international traffic have been considered, and a high-speed rail link with the Springfield-Branson Regional airport is being looked into.

Where does the Ozarks story of rivers, railroads and roads end? Probably never. There will be just another chapter.

High Dams, High Hopes: Branson Grows

Just as important as roads to the development of the Branson area were dams. Substantial rainfall could bring the creeks up quickly, and they poured their flow into the White River, resulting in floods of devastating destruction to homes, towns, livestock, as well as a disruption of travel and transportation. It would be impossible for months at a time to cross the White, resulting in today's oddity of two schools just across the river from each other, Branson and Hollister Public Schools. There had been plans since the middle of the 19th century to build locks or dam the White River. In fact, it was a series of locks authorized by Congress on the middle section of the White which spurred railroad interests to build the railroad up the White River Valley.

Such projects were opposed by farmers (who would see the area's most fertile land inundated) and the developing float trip industry, headed up by successful entrepreneur Jim Owen and others, who would see business and way of life dependent on shoals, rapids, gravel bars, and bluffs disappear under a lake.

The first dam was Powersite Dam in 1913 which created Lake Taneycomo (named for Taney Co. Mo.) Authorized in 1911, it was the largest power dam in the country at the time: 50-feet high and 1,200-feet long. Though small by today's measures, its impact was large. It brought electricity to the Ozarks and made a river without rapids, backing up water for 22 miles to what is now the base of Table Rock Dam. It created the area's newest scenic view, and it caused the development of resort town Rockaway Beach, modeled and named for the Adirondack New York resort town. It catered to people who came for a taste of the Ozarks and to fish, boat, swim, and ski its warm waters. The dam changed the tourist industry, but it did nothing to hinder the devastating floods that periodically swept the Ozarks. When the White went on a rampage, 600,000 acres of cotton, tobacco, corn, and beans were flooded. In the 1930s, farmers had only one year of every three in which their crops weren't wiped out by high water. Low-lying areas of Branson and Hollister were frequently inundated by high water of the White.

Through the efforts of U.S Representative Dewey Short, a series of flood control dams were authorized. The first flood dam, in Arkansas, completed in 1951 was Bull Shoals Dam, which backed up water to the base of the earlier Powersite Dam in Missouri. Most of Forsyth was relocated from beside the White River, where it had existed for over a hundred years, to the top of Shadow Rock Bluff. Next was Table Rock Dam, completed in 1958. Gone was the threat of floods to Branson and Hollister, but the tourist industry developed over a half a century based on Taneycomo's warm waters also was gone. Water entering Taneycomo came from the bottom of the impounded lake, and it was a chilly 50 degrees—too cold for swimming, too cold for skiing, and too cold for the many species that had developed a thriving sports fishing industry. But it was just right for trout, and Taneycomo became a major trout attraction, with a large trout hatchery at the base of Table Rock Dam. (See our Recreation and the Great Outdoors chapter.)

The fourth dam, number three of the flood dams, was Beaver Dam, again in Arkansas, completed in 1965. The White River, beginning in Arkansas and making a huge oxbow in Missouri before again flowing back into Arkansas, no longer existed as a river in Missouri. It was now a series of lakes. It prevented the devastating floods that ravaged the upper White River valley, but it destroyed a meandering river, and it changed forever the makeup, character, and development of the Ozarks.

No longer did people come to the area for float fishing, but other types of fishing attracted even more fisher-tourists. In the 50s and 60s, these anglers brought their wives and children, in part because of the opening of the tiny theme park in 1960, Silver Dollar City, by Mary Herschend and her sons Jack and Peter. The musical entrepreneurial Mabe family filled a need by providing evening entertainment in an old building in downtown Branson. The Presley family opened their family music show in 1967 on what was to develop into The Strip. Their success brought others, including Roy Clark, the first nationally known artist to hang up a shingle on a Branson theater in 1983. Other stars found that having a permanent theater as a home was attractive; rather than being on the road going to audiences, it was easier to have the audiences come to them, and it allowed entertainers have some home life instead of a series of motel rooms on the road. Soon stars like Conway Twitty, BoxCar Willie, Kenny Rogers, Merle Haggard, Moe Bandy, and Mel Tillis were making Branson a rival of Nashville. They were joined by pop singers such as Andy Williams, Wayne Newton, The Platters, and Bobby Vinton. The fact that Branson was a country music Mecca inspired *60 Minutes* to do a feature on the boom town atmosphere, and the resulting national publicity produced what we call the Branson Boom and opened the way for other venues of entertainment, spawning the huge entertainment industry which now dominates Branson. The primary industry of sports fishing, though still an important reason for folks coming to Branson, is now secondary.

The growth and the publicity of the Branson Boom of the early 1990s produced another attraction: shopping. Now, as many people come to Branson to shop as come for the live music, and they frequently indulge in a little of both.

Branson has always been changing or developing in odd and unexpected ways. Cotton and tobacco growing are no longer important, and the gins and mills on the rivers are historic relics. The tie and lumber industry is of little importance. The mussel shell industry has come and gone. The canneries spawned by growing beans and tomatoes are vacant or have already disappeared. The old industries would boom, and then there would be a bust—until replaced by a different industry. At the core since the publication of Wright's *The Shepherd of the Hills* in 1907, however, has been the ever-growing, ever-developing, and ever-changing tourist industry. That primary industry is bigger than ever and much more diversified.

What does the future hold for Branson? Will it go the way of Eureka Springs after the spa boom of the 1890s or the tourist-attracting English village of Hollister at the turn of the last century or the Adirondacks-style Rockaway Beach and enter a long bust phase before another big boom? Who knows, but it will be a long and meandering path, much like the creeks and rivers which characterize the Ozarks.

Come and visit and observe. Come and stay—and meander with us.

HISTORY

Accommodations

LOOK FOR:
- On the Strip
- Off the Beaten Path
- Lake Resorts
- Kid-friendly Spots
- Sites for Large Groups

Price Code

Our price code is based on the average rate for a double occupancy room in peak season. You can expect to pay these rates September through December at hotels and motels. The resorts charge in-season rates June through August.

$	Less than $50
$$	$51 to $85
$$$	$86 to $110
$$$$	$110 and higher

The Tri-Lakes area now has more than 23,000 hotel and motel rooms, more than Kansas City with 17,000 and St. Louis with 15,000. A few years ago it was tough to find a room on the spur of the moment during peak season in the summer and fall. With an annual visitor count of more than 3.5 million in 1990 and fewer than 10,000 rooms, you had to make reservations well in advance in order to ensure space. Since 1990, however, the number of rooms has grown by 150 percent, but the number of visitors has only gone up 87 percent. Only rarely do visitors now have trouble finding a place to stay. The facilities on The Strip usually fill up first, but motels just a couple of blocks away may have plenty of rooms available even during our busiest months, October through December.

Some of the condominium resorts are still adding a handful of units, but other than that there has been relatively little new motel construction since 1995. One of the new facilities is the 304-room, upscale Chateau on the Lake, which opened in 1997. You can still find plenty of mom-and-pop places, most of them with fewer than 30 units. The owners are usually retired couples who came to the area 20 years ago from some place up north and decided to live out their years making friends with their overnight guests. Their places may not have a list of amenities as long as the major chains, but they take your business seriously and will go out of their way to see that you leave with a good impression of our town.

Visitors today also have a variety of national chains to choose from including Howard Johnson's, Sleep Inn, Holiday Inn, Comfort Inn, Travelogue, Best Western, Quality Inn, Residence Inn, Days Inn, Hampton Inn, Econo Lodge, and Super 8. We have profiled a few of them here, but you know what to generally expect.

Since they are located in the Live Music Capital of the World, many accommodations offer to set you up with show tickets. They find out what shows you want to see, then they call the theater box office to make your reservations. They hand you a voucher and charge the tickets to your room. You present the voucher at the box office and voila, you've got your seats. A few of the hotels charge a $2 to $3 fee per ticket for this service.

If you came to town more than 5 years ago in January or February trying to avoid peak season rates, you may not have found a soul in sight. That's all changed now with the efforts of a group of local businesses and the Branson/Lakes Area Chamber of Commerce. Their Hot Winter Fun promotion has really taken off in the last few years. Now more than 20 shows and dozens of attractions and major shopping centers stay open during the winter months including plenty of hotels. For a complete list of all Hot Winter Fun business members log on to www.hotwinterfun.com. Unless otherwise noted, the ones we have listed here stay open year round.

The room rates are very affordable in the winter months with some properties slashing their prices by as much as 40 percent. There's no such thing as a traffic jam in January, but you'd better come now before the whole world finds out.

Branson motel owners are setting their sights on families with children these days and have constructed playgrounds, miniature golf courses, volleyball, and basketball facilities as well as video arcades and small water parks as enticements. The biggest enticement of all is the kids-stay-free plan. A few places let children up to the age of 12 stay free in their parents' room. We have noted those that do. You can get baby cribs for free at some places and for as little as $5 at others. Little junior may have to leave Fluffy at home, though, since most places do not allow pets. Some charge extra for pets. Call first if you're thinking about bringing an animal friend.

Because many of the newer establishments were constructed after the Americans with Disabilities Act was implemented, you should be able to find handicapped accessible facilities. Unless otherwise noted, all the structures in this section with more than one floor have elevators.

All of the establishments listed here have both smoking and nonsmoking rooms unless otherwise noted. The Gazebo Inn, for one, is entirely smoke-free.

This chapter offers a representation of the full range of facilities available in the Tri-Lakes area. We can't tell you about them all, so if you need a little more help in deciding where to stay, we suggest you call the **Branson/Lakes Area Chamber of Commerce Welcome Center** at (800) 214-3661 or (417) 334-4136. Their computerized locator system allows them to pull up a list of all available lodging facilities with current vacancies. The system makes immediate reservations and prints driving directions to the facility. The system can also be used to make same-day attraction and show reservations. The one drawback to the system is that it is not an advance reservation system. If you need a room or ticket on a same day basis, it is a good system to use. After 5 PM call (417) 336-4466 for access to the Lodging Locator system. For advance reservations you may call the **Branson Lakes Area Lodging Association's Centralized Reservation System** toll free at (888) 238-8782. They have a comprehensive list of all the association's members with information on each establishment's rates, amenities, and policies.

Rates

The average rate for a room in Branson is a little more than $55 depending on whom you ask. Rates at individual properties can vary as much as 100 percent depending on what kind of room you choose. If you're looking for a package deal, many of the motels, resorts, and nightly condo rentals offer lodging, show tickets, and meals for one price. Some of them will even throw in show tickets if you stay a minimum number of nights.

In addition to offering a reduced rate for children, many of the places offer a senior citizen discount, an AARP discount, or an AAA discount. Be sure to ask when you make your reservations. When you get in town, stop at a brochure rack to pick up brochures for motels. Some of them contain coupons.

Checkout time for most of the hotels and motels is 11 AM or noon. The resorts ask that you be out a little earlier, at 10 AM.

A free continental breakfast is more the norm than the exception, but the fixings do vary from your standard cold cereal to homemade breads and muffins. Unless otherwise noted all continental breakfasts in this chapter are free. You can find a swimming pool at most every location and some of the suites come with Jacuzzis. One nice thing about Branson motels is that the majority of them don't charge for local calls.

If you want to compare amenities at a glance, you can request the free *Slip Away* magazine from the Branson/Lakes Area Chamber of Commerce at (417) 334-4136. They have a chart with all of their member properties listed.

ACCOMMODATIONS

Location

We have divided this chapter into two categories: Hotels and Motels, then Resorts and Condominiums. Within each category the facilities are arranged by location. The six subcategories in the Hotel and Motel section are North of Town, Shepherd of the Hills Expressway, East Half of The Strip, West Half of The Strip, Green Mountain Drive, and Just Off The Strip. The east-west dividing line we used is Wildwood Drive, which runs north and south and crosses The Strip beside the Bobby Vinton Blue Velvet Theatre and The Grand Palace.

If you know you'll be spending a lot of time at Silver Dollar City or Shepherd of the Hills

Homestead, it makes sense to stay on the west end of The Strip. Green Mountain Drive runs parallel to The Strip on the south. The properties in the Just Off The Strip category are mostly located near the west end of The Strip on Keeter Drive, Shaefer Drive, and Arlene Drive.

There are three categories for Resorts and Condominiums: Table Rock Lake, Lake Taneycomo, and Miscellaneous, which covers those that are not associated with one of the lakes.

We've put all the bed and breakfast facilities in their own chapter and campers will have to turn to the Campgrounds and RV Parks chapter for a list of amenities.

Hotels and Motels

North of Town

Branson Inn
$$ • U.S. Hwy. 65 and Mo. Hwy. 248
• (417) 334-5121, (800) 334-5121

West of U.S. Hwy 65 the Branson Inn's driveway meets Mo. Hwy. 248, just west of Planet Branson restaurant and nightclub (see the Nightlife chapter). You can walk to the Wayne Newton Theatre or if you want to check out the nightlife at Planet Branson, they will send their shuttle bus over to get you on weekends. Each of the Branson Inn's 270 rooms comes with two double beds, two queen beds, or one king bed; cable TV; a phone and a coffee pot. They serve continental breakfast. The hotel has baby cribs and rollaway beds for $5 extra. Facilities include an outdoor swimming pool, a kiddy pool, a hot tub, and laundry facilities. Right next door is the China Garden restaurant. (See our chapter on Restaurants for more information.)

Super 8 Branson North
$$ • 150 Church Rd.
• (417) 335-2543, (800) 335-2543
• www.bransonsuper8.com

From U.S. Hwy. 65 take the Bee Creek Road exit and go east. Follow Bee Creek Road to Church Road and turn left. You can't miss Super 8. They don't charge for the privacy at Super 8, but you'll still get plenty of it. Each of the 60 units comes with either two double beds, two queen beds or one king bed; cable TV; phone and front-door parking. A kitchenette unit has a king bed, full-size refrigerator, stove, and sink. You can get a free baby crib or a rollaway bed for $5 extra. There is an outdoor swimming pool with a slide and a picnic area with a barbecue grill. You can park your RV at Super 8 and

they serve complimentary coffee and muffins for breakfast. The motel offers vacation packages starting at around $275 for their couples' package, which includes three nights' lodging and tickets to three music shows. Kids stay free.

Shepherd of the Hills Expressway

Barrington Hotel
$$ • 263 Shepherd of the Hills Expy.
• (417) 334-8866, (800) 760-8866

Situated just west of the intersection of Shepherd of the Hills Expressway and Mo. Hwy. 248, the Barrington Hotel is easy to miss if you're not looking. It's easier to see if you're coming from Mo. Hwy. 248. Just look for the large pink letters on the brick four-story building. The lobby looks more like that of a winter lodge than a hotel with its stone fireplace, plank wood floor, green marble tile, and hanging tapestries. The rooms are decorated in burgundy and turquoise; each comes with queen bed, cable TV, and free local calls. There is an outdoor pool, hot tub, and some rooms come with Jacuzzis. Children under the age of 18 stay free. Coffee is served all day and you can get a deluxe continental breakfast in the morning.

Cascades Inn
$$ • 3226 Shepherd of the Hills Expy.
• (417) 335-8424, (800) 588-8424
• www.cascadesinn.com

Located just a stone's throw east of the Braschler Theater and not too much farther from the Shoji Tabuchi Theatre, Cascades Inn is a four-story, 160-room complex with an indoor pool and whirlpool, sauna and steam room, gift shop, game room, exercise room, and conference room for up to 100 people. The spacious rooms are outfitted in turquoise and pink

> **INSIDERS' TIP**
>
> While the summers don't generally get too hot in the Tri-Lakes area (a few days hover around 95 degrees in August) all of the listings in this chapter have air conditioning.

decor, matching their tropical theme. Each comes with two queen beds or one king bed. Each morning you can enjoy the inn's extended continental breakfast in the hospitality room. Children stay free.

Classic Motor Inn
$$ • 2384 Shepherd of the Hills Expy.
• (417) 334-6991, (800) 334-6991

What would you expect to find at the Classic Motor Inn? Classic cars perhaps? You can usually find some kind of '50s model on display in the lobby and occasionally even a few parked outside. That's basically where the theme ends. A room at the Classic Motor Inn has either two queen beds or one king bed. Some of their 62 rooms come with hot tubs. The inn has an outdoor pool, gift shop, coin laundry, and continental breakfast. All three outlet malls are no more than a five-minute drive away. The inn is closed in January.

Foxborough Inn
$$ • 235 Expressway Ln.
• (417) 335-4369, (800) 335-4369
• www.foxboroughinn.com

Located just off the east-end of Shepherd of the Hills Expressway, the Foxborough Inn's 175 rooms have spectacular views of an as-yet-undeveloped wooded hillside. Because it's off the main road, you may miss the inn if you're not watching carefully. From Mo. Hwy. 248 turn left at the second stoplight on Shepherd of the Hills Expy. It's on the left just past The Grand Mansion. If you're traveling east on Shepherd of the Hills, turn left on Expressway Ln. before you come to the stoplight at Mo. Hwy. 248. The inn will be on the right just before The Grand Mansion.

The Foxborough features a snack bar that is open from 6 AM until midnight serving a continental breakfast and a light dinner after the shows. There is a coin-operated laundry, outdoor swimming pool, and a gift shop. A room comes with two queen beds or one king bed, cable TV (close-captioned), and phone. Some rooms have Jacuzzis. The Foxborough is closed in January.

Orange Blossom Inn
$$ • 3355 Shepherd of the Hills Expy.
• (417) 336-6600, (800) 753-3711

If you're coming to see the man with the fiddle, Shoji Tabuchi that is, you can stay right across the street from his theater at the 77-unit Orange Blossom Inn. It's closed January through March, but so is Shoji's theater. Each room has two queen beds or one king bed, a color TV, and phone. Some rooms have two-person Jacuzzis. There is an outdoor pool and hot tub. Coffee is served in the lobby along with a free continental breakfast. If there's a long line at the Shoji Tabuchi Theatre, you can ask the front desk to help you make reservations for his show and many others. The level parking lot has a dump station for motor coaches.

Tara Inn
$$ • 245 Shepherd of the Hills Expy.
• (417) 334-8272, (800) 525-8272

If you can get to the Barrington Hotel, you can find the Tara Inn. It's located right next door. Since it's off the beaten path, there is very little drive-by traffic. The rooms are tastefully decorated with deep purples and greens. The four-poster bed in the king suite even has a satin bedspread. Dried flower arrangements are scattered about the dark cherry furniture. All king suites come with Jacuzzis and dark wood-beamed ceilings. The king suites have honeymoon appeal and families fit nicely into their two-room suites featuring a living area with large windows and French doors opening to the outdoor swimming pool area. A standard double room has a color TV, a sitting area, and phone. The inn serves a deluxe continental breakfast each morning. The Tara Inn is closed January and February.

The Guest House Hotel
$$ • 165 Expressway Ln.
• (417) 336-3132, (800) 383-3132

The first thing you'll notice when you step inside The Guest House is the detailed foxhunting scene painted on the wall behind the front desk. The lobby has a massive fireplace and beautiful wood bookshelves reaching to the ceiling. The décor throughout the 98 rooms is equally impressive. The color scheme includes rich hunter green and cranberry. A standard room comes with one king or two queen beds, cable TV, and phone. Some suites have Jacuzzis. Each of the furnished apartments has two bedrooms, two baths, a kitchen, a Jacuzzi, and a washer and dryer. Ask about long-term rates. There is an outdoor swimming pool and

INSIDERS' TIP
Need a place to sit down? Branson has a combined total of 106,250 motel rooms, restaurant seats, and theater seats.

hot tub. The hotel serves a continental breakfast in the breakfast room. Children under the age of 18 stay free. The Guest House is closed January and February.

East Half of The Strip

Edgewood Motel and Reunion Center
$$ • 1700 76 Country Blvd.
• **(417) 334-1000, (800) 641-4106**
Nestled on 27 wooded acres across from the Dixie Stampede dinner attraction (see our Attractions Chapter), the Edgewood Motel and Reunion Center has 297 rooms, two swimming pools, a gift shop, coin-operated laundry, and an outdoor picnic area with a meeting room/reunion center for up to 75 people. A deluxe room comes with a king-sized bed or two queen-sized beds, a sofa bed, and a sitting area. For breakfast you can walk on over to the Home Cannery Restaurant, which is adjacent to the motel (see our chapter on Restaurants). If you need assistance with show tickets, meals, or attractions, Edgewood Receptive Services can put together a package vacation tailored to your specifications. You can ask the front desk clerk for help or call (800) 627-4596. The motel is closed in January.

Gazebo Inn
$$ • 2424 76 Country Blvd.
• **(417) 335-3826, (800) 873-7990**
The Gazebo Inn looks more like a quaint little bed and breakfast than a hotel. The pale pink and green Victorian decor is carried throughout all 73 rooms. The honeymoon suites feature marble Jacuzzis with separate showers, sitting areas, and balconies overlooking The Strip in front, or the outdoor swimming pool in back. The family suite has two bedrooms and a kitchenette. The standard room comes with two queen beds, a writing desk, cable TV, and a phone. All rooms are non-smoking.

Grand Country Inn
$$ • 1945 76 Country Blvd.
• **(417) 335-3535, (800) 828-9068**
• **www.grandcountry.com**
Who needs to fight the traffic on The Strip when you can stay at the Grand Country Inn?

You can do your shopping at the Grand Country Market (see our chapter on Shopping), take in one of four live music shows at the 76 Music Hall (see our chapter on The Shows), eat at the Grand Country Buffet, and play a round of indoor miniature golf. The Splash Country Water Park, free to Grand Country Inn guests, features a huge wading pool, water slide, and lots of other neat water elements the kids will enjoy, plus shaded seating areas for mom and dad. You can do it all at Grand Country adjacent to the 319-room Grand Country Inn. Each room comes with one king bed or two queen beds, cable TV, telephone, and a beautiful view of the hillside. Relax year round in the indoor pool or cool off in the outdoor pool and spa in the summer. The staff will customize a vacation package including show tickets, meals, lodging, and attractions for one price.

> ## INSIDERS' TIP
> Some of the resorts post flyers about upcoming fishing tournaments on Table Rock Lake and Lake Taneycomo. They may even offer free registration if you stay a minimum number of nights.

Outback Roadhouse Motel & Suites
$$ • 1910 76 Country Blvd.
• **(417) 334-7200, (800) 562-0622**
• **www.outbackbranson.com**
Can't afford a secluded lakeside resort? The Outback Roadhouse Motel & Suites is affordable and secluded. You'll have to settle for a heated outdoor pool, though. Located a good 500 yards off The Strip next to the Outback Steak & Oyster Bar (see our Restaurants chapter) and the Outback Pub (see our Nightlife chapter), the motel sits on 15 private acres. There are no hiking trails but the motel encourages guests to explore the wooded terrain. The complex features Jacuzzi suites with two bedrooms, family suites with three beds, a kitchenette, Whirlpool tub, wet bar, refrigerator, and microwave. The standard room comes with one or two queen beds, cable TV, and phone. They serve a hot continental breakfast. After your hike around the property relax in their hot tub and sauna. Get 10 percent off your room if you make your reservations online through the motel's website.

Shadowbrook Motel
$$ • 1610 76 Country Blvd.
• **(417) 334-4173, (800) 641-4600**
One of the Edgewood Motel and Reunion Center properties, the 60-room Shadowbrook Motel sits at the corner of Mo. Hwy. 76 and Fall Creek Road. All of the rooms have a view

The Dutch Country Inn features Jacuzzis for Mom and Dad, and a nearby play area for children called Kids Kountry.

of the 27-acre park complete with picnic tables. You can get a complimentary continental breakfast or take the shuttle to the Home Cannery Restaurant. The motel is closed in January and February. Since the motel sits off the busy Strip, you won't have to worry too much about noise.

West Half of The Strip

BoxCar Willie Motel No.1 and No.2
$ • 3454 76 Country Blvd.
• (417) 334-8873, (800) 942-4626
$ • 360 Schaefer Dr.
• (417) 336-3878, (800) 942-4626

The BoxCar Willie Theatre has become The Dutton Family Theatre, but the BoxCar Willie Motels still remain a popular place for folks to come and feel a little closer to their favorite hobo who is no more. BoxCar Willie Motel No.1 is right behind The Dutton Theatre and No.2 is just one block south on Schaefer Drive. The rate is the same at both places, so take your pick. No.1 doesn't have a pool, but No.2 has one inside. A room at either place comes with two queen beds or one king bed, cable TV, and phone. No.2 has Jacuzzi suites. Both places offer a continental breakfast. It's served in a caboose at No.1. Guests at No.2 can park at No.1 and walk to the many attractions on the west end of The Strip.

Dutch Kountry Inn
$$ • 2425 76 Country Blvd.
• (417) 335-2100, (800) 541-5660

Step into a Dutch villa atmosphere at the Dutch Kountry Inn right next to the Tanger Outlet Mall, Kids Kountry, The Track, and The Lost Silver Mine miniature golf course. While the kids are out entertaining themselves, mom and dad can relax in the honeymoon suite's two-person Jacuzzi or take a snooze in its king waterbed. If togetherness is what your family is all about, you can stay in the two-bedroom, 1½ bathroom family loft suite. A standard room comes with two double beds or a king-size bed, cable TV, phones, and a sitting area. There is an outdoor swimming pool, and Peppercorn's Restaurant and Bakery is right next door (see our chapter on Restaurants) or you can enjoy their continental breakfast. With 150 rooms and a windmill above the lobby, you can't help but notice this one.

Fiddlers Inn
$$ • 3522 76 Country Blvd.
• (417) 334-2212, (800) 544-6483

The Fiddlers Inn is right next door to the Legends Family Theatre and has 78 units that come with double beds, two queen beds or one king bed, cable TV, and phones. There is an outdoor swimming pool and an above ground hot tub. They serve a free deluxe continental breakfast and they have a coin laundry facility. The front desk staff will help you make your show ticket reservations as well.

Hi-Ho Motor Inn
$ • 3325 76 Country Blvd.
• (417) 334-2204

The Hi-Ho Motor Inn has the right location and a good price. It's within easy walking distance of the Jim Stafford Theatre, the Mickey Gilley Theatre, and dozens of restaurants and retail stores. This 56-unit inn has two-room family units that come with two double beds and one king bed. Each standard room has two double beds, cable TV, and phones. The inn even has honeymoon Jacuzzi suites. There is a good-sized outdoor pool and plenty of level parking. Kids will be happy to know that The Track is right next door. (See our Kidstuff chapter.)

Hotel Grand Victorian
$$$ • 2325 76 Country Blvd.
• (417) 336-2935, (800) 324-8751

Just as the name implies, the Hotel Grand Victorian abounds with Victorian style from the Italian marble in the two-story lobby, to the four-poster bed in the Presidential Suite, to the rich green and burgundy room decorations. Tasteful flower arrangements and green plants fill the lobby and sitting room. The Presidential Suite has a marble Jacuzzi, four-poster bed, couch, refrigerator, and microwave. Some of the 152 rooms have private balconies and Jacuzzis. There are indoor and outdoor swimming pools, an exercise room with video games and a breakfast area where you will find muffins, bagels, donuts, fresh fruit, juice, and coffee each morning. There's even a fireplace in the gazebo pool house. The Tanger Outlet Mall, The Grand Palace, Andy Williams Moon River Theatre, Bobby Vinton Blue Velvet Theatre, Ride the Ducks, and Wal-Mart are within a stone's throw.

Lodge of the Ozarks Entertainment Complex
$$$ • 3431 76 Country Blvd.
• (417) 334-7535, (800) 213-2584
• www.lodgeoftheozarks.com

Built more than 15 years ago, the Lodge of the Ozarks has been called the "classiest hotel in Branson" by *People* magazine. When you step inside the two-story lobby, you are surrounded by elegance. Just down the corridor you'll find the hair salon, three gift shops, The Rafters Restaurant, Club Celebrity, and the Hughes Brothers Celebrity Theatre. (See our chapters on Nightlife and The Shows.) The Lodge has 190 rooms with a meeting facility that can hold up to 800 people. This is one of the largest convention sites in Branson with three large meeting rooms and on-site catering.

The hotel rooms are spacious and each has queen-size beds, cable TV, and a couch. Some rooms have Jacuzzis, refrigerators, wet bars, and extra vanities. You can look down on the indoor pool and hot tub from the second and third floors. During your stay you can enjoy room service, a continental breakfast, or make an appointment with their massage therapist. Bob and Elizabeth Dole stayed at the Lodge on his first full day of presidential campaigning after resigning from the Senate in 1996.

Melody Lane Inn
$$ • 2821 76 Country Blvd.
• (417) 334-8598, (600) 338-8598
• www.palaceinn.com/melodylane

Right next door to the Baldknobbers Jamboree Theatre and across the street from The Palace Inn, the Melody Lane Inn has 140 spacious rooms, each of which comes with either a king or two queen beds, cable TV, and a phone. There is a coin-operated laundry facility and all rooms have a view of the outdoor swimming pool and Jacuzzi. Some rooms adjoin so you can keep an eye on the kids. The inn provides shuttle service to local attractions. The Melody Lane Coffee Shop serves a light breakfast each morning. The inn is closed in January and February.

Queen Anne I and II
$$ • 3510 76 Country Blvd.
• (417) 335-8100, (800) 229-3170
$$ • 245 Schaefer Dr.
• (417) 335-8101, (800) 229-3170

Queen Anne I sits right on The Strip near The Dutton Family Theatre across from White Water, and Queen Anne II is just two blocks south on Schaefer Drive. No.2 offers a little more privacy but all the amenities of No.1. During the Ozark Mountain Christmas season, both motels are decorated with white lights to show off their Victorian rooflines. Both motels have small but clean rooms with two doubles,

INSIDERS' TIP

Trying to decide which to pack—long sleeves or shorts sleeves. Call the WeatherFone at (417) 336-5000 anytime to get a current temperature in Branson.

Guests at The Palace Inn enjoy a bird's eye view of The Strip from private balconies.

Photo: Branson/Lakes Area Chamber of Commerce

two queens, or one king bed. Both also have cable television, outdoor swimming pools, and free coffee. The suites at both places have full kitchens. Guests at No.2 may park at No.1 and walk to the shows and attractions on The Strip. Children stay free.

The Palace Inn
$$ • 2820 76 Country Blvd.
• **(417) 334-7666, (800) 725-2236**
• **www.palaceinn.com**

One of Branson's tallest hotels, the five story pink and white Palace Inn is quite an impressive sight. From your private balcony overlooking The Strip you can conduct your own study of Branson traffic numbers.

The two-story lobby gets the award for having the largest flower-patterned wallpaper of any in town. Those pink flowers will really catch your eye. They caught the eye of President George Bush when he stayed there in '92, and the late presidential hopeful Pat Paulsen even announced his candidacy from the lobby during a press conference in '96. In 2000 the Miss USA delegates stayed here.

The 101 hotel rooms have king or queen beds, cable TV, phones, coffee machines, and very high ceilings. Some rooms have Jacuzzis. The 65 less expensive motel units in the South Tower all have refrigerators. The Palace Inn has a penthouse and a two-bedroom family suite that sleeps eight and a honeymoon suite. There is an indoor pool with a whirlpool and an outdoor pool with a whirlpool and sun deck. You can order from room service, visit the cocktail lounge, and enjoy a continental breakfast. They also have coin-operated laundry facilities, a beauty shop, and a massage therapist on staff.

When you're ready for a fine casual dining experience, check out Buckingham's Restaurant and Oasis Lounge, which is in the hotel. (For more information about Buckingham's and the Oasis Lounge, check our Restaurants and Nightlife chapters.) Even if you're not hungry you've got to see the safari themed décor.

The hotel owns a limousine so you can get a ride to just about any place in town. They'll even shuttle you to and from the M. Graham Clark Airport at College of the Ozarks.

The Plantation Inn & Restaurant
$$ • 3460 76 Country Blvd.
• **(417) 334-3600, (800) 324-6748**

The Plantation Inn has 78 spacious rooms, each with one or two beds, cable TV, and free local calls. The inn also has an outdoor swimming pool. Children stay free. You can get complimentary coffee in the lobby or hop on over to The Plantation restaurant for an all-out break-fast feast. (See our chapter on Restaurants for more information.) If you need assistance with your vacation plans, The Plantation will put together a package for one low price. The Plantation Inn is closed in January and February.

Green Mountain Drive

Alpenrose Inn
$ • 2875 Green Mountain Dr.
• **(417) 336-4600, (800) 324-9494**

An enchanting Bavarian setting is what you'll find at the Alpenrose Inn. In addition to the Alpine mural, you'll see a number of original pieces of art colorfully decorating the two-story lobby. Created by local artists, the works are all for sale. Each of the 50 rooms at the Alpenrose Inn comes with cable TV, phones, and king or two queen beds. In the summer you can enjoy the outdoor pool and sun deck. Children aged 11 and younger stay free and they'll be happy to know that the Pirate's Cove miniature golf course is right next door. (See our Kidstuff chapter for more on Pirate's Cove.) Alpenrose Inn is closed in January and February.

Branson's Best
$ • 3150 Green Mountain Dr.
• **(417) 336-2378, (800) 404-5013**
• **www.branson.net/best**

For you late risers, Branson's Best has a 1 PM checkout time. You'll need it if you stayed up all night drinking the free coffee they serve 24 hours a day. Each of their 65 rooms comes with two queen beds or one king bed, cable TV, and phones. Baby cribs are no extra charge and children under the age of 18 stay free with a parent. The inn has an outdoor swimming pool and a 16-item continental breakfast, including donuts, bagels, juice, and cereal. Each evening you may enjoy free ice cream and hot cobbler. Branson's Best is located on Green Mountain Drive near the intersection of Mo. Hwy. 165. The inn is closed in January and February.

Grand Oaks Hotel
$$$ • 2315 Green Mountain Dr.
• **(417) 336-6423, (800) 553-6423**

This 112-unit hotel is within walking distance of the 18-hole Thousand Hills Golf Course (see our chapter on Recreation and the Outdoors). Situated on Green Mountain Drive just south of The Strip, the Grand Oaks Hotel is close to the Andy Williams Moon River The-

atre, The Grand Palace, the Grand Village, Tanger Outlet Mall, and dozens of restaurants. A deluxe room comes with a king bed or two queen beds, two sink vanities, Jacuzzi, and living room. The family suites sleep up to six. If you're waiting on your clothes to dry in the coin-operated laundry facility, you can check out the game room or burn off a little Ozark cookin' in the exercise room. The formal meeting room, with its audiovisual capabilities, makes the Grand Oaks Hotel a great corporate conference site.

Hampton Inn
$$ • 2350 Green Mountain Dr.
• **(417) 334-6500, (800) 443-6504**

Located behind The Grand Palace and the Andy Williams Moon River Theatre, the Hampton Inn is a two-story 113-room motel with an impressive lobby featuring a crystal chandelier, huge windows, and rich green walls and floor tile. The rooms are quite large, and each comes with two queen beds or one king bed, cable TV, and phone. Some rooms connect and the king suites have hot tubs. There is an indoor pool. The inn serves a continental breakfast and boasts a 100 percent satisfaction guarantee or you receive a free night's stay.

Settle Inn Resort and Conference Center
$$$ • 3050 Green Mountain Dr.
• **(417) 335-4700, (800) 677-6906**
• **www.bransonsettleinn.com**

As you drive along Green Mountain Drive just look for the white castle on the hill. With 300 rooms it's hard to miss the Settle Inn. Known for its 40 themed suites, the Settle Inn is an attraction all its own. If you're willing to pay a little more than the basic rate, around $100 or so, you can stay in the Safari suite complete with huge green plants, an African mural, and bamboo furniture. Or you can take a trip to New York in the Big Apple suite with its Statue of Liberty mural. If you're looking for a period theme, try the Garden of Eden suite. Adam and Eve would feel right at home. Or if you're into something a little more contemporary, try the Medieval suite complete with armored knight. If you haven't remodeled your home in the last 30 years, you'll feel at ease in the 1970s Saturday Night Fever suite. Each suite comes with a whirlpool, plenty of furniture, color TV (even though somewhat out of place in the Garden of Eden and Medieval suites), and a phone. The regular rooms come with queen or king beds and cherry wood furniture.

The list of amenities at Settle Inn runs the full range and includes a deluxe continental breakfast, 24-hour coffee service, two indoor pools and spas open 24 hours, tanning beds, video arcade, guest laundry and dry cleaning service, and an outside gazebo and sun deck. You can get an evening snack in the Garden Cafe and Lounge, or if you're an early riser, you can catch the free morning musical variety show at 8 AM in the Stonehenge Banquet Room. Settle Inn's 7,000 square-foot conference center has meeting space for up to 500. They'll be happy to have your event catered.

Each week Who Dunnit? Productions presents a comedy Murder Mystery Dinner Theatre. Guests try to catch the culprit by analyzing clues, interviewing suspects and voting on whom they think perpetrated the crime.

Just Off The Strip

Days Inn Branson
$$ • 3524 Keeter St.
• (417) 334-5544, (800) 334-7858
With 425 rooms conveniently located just off the west end of The Strip on Keeter Street, the Days Inn is one of the largest facilities in Branson. The Inn's acreage is nicely landscaped and the rooms all have a view of the south side of The Strip. Each room has two double beds or one king bed, cable TV, and phones. Some rooms connect. There is an outdoor swimming pool, wading pool, spa, and children's playground. There is a guest laundry facility, and you can get a room with a refrigerator and microwave if you desire. A continental breakfast is served in the lobby or you can get a hot meal at The Green Mountain Cafe, which is located on the property. The cafe serves standard American fare for breakfast, lunch, and dinner. Children stay in the motel and eat for free at the cafe.

Econo Lodge
$$ • 230 S. Widwood Dr.
• (417) 336-4849, (800) 553-2666
• www.econolodge.com
The Econo Lodge is just far enough off The Strip not to be bothered by the flashing neon theater marquees but close enough to walk to The Grand Palace, Andy Williams Moon River Theatre, and the Bobby Vinton Blue Velvet

Theatre. If you get hungry you can take an even shorter stroll to the Lone Star Steakhouse or The Pasta Grill. Each of the 67 rooms comes with two queen beds or one king bed, cable TV, and a phone. Some rooms have Jacuzzis. There is an outdoor swimming pool and spa as well as a guest laundry facility. The continental breakfast is served in the lobby each morning. Children under the age of 18 stay free with their parents.

Mountain Music Inn
$$ • 300 Schaefer Dr.
• (417) 335-6625, (800) 888-6933
• www.mountainmusicinn.com
Located just two blocks off The Strip, the Mountain Music Inn is a three-story 140-room complex with large windows and a huge indoor pool. The 75-person meeting room and coffee shop overlook the pool and Jacuzzi. The coffee shop stays open until midnight. The rooms feature a double vanity, two queen beds or one king bed, cable TV, and phones. Some rooms have Jacuzzis. There is an exercise room and an outdoor pool. The deluxe continental breakfast includes fresh homemade muffins, cinnamon rolls, bagels, toast, cereal, fruit, oatmeal, and juice. Children stay free with their parents. The parking lot is flat and tastefully landscaped. The concierge will reserve tickets to your favorite show.

Polar Bear Inn
$$ • 3545 Arlene Dr.
• (417) 336-5663, (800) 699-2327
• www.polarbearinn.com
This 40-unit inn carries the polar bear theme to new heights. All of the rooms have framed polar bear art hanging on the walls, and you may even run into the bow tie wearing polar bear roaming through the halls chatting with guests. You can get your polar bear T-shirt in the gift shop. The standard room comes with two queen beds or one king bed, cable TV, VCR, and phone. You can rent movies in the lobby. Refrigerators and rollaway beds are available for $5. Children aged 16 and younger stay free with an adult. There is an indoor heated pool and spa as well as an outdoor pool nestled against a wooded lot. A continental breakfast is served each morning in the TV area. The

INSIDERS' TIP
Most of the area's motels receive The Vacation Channel programming (see our Media chapter). It's on Branson cable channel 6 24 hours a day and is a great source of information on the music shows, traffic routes, and local history.

ACCOMMODATIONS

Polar Bear Inn took the first-place award in the Branson Area Festival of Lights animated display category in 1996.

To get there from The Strip, turn south on Keeter Street across from White Water. Turn right at the first stop sign (you'll still be on Keeter Street). The Polar Bear Inn is just around the corner from Shenanigans RV Park and is closed in January.

Radisson Hotel
$$$ • 120 S. Wildwood Dr.
• (417) 335-5767, (800) 333-3333
• www.radisson.com

The Radisson Hotel towers above the Branson skyline with 10 stories and 500 rooms. Within easy walking distance are The Grand Palace, Bobby Vinton Blue Velvet Theatre, and the Andy Williams Moon River Theatre. The Branson Strip Bar and Grill is located on the ground floor and provides room service. The 76 Saloon is right next door and is a great place to go to have a drink and watch a little TV. The 76 Café features desserts and specialty coffees.

Each spacious room has a coffee maker, dataport, hair dryer, ironing board, voice mail telephone, and satellite television with in-room movies. The top floor houses the penthouse, presidential, and executive suites, which go for around $200 a night. Each suite has its own Jacuzzi. You also get a complimentary continental breakfast, evening cocktails, and hors d' oeuvres in the pricier suites.

The hotel has a swimming pool with half of it inside and half of it outside. Other upscale amenities include a hot tub, sauna, exercise room, gift shop, game room, salon, and boutique. If you're feeling tense after your trip you can ask for a massage at the salon. The desk personnel will be happy to arrange show reservations for you and you can also visit the concierge desk to find out what's going on in town during your visit.

The ground floor is designated as meeting space and can accommodate up to 600 people for catered banquets. The sunken lobby has a number of overstuffed chairs and couches as well as a piano if you're in the mood to entertain.

Sleep Inn
$$ • 210 S. Wildwood Dr.
• (417) 336-3770, (800) 221-2222

This 68-room facility is just 5 miles from Silver Dollar City. Each room comes with two queen beds or one king bed, cable TV, phone, and oversized shower. There is an outdoor swimming pool and courtyard. You can get a hearty continental breakfast in the lobby each morning and then head on over to one of the nearby souvenir shops for some down and dirty shopping. If you're interested in shows, you can ask the front desk staff to help make your reservations.

Spinning Wheel Inn
$ • 235 Schaefer Dr.
• (417) 334-7746, (800) 215-7746

The Spinning Wheel Inn has all the amenities a family on a budget might want. There is a large fenced-in outdoor swimming pool, a children's playground, and a shaded park with picnic tables. Some of the rooms even come with three beds. Plus, children under the age of 16 get to stay in their parents' room for free. The rooms are a bit small but well kept. Each room has cable TV, a phone, and either two queen beds or one king bed. The inn provides a continental breakfast in the lobby consisting of donuts, coffee, and juice. The staff will help you make your show ticket reservations. Be sure to pick up one of their brochures. Sometimes they have coupons attached to the back worth as much as $5 off. The Spinning Wheel Inn is closed January through March.

Resorts and Condominiums

Resorts and condominiums in the Branson area cater to anglers, golfers, children, and show buffs alike. The range of amenities at these places runs the full range. The only thing they don't offer is salt water. You can rent fishing boats, pontoon boats, Jet Skis, or canoes from the resorts with marinas. They have professional fishing guides who will go along to help you

INSIDERS' TIP

Nearby Eureka Springs, Arkansas has long been known as a major honeymoon destination. Now the Branson/Lakes Area Chamber of Commerce is working to attract more newlyweds. Give them a call at (417) 334-4136 and they'll pass along tips for planning a wedding or honeymoon in Branson.

navigate unfamiliar territory while telling you stories about the good old days.

The rooms at these places range from your basic cabin to 1,000-square-foot deluxe condos with Jacuzzis, VCRs, and cherry wood furnishings. The outdoor activities range from sand volleyball to basketball to shuffleboard to horseback riding. Many of the places have exercise facilities for the truly disciplined and free deluxe continental breakfasts for the truly undisciplined. Whatever your taste, the Branson area's resorts and condominiums hit the spot.

Lake Taneycomo

Lakeshore Resort
$$ • 1773 Lakeshore Dr.
• (417) 334-6262, (800) 583-6101

Lake Taneycomo has been ranked one of the top five trout lakes in the nation and the popularity of the fishing resorts on Lakeshore Drive attest to that fact. Lakeshore Drive runs parallel along the bank of Lake Taneycomo just across from downtown Branson. Follow Mo. Business 65 (Veterans Blvd.) east across the Taneycomo Bridge and look for Lakeshore Drive immediately on your left. Lakeshore Resort, as it is appropriately called, is the place of choice among die-hard anglers. It has a marina with boats for rent, and it also provides guide service. The units can hold a family of up to 10 in their 3 bedroom cottages. Some of the cottages have fireplaces, living rooms, kitchenettes, and Jacuzzis. They all come with cable TV. Outside there is a children's play area and a swimming pool. The picnic tables are just a stone's throw from the water.

Sammy Lane Resort
$$, no credit cards • 320 E. Main St.
• (417) 334-3253

Many businesses in the Branson area are named after characters from Harold Bell Wright's famous novel, *The Shepherd of the Hills*. The Sammy Lane Resort took the name of the book's heroine when it opened in 1924, which makes it the oldest resort in Branson. With 800 feet of Lake Taneycomo shoreline, the resort offers visitors a night's stay in the Log Lodge with its two-room suites plus kitchenette, the cozy two-bedroom cottages, or the cabins, which sleep up to eight. Each unit comes with cable TV, a barbecue grill, and phone. Baby cribs are $1. Since Lake Taneycomo is a cold-water lake, you'll probably want to cool off instead in their 150' x 60' 330,000-gallon swimming pool,

the largest private pool in the Ozarks, or relax in the whirlpool.

The grounds at Sammy Lane are perfect for strolling on a hot summer's afternoon. You can take refuge under one of the many large shade trees if you get too hot or you can rent a boat at their boat dock and go for a spin on the lake. Be sure to examine the masonry work on the log cabins. Sammy Lane Resort was entered into the National Register of Historic Places in 1993. It is located just across the railroad tracks in downtown Branson. Just look for the rock entry sign. The resort is closed in January and February.

Sunterra's Fall Creek Resort
$$$ • 1 Fall Creek Dr.
• (417) 334-6404, (800) 562-6636

Follow Mo. Hwy. 165 south from The Strip past the intersection of Fall Creek Road (notice that we have a Fall Creek Drive and a Fall Creek Road). Fall Creek Drive will be on your left before you get to the Welk Resort Center.

With 250 condominiums and motel rooms and a long list of lake amenities, Fall Creek Resort is one of the most popular in town. The Fall Creek Marina, (417) 336-3611, (800) 480-3611, rents all kinds of fishing boats and pontoon boats. They even provide fishing guides. Fall Creek Resort has an indoor and outdoor swimming pool, whirlpool, a fitness center, children's playground, miniature golf course, tennis court, shuffleboard, basketball court, and guest laundry facilities. A standard room comes with two beds, cable TV, and a phone. The more deluxe accommodations include Jacuzzis, one-, two-, or three-bedrooms, fully equipped kitchens, and family-size living areas. Some units are two stories. You can get a deluxe continental breakfast in the clubhouse or hop on over to the Fall Creek Steakhouse just down the road and catch a flying roll. (See our section on Restaurants.)

Trout Hollow Lodge
$$ • 1458 Acacia Club Rd., Hollister
• (417) 334-2332, (800) 328-1246
• www.trouthollow.com

To get there from Branson, take U.S. Hwy. 65 south to Mo. Hwy. V. Look for the signs directing you to College of the Ozarks. Go nearly a mile and make a right on Acacia Club Road. The lodge is 1 mile down the road on your right. Trout Hollow Lodge has recently remodeled its 20 one-, two-, and three-bedroom cabins. Each comes with a fully equipped kitchen, cable TV, and phones. All of the well-shaded

Big Cedar Lodge, just 10 miles south of Branson is one of the area's premier resorts.

cabins have a lake view and are within walking distance of the full-service Trout Hollow Marina. There is a swimming pool, picnic area with playground, a 260-foot fishing dock and a bait and tackle shop that also stocks people food. If you stay six nights, the seventh night is on the house.

Table Rock Lake

Big Cedar Lodge
**$$$ • 612 Devil's Pool Rd., Ridgedale
• (417) 335-2777 • www.big-cedar.com**
The Bass Pro Shops of resorts is the 305-acre Big Cedar Lodge located just 10 miles south of Branson on Mo. Highway 86. With its Adirondack-style architecture and its wilderness-themed landscaping, Big Cedar is an attraction all its own. Developed by Bass Pro Shops owner Johnny L. Morris, Big Cedar has been attracting the attention of the rich and famous since its initial creation more than 70 years ago by two wealthy Missourians, Jude Simmons, and Harry Worman, who incidentally now have buildings named after them. The two men built resort homes in what was then known as Big Cedar Hollow. In 1947 a real estate executive bought the property and added the Devil's Pool Ranch guest resort. Since

that time, the White River was dammed to form Table Rock Lake. Morris later bought the property and the rest is history.

With a list of amenities a mile long, a five-season rate card and upwards of 30 different types of rooms, it is impossible for us to mention them all. We will tell you that the price for their basic room in peak season is around $120. That includes two beds, a phone, and cable TV. You can get the same room for around $80 in January. On the other end of the spectrum is the 2,500-square-foot Governor's Suite. It goes for approximately $1,000 a night in peak season and includes four bedrooms, four baths, private balconies, remote-controlled fireplaces, TVs, VCRs, a kitchen, bar, and boardroom.

The list of amenities includes riding stables, tennis courts, a swimming pool, Jacuzzis, private log cabin suites, a playground for children ages 4 through 12, three restaurants and all the fish you can catch from their private marina on Table Rock Lake (you'll have to abide by Missouri fishing regulations, however.) You can rent fully equipped Tracker bass boats, ski boats, pontoon boats or canoes by the hour or by the day. If it's a guide you need, they'll supply that too.

Their Top of the Rock executive nine-hole, par 3 golf course was designed by Jack Nicklaus himself and is a member of the Audubon Signature Cooperative Sanctuary program for natural habitat conservation.

Just down the road 20 minutes is Dogwood Canyon, a 10,000-acre private wilderness refuge owned by the same folks. You can walk, rent a bicycle, or take the guided tram tour. Along the way you may spot Texas longhorns, American bison, Whitetail deer, and wild turkeys. For trout anglers who don't like much of a challenge, they even have well-stocked trout streams.

The restaurants at Big Cedar run the full gamut. At the Truman Smokehouse Restaurant you can grab a barbecue sandwich, or you can get prime rib at the Devil's Pool Restaurant, a local favorite. The Worman House restaurant serves gourmet cuisine. (See our Restaurants chapter.)

If you're serious about visiting Big Cedar call (800) 227-7776, and for $10 they'll send you a VHS videotape of the entire complex.

Chateau on the Lake Resort Hotel and Convention Center
$$$$ • 415 N. Mo. Hwy. 265
• (417) 334-1161, (888) 333-5253
• www.jqh.com

Local business owners have long awaited the opening of the Chateau on the Lake's convention facilities. The one thing Branson had lacked was a facility large enough to accommodate large groups. With 40,000 square feet of meeting space, the Chateau can accommodate groups up to 4,000. Since it opened in 1997, other area hotels and restaurants have felt the ripple effect of the Chateau's convention business.

The most striking feature of the hotel, besides its imposing presence on a large mountain overlooking Table Rock Lake, is the 10-story atrium courtyard draped with a plethora of foliage, trees, and waterfalls. The glass elevators on either side of the atrium take visitors to their rooms on the third through 10th floors, which all have private balconies, some with a lake view. Each room is decorated in deep purples and mauves. The hallways are lined with cherry furniture, plants, and artwork. It is one of John Q. Hammon's best creations yet. He owns numerous resorts and hotels around the globe including the Holiday Inn-University Plaza Hotel and the University Plaza Trade Center in Springfield.

The hotel has 302 rooms and two 1,000 square-foot Presidential Suites, which are located on the top floor. Besides the best view, these suites have just about every amenity you can think of: TVs, phones, Jacuzzis, king beds, and kitchenettes just to name a few.

The grounds of the resort are as impressive as the interior. They have a hiking and biking trail, tennis courts, indoor and outdoor swimming pools, a spa, fitness center, hair salon, full service marina, and a supervised children's program, called Crawdaddies Kid's Club, which is open daily and lets kids enjoy a place all their own. If you can't decide what to do, ask the full-time recreation coordinator to help you plan your day. After a hard day relaxing at the resort, you can pop into The Library for a cocktail and gawk at its massive stone fireplace. Or you can try out the Chateau Grille, a fine dining restaurant. For dessert try The Sweet Shop, which is also a gift shop.

To get to Chateau on the Lake from The Strip, take Mo. 165 south until you come to Mo. 265. Turn left and look for the entry signs. Or, if you're coming from Silver Dollar City, turn right on Mo. Hwy. 376 across from the Country Tonite Theatre, follow it to Mo. Hwy. 265, turn left and wind around the two lanes until you see it on your right.

Eagle's View Cottages
$$ • Indian Point Rd.
• (417) 338-2227, (800) 888-1891
• www.indianpoint.com

Eagle's View Cottages come in pink, green, or yellow. Take your pick. The basic cottage comes with two double beds or one queen bed, a full bath, a refrigerator, sink, cook top, and microwave. They start at around $60 a night. Some cottages have ovens and dishwashers. Their largest unit can accommodate 10 to 12 people. Eagle's View condo units have fireplaces and whirlpool tubs, but start at around $90 a night. You also get a view of Table Rock Lake, boat access, a swimming pool, and picnic area.

Indian Point Lodge
$$ • Indian Point Rd.
• (417) 338-2250, (800) 888-1891
• www.indianpoint.com

You can choose from two-bedroom condos, resort units with up to four bedrooms or lakeside cabins at Indian Point Lodge on Table Rock Lake. The basic unit starts at $70 for two double beds and works its way up from there. Each room includes cable TV, a telephone, a kitchen, a fireplace, a lakeview patio, and a barbecue grill. A resort unit features wood-beamed ceilings, a sitting area, and a view of the outdoor swimming pool. The condos come fully furnished. There is a children's play area, game

ACCOMMODATIONS

room, and a full-service marina with bass boats and pontoon boats starting at $30 a day for a basic boat and motor. The lodge offers vacation packages including show tickets for around $295 for a three nights' stay and Angler's Adventure Package Trips.

Rockwood Resort
$$ • Indian Point Rd.
• (417) 338-2470, (800) 276-6667
• www.rockwoodresort.com

Located on Indian Point Road just 1½ miles south of Silver Dollar City, Rockwood Resort features standard motel units with a view of either the swimming pool or the lake. Lake units run a little more. The units come with fully equipped kitchenettes, cable TV, and phones. Their largest unit has a living room, a balcony overlooking the lake, three bedrooms, two baths, one queen bed, one full bed, and two twin beds. The resort rents boats and motors by the day or half-day, and prices start at $12.50 per day for your basic 16-foot aluminum-hull boat. They have a paved boat ramp, freezer service for your day's catch, a cleaning station and lockers (bring your own lock). They have guides available to help you find the biggest fish. If you visit Rockwood in the early spring when their rates are the lowest, you can get a room for $39 with a three night minimum stay. Rockwood is closed in January and February.

Still Waters Condominium Resort
$$ • Indian Point Rd.
• (417) 338-2323, (800) 777-2320
• www.branson.net/stillwaters

Except for a live music show, Still Waters has it all. If you're into watersports you've come to the right place. Still Waters has its own full-service marina and boat launch. You can rent Jet Skis, fishing boats, ski boats, or take a leisurely tour of Table Rock Lake in one of their free paddleboats. If land activities are what you're after, the resort has a tennis court, sand volleyball court, bicycles, a hiking and jogging trail, horseshoe throwing pit, and a covered pavilion with a huge barbecue grill. The kids can hang out in the video arcade, burn off some energy at the playground, or cool off in one of the three swimming pools. In 1998 the resort added Zoom The Flume, a water slide free to guests of all ages. There's also a kiddy pool for the littlest ones—children under the age of 5 stay free.

You can choose from basic motel units, cottages, and one-, two-, or three-bedroom luxury condos. Many of the units have two bathrooms,

full kitchens, and Jacuzzis in the master bedroom. Each unit comes fully furnished and has cable TV and a phone. If there's nothing on to watch, you can rent a video. The units are decorated with modern furnishings and have large windows overlooking the swimming pools. If you really want to go to town to see a show, Still Waters will make your reservations for you.

Other Areas

Grandvista Resorts at The Woods
$$ • 2201 Roark Valley Rd.
• (417) 334-2324, (800) 935-2345

The Woods has one of the best out-in-the-country-but-still-in-town locations in Branson. To get to it, look for the signs at the intersection of Roark Valley Road and Shepherd of the Hills Expressway. It's located high on a hill just north of the intersection. As you drive along the expressway, you may be able to catch a glimpse of the log cabins through the trees. Never fear, though, because The Woods Resort is as private as it is charming. You can choose from their 200 guestrooms or from their 25 one-two- or three-bedroom cabins. A standard motel room comes with two king or two queen beds, cable TV, and phones. Each private cabin has a fully equipped kitchen, fireplace, Jacuzzi, and deck.

Outside, there is a large swimming pool, a covered pavilion, shuffleboard, basketball, volleyball, and children's play area. You'll see a natural waterfall on the walking path. The resort serves a continental breakfast.

Holiday Hills Resort & Golf Club
$$$ • 620 Rockford Dr.
• (417) 334-4013, (800) 225-2422
• www.holidayhills.com

Just 3 miles east of downtown Branson just off Mo. Hwy. 76, Holiday Hills is a golfer's paradise. The 18-hole golf course has bentgrass greens, shade trees, and plenty of Ozark Mountain twists and turns. If aliens beamed up your clubs, they'll rent you some (We know you wouldn't forget to bring yours on vacation, now would you?) See our Recreation and the Outdoors chapter for more on the golf course. You can also try a little shuffleboard, miniature golf, tennis, basketball, or horseback riding. For those a little more daring there's an archery range. If fishing is more your speed, they will hook you up with a fishing guide.

The condos at Holiday Hills come with one-, two-, or three-bedrooms and can sleep up to six adults. The basic unit has a private patio or balcony, cable TV, phone, fully furnished kitchenette, ceiling fans, plenty of comfortable furniture, and front door parking. Some of the units feature Jacuzzis. Be sure to check out their restaurant, The Grille on the Greens for light lunch after a few holes of golf.

Pointe Royale Condominium Resort
$$ • 158-A-SA Pointe Royale Dr.
• (417) 334-5614, (800) 962-4710
• www.pointeroyale.com

To get to Pointe Royale take Mo. Hwy. 165 south from The Strip. It's just across the street from the Welk Champagne Theatre and only 2.5 miles from the *Showboat Branson Belle*. Many of the area's entertainers either have homes in the Pointe Royale residential community or rent condos on a long-term basis. You never know whom you may run into around there. Andy Williams often takes advantage of the resort's 18-hole championship golf course (see our chapter on Recreation and the Outdoors).

Many of the 300 condos have a view of the fairway and rent for slightly higher than the units off the fairway. The basic unit comes fully furnished with linens, kitchen appliances and utensils, and patio furniture. The basic unit has one queen bed in the bedroom and one queen sleeper sofa in the living room. Each unit has cable TV, a phone, and private balcony. Other units come with two and three bedrooms, fireplaces, and washers and dryers. The outdoor amenities include a tennis court and swimming pool. Guests receive priority tee times and discounted rates for golf carts. Children under the age of 12 stay for free. If you stay six nights, the seventh night is on the house.

Thousand Hills Golf and Conference Resort
$$ • 245 S. Wildwood Dr.
• (417) 336-5873, (800) 864-4145
• www.thousandhills.com

Thousand Hills is better known for its 150-acre 18-hole, par 64 golf course than its condo rentals. (Golfers see our chapter on Recreation and the Outdoors). Nevertheless, if you're going to play golf, it's best to be as close to the green as possible, right? It is located just off Green Mountain Drive, the street that runs parallel to The Strip south of The Grand Palace. Thousand Hills has standard hotel units, one-,

two-, and three-bedroom condos. The resort also has rooms with a bedroom, bath, and kitchenette that lock off from the living area. Some of the pricier units have private outdoor hot tubs overlooking the golf course. All the units come fully furnished with tasteful and subdued decor. Each unit features cable TV, phones, and a balcony with patio furniture. There is an indoor and outdoor swimming pool, hot tub, clubhouse, exercise center, tennis court, laundry facility, and meeting space for up to 200 people. Check-in is at the clubhouse on Wildwood Drive, but the 175 units are on Green Mountain Drive.

Welk Resort Center
$$$ • 1984 Mo. Hwy. 165.
• (417) 336-3575, (800) 505-9355

Is it a resort with a theater or a theater with a resort? Turn to our chapter on The Shows if you're interested in the Welk Champagne Theatre or the Lennon Brothers Breakfast Show. Read on here if you're looking for a place to stay.

With 158 good-sized rooms, an outdoor swimming pool, restaurant, gift shop, laundry facility, and hand-held video games for the kids, it is hardly just a place to catch some Zs. Throughout the year the resort hosts a number of special events, and from 1997 to 1999 it was the home to the annual season kick-off festival, Branson Fest. (For more on these events see our Annual Events chapter.) You can play horseshoes, croquet, and board games with the other guests at the resort or you can dance the night away at the Stage Door Canteen Restaurant. The restaurant has a small dance floor and provides live music in the evenings. Their huge breakfast buffet is served before the Lennon Brothers Breakfast Show—you can buy a ticket to the show that includes breakfast or enjoy their expanded continental breakfast.

The basic room comes with two queen beds, cable TV, a phone, and country style furnishings. Some units have Jacuzzis. Children stay free with their parents.

If you are interested in a little Welk family entertainment, you can buy a vacation package that includes lodging at the resort, tickets to the shows, meals, and an autographed photo of the cast. They will even help you get tickets to other Branson shows as well. The resort is closed January through March.

Bed and Breakfast Inns

Price Code

$	$65-$85
$$	$86-$100
$$$	$101-$130

Bed and breakfast inns, or B&Bs as they are called in the British Isles where they are a time-honored option for travelers and sightseers, are beginning to catch on as an option in this country, even here in the Ozarks. One local inn owner estimates that 80 percent of her guests are first-time bed and breakfast visitors. The homey, often quaint accommodations with individually appointed and themed rooms, offer a refreshing departure from what some would consider the cloned cookie-cutter sameness of motels. You can expect bed and breakfast inns in the Ozarks to be sprinkled with romance, a sense of quiet retreat, local history, and splendor.

Often large, older homes in the British Isles are converted into bed and breakfast inns, but the Branson area does not have the lengthy history of the mother country nor a legacy of old, elegant architecture. Some of the area's old homes have made the bed and breakfast conversion, though most area bed and breakfast inns are newly built for that purpose. There are also quite a number of nice "regular" homes, owned by people who like people and whose kids have flown the nest. These folks operate the extra space in their home as a bed and breakfast inn "just for the fun of it," and they lavish attention on detail and their small number of guests.

Unlike their counterpart in the British Isles, Branson bed and breakfasts have private baths as the rule rather than the exception. Some inns are almost decadent in their luxury: fireplaces, private spas, libraries, king-size beds and neat, one-of-a-kind appointments. Some of the inns are furnished with antiques. Many of the inns are off the beaten path, a plus for some visitors, and often feature a peaceful river valley or a mountain hillside with a panoramic view. They can be romantic and peaceful, and the personal service one gets transcends that of chain motels. Quite a number are built on Table Rock Lake and offer docks for fishing and swimming, and some can accommodate boats overnight, so you can arrive to your destination via water if you want!

And of course there are the famous breakfasts you expect, a meal so substantial that it should tide you over the entire day. The heart of the bed and breakfast inn is the personal care and attention for guests at reasonable rates, with breakfast. Many Ozark bed and breakfast innkeepers seem to believe that the way to your heart is through your stomach! While bed and breakfast inns may have

INSIDERS' TIP

You can get a free Missouri Travel Guide which contains a list of bed and breakfast inns for the entire state, as well as other interesting and helpful travel information for your Show Me state vacation, by calling the Missouri Division of Tourism, (573) 751-4133.

smaller buildings than hotels and motels, they definitely have big hearts.

There is a good deal of variety within the realm of bed and breakfast inns in Branson. Some are new, like the Bradford Inn; some are old, like the historic Branson Hotel that dates from 1903. Some allow children, but not pets—and vice-versa. Some have showers, some don't. Some allow smoking; others are smoke free. Most of them are wheelchair accessible. Whatever your individual concern, ask when you make your reservation.

There are so many inns in the Branson area now, space limitations preclude describing each, but we list the best which offer good rooms, an interesting décor or location, and a friendly atmosphere. We've given you a price guide for a one-night stay for two with a double bed and breakfast, though some offer only a continental breakfast or a reduced rate for a continental breakfast. We've given directions for some inns; others said they don't take drop-ins and indicated they would give directions when reservations were made. Unless otherwise noted, all accept credit cards.

An Ozark Country Inn
$$ • 23765 Stonington Road, Omaha, Ark.
• (870) 426-6942, (888) 310-6128
• www.ozarkinn.com

An Ozark Country Inn is a picturesque bed and breakfast nestled in the majestic oaks, dogwood, and redbuds of the Ozark Mountains just south of Branson in Omaha, Arkansas. It's a secluded town for writers, lovers, photographers, or those seeking pure tranquility, but it's only 35 minutes from both Branson and Eureka Springs.

Innkeepers Charles and Pamela McNeel look forward to filling their happy home with happy guests seeking restful getaways, outdoor excursions on their 112 acres of woodland, and country romance in a rural setting. A garden patio offers a chance to steal a breath of fresh country air and rest in the hammock with a large refreshing glass of pink lemonade. Play a round of croquet or horseshoes, maybe a game of badminton. Enjoy the starlit hot tub and listen to the whippoorwills come evening.

Beautifully decorated accommodations include four rooms with a queen or full size comfortable bed, private bath, sound spa radio, 4-cup coffeemaker with all the condiments, satellite TV, and lovely views of the country from each room. The large Gathering Room has tall, open windows to draw you into the outdoors. It's not unusual to see deer and wild turkey visiting the grounds. Bird watching has never been easier. You can see cardinals, bluebirds, pileated woodpeckers, just to name a few!

The kitchen is the heart of activity, where fancy homespun country breakfasts are prepared for your enjoyment. Pam uses her own "home grown eggs" in the Quiche Lorraine. Expect homemade jams, jellies, and applebutter made from their own fruit to spread over Pam's large country buttermilk biscuits. An Ozark Country Inn is located 35 minutes south of Branson. Take U.S. 65 south to Ark. 14 east at Omaha. Travel approximately 5 miles to

---

Want the bed and breakfast experience in the Ozarks? You might first check out Bed and Breakfast Inns of Missouri, the state's only organization of inspected and approved inns at www.bbim.org. Many Branson area B&Bs will be listed and have a web page with information.

There are also three free local reservation agencies you can call.

Bed & Breakfast Get-A-Way Reservation Service can book you at a number of 4 star and premiere Branson bed and breakfast inns—Victorian, contemporary, historic or rustic. One call does it all at no cost to you. Call 877-BNB-Getaways (877) 262-4382.

Show Me Hospitality books for 18 area bed and breakfast inns. Linda Hovell is familiar with all the inns and will match what you're looking for with the inn that has it. Call (800) 348-5210.

Ozark Mountain Bed & Breakfast Service can book you at any one of more than 100 inns, cottages and suites in southern Missouri and northern Arkansas. Call (417) 334-4720 or (800) 695-1546. A descriptive list of all the bed and breakfast inns can be mailed to you in advance by calling the above number.

Ozark-speak

Food or drink that's spicy is described as being "strong enough to raise a blister on a rawhide boot."

Stonington Rd. and travel 5 more miles. The Inn is on the left. Watch for the sign.

Aunt Sadie's Garden Glade Bed & Breakfast
$$$ • 163 Fountain St.
• (417) 335-4063, (800) 944-4250
•www.auntsadies.com

Just a few miles north of Branson, Aunt Sadie's country Victorian style inn is on 7 wooded acres overlooking Bee Creek Valley. Aunt Sadie's is obviously using glade as "a bright open space in the forest," which aptly describes her establishment, not the "rocky, barren, semi-desert environment" that we typically mean here in the Ozarks. The inn, owned and operated by Linda and Dick Hovell, has four suites—three with private hot tubs, two with fireplaces—and a two bedroom cottage with private bath and shower, hot tub, TV, microwave, refrigerator, and coffee maker. The cottage will sleep five adults comfortably and is perfect for two couples or guests traveling with kids.

Sadie's furnishes a hearty home-cooked breakfast; homemade biscuits and gravy, an egg dish, two meat dishes, fresh-baked pastries, and juice—a perfect way to start the sightseeing day. You're only 1 mile from the Will Rogers Theatre and minutes from Mo. 248.To get to Sadie's Garden Glade, take U.S. 65 north of Branson and take the Mo. Highway F exit. Turn left and go under U.S. 65; then take the second left on the outer road, named West Outer Road South, and go 1.3 miles to the end and turn right on Fountain Street.

Barger House
$$ • 621 Lakeshore Dr.
• (417) 335-2134, (800) 266-2134

A charming Parson Capen Colonial on Lake Taneycomo, this three-unit inn is close to historic downtown Branson and only minutes from the shows on the Strip. There is dock access on the lake, as well as a view of Taneycomo. The inn also has a swimming pool and hot tub. Beds are queen-size, and units have private baths; the large honeymoon suite has a heart-shaped Jacuzzi. Full breakfast, country style (ask for the steak and eggs), is offered by host Ralph Barger.

Barn Again Bed and Breakfast
$$ • 904 W. Church St., Ozark
• (417) 581-2276, (877) 462-2276

Located in Ozark, close to antique stores yet within easy driving distance of both Branson and Springfield attractions, this five unit bed and breakfast inn features 1910 "farmhouse suites," two in the barn and three in the original milking parlor, all near the swimming pool. Units are large (big as a barn!) and have private entrances and full baths (some units have a Jacuzzi), and all are within easy walking distance of the network of walking paths by the Finley River. Built in 1910 and restored by the Amish community, the inn, now listed on the Ozark Historical Register, has one unit named the Amish Room furnished with Amish antiques, furniture, and quilts. The inn has a full gourmet farm breakfast served in the main house, the original barn of this turn-of-the-century homestead.

Bradford Inn
$ • HCR 9, Box 1276-10 • (417) 338-5555

The Bradford features decks with a spectacular view of the mountains, and it brings in the out-of-doors with more than 200 windows so you can enjoy the lake, mountains, sunrises, and sunsets, even inside! The Bradford is only a few miles from Silver Dollar City, the Shepherd of the Hills Homestead and Outdoor Theatre, and the Strip theaters. It has 32 individually themed units, (Gothic Room, Golf Room, Rustic Room, Secret Garden Room with its own stone wall and gate) all with private bath, Jacuzzi, fireplace, cable TV, phone, king or queen beds, writing desks, and deck or patio. There are two multi-bedroom units that sleep six and nine. Lucyanna and Bob Westfall, owners and operators of the Bradford, serve full breakfast: sausage and eggs, homemade Belgian waffles, fresh-baked breads, and fresh fruit.

To get to the Bradford, take Mo. 76 west from Branson to Mo. 265 and turn left (south) and you'll find the inn on your left after two miles.

Branson Hotel
$$ • 214W. Main St. • (417) 335-6104

You can stay in the same hotel where Harold Bell Wright stayed and wrote much of *The Shepherd of the Hills,* the book that helped launch Branson's tourism. The hotel dates back to 1903 and was built in anticipation of the St. Louis Iron Mountain & Southern Railroad arriving in town—which it did, but two years later. Interestingly, the hotel housed Branson's first town library, started by the Maids and Matrons Study Group. The hotel was used continually, but gradually fell into decay until new owner Teri Murgia rebuilt and refurbished the hotel. The nine guest rooms are a bit small according to modern standards but are interestingly themed,

The Ozarks has nature in a more formal setting, too!

Photo: A.C. Haralson/Arkansas Dept. of Parks & Tourism

mostly in Victorian decor: the English Garden Room, the Rose Room, the Vintage Room, and the Wicker Room. An interesting room is the Fox's Den, a lair of fox paraphernalia, with pictures, prints and appointment that reflect Reynard, the fox of fairy tales old. The Duck Club has duck prints, duck lamp bases, and enough antique decoys and duck decor to make Donald Duck himself feel at home. All rooms have cable TV, phones, plush carpeted floors, and beds of varied style and interest including canopied or high-backed oak. There is a comfortable parlor with vintage Godey prints and two large verandas shaded by a gnarled oak, with Adirondack chairs for guests to sit and visit.

In the entry of the hotel is a photograph taken around 1905 that shows Branson notables and Harold Bell Wright (who stayed in what is now the Fox's Den). Beneath the photo is the old hotel register lying on its oak stand, with an original advertising strip listing area merchants of the era, part of the nice historical touches of the new, old Branson Hotel.

INSIDERS' TIP

The Dairy Hollow House is a bed and breakfast inn in nearby Eureka Springs, and proprietor Crescent Dragonwagen is a noted writer and cook. (She was caterer for one of President Clinton's inaugural parties.) When in our local bookstores, check for her books, including *The Dairy Hollow House Cookbook.*

Breakfasts are big and varied: fresh fruits, juices, home-baked muffins (the apple walnut is our favorite) and bread, eggs of various styles, sausage, bacon, and hash browns served in the glass-enclosed Breakfast Room. The meal is something to bring you out of bed with a bounce in your step. The hotel is close to the historic downtown near the intersection of Main Street and U.S. Business 65.

The Brass Swan Bed and Breakfast
$$ • 202 River Bend Rd.
• (417) 336-3669, (800) 280-6673

Dick and Gigi House make their house your house. Just off Fall Creek Road, it's an elegant contemporary home near Lake Taneycomo, only minutes from historic downtown Branson and the attractions on The Strip. Each of the four rooms has a sitting area, phone, TV, VCR, AM-FM clock radio, and private bath. One unit has a private, mirrored hot tub, and there is also an outdoor hot tub against a background of majestic shade trees. Some rooms have hot tubs, and the Branson Suite has a fireplace and whirlpool tub. Breakfast is full, family style and includes fresh fruit, juices, and assorted home-made breads.

Cameron's Crag
$$ • 738 Acadia Club Rd., Point Lookout
• (417) 335-8134, (800) 933-8529

This contemporary home is perched high on a bluff overlooking Lake Taneycomo and the Branson skyline. All three guestrooms have wonderful views, king-size beds, private baths, and hot tubs. The area is quiet and secluded but only minutes from Hollister, Branson, and the attractions on The Strip. School-age children are welcome. Kay Cameron provides a hearty breakfast with something different every day. Ask her about her cookbook!

To find Cameron's Crag, take U.S. 65 south from Branson. Turn right on Mo. Highway V, go past the College of the Ozarks entrance, and turn right on Acacia Club Road. You'll find the Crag about 1½ miles down the road on your right.

Cinnamon Hill Bed and Breakfast
$$ 24 Wildwood Ln., Kimberling City
• (417) 739-5727, (800) 925-1556

Shirley DeVrient, owner-operator, has a modern, contemporary house with three units in Victorian Country décor, all with private baths. She serves a full country breakfast, family style, with an egg dish, meat dish, and home-made muffins and breads that you can top with her homemade jams—raspberry, blueberry, or strawberry from locally picked fruits at the Persimmon Hill Berry Farm. Cinnamon Hill is only 8 miles from Silver Dollar City and is within easy driving distance of Eureka Springs.

Emory House Bed & Breakfast
$$ • 143 Arizona Dr.
• (417) 334-3805, (800) 362-7404
• www.emorycreekbnb.com

Located 3 miles north of Branson, this inn, built in 1993, overlooks Emory Creek where it joins Bull Creek. You can relax in a porch swing and perhaps see a deer as you walk down the wildlife trail to Emory Creek. The large, blue and white Victorian house has modern conve-niences, including private Jacuzzi-tub baths in

each of the seven guest rooms, TVs, and good lighting. Forget your own robe and slippers? Owners Beverly and Sammy Pagma provide such luxuries for you. Rooms are not equipped with individual phones, but there is a dedicated line for guests, and local calls are free. A grand staircase rises to the open second story from the main salon of the house. The decor is Victo-rian: old horse prints, a giant carousel rocking horse, cut-glass and stained-glass lamps, overstuffed chairs, carved beds with huge head-boards, upright Chickering pianos, and a library of classics and bestsellers. Rooms are named after writers and historical people of Missouri: Harry S. Truman, Laura Ingalls Wilder, Sammy Lane, and Rose O'Neill. Breakfasts are big with pip-ing hot breads and muffins; pumpkin streusel; stuffed blueberry French toast; ham, potato and cheese quiche; and creamed eggs in pastry puffs. Wash it down with Beverly's eye-opening Sunrise Surprise, a refreshing drink of freshly squeezed orange juice, lime juice, and local wildflower honey.

INSIDERS' TIP

Nearby Eureka Springs, just over the line in Arkansas, has more bed and breakfast inns than any city in the United States, according to *USA Today*. Eureka Springs boasts 125 B&Bs, while San Francisco, CA comes in second with 119.

Fall Creek Bed & Breakfast
$$ • 4988 Fall Creek Rd.
• (417) 334-3939, (800) 482-1090

If you need pampering, the place to get it is at the Fall Creek Bed & Breakfast. Only min-utes from the shows on The Strip, this newly-built Victorian-motif facility that looks like a Victorian Castle has 19 units which feature queen beds, room phones, and remote cable TV. Also available are a big TV and VCR room, an exercise room, whirlpool room, barbecue and picnic area, swimming pool, and washer and dryer facilities. Fall Creek serves up a full break-fast, country style—three meats, scrambled eggs, hash browns, biscuits and gravy, juice, and a full complement of breads and muffins.

The Free Man House
$$ • 1773 Lakeshore Dr., Branson
• (417) 334-6262, (800) 583-6101

Only 3 miles from downtown Branson, the Free Man is on the banks of Lake Taneycomo. Each uniquely decorated suite offers its own private entrance and bath with breakfast (waffles are a specialty) served in your room— or next to the cascading waterfall. There are three rooms: The Rose Suite has two rooms and a private hot tub. The Dogwood Suite has a small kitchen, for those interested in doing some of their own cooking while on vacation. A large deck overlooks the lake and a swimming pool is also available for guests.

Gaines Landing Bed & Breakfast
$$$ 521 W. Atlantic St.
• **(417) 334-2280, (800) 825-3145**

Gaines Landing is a spacious contemporary home featuring three separate units with private entrances, baths, and outdoor hot tubs. There is also a common sitting room for all guests with a fireplace, TV and VCR, video library, wet bar, refrigerator, microwave, and comfortable chairs. A full breakfast is served family style in an elegant dining room. The inn is a smoke-free home and is in a quiet neighborhood of Branson, but only blocks from historic downtown Branson and minutes from The Strip's attractions.

Josie's Peaceful Getaway
$$$ • On Indian Point
• **(417) 338-2978, (800) 289-4125**
• **www.bbonline.com/mo/josies**

Indian Point is the peninsula that juts out into Table Rock Lake south of Silver Dollar City, and Josie's Getaway, owned and operated by Bill and Josie Coats, is near the tip of the Point right on the lake. It's a great place to stay if you're going to be doing lake activities or taking in Silver Dollar City, though it is only 8 miles back to The Strip. Josie's has three guest rooms and a suite, all with private baths. The inn is new with Victorian decor, a hot tub, and fireplaces. Enjoy a walk along the lakeshore in the morning and come back to Josie's candlelight breakfast.

To get to Josie's, from Mo. 76 take Indian Point Road to Coleman Junction (on your left). Turn left at street sign 60H. Then make an immediate right following 60H and go a half-mile. You'll see Josie's sign and parking lot.

The Martindale Bed & Breakfast
$, no credit cards • HCR 4, Box 3570, Reeds Spring
• **(417) 338-2588, (888) 338-2588**
• **www.tablerocklake.net/lodging/martindale**

Lucille and Ellis Martin provide good, old-fashioned Ozark hospitality in their lakeside home. The two units have private balconies and overlook the great room with its massive fireplace. Units have mirrored cherry armoires with TVs, scroll queen-size beds, and private

bathrooms. You can expect your native Ozarkian hosts to provide a full breakfast that is "sumpt'n special"—country omelette pie, savory sausage, biscuits and gravy, Amish bread, and fruit.

The Martindale is in the Kimberling City area, a perfect place to enjoy that area of Table Rock Lake and only 15 minutes from Silver Dollar City. To get there from Branson West, take Mo. 13 south toward Kimberling City. Turn left on Mo. Highway DD and go 4½ miles, turning left on DD-20. Keep to the left, and you'll see The Martindale on your left. All lefts, right? Watch for the purple signs for The Martindale.

Red Bud Cove Bed & Breakfast Suites
$$ • 162 Lakewood Dr., Hollister
• **(417) 334-7144, (800) 677-5525**

Red Bud Cove is one of the quietest coves on Table Rock Lake. If you come in early April, you can see the pink mist of the red buds in bloom on the hills and you'll know how the cove got its name. Each suite has a private entrance, and includes bedroom, living room, kitchenette, dining area, and private bath. Some come with a spa for two and some with a fireplace. You can expect a queen or king bed in each bedroom, as well as a sofa bed in the living room. You'll enjoy your hearty full breakfast served in the dining room in the main house overlooking the lake. Hosts Rick and Carol Carpenter will give you hints on how to best enjoy the Ozarks. There's an outdoor hot tub, and you can rent a fishing or pontoon boat. Swim, fish, or just watch the sun set at the lake's edge.

Red Bud Cove is at the end of Table Rock Lake Road 65-48. Go south on U.S. 65 past the 265 junction and look for the turnoff on 65-48, which becomes Lakewood Drive on your right.

Rhapsody Bed & Breakfast Inn
$$ • 296 Blue Meadows Rd.
• **(417) 335-2442, (800) 790-3892**
• **www.rhapsodyinn.com**

Hosts Patti and Duane Scott offer you the serenity and peace of our mountains with the elegance of the finest hotel. They are away from the traffic of Branson but close to the thick of things, right off Fall Creek Road. You can pamper yourself in the exquisite Victorian interior graced with rich mahogany wood and glorious tapestries. Each room is appointed with a queen-size bed and private bath with two pedestal sinks. During the summer, you can cool off in "the pool with a view." They suggest you come hungry and enjoy the luscious home-cooked breakfast.

Schroll's Lakefront Bed & Breakfast
$$ • 418 N. Sycamore St.
• (417) 335-6759, (800) 285-8833
• www.schrollsbandb.com

The Schroll family has three units, each with distinctive decor. All have cable TVs, in-room phones, queen or king beds, private entrances, and private baths with Jacuzzi tubs. Branson's North Beach Park is "your back-yard." You'll find yourself right on the banks of Lake Taneycomo where you can enjoy the wildlife and fish for trout only blocks from the downtown shops. You're only minutes from the shows on The Strip. The full breakfast is a gourmet's delight, or you can have continental if you prefer, in the breakfast room or outdoors on the deck.

The Thurman House Bed and Breakfast
$$ • 888 Mo. Hwy. F
• (417) 334-6000, (800) 238-6630

Owners Carolyn and Pat Thurman invite you into their peaceful getaway, surrounded by flowers and rock gardens. It can be your quiet place before exploring the excitement of The Strip. There are two guest rooms for a private getaway, honeymoon, or family vacation. Rooms have a private bath and entrance and there is a patio where you can swing in the rocker glider or enjoy the large six-person hot tub. Expect a full country breakfast each morning: homemade biscuits, savory sausage gravy, waffles, and muffins. You can call ahead and let Carolyn know if you have special dietary requirements.

BED AND BREAKFAST INNS

Ozark-speak

A nervous person is described as being as "jumpy as a man with a pacemaker at a microwave cookoff" or "as nervous as a long-tailed cat in a room full of rocking chairs."

Restaurants

If you've come to Branson and are on a diet, put it on the back burner until you get back home. The selection of places to eat rivals the selection you have to make at the area's ubiquitous buffets. Because the competition for your food dollar is so fierce, food is relatively inexpensive—and it can be good.

A bit of history—it wasn't always like that. We can remember when there were only three cafes in town, and not a single stoplight. Now it seems like there are almost 3,000 eating establishments in the area, and we have stoplights now, too. Some of us joke about our eating habits and culinary tastes by saying, "If it ain't fried, it ain't food." And although Branson may be the cholesterol capital of the world, you can eat healthful, sensible, and enjoyable meals, too. We'll point out places that have health-conscious menus. But, as we've said, Branson is the place to backslide on that diet of yours.

Ozarkers, culinary-wise, could be divided into two types. The first is the basic meat and potatoes type with a mind closed to outside food influences. The other type follows the philosophy, if it grows and God made it, it can be eaten. This type's table would be graced with scrambled eggs and squirrels' brains, barbecued 'coon, woodchuck ragout, venison, paw-paw and persimmon bread, fruit pies and cobblers, and jams and jellies from the cornucopia of local plants such as blackberry, pokeberry, mulberry, raspberry, gooseberry, wild grape, plum, and elderberry. In short, anything that could be picked and prepared. It was this type of Ozark eater who embraced, lovingly, the outside food influences that better transportation and tourism brought. You won't be fed this local fare in restaurants, but native fruit pies and cobblers are available and even featured in most area eating establishments. An influx of tourists and new residents brings various ethnic culinary possibilities but the area is still pretty homogeneous when it comes to food. You'll also find the usual chain gang of fast food establishments, from Applebee's and Blimpie's all the way to the end of the alphabet. We don't cover them in this book, unless they have a unique local feature or you might not have yet experienced them in your neck of the woods, because you know what to expect from them. But don't allow yourself to be manacled to the sameness and security of fast food. Check out local eateries. If you don't like one, you can find a dozen others you do like.

This chapter will guide you to what we think are the best of the lot, and that includes some that you may have second thoughts about when you first drive up. One of the things we have learned over the years: Never judge a book by its cover, people by their dress, or a restaurant by its facade. Some of the hole-in-the-wall and divey-looking joints serve the best food. You may find that the friendliness, food, or convenience of a particular place bring you back time after time during your stay, but we encourage you to experiment and spread your dollar more broadly. We locals think nothing of driving over to Hollister to lunch at the Red Lion or out to the boondocks toward Blue Eye to sample the fare at the Devil's Pool Restaurant at Big Cedar Lodge. The better roads and greater restaurant choices have broadened our diets and probably our girths. So, follow our advice and you'll leave Branson a better (and probably bigger) person for it!

LOOK FOR:
- **Buffets**
- **American**
- **Fine Dining**
- **A Meal with a View**
- **Ethnic Delights**
- **Sweet Treats**
- **Dinner and a Show**
- **Gourmet Brunch**

Price Code

$	Less than $20
$$	$21 to $40
$$$	$41 to $60
$$$$	More than $60

One point to keep in mind, many restaurants do not serve beer, wine or mixed drinks. Some serve only beer, some only wine. There doesn't seem to be any rhyme or reason to the alcohol-serving situation. If drinks are in your dining plans, it might be wise to call and ask what the place serves. What about dress? We Ozarkers believe in being comfortable and making others feel comfortable. Dress in most establishments is country casual and typical tourist garb, just be clothed. A few of the more upscale spots might like you to wear slacks and even a tie and coat, but they aren't likely to refuse you service if you come in wearing shorts and a tank top. Common sense and the weather will dictate your choice of clothing.

As for when to eat, the rule seems to be: If you're hungry, they'll feed you. The schedules of those in the service industries and of the entertainers make for meals that are often on a catch-as-you-can basis. And there is no telling when a tourist will want to have the feed bag put on. Some restaurants are all-nighters; some are early birds and specialize in morning meals, often the bargain meal of the day. Some even serve breakfast at any hour. Your server can answer any questions about the food or the area.

If you have kids in tow, you'll find most restaurants are very child-friendly, and if they don't have a kids' menu, they are usually more than willing to bring out something that will please a picky youngster. Let price be your guide. The less expensive the restaurant, the more likely it will cater to kids. Accessibility for the physically challenged varies greatly, but since many of the restaurants were built during the "boom period," they are readily accessible for the handicapped. Older establishments may have narrow doors, steps, or other obstacles, or bathrooms too tiny to accommodate wheelchairs. If handicapped facilities are of concern to you, be certain to call the restaurants to see what arrangements might be made to fit your needs.

Most restaurants are open seven days a week during the busy season (April through Christmas), and the season has gotten longer over the years. When things slow down during January and February, many restaurants cut back on their serving hours or close completely. If you're in town the first three months of the year, it would be a good idea to call ahead, just to make certain where you want to eat is open. That also goes for reservations. Hardly any place requires them, but it's smart to call the nicer restaurants during the busy season or if you're trying to catch a show right after dinner.

Most establishments will accept major credit cards (MasterCard, Visa, Discover), cash or travelers checks. Some even accept personal checks, though others won't accept personal checks at all, not even from locals. Unless otherwise noted, your plastic is accepted at the restaurants we list. Note the price code assigned to each restaurant listing. The little dollar signs are a hint at the bottom line for your evening dining—an indicator of the usual amount you can expect to pay for dinner for two, not including appetizers, dessert, drinks, or gratuity. You can expect lunch prices to be a third to half as much.

We've grouped restaurants according to major fare offered (American, Asian-American, Italian and Pizza, Steak Houses and Barbecue, Tex-Mex, More than a Meal, and Fine Dining), though some establishments offer fare from more than one category. We've also included a category called "A Bit of a Drive, But Worth It" for places that you'd have to work to fit into your schedule. And for your sweet tooth, we've created a category called Snacks and Sweets.

American

Branson Café
$ • 120 W. Main St., Branson
• (417) 334-3021

A sign reads, "If the Colonel had our fried chicken recipe, he'd be a General now!" says something about the food served and the ego of the owner. And the Better Business Bureau hasn't made them take it down for false advertising. The Branson Cafe is one of our down-home cafes that serves "comfort food." Breakfast is a specialty. It's a hangout for the locals who have a shelf for their own mugs and a gossip circle to sit at, but it handles the tourists quickly, too. Coffee is a bottomless cup for 65 cents, and the fruit and meringue pies are good and good looking. You can even buy whole pies with meringue as high as Dolly Parton's hair.

Branson Strip Bar & Grill
$$ • 120 S. Wildwood Dr., Branson
• (417) 335-5767

Elegance and casualness are combined at the Branson Strip Bar & Grill located in the Crowne Plaza Hotel. (And yes, folks joke about the name, but don't expect any strippers from your Strip waitresses!) The menu has a variety of steaks, chops, fish, seafood, and pastas. One of our favorites was penne pasta with roasted chicken, tender roasted chicken tossed with garlic, tomatoes, and mushrooms in a light alfredo sauce, a real bargain at $10.95. Other great eats are fresh Ozark trout and the Missouri state chops, two seasoned, char-grilled pork chops topped with fresh sauteed mushrooms.

The Downtown Restaurant
$ • 103 S. Commercial Street, Branson
• (417) 334-4444

Classic dinner cuisine in the center of downtown Branson makes this cafe a great place to pause for eats or treats in your downtown Branson sight-seeing. This bright and clean cafe has daily specials for breakfast, lunch, and dinner as well as great menu choices. Locals like the custom-built, home-style burgers built for your individual taste. They have hot and deli-style sandwiches; the pork tenderloin sandwich is a favorite. Desserts include cakes, cobblers, and pies, with or without ice cream. One nice aspect about The Downtown is that they have fare for the health conscious: egg-substitute omelets, a variety of salads, several light-type specials and sugar-free pie. The menu is impressive for its variety and for its inexpensiveness: Nothing on the menu in 2000 is more than $11.

Farmhouse Restaurant
$ • 119 W. Main St., Branson
• (417) 334-9701

From early morning to late at night, the Farmhouse feeds Branson. Come at 7 AM and you can get a great breakfast; arrive after the shows for a late night snack. The Farmhouse is one place you can get breakfast anytime, and the lunch and dinner menu lists catfish, shrimp, chicken-fried steak (their specialty), and ham steak. They also have daily specials. Save room for the blackberry cobbler, the dessert they're famous for. A close second is the apple dumpling—great with cinnamon ice cream and tea, our favorite snack after shows. You can talk over a treat like that for a long time, but they drive you out at midnight.

Planet Branson
$$ • 440 Mo. Hwy. 248 , Branson
• (417) 335-7881

Planet Branson, often just called PB by the locals, is the place to go line dancing. You can have Dinner with Di from 5 to 7 PM, one of the area's most popular lounge/dinner entertainers. (See our Nightlife chapter.) Though Planet Branson has an 1,800 square-foot oak dance floor

and a game room with a big screen TV, PB is known for more than just the dancing and fun and games: it serves great food for dinner every day except Monday when it's closed. The hickory-smoked ribs and the Kansas City strip are the bestsellers at PB, but you can get soups and salads as well as pastas and sandwiches. One of their sandwich greats is an open-faced prime rib on French bread with a tangy horseradish sauce. The restaurant is known for its "starters," almost meals in themselves. Popular selections are nachos, fried potato skins, shrimp, and quesadillas (grilled chicken fingers and salsa topped with Monterey Jack and cheddar cheeses wrapped in a flour tortilla). They also have a children's menu.

Home Cannery Restaurant
$$ • 1580 76 Country Blvd., Branson
• (417) 334-6965

If you've been feeding folks coming to Branson for nigh on to 15 years, you have to be doing something right! The Home Cannery prides itself on the fact that "everything's homemade—even the mashed potatoes are real." It offers buffets at all three meals, but you can get a good sandwich from the menu, a Reuben or a cold roast beef with horse radish. The menu lists steaks and seafood, and they also have a "light menu" for those with a mini-appetite. Another feature is delectable desserts such as cobblers (with or without ice cream) and bread pudding with lemon sauce. The restaurant also offers "plate specials" for all three meals. The meatloaf and pork loin specials are bestsellers.

Jimmy's Keyboard Restaurant & Lounge
$$ • 1847 76 Country Music Blvd., Branson • (417) 332-0001

Formally located in the Branson Meadows Mall, Jimmy's was new in 1997 but has rapidly become a mainstay of the Branson dining experience at the new location on The Strip. Owner Jimmy Nicholas is a keyboard comic who also happens to be an artist with a keen delight in eating. He performs during breakfast, lunch, and dinner. Coming from Ft. Lauderdale, he brings some Floridian cosmopolitanism to the Ozarks. Jimmy's has a great prime rib sandwich for lunch, but our favorite is the Jimmy Burger, a half-pound burger with grilled onions and mushrooms. Dinner delights are the prime rib made special with some seasonings we aren't quite able to identify and Burgundy beef tips with linguine. Jimmy's serves till midnight. Desserts are made on the premises, and the full bar and the extended hours are making Jimmy's a favorite after-the-shows gathering place.

McFarlain's Restaurant
$ • 3562 Shepherd of the Hills Expy., Branson • (417) 336-4680

In two short years in the IMAX Mall complex, this restaurant has established a strong reputation for good food. McFarlain's says there is no secret to their great food, they just make it the old-fashioned way, like it was made at home—breakfast, lunch, and dinner. That means gathering fresh-as-you-can-get ingredients and serving them in great menu selections, delivered as soon as the food is done. That means no buffet lines. It may take a bit longer, but McFarlain's believes life's too short to eat bad food. The restaurant is known for fried green tomatoes, sweet potato fries, pot roast, and chicken pot pie. They make great desserts and pies are their specialties: apple, cherry, strawberry-rhubarb, coconut, chocolate, and even some sugar-free varieties. When it comes to pie, McFarlain's motto, on a prominently placed sign, is, "Life's too short. Eat pie first." Not bad advice. Try the Branson Traffic Jam pie!

McGuffey's
$$ • 2600 76 Country Blvd., Branson • (417) 336-3600
$$ • 1464 W. Mo. Hwy. 248, Branson • (417) 335-8680
$$ • 3265 Falls Pky., Branson • (417) 337-5389

The McGuffey's Readers used in our area's early one-room schools inspired the theme for these restaurants. When you open the menu modeled on those readers, you can go back in time to good food. McGuffey's is also interesting because the walls are a veritable local museum with photographs of early Branson and its citizens. It actually was Andy Williams who convinced McGuffey's owners to open their first restaurant in Branson (next to Andy's Moon River Theatre), and he often dashes over for a snack. The other two McGuffey's feature much the same menu, but the Falls Parkway restaurant has more of a steakhouse atmosphere and features more steaks. The area is proud of McGuffey's for being so environmentally conscious as well as being the purveyor of fine, fresh food. McGuffey's makes a good Thai chicken salad, and the blackened grilled chicken with Alfredo sauce over a bed of spiral pasta is another one of their award-winning dishes. The spectacular menu also includes heart and diet-conscious items. You can get basic burgers, chicken fingers, steaks, and ribs (slow-cooked for eight hours in their special sauce). But there are also some unusual specialty items such as the pepper-steak sandwich: a hoagie bun filled with sliced prime rib that has been sauteed in wine with mushrooms, peppers, and onions. The sandwich is then topped with melted cheese. Another tasty dish is the New Orleans Seafood Delight, which is a blackened albacore tuna steak over pasta, topped with a creamy Cajun sauce and accompanied with veggies. You can order a drink in this schoolroom atmosphere from the Faculty Lounge Bar, which really livens up after the shows let out and area entertainers and workers stop by.

Penelope's Family Restaurant
$ • 3015 76 Country Blvd., Branson • (417) 334-3335

Convenient to most of The Strip theaters, Penelope's has a great buffet for those who are touristing in the fast lane, along with inexpensive menu selections. Penelope's takes great pride in "scratch cooking" and disdains prepackaged "heat-ups." The meatloaf is a recipe you would like to have for your own. House favorites are a 10-ounce rib-eye steak and a six-ounce prime rib. They have hot and deli-style sandwiches, and they offer a children's menu. It's a favorite lunch place for the locals who work in the immediate vicinity. Desserts seem a specialty here, as there is a large selection of cheesecake, pies, cakes, and cobblers. We recommend the carrot cake as a great way to get your vegetables.

Peppercorn's Restaurant and Bakery
$$ • 2421 76 Country Blvd., Branson • (417) 335-6699

This local eatery was named after the green berries produced by a climbing shrub in the East Indies. As the berries ripen, they turn red and are picked and dried. The resulting "peppercorns" have been used to indicate a small token or a nominal fee. When ground and sifted they become black pepper used for seasoning. You can grind your own peppercorns on your meal there, but we find the food just fine as is. We also like the roomy booths and large tables. Peppercorn's breakfast buffet features a fresh fruit bar, homemade cinnamon rolls, hot apple butter, biscuits and gravy, hash browns, scrambled eggs, bacon, ham, sausage, grits, pancakes (with hot syrup and strawberries), and hot muffins from the bakery. The lunch and dinner buffets have a variety of Peppercorn's homemade entrees, hot vegetables and a fresh-from-the-garden salad bar. You also will find homemade soup, freshly baked bread, and delicious hot cobbler for dessert. We like to top ours with ice cream!

The Plantation
$$ • 3460 76 Country Blvd., Branson • (417) 334-7800

The Plantation offers southern cookin' at its best. Perhaps that's why theater folks drop in to enjoy the fried chicken, all-you-can-eat catfish, hush puppies, and fried okra at its lunch and dinner buffets. You may like it so much you'll want to come back for breakfast. The southern breakfast buffet offers pancakes, eggs in a variety of ways, bacon and sausage, hash browns, biscuits and gravy, and various fruits. If you're not in the mood for the delights of the buffets, you can always order from the menu: breakfasts, steaks, and seafood. And The Plantation has a full bar for before or after dinner drinks. The favored drink? Southern Comfort, of course!

Pzazz
$$ • 158 Pointe Royale Dr., Branson • (417) 335-2798

The sports bar and eatery features "All-Pro Stir-Fry Veggies" and "World Series" pizza and "Birdie" sandwiches. But what would you expect from owner-operator Jack Hamilton, who spent two decades on the pitcher's mound playing in the majors. Now he pitches a good line of gab (Ask him how he got his nickname of "Hairbreath Harry") and lunch and dinners that have pzazz. The restaurant is right at the entrance to the Pointe Royale development and overlooks the golf course. You can have a turkey breast sandwich or fajitas. Or you can sip a drink at the full-service bar and watch ESPN on the big-screen TV while munching on Jack's famous World Series pizza, crispy and crusty with a prime rib topping smothered with four cheeses. Then you'll know why Pzazz is a local favorite stopping off place.

The Red Lion Pub
$, no credit cards • 1865 U.S. Bus. Hwy. 65, Hollister • (417) 334-8684

In England, The Green Man and The Red Lion are common names for pubs, but we have no Green Man and only one Red Lion in our area, an uncommonly good but small pub in Hollister. At the old stone building on the banks of Turkey Creek, you can have your favorite brew and a lunch or dinner that is substantial, good and inexpensive. For more than 10 years,

owners Bob and Carol Voight have made us great sandwiches (the Reuben is popular) and burgers for lunch, as well as traditional fish and chips. Thursday is Mexican day with a variety of Mexican dishes available. The Friday night prime rib special always packs the place. For dinner, the fried chicken is a popular entree, and the salmon with caper sauce is good. The Red Lion is famous for its french-fried onion rings.

The Shack Café
$, no credit cards • 108 S. Commercial St., Branson • (417) 334-3490

The Shack is the oldest cafe in town, though it moved years ago from a shack across the street (now part of a bank's parking lot) to bigger and better quarters, the food is still the same good homemade comfort cookin'. Your friendly waitress takes your order and puts it on the cooks' spin wheel, who takes the requests in order. Dishes come out, usually with an accompanying bellow from the cook in "restauranteeze," and the waitress delivers your meatloaf or fried chicken with a smile and a, "Here you are, honey." You can have a ringside seat for this Branson show at the counter in the back, where locals gather for coffee and conversation or to read the newspaper. More deals have been struck in The Shack than on all the golf courses and in all the real estate offices in town. The Shack offers breakfast, lunch (with daily specials), and dinner (the pan-fried chicken is our favorite). For dessert, try the gooseberry cobbler or the raisin cream pie.

Sir Jed's Banjo's Pub & Eatery
$ • 20 Downing St., Hollister • (417) 334-5164

You can check out downtown Hollister, just across the Taneycomo bridge from Branson, when you have lunch at Banjo's. Its friendly pub atmosphere is a plus, and you can get the lunch special during the week for less than $4— also a definite plus. Favorites are chicken-fried steak, catfish, and the tuna cobb salad. A dinner menu favorite is Banjo's famous half-pound wineburger. With the seven pool tables and a dart board, there's always some action in the sports section of the pub.

Stage Door Canteen
$$ • 1984 S. Mo. Hwy. 165, Branson • (417) 336-3575

Located in the Welk Resort Center, the Stage Door Canteen is decorated like a WWII canteen with lots of memorabilia from local Ozark vets. For some, it brings back memories; for others, it's a tasty way to learn a bit of history. The Canteen is where The Lennon Brothers host breakfast before their show in the Welk Theater. The restaurant also serves lunch and dinner. The German-American menu (what would you expect at the Welk complex?) features sauerbraten and a German platter with smoked pork chops. Other popular menu items are the roast turkey with walnut dressing and the chicken and dumplings. You can also order pan-fried trout or prawns and pasta as well as a good Kansas City strip. They also make some fine salads topped with blackened chicken. And there's a buffet. It's a convenient place to eat before the Welk Show. Evenings from 5 to 7 PM and Sunday brunch features Luis Rojas at the piano, a classical pianist who's taken up "playing in a club again" for fun as he did years ago in Havana.

Uptown Café
$$ • 285 Mo. Hwy. 165, Branson
• (417) 336-3535

Art deco and chrome, lots of it, is the motif for this theme cafe that serves favorites from the '40s and '50s. People go to the Uptown as much for the unique atmosphere as the delicious food, and everyone has to check out little yellow taxi (a '53 Henry J. Kaiser). It's a classy and classic diner from that time, but with a contemporary touch. The Uptown is known for its Kansas City steak burgers, patties fixed on a greaseless griddle. They also serve a great baked trout almondine; other fish dishes included fried catfish and clam strips. Broiler favorites are the beef kabob, twin skewers of tenderloin, onions, peppers and tomato that are char-grilled to perfection, and Hawaiian chicken. The breakfast buffet has all you want or need for breakfast plus fruits and right-from-the-oven breads, biscuits, and rolls.

Asian-American

China Garden
$ • 448 Mo. Hwy. 248, Branson
• (417) 339-4311

Lily Quiko offers authentic Chinese cuisine (Hunan, Canton, and Mandarin) for lunch and dinner from an a la carte menu and a buffet, seven days a week. For those who like fried, it's here, but those who like crisp and tender vegetables served in exquisite offerings will be equally pleased. The shrimp and snow peas is tasty and mild; the Dragon and Phoenix (lobster and chicken with a spicy sauce) is more than hot. China Garden is famous for the "general chicken," and it usually is found on the buffet. Try a pot of jasmine tea with your meal, and top your dining experience off with a glass of plum wine. China Garden has a full-service bar and features a variety of beers, including Oriental offerings. If you're daring, try the Flaming Volcano. The China Garden is in the Branson Inn complex. The easiest way to get to it is the "back way"; turn north on to Mo. 248 at U.S. 65 and then turn right at the sign just past Planet Branson.

Hong Kong Buffet
$ • 1206 76 Country Blvd. Branson
• (417) 334-2727

Only in Branson! Chinese cuisine right next door to the Ozark cooking of the Hillbilly Inn. This small but efficient restaurant packs a lot of variety in its limited space: moo goo gai pan, shrimp and pea pods, Hong Kong Delight (shrimp in a sweet and sour sauce), and beef with oyster sauce. There are more than 100 Chinese dishes, from the well-known to the exotic.

Lotus Valley
$ • 3129 76 Country Blvd., Branson
• (417) 334-3427

Serving the same menu as the Hong Kong Buffet, this restaurant attracts a number of workers from The Strip in that area and pulls in crowds from nearby theaters. The buffet has lots of fried entrees but there are lighter, low-fat dishes as well. Lunch and dinner are served daily.

Tran's Chinese Buffet
$ • 1305 76 Country Blvd., Branson
• (417) 334-4652

Dung Tran taught us Bransonites to like "Oriental food" when he came here in 1979 as a Chinese refugee from Vietnam with absolutely nothing but the clothes on his back. Sponsored

Ozark-speak

During the spring rains, bottom land gets so muddy it will bog down a buzzard's shadow.

by the local First Presbyterian Church, the Tran family worked at an area restaurant, saved and started their own small restaurant downtown. They built a loyal following. When they moved out on The Strip, we regulars followed the family. We like moo goo gai pan, sweet and sour, and the wide range of Chinese food. Tran's is known as "a place where you can eat good but cheap"—and that's with dessert. Tran's has both menu and buffet service, with a buffet that has an amazing variety.

Fine Dining

Buckingham's
$$$ • 2820 76 Country Blvd., Branson
• (417) 337-7777

Buckingham's, in the Palace Inn next to the Grand Village, is our nod to Africa with its safari décor forest plants, animal skin prints, and carved wood totems. The cuisine might be labeled as modern continental. Appetizers are good and big enough to serve as light fare for those with a modest appetite. The menu is clever, and food ranges from what you would expect (steak, fish, and prime rib) to the exotic, such as wild game (ostrich and quail). The wine list is probably the longest in town with more than 30 selections. Desserts are rich and flamboyant, so expect to see flaming dishes even if you don't order them. Buckingham's serves only dinner. (See our Nightlife chapter.)

Candlestick Inn
$$$ • 127 Taney St., Branson
• (417) 334-3633

One of the oldest restaurants in the area, the Candlestick has an established reputation. Its the place we locals go to celebrate a special occasion because of the food and the view. Perched atop Mt. Branson, it offers a panoramic view of Lake Taneycomo and the city of Branson, especially nice during the Christmas season. When the weather is nice, you can eat out on the large deck. Chef Dave Gilderson describes his cooking as "a little bit French with some Creole and Cajun food and a lot of other styles" and serves up delectables like crab cakes, grilled rack of lamb with apple-mint chutney and cassis juice. There's a roasted Long Island

duckling that locals rave about. The antique bar always has the right wine for your meal, and you can top the evening off with one of Chef Gilderson's famous desserts. Lunch and dinner are the only meals served at the Candlestick. To dine at the Candlestick, cross the Lake Taneycomo bridge and turn left on Missouri Highway 76 east towards Forsyth. When you start up the steep hill, look for the sign on the left about halfway up and turn left on Candlestick Road.

Chateau on the Lake Resort, Hotel, and Convention Center
$$$ • 415 N. Mo. Hwy. 265 , Branson
• (417) 334-1161, (888) 333-LAKE
• www. jqh.com/chateau.html

The Chateau Grill in Branson's newest luxury hotel overlooking Table Rock Lake features fine dining for breakfast, lunch, and dinner. The plush carpet, fine stonework, and cherry paneling absolutely reek of richness and elegance. The hotel has been awarded AAA's four diamond rating, the only hotel in Branson and one of only four in Missouri to achieve the rating. (See our Accommodations chapter.) The Atrium Lounge Bar provides full service for any drinks with your dinner. The 10-story Chateau, on a high ridge just north of Table Rock Dam, offers a dining room with a view—and what a view! The restaurant, on the entry level, provides a panoramic and serene view of the lake, but you may want to see the landscape from higher up after you finish dining. Chef Doug Knopp creates an equally spectacular menu of what he calls "American Melting Pot," a melding of the best of various cultures and nationalities. One of the Grill's many outstanding appetizers is fruit de mer: smoked scallops, shrimp, and Alaskan crab meat, with three different types of caviar in lemon vinegar. One of Chef Doug's creations that has gained a national reputation is his sorghum-glazed salmon with caper-whipped potatoes, and candied beets (glazed in butter and honey with lemon butter sauce). Another popular selection is the pecan-seared Colorado rack of lamb with pancetta potato tower and porcini mushroom pan juices. For those who want to "eat rich," the mushroom dusted veal tenderloin with pan-seared frois gras in ox-tail cabernet

INSIDERS' TIP

Restaurants with a view: For a panoramic view of Table Rock Lake, Top of the Rock is tops. For a close-up, on-the-water view of Lake Taneycomo, try Dimitri's at the foot of Main Street. For a night view of Branson, the place to be is the Candlestick Inn.

reduction is one of his creations that doesn't count calories. There are also lots of vegetarian items—including roasted vegetable fritatta with wilted greens in a balsamic reduction. Desserts are made in-house and our favorite is the choco-late-raspberry truffle with a vanilla bean sauce and anglais glaze. The Grill's signature dessert is a rich Southern pecan tort with chocolate-caramel sauce. Reservations are suggested for this one!

Devil's Pool Restaurant
(Big Cedar Lodge)
$$$ • Devil's Pool Rd., Ridgedale
• (417) 335-5141 • www.big-cedar.com

You don't have to be a member of the oc-cult to dine at the Devil's Pool. The restaurant gets its name from the nearby Devil's Pool Spring, reputed by locals to be bottomless and, according to some, the place where several "revenooers" met their end after meddling in area moonshine making. The restaurant is on the grounds at Big Cedar Lodge, and it is well worth the drive out to it, if only to have a drink at the Buzzard's Bar. We like it for the fresh shiitake mushrooms and goat cheese from nearby farms and the smoked trout appetizer (great with horseradish). Chef Robert Stricklin curries good food contacts and makes them into memorable dishes. If you're a trout lover, you'll like the Devil's Pool's specialty-trout fixed in a variety of ways, that they order in the morning and serve that night. You can also get steaks, pastas, and soups (a different one every day). The Devil's Pool is famous for its smoked prime rib. They serve all three meals, and some people go there just for the old hunting lodge decor. You can admire the antiques and the spectacu-lar stonework while enjoying a drink from the full-service Buzzard's Bar. When you see it and taste the food, you'll know why St. Louis and Kansas City folks come down here just to dine.

To get to the Devil's Pool, take U.S. 65 10 miles south to Mo. 86. The turnoff to the res-taurant, about a half mile down Mo. 86, is well-marked.

Dimitri's
$$$ • 500 E. Main St., Branson
• (417) 334-0888

A trip to Branson is not complete unless you dine at Dimitri's. You can't miss it. Drive down Main Street until you're about to drive into the lake, then walk out onto the lake in this floating restaurant with an Old Grecian design. Owner Dimitrios Tsahiridis believes dining is more than just good food, it's also

good atmosphere. When you dine here you are the star, Dimitri would have it no other way. Romance is on the menu in an atmosphere of spotless crystal, fine china, polished silver, and waiters in tuxedos at your elbow. Dimitri's high-quality standards are illustrated by his choice in prime meats. He buys Black Angus beef, the highest quality you can buy in the United States. Whether you select the Steak Diane, prime rib, or Dimitri's personally rec-ommended filet mignon, you will certainly be satisfied. Expect great dishes in the interna-tional cuisine tradition: spanakopita, Grecian-style lamb chops, and rich desserts. Desserts are dramatic and served with flare, often liter-ally. Try the ambrosia flambe for the dramatic or the baklava for just plain tasty, and top off the meal with one of Dimitri's famous liquor-laced coffees. Dimitri's is a four-time winner of the Gourmet Diners Club Silver Spoon Award.

The Worman House Restaurant
(Big Cedar Lodge)
$$$ • Devil's Pool Rd., Ridgedale
• (417) 339-5214 • www.big-cedar.com

Once the home of railroad magnate Harry Worman and his wife, Dorothy, the restaurant is one of the newest and swankiest in the area, but only open for Sunday brunch (perhaps the finest in the area) and special occasion parties and gatherings. The menu features American Harvest cuisine, perhaps because it presents the best of our bountiful land: hot waffles with a variety of syrups (pecan is one of our favorites), omelettes to order (and they can put just about anything in it, from ham and cheese to mush-room and jalapenos). There's a great view of Table Rock Lake, and the mood and the decor is right out of the roaring '20s.

The Worman House is located on the grounds of the Big Cedar Lodge. Take U.S. 65 10 miles south to Mo. 86. The turnoff to the restaurant, about a half mile down Mo. 86, is well marked.

Italian and Pizza

J. Parrino's Italian Café
$ • Hwy. 13 at Oak St., Kimberling City
• (417) 739-1266

When we think pasta, we think Parrino's. Their Springfield restaurant was such a success with Branson folks, they opened one in the lakes area so we wouldn't have to drive so far! J. Parrino's features a broad range of Italian specialties, using original old family recipes, served in a cozy family oriented atmosphere. Portions are generous, with unlimited house salad and warm rolls, and the price is reasonable: nothing over $8.50. One of our favorites is shrimp vende, shrimp sauteed in a white wine lemon butter sauce with diced tomatoes and mushrooms and tossed with angel hair pasta. For those in a rush or who are just too tired to go out, Parrino's delivers.

Mr. G's Chicago Style Pizza
$ • 202 N. Commercial St., Branson • (417) 335-8156

If you're a Chicago fan, you'll enjoy the ambiance of the sports memorabilia, pictures and newspaper clippings as well as the food at Mr. G's. Pizza styles include both thin-crust and panstyle, with homemade sauce and Italian sausage. Large and mini pizzas are available for big or small appetites, with toppings as exotic as pineapple and jalapenos. Try the tomato bread, Italian bread with tomatoes, oregano, basil, and Parmesan cheese. Mr. G's also serves pasta dishes, sandwiches, soups and salads, and beer from the bar.

Rocky's Italian Restaurant
$$ • 120 N. Sycamore St., Branson • (417) 335-4765

Rocky's is a great place for the locals for lunch and dinner, many of whom can remember when it was a feed store. You can still see evidence of the plank loading dock at the entrance. Its limestone creek rock exterior has a rustic, continental interior that is interesting and homey without being pretentious. Before you order, notice the local artwork on the walls and the sculptures, including the blue heron fountain, by artist Tim Cherry. Rocky's has a full range of good pasta dishes, and you can sip a variety of wines (no Missouri or Arkansas wines, though) and mixed drinks from the bar. We recommend the chicken noodle soup, simply because it has an Italian zest in what is often thought of as a rather bland dish. Also good are the salads, especially Rocky's special salad and the tortellini salad. If it's Italian, you can order it at Rocky's: spaghetti, lasagna, fettuccine, and ravioli. Service is so quick, you probably won't have time to have a game of darts at the bar, but it's great fun to watch. Rocky's also has live music entertainment.

Top of the Rock
$$ • Top of the Rock Rd. • (417) 339-5320

When you get to the Top of the Rock, you'll know how it got its name, it has the grandest view for dining that we know. Lots of locals go there just for a snack and a beer in the summer and sit out on the patio to watch the wind patterns on Table Rock Lake. It's a great experience at sunset, too, especially if you can catch the *Showboat Branson Belle* with the sun behind her. Be sure to bring your camera. You can get more than just a great view. Top of the Rock is famous for its wood-fired pizza (wood-roasted chicken, barbecued chicken, Italian ham, and vegetarian are just some of the options), pastas, and great desserts. The Jack Nicklaus Signature Golf Course is right off the restaurant, so attire is "golf course casual." It can still be a special occasion, romantic dining experience, though, especially in the evenings.

To get to Top of the Rock, take U.S. 65 south and turn right on Top of the Rock Road, just before you come to the 86 junction. The restaurant is about a half-mile along on Top of the Rock Road.

Seafood

Happy Days Steak and Seafood
$$ • 2206 76 Country Blvd., Branson • (417) 334-6410

We didn't quite know just where to put Cajun Chef Bob Champagne in our categories. Certainly his fresh, homemade seafood gumbo, shrimp Creole, crawfish, and catfish fit the seafood category, but the aged prime beef could put him in our steakhouse category. Try entrees from both and see what you think. Chef Bob brags about having the "best catfish in the world" and advertises as specializing in seafood and Louisiana cooking. His Cajun recipes are not hot, just tangy, and there is always extra Tabasco for those who like it steaming. Cajun

INSIDERS' TIP

"If it Ain't Fried, It Ain't Food" is a song by country star Ray Jones. Ever hear of him? He's the fictional creation of detective novelist Donald E. Westlake whose *Baby, Would I Lie?* takes place in Branson. It's a fun read to check out the landmarks and places he mentions and to take in his elbow-in-the-ribs humor about Branson and our tourists.

music accompanies dinner on Friday and Saturday nights.

Landry's Seafood House
$$$ • 2900 76 Country Blvd., Branson
• (417) 339-1010

Landry's has the atmosphere of an old time 1940s coastal seafood house, a bit of the seashore here in the Ozark hills. The Landrys come here from Katy, Texas, down near Houston, and they bring their reputation for great seafood inland. You'll enjoy their special recipes for tasty appetizers and they have entrees like red snapper, stuffed flounder, lemon pepper catfish, crawfish etouffee, gumbo, and spicy crawfish all served in a laid-back atmosphere. Their specialty is shrimp, and you can have it your way: fried, boiled, chilled, served in gumbo, combined with pastry stuffed in a po-boy. In fact, depending on the season, shrimp lovers will go through 80 to 275 pounds of shrimp a day! For those who aren't the seafarin' type, Landry's offers certified Angus steaks and tempting chicken delicacies. They're open for lunch and dinner, and you can call ahead for carry-out.

The Rails
$$ • 433 Animal Safari Rd., Branson
• (417) 336-3401

Nearly every place to eat in Branson, it seems, has a buffet, but The Rails is one of the best all-you-can-eat fish and seafood buffet we know of. For less than $10 you can fill up on both boiled and fried shrimp, delectable catfish, Cajun fries, clam strips, seafood gumbo, stuffed crab, clam chowder, grilled chicken breasts, and barbecue ribs. Then top it off with a dessert of fruit cobbler and ice cream. It's all Southern comfort food, but what do you expect: owners Buddy and Jane Hurst came to the Ozarks from southern Arkansas, and they were close enough to Louisiana to have a major Cajun influence. The Rails is on the left just after you turn off on Animal Safari Road from Mo. 165, just down from where Green Mountain Road joins Mo. 165.

Steakhouses and Barbecue

Beverly's Steakhouse & Saloon
$$ • 225 Violin Dr., Branson
• (417) 334-6508

Beverly's is one of the few places that offers some nightlife other than the shows. They have an open stage every night, and the pros jam here after their shows. Locals love the place, but don't go for the decor. Beverly's features daily luncheon specials, and the lounge is open from 11 to 1:30 AM. It's a great place if you're looking for good food, cold beer, and local color. Steaks, fried chicken, and prime rib sandwiches are favorites. Chunky cheese potatoes is the popular veggie, but they toss a mean salad for the lean, too.

B. T. Bones
$$ • 2346 Shepherd of the Hills Expy., Branson • (417) 335-2002

"A Little Taste of Texas in Branson" and "Great Steaks! No Bull!" are accurate B. T. Bones' slogans. The ranch decor fits the steaks, prime ribs, and fajitas that are the favorites. You can also get shrimp, trout, catfish, salmon, and mahi-mahi, which doesn't sound very western, but neither does the meatless, cholesterol-free garden burger. It's that influence by outsiders! Although B. T. Bones doesn't advertise it, the meals come with a show, as there is always dancing to live music by some good Off-the-Strip talent. The bar is raised so you can get a better view, and it has typical finger food: nachos, buffalo wings, "Texas bullets" (stuffed and fried jalapenos). Locals come by after the show, and B. T. Bones attracts the college crowd, not only locally but also from Springfield. Sunday is karaoke night.

Fall Creek Steakhouse
$$ • Mo. Hwy. 165 at Fall Creek Rd., Branson • (417) 336-5080

Bring your catcher's mitt here, as you have to catch your high-rise, softball-size rolls. It's all part of the fun of eating steaks grilled with real hickory chips. The restaurant has baked sweet potatoes as well as traditional spuds served every way imaginable. You can also try fried dill pickles and fried green tomatoes. Lunch and dinner are served daily, and a kids' menu is offered. Cocktails are available. The back porch overlooking Fall Creek is a great place to enjoy a drink or eat and watch the raccoons that come up for a free handout.

Mesquite Charlie's
$$ • 2849 Gretna Rd., Branson
• (417) 334-0498

You can't miss Mesquite Charlie's. It's the big brick restaurant at the corner of Gretna and Roark Valley roads and one of Branson's newest. The decor is expensive antiques and the central lobby is paneled in antique wood with etched-glass windows. The crystal chandeliers that you see hang from a 30-foot ceiling. With its four dining rooms (each with its own kitchen) on two floors, it's the largest restaurant this side of Texas. The restaurant is something of a show as well as a showplace: each dining room has windows looking into the kitchen so you watch their famous mesquite-broiled cowboy steaks being prepared. There's a full-service bar with antique paneling and fixtures and a large dance floor, where Miss Kitty would feel right at home. If you eat there, you won't see it, but their employees appreciate the on-premise housing of 33 apartments on the building's bottom floor.

Outback Steak and Oyster Bar
$$$ • ·1914 76 Country Blvd., Branson • (417) 334-6306

You'll almost pick up an Aussie accent with the meal and atmosphere of the Outback. There are down under favorites like lamb chops, snaggers (large spicy sausages), steaks, oysters, and even alligator tail. The food is served in an atmosphere of flags, tools, musical instruments, signs, and Australian antiques with primitives on the weathered barn board interior. Bread is served in the metal buckets it's baked in, and you'll swear the khaki-clad servers look like they're ready for a safari into the outback. (They even have the accent right!) The menu has interesting alligator and oyster "teasers" (appetizers) and drinks from the full-service bar, including a number of Australian brews. Locals have found it's a great place for after-the-shows gatherings, especially when you can eat, sit, drink and talk on the deck during summer nights or hang out in the Outback Pub next door. It seems to be a local favorite of college students, perhaps because they have noticed there actually are 99 bottles of beer on the wall (count 'em if you don't believe us)—and all of them different. (See our Nightlife chapter.)

Shorty Small's
$$ • 3270 Yellow Ribbon Rd., Branson • (417) 334-8797

"Short on name, but big on barbecue," Shorty's has juicy burgers (a favorite is the mushroom cheeseburger), steaks, macho nachos, "jumpin' off the bone barbecue ribs," tender barbecue brisket, and tasty salads, including a heroic-size taco salad. Proportions are generous at Shorty's, perhaps to make up for the diminutive name and perhaps to make you want to buy a "I Pigged Out at Shorty Smalls" T-shirt. Shorty's serves lunch and dinner daily

in a plain Southern smokehouse atmosphere just down from The Falls shopping center before Fall Creek Road.

Uncle Joe's Bar-B-Q
$$ • 2819 76 Country Blvd., Branson • (417) 334-4548

Uncle Joe's is probably the oldest place out on The Strip, and we can remember when it was just a shack where the locals drove out for great barbecue with the slaw and beans to accompany it. Times change, but good barbecue doesn't. It's the same, slow-cooked, hickory-smoked recipe, and it attracted the interests of George and Barbara Bush when they were in town in 1992. Ask owner Maria Wilson about the visit and she can tell you exactly what they ordered. You can try the brisket dinner, which Barbara had, or a slab of ribs, which George ate. Or you can not trust their tastes and order something different, but you'd think Texans would know a thing or two about barbecue! If you like the sauce, you can pick up a bottle on the way out.

Tex-Mex

Casa Fuentes
$ • 1107 76 Country Blvd., Branson • (417) 339-3888

This casual cantina offers authentic Mexican cuisine, and locals like it for lunch. Quite a few have even been convinced to try spicy for breakfast, and, of course, the good food attracts the evening crowd. The Casa Fuentes was actually established in Mexico City in 1920 by Manuel Fuentes Martinez, who had worked as head chef in hotels and restaurants in New York, Chicago and Dallas for more than twenty years. His son Manuel Fuentes Alvarez continues his tradition in Mexico City, and Puebla, and now his son Manuel Fuentes Rodriquez continues the tradition in Branson, somewhat adapted to American tastes. We're learning to desert our traditional biscuits and gravy for Huevos con Chorizo (eggs with Mexican sausage, rice, and beans) or the Enfrijoladas (soft tortillas rolled in bean sauce and topped with onion, cheese, and sour cream) and other delectable day-starters. For lunch, there is a variety of traditional specials, or you can order a la carta: Chiles Rellenos (poblano peppers stuffed with beef and cheese and served with rice and beans), or the Taco Loco (three tacos with shredded beef, rice and beans). Dinner can be one of a dozen Casa Fuentes specialities. A favorite is Bisteck a la

RESTAURANTS

Mexicana—thinly cut steak, stir-fried with tomatoes, onions and jalapeno peppers and served with refried beans, Mexican rice, guacamole and hot tortillas. •If any of this fare proves to be too hot, the fire department is only two doors down The Strip from you! Good to know.

Gilley's Texas Café
$$ • 3457 76 Country Blvd., Branson
• (417) 335-2755

Mickey Gilley eats here. He says the food's good and it's good for business. It's his restaurant, next door to his theater. His usual is Hot Tex buffalo wings with iced tea or a light draft beer. Locals like Mickey's chili and buy Gilley's chili seasoning mix to replicate their restaurant favorite in their own kitchen. Beef or chicken fajitas, homemade enchiladas, and Texas nachos are popular menu items, but other options include steaks, burgers, ribs, and salads. Gilley's frozen Margaritas are popular during the heat of the day and after the show.

Garcia's Mexican Restaurant
$$ • 3016 76 Country Blvd., Branson
• (417) 334-5801

We can remember when Garcia's had a small restaurant near where the old Branson grass and gravel landing strip used to be and White Water is now. (Can you believe that?) But they have been serving authentic Mexican dishes long before that time, since 1933 to be precise. Rafael y Conseulo Garcia fixes enchiladas, chimichangas, burritos, tamales, and sopapillas, all the real thing. Garcia's has great deals for lunch, and they have a children's menu. You can enjoy a dynamite dinner with a full range of domestic and imported beers.

Pepper Bellies
$ • no credit cards • 305 Main St., Branson
• (417) 339-4096

Debra Gardner has been slinging Tex-Mex food on Branson's Main Street since 1996, and in that short time has attracted a devoted clientele. She comes by her taste and abilities naturally, her mother-in-law is from the Jalisco area of Mexico and she grew up on western Oklahoma Tex-Mex cooking. The great feature of Pepper Bellies is the made-fresh-every-day salsa, and you must have great self-control not to eat so much you ruin your appetite for the meal that follows! Whether on the homemade flour or corn tortilla chip, this is salsa and chips to kill for. Pepper Bellies uses mother-in-law's recipe for the enchiladas and the rice and beans well as the pork carnitas and the tamales. Pep-

per Bellies has beer and wine, so you can "sip and sample the salsa" and enjoy the authentic 1920s to 1950s vintage Mexican decorations while waiting for your meal. Pepper Bellies is across from the Sammy Lane Resort on the Branson lakefront, a great, cool place for an evening's walk during the summer.

More than a Meal

For you Type A people who like to cram in as much as you can and do something while eating, here in Branson you can take a cruise, watch a horse show, or see the antics of some redneck good ole boys (and their gals). You have to be able to rubberneck, laugh, clap, chew, and swallow at the same time at these places. Note that our price guide includes your meal and the show or attraction.

Branson Scenic Railway
$$$ • 206 E. Main St., Branson Depot
• (417) 334-6110

Take a train ride up Turkey Creek Valley or the Roark Creek Valley on this candlelight excursion into our Ozarks past. The dinner train is Saturday evening only, leaving at 5 PM and returning at 7:15 PM, just in time for you to make a show. This sit-down dinner offers traditional train fare, which includes a salad, a beef, fish, or chicken entrée, plus vegetables and drink. The train will take you back in time to when the railroads set the standard for luxury. You'll see the seasonal splendor of the Ozark Mountains. The conductor will point out some of the interesting highlights along the 50-mile round trip and let you know when you'll plunge into the darkness of a tunnel. With the fine china and linen in candlelight, it's what we call romance. It's an Ozarks version of the Orient Express without the murder. If you get time, you may want to take in the sights from one of the dome cars. Train cars are available for private parties if you're interested. Make your reservations for dinner 24 hours in advance.

Dixie Stampede
$$$ • 1527 76 Country Blvd., Branson
• (417) 336-3000
• www.dixiestampede.com

"The most fun place to eat in Branson," says Dolly Parton of her 1,000-seat restaurant. You get a four-course meal of hickory-smoked barbecue ribs and rotisserie chicken, plus veggies, dessert, and drinks served while you watch a horse show. The service for that many people is

Kids get a kick out of the trick riding at the Dixie Stampede dinner attraction.

Photo: Dixie Stampede

fast, and if you get so caught up in the show that you forget to chew and swallow, you can take the rest home in a doggy (make that a horse) bag. The architecture of the Dixie Stampede theater gives an idea of the theme. It's antebellum "Old South" with horse races, roping, trick riding, chicken races, (and races with birds bigger than chickens—would you believe ostriches?) and a fireworks finale. Dolly does it big for you. Of course, she's had some experience, with similar venues in Pigeon Forge, Tennessee and Myrtle Beach, South Carolina. We suggest reservations for this one, and get there in time for the pre-show entertainment in the alcohol-free saloon. There are two Stampedes each night, at 5:30 PM and 8 PM, with the preshow starting at 4:30 and 7 PM. This Southern spectacle with food is served up nightly March through December with some exceptions. Call for show nights and times for a gallopin' good evening!

Lake Queen Dinner Cruise
$$$ • 280 N. Lake Dr., Branson
• (417) 334-3015

For more than 30 years, the Lake Queen has made its home on Lake Taneycomo and carried more than a million passengers for its sightseeing, breakfast, and dinner excursions. It's a 22-mile 1½ hour cruise with a running commentary of the sights and sounds along the route, plus some Ozark tall tales called "stretchers," all served up with a full buffet. (See our Attractions chapter.) Buffet items vary, but the fixins are good, and if you go away hungry, it's your own fault. Daily cruises are scheduled from April through October, with only weekend cruises in November and early December. Call for times and prices. (See our Attractions chapter.)

Lennon Brothers Breakfast Show
$$$ • 1984 S. Mo. Hwy. 165, Branson
• (417) 337-SHOW
• www.welkresort.com

Take a musical journey through the fantastic '40s and beyond with Dan, Joe, Bill, and Gail Lennon as they serenade you after breakfast at the Stage Door Canteen. Breakfast is at 8 AM, the show is at 9:30 AM. (See Stage Door Canteen of this chapter.)

Polynesian Princess
$$$ • 1358 Long Creek Rd.
• (417) 337-8366
• www.polynesianprincess.com

Early in the morning or late in the evening, cruise Table Rock Lake while you eat. This sightseeing yacht serves breakfast (9 AM), sightseeing only (11 AM), and dinner (5 and 8 PM) for some sights in the area you'd never see by land. There's hula fun for everyone, and you learn interesting lake facts as the captain narrates part of your cruise, telling tales of towns buried beneath the waters. The menus are set, with breakfast being eggs, meat, hash browns, and toast with jelly. For dinner you have two entrees, Hawaiian fruit and ginger chicken and Kahlua pork tenderloin, plus fixings to go with them: fresh garden salad, rice pilaf, honey glazed carrots, and dill rolls. It may seem a bit incongruent with the Ozark lake scenery, but folks like the Hawaiian music and the hula dancer.

She'll even teach you how to dance! The yacht docks at Gage's Long Creek Marina and cruises seven days a week during the season and on select weekends during the winter. You can charter the Princess for private parties and gatherings.

To get to the dock, take U.S 65 south to Mo. 86 west. As you come down the long hill to the Long Creek Bridge over Table Rock Lake, watch for the sign for Gage's Marina on your left.

Showboat Branson Belle
$$$ • 4800 Mo. Hwy. 165,
near Table Rock Dam
• (417) 336-7171, (800) 227-8587

Ride the biggest boat in the world launched on bananas. (Get the captain to tell you how they got that big sternwheeler off the bank and on to the lake!) You can have a cruise, meal, and show all in one to pack lots into a short time on your vacation. You can do breakfast, lunch, or dinner (two evening cruises) or Sunday brunch. Meals aboard the *Branson Belle* come right from the ship's galley and the various courses are served by the singing and dancing servers while you watch the current stage show. The menu is set, with breakfast of ham, egg and cheese casserole, muffins, fruit, juice, and coffee. Lunch and dinner both feature a green salad, hot bread, vegetables, chicken and brisket, plus dessert and coffee. The ship has no bar so go expecting tea and soft drinks. Plan a block of two hours for the cruise, dinner, and show. There is time before and after the meal to go out on deck and take in some of our magnificent scenery. Cruise times vary according to the season, so call ahead for departure times. (See our Attractions chapter.)

Out of the Way, But Worth the Drive

Chez Charles
$$$ • 37 North Main St.,
Eureka Springs, Ark.
• (501) 253-9509, (888) 253-1003

Dining at Chez Charles is a feast for the eye as well as the mouth, and as much energy and effort are put into making the food look good as well as taste good. If you're taking a daytrip to Eureka Springs (see our Daytrips chapter), you may want to make Chez Charles a stop to cap off a perfect day. Chef Charles Clark calls his own individual style of preparation and presentation "a combination of California and France." Chef Charles has been called stubbornly individualistic and wildly artistic with his menu items and with himself. He has worked under award winning chefs and was himself Executive Chef for a 250 room resort casino on the Dutch Island of Curacao. Chez Charles is a dining experience in which you can be involved, talking with Chef/Owner Charles Clark in the open kitchen area and observing him as he masterfully practices his art. Located in the newly restored Grand Hotel, Chez Charles won the Arkansas Times Best New Restaurant award for the station in 1997 and the Best Dessert Award in 1998. Though a relatively new gourmet venue for the Ozarks, the restaurant has quickly established itself as a leading contender as one of the places to go for those who want to taste the best of the Ozarks. We recommend the smoked trout and tortellini with garlic cream sauce for a starter. Our favorite entrees are the roast duckling with lingonberry sauce and the rack lamb with rosemary sauce. Don't be surprised when your food comes decorated with flowers and leaves: marigold, hibiscus or anise blossoms, sage or tarragon leaves. All are organically grown, edible, and are very tasty, making a great "palate cleanser" between bites of the main course. Desserts are a real production number, served in a large, shallow white bowl with abstract Mondrian-inspired artwork in the array of sauces and colors and presented with fireworks! Our favorite was the sponge cake with chocolate-amaretto ice cream, dark and white chocolate, caramel, and creme anglais and orange sauces. Dinner is served by reservation only daily 5 PM to 10 PM and Sunday 6 PM to 10 PM. Chez Charles is closed Tuesday and Wednesday. Chez Charles does not accommodate children under 10 years of age.

Hillside Caterers
$$, no credit cards • 920 Craig St., Reeds Spring • (417) 272-1581

Mentioning this restaurant in a guidebook may be about as foolish as broadcasting on the radio your favorite fishing hole, but when you know something is good, you just want to share it. Let it be known, though, that you don't order food here, you eat what Rab and Kathy prepare for you, and they prepare what interests them, what is in season, and fresh, and what happens to catch their eye when they go out shopping for your particular dinner. When we want to show off and play up our hillbilly image, we take guests to Rab and Kathy's.

Let's explain. You have to plan ahead and bring enough people to fill the entire single table as you will be the only people there. That will be a group of 8-16 people. Don't plan on catching a show or doing anything but enjoying a great meal that evening. Try to plan at least five days in advance, but don't be surprised if the evening of your choice is already taken by another group. They do have occasional "open dinners" that you can join if you call ahead and they still have room.

For $18 per person plus gratuity, you can expect an exquisite menu of soup and 10 other dishes, including two meat entrees and a non-meat entree, several salads, vegetables, bread, two desserts, and coffee and tea. If you want wine with your meal, bring your own. You might ask if Rab would fix certain dishes we have found to be spectacular: the rich and creamy mushroom soup, the jalapeno puffs, spanakopita (spinach and feta cheese in phyllo leaves) or the stuffed pork chops. The banana cream pie or eggnog pie could be one of your great desserts. But whatever they fix, it will be good and there will be enough variety to make some buffets pale in comparison. It will be all "scratch cooking"; Rab quit cooking at a major area restaurant when it went to too much prepackaged, preprepared food. Don't let the difficulty of finding the place, the "outback" appearance, or the lack of parking space deter you when you pull up. You're in for a gastronomic gourmet gala!

To find Hillside Caterers, take 76 west to Branson West, take Hwy. 13 into Reeds Spring. Take a right at the caution light in town onto Spring Street. Just past the spring (you can't miss it, it's right in the middle of the street), turn right on Claybough Street and after a short distance, turn left on Craig Street. The restaurant will be about halfway up the hill on your left. Remember to make reservations well ahead of time. They'll even send you a map on request.

Ozark-speak

At those Branson buffets, one Ozarker commented, "a fellow can eat so much it keeps him skinny just carryin' the weight around."

Rose Garden Restaurant

$ • 485 Rose O'Neill Rd., north of Branson on U.S. Hwy. 65
• (417) 561-2250, (800) 539-7437

Enjoy the elegance of a champagne brunch on Sunday with background musicians. The Rose Garden Restaurant is part of Bonniebrook Park, and the brunch includes a complete breakfast line with fruit and salad bar, several soups, meats, and vegetables. The $12.95 price includes park admission, as well as a tour of Rose O'Neill's home and the museum. (See our Attractions chapter.) They also have a daily lunch buffet, but call regarding dinner. You'll find this elegant spot nine miles north of Branson on U.S. 65, but you may think we're sending you on a wild goose chase. Turn right just after you cross the Bear Creek Bridge, follow the road as it wanders along Bear Creek and then back to the secluded hollow that Rose O'Neill so cherished.

Lambert's Café

$$ • U.S. Hwy. 65 and County Rd. J/CC, Ozark • (417) 581-7655

Here's another road show, but you have to go up the road almost to Springfield for this one! The Ozarks now has its own version of the famous bootheel cafe in Sikeston. The first one opened in 1942 and made famous the "throwed roll" originated by a customer who yelled to a server, "Just throw it to me!" You'd think a lot of great yeast rolls would be dropped by butterfinger catchers, but not many are. Now #2 has the same good food, in a barn-like structure decorated with Missouri roadside advertising art from the '30s, '40s, and '50s, and with items from barns and toolsheds. Lambert's features downhome comfort food—steaks, ribs, pork chops, ham, and meatloaf—for lunch and dinner. Not everyone would agree, but high on our list is liver and onions. Keep filling your plate with "pass-alongs," helpings of fried okra, black-eyed peas, and fried apples until you're filled and just have to pass them along. This place is so popular and so famous that the line can be long (30 to 45 minutes) during the busy season, but people don't seem to mind the wait.

Papouli's

$$$ • Mo. Hwy. 248, Reeds Spring
• (417) 272-8243

Tom and Bessie Haldoupis came here from Greece so many years ago that they almost have a hillbilly accent, and they've been cooking most of those years using old family recipes. They had other restaurants, but Papouli's has been attracting those who take eating seriously since 1986. It's said that St. Louis and Kansas City have "Papouli Clubs," groups of devoted diners who meet and talk about the food they've eaten at this Reeds Spring restaurant. The Greek salad is legendary, loaded with feta cheese and covered in a family recipe dressing that is out of this world. The lamb kabobs are also famous. The menu includes more traditional American fare as well. The plain blue exterior of the restaurant (a remodeled bait shop, Tom told us) doesn't prepare you for the fine dining experience inside, but you know something is up because the parking lot is always packed.

The Riverside Inn

$$$ • 2629 N. Riverside, Ozark
• (417) 581-7051

Those interested in fine dinning have been coming to The Riverside since 1923 when rumors circulated that people drove down from St. Louis and Kansas City just for famous fried chicken, corn fritters, and "Taney County scotch," the local moonshine from the hills south of Ozark. The Riverside and its food have stood the test of time. In its 75-year history, the Riverside has been flooded several times by the Finley River, most recently in 1993, but it has always reopened. Owner Eric Engel doesn't like to think about floods, but he keeps his flood insurance paid! With the Finley River flowing just outside your window, friendly for the moment, you can enjoy steaks, frog legs, seafood, that famous fried chicken, and sinful desserts. A great favorite is Chateaubriand for two ($48) with Rutherford Hill merlot; the steak is a 24-ounce choice cut, and they carve it for you at the table. Enjoy the ambiance of The Riverside's antiques, stained glass windows, mirrors, and the greenhouse, home to the mint plants that add zing to your tea, salads, and sauces. Ask your server

INSIDERS' TIP

Want to prevent your child from spilling a water glass at your table, and yourself from a mess and embarrassment? Restaurants are generous with king-size water glasses, but many haven't caught on to the fact that toddlers can't easily handle those monster glasses. Unless your youngster has hands like a professional basketball player, request a smaller size glass.

about the restaurant's famous floods and you'll be shown the high-water marks on the wall and told stories of bygone days. The wall murals by original owner, artist-businessman Howard Garrison, make for some interesting yarns, too. You can get fine food and an easy local history lesson in a single evening at this dinner-only classic.

Sweets

This is the dessert section of our list of local eateries, and it is only a small gathering of the best, and new ones pop up each season like spring Ozark wildflowers. Being a tourist must be hard work because we have so many restaurants and even more stands and kiosks for snacks and sweets. Indulge your sweet tooth at a couple of them.

How much is your sweet tooth going to cost you in Branson? That depends on you and the number of kids you have in tow. You can get a foot of chocolate at The Fudge Shop for 99 cents (a great gag gift for chocoholic friends), but if you're paying by the pound for fudge and nut candies, expect to pay $2.50 to $4 at most places.

Hard ice cream runs about $1.50 a scoop, and you get a big one. A double is about $2.90, and a triple may cost $4.25. A malt, shake, or sundae can cost $2.75-$2.90. So, all things considered, you can get by as cheap as a buck and a half a head (or should that be mouth?), but count on spending more like $2.75 per mouth. Now you look at the kids in tow, judge their appetites, and you do the multiplication!

Branson Main Street Ice Cream Parlor
104 Main St., Branson • (417) 334-4423

Small and intimate, this ice cream parlor provides cones, splits, and sundaes. It's a great place to stop for a break in your downtown shopping. Our favorite is a double scoop of black walnut ice cream, but they have about every flavor you could want—and a few you wouldn't ever think of.

Cakes 'N' Cream Dessert Parlor
2805 76 Country Blvd., Branson
• (417) 334-4929

Half the fun of this place is the atmosphere which is decidedly '50s, with vintage records on the wall, a Wurlitzer jukebox with tunes of the time and intimate round tables with sweetheart chairs. You can get homemade cobblers, pies, cakes (try the Black Forest cake), funnel cakes (topped with vanilla ice cream, fresh strawberries, and whipped cream), banana splits, and sundaes. They serve 'em up from midmorning to midnight seven days a week during the busy tourist season. They also have sugar-free ice cream and fruit pies for those with special diet needs. When you see the costumed servers work at getting that rock hard ice cream out of the containers, you'll know why we wouldn't wager anything on a blacksmith who might get into an arm-wrestling contest with one of them.

Cheese Please & Umm-More
104 W. Main St., Branson • (417) 339-1782

Cheese crazy describes owner Judy Watson, and she aims to please with cheese. You can get deli sandwiches that are big on cheese. (The pimento cheese sandwich is our favorite!) But also try the cheese and nachos, the cheese soup or chili with cheese. For dessert, there's cheese cake of course—with toppings most folks only dream of: cherry, raspberry, and strawberry. If cheese doesn't please, they have a variety of fruit cobblers and over 16 locally made ice creams. Our favorite was the pistachio-almond, but a close second was the Ozark black walnut. They also have a variety of flavored popcorns, chocolate golf balls, and other snacks that make great gifts or take-with-you's. You'll find Cheese Please right across the street from Dick's Five and Dime.

Delicious Delights
2925 76 Country Blvd., Branson
• (417) 334-5494

Hot dogs, funnel cakes, ice cream, and delicious strawberry shortcake are the hot items for people with a sweet tooth. It's a busy place, because they also established a reputation for great deli sandwiches, but while you're indulging your sweet tooth, you may want to check out some of the gift items for friends back home.

The Fudgery
1335 76 Country Blvd., Engler Block
• (417) 336-7254
3562 Shepherd of the Hills Expy.,
IMAX Entertainment Complex
• (417) 336-3887
300 Tanger Blvd., Tanger Mall
• (417) 337-9899

The Fudgery promises (and provides) fudge and fun, the only free show in town. Watch the singing, wise-cracking candy-makers make up a batch and roll it out on the big marble slab. They might even offer you a free sample. The

Fudgery gives you three chances to indulge that sweet tooth while you're here in Branson. They have the richest, creamiest fudge around including New Orleans praline fudge, vanilla, chocolate, peanut butter, and other types you could only dream of.

The Fudge Shop
106 S. Second St., Branson
• (417) 334-5270

For more than 28 years Barry and Pat Dautrich at The Fudge Shop have satisfied Branson's sweet tooth. You can get a variety of homemade hard candies and fudge, including peanut clusters, pecan logs, caramels, and taffy. Order a foot of chocolate—a great gag gift to take back, if you don't eat it first. Take a look at their famous Dolly Parton suckers. Sample their creamy, rich fudge and you'll know why everyone who goes in comes out carrying a box.

INSIDERS' TIP

Cy Littlebee's Guide to Cooking, published by the Missouri Department of Conservation, and found in many local book stores, offers great recipes for game and native foods. You'll also find the cream-of-the-crop recipes, the best of area cooks and even "pioneer recipes" in cookbooks published by our local churches, societies, and service organizations. Watch for them in gift shops and bookstores.

Mr. B's Ice Cream Parlor
102 Second St., Branson • (417) 336-5735

A cheerful red and white checked decor is splashed around this small, old-fashioned ice cream shop at the corner of Main Street and U.S. Business 65. It's not just desserts though. You can get hot dogs, chili dogs, and deli sandwiches. But it's the ice cream that Ron and Virginia Garrison are famous for. They serve up old-fashioned ice cream sodas, malts, and shakes. They have hand-dipped ice creams (over 23 flavors) and yogurts. Favorites are apple pie, cherry-almond, and "death-by-chocolate." They even have no-sugar/no-fat ice creams for the diet conscious. Let them know it is your birthday, and you'll get a free ice cream cone. They

also have fruit cobblers and real stirred-in-copper-kettles fruit butters—apple, plum, peach. If it takes more than ice cream to satisfy that sweet tooth, The Fudge Shop is right next door!

Scoops
7900 Mo. Hwy. 165 • (417) 337-9744

Scoops has sandwiches as well as ice cream, but they're famous for their ice cream cones, splits, and sundaes. Located right across the scenic view on 165 south of Hollister, it's a great place to get a double scoop of chocolate-mint ice cream and check out the view and watch the activity on the golf course at Pointe Royale or the boats on Lake Taneycomo hundreds of feet below you. Scoops is a bit isolated from everything else, but if you're going toward the Dam, it's worth a stop. We know people who make it a point to drive out there just for a cone when the urge hits them.

Sweet Dreams
3044 Shepherd of the Hills Expy., Branson
Victorian Village Shops • (417) 335-8468

One of 25 shops in the Victorian Village, Sweet Dreams has 24 kinds of fudge and the area's largest selection of sugar-free candies. Our favorite fudges (after chocolate, of course) are root beer float fudge and red, hot and blue fudge, named for the hot Red, Hot & Blue Show. (See our Shows chapter). This colorful fudge is as fun to eat as the show is to watch. Sweet Dreams also has an assortment of coffees, including a special Sweet Dreams blend that is as good 6 hours after it is brewed as it is freshly brewed. For the kids there are Gummi candies, including colorful worms and caterpillars.

Nightlife

If you ask locals what kind of nightlife there is in Branson, they'll probably tell you to see an 8 o'clock show. That's because most folks go to bed fairly early around here. Those of you who are looking for action even after the shows have let out will find a fair mix of local taverns and glitzy nightclubs. Up until the last couple of years, the choices for late night entertainment in Branson were slim. However, as the number of annual visitors steadily increases, so does the demand for more late night establishments.

Most of the nighttime activity in Branson actually takes place in about a dozen or so restaurants with full-service bars. We have grouped them together in this chapter, but you'll also find most of them listed in our Restaurants chapter. Some have live entertainment from time to time, but most of them do not. Unless otherwise noted there's never a cover charge at these places. If you're really looking to kick up your heels and are under the age of 30, you should probably head on up to Springfield where there's a plentiful supply of dance clubs and taverns that are frequented by mostly twenty- and thirty-somethings. Check out the *Springfield News-Leader*'s weekend section that comes out on Fridays for a list of the places hosting live bands or other special events. Branson does have a few places where you can go to cut a rug. Most notable are B.T. Bones and Planet Branson. They both have live bands, and Planet Branson even brings in nationally known acts each week.

The legal drinking age is 21 in Missouri, and many of these places will ask for identification. Non-drinkers will find a few places that serve a selection of non-alcoholic concoctions.

If you've had one too many of the altering kind, ask the bartender or waitperson to call a cab for you. Why spoil an otherwise perfect vacation?

During the winter months, most of our bars and nightclubs close up well before midnight, and even during the busy summer and fall not too many stay open past then. After 1 AM you may have to settle for cable TV.

Local entertainers like to frequent the nightspots after the shows. They catch up on gossip while enjoying a beer with their evening meal. At Beverly's Steakhouse & Saloon you never know whom you might see at the bar or at the microphone.

If you belong to the under-21 dating crowd, and want to cuddle up to your sweetheart in the dark, see a movie at Branson Movies 4 or at IMAX. Skateworld stays open until 10 PM, and some of the go cart tracks stay open until midnight in the summertime, which can be great fun for a date (see our Kidstuff chapter). If all else fails, take your other half down to the lakefront in downtown Branson. A midnight stroll along Lake Taneycomo may do more for your love life than some loud, smoky evening spent in a bar.

LOOK FOR:
- **Eats and Drinks**
- **Live Entertainment**
- **Dancing**
- **Movies**

INSIDERS' TIP

Although Branson police officers may be friendlier than most, they do enforce the law. Don't drink and drive.

Eats and Drinks

Applebee's Neighborhood Bar & Grill
1836 Country Blvd. • (417) 336-5053

This one's got everything you would expect to find at any other Applebee's franchise, but what sets it apart is its location—right next door to another nightlife hot spot, Branson Movies 4. You can pop over and grab a beer after the movie while watching cable TV at the bar. This is a popular hangout for local college students and other barely 21 guests.

Buzzard Bar (Big Cedar Lodge)
612 Devil's Pool Rd., Ridgedale
• (417) 335-2777

This is the kind of place where you might have found Teddy Roosevelt after one of his hunting trips, if it had been around back then. In keeping with true Big Cedar Lodge style, the Buzzard Bar is a dark and cozy place where you can enjoy Irish coffee and other imported alcoholic beverages. Head on upstairs to the Devil's Pool restaurant (see our Restaurants chapter) for a dinner feast or skip dinner altogether and get to know the bartender on a first name basis. Be sure to check out the view of Table Rock Lake out the west side of the building.

Candlestick Inn
127 Taney St. • (417) 334-3633

Thinking of popping the question? You won't find a more romantic spot than the Candlestick Inn. And that's no bluff, because it's perched 250 feet above Lake Taneycomo just east of downtown Branson. This casual but gourmet restaurant boasts the best sunset scenery in town. You and your special someone can choose from a long list of fine wines, liquors, and imported beers to celebrate the occasion (assuming the answer is yes). You won't find any loud bands or karaoke at Candlestick, just great atmosphere, food, and service.

Happy Days Restaurant & Lounge
2206 76 Country Blvd. • (417) 334-6410

Located inside the Branson Mall, next door to the Branson Mall Music Theatre, Happy Days serves breakfast and lunch as well as dinner before and after the 50's At the Hop show,

which means you can stop in after 10 PM for food, drinks, or a little late night CNN. The theme here is the fabulous 50's; so that lingering ducktail you just can't stand to part with will look completely appropriate amidst the other rock 'n roll era memorabilia. If you're ordering off the menu, we recommend the "You Ain't Nothin' But a Hop Dog" or the "I Only Have Fries for You."

Dillon's Pub
309 E. Main St. • (417) 334-9651

It's all about drinkin', talkin', and shootin' pool at this local pub. With just enough room for about 75 people, this is where locals go to catch up on gossip or hear the latest fishing tales. The bar has a jukebox that pipes out one rock 'n' roll tune after another. They're known for their burgers but you've got to get there before 6 PM, after that its drinks only. If you don't want them to know you're from out of town, say hello to everybody as you walk in the door. They'll spend the rest of the night trying to decide whom you're related to.

> ## INSIDERS' TIP
> If you get lost easily and suffer from insomnia, by all means hop in the car and check out the town after 1 AM. There's hardly any traffic, so it's a great time to get to know your way around.

Fisherman's Roost
313 E. Main St. • (417) 334-1363

Need a hair-of-the dog after a big night on the town? This place opens bright and early at 8 AM, taps and all Mondays through Saturdays. Another one of Branson's pre-boom relics, the Fisherman's Roost is a great place to go to jaw and rub elbows with the locals after dark. Anything more than that and you'll have to take it outside. They stay open until 1:30 AM 6 nights a week.

Lone Star Steakhouse
201 Wildwood Dr. • (417) 336-5030

Popular with tourists and locals alike, Lone Star Steakhouse serves up food and liquor in the Texas tradition: big. If you've just come to drink, try one of their giant Margaritas. You may only need one. Their grilled chicken is out of this world and unless you have a Texas-sized appetite, you'll have plenty to take home. You never know who you might run into at Lone Star. Many of our local entertainers stop by after the shows for a well-earned steak dinner. If you're looking for a place to celebrate a birthday, the staff at Lone Star will make enough

The Grand Palace with 4,000 seats is Branson's largest theater.

Photo: Branson/Lakes Area Chamber of Commerce

noise to let everyone in the place know you're there.

McGuffey's
2600 76 Country Blvd. • (417) 336-3600
1464 W. Mo. Hwy. 248 • (417) 335-8680
3265 Falls Pkwy. • (417) 337-5389

There's always a big late-night crowd at McGuffey's restaurants, except for maybe in January and February. The lounges at these popular hangouts serve signature drinks like the Orangutang and the Twister, frozen tropical concoctions served in tall iced mugs— um, um good! During peak tourist season McGuffey's bars stay open until 1 AM. The bartenders are a great source of information about what's going on in the area and are more than willing to lend an ear to a talkative customer. Even when there's a line at the front door, you can usually slip into the lounge for table service. The McGuffey's on The Strip, next to the Andy Williams Moon River Theatre, has a quaint little outdoor patio with occasional entertainment.

Oasis Lounge
2820 76 Country Blvd. • (417) 337-7777

It's OK to bring your camera to the safari-themed Oasis Lounge. More than one local has

been known to do it. You'll see why when you step into this upscale bar, adjacent to The Palace Inn. From the wicker ceiling fans to the wall murals to the palm trees and zebra-print upholstery, this place carries the term "themed decor" to new heights. They keep a well-stocked bar of imported wines and liqueurs on hand for the most discriminating palates. The food comes picture perfect and tastes just as good. Food is served until 9 PM and the Lounge stays open until 11 PM Monday through Saturday.

Outback Pub
1922 76 Country Blvd. • (417) 334-7003

Name your favorite brew and the Outback Pub probably has it. With more than 100 beers, wines, and beverages, the hard part will be in making the decision. Aside from the beer, this is a great place to go for big time Australian atmosphere. They've got live entertainment, darts, billiards, and unique appetizers and sandwiches for lunch and dinner. We like the alligator tail. It's a little like chicken, but more like fish. When the weather's nice you can sit outside on the veranda or, on cool evenings, cozy up to the fireplace. If you're looking for a more substantial meal try the Outback Steak and Oyster Bar next door (see our Restaurants chapter).

Red Lion Pub
1865 U.S. Bus. Hwy. 65, Hollister
• (417) 334-8684

Another local favorite, the Red Lion Pub in Hollister is a great place to grab a quick late-night sandwich (the Rueben is our favorite) or shoot a game of pool. Happy Hour is from 3 PM to 6 PM everyday except Sunday. On Fridays you get the happy hour discount, 25 cents off each drink, all day long. No credit cards accepted.

Rocky's Italian Restaurant
120 N. Sycamore St • (417) 335-4765

This is where the downtown business crowd gathers for lunch and where they unwind after 5 PM. You can order from their full-service bar any time of day. In the evening, test your hand-eye coordination with a game of darts, and then decide if it's time to call a cab. From time to time Rocky's brings in a local combo band for weekend evening entertainment. The atmosphere is great, and the food is even better. By the time you finish with the homemade bread they bring to your table, you'll be lucky to have room for anything else.

Live Entertainment

Beverly's Steakhouse & Saloon
225 Violyn St. • (417) 334-6508

If you're looking to run into a local musician, this is the place to go. Every night the saloon has an open stage, and the entertainers gather to jam, dance, eat, and drink. Since there's never a cover charge, you may get to hear for free the same musicians you just paid $25 to see at one of the music shows. The only difference at Beverly's is that they've got on blue jeans and T-shirts instead of rhinestones and sequins. In 1997 Beverly's moved from their location on Mo. Highway 248 south a block to the old McGuffey's Diner building between the Barrington Hotel and The Grand Mansion theater; same neighborhood, fancier joint.

Charlie's Steak, Ribs & Ale
3009 W. 76 Country Blvd.
• (417) 334-6090

Drop by this local favorite across from the Hollywood Wax Museum for a little late night big band and swing dancin' with bands like Ain't Misbehavin', known as Branson's little big band. There's a $3 cover charge, but you'll get to hear music performed by members of the Bobby Vinton Glenn Miller Orchestra, Lawrence Welk show, Andy Williams show, and Lennon Brothers' show. The great thing about our local bands is that they're made up of top musicians and singers from the theaters. If you arrive early for dinner you'd better come hungry, because the food at Charlie's is piled high. We like the ribs best.

Club Celebrity
3431 W. 76 Country Blvd.
• (417) 334-7535

This 175-seat Las Vegas-style showroom in the Lodge of the Ozarks complex features live entertainment every evening from 9 PM to 1 AM except Sunday. Regional bands like the 50 Cent Millionaires and others take the stage on a rotating schedule. There's a dance floor right in front of the stage and on any given night you'll find a hand full of serious ballroom and swing dancers burning up the floor. The entertainment schedule is scaled down a bit in the winter months. There is a full bar at Club Celebrity, and they'll even cater a dinner or special event for large groups.

Down Under Sports Bar & Grill
1580 76 Country Blvd. • (417) 334-1207

Bring your ID to this place. They have a strict policy about carding those who look even remotely under 21. This intimate little joint has live entertainment on a stage so tiny the band is practically in your lap. They feature a number of regional rock, R&B, and country bands. They have even been known to bring in an alternative rock group or two. Expect to pay a $3 to $6 cover. If the music is a little loud right next to the dance floor, you might want to step into the back room where you'll find pool tables and a TV. If you're into karaoke, they have that too.

Jimmy's Keyboard Restaurant and Lounge
1847 76 Country Blvd. • (417) 332-0001

It's just what the name implies—a full-service restaurant and lounge with keyboard en-

---

INSIDERS' TIP

If you know you'll be out partying late and will need a ride home, check with the front desk of your hotel to find out if they offer shuttle service. Many of the area's hotels will be happy to bring you back in for the night.

An unusually quiet moment for raucous ragtime pianist, Jo Ann Castle.

Photo: Branson/Lakes Area Chamber of Commerce

tertainment. Jimmy's, across from Branson Movies 4 on The Strip, stays open long after the movie-goers have gone home. During the busy season there is live entertainment every night. The owner himself, Jimmy Nicholas, is the attraction. His unique style of comedy coupled with his talented musicianship make for a great evening's fun. The food is not too bad either. We recommend the Oriental Chicken, or just skip it and have some of their homemade dessert.

Dance Floors

B. T. Bones
2346 Shepherd of the Hills Expwy.
• (417) 335-2002

If you can find a spot on this dance floor, cowboy hats off to you. You'd better get there early, because floor space is rare after about 8 PM when the band strikes up and the two steppers and line-dancers take over. Joni Carter, Carl

Bird, and the Route 66 Band cover all your favorite country songs plenty loud enough for you to hear 'em. Sundays are karaoke night, and folks from all over come to make their Branson debut. It's not unusual for this 300-seat place to be packed right up until closin' time (1 AM Monday through Saturday, 12 PM on Sunday). There's never a cover charge here, but they make it up on steaks and cocktails.

Mesquite Charlie's
2849 Gretna Rd. • (417) 334-0498

Mesquite Charlie's is not only known for being the largest restaurant in the state, but its Blazing Star Saloon has one of the largest dance floors as well. On the weekends the saloon brings in different bands that perform big band, country, and rock 'n' roll standards (usually only one style per night). The band gets started at around 7 PM and plays until around 11 PM. You don't have to pay a cover charge except on special occasions such as Mother's Day. They serve appetizers in the saloon while the entertainment is going on, but for dinner you'll have to find a seat in one of their four dining rooms. For a non-alcoholic treat, try a Sidewinder or Six-shooter. The place is filled with large pieces of antique furniture, crystal chandeliers, and hand-painted wall murals. Peek into the kitchen through a large glass window and watch as they prepare your 32-ounce Porterhouse.

Planet Branson
440 Mo. Hwy. 248 • (417) 335-7881

Formerly known as Guitars and Cadillacs, this joint is the Cadillac of nightclubs in Branson. With a total capacity of 960 and a dance floor large enough to hold the entire Osmond family, cousins and all, you can dance the night away or sip Margaritas while you watch music videos on the big screens. Each week they host a concert with different name acts. Recent bands include So Far Gone, 38 Special, Bad Company, Dr. Hook, The Little River Band, and others. Tickets range from $5 to $25 for these frequently sold-out shows. They also bring in local bands from time to time who play everything from country to rock to R&B to alternative. On nights when they don't have a live band, a deejay plays popular country, rock, and dance music and will take requests. The cover charge is around $4 on DJ nights. They've recently added a Karaoke night with occasional prize contests. The bar opens at 4 PM, and the full-service restaurant is open from 5 to 9 PM. You can get prime rib, chicken, salads, and other standard fare seven days a week. If you come for dinner you don't have to pay a cover, except on concert nights. They close at 10 PM on Sundays.

> ## INSIDERS' TIP
> Trying to watch your weight? Better pass on that drunk-munchies-inspired cheese-smothered, fried potato skin chili-nacho-bacon appetizer. That's where all that fat comes from.

Sportsbars

Dockers Restaurant & Sports Bar
3100 Green Mountain Dr.
• (417) 332-0044

You can't miss this dry-docked riverboat on Green Mountain Drive. Dockers really does look like a riverboat on the outside. Inside you'll find the shipyard theme carried throughout the restaurant seating area and sportsbar. The sportsbar features plenty of TVs so there's no fighting over which channel to watch. You can

order off the menu in the sportsbar or enjoy their huge evening seafood buffet that includes peel-n-eat shrimp, baked white fish, fried catfish, fried shrimp, and crab legs all served out of a canoe turned buffet table.

Pzazz
158 Pointe Royale Dr. • (417) 335-2798

This is the place to go when you want to watch that big game on the big screen. Pzazz serves a mean pizza too. It's just inside the gates of Pointe Royale housing development and across from the Welk Resort, and it's a well kept secret among locals. You may run into any one of a handful of celebrities who live at Point Royale.

Shotgun Willie's Steak House & Sports Pub
W. Mo. Hwy. 76, Notch • (417) 338-2141

If you're looking for a little down time after a long day with the family at Silver Dollar City, go a half mile west from Indian Point Road on Mo. Highway 76 to Shotgun Willie's, in the Best Western Branson Lodge (see our chapter on Accommodations). It's one of Branson's newer sports bars with a 10-foot big screen TV and 6 satellite receivers tuned in to all the big games. There's a jukebox and happy hour is from 4 to 6 PM daily. They have a full service restaurant that serves until 9 PM.

Movie Theaters

Branson Meadows Cinemas
4740 Gretna Rd. • (417) 332-2884

Branson's newest and largest first-run movie theater opened in March 2000 at the Factory Shoppes at Branson Meadows. This Shopro Theatre features 11 screens and each theater has plush continental stadium seating and digital sound. They're calling it "stealth cinema design" and saying it's the first one of its type in Missouri. All we know is that the new design provides for a great movie-going experience. The seats are comfortable and you have no trouble seeing over the person in front of you. The theaters are so small, that every seat is close to the screen. They even have cup holders and we know how important those are when you're trying to juggle popcorn, soft drinks and hold hands at the same time. There's an arcade room and a private party room as well. Tickets for movies beginning before 6 PM are $4.25 per person. Movies starting after 6 PM are $6.50 for adults, and $4.25 for adults aged 55 and older, and children aged 3 through 11. Children aged 2 and younger always get in for free. Each Tuesday is "bring your own bag" night. They'll fill it with popcorn for free.

Branson Movies 4
1840 76 Country Blvd. • (417) 334-6806

Branson's oldest 35-mm first-run movie theater has one or two new movies each Friday. They offer three matinee show times daily before 6 PM for $4.25 per person. Adult tickets to the evening shows are $6.50 on Friday, Saturday, and Sunday and $6.25 on Monday, Wednesday, and Thursday. Children ages 3 through 11 and adults aged 55 and older get in for $4.25 every day. Tuesday is discount day with all seats $4.25 unless restricted. To find out what's playing, check the *Branson Tri-Lakes Daily News* or call the theater's recorded message at (417) 334-INFO. This is a Goodrich Quality Theater.

IMAX Entertainment Complex
3562 Shepherd of the Hills Expwy.
• (417) 335-4832, (800) 419-4832

For the ultimate movie-going experience try IMAX. Its six-story screen and surround-sound system will knock your socks off. Beginning at 9 AM each day, the theater runs a different IMAX film every hour. Recent films we saw include *Grand Canyon: The Hidden Secrets, Ozarks Legacy & Legend, Alaska: Spirit of the Wild*, and *Everest*. At 8 PM they run a major motion picture. We saw *Sixth Sense* with Bruce Willis and what a fright that was. There's a new full-length movie every week, so be sure to call ahead to find out what's playing. Adult tickets for the regular IMAX films are $8 plus tax and $4.95 for children ages 4 through12. Feature film prices are $7 plus tax for adults and $4 plus tax for children. Purchase tickets to more than one film in a day and you get the second ticket for half price. (See our chapter on Attractions for more information.)

The Shows

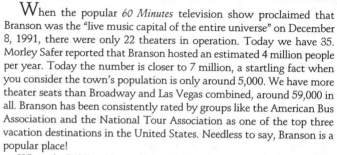

When the popular *60 Minutes* television show proclaimed that Branson was the "live music capital of the entire universe" on December 8, 1991, there were only 22 theaters in operation. Today we have 35. Morley Safer reported that Branson hosted an estimated 4 million people per year. Today the number is closer to 7 million, a startling fact when you consider the town's population is only around 5,000. We have more theater seats than Broadway and Las Vegas combined, around 59,000 in all. Branson has been consistently rated by groups like the American Bus Association and the National Tour Association as one of the top three vacation destinations in the United States. Needless to say, Branson is a popular place!

When the Baldknobbers started the first show four decades ago, little did they know that their show would be joined by more than 80 others in the years to follow. Today the entertainment offerings in Branson range all the way from community theater productions and amateur talent shows to extravagant Las Vegas-style productions complete with 3-D special effects, dazzling costumes, laser lighting systems, and surround sound. And who can forget the big-name stars! Over the years Branson has played host to some of the biggest names in country and pop music both past and present—mostly past, but nevertheless still some of the most famous. Try getting a ticket to Andy Williams' Christmas show after about November 1 and then decide if the term "has been" isn't a little premature.

If you ask people why they come to Branson, the majority of them will say to see the shows, but what they really enjoy is getting to meet the stars face to face. You see, in Branson there are no walls between the entertainers and their audiences. They sign autographs, pose for pictures, board motor coaches and listen intently as people tell them stories about hearing their songs for the first time. If it's your birthday or your anniversary, the stars will announce your name from the stage, or they might even invite you to come up and join them. Veterans are recognized routinely from the stage of almost every theater in town, and no matter what state you're from, you'll be made to feel as if it were the only one in the union.

Since most of the entertainers have homes in Branson and live here at least nine months out of the year, you're as likely as not to run into Yakov Smirnoff at Wal-Mart or see Jennifer Wilson working out at the health club. Mel Tillis and Shoji Tabuchi are regular Table Rock Lakers, and Moe Bandy spends most of his free time on one of the area's golf courses. If you see a really good-looking group of 20-something guys and gals at one of the area's restaurants, you can probably bet they make up the chorus or dance troupe at one of the shows. Go over and say hello, they'll be glad to shake your hand and tell you about their show. Branson is a small town, and the entertainers don't have many places to hide, not that too many of them even try.

One of the best things about the shows in Branson is that because the entertainers are not constantly packing up to get to their next gig, they have time to really work on their presentations and develop new and creative ways to show off their talents. Comedian, musician, and all-around creative genius Jim Stafford is the perfect example of someone who takes full advantage of the time he has to develop his product. His show is constantly changing through the addition of new numbers, special effects, cast members, jokes, and other neat tricks. You could go to his show five times a year and see something new every time.

Most performers do two shows a day. The most common showtimes are 9:30 AM, 2 PM, 3 PM, 7 PM, and 8 PM. The shows usually last around two hours with a 15-minute intermission. Some of them have preshows that begin as much as 30 minutes ahead of the main show. Preshows generally feature some type of specialty act, emcee, or comedian.

The theater season in Branson runs from March through December; however, many of the shows are staying open during January and February for Hot Winter Fun (see our Annual Events chapter). For a list of these shows, call the Branson/Lakes Area Chamber of Commerce, (417) 334-4136. Most of the theaters offer Christmas shows that begin around the second week of November and run through the end of the week before Christmas. Ticket prices may be slightly higher for some shows during this time. The custom in Branson is for the shows to devote the second half entirely to Christmas-themed entertainment, while the first half remains the same as their regular season show. There are some exceptions. We have not included specific information for Christmas shows in this book, so your best bet is to call the theater directly to find out what's in the works.

Holidays are a big deal in Branson, especially Veterans Day. Veterans receive discounts to most shows during the week of Veterans Homecoming each year and are treated to some type of special recognition at each. (See our Close-up in the Annual Events chapter for more information.) New Year's Eve is fast becoming another biggie. Many of the theaters present special late shows to ring in the new year and offer additional shows on New Year's Day.

The showtimes and dates listed in this section are intended to give you a general idea of the days and times a particular show plays. Most shows run six days a week, one or two times a day. Specific dates and times vary frequently throughout the year, so be sure to call the box office if you have a particular date in mind. Also remember that if you call in April to find out what the dates and times are for a show in October, you'd best call back to confirm the information two to three weeks out.

Not only do the entertainers change their show schedules during the year, they also have been known to change theaters as well. Don't panic if you dial the number of a theater only to find out that the show you were looking for is no longer playing there. Again, your best bet is to call the Branson/Lakes Area Chamber of Commerce to find out who is where. (See our Close-up in this chapter on Branson's game of musical chairs.)

The ticket prices we have listed here include tax unless otherwise noted and are subject to change. Each year the prices go up anywhere from 50 cents to $1.50 per ticket. Fortunately, more shows are now allowing children ages 12 and younger in for free. The children's ticket prices listed here generally applies to those ages 12 and younger. There are some exceptions so be sure to call the box office for specific information. Some of the theaters admit children for free during the summer months but charge at other times of the year. Babes in arms are usually always admitted free.

The easiest way to purchase tickets is to call the box office directly. Some theaters ask for a credit card number before they will reserve your seats, while others simply require you to pick up and pay for your tickets 30 minutes to one hour before showtime. If you don't show up in time, you risk losing your reservation unless it has been guaranteed with a credit card. The earlier you call, the better your chances of getting good seats. Good seats vary widely from theater to theater. Front row center may be great in one venue but too close to the stage in another. If you have time, you might want to stop by the box office the day before the show and ask to see a seating chart, or if you have special needs, you can ask to take a peak inside the auditorium. Let the box office staff know if you have seriously impaired vision, need a wheelchair space or require hearing assistance equipment. Staff members will do their best to accommodate you.

INSIDERS' TIP

To find out more about Branson entertainment on the Internet, log on to some of these websites for links and other great information:
www.branson.com,
www.bransoncourier.com,
www.bransonusa.com,
www.bransonchamber.com,
www.bransonwebzine.com

A number of ticket brokers and tourist information centers in town will be happy to make all of your show reservations for you. Some of them charge a small fee, and others purchase tickets from the theaters at a wholesale price and then mark the tickets up. These companies are a good source of information about the shows and will even deliver your tickets to your hotel room. Hotels, campgrounds, RV parks, resorts, and other overnight lodging facilities also make reservations for guests. If you know what shows you want to see at the time you make your lodging reservation, the place will often have the tickets waiting for you when you check-in and simply add the cost of the tickets to your final bill. If you have tickets in your hand before you arrive at the theater, you can avoid the line at the box office right before showtime.

Most all of the theaters have some type of concessions area where you can purchase soft drinks, popcorn, candy bars, coffee, and water. A few serve hot dogs, muffins, and cookies, but that's about it. You can take food and drinks into all the theaters, but listen closely for their audio and video recording policies, usually mentioned at the beginning of each show. Some magic shows even ban the use of flash cameras inside the auditorium.

76 Music Hall
Grand Country Resort
1945 76 Country Blvd.
• (417) 335-2484
• www.grandcountry.com

Wouldn't it be neat if there were a place where you could see a show any season of the year, any day of the week, and any time of the day? And if you could do a little shopping and enjoy a meal while you're there?

There is such a place, and it's called the Grand Country Resort. Previous visitors might know it as the 76 Mall Complex, but that was before a series of renovations. And yes, it's still got the indoor miniature golf, video arcade games, and plenty of motel rooms. (See our chapters on Kidstuff and Accommodations.)

The first of the four shows at the 554-seat theater each Monday through Saturday is the Brumley Music show at 10 AM. It features two generations of Brumleys: Tom, known for his pedal-steel performance on hits dating back to Rick Nelson's "Garden Party," and his sons Todd and Tommy. A third generation is represented by the songs of Tom's father, songwriter Albert E. Brumley, famous for hits such as "I'll Fly Away" and "Turn The Radio On."

Next up at 1 PM is the Down Home Country music show. Splinter Middleton and his band, the Straightshooters perform Western swing music like the second coming of Bob Wills himself. Fiddler and emcee Wade Benson Landry offers a taste of Cajun country, and the very talented Lori Locke covers popular country hits by female performers.

Then it's 76 Country U.S.A at 3:30 PM and 8 PM starring the Pierce Arrow quartet. The high point of the show has to be funnyman Paul Harris, who as hillbilly "Barely Made-It" is definitely one of our favorite Branson comedians. The "low point" is bass singer Dan Britton, who, according to the *Guinness Book of World Records*, holds the world record for the lowest vocal note ever recorded.

But wait, there's more! On Sundays, catch the Sunday Gospel Jubilee at 2 PM and the Ozark Mountain Jubilee at 7 PM. Admission to all shows is $19.50 for adults and children get in free. The 76 Music Hall offers special discounts if you purchase tickets to more than one show. The place is open year round.

Ain't Misbehavin' Supper Club
Mo. Hwy. 165 at Green Mountain Dr.
• (417) 335-2654, (888) 234-SHOW
• www.redhotblue.com

Nobody beats the cast members of Red, Hot…& Blue for sheer energy and enthusiasm in putting on a show. Dubbed "Branson's All-American Ambassadors of Entertainment," these six singer-dancers have jumped from one venue to the next in an effort to accommodate their growing audiences since first bringing their own brand of diplomacy to Branson in 1996.

Finally landing at the Ain't Misbehavin' Supper Club (formerly known as Pump Boys and Dinettes) has at last given the show a big enough stage to do justice to the zesty dance numbers. The show is a song-and-dance tribute to the best music of the Ragtime era, the Roaring '20s, the big band years, and even the '50s and '60s. No wonder they have to change costumes so fast. And what costumes they are! The show is worth seeing just for the fancy duds and outrageous wigs.

Red, Hot… & Blue plays April through December, Sundays through Thursdays, at 9:30 AM. Tickets are $20 for adults and free to children aged 12 and younger. Breakfast is served before each show at 8:30 AM and costs and additional $8 for adults and $5 for children aged 12 and younger. You get ham and cheese quiche, a muffin, fruit, beverage, and the price even includes the tip.

THE SHOWS

The cast of the Red, Hot...& Blue show are known as Branson's ambassadors of entertainment.

Photo: Red, Hot...& Blue

THE SHOWS

Andy Williams Moon River Theatre
2500 76 Country Blvd.
• (417) 334-4500, (800) 666-6094

You've heard the saying, "everything old is new again"? Well, maybe Andy Williams, who turned 71 in 1999 isn't old (and never will be, in our opinion), but he's certainly enjoying a career renewal in Branson. It's not like he ever disappeared from the entertainment scene. He had a string of gold records and silver screen appearances in the early '60s, followed by a very popular TV variety show that ran from 1963 to 1971 on NBC. In the decades that followed, his annual Christmas special on television became an institution. In between he played to audiences all over the world, because as the song says, "there's such a lot of world to see."

Having his own theater in Branson, though, has put Williams back in the spotlight in a big way, and what's good for Andy is good for Branson. By now you've probably figured out that Branson isn't just about country music anymore, and frankly Andy Williams is a large part of the reason why. Most folks consider him to be the first pop music star to call Branson home, and his arrival in 1992 helped pave the way for other non-country performers such as Wayne Newton, Tony Orlando, and the Welk show.

It's been some 40 years since "Moon River" became a hit song, and the fact that it now has its own namesake theater is a testament to the influence that a mere piece of music can have on our popular culture. It also has its own little stream of the same name, flowing over the limestone in front of the theater.

Inside, the lobby boasts some impressive pieces from Andy's private art collection, including an original Henry Moore and three from Willem de Kooning. The most important place to visit in the lobby before the show is the restroom: the show is more than two hours long, and there's no intermission.

Backed by a dozen-member orchestra, Andy delivers all his hits, just like you'd expect. But what you might not expect are the lavish production numbers and costume changes, such as the now famous Andy-as-Carmen-Miranda getup that had audiences roaring a few years back. A guy who'll put on a dress and an enormous fruit-covered hat just for laughs is more than just a classic, he's hip. The theater's ushers, many of them budding singers and dancers themselves, join Andy on stage for some big production numbers from time to time.

The man who brought the Osmonds to the world's attention is still bringing us a Christmas show that's a virtual sellout, year after year. The show changes each season, and it includes contemporary songs as well as oldies. In 2000 Andy's Christmas shows run from the beginning of November through the second week in December. During September and October Andy shares half of his show with country music superstar Glen Campbell. A new show in town called Broadway on Ice opens the season at the theater in April and plays through August. Showtimes at the Moon River Theatre are 3 and 7 PM Mondays through Saturdays. Tickets start at around $29 for adults and $12 for children.

Baldknobbers Hillbilly Jamboree
2845 76 Country Blvd.
• **(417) 334-4528**
• **www.baldknobbers.com**
The Baldknobbers celebrated their 40th year

in Branson in 1999. They've been here longer than any other show and don't show any signs of slowing down. If you know anything at all about Branson, you've probably heard their story, but just in case you haven't, we'll recap it for you. In 1959 four brothers—Bill, Jim, Lyle, and Bob Mabe—started a little show in downtown Branson on the second floor of City Hall. The room had 50 folding chairs and a small stage where the brothers entertained locals and visiting anglers and others who had come to enjoy Lake Taneycomo and the Ozarks outdoors. The group's instruments—a washtub bass, a banjo, a Dobro, and a washboard with a jawbone for rhythm—were mostly homemade. Tickets were 50 cents for kids and $1 for adults. After they outgrew City Hall, they moved to the 200-seat Sammy Lane Pavilion on the lakefront and then on to an old skating rink that accommodated 600 people. In 1968 they built their current theater on The Strip and put in 864 seats. After five remodelings, a lobby renovation and the addition of 836 seats to total 1,700, the Baldknobbers' nest was made.

Bill and his wife, Joyce, and Jim and his wife, Katie, still run the business operation of the theater while the younger Mabes now dominate the stage. Guitar player Dennis Mabe, son of Bill and Joyce, is the lead male vocalist. Brent Mabe, Lyle's son, plays bass guitar and Tim Mabe, who is Jim and Katie's son, carries on his father's legacy as Droopy Drawers Jr. Veteran performers like Mike Ito, who grew up in Tokyo, Japan, and joined the group in 1979, Gene Dove, emcee, singer, and guitar player, and Howard Hale, vocalist and piano player with the group since 1967, along with several other seasoned musicians and singers round out the cast.

The show's formula has deviated little from its humble beginnings. The instruments are fancier, the costumes are flashier and the sound and lighting systems are high-tech, but the musical styles and comedy routines are much the same. Each year the show gets completely overhauled, and new songs are added and old ones are taken out. Don't be surprised to hear the "Orange Blossom Special" though. It seems to be a mainstay. They do old country songs by the greats and hot new country songs by current chart toppers. The comedy skits evoke riotous laughter show after show. Droopy Draw-

INSIDERS' TIP
Some of Jim Stafford's front-of-house workers later appear in the show.

The Baldknobbers presented the first music show in Branson in 1959.

Photo: Branson/Lakes Area Chamber of Commerce

ers Jr. and Stub Meadows fire off one hillbilly joke after another.

Life magazine wrote, "Branson is the Baldknobbers." To find out where the name Baldknobbers came from, check out our History chapter. You can see the Baldknobbers Mondays through Saturdays at 8 PM March through December. Ragtime Joe's preshow starts at 7:15 PM. Tickets are $20 for adults and $10 for children ages 11 and younger.

Bobby Vinton Blue Velvet Theater
2701 76 Country Blvd.
• (417) 334-2500, (800) US-BOBBY
• www.bobbyvinton.com

Billboard magazine called Bobby Vinton "the all-time most successful love singer of the Rock era." It's easy to see why since he had more number one hits during rock 'n' roll's first 10 years than any other male vocalist including Elvis Presley and Frank Sinatra. His first big hit, "Roses are Red," along with others like "There! I've Said it Again!," "Please Love Me Forever," "I Love How You Love Me," and "Blue Velvet" have sold more than 75 million albums and earned him more than a dozen gold records.

Destined to be a musician, Bobby was born in Canonsburg, Pennsylvania, a suburb of Pittsburgh, to a locally popular bandleader named Stan Vinton. Bobby grew up studying music and had his own band by the time he was 16. During his show at the Blue Velvet Theater he often tells the story of how his mother used to pay him a quarter to practice the clarinet. So today he says he pays his mother, Dorothy, a quarter to perform in his show. It always gets a good laugh. If you're wondering, yes, Dorothy does make an appearance in the show. Bobby's family is involved in his Branson enterprise. Wife Dolly and son Chris manage the theater, and daughters Kristin and Jennifer perform on stage.

The Glenn Miller Orchestra backs Bobby's eloquent vocals. When it's their turn to play the tunes that made the late Glenn Miller famous, like "In The Mood" and "String of Pearls," Bobby joins in on the clarinet, piano, saxophone, trumpet, drums, and oboe to demonstrate that all those years of practice really did pay off. Bobby really gets involved with his audiences. He and the band have been known to parade up and down the aisles, all the while not skipping a beat. He even invites couples from the audience on stage to dance from time to time.

Even if you don't have time to see his full two-hour show, we recommend a quick peek inside the lobby of his 1,600-seat theater, which is located right across from The Grand Palace.

The two-story lobby is blue all right, from the Italian floor tile to the cherubic ceiling and wall murals. The carpeting inside the auditorium is patterned with blue and gold albums bearing the initials BV. As with many of the buildings in Branson, the Bobby Vinton Theater was built on the side of a hill, a very steep hill. The parking lot in back can be difficult to maneuver, especially if you're in a wheelchair or have trouble walking up an incline. There's a nice flat spot right in front of the front door where you can be dropped off, though.

Bobby's shows are at 3 and 8 PM Tuesdays through Sundays, April through December with a number of exceptions. Bobby takes July off completely.

Sharing the theater with Bobby in 2000 is the Spirit of the Dance show. If you've seen or heard of Riverdance, then you have a pretty good idea of what to expect. This touring group presents traditional lightning-fast Irish dance numbers that'll leave you dizzy if you try to watch the dancers' feet. It's worth the trouble to keep up, though, because these men and women have the talent and energy to carry a full two-hour show. Spirit of the Dance is presented May through December at 10 AM, 3 PM, and 8 PM on select days. Call for the exact schedule. Tickets to the Bobby Vinton show and Spirit of the Dance are $26 for adults and $10 for children ages 16 and younger.

Branson Mall Music Theatre
2206 76 Country Blvd.
• (417) 335-5300, (800) 434-5412
• www.50satthehop.com,
www.bransonclassics.com

Let's go to the hop—the fabulous '50s At the Hop show, that is. It plays at the 500-seat theater in the Branson Mall. If you're old enough to remember the music of Roy Orbison, Buddy Holly, the Beach Boys, and Jerry Lee Lewis, this energetic cast is young enough to bring it to life, complete with poodle skirts and all those crazy dance styles. The king of rock n' roll may be dead, but here Elvis still rules. Branson All-American Music Awards two-time Female Vocalist of the Year, Nedra Culp commands a lot of "R.E.S.P.E.C.T." when she sings "Baby, Baby I Love You" and if you can't hear her amazingly powerful voice, she'll "Shout" it for you. Nedra, the Hoppettes, and the Dream Dates, sing, dance, and play all kinds of musical instruments.

Tickets are $22.25 for adults and $8.50 for children ages 6 through 11. Kids under 6 get in free. Showtimes are 2 and 8 PM Tuesdays through Sundays, April through December.

January through March, the show plays select days.

Taking nostalgia even further back is the Breakfast With The Classics show at 9:30 AM, Tuesdays through Sundays. This is a mellow, song-and-dance return to the songs of the 1940s and 1950s with a good-sized cast and a live band just like its sister show. Plus, you'll get to see more of Nedra Culp along with male vocalist Bill Brooks. Ticket prices are $17.50 for adults and free to children aged 11 and younger. If you want to have breakfast before the show at 8:30 AM in the Happy Days restaurant located inside the mall, combo tickets are $22.50 for adults and $5 for children aged 11 and younger. Shows run April through December.

Braschler Theatre
3044 Shepherd of the Hills Expy.
• (417) 334-4363, (800) 789-7001
• www.barbarafairchild.com

The Braschler family came to Branson in 1984, which, as far as music shows go, practically makes them natives. The Braschlers and Branson are like a match made in heaven, which may explain why they're known as Branson's favorite gospel group. They even do a special matinee on Thursdays at 2 PM that's all gospel. After all, patriarch Cliff Braschler is a former preacher.

But don't worry, their regular 8:30 PM show, Tuesdays through Sundays, has plenty of country, patriotic, and pop music too. It's also got comedian Terry Sanders, better known as Homer Lee. Some people say Homer is a Branson institution (or do they mean he should be in a Branson institution?). Either way, his Joan Rivers impersonation will have you rolling in the aisles. Admission is $19.50 for adults and free to children. The Braschlers play April through December.

Also appearing at the Braschler Theatre is Branson's sweetheart of laughter and song, Barbara Fairchild. In 1998 Barbara celebrated the 25th anniversary of the release of "The Teddy Bear Song," which hit number one on the country music charts in 1973. She was twice nominated for a Grammy award in the 1970s, but then dropped out of the limelight for a number of years. She gradually emerged from her hiatus with limited engagements in Branson in the late 1980s. A few years ago she sold her home in Nashville and became a permanent resident here. In 1997 she opened her show at the former Campbell's Jubilee Theater and renamed it the Barbara Fairchild Theater. In 1999, the building's owner demolished the aging theater and built the Starlite Theatre in its place (see its listing in this chapter). Barbara moved her show over to the Braschler Theatre where she performs at 10 AM, Monday through Saturday, April through December. On Sundays Barbara does a 10 AM worship service at the Welk Theatre (see the Worship chapter). In July and August, Barbara hits the road during the week for her "We Want America Back" rallies. Tickets to Barbara's shows are $19.50 for adults and free to children ages 12 and younger. For more information about Barbara Fairchild's show and her campaign to influence politicians to support prayer in schools through her "We Want America Back" rallies, you can visit her website listed above.

Country Tonite Theatre
4080 76 Country Blvd.
• **(417) 334-2422, (800) GO-TONITE**
• **www.countrytonite.com**

This show packs one punch of country—country music, country-looking sets, country-style clothing, and country dancing. The cast is an ensemble crowd, and we do mean crowd. With 30 or so members including a large band, featured vocalists, dancers, a comedian, and trick roper and gunslinger, this show is one of the liveliest in town. This crew performs all the hot new country songs along with some of the older classics. The dancers clog, square dance, and do some mighty fine jumps and lifts. In 1999 the Branson All-American Music Awards named the show Show of the Year and in 1997 it won more awards than any other show in Branson. Fiddler Wayne Massengale received the BAAMA Fiddler of the Year award in '95, '96, and '97.

The show originated in 1992 at the Aladdin Hotel in Las Vegas and has been dubbed the best live country show in America by the Country Music Association. In 1994 the show opened in Branson at the old Ray Stevens Theatre. Although the show doesn't claim to have any big-name stars, performers like 8-year-old Jenna Rene Crispin may soon reach star status. She has won a number of awards for her vocal talent. Clint Johnson, the pre-teen singing sensation, is also one to watch. Expert yodeler David Bradley covers cowboy songs like "Cattle Call," "Tumbling Tumbleweeds" and "Ghost Riders in the Sky." Other performers in the show include Branson's '97 Bass Guitarist of the Year Clay Cooper, comedian John Wesley, and Johnny Lonestar, who dazzles audiences with his gun twirling and championship rope spinning.

The Country Tonite show is open March through December. Showtimes are 3 and 8 PM every day except Thursdays. Tickets are $25.50 for adults and $11 for children aged 4 through 12. Children under 4 get in free.

Dinner Bell Restaurant
Buck Trent Breakfast Show
• **200 Wildwood Dr.** • **(417) 335-5428**
• **www.bucktrent.com**

You may have seen Branson morning show pioneer Buck Trent when he performed mornings at the Pump Boys and Dinettes Dinner Theatre in Branson several years ago. He moved around a couple of times since then, but in 1998 he settled at the Dinner Bell Restaurant. Mr. Banjo, as folks like to call him because of his amazing skill on the five-string banjo, twice has been named the Country Music Association's Instrumentalist of the Year. Buck's show features vocalists Kenny Parrott, Tonyia Landry, Beverly Dillard, and fiddle players Bruce Hoffman and Wade Benson Landry. The sit-down, home-style breakfast comes complete with all the fixins including eggs, bacon, sausage, gravy, coffee, and many extras. Breakfast starts at 8 AM and the show kicks off at 9 AM. Tickets to the show and breakfast are $18.95 for adults and $2 to children accompanied by an adult. Tickets to the show only are $16 for adults and free to children. Shows run Mondays through Saturdays from April through December.

Dixie Stampede
1527 76 Country Blvd. • **(417) 336-3000, (800) 520-5544** • **www.dixiestampede.com**

Whether you go there for the food or the show (you can't get one without the other) you'll leave plenty happy with both. The Dixie Stampede is a 35,000-square-foot arena with seating for 1,000. Audience members dine at tiered tables that surround the 12,000-square-foot dirt floor on three sides. The show and the meal kick off at the same time. Thirty-six costumed servers bring out huge tubs of chicken, ribs, potatoes, corn, soup, and dessert. The catch is that they don't bring out any flatware. That's right, no knives or forks. They do offer a moist towel for cleaning up after the meal. (See its listing in the Restaurants chapter for more information about the meal.)

The cast of more than 30 performers presents a show reminiscent of the days when folks hosted parties on the grounds of grand Southern plantations. Singers dressed in 1850s-style costumes enter via horse-drawn carriages.

THE SHOWS

Guests at the Dixie Stampede enjoy the show.

Photo: Branson/Lakes Area Chamber of Commerce

There's plenty of flirting and singing between the belles and their beaus. The action really heats up though when the riding competitions start. Trick riders race their horses around the arena, all the while flipping, turning, and standing in the saddles. The Calvary charge features six riders with swords who attempt to spear hanging 3-inch rings. There's even an ostrich-riding competition. Audience members can get in on the fun when they are invited to toss horseshoes, chase chickens, and ride the horses. The patriotic musical finale features a 35-foot Statue of Liberty, a 30-by-50-foot American flag, and 30 white doves.

There's a music and comedy preshow in the Carriage Room adjacent to the arena that starts one hour before showtime. You can purchase a nonalcoholic tropical beverage or soft drink while you wait for the arena doors to open. The 32 horses at the Dixie Stampede are held in stalls along the west side of the building from 10 AM right up until showtime. You are welcome to stop by and visit them anytime, and you don't need a ticket.

Tickets to the meal and show are $39 for adults and $21.50 for children. Showtimes are 5:30 and 8 PM seven days a week March through December, with some exceptions.

Dockers Restaurant & Sports Bar
Danny Davis & The Nashville Brass
3100 Green Mountain Dr.
• **(417) 332-0044**

Each Monday through Saturday at 11 AM April through December you can catch the Danny Davis & The Nashville Brass show at Dockers Restaurant. Danny Davis is a Grammy-Award winning performer and has received several honors from the Country Music Association. In addition to his own performing career, Davis served for several years as an artist and repertoire director for RCA and MGM where he was instrumental in making Connie Francis a household name. He also worked with artists like Willie Nelson, Dottie West, and Don Gibson while at RCA.

Danny's show at Dockers lacks some of the razzle and dazzle of the typical theater shows, but the music is just as good if not better. He and his group of musicians play songs like "The Wabash Cannonball," "I Saw the Light," and "Unforgettable." Tickets to the show and lunch afterwards are $18 for adults and $9 for children. Lunch is served at noon. (See our Nightlife chapter for more on Dockers Restaurant & Sports Bar.)

The Dutton Family Theater
3454 76 Country Blvd.
• **(417) 332-2772, (888) 388-8661**
• **www.theduttons.com**

BoxCar Willie entertained audiences from his theater at 3454 76 Country Boulevard for more than 10 years before losing his battle with leukemia in April of 1999. The Dutton Family, who first performed in Branson at the Barbara Fairchild Theatre, took over the BoxCar Willie Theatre in 1998 when BoxCar became too ill to perform and now they call it their permanent home.

While the outside of the building still bears reminders of the world's most famous hobo, the Duttons have begun a transformation to make the venue look and feel more like their place.

BoxCar Willie would be proud to know that country music is still being performed in his theater and Dean and Sheila Dutton, parents of Benjamin, Abigail, Timothy, Judith, Amy, and Jonathan, go the extra mile to present the same kind of heart-warming, hand-clappin' feel-good show that BoxCar was known for.

The Duttons are a mighty talented bunch of musicians, singers, and dancers. The kids, (who are hardly kids anymore) play a variety of instruments like the violin, guitar, bass, viola, cello, banjo, mandolin, keyboard, harmonica, and drums. Sheila and Dean are right there on stage with them plucking out traditional country, gospel, pop, and patriotic songs. Before settling in Branson, the family traveled throughout the world performing hundreds of dates each year. In the off-season, they still manage to squeeze in a few concert dates as well. They've performed on PBS and don't show any signs of slowing down. Their shows are at 10 AM, 2 PM, and 8 PM Mondays through Saturdays from April until December. The exact days and times vary throughout the year. Tickets are $19.50 for adults and children aged 12 and younger get in free.

The Grand Mansion
187 Expressway Ln.
• **(417) 336-1220, (800) 884-4536**
• **www.thegrandmansion.com**

One of the theaters operated by Syncor Entertainment, The Grand Mansion, formerly known as The Magic Mansion and the Wayne Newton Theatre, now hosts piano showman Dino Kartsonakis. His production show features a cast of 25 dancers, all lavishly costumed, and some very expensive-looking sets. Dino's wife, Cheryl, a vocalist, co-stars in the show. Dino plays a rhinestone-studded 94-foot concert grand piano, and he's a master.

Although Dino was originally best known for his popular albums in the field of Christian music, his many seasons in Branson at various venues have exposed him to a much broader

INSIDERS' TIP

At Bobby Vinton's concession stand you can purchase a chocolate candy bar covered in a blue wrapper with the initials BV stamped on it. Take this back to grandma. She'll love you for it.

Early Birds can Choose
from Multiple Morning Shows

What Las Vegas is to late night entertainment Branson is to early morning entertainment. While other cities around the country may host a breakfast show or two, Branson has more than 15 full-blown live production shows that all start before 10 AM. Many of these shows feature local entertainers as well as nationally known stars like Buck Trent, Jim Owen, the Lennon Brothers, Barbara Fairchild, Ronnie Prophet, and Yakov Smirnoff.

The popularity of the morning show in Branson has grown steadily over the past five years. Many people who come to Branson have one goal in mind and that is

to see as many shows as possible. Before the advent of the morning show, folks could only see two shows a day, one in the afternoon and one in the evening. When morning show pioneers like Bob Nichols and Buck Trent realized that people who might otherwise miss their shows would get up early to come see them, they started doing morning shows. The idea caught on and other entertainers began moving their shows from evening time slots to morning time slots. Now you can see three shows a day, seven days a week, year round in Branson.

Almost all of the theaters have hosted a morning show at one time or another in addition to their marquee headliner. For example, during the 2000 season Jim Owen is at the Mickey Gilley Theatre, Doug Gabriel is at the Starlite Theatre, Barbara Fairchild is at the Braschler Theatre, Philip Wellford is at the Osmonds Theater, and the Lennon Brothers are at the Welk Champagne Theatre. Morning stars Yakov Smirnoff, The Hughes Brothers, and Jennifer Wilson headline theaters bearing their own names.

The one name that is synonymous with morning shows in Branson is Jennifer Wilson. She was virtually unknown before making her morning show debut at the Roy Clark Celebrity Theatre in 1993. While headliners like Buck Trent and the Sons of the Pioneers were able to capitalize on their name recognition to attract crowds to their morning shows, Jennifer was faced with the twofold task of alerting the public about her new show and enticing people to show up at 9:30 AM to

Jennifer Wilson was virtually unknown until she opened the Jennifer in the Morning show. Now she frequently sells out her 900-seat Jennifer's Americana Theatre.

Photo: Jennifer's Americana Theatre

see it. Jennifer's manager, William Dailey, embarked on an aggressive ad campaign that not only helped make Jennifer a celebrity, but that increased awareness of morning shows altogether. Billed as "Jennifer in the Morning," Jennifer helped pave the way for other up-and-coming morning show performers like Doug Gabriel and the Hughes Brothers. After two successful seasons at the Roy Clark Celebrity Theatre, Dailey purchased the 900-seat Americana Theatre for Jennifer from Moe Bandy. By 1996 Jennifer's morning shows were so frequently sold out that she added afternoon and evening shows as well.

Doug Gabriel and The Hughes Brothers perform morning shows as well as select evening shows. Not too many performers besides Jennifer, Doug, and The Hughes Brothers attempt this kind of schedule. Two shows a day spread so far apart can be quite grueling. Some of the morning show performers like Yakov Smirnoff and Mike Radford do two shows a day, one in the morning and one in the afternoon, but for the most part, morning shows are just that. If you want to see Jim Owen belt out those old Hank Williams Sr. tunes, you have to show up at 10 AM because the rest of the day he's out on the golf course or puttering around town in his antique cars. You only get one chance a day to see Barbara Fairchild. Her show is at 10 AM.

If you like to start your day off with a hearty breakfast, many of our theaters offer meals either just before or during the show. The Welk Stage Door Canteen serves breakfast at 8:30 AM and the Lennon Brothers take to the stage with their swingin' sounds of the '40s at 9:30 AM. Buck Trent moved his show to the Dinner Bell Restaurant in 1998 where breakfast is served at 8 AM and the show starts at 9 AM. Red, Hot...& Blue performs at 9:30 AM at the Ain't Misbehavin' Supper Club with breakfast starting at 8:30 AM. Ronnie Prophet and his wife Glory-Anne perform at the Pickin' Parlor Theater at the Shepherd of the Hills Homestead at 9:30 AM just next door to Aunt Mollie's Restaurant. (See our listing for Shepherd of the Hills Homestead and Outdoor Theatre in the Attractions Chapter for more on Ronnie Prophet.) Most of the shows will allow you to purchase tickets for both breakfast and the show or just the show. Most of the theaters that don't offer a full-course meal do open their concession stands bright and early so you can get popcorn, hot dogs, candy, coffee, and colas.

The average ticket price for a morning show runs around $21, a few dollars less than the evening shows, but the quality in terms of production values is basically the same. Yakov Smirnoff's show at Yakov's American Pavilion features a large cast of singers and Russian dancers along with a horse. The cast of the Red, Hot... & Blue show has some of the best

Doug Gabriel's morning show at the Starlite Theatre features a live band, back-up singers and a variety of country, gospel and pop tunes.

Photo: Starlite Theatre

(Continued on next page)

THE SHOWS

costumes in town and the band in the Philip Wellford Comedy Show features musicians from the Welk Orchestra.

As with many of the shows in Branson, morning shows frequently move from theater to theater, so be sure to call ahead before arriving for a show. The staff at the Branson/Lakes Area Chamber of Commerce, (417) 334-4136, should be able to tell you where a particular show is currently playing.

If you're an early riser and like to wake up to the sound of music, give a morning show a try. The performers get all dolled up in their rhinestones and sequins and once the curtain rises everyone just sort of forgets what time it is.

audience. There's still a strong religious element in the show, which is tastefully done, and Dino's sincerity is evident. The religious underpinnings are particularly appropriate for his Christmas extravaganza, which is always a popular ticket. Dino's honors include winning a Grammy award and eight Dove awards.

Dino plays Mondays through Saturdays at 3 and 8 PM from April to December with some exceptions. Adult tickets are $26 and children's tickets are $9.50.

The Grand Palace
2700 76 Country Blvd.
• **(417) 336-1220, (800) 884-4536**
• **www.thegrandpalace.com**

At 4,000 seats, The Grand Palace is the largest auditorium in Branson. But just how big is it really?

The numbers tell the story. The total floor area inside equals 1½ football fields. The ceiling is 88 feet high. The custom-made chandelier in the lobby weighs 1,250 pounds, is composed of 10,000 pieces including the crystals and is 10 feet, 4 inches in diameter. The cost to build all of this—a cool $13 million.

The design of the lobby, inside and out, recalls the fabulous antebellum mansions of the South, right down to the grand staircase. The auditorium behind the lobby is painted sky-blue on the outside. The reason, so the story goes, is so that when viewed from a distance, the auditorium shell will blend into the sky and leave only the impression of a magnificent mansion.

To understand how and why such a colossus would be built, you have to look back to the heady days of the Branson boom. Thanks to widespread television exposure, Branson was being discovered by the masses, and it was the hot vacation spot (it still is, of course, but today it's neither such a secret nor a surprise.) Silver Dollar City, the long-reigning big dog in Branson, was looking to expand from theme parks into live entertainment, and the owners

wanted a prestigious place to showcase the biggest stars in country music. So they teamed with singer Kenny Rogers, and The Grand Palace was born in 1992.

During the next five years, The Grand Palace hosted every big name you can think of: Reba McEntire, Vince Gill, Lorrie Morgan, Barbara Mandrell, Glen Campbell, George Jones, Jay Leno, Regis and Kathie Lee and, of course, Kenny Rogers. In 1995 Kenny withdrew from the venture, and after the 1996 season Silver Dollar City announced it was selling the theater and returning full time to the theme park business that it knows best.

The Lynn Hall family, operating as Syncor Entertainment, Inc., bought the theater and opened with pianist Dino Kartsonakis in 1997. Dino's flamboyant style fit right in with the palatial venue. In 1999 Syncor moved Dino over to another palatial venue, what is now known as The Grand Mansion (see its listing in this chapter). Syncor then focused on bringing big name stars to The Grand Palace like Leann Rimes, Tony Bennett, Martina McBride, Randy Travis, Bill Engvall, Dwight Yoakam, Bryan White, Suzy Bogguss, and K.C. & The Sunshine Band. In 2000 the concert series continues with names like The Oak Ridge Boys, Charley Pride, and Jeff Foxworthy. The stars usually come in for one to five days and perform one show a day. Ticket prices vary for each performer. The theater is open from April through December.

The Grand Palace's greatest claim to fame to date is hosting the 1999 and 2000 Miss USA pageants. With a lot of help from private businesses, the city, and a host of other sponsors, pre-recorded video clips of Branson, and live footage of the pageant from The Grand Palace were shown to millions of viewers worldwide when CBS aired the pageants in February of both years. Big stars like Donald Trump, Carson Daly, Christina Aguilera, Brian McKnight, Mark Wills, Lou Bega, Julie Moran, and Ali Landry were on hand in Branson for the 2000 pageant.

THE SHOWS

The Hughes Brothers purchased the Celebrity Theatre in 1999
and now perform morning shows there.

Photo: The Hughes Brothers Celebrity Theatre

Chateau on the Lake Resort and Conference Center (see its listing in the Accommodations chapter) hosted the big after-the-pageant bashes both years where guests got to rub shoulders with the contestants and feast on elegant hors d' oeuvres. Tickets to the pageant in 2000 went for up to $125 per person, but were well worth the price. Watching the live network television production from the fifth row was quite a memorable experience. While there are no plans on the drawing board to bring the pageant back to Branson in the foreseeable future, talks are underway to bring in the Miss Teen USA pageant. We'll have to wait and see on that one.

The Radio City Christmas Spectacular starring the world-famous Rockettes continues to be a Christmas-time favorite when it comes to town each November and December. The show's schedule changes from year to year so

call The Grand Palace for exact dates and times. Prices range from $20 to $50 per ticket depending on seat location.

The Hughes Brothers Celebrity Theatre
3425 76 Country Blvd.
• **(417) 336-3688, (888) 518-9925**
• **www.hughes-brothers.com,**
www. theplatters.com

Up until The Hughes Brothers purchased the theater from its original owner, Jim Thomas in early 2000, it was the one theater in town that had managed to stay out of the name game for the most part. That is—the name had changed just twice since 1983. First it was the Roy Clark Celebrity Theatre and then just the Celebrity Theatre. In the early years the theater hosted some of the biggest names in entertainment, like Tanya Tucker, T.G. Sheppard, Ray Price, Lucy Arnaz, and Roy Clark, of course. A few of the stars who now have their own theaters first played in Branson at the Roy Clark Celebrity Theatre. Jim Stafford, Bobby Vinton and the late BoxCar Willie all met with such success during their limited runs here that they decided to put down roots in the little town none of them had heard of before. In 1997 Roy Clark announced that he was cutting back his performance schedule in Branson to pursue other interests; however, from time to time he comes back to town for a limited run.

The Platters moved in to take Clark's place in 1998. They'll continue to play the 2 PM and 7 PM time slot while The Hughes Brothers take the stage at 10 AM.

The five-member Platters gained popularity in the '50s with hits like "Smoke Gets in Your Eyes," "Only You," The Great Pretender," and "My Prayer." They produced 38 top hits and 16 gold albums. In 1997 the group recorded a new album, which contained many of their old hits plus Billy Ray Cyrus's "Achy Breaky Heart." Their version gets our vote. Watch out Billy Ray, The Platters are hip again.

The Platters perform March through December at 2 and 7 PM every day except for Sunday. Tickets are $22 for the show for adults and free to children aged 16 and younger. If you want dinner in the upstairs dining area before the show, the price is an additional $17 per person. Dinner starts at 5 PM.

The Hughes Brothers show is packed with hot country songs, gospel favorites, Broadway show tunes, and even some patriotic music to boot. Their vocal harmonies and smooth dance moves, not to mention their instrumental talents, are quite impressive. The brothers even work their wives and children into the show. Six-year-old Kristina Marie is quite a showstopper.

The Hughes Brothers perform from March through December, Mondays through Saturdays, with adult tickets priced at $20. Children 12 and younger get in free.

Jennifer's Americana Theatre
2905 76 Country Blvd.
• (417) 335-3664 (888) 4-JENNIFER
• www.jennifer.com

One of Branson's most popular morning performers, Jennifer Wilson has been waking up audiences since 1993 when she opened the Jennifer in the Morning show at the Roy Clark Celebrity Theatre. Originally from the Huntsville/Moberly area of Missouri, Jennifer was dis-

covered by businessman William Dailey, husband of famous romance novelist Janet Dailey, when she came to town as a guest performer in the That's Showbiz Talent Show. Dailey immediately recognized Jennifer's singing and dancing talents and was determined to make her a star.

At the time when morning shows were just beginning to catch hold, Dailey gambled that Jennifer would be well received by morning audiences. Two seasons later Jennifer was doing so well that Dailey moved her into Moe Bandy's Americana Theatre, where she shared the marquee until Bandy left at the end of the 1996 season. In 1996 the theater was renamed Jennifer's Americana Theatre, and the Jennifer in the Morning show became the Jennifer show. Since many of her morning shows were selling out, afternoon and evening shows were added and the "Jennifer in the morning" slogan was dropped. Folks around here still refer to her as Jennifer in the morning and probably always will. She has been named Female Entertainer of the Year, Female Vocalist of the Year, and Morning Show of the Year winner numerous times by the Branson All-American Music Awards.

Jennifer's popularity has not been limited to the boundaries of Branson. As the official USO worldwide spokesperson, Jennifer spends the months of January and February touring the world entertaining troops stationed at military bases. Her theater has been designated the official home of the USO in Branson. Jennifer has performed on numerous national television programs like The Ralph Emory Show, Prime Time Country, The Statler Brothers Show, and Crook and Chase. At one time Jennifer was ranked one of Missouri's top models. Jennifer has released four albums of country, pop, and gospel songs, some of which were written by her mother, Peggy Wilson, and one Christmas album.

In 1997 Jennifer released an album containing a country version of Elton John's "Candle in the Wind 1997." The Asian and European Country Music Association ranked her second only to Garth Brooks on the country music charts soon after the song was released. Her album contained 17 other songs and received airplay on country music stations in the United States as well. All of the proceeds from the sale of the album go to the Princess of Wales Memorial Fund.

A tireless perfectionist, Jennifer spends every moment off stage preparing for the time she spends on stage. Her two-hour show is packed with dozens of dance routines that range from tap to jazz to the Charleston to her own creation, the Missouri Clog. The Prime Time Pickers band, a group of well-seasoned musicians backs Jennifer. She sings everything from Broadway to gospel to '40s big band songs and, of course, country.

Jennifer performs at 9:30 AM and 7 PM Mondays through Saturdays from April to December. The schedule varies somewhat so call for specific times. Tickets are $19 for adults and children ages 15 and younger get in free.

For the past several years Jennifer's theater has hosted the most successful easy listening-country entertainer in Great Britain and Ireland, Daniel O'Donnell, whose credits include being named Ireland's Entertainer of the Year multiple times. He has had numerous number one hits on the British country music charts and has sold more than 3 million records worldwide. Mary Duff, Ireland's top female vocalist, joins Daniel. Shows run November and December at 2 PM Monday through Saturday. Tickets are $21 for adults and free to children aged 15 and younger.

Jim Stafford Theatre
3444 76 Country Blvd. • (417) 335-8080
• www.jimstafford.com

When vaudeville went out of fashion decades ago, it seemed that the days of an entertainer who could do it all were past. And so it remained until Jim Stafford hit town.

Reasonable people could disagree on whether Jim is a singer-songwriter who does comedy, or a new American humorist who is also a musician. Reciting a list of his credits would do nothing to settle the argument, because he's done so much in both fields. Even so, it's worth noting that he's had hit records such as "Spiders and Snakes" and "Cow Patti," his own TV show (The Jim Stafford Show in 1975) and served as head writer for the Smothers Brothers Comedy Hour.

Nothing can prepare you for seeing the Jim Stafford show at his theater in Branson. Most people are surprised to see whirling blimps and flying saucers and 3-D movies in a town full of music shows. They do however, get a good dose of music, and Jim delivers that on guitar, fiddle and harmonica, just to name a few.

The show has something new every year, and that's what keeps folks coming back. Our favorite part is the black-light segment, but in 1998 it was the real-live tornado effect that really blew us away. Now Jim's added a 3-D movie he created, shot, and edited all at his theater. It's shown on a stereoscopic 3-dimen-

sional rear projection screen. Sounds high-tech, huh?

Jim talks a lot about family during the show, and his own is incorporated in a major way. His wife, Ann, who is the theater manager, joins him on stage, and his 6-year-old son Sheaffer demonstrates budding prowess on the drums, fiddle and guitar. Even little G.G. gets into the act. It's all calculated to tug at the audience's heartstrings, and it works. It's shameless, really, but Jim knows it's shameless, and we know he knows—and that's part of the fun of it. Corn is okay if it's well tempered with cleverness.

By the time you add up the jokes, stories, songs, and a 22-piece marching band, you've got what we consider the rebirth of the vaudeville-type variety show, with a definite technological twist. Unlike most entertainers, Jim plays seven nights a week and does matinees on Sundays. The bulk of his season is March through December, but he also plays many dates from late January through February. Showtime is 2 and 8 PM. Adult tickets are $27.50, and kids aged 6 through 11 are admitted for $8.50. Kids 5 and under get in free.

Before or after the show, check out Pie-Annie's upstairs at the theater. It's a sandwich and dessert shop with an old-fashioned soda shop feel. It's also a gift shop, which is very convenient since that's where Jim signs autographs after the show.

Kirby VanBurch Theatre
U.S. Hwy. 65 at Mo. Hwy. 248
• (417) 337-7140, (800) 60-MAGIC

First it was Berosini and VanBurch at the Five Star Theatre (now known as the Remington Theatre), then it was VanBurch and Wellford at Branson's Magical Mansion (now known as The Grand Mansion). After that it was The Kirby VanBurch Show at the Palace of Mystery (previously the Gettysburg Theater) and now, it's Kirby VanBurch at the Kirby VanBurch Theatre, formerly known as the Will Rogers Theatre. You might think Kirby VanBurch spends more time packing up and moving from theater to theater than he does performing, but that's really not the case. The Prince of Magic, as he is known, has simply had a hard time settling into one venue. His show, however, is equally impressive on any stage, since he's been working on perfecting his craft for a number of years in Branson and before that in Las Vegas casino showrooms. In 1999 Kirby won the International Magician of the Year title.

The show features Kirby performing his traditional illusions and magic tricks aided by his dancers and various lions, tigers, and leopards. Most people's favorite is a rare royal white Bengal tiger named, imaginatively enough, Branson. He and the rest of the unique menagerie reside in the animal compound on the premises. Showtimes are 2 PM and 8 PM Tuesdays through Sundays from April through December. Tickets are $25 for adults and $16 for kids.

Legends Family Theatre
3600 76 Country Blvd.
• **(417) 339-3003, (888) 374-7469**
• **www.legendsbranson.com**

After several years in Branson at somebody else's theater, Legends In Concert has a place of its own on The Strip, the former Cristy Lane Theatre, across from Western Sizzlin'. Night after night, in nearly a dozen locales all over the world, Legends is renewing its reputation as the best of the great pretenders.

"Dolly Parton," "Marilyn Monroe," "Roy Orbison," "Michael Jackson," "Garth Brooks," "Reba McEntire," "Shania Twain," "Elvis Presley," "Little Richard," "Frank Sinatra," "Bette Midler" and "Judy Garland" are among the superstars of the past and present who might make an appearance at any given performance. Remember, they're not the real things, but as you watch the show you may find yourself forgetting that little point. "Elvis," of course, almost always gyrates on stage to close out the show. What makes this presentation so eerily realistic is the fact that not only do the impersonators look like the stars, they also can sing like them or play their instruments. Many are called but few are chosen, and those few are usually quite talented in their own right, apart from the coincidence of being a look-alike.

Among the highlights of the show are the Legends dancers, whose beauty and precision makes them the closest thing Branson has to show girls. Rounding out the talent pool is the Legends Tribute Orchestra. The "star" line-up changes four times a year to coincide with audience preferences. The summer-time show is geared more for younger crowds with "Madonna" and "Shania" and in the spring and fall older audiences are treated to the likes of "Marilyn" and "Frank Sinatra."

Showtimes are 2 and 8 PM Thursdays

through Tuesdays, March through December. Head on over with the family, as kids are admitted for $5.56 (ages 4 through 16) and adult tickets are $24.41 Kids under 4 get in free.

The Bob Nichols Show with The Brett Family plays at the Legends Theatre every day except Sunday at 9 AM March through December. Tickets are $17.95 for adults and $5 for children aged 16 and younger.

Mel Tillis Theater
2527 Mo. Hwy. 248 • (417) 335-6635
• **www.meltillis.com**

Like many of the shows in Branson, the Mel Tillis show is truly a family affair. In 1998 and 1999 Mel brought in his daughter Pam Tillis to perform with him on select days of the year. It was such a hit that for the 2000 season, Pam joins in the Christmas shows in November and December as well. The father/daughter duo is a big hit with fans of country music past and country music present. In recent years Pam has had a string of chart-topping hits like "Don't Tell Me What To Do," "Cleopatra, Queen of Denial," "Maybe It Was Memphis," and "Mi Vida Loco." She was named Female Vocalist of the Year in 1994 by the Country Music Association and has received a string of gold and platinum albums. She even appeared on Broadway in 1999 in "Smokey Joe's Café." Pam, the oldest of Mel's children, was born in Plant City, Florida, in 1957 and raised in Nashville where she learned early on the workings of the country music business. It was not until the mid-'80s that Pam decided to pursue a music career full-time. In 1990 she received a recording contract from Arista and a year later produced the breakthrough album, "Put Yourself In My Place." She has been in constant demand as a concert performer and television personality ever since. She has appeared on *The Tonight Show with Jay Leno* and *The Late Show* with David Letterman, and she has hosted episodes of TNN's *Live at the Ryman* series.

Joining sister Pam and dad Mel in the show are singer Connie Lynn; Mel Jr., a singer and songwriter; Carrie April, a classically-trained opera singer; and grandson Marshall, who is not yet old enough to drive but is cute enough to dazzle a crowd. A 20-piece band and The

INSIDERS' TIP

Many of the area's music shows have coupons in local guidebooks. A few good ones to check out are Best Read Guide, Take-1, Travel Host, and Sunny Day Guide Book, all usually available in stands or at your hotel front desk.

THE SHOWS

You'll find a dance ensemble in most of the large production shows in Branson.

Photo: Branson/Lakes Area Chamber of Commerce

Stutterettes, Mel's appropriately named backup trio backs the family. You won't notice Mel's characteristic stutter when he sings "Ruby, Don't Take Your Love to Town," "I Believe In You" or "Take Me Back to Tucson," but when he starts to tell a joke, you can usually bet that the punch line will be somewhat delayed.

Mel's been in the music business some 44 years and has spent the past 11 full-time in Branson. He's no longer and old road dog that's for sure, but he and pals Waylon Jennings, Jerry Reed, and Bobbie Bare released an album lamenting the aspects of growing older called "Old Dogs." The Country Music Association nominated it for vocal event of the year in 1999. In the early 1950s Mel performed with a band called the Westerners while serving as a baker in the U.S. Air Force. In 1956 he wrote the song "I'm Tired," which was recorded by Webb Pierce, and his career took off. In 1976 he was inducted into the Nashville Songwriters International Hall of Fame and named the Country Music Association's Entertainer of the Year. Mel's songs have been recorded by artists like Brenda Lee, who appeared with Mel at the Mel Tillis Theater throughout the 1997 season, Charley Pride, Ricky Skaggs, George Strait, and the Oak Ridge Boys. He has starred in more than a dozen feature films including "Every Which Way But Loose," "Smokey and the Bandit II," and "Uphill All the Way" with Roy Clark.

The Mel Tillis Theater, which sits on 25 acres on the northwest side of town, is one of the largest in Branson with 2,700 seats and a 35,000-square-foot lobby. Mel even hosts conventions and other special events in the building.

Mel performs at 2 and 8 PM every day except Monday from April through December. Exact days and times vary. Pam Tillis plays select dates in April, May, June, November, and December in 2000. Tickets are $29 for adults and $15 for children to see Mel and Family and tickets to the shows with Pam Tillis are a couple bucks more.

Mickey Gilley Theatre
3455 76 Country Blvd.
• **(417) 334-3210, (800) 334-1936**
• **www.gilleys.com**

When people talk about Mickey Gilley's music show, one of the first things they mention is the comedy. And it's no wonder. Throughout the show, Mickey and his steel guitar player, Joey Riley, swap barbs and jokes and stories until you think you're gonna bust.

Mickey may have been an Urban Cowboy in the 1980 movie that made him famous, but today he is as urbane as he is witty. He strolls on stage decked out in a tuxedo and some serious jewelry, including a necklace bearing a diamond pendant that spells out "MG." But then he mentions that his cousins are Jerry Lee Lewis and Jimmy Swaggert, and we realize the joke's on him after all.

Still, Mickey has come a long way from the rough-and-tumble days of growing up in Texas. His mama, he says, bought the piano that he and his famous cousins all learned to play on because she hoped Mickey would take a shine to gospel music and become a minister. We don't know why or when he went astray, but we're glad he did. For more than two decades, Mickey has been preaching about the heartaches and hard breaks of the honky-tonk life. Among his 39 top 10 country hits, and 17 number one hits are "Don't the Girls All Get Prettier at Closing Time," "Stand By Me," and "Room Full of Roses."

No one knows more about honky-tonks than Mickey. His nightclub in Pasadena, Texas, Gilley's, was an institution long before the movie cameras dropped in to capture John Travolta ridin' the mechanical bull. And speaking of hard breaks, both the Gilley's nightclub in Texas and Mickey's first theater in Branson were destroyed by fire, the latter in 1993. (Maybe that's what cousin Jerry Lee was forecasting when he sang about "Great Balls of Fire.")

Undaunted, Mickey rebuilt in 1994, and his 996-seat theater is frequently sold out. During most of his season, Mickey does an 8 PM show only, but on a few dates in September, October, and November he also does a 2 PM matinee. Ticket prices are $23 for adults and $5 for children. The theater is open from March through December.

Also presented at the Mickey Gilley Theatre is the Jim Owen Morning Show. Jim is perhaps best known for capturing the essence of Hank Williams Sr. (a role he played many years ago for one of John Stuart's Legends In Concert productions). Besides, a big dose of classic country, Jim also performs some of the hits he has penned for other artists, including "Louisiana Woman, Mississippi Man" done for Conway Twitty and Loretta Lynn.

The show also includes tributes to Dottie West and Faron Young, with the help of Jim's female backup singers, Sunshine Express and his band, the Last Cowboy Band. But thanks to the recent release of a new pop music album, Jim has added numbers such as "I Left My Heart in San Francisco."

The Jim Owen morning show is presented at 10 AM from March through December. Exact dates vary. Ticket prices are $16 for adults and $6 for children.

Moe Bandy Theatre
3446 76 Country Blvd.
• (417) 334-5333, (888) 322-6394
• www.moebandy.com,
www.sonsofthepioneers.com

In 1998 Moe Bandy moved from the matinee time slot at the Mickey Gilley Theatre to the headliner spot at the former Anita Bryant Theatre. It wasn't the first time Moe had his own Branson theater, though. Before his two seasons at Gilley's, Moe was in the Americana Theatre, which is now home to Jennifer Wilson.

Moe was raised in San Antonio, Texas, and labored as a sheet metal worker while playing the local nightclubs. After a stint in the rodeo, he began to hit it big with such chart-toppers as "Bandy the Rodeo Clown" and "Americana." Like many of his Branson colleagues, he's won numerous awards from such prestigious outfits as the Academy of Country Music and the Country Music Association.

After more than a decade in Branson, Moe's blend of country and patriotic music is as well received as ever. His show includes all his country hits as well as the comedy of his sidekick, "Hargus Marcel." Moe likes to sign autographs after the show, and that might be a good time to ask him about his fishing exploits. He enjoys relating the story of how he once took Mel Tillis and Shoji Tabuchi out fishing, but had to bring them back after only 15 minutes because, "I couldn't understand either one of them."

Moe Bandy's show is presented March through December at 8 PM every day except Mondays. Tickets are $21 for adults and free for children aged 12 and younger.

Also appearing afternoons at the Moe Bandy Theatre is the Sons of the Pioneers. This group has been making music since the early 1930s. You may remember them from Roy Rogers

INSIDERS' TIP

Many of the listings in this chapter reference the Branson All-American Music Awards. This awards program is held each year usually in November and is compiled of a large pool of local residents and fans who select winners in a variety of categories including Best New Show, Entertainer of the Year and others.

The Osmond brothers' family show includes on-stage ice skaters.

movies (he was one of the group's founders) or have heard one of their classic records, like "Cool Water" or "Tumbling Tumbleweeds." The Pioneers have called Branson home for well over a decade, and the current members, Dale Warren, Luther Nallie, Sunny Spencer, Gary LeMaster, John Nallie, and Ken Lattimore, sound as smooth and harmonious as their famous forebears. One of our favorites is Gary LeMaster, who is only the third lead guitarist in the group's history. We won't try to list all the different instruments he can play, or the funny ways he plays 'em, but make sure you get his autograph after the show, he's always got a tale to share. Remember, these guys are the real thing—the Pioneers practically invented Western music, and nobody in town does it better.

The Pioneers ride the range Tuesdays through Sundays at 2 PM. Tickets are $19 for adults and free to children aged 12 and younger. Shows run from May through December. The Sons of the Pioneers still perform a number of shows in different locations around the coun-

try each year, so call the theater or visit their website if you want a copy of their road schedule.

"The Cowboy Ain't Dead Yet," a musical comedy, plays at 10 AM Tuesdays through Saturdays March through December. The show features Joe Vandygriff, an actor, singer-songwriter who portrays Joe Texas, a cowboy whose mission it is to demonstrate that cowboys of days past are indeed still alive and well. His story is told through music, poetry, and comedy. Tickets to this show are $19.75 for adults and $9.50 for children.

Osmond Family Theater
3216 76 Country Blvd.
• **(417) 336-6100, (800) 477-6102**
• **www.osmond.com,**
www.wellfordshow.com

Perhaps Branson's most well known family and certainly one of the largest, the Osmonds have been in the entertainment industry for more than 40 years. First discovered by Walt Disney, brothers Alan, Wayne, Merril, and Jay became household names when they appeared as regular guests on Andy Williams' NBC television specials in the 1960s, but they started performing ten years before then. Their string of hit records, 47 gold and platinum in all, include songs like "One Bad Apple," "He Ain't Heavy, (He's My Brother)" and "Yo Yo." Their performances of these songs and others are just as good today, if not better, than when first recorded. Their voices have matured a little, needless to say, but along with age comes experience. The Osmonds are an outstanding example of flawless talent and showmanship.

In 1996 the Osmonds transformed the surface of their stage into an ice-skating rink. You can see world championship ice-skating performed during each show by the Ice Angels. The Osmond brothers wear special no-slip shoes during their numbers. The magical illusions of Anthony Reed and the comedy of ventriloquist Jim Barber along with vocalist Babette Young round out the cast. Oh, and we must not forget about the fabulous Jay Osmond Band.

Youngest brother, Jimmy, is the mastermind of the business, but still finds time to join his older siblings on stage on a regular basis. You won't see Donnie or Marie in this show. They're busy with their own show these days on network television. The duo is enjoying phenomenal success with their daytime talk show and we wish them the best of luck.

Before the 2 and 8 PM shows you can enjoy candlelit lunch or dinner served inside the Osmond Theater. Lunch seating begins at 12:30 PM and includes a hot turkey or beef sandwich, beverage, garden salad, potatoes, green beans, and apple cobbler a la mode for $12 for adults and $6 for children. The evening meal is served at 6:30 PM and consists of prime rib and a variety of side items for $17.50 for adults and $8 for children. These prices are in addition to the show ticket prices.

The Osmonds perform at 2 and 8 PM March through June and September through December, Monday through Saturday with some exceptions. Tickets start at $27.50 for adults and $5 for children.

In July and August the Osmonds take a break from the theater, but you can see Jim Barber, Babette Young, Anthony Reed, the Ice Angels and others in a new high-energy Jimmy Osmond production called Flashback. The show traces the best music from the '50s to the present. The show plays at 8 PM Monday through Saturday. Tickets are $22.50 for adults and $5 for children.

Tony Orlando knocked three times at the theater and now he's doing select dates in May, June, October, November and December. Call early if you want tickets to his ever-popular veterans tribute shows during the week of Veterans Homecoming. Tickets start at $27.50 for adults and $5 for children.

As if there weren't already enough going on at the Osmond theater to spend your entire vacation there, Branson's only Emmy award-winning funnyman Philip Wellford presents his hilarious show at 10 AM Mondays through Saturdays from April through June and October through December. In July and August he does a 2 PM only show.

Philip's two-hour show is one side-splitter after another. Philip will do anything to get a laugh. He'll ride a unicycle, juggle fire, swallow ping pong balls, dance, invite audience members on stage, and he'll even fall down (more than once). Joining Philip on stage is his lovely wife Susan, ventriloquist Patty Davidson and his band, Five Guys Named Moe. There's plenty of music in Philip's comedy show. It's largely of the jump jivin' swing style. Tickets to his show are $17.99 for adults and $5 for children not including tax.

Owens Theatre
205 S. Commercial St
• **(417) 336-2112, (800) ELVIS-95**
• **www.elvisinbranson.com**

If the king were alive he'd probably have his own theater in Branson by now, but fortunately for us we have Dave "Elvis" Ehlert to stand in for him. Ehlert's show, called Elvis and the Superstars, has played at the historic Owens Theatre in downtown Branson for the past few seasons. Ehlert has been impersonating Elvis for nearly three decades. Before coming to Branson he performed on the Legends in Concert stage in Las Vegas and a variety of other venues. He has even appeared on the Oprah Winfrey show. Ehlert, who is originally from Chicago, was an original inductee into the Elvis Performers World Wide Hall of Fame in California.

The show in Branson not only showcases Ehlert's ability to move, gyrate, and sing like the King, but also his impressions of the Blues Brothers, Roy Orbison, Liberace, Willie Nelson, Julio Iglesias, Tom Jones, Johnny Mathis and Michael Jackson—just to name a few.

The theater is open February through December with showtimes at 2 and 8 PM Friday through Tuesday. Tickets are $22.25 for adults and $8 for children ages 6 through 11. Kids ages 5 and younger are admitted for free.

Presleys' Country Jubilee
2920 76 Country Blvd. • (417) 334-4874
• www.presleys.com

The Presley family is truly an icon for Branson. They built the first theater on The Strip in 1967 and have entertained millions of visitors every year since. Their show stars three generations of incredibly talented musicians, singers and comedians.

It all started when the patriarch of the family, Lloyd Presley, made somewhat of a name for himself in the 1940s with his live performances on KWTO radio in Springfield. In the 1950s he and his family performed in the Underground Theater, a cave just north of Kimberling City. In 1967 Lloyd and his wife, Bessie May, their son, Gary, and his wife, Pat, paid $15,000 for 10 acres on The Strip. The building they designed had a level concrete floor and no permanent seats. In the event that their music show idea didn't float, they planned to turn it into a boat storage facility. Slowly but surely folks did come to see their show. They sat in folding chairs and purchased their tickets out of Gary's home just behind the theater. The family continued to keep their day jobs while the audiences grew. Lloyd worked as a professional fishing guide on Table Rock Lake. Gary commuted to Springfield where he worked at a typewriter factory.

Bessie May kept her job as a secretary, and Pat worked for Security Bank. By 1975 the theater had been expanded to hold 1,300 people, and the shows were selling out. After a total of six expansions including the addition of a balcony and wings, the total capacity reached 2,000 and the shows still continue to sell out.

With 20-plus cast members, the Presleys' show is one of the hottest tickets in Branson. The 30-minute comedy preshow is worth the price of admission alone. Gary, also known as the sequined, overall-clad "Herkimer," gets out and works the crowds. The show that follows features a variety of hot new country music and old favorites along with Southern gospel and swing all performed on instruments like the banjo, fiddle, guitar, bass guitar, drums, and harmonica. Greg Presley, Lloyd's grandson, gets our vote as one of the best harmonica players in town. The entire cast wears superb-looking costumes complete with fringe, sequins, and beads. What started out as a homemade show in a metal warehouse is now not only one of Branson's best but also as good of a show of its kind as you'll see anywhere.

The Presleys play March through December at 8 PM Mondays through Saturdays. Tickets

are $19.75 for adults and $9.50 for children, not including tax. In 1998 the Presleys installed an amazing-looking new sign in front of their theater that projects video footage of the show. If you're driving along The Strip, you can't miss it.

The Promise Theatre
755 Gretna Rd. • (417) 336-4202
• www.thepromise.com

Down in the Ozarks, if one is good, then two is better. That seems to be the premise of The Promise, which like its famous long-running neighbor the Great Passion Play in nearby Eureka Springs, Arkansas, has Jesus Christ as its subject matter. Well, after all, Branson is in the heart of the Bible Belt, and folks around here aren't shy about proclaiming their faith.

The Promise opened here in 1996 after playing for several years in an amphitheater in Glen Rose, Texas. It's billed as a musical drama based on the life of Christ. There's plenty of spectacle and special effects, with fancy period costumes and sets to match. The cast of more than 50—not including the live sheep, horses, birds, and camels—features men, women, and children of all ages who act and sing out trials and tribulations of His life. Some of the songs are Dove Award winners. The show has proven to be popular with the many church groups and motorcoach travelers who come to Branson.

The Promise is presented at 3 PM and 8 PM Mondays through Saturdays from April through December. The adult ticket price is $27.50 and $14.50 for children aged 7 through 12. Children younger than age 7 get in free. Tickets for adults aged 55 and older are $26.50.

A sister production to The Promise, called Two from Galilee tells the story of Mary and Joseph before the birth of Jesus. With equally impressive production value, Two from Galilee is presented Monday through Saturday at 3 PM November through December. Ticket prices are the same as for The Promise. You can save a few bucks on a combo ticket, so call the box office for more information.

Remington Theatre
3701 76 Country Blvd.
• (417) 336-6220, (888) 371-3701
• www.remingtontheatre.com

This exquisite-looking theatre named after artist Frederic Remington whose sculptures and other artwork decorate the lobby has 2,700 seats and boasts the largest ice rink on any theater stage in the United States.

The ice rink is quite an impressive sight and

Performers Play Game of "Musical Theaters" in Branson

Imagine this. You've finally saved up enough money for the ultimate Branson vacation. You've plotted your route to town, made hotel reservations, received the information you requested from the Branson/Lakes Area Chamber of Commerce, gassed up the vehicle, and set off on your merry way. Along the stretch of U.S. Highway 65 between Springfield, Mo and Branson you see billboard after billboard adorned with the faces of entertainers you grew up listening to on the radio. By the time you get into town, you have your mind made up which shows to see and which to save for next year.

You arrive at your hotel at 7:15 PM, in plenty of time to make it to that 8 PM show over at the such-and-such theater. You break out the city map, locate your destination and rush out the door. When you arrive at the theater, you notice something strange. The marquee lists the name of a different performer. "That's okay," you think to yourself, "maybe they've got two stars playing here." You approach the friendly box office clerk and ask for four tickets to your all-time favorite singer. Instead of handing you the tickets, she flashes you a puzzled look.

"I'm sorry, so and so has moved down the street to the so and so theater," the friendly clerk replies.

A lump rises in your throat as you realize you don't have time to make it to the so and so theater before the curtain rises.

Welcome to Branson. The entertainers here have come up with a new game called musical theaters. It's a slightly modified version of musical chairs. Every so often, some of them pack up their bands and move two or three doors down the street. At the beginning of every new game—or season as we call it—some of them end up without a place to sit down. They're usually replaced with new, faster-moving players. Since the Baldkobbers opened the first show in Branson in 1968, lots and lots of players have come and gone. Big name stars like John Davidson, Glen Campbell, Cristy Lane, Ray Stevens, and Anita Bryant all had theaters bearing their names at one time. Headliners like Willie Nelson, Kenny Rogers, Louise Mandrell, Larry Gatlin, and Ray Price even had their own shows here, but they are no more. They've been replaced by other big name stars and ensemble production shows like Country Tonite, The Promise, Spirit of the Dance, and Dino Kartsonakis.

As with life, just about the time you get used to something, it changes. The theater business in Branson is no exception. It is dynamic and that's what makes it interesting. While entertainers like Bobby Vinton and Andy Williams own their own theaters, many do not. When they get a better offer from another theater owner, they do the smart business thing and move. Occasionally, as was the case with Tony Orlando and Wayne Newton, who moved from the Tony Orlando Yellow Ribbon Music Theater to play at the former Glen Campbell Theatre from 1998 through 1999, the owner of a theater will file bankruptcy. The same thing happened with the Charley Pride Theatre in 1997. As of yet Pride has not found a new place to sit down in Branson. After the owners of Mutton Hollow Entertainment Park and Craft Village filed bankruptcy and closed the park, The Platters moved their show to the Roy Clark Celebrity Theatre, which is now the Hughes Brothers Celebrity Theatre.

Critics often try to use the announcement of a Branson theater bankruptcy to conclude that the town is drying up and that the big name stars are on their way out. This couldn't be further from the truth. As with any industry, there are businesses that come and go. Restaurants around the country go out of business, motels go out of business, and T-shirt shop owners file bankruptcy. The only difference is that they don't make the front page of the newspaper and theater closings do. The Branson boom of the early '90s is now only an echo, but the economy it generated is alive and well. Enough said.

The overall face of entertainment in Branson is beginning to change, however. When Roy Clark first moved to town in 1983, he was the first nationally known entertainer to call the place home. Up until that time the Baldknobbers and Presleys and other family shows ruled. Some said Clark would never last, that Branson was no place for stars. Well, Clark and others who joined him like the late BoxCar Willie, Mel Tillis, and Jim Stafford proved them wrong. Then, when Andy Williams opened in 1992, some said his style of pop music wouldn't appeal to the country fans that were coming to see Roy Clark and BoxCar Willie. Williams and others like Bobby Vinton and Tony Orlando proved them wrong. Today, variety productions shows like Country Tonite, Legends in Concert, Dixie Stampede, and Magic of the Night are testing the waters and enjoying substantial success. They seem to be the wave of the future for Branson.

Jim Thomas, former owner of the Roy Clark Celebrity Theatre and the Remington Theatre, said he believes the days of stars in concert are over in Branson. A bare stage and a lonely spotlight used to do the trick, but not today. What he means is that audiences want to see the stars surrounded by glitz, flash, fancy costumes, dancers, props, ice skating, variety acts, comedy, pyrotechnical stunts, animals, and other bells and whistles. When Thomas produced the show, Branson City Lights, in 1997 at the Remington Theatre, (formerly known as the Wayne Newton Theatre and the Five Star Theatre), he put in all those things plus the kitchen sink. The show played for three years, but was replaced by an even hotter production show in 2000 called Magic of the Night. Director Gary Ouellet brought to the Remington Theatre his experience as a network television producer of shows like NBC's "World's Greatest Magic" and "World's Most Dangerous Magic." Gone not only are the days of stars in concert, but of mom-and-pop shows with small-time production values. Shows that come to Branson today must be bigger, better and more spectacular than their predecessors if they expect to draw the crowds.

While the nationally known name acts may not be showing up on Branson marquees quite as much as they used to, entertainers like Andy Williams, Bobby Vinton, Jim Stafford, Mickey Gilley, Mel Tillis, and other Branson veterans know that in order to appeal to audiences year after year, they have to give them what they want—fancy

(Continued on next page)

Mel Tillis is one of the few performers in town that you can count on to be at the same place year after year. He owns his own theater on Mo. Hwy. 248 just a few miles off The Strip.

Photo: Mel Tillis Theater

THE SHOWS

productions. And these guys do. This is not to say that traditional shows like the Baldknobbers and Presleys don't offer big production value. Drive by the Presleys' theater and take a look at their new marquee with its enormous video screen or stop in and check out the Baldknobbers' sound and lighting systems. You'll quickly see that these shows have found a successful recipe that tempers hillbilly charm with showbiz glitz.

The stars and production shows that have been here the longest are the least likely to participate in the game—of musical theaters, that is. It's the newer players or the locally-known shows like Red, Hot...& Blue, Philip Wellford, The Hughes Brothers, and Kirby VanBurch whom you might have a hard time locating from season to season. In time, they too will settle into more permanent homes. Wayne Newton is one big star who hopped from theater to theater year after year. His first home was the Wayne Newton Theatre, which is now The Grand Mansion. From there he moved to the next Wayne Newton Theatre, which is now the Remington Theatre. From there it was on to the Tony Orlando Yellow Ribbon Music Theater, which is now dark. After that, he and Tony Orlando moved into the current theater, which was named the Talk of the T.O.W.N. Theatre. However, after Tony left in 1999, it became the third building in Branson bearing the name, Wayne Newton Theatre. In 2000, Wayne Newton announced he wouldn't be performing in Branson, though the theater still bears his name.

The old switcharoo usually takes place between December and March, when many of the theaters are closed for the winter and entertainers are most likely to make their move. Occasionally some move in the middle of the season, but not too often. Your best bet for finding out who is where is to call the Branson/Lakes Area Chamber of Commerce (417) 334-4136 before you leave home. Since the information in this guide is compiled well before it makes it into your hands, some of our listings may even be out of date.

When you're driving down The Strip or U.S. 65 don't believe everything you read. Billboard companies don't always paint over old copy in a timely fashion. One billboard we saw at the corner of Mo. Highway 248 and Shepherd of the Hills Expressway read, "There's only one Wayne and there's only one Wayne Newton Theatre" and directed people to what is now the Remington Theatre. The billboard went up when Wayne Newton was playing there and the theater's name was the Wayne Newton Theatre, but it didn't come down until long after he'd left that building and had started playing with Tony Orlando over at the Tony Orlando Yellow Ribbon Music Theatre. For much of the time the billboard was up, there was no Wayne Newton Theatre. If you're wondering why the streets in Branson are so jammed just before showtimes, now you know—it's from all the people still trying to find the Wayne Newton Theatre.

the new Magic of the Night show takes full advantage of all that space. The show stars illusionists The Hamners, a husband and wife team who have appeared on NBC's World's Greatest Magic series as well as a variety of specialty performers who rotate in and out of the show throughout the year. Some of the acts you are likely to see include T.J. Howell, whose comedy juggling on ice skates leaves audiences in stitches every time, and even T.J. occasionally. For summer audiences The Hamners cause a 4-ton elephant to disappear on stage. And the adagio ice skating team of Jeb Rand and Jennifer Bayer makes the most complicated jumps and spins seem effortless. Magician and comedian Lex Pearson offers up a delightful preshow and the Magic of the Night dancers round out the cast. The show was created and directed by Gary Ouellet, the well-known writer-director of NBC's World's Greatest Magic series and dozens of other network specials. Ouellet's long list of credits also includes ABC's Champions of Magic series, NBC's World's Most Dangerous Magic series, and NBC's Lance Burton magic specials.

Andrew Marsh, general manager of the theater and producer of Magic of the Night, says Ouellet is one of the first to bring theatrical excitement to the variety and magic format. There's plenty of excitement all right. When

Dave Hamner impales wife Denise on a 6-foot syringe to demonstrate the perils of illegal drug use, you can hear a pin drop in the audience. The death-defying illusion Vertigo places Denise high above a bed of razor sharp spikes until Dave, who has to free himself from his own jail cell full of spikes, comes to rescue her. The finale of the show is as inspiring as it is beautiful. Without giving away the ending, we'll just say it involves birds, about 80 of them. Dave and Denise Hamner use exotic birds throughout the show and Dave even sings and plays musical instruments. There's plenty of audience participation in this show and one lucky couple even gets a chance to win a big prize in the "Who Wants to Win a Million Dollars" segment.

Magic of the Night plays February through December at 3 and 7:30 PM Monday through Saturday. Tickets are $19 for adults and $11 for children aged 16 and younger.

Shoji Tabuchi Theatre
3260 Shepherd of the Hills Expy.
• **(417) 334-7469** • **www.shoji.com**

Guess who's the most talked-about entertainer in the live country music capital of the world? Nope, it's not some Nashville recording artist, it's a violinist from Japan.

If you don't know who Shoji is, don't feel bad. He's the biggest star nobody ever heard of. He's never written or recorded a hit song, and outside of Branson he's virtually unknown. But here he's the Godzilla of the Ozarks, attacking all our preconceived notions of what a music star looks and sounds like.

We might as well tell you about the theater bathrooms first, because that's probably one of the first things a visitor hears about anyway. The women's room features live cut orchids at every granite and onyx pedestal sink. There's stained and jewel-adorned glass and exquisite chandeliers. The men's restroom contains a hand-carved mahogany billiard table, black leather chairs, a marble fireplace, a walnut mirror built in 1868 and black lion head sinks. Those who forget to take their camera into the bathroom with them needn't worry, because the restrooms are featured on picture postcards in the gift shop.

On the other hand, though, perhaps the lavish lounges aren't so unusual when you consider that the exterior of the building is decked out in purple neon. It's our guess that this particular shade did not exist on the planet before Tabuchi, or perhaps it's just that so much of it has never been assembled all in one place. Those

who might complain that the decor of the theater exceeds the bounds of acceptable ostentatiousness should be reminded that this is not a museum, it's an entertainment hall.

What we like most about Shoji is that his success epitomizes the American Dream. He immigrated to the United States after being inspired by a Roy Acuff concert in Osaka, then waited tables in San Francisco while waiting for his big break. Eventually he landed in Branson in 1981 and steadily worked his way up from theater to theater. In 1990 he built his showplace at a convenient location on Shepherd of the Hills Expressway, where he has enjoyed unfathomable success.

It's evident that the show is a million-dollar production. The laser effects are state-of-the-art, the costumes are lavish and chorus members always seem to be flying about. The orchestra numbers approximately 18, and there are probably that many singer-dancers as well.

Shoji fiddles in every style of music you can think of. Besides the obligatory "Orange Blossom Special," Shoji does classical, Cajun, Broadway, and bluegrass. Each season brings something new to the production, due in large part to his wife, Dorothy, who is credited as producer and choreographer. She often sings and emcees as well.

In recent years Shoji's teenage daughter Christina, also a singer, has been featured in an increasingly prominent role. Shoji sings some too. His Japanese accent is still cute as ever, even when sung, but we think this would be a good time to point out again that Shoji is a first-rate fiddler. By the way, it's pronounced SHOW-gee Ta-BOO-chee.

You can see him March through December at 3 and 8 PM, Mondays through Saturdays. During the fall and Christmas season he also performs on select Sundays and adds 10:30 AM shows as well. Tickets are $31 for adults, $30 for adults aged 60 and older and $20 for children March through October. In November and December add $5 to the adult prices and $2 to the children's price. That makes it practically the most expensive ticket in town, but on other hand, the show itself is one of the longest too. Clocking in at 2 hours, 30 minutes give or take a little, you'll get your money's worth.

Starlite Theatre
3115 76 Country Blvd.
• **(417) 337-9333, (877) 336-7827**
• **www.starlitetheatre.com,**
www.douggabriel.com

Out with the old Barbara Fairchild Theatre

and in with the new Starlite Theatre. This brand new venue on The Strip was erected in 1999 on the very spot the Barbara Fairchild Theatre used to sit. The building's owners, Ron and Judy Layher, decided the old venue had seen all of its better days so down it came and up went the 900-seat Starlite Theatre, with an 11,000 square-foot glass enclosed five-story lobby that sits so close to the street, you can see your reflection in the glass as you drive by. The Layhers have attempted to recreate the look and feel of a '50s main street America inside the atrium complete with a gazebo, a park area, and some nifty classic cars. The '50s-themed Starlite Diner, located inside the lobby serves up traditional diner fare and very yummy shakes. (See our Restaurants chapter for more information.)

The signature show at the Starlite Theatre is called Lost in the Fifties and was voted best new show in 1999 by the Branson All-American Music Awards. The cast of 16 includes 6 band members and 8 singer-dancers who perform the hits of the 1950s rock 'n' roll era in period costumes. This is a fast paced show that'll have you singing along and tappin' your toes to the music. Eight-year-old Branson veteran Matthew Matney does an Elvis impersonation complete with mini-bellbottoms. Matthew has been performing on stage in Branson since he could talk, which was about the same time he learned to sing. You can also see him and his 5-year-old sister, Molly, in the Starlite Kids Revue show at 5:30 PM. The 9 cast members of this American Kids spin-off show are the cream of the crop in young talent today. We're not talking your local talent show winners here, folks. These kids who range in age from 5 to 16 sing and dance their way through the most popular music of the modern era. Each week or so during the summer guest performers join the cast. Tickets to the Starlite Kids Revue show are $20 for adults and $6.50 for children. Tickets to Lost in the Fifties are $26.50 for adults and $6.50 for children. These shows run February through December every day except Friday with some exceptions. Showtimes for Lost in the Fifties are 2 and 8 PM.

Branson favorite, Doug Gabriel performs mornings at the Starlite Theatre. His shows start at 9:30 AM Mondays through Saturdays March through December with some exceptions. Doug has been wowing morning crowds with his tremendous vocal abilities and his master musicianship for almost a decade. He was named Branson's All-American Music Awards Morning Show of the Year in '97 and '98 and has been named Male Vocalist of the Year five times. Doug is also quite the all-around personality. He likes to get out and mingle with the crowd early

Award-winning male vocalist, Doug Gabriel stars in his own morning show at the new Starlite Theatre.

Photo: Doug Gabriel

on in the show. He performs everything from country to gospel to old-fashioned rock 'n' roll. If his rendition of "Malaguena" won't get your heart pumping, nothing will. When Doug was 10 years old his father crafted what he calls a "mufftar" from a 1969 T-Bird muffler and guitar parts. The musical instrument actually produces pretty good sound, and Doug still uses it in his show. Branson's Ripley's Believe It or Not! Museum added a replica of the mufftar to its collection in December of 1997 (see our Attractions chapter). Doug's wife, Cheryl, joins him on stage for touching vocal duos as do their children Joshua, Jordan, and Jasmine. Doug is backed by what is possibly one of the best bands in Branson. His horn section adds a special flare to many of the musical numbers. Doug is quite the songwriter and performs a number of his original works in the show. Tickets are $21 for adults and free to children aged 16 and younger.

Wayne Newton Theatre
464 Mo. Hwy. 248
• (417) 335-2000

Previous visitors to Branson know this 2,000-seat theater as the Talk of the T.O.W.N. Theatre as it was called in 1998 when Tony Orlando and Wayne Newton shared top billing. When Orlando left Branson at the end of the season, it became the Wayne Newton Theatre. It was originally built for Glen Campbell and was called the Glen Campbell Theatre for several years. If you're getting this theater's exact location confused with the previous two Wayne Newton Theatres that's easy to understand (see our close-up in this chapter on Theater Musical Chairs). It's located right off U.S. 65 on Mo. 248. As we mentioned in the Getting Here, Getting Around chapter, Mo. 248 is now a fabulous multilane highway, so you usually don't have to worry about the traffic. You can see the east end of the theater as you enter town from the north on U.S. 65.

In March of 2000 Wayne Newton announced he would not be performing in Branson. Performing the bulk of the schedule at the Wayne Newton Theatre are the Incredible Acrobats of China. This group of Shanghai Circus performers twist, turn, and contort their small bodies into unimaginable positions while performing difficult balancing routines, strength maneuvers, and other bizarre feats. They are a real favorite. Tickets are $20 for adults and $12 for children. The Acrobats perform May through December every day except Sundays with a few exceptions. Showtimes are 10 AM, 3 PM and 8 PM.

Welk Champagne Theatre
1984 Mo. Hwy. 165
• (417) 337-SHOW, (800) 505-WELK
• www.welkresort.com

For years millions of people sat glued to their television screens every Saturday night to watch the popular Lawrence Welk TV Show and those darling little Lennon Sisters. Today you can see the Lennon Sisters and a host of other featured Lawrence Welk TV stars at the 2,300-seat Welk Champagne Theatre. The Welk Resort Center is a destination in and of itself. The complex includes a 160-room hotel, the Champagne Theatre, the Stage Door Canteen Restaurant and Lounge, nearby retail shops, and all the nostalgia you could ask for. (See our chapters on Accommodations and Restaurants for more information on these places.)

Larry Welk, son of the late band leader Lawrence Welk and president of The Welk Group, Inc., recognized that Branson was the perfect place to reassemble the former Welk cast members for a live show. So when the theater opened in 1994, the Lennon Sisters and Lennon Brothers moved to Branson. Most of them came from California, where they had spent the past 20 years or so pursuing individual interests and raising their children.

The Welk Show in Branson is presented with all the grandeur and spectacle reminiscent of the television show. The Lennon Sisters perform songs like "Falling Leaves," "My Favorite Things" and "Boogie-Woogie Bugle Boy." In 2000 the show salutes a century of American music, and is produced by Tom Bahler and Mary Lou Metzger who have created a musical journey through the 1900s accompanied by the 20-piece Lawrence Welk Orchestra.

The Lennon Sisters, pianist Jo Ann Castle, the Lennon Daughters, the Cathcart Brothers, Jack Imel, Ava Barber, Russian adagio team Paul Riazantzev and Elena Lopatnicova, and the Welk singers and dancers are regular cast members. Throughout the year they are joined by former Welk TV stars like Ken Delo, Myron Floren, Ralna English, Bobby Burgess and Elaine Balden, Joe and Chris Feeney, Guy Hovis, and others. The performers rotate in and out of the show at different times of the year. They usually come to town for around two weeks at a time. Call for specific dates of these guest performers.

The set of the Welk show in Branson looks just like the one from the television show. A huge crystal chandelier hovers above the stage and the letters LW hang against the backdrop. There's even a bubble machine. The Welk show gets our vote for having one of the best lighting designs in town. The costumes are fantastic too. And yes, the Lennon Sisters (Mimi, Janet, Kathy, and Dee Dee) still dress in matching dresses with different necklines.

Tickets to the Welk Show are $29 for adults and $12 for children ages 6 through 12. Children 5 and younger get in free. The Welk resort offers complete vacation packages that include tickets to their shows, plus lodging, meals, and tickets to other shows and attractions. Shows start at 2 and 8 PM six days a week from April through December with a few exceptions. There are no shows on Sundays except for a few dates in October, November, and December.

Throughout the year the Welk Resort Center hosts a variety of special events. In 2000, the Fifth Annual Lawrence Welk Polka Festival is held in June and features polka bands from across the country performing on stage. In years past the center has hosted the Welk Square Dance Jamboree where square dance groups got a chance to show off their fancy footwork and Branson Fest, the annual kick-off of the year's shows and attractions. Call the box office for specific dates and prices for special events.

The Lennon Brothers Breakfast Show stars the brothers of the Lennon Sisters—Dan, Joe, and Bill, and Bill's wife, Gail. This group brings to life the sounds of the World War II era with songs by groups like the Modernaires, the Pied Pipers, and the Delta Rhythm Boys. The group has received the Branson All-American Music Awards Breakfast Show of the Year honor numerous times and has been called the "best show in Branson" by the Chicago Tribune. The show started out at the Stage Door Canteen, but because the audiences have grown so much over the past few years, The Lennon Brothers now perform on the Champagne Theatre stage. Veterans be sure to catch this show during Veterans Homecoming each year.

Breakfast is served in the Stage Door Canteen, which is located inside the theatre at 8:30 AM, and the show starts at 9:30 AM. Tickets to the show only are $19.50 for adults and free for children. Tickets to the show and breakfast are $24.50 for adults and $5 for children. The Lennon Brothers can be seen April through December.

Yakov's American Pavilion
3750 76 Country Blvd.
• (417) 33-NO-KGB, (800) 33-NO-KGB
• www.yakov.com

After five seasons in Branson with shows at the Cristy Lane Theatre, the Osmond Family

Theater, and The Grand Palace, Russian comedian Yakov Smirnoff finally got a theater bearing his own name in 1997. The 1,300-seat former Ozark Theater, at the west end of The Strip near the Country Tonite Theatre is now known as Yakov's American Pavilion. The outside of the building was remodeled when Yakov took over and a new street sign was erected in the likeness of Yakov himself. You can't miss his huge 3-dimensional face as you drive down The Strip.

Yakov's show is full of comical yet touching stories about growing up in Russia and adjusting to life in America. In 1977, shortly after Yakov graduated from college in Russia where he studied art, he and his parents traveled to New York in search of their freedom. One of Yakov's first jobs was as a bartender in a hotel with a 2,000-seat theater. With a little encouragement from one of his coworkers, Yakov soon mustered up the nerve to take the stage. While in Russia, Yakov had spent a few years as the emcee of a band that worked cruise ships in the Black Sea. He wasn't exactly a stranger to the stage, but most of his jokes he only knew how to tell in Russian. Nevertheless, Yakov was a hit at the hotel.

This experience led to a move to Los Angeles, where he found work in comedy houses before being cast in the 1984 movie "Moscow on the Hudson" starring Robin Williams. Two more feature films followed in 1986, "Heartburn" with Jack Nicholson and Meryl Streep and "The Moneypit" with Tom Hanks and Shelley Long. A few years later while he was performing at a Farm Aid concert in Iowa, Yakov ran into Willie Nelson, who told him about Branson. In 1993 Yakov opened at the Cristy Lane Theatre and has been in town ever since.

Yakov's particular brand of comedy pokes fun at communist Russia and at the idiosyncrasies of his everyday life as a husband, father, and now an American. His show includes comedy, music, and Russian dances. Comedian David Hirschi, a.k.a. Slim Chance, who is also a fantastic juggler, defected from the Country Tonite show and joined Yakov in 1998. Yakov's is so sure you'll like his show, that he offers a money back guarantee if you're not satisfied with it.

The gift shop inside the lobby of the theater contains items imported from around the world. You'll see hand-painted glass collectibles from Holland, breakfast teas from Ireland, pottery from South America, hand-carved wooden boxes from Poland and beer steins from Germany. You can also get a copy of Yakov's book, "America On Six Rubles A Day" which is now in its fifth printing, and has sold upwards of a quarter of a million copies.

Yakov's shows play at 9:30 AM and 3 PM April through December, Tuesdays through Sundays with some exceptions. Tickets are $25.25 for adults and free for children.

Attractions

From the bottoms of our caves to the tops of our hills, the Ozarks is packed with a huge selection of attractions both natural and manmade. Long before there were automobiles and airplanes, folks came on horseback and in wagons to see the rivers, caves, and wildlife. Thanks to a little modern technology now you can see our oldest attractions from our newest attractions. Railway cars will take you through tunnels and over natural bridges deep into the Ozarks outdoors. Paddlewheel boats will take you down Lake Taneycomo and across Table Rock Lake. Hot-air balloons will take you 2,000 feet above the hills. Ducks (WWII amphibious vehicles) will take you across both land and lake. And from the 230-foot tall Inspiration Tower you will see a far wider view of the Ozarks than Harold Bell Wright ever did.

Not only do our attractions let you see the Ozarks from all possible angles, but also at the same time you can see a live music show, enjoy a meal, or sit in a high-tech IMAX movie theater. Our two largest theme parks will show you a view of the Ozarks' past. Silver Dollar City and the Shepherd of the Hills Homestead have preserved turn-of-the-century pioneer life in their shops, live shows, crafts, music, and hospitality. These two world-class attractions offer much more than a history lesson. Silver Dollar City has sensational thrill rides, full production shows, fine gift items, and great new water attractions for kids. At the Shepherd of the Hills you can watch the outdoor drama with its pyrotechnical special effects, and modern sound and lighting systems.

Although many of the area's attractions are deeply rooted in the Ozarks past, places like the Hollywood Wax Museum and Ripley's Believe It or Not! Museum rely on the appeal of their bizarre contents and wax movie star figures, to attract visitors. These places, along with the IMAX Entertainment Complex are real hot spots with the younger generation. You might want to flip to our Kidstuff chapter for other great attractions for kids. You'll find a listing for White Water, Sammy Lane Pirate Cruise, Cool Off Water Chute, and The Tracks in that chapter. Nearby Springfield also has a number of great attractions like Bass Pro Shops, the Discovery Center, and Dickerson Park Zoo. You'll find them listed in the Daytrips chapter.

The attractions listed in this chapter range from a free stop at the Shepherd of the Hills Historical Evergreen Cemetery to the $180 hot-air balloon ride and everything in between. Many of the places offer season passes, combo tickets, and group discounts. The hours of operation can change during the year, as can available space. Be sure to call in advance before your trip to town so you won't wind up like Clark Griswold at Wally World in *National Lampoon's Vacation*.

Most of the attractions publish their ticket price excluding tax. We have noted those that include tax in the published price. While Branson is still a seasonal town, many of the attractions are extending their winter hours and some of them even stay open year round. They often close earlier in the winter, however, so again, call ahead.

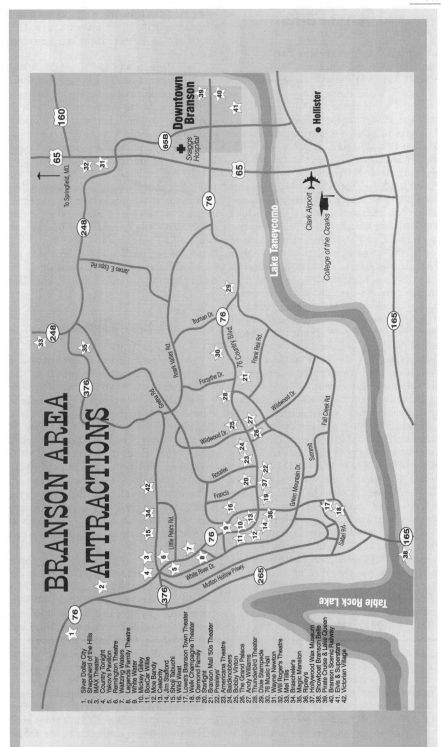

ATTRACTIONS

BRANSON AREA
ATTRACTIONS

1. Silver Dollar City
2. Shepherd of the Hills
3. IMAX Theater
4. Country Tonight
5. Yakov's Pavilion
6. Remington Theatre
7. Waltzing Waters
8. Legends Family Theatre
9. White Water
10. Mickey Gilley
11. BoxCar Willie
12. Moe Bandy
13. Celebrity
14. Jim Stafford
15. Shoji Tabuchi
16. Wild West
17. Lowe's Branson Town Theater
18. Welk Champagne Theater
19. Osmond Family
20. Starlight
21. Branson Mall '50s Theater
22. Presleys'
23. Americana Theatre
24. Baldknobbers
25. Bobby Vinton
26. The Grand Palace
27. Andy Williams
28. Thunderbird Theater
29. Dixie Stampede
30. 76 Music Hall
31. Wayne Newton
32. Will Roger's Theatre
33. Mel Tillis
34. Braschler's
35. Magic Mansion
36. Ripley's
37. Hollywood Wax Museum
38. Showboat Branson Belle
39. Pirate Cruise & Lake Queen
40. Branson Scenic Railway
41. Elvis & Superstars
42. Victorian Village

Theme Parks

Branson USA Amusement Park
Mo. Hwy. 376 and Mo. Hwy. 76
• (417) 335-2396 • www.branson-usa.com

Located at the corner of Mo. 376 and The Strip just south of the Country Tonite Theatre, the 110-acre Branson USA Amusement Park encompasses what used to be known as Mutton Hollow theme park. You won't find much resemblance between the two parks except that the old 800-seat theater still exists, as do some of the retail shops. The new park opened in 1999 with a completely overhauled look, more suited for children and young adults. You'll find thrill rides, kiddy rides, an elevated go-cart track, an 18-hole miniature golf course, and in 2000, an additional 10 new rides. Also in 2000, the park plans to add a 15,000-square foot raised boardwalk designed to include new rides, an evening music entertainment center, games, food, retail shopping, and more space for folks to hold private parties and picnics. There are plenty of places to grab a quick bite to eat at any of the eight eateries and you can pick up a Branson souvenir T-shirt or handcrafted gift item at one of the twenty shops. Large groups are welcome to reserve one of the large outdoor pavilions for reunions or parties. The park will provide catering service. The admission to the park is free, however, the rides and live entertainment have individual prices. In 1999, guests purchased tickets for $1 each and cashed them in at the various rides. Rides had ticket values posted. For example, the Wind Storm Roller Coaster required 4 tickets. The Sky Chaser Ferris Wheel required 3 tickets. The Branson USA Live Show required 8 tickets. The park is open from April through December from 11 AM until midnight. During the Christmas season the park features 500 lighting displays with more than 1 million lights.

Silver Dollar City
Indian Point Rd.
• (417) 338-2611, (800) 952-6626
• www.silverdollarcity.com

From the moment you step off the tram at the entrance gate you'll be transported back to a day and time when folks lived simpler lives free from modern day stress. There's plenty of hustle and bustle at Silver Dollar City, only it's of the 1890s type. You'll see "citizens" dressed in authentic-looking pioneer outfits rushing to and from their craft stations, musicians roaming the streets playing fiddles, guitars and other home-made instruments and wide-eyed children taking in the sights, sounds, and smells in a kind of place many of them have never seen before.

Over the past 40 years Silver Dollar City has grown from a small family operation into a booming commercial enterprise. It has been voted one of the top theme parks in the world (1998-1999) by the International Association of Amusement Parks & Attractions and it plays host to more than 2.5 million visitors each year. Even with the addition of five annual festivals, a 1,800-seat exhibition and performance center, new attractions including BuzzSaw Falls in 1999 and Splash Harbor in 1998, and more than 50 live shows each day, Silver Dollar City has consistently maintained its commitment to old-fashioned authenticity and style. No trip to Branson would be complete without at least a peek into Ozarks pioneer life and there's no better place to experience it than at Silver Dollar City.

A Short History

What started out simply as a geological wonder is now a booming tourist attraction. Marvel Cave, as it is now known, was discovered by the Osage Indians around 1500. After hearing unusual noises coming from within the cave, the Indians opted not to enter it, but they did give it the name The Devil's Den. A group of miners, led by Henry T. Blow ventured inside the cave in 1869 hoping to find lead. While they discovered no lead ore, they were convinced the cave must be full of marble. When word spread, the locals began referring to it as Marble Cave. After Blow died in 1927 the cave was renamed Marvel Cave since no marble was ever mined from its walls.

In 1894 archeologist William Henry Lynch bought the cave and opened it to tourists. After Lynch's death in 1932 his two daughters took over the business and by the late 1940s were entertaining 5,000 guests a year. In 1946 two vacationing tourists from Chicago, Hugo and Mary Herschend, fell in love with the cave and in 1949 signed a 99 year lease on the property. They planned to turn the cave into an entertainment center with live music and square dancing since the constant 58-degree temperature in the cave made it a perfect summertime retreat. But, just four years later Hugo died at the age of 55 and left the task of operating the business to his wife and two sons, Jack and Peter.

Their entrepreneurial skills served them well.

Acting on a tip from a traveling salesman who claimed to have been born in the general store of the town that had once stood near the cave, the Herschends decided to recreate an 1880s Ozark Mountain village in order to encourage more tourists to visit the cave.

In 1960 Silver Dollar City opened with a blacksmith shop, general store, ice cream parlor, a doll shop, and a stagecoach ride. As a marketing ploy, each park visitor received his change in silver dollars. When they left the area and spent the silver dollars people would ask where they got them. The idea worked. In its first year, Silver Dollar City attracted more than 125,000 people.

Getting Around

After you pass the entrance gate and pick up a map of the park, the first thing you'll come to is the Hospitality House. Here you'll find an abundant assortment of souvenirs and snacks as well as the line that forms for Marvel Cave. The Mine Restaurant is not far inside the park on the right as you exit the Hospitality House. This is a good place to stop for breakfast or lunch before you begin the hike through the park. The "streets" at Silver Dollar City twist and turn amidst the trees and hills, but just remember as a general rule, if you're walking downhill, you're going deeper into the park, and if you're walking uphill, you're heading back to the entrance. Strollers, wheelchairs, and electric carts are available for a nominal fee and the latter two can be reserved by calling (800) 225-0222. Ask for the stroller booth. Strollers are available on a first-come-first-serve basis. Fortunately there are many places to sit and catch your breath at SDC and the trees that Mary Herschend insisted be spared more than 30 years ago shade many of them. Pets are allowed at the park but must be kept on a leash at all times. Only service animals are allowed on rides and in the restaurants. The average visit to Silver Dollar City takes at least one day, two if you come during a festival or are one of those types who likes to see and do it all.

Shows

With 50 live shows a day at Silver Dollar City, you're never more than a few feet away from some of the liveliest entertainers in the Midwest. Most of the shows feature performers who can sing, dance, play a musical instru-

ment, and tell a quick joke to boot. Some of the shows move from venue to venue during the course of the season. The days and times for a particular show also change frequently, so be sure to call in advance or stop by the Hospitality House if you are interested in seeing a specific show. The shows change from year to year and here we've listed a few of the SDC venues with examples of the types of shows they feature. The Silver Dollar Saloon show is usually one of the best at the park. In 1998 the show featured a large cast of young men and women in a musical review celebrating the venue's 25th anniversary. In 1999 the "How The West Was Wed" show invited the audience to participate in an Old West wedding. The "Harmonies from the Hollow" show was in its third year at the 4,000-seat Echo Hollow Amphitheater in '99. The show begins each day when the park closes. The Haygood Family has performed at the Riverfront Playhouse as well as at other venues throughout the park. They were voted SDC's highest-rated show in 1997, and once you've seen these youngsters perform, you'll probably agree. The seven brothers and one sister (ranging in age from 5 to 22- years- old) sing, dance, and all play the fiddle. The Horsecreek Band combines bluegrass, Western swing, and Ozarks hospitality at the Gazebo. During the summer months championship cloggers from all over the United States perform at the Gazebo stage. One of Branson's favorite performers, Keith Allen also known as Redneckers, performs his one-of-a-kind, one-man show at the Boatworks Theater and at the Dockside Theatre. In 1999, the Boatworks Theater hosted the "Wings Over America, Birds of Prey" show featuring eagles, falcons, owls, and other birds. New in 2000 is the 1,800-seat Red Gold Heritage Hall, a performance and exhibition center themed to reflect the Ozarks tomato canning and shipping history. The venue will host special shows during each of the park's festivals including the Nickelodeon Double Dare 2000 show, a version of Nickelodeon's popular obstacle course game show during the Children's Festival.

Rides and Attractions

Adrenaline junkies rejoice at the many opportunities to catch a buzz at Silver Dollar City's rides and attractions. From the Thunderation roller coaster to the eight-story tall, high-speed Wilderness Waterboggan flume, there are plenty of ways to raise your blood pressure at Silver Dollar City. In 1999 the park debuted its new-

*Marvel Cave at Silver Dollar City has the largest entrance room in the United States:
204 ft. tall, 225 ft. wide, and 411 ft. long.*

Photo: Silver Dollar City

est adventure ride called BuzzSaw Falls. The wet-dry coaster combines sharp twists and turns at speeds of approximately 50 mph with a 9-story plunge right into a reservoir. Other thrill rides include Lost River of the Ozarks, where passengers are taken on a whitewater adventure through the Ozark hills; Fire in the Hole, a ride through a burning town; and the Great Shoot-Out at the Flooded Mine, a float through a flooded mine full of bandits and outlaws. Another favorite is the American Plunge, where passengers board a hollowed-out log and ride it to the bottom of a water chute. (It's just a fancy way to get wet, really.) The good news for some of us is that not all of Silver Dollar's City's 17 rides and attractions will scare the living daylights out of you. The Frisco Silver Dollar Line Steam Train is about as tame as they come.

You'll be treated to a 20-minute trip through the woods as a narrator provides commentary on the scenery. Watch out, though—it seems bandits like Alf Bolin are still a hidin' out in them thar Ozark hills (see our History chapter for more about Mr. Bolin). They usually don't take any prisoners, and their robbery attempts are comical at best.

The Cave

Early Spanish explorers came to the cave looking for the Fountain of Youth. Miners hoping to find marble called it Marble Cave but were surprised to find nothing but a plentiful supply of bat guano. The guano was mined, however, for fertilizer. Open for more than a century as Missouri's oldest continuously operating cave tour site, Marvel Cave was once home to the Ozark Jubilee, the Presley family music show, and hundreds of square dances. Jack Herschend was married in it. The gigantic Cathedral Room has even seen hot-air balloon competitions. That's right, it's that big. A complete tour of the cave is included in the admission price to the park. There are a few tight squeezes, but for the most part it's not a bad hike, around 60 minutes. If you have a special medical condition, we suggest you talk to a cave guide before attempting the tour. There are 600 stairs you'll have to maneuver. The good news is that you go in on foot and come out on a train. The cave is fully lit and a great place to cool off on a hot summer's day. Tours depart a number of times a day from the Hospitality House just near the entrance of the park.

Kidstuff

Tom Sawyer's Landing is a play area designed especially for kids too young for the thrill of Thunderation. Inside Tom Sawyer's Landing are a number of mechanical rides such as the Runaway Ore Cart Coaster and the Skychase Balloon Ride. There is a four-story Rope Tower for the aspiring climber, a Ball Room for the hide-and-seekers, a Critter Corral petting zoo with goats and chickens for the animal lover, and a bubble-making machine for kids of all ages who still find wonder in creating such things. Children with boundless energy appreciate Geyser Gulch, the world's largest treehouse with three towers of mazes, rope crawls, foam blasters, and water cannons as well as Splash Harbor, a three-story boat and

four-level dockside tower outfitted with enough water toys to douse the entire state. (See our close-up in the Kidstuff chapter for more on the annual Children's Festival at SDC.)

McHaffie's Pioneer Homestead

Experience life in the 1890s firsthand at McHaffie's Pioneer Homestead, where you'll see authentic-looking pioneers tending the animals, carving wood, sewing, square dancing, cooking over an open fire, and more. The homestead is an authentic Ozark log cabin built in 1843 at Swan Creek near Forsyth. Opal Parnell donated it to the Herschends and insisted that it be used only as a working homestead. The inhabitants will be happy to answer questions, and they'll even throw in a tall tale or two. At 4 PM daily you can stop by for the musical jam session. The nice thing about a visit to Silver Dollar City is that the entire staff is ready, willing, and able to interact one-on-one with visitors. No one leaves a stranger.

Wilderness Church

Authentic is the name of the game at Silver Dollar City, and the Wilderness Church is no exception. The walls of this 1800s-looking structure are made out of old logs. The pews are carved out of logs and the podium is even made out of a huge old tree. Guests are always welcome to stop in for a little spiritual reflection or to peer out the large window overlooking a garden. Church services are held on Sundays at 9:30 and 11 AM. Drop in to join the hymn singing a number of times each day. If you've finally found that special someone, Wilderness Church has served as the setting for hundreds of weddings over the years, and if you make your reservation early, it can host yours too. Call the central reservation number listed for SDC for information. You can renew your vows Monday through Saturday at 4 PM. You must sign up at the Angel Shop to participate.

Shops and Crafts

There are a few places where you will find a selection of run-of-the-mill souvenir items at Silver Dollar City, but for the most part each shop carries entirely unique handcrafted items.

The Hospitality House and Ozark Marketplace carry an assortment of T-shirts, trinkets, and seasonal merchandise. The other 60 shops carry the products of Silver Dollar City's 100 craftspeople. You'll find painted folk art designs along with wood heirloom keepsakes and antiques at Mary Sue's Pioneer Paint Cabin. Choose from a variety of dried meat jerky, mustards, sauces and panned fried potatoes at Canaday's Smoked Meats. At the Silver Pick Rock shop you can pan for gems and take home beautiful stones. At Wild Lilly Floral & Naturals you can get a seasonal floral arrangement and choose from their selection of aromatherapy products, handcut soaps, stationary, and books. The Leather Moccasin Shop features what else—handmade moccasins. If you're worried about carrying all those treasures around with you all day, you can arrange to have them delivered to the entrance of the park. Just remember to pick them up on your way out.

The Society of Demonstrating Craftsmen at Silver Dollar City helps ensure that there is a plentiful supply of young craftspeople being trained in the variety of arts displayed at the City. Many of the craftspeople employed at Silver Dollar City are retired business owners, executives, and laborers who came to the Ozarks to enjoy their golden years. They picked up their skills from watching other craftspeople and now pass on their knowledge to others.

Food

After a big meal at The Mine Restaurant you probably won't have room for much else for a few hours, but when you are ready there are a number of places to grab a snack or sample old-fashioned pioneer cooking. When we say snack we don't mean a bag of chips. All the food served at Silver Dollar City is supervised by renowned chef Doug Zader, who was trained at the Culinary Institute of America. His barbecue sauces are so popular they are bottled and available for sale. If you are looking for a snack, you can get a bag full of fresh corn popped in a cast-iron kettle over an open fire at the Sawmill Kettle Corn shop. The pastries at Eva and Delilah's Bakery are to die for, and the Black Angus chargrilled burgers at the Garden Café are a real treat. The Tater Patch serves up calico fried potatoes, curly fries, chicken strips, and pork tenderloin sandwiches. During the festivals you will find additional food offerings according to the season. Our favorite is the hot wassail served during the Christmas festival. For a more substantial meal try Mary's Springhouse Restaurant where you'll find spaghetti, chicken-fried steak, and Italian sausage sandwiches. The Riverside Ribhouse has barbecued ribs, barbecued chicken, and hand pulled pork sandwiches.

Festivals

With the exception of a few weeks between the five festivals, there is always something special happening at Silver Dollar City. (See our Annual Events chapter for more information.) The fun starts in mid-April each year with World-Fest, a four-week festival featuring 400 performers from around the globe who bring their music, dance, costumes, and culture to the park. During World-Fest craftspeople from around the world demonstrate their techniques for glassblowing, armor construction, egg decorating, and blacksmithing. Chefs from other countries give daily demonstrations on how to prepare items unique to their cultures.

The Great American Music Festival begins each year a few days after World-Fest ends in mid-May and lasts until the first week in June. More than 200 musicians perform throughout the park. They play bluegrass, country, gospel, and Dixieland music on a variety of instruments, some of them homemade.

The National Children's Festival held each year from mid-June through the end of August is fast becoming one of the park's top draws. Silver Dollar City routinely brings in special displays and interactive exhibits for kids as well as new shows and hands-on crafts and games.

The Festival of America which begins each year in early September and lasts through October, features the creations of visiting craftsmen and women from around the country who specialize in such art forms as raku pottery, coppersmithing, carousel horse carving, and stained glass

The lobby of the Bobby Vinton Blue Velvet Theatre is adorned floor to ceiling with hand painted murals.

Photo: Branson/Lakes Area Chamber of Commerce

artistry. The park serves delicacies from across the country.

One of the most popular seasons in the Ozarks and one of the most popular festivals at Silver Dollar City takes place as Christmas approaches. The Old Time Christmas Festival begins in early November and runs through the end of December. Each evening at 5:30 PM guests can watch the lighting of the five-story Christmas tree on the Square. The tree has over 160,000 lights. Guests may sing carols at Wilderness Church or catch a special Christmas show at the Silver Dollar Saloon. Perhaps the best part of the entire celebration is the fact that the entire park is filled with tiny lights, Nativity scenes, traditional Christmas ornaments and the smell of hot mulled cider and wassail as well as other tasty holiday treats.

Vital Statistics

How to get there: Silver Dollar City is 4.5 miles west of the Country Tonite Theatre just off Mo. 76 on Indian Point Road. Turn left at the entrance sign at the intersection on Mo. 76 and Indian Point Road.

Parking: The first parking lot you'll come to is for handicapped licensed vehicles. Just show the parking attendant your tag. The other lots sit on both sides of Indian Point Road just past the main entrance to Silver Dollar City. There is no charge to park. Trams run every few minutes to and from the lettered lots. Be sure to remember which lot you parked in to save time at the end of the day searching for your car.

Admission prices (including tax): A one-day admission is $32.85 for adults ages 12 and up, $22.25 for children ages 4 to 11 and free for children aged 3 and younger. Seniors aged 55 and older get in for $30.75. During the Old Time Christmas festival Nov. 4 – Dec. 23, adult admission is $27.55, senior admission is $25.45, and children ages 4 to 11 get in for $16.95. Children aged 3 and younger get in free. Season passes are $45 for adults and $35 for children if purchased before June 1. After June 1 season passes are $55.65 for adults and $45.55 for children. If you also plan to visit White Water, you can save money by purchasing combo season passes to both attractions starting at $75 for adults and $65 for children ages 4 through 11.

Hours of operation: Silver Dollar City is open April 5 through the end of December. The week after Christmas is a great time to pick up sale items at the more than 60 shops. From opening day in April to mid-May the park is open Wednesdays through Sundays from 9:30 AM to

6 PM. On Saturdays the park is open from 9 AM to 7 PM. From mid-May to the end of August the park is open daily from 9:30 AM until 7 PM. From late August to late October the park closes at 6 PM every day except Saturday when it stays open until 7 PM. There are a few exceptions so be sure to call for exact dates. Beginning on Labor Day the park is closed on Mondays for the rest of the year. From early November until the end of December the park is open from 1 to 10 PM Wednesdays through Sundays. There are a few exceptions to this schedule so be sure to call in advance to check exact dates and times.

Shepherd of the Hills Homestead and Outdoor Theatre
5586 W. Mo. Hwy. 76
• **(417) 334-4191, (800) OLD-MATT**
• **www.oldmatt.com**

No visit to Branson would be complete without a visit to Shepherd of the Hills Homestead and Outdoor Theatre. The traditional sights, sounds, and smells of the Ozarks are alive and well at this turn-of-the-century theme park. You won't find the commercialism you might expect at one of the country's most popular attractions. (More than 7 million people have seen the outdoor drama to date.) You will find gentle rolling hills, mature trees, flowers in the summer and fall, and the same kind of hospitality Harold Bell Wright encountered more than a century ago. What you get from a visit to Shepherd of the Hills is more than a history lesson. It's a trip back to a state of mind when families thought nothing of opening their homes to strangers and even less of defending their farms with their very lives. The best part of Shepherd of the Hills Homestead and Outdoor Drama is the people who steadfastly perpetuate its wholesome environment and take pride in their Ozarks heritage.

A Short History

What tourists know today as Shepherd of the Hills Homestead and Outdoor Theatre all began with a minister, a farmer, and a flood. The minister was a man by the name of Harold Bell Wright, who traveled from his home state of New York to the Ozarks in 1896 to contemplate his diminishing career and improve his

INSIDERS' TIP

Parking lot thefts aren't generally a problem in Branson; however, never leave your doors unlocked and be sure to cover up valuables.

ailing health. During his journey into the Ozarks on horseback, Wright was stopped short by the flooded White River. Farmers John and Anna Ross offered to let Wright stay a night on their farm (which would today be located just east of the Country Tonite Theatre on Hwy. 76 near Mutton Hollow, the current site of Branson USA Amusement Park) until the river subsided, but his visit extended for an entire summer. During the next eight years Wright returned to the Ross home each summer, where he began compiling the events and characters for his novel, *The Shepherd of the Hills*. The book was published in 1907, and its success was immediate.

When the Missouri-Pacific Railroad completed the track of the White River Line through the Roark Valley in 1906, the area became more accessible to tourists. By 1909 travelers stopping in Branson or Reeds Spring began asking to see Old Matt's Cabin, as the Ross homestead was called in the book. After the deaths of John and Anna Ross around 1923, the daughter of a Springfield banker, Lizzie McDaniel, bought the homestead and set about the task of restoring the cabin. The first dramatizations of Harold Bell Wright's story were told on the cabin's lawn. She also named the cornfield where Wright had once camped, Inspiration Point. Dr. Bruce Trimble and his wife, Mary, acquired the property in 1946 after McDaniel's death and added a number of attractions including a gift shop called Aunt Mollie's Cupboard, and the outdoor amphitheater called the Old Mill Theatre. In 1941 a film was made of the story, which starred John Wayne in his first Technicolor film.

Performances of *The Shepherd of the Hills* play began in 1960. The drama became the leading outdoor performance in the country under the direction of the Trimble family. In 1985 the son of Mary and Bruce Trimble, Mark, and his wife, Lea, sold the property to its current owner Gary Snadon. During the late 1960s Snadon played the villainous Wash Gibbs in the outdoor drama while maintaining his day job as a teacher and football coach at Branson High School. In 1989 Snadon added Inspiration Tower, and in 1990 he had the Morgan County Church relocated to the homestead to signify the churches where Wright used to preach. Each year since, Snadon and his family have added new attractions to the park to reflect the growing and ever-changing demands of the public. In 1997 the 90-member cast of *The Shepherd of the Hills* play celebrated its 5,000th performance.

Touring the Park

The Jeep-drawn guided tours of the homestead take visitors on a journey back to the days of Bald Knobbers, traveling preachers, and subsistence farming. Among the stops is the Morgan Community Church, built in 1901, where visitors spend a few moments with a recorded impersonation of Harold Bell Wright in an inspirational presentation.

The national historic landmark Old Matt's Cabin is a highlight of the tour. A photographer will take your photo on the front porch steps. Along the tour you'll also see Inspiration Point, Harold Bell Wright's Circle of Legends, Lizzie McDaniel's home, a moonshine still, the backstage area of the amphitheater, and the Waves of Glory Flag Museum.

No visit to the homestead would be complete without a trip to the top of Inspiration Tower. Built in 1989, the structure is 230 feet tall and weighs more than 3 million pounds. Its flagpole is 1,608 feet above sea level. As you look through a telescope on the open-air observation deck, you can see people in boats on Table Rock Lake. The enclosed observation deck contains 4,400 square feet of glass—enough to cover a third of a football field. The ground level houses a gift shop, snack bar, and restrooms. The tower has 225 stairs and two elevators. During the Christmas season the tower is adorned with 25,000 lights, transforming it into one of the Ozark's largest Christmas tree-shaped displays.

Other attractions at the homestead include the Shepherd of the Hills Clydesdales. In 1997 they made an appearance in the Macy's 71st Annual Thanksgiving Day Parade. There are pony rides for the kids and a City Kids and Country Cousins playground where little ones can burn off energy. The Precious Moments Animated Gallery and Gift Shoppe contains creations from internationally known artist Sam Butcher. There are demonstrating craftspeople scattered throughout the park and live musical entertainment all day long. Ronnie Prophet, a 1999 inductee into the Canadian Country Music Hall of Fame, performs at the Pickin' Parlor Theatre next to Aunt Mollie's Restaurant at 9:30 AM April through December. Breakfast is served before Prophet's show in the restaurant

and lunch immediately follows. Tickets for the show and a meal can be purchased together. Aunt Mollie's is a buffet style restaurant serving three meals a day. You'll find Ozarks' favorites like fried chicken, mashed potatoes, gravy, beans, roast beef, corn, salad, and hot breads.

The Outdoor Drama

The original goal of *The Shepherd of the Hills* outdoor drama was to bring to life the characters, the events, and the setting of The Shepherd of the Hills novel. When the play was first presented in the 1960s, it was considered one of the most ambitious theater projects in the Midwest. Through the use of "living" props such as horses, a functioning steam engine, a mill, and a dirt stage, the theater concept called ultra-realism came to the Ozarks. Set against a natural backdrop of stars, trees, moonlight, and the echo of frogs and crickets in the nearby woods, The Shepherd of the Hills play would have made Harold Bell Wright proud. Many generations of cast members have grown up playing the characters Wright described in his novel. Some of the current cast members have been in the show for nearly 30 years and now share the stage with their children and grandchildren. The story has all the elements of a good old-fashioned romance—conflict, young love, music, dancing, tragedy, fighting—you name it, it's there. The current production has a cast of 90 actors and actresses, 32 horses, 28 single action Ruger revolvers, 22 double-barreled shotguns, and a nightly pyrotechnical display of Dad Howitt's cabin. The play is presented nightly at 8:30 PM from April through August and at 7:30 PM from late August until October. When it's raining, there's no show.

Special Events

Each year Shepherd of the Hills Homestead offers a number of special events. A few of the ones presented in recent years include the Bluegrass Festival where musicians from Branson and around the country converge on the homestead to present traditional Bluegrass music. This event is usually a week long and takes place during the summer. Pioneer Days, held in May, celebrates the anniversary of Harold Bell Wright's historic visit to the area. The Fall Harvest Festival features guest craftspeople demonstrating their unique trades as visitors watch.

ATTRACTIONS

Harold Bell Wright: Shepherd to the Opening of the Ozarks

"This, my story, is a very old story.

"In the hills of life there are two trails. One lies along the higher sunlit fields where those who journey see afar, and the light lingers even when the sun is down; and one leads to the lower ground, where those who travel, as they go, look always over their shoulders with eyes of dread, and gloomy shadows gather long before the day is done.

"This, my story, is the story of a man who took the trail that leads to the lower ground, and of a woman, and how she found her way to the higher sunlit fields.

"In the story, it all happened in the Ozark Mountains, many miles from what we of the city call civilization."

So begins the novel that opened up the Ozarks to the tourist industry. What *Midnight in the Garden of Good and Evil* did for tourism in Savannah, Georgia, in the 1990s, *The Shepherd of the Hills* did for the Ozarks in the first two decades of the 20th century. The book by minister Harold Bell Wright was part of the social gospel of the time, spread as much by fiction as by sermons from the pulpit during the Third Great Awakening, a middle-class response to a nation worried about the rising tide of immigration and the theories of Sigmund Freud, Karl Marx, and Charles Darwin.

The inspiring story of the muscular Young Matt, the lovely Sammy Lane, and the wise Old Shepherd, set in the purity of the isolated Ozarks was not greeted with praise by the critics but it struck a responsive chord with the book-buying middle class. It still does.

After its publication in 1907, it quickly became a bestseller, selling a phenomenal 1.2 million copies. Railroads cars loaded with the book departed daily from Chicago to satisfy the public's reading appetite. Action-packed with vividly drawn characters and a moral that many can still believe in, the novel is quite readable today. Fueled in part by the popularity of the Ozarks tourism industry, an interest in history and the early Ozarks, and the outdoor drama based on the play (see our Attractions chapter), the book still sells enough copies to keep it in print, and it has sold enough copies over the years to make it one of the bestsellers of all time.

Wright, who became the John Grisham of his day, studied for the ministry two years at Ohio's Hiram College, but left in 1884 because eye trouble and pneumonia prevented him from working to pay for his tuition. During the next three years, Wright made his way westward, earning his keep by doing farm work and painting landscapes on the sides of delivery wagons. He ended up in the Ozarks, having come by horseback from Marionville, where the railroad ended. Turned back from a flood-swollen White River, he took shelter at the homestead of John and Anna Ross on a ridge above Mutton Hollow. He intended to only spend the night, but stayed the summer. He returned to the Ross homestead each summer for the next eight years.

It was in the Ozarks where he first began preaching, initially because the local minister missed a community Thanksgiving dinner. According to Wright in a 1917 account, "A long, lean hill-billy approached me. 'You got edication, mister, why can't you preach to we-uns?'" Wright took the pulpit, delivered a successful message and began preaching regularly. He was soon offered a pastorate at a Disciples of Christ Church in Pierce City, Missouri. Wright preached there from 1897 to 1898, and he had other pastorates in Lebanon and Kansas City, but he was always drawn to the Ozarks and to writing.

It was at the Ross homestead that he met some of the hill folk that would be transformed into the characters of his novel. John and Anna became Old Matt and Aunt Mollie, and their son, Charles, is the acknowledged Young Matt. Several local women later claimed to be the model for Sammy Lane, but it seems that Grace Shear may have been Wright's model. Truman Powell was the prototype for the Old Shepherd. Levi Morrill, a general store operator at Notch, provided the pattern for Uncle Ike. It's easy to see that Wright's characters were deeply rooted in the Ozark hills and its people. If you stop at the Evergreen Cemetery beside Mo. 76 near Silver Dollar City today, you can find the final resting spot for many of Wright's models. You can also find the names of the characters from the novel embedded in the names of dozens of businesses and place names in the area.

Whether they shaped or reflected American values, Wright's bestsellers certainly embody the values of his readers, a group who represented a mainstream in the American culture. They still do. Wright pitted the corruption of cities and civilization against the purity of person and environment found on the vanishing American frontier. The Ozarks was isolated enough to be uncorrupted.

The Old Shepherd, who finds strength in the hills and regeneration after leaving Chicago, says at the end of the book that the coming railroad will taint the mountains with city ways. "Many will come and the beautiful hills that have been my strength and peace will become the haunt of restless idlers and a place of revelry." Many people, looking at the phenomenal growth of the Branson area and the live entertainment industry, with its Vegas-style lights on The Strip, would say that the Old Shepherd's prediction came true. But as he preached the purity of the isolated Ozarks, Wright himself was the initial impetus of a string of events that opened up the Ozarks, the others being better roads and the building of the White River dams. The book's popularity caused visitors to flock to the area to see first

hand what they had experienced vicariously in the book.

Ironically, they came on the newly opened White River railway.

By 1920 the novel's influence in bringing travelers into the region had slowed. Pearl "Sparky" Spurlock helped keep the legend alive with her taxi service from Branson, taking visitors to the former Ross homestead over the rugged Dewey Bald Road, later to become Mo. 76 and The Strip. Lizzie McDaniel, the daughter of a Springfield banker, bought the homestead in the 1920s and hunted for memorabilia connected to the Ross family and Wright. Dr. Bruce Trimble, a professor at the University of Kansas, and his wife,

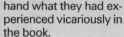

ATTRACTIONS

(Continued on next page)

Mary, and their son Mark acquired the homestead after McDaniel's death. Their operation of an outdoor theater on the site that told the story of Wright's novel soon became a major area attraction and one of the largest outdoor theaters in the nation.

A Branson football coach, Gary Snadon, who played the evil Wash Gibbs in the play, bought the Shepherd of the Hills Homestead and Outdoor Theatre from Mark Trimble and his wife, Lea, in 1985. By that time the outdoor drama and the combined attractions in the area were putting such a burden on the section of Mo. 76 between Branson and Silver Dollar City that Snadon built his own road (see our History chapter).

Wright had resolved that if *The Shepherd of the Hills* was successful, he would give up the ministry. It was his most successful book, and Wright became a full-time novelist. His book was so popular that he even directed a film based on his novel in 1919. The book has been filmed as a movie several other times, once with John Wayne in the early '40s, his first Technicolor movie. Copies of it are readily available, and it is interesting viewing, but anyone who knows the Ozarks can recognize that it wasn't filmed in the Ozarks!

Wright's novel allowed him to leave the ministry and become a major popular writer in the early decades of this century. Its success brought the first wave of tourists to the isolated Ozarks, and many people still refer to the area as "The Shepherd of the Hills Country."

Wright died in 1944. Though he could see at that time the effect his novel had on opening the Ozarks to the outside and its influences of the big city, one can only wonder what he would think today were he to travel the old trail as he did a hundred years ago as it leaves the White River Valley and begins its climb into the hills and skirts around Dewey Bald. It was the trail that became Mo. Highway 76 and The Strip. Would he recognize it?

What hath Wright wrought?

For the past several years, Shepherd of the Hills has hosted the annual Cruisin' Branson Lights Automotive Festival in August. Thousands of classic, custom, and hot rod vehicles dot the landscape of the park while Branson performers treat onlookers to a variety of entertainment in outdoor tents. There's a car auction, an awards program, and plenty of vendors waiting to sell you those hard to find car accessories and keepsakes. One of the most popular events each year at the park is the drive through Trail of Lights display, held from November to January. It's the only time visitors are allowed to drive their own vehicles through the homestead. You'll see animated characters like elves and animals amidst Christmas sets adorned with thousands of sparkling lights. This is a real treat for the kids and the price is right too.

Vital Statistics

To get there, go 1 mile past the Country Tonite Theatre on Mo. 76. The parking lot is on the south side of Mo. 76. There is a walk-way underneath the highway that leads to the entrance to the park. Parking is free.

Admission to the site is free, but the various attractions have individual prices. A Jeep-drawn day tour plus a visit to Inspiration Tower and a ticket to the play is $27 for adults and $12 for children ages 4 to 16. Children younger than 4 get in free. Tickets just to Inspiration Tower are $5 for adults and $2 for kids ages 4 to 16. Tickets to the play are $21 for adults and $10 for children younger than 16. Children younger than 4 get in free. Clydesdale-drawn wagon rides are $5 for adults and $3 for children aged 4 through 16. Trail rides on horses are $10 for adults and children aged 7 and older. Kids aged 6 and younger can ride the ponies for $2. Prices for the Trail of Lights are $7 for adults and $3 for children younger than 16. Season passes are $39.95 for adults and $24.49 for children aged 4 to 16. Children younger than 4 get in free.

Tickets to the Ronnie Prophet show are $15 for adults and free for kids younger than 16. If you want to have breakfast before the show at Aunt Mollie's Restaurant, the combo tickets are $19 for adults and $2 for children younger than 16. A ticket to the show plus lunch afterwards is $22 for adults and $3 for children.

The park is open from the last Saturday in April through October Monday through Saturday. Jeep-drawn tours run from 9:30 AM to 5:30 PM. The ticket office opens at 8 AM and the gift shop opens at 9 AM. The park closes for about 10 days at the end of October and opens back up for the Christmas season through December. During the Christmas season the park is open seven days a week. The Trail of Lights is open from early November until the first week in January from 6 PM until midnight. Admission is $7 for adults, $3 for children aged 4 through 12 and free to kids younger than 4. The Inspiration Tower is open 7 days a week all year long and stays open until midnight during the Trail of Lights. During January and February the tower closes at 4 PM.

Museums

BoxCar Willie Museum
3454 76 Country Blvd.
• **(417) 334-8696, (800) 942-4626**

The world's most famous hobo, BoxCar Willie, lost his battle with leukemia in April of 1999, but his memory is alive and well in Branson. Lecil Travis "Marty Martin," a.k.a. BoxCar Willie, was one of the first nationally known performers to make Branson his permanent home in 1987. While his theater is now home to the Dutton family and his motels accommodate visitors who will never again hear him perform his signature "train whistle," BoxCar Willie continues to make an impression on Branson visitors and will for years to come. If you get a chance to visit downtown Branson, you'll probably happen upon BoxCar Willie Drive, located just east of the lakefront next to the train depot. The BoxCar Willie Museum is an eclectic mix of items he collected throughout his own life as well as memorabilia from famous personalities he admired. You'll find photos of Roy Rogers and Trigger, Mickey Mantle baseball cards, and items owned by Elvis Presley. One of BoxCar's most prized possessions was the cockpit of a KC-97 tanker. The quaint museum houses numerous buttons, pins, and other military collectibles, and of course a large collection of railroad artifacts. BoxCar spent a portion of his youth riding the rails with his father, who was a track foreman for a railroad. It was during this time that BoxCar began imitating the sound of a train whistle with only his voice. His voice and his pure country music made him a star. BoxCar's numerous gold and platinum albums are on display in the museum along with an assortment of cassettes and CDs of his music. Admission to the museum is free if you stay at one of the BoxCar Willie motels. If you show your ticket stub from the Dutton Family show, they'll knock $1 off the $3 admission price. Children younger than 12 get in free with an adult. The museum is open from 9 AM to 9 PM Mondays through Saturdays from early spring until late December.

Hollywood Wax Museum Branson
3030 W. 76 Country Blvd.
• **(417) 337-8277, (800) 720-4110**
• **www.hollywoodwax.com**

The facade of the Hollywood Wax Museum is fashioned after Mount Rushmore, except that the larger-than-life faces are of dead movie stars, not presidents. The 115-foot-long, 50 foot-high stone front is adorned with the likes of Marilyn Monroe, Charlie Chaplin, John Wayne, and Elvis Presley. If you happen not to see that, you surely won't miss the marquee of a man and an old-time movie camera perched high on a beam facing the building. The collection of 170 wax figures inside the building is equally impressive. From the 60 foot-tall King Kong in the entry, to the Hall of Presidents to the moving display of the Last Supper, the museum is packed with uncanny likenesses of dozens of notable TV, movie, sports, political, and historical figures. There's a Land of Oz display complete with Dorothy, a set from the Tonight Show with Johnny Carson and even a display of Grand Ol' Opry stars. The crypt room houses the Alien, Dracula, Elvira, and a dead ringer for Jason of the *Friday the 13th* movie series. (No pun intended.) You'll find Kate Winslet and Leonardo DiCaprio figures from *Titanic* and there's even a Mark McGwire figure poised for a home run. The Hollywood Studio Store, located inside the museum contains officially licensed Star Wars merchandise. The self-guided tours usually take 1 hour. The museum is open seven days a week, year round, from 8 AM until midnight. Tickets are $9.95 for adults and $6.95 for children ages 6 to 11. Kids younger than 6 get in free.

Ralph Foster Museum
College of the Ozarks, Point Lookout
• **(417) 334-6411, Ext. 3407**

Known as the Smithsonian of the Ozarks, this museum contains the lifetime collections of radio pioneer and philanthropist Ralph D. Foster, who donated much of the museum's contents to the college. Housed in a former boys dormitory on the campus of the College of the Ozarks, the museum takes up three floors and includes objects representing archaeology, history, antiques, numismatics, natural history, fine arts, geology, and mineralogy. A collection of Foster's 1,500 guns fills the second floor and includes a Thompson submachine gun, Poncho Villa's pistols and a handgun once owned by Hollywood cowpoke Slim Pickens. Natural history exhibits, mostly taxidermy animals from Africa and North America, line the walls. On the third floor you can see rocks, minerals, and preserved birds and butterflies.

Other exhibits in the museum trace the history of the Ozarks and the more recent Branson boom. The famous jalopy owned by the Clampett family in the 1960s TV series *The Beverly Hillbillies* can be found on the first floor. The collection of fine art at the museum ranges from Kewpie dolls created by Rose O'Neill to paintings by Thomas Hart Benton, M.E. Oliver, and others. There's also a collection of Native American art (see also our Arts and Culture chapter). Admission to the museum including tax is $4.50 for adults and $3.50 for adults aged 62 and older. Children younger than 18 get in free. The museum is open year round Mondays through Saturdays from 9 AM to 4:30 PM with a few exceptions.

Ripley's Believe It or Not! Museum
3326 76 Country Blvd.
• **(417) 337-5300, (800) 998-4418 ext. 2**
• **www.ripleysbranson.com**

If the first thing you saw when you arrived in Branson was Ripley's Believe It or Not! Museum, you might think the New Madrid fault had finally given way. The building is as much of an attraction as the weird collection inside. There's a crack right down the middle of it, and the marquee lays half-cocked on one side. Huge chunks of missing mortar reveal the wood framing, and the water fountain out front is even split in half. Inside the second floor, the faux-earthquake theme continues with exposed ceiling beams and cracked sheet rock. Once you finally dare to enter the building, you'll encounter an immense collection of odd artifacts and unusual art based on the findings of Robert Ripley.

Ripley spent 40 years traveling the world from New Zealand to Tibet in search of the unbelievable and inexplicable. A self-taught artist, Ripley started his "Believe It or Not" cartoon feature in 1918, and at the height of his popularity the cartoons could be found in more than 300 newspapers with a combined readership of 80 million—a feat Ripley himself would have been amazed to report. In 1933 he opened his first Odditorium at the Chicago World's Fair, and nearly 2 million people came to view such objects as a shrunken head from Ecuador, a two-headed calf, and photos of the world's tallest man.

Today, people's fascination with incredible facts, strange artifacts, and "impossible feats" continues to thrive. There are 26 Ripley's museums around the world, each with a different list of contents. In Branson you'll find cool collectibles from many of the local celebrities. Doug Gabriel's first mufftar, a musical instrument crafted by his father out of a muffler and guitar parts, is on display as well as one of Shoji Tabuchi's fiddles. There's even an intact candy bar that survived scorching temperatures in the Mickey Gilley Theatre fire in 1993. Richard Clark's original Highrise drawing is also on display.

In April of 1998 the museum added a gallery with 45 new exhibits including a replica of an ancient Chinese emperor's dragon ship. It is one of only eight existing hand-carved jade ships in the world. It stands 9 feet tall, 12 feet long, and weighs more than 1,800 pounds. The new gallery also contains a carving called Universal Celebration that is almost as large as the jade ship. Made out of camel bones, the carving contains intricately detailed pagodas, flying cranes, and Bonsai trees. There's also a rice-grain painting of the four Beatles, a Last Supper painting on a coin, a toothpick carving made to look like Dracula, hand painted potato chips, and a purse made out of cigarette wrappers.

Robert Ripley makes an appearance on each self-guided tour in a short holographic presentation from his study. There are plenty of other high-tech interactive displays at the museum, such as the tongue-rolling test. Kids will get a kick out of the giant jellybean portrait of Mary Poppins, the figure of Liu Ch'ung (the man who had two pupils in each eye), and the stretch limousine with its heart-shaped hot tub. From time to time Ripley's rotates some of its more popular exhibits among the various locations around the world. One of the most popular exhibits ever to go on tour was the African fertility statue. When it was on display in the Branson museum a few years ago, women who touched it were asked to fill out a card to send back to the company if they found themselves pregnant in the months following the encounter. While the statue was on tour, Ripley's headquarters reported attendance was up 30 percent, and during a 14-month period, 14 women became pregnant after touching the statue. Was it coincidental or did the statue really have magical powers? Believe it or not!

Plan to spend at least two hours at the museum in order to get the full flavor of the place. There's a candy shop at the end of the tour where you can pick up jellybeans, taffy, chocolate, cookies, and other sweet goodies for the trip home. Tickets are $11.95 for adults, and children ages 4 to 12 get in for $7.45. Children younger than 4 get in free. The museum is open daily from 9 AM until 11 PM March through December and from 9 AM until 7 PM January and February.

Historic Sites

Bonniebrook Park
485 Rose O'Neill Rd., Walnut Shade
• (417) 561-2250 or (417) 561-2265
•www.bonniebrookpark.com

One of Missouri's most famous residents, Rose O'Neill was also one of the early 20th century's most remarkable women. By 1914 her illustrations and cartoons in such magazines as *Harper's Monthly, Harper's Bazaar, Good Housekeeping*, and *Twentieth Century Home* along with her novels and poems had earned her $1.4 million. She is perhaps best known for her Kewpie drawings and sculptures, which have been collectors' items since the early 1900s. The annual Kewpiesta festival sponsored by the International Rose O'Neill Club is held in Branson each April to commemorate O'Neill's works (see our Annual Events chapter). O'Neill's reconstructed home, Bonniebrook, just north of Branson, is one of the area's most visited places. The impeccably maintained grounds, restaurant, gift shop, and nature trails provide a glimpse into the life of this enormously talented and unique individual.

The original home burned to the ground three years after O'Neill died in Springfield in 1944, but thanks to the Bonniebrook Historical Society, Inc. and other collectors around the world, the home has been restored and filled with O'Neill memorabilia, including illustrations, sculptures, and numerous Kewpie pieces. It is listed on the National Historic Register. The top floor of the home was O'Neill's studio, where she spent hours contemplating new creations and even designing her own clothing. She was often seen wearing her own designs when she visited the local movie theater, as she did often. A short distance from O'Neill's home

and just across the "bonnie brook" for which the house is named, lies the family cemetery where Rose, her siblings Callista and James, and their mother, Meemie, are buried.

Also on the park grounds is the Rose Garden Restaurant, which serves lunch seven days a week from 10 AM to 3 PM. Sunday champagne brunch is served from 10:30 AM to 3 PM and costs $12.95 per person. Champagne is served beginning at 11 AM. On Sundays the home tour is complimentary with the purchase of brunch. Admission to the home tour, museum, and grounds is $5 per person. Children under the age of 12 get in free. The 20-minute home tours are given seven days a week between 9 AM and 4 PM except from noon to 1 PM. The museum and grounds are open from 9 AM to 5 PM daily. The site also has eight Bonniebrook label wines and a gift shop with copies of O'Neill's illustrations, art, books, poems, and dolls.

The private setting of Bonniebrook park lends itself to private parties, weddings and banquets. Bonniebrook is approximately 9 miles north of Branson just off U.S. 65. Rose O'Neill Road is on the right just past the bridge at Bear Creek. Once you turn on Rose O'Neill Road, look for a sign leading you left to the park entrance.

Shepherd of the Hills Historical Evergreen Cemetery
Mo. Hwy. 76 W., between Indian Point Rd. and Mo. Hwy. 265

After you've seen The Shepherd of the Hills outdoor drama and gotten to know the characters who formed the basis for Harold Bell Wright's wildly famous novel *The Shepherd of the Hills*, you can visit their final resting places at the Shepherd of the Hills Historical Evergreen Cemetery. A small sign just west of Indian Point Road on Mo. 76 marks the entrance to the cemetery. If you get to the intersection of Mo. 265, you've gone too far.

You'll see the graves of J.K. and Anna Ross (Uncle Matt and Aunt Mollie), Levi Morrill (Uncle Ike), and his wife, Jennie, and Truman Powell (the Old Shepherd). Morrill donated the land for the cemetery in 1894, and a memorial stone was erected in 1925 in memory of these legendary Ozarkians whose mark on the area remains alive and well today. In an appropriately tree-shaded portion of the cemetery at the easternmost corner lies a granite stone bearing the names of Mary R. (1899-1983) and Hugo Herschend (1899-1955), founders of Silver Dollar City.

ATTRACTIONS

See the Sites

Branson Scenic Railway
206 E. Main St.
• (417) 334-6110, (800) 2-TRAIN-2

Take a trip back in time to the days when rail travel was one of the best modes of transportation in Branson Scenic Railway's restored 1940s dome cars. Their 105-minute excursions take you 20 miles from the depot in downtown Branson south to Arkansas or 20 miles north to Galena, depending on the schedule. The glass-bubble topped cars offer a great view of the rugged countryside especially during October, the railway's busiest month, when the leaves have turned their fall shades of orange, gold, and red. Along both routes you pass through tunnels, over bridges, and next to meandering streams. You may even see a bobcat, a bald eagle, or a deer along the way. Branson Scenic Railway offers theme excursions on holidays including Easter and Christmas.

INSIDERS' TIP

Traffic really stacks up on Mo. 76 coming back into Branson at the close of Silver Dollar City each day. To avoid the snarl, you might want to leave a little early or take the scenic route east from Indian Point Road on Mo. 76 to Mo. 265 and then to Mo. 165 where it intersects U.S. Highway 65 south of Branson. From there it's a straight shot north back into town.

Up to four trips are offered Mondays through Saturdays from late March to mid-December. Trips are added on Sundays in October and on select holidays during the year. From March through December, departures are at 9 AM, 11:30 AM, and 2 PM. From May through December a 5 PM run is added on select dates. During the Saturday 5 PM excursions, passengers are treated to a full-course prime rib dinner for $42 per person. This trip lasts 135 minutes. A concession car offers sandwiches, coffee, and sodas on all other trips for an additional charge. Tickets for the regular trips are $19.75 for adults and $9.75 for kids aged 3 through 12. Children younger than the age of 3 ride for free.

Lake Queen
280 N. Lake Dr. • (417) 334-3015

The Lake Queen is a genuine paddle-wheel riverboat that has been cruisin' up and down Lake Taneycomo for more than 30 years. More than 1.5 million folks have called themselves passengers during that time, and many of them come back year after year. Besides the scenery on the banks of Lake Taneycomo, folks are treated to a huge buffet meal when they step

on board. The Coast Guard-licensed captains provide comical commentary on the history of Lake Taneycomo and point out several landmarks, including the former estate of romance novelist Janet Dailey, and Kamp Kanakuk and Kanakomo. There's usually some form of live music on the top deck for passengers to dance to after the meal. The breakfast cruise features scrambled eggs, bacon, and fresh-baked pastries for $15.73 for adults and $9 for children ages 4 through 12. The lunch cruise is $19.96 for adults and $9.48 for children. The dinner cruise is $19.96 for adults and $9.75 for children. A sightseeing-only cruise is $9.84 for adults and $6.29 for children no meal is included. Breakfast cruises depart at around 9 AM, lunch cruises at 11 AM, and dinner cruises at 5 PM. The sightseeing cruises depart at 11 AM, 12.30 PM, and 2:30 PM. Reservations are recommended for the meal cruises. The Lake Queen operates from April through mid-December. They'll be happy to host a special event such as a wedding, anniversary, or family reunion.

Ozark Balloon Port
2235 Smyrna Rd., Ozark • (417) 581-7373

Ozark Balloon Port owner Jim Herschend says a ride in a hot-air balloon is a popular gift idea, according to his customers who often come to celebrate anniversaries, birthdays, and other notable occasions high above the Ozark hills. Since the experience is a bit pricier than, say, a trip to Waltzing Waters—it costs $180 per person for a typical flight—you'd better make sure your gift recipient would approve of the idea before plunking down that 50 percent deposit, which is due at the time the reservation is made. For the past 16 years Herschend has been taking folks up, up, and over the treetops 2,000 feet in the air in his five hot-air balloons. The visibility factor and wind speed makes each ride unique. Herschend says he has a perfect safety record and won't go up if there's any precipitation or too much wind. If it's windy enough to fly a kite, it's too windy to go up in a balloon, he says.

An award-winning pilot himself, Herschend knows all about balloon safety. In 1992 he and a copilot won the oldest hot-air balloon race in

Get a birds-eye view parasailing on one of the area's lakes.

Photo: Branson/Lakes Area Chamber of Commerce

Europe to take home the Gordon Bennett Cup. This marked the first time Americans had won the contest in 33 years. He will compete again for the title in 2000. In 1994 he was entered in the National Aeronautic Book for inflating and flying five hot-air balloons underground in Marvel Cave at Silver Dollar City.

There are about a dozen sites in and around Ozark from which Herschend launches his balloons. Many of the flights take passengers near the banks of the Finley River, where whitetailed deer and beaver are often spotted. Each balloon holds two to four passengers, and children are welcome as long as they are old enough to follow directions, Herschend says. Balloons may be launched seven days a week, 12 months a year conditions permitting. The typical flight takes about three hours total with half of the time being spent setting up and the other half in the air. The Ozark Balloon Port business office is open Monday through Friday from 9 AM to 5 PM except for January through April when the office is closed on Monday, Wednesday and Friday.

Polynesian Princess
1358 Long Creek Rd.
- **(417) 337-8366, (800) 653-6288**
- **www.polynesianprincess.com**

This luxury sightseeing yacht combines good food and musical entertainment with a cruise on beautiful Table Rock Lake. The *Polynesian Princess* seats 114 passengers in the plush dining area where three meals a day are served. There's a small stage at one end of the room where a hula dancer performs and a guitarist plays Polynesian music during each cruise. The entire dining area is lined with large windows, and every table has a great view of the lake. Breakfast is served aboard the morning cruise, which leaves the dock at 9 AM. The early dinner cruise departs at 5 PM and returns in plenty of time for you to make an 8 PM music show in town. The 5 and 8 PM dinner cruises come with either Hawaiian chicken or Kahlua pork and a number of side items (see our listing for the *Polynesian Princess* in the Restaurants chapter). There's also an 11 AM sightseeing only cruise.

Prices for the breakfast cruise are $16 for adults and $8 for children younger than 16. The dinner cruises are $29 for adults and $14 for children. The sightseeing only cruise is $13 for adults and $7 for children. The *Polynesian Princess* sails April through October, every day except Monday. Reservations are strongly suggested in the summer and early fall. If you arrive at the dock early, you can sip a soft drink on the lakeside patio or take a peek inside the Long Creek Lagoon gift shop where you'll find a number of souvenir items. If you've got a special event in mind like a wedding, private party, or business meeting, you can charter the entire boat. To get to the *Polynesian Princess* follow U.S. 65 south of Branson to Mo. 86. Go west on Mo. 86. Before you cross the Long Creek Bridge, a sign directs you left to Long Creek Road and Gage's Long Creek Marina where the boat is docked.

Ride the Ducks
2320 76 Country Blvd. • (417) 334-3825

One of the best ways to orient yourself to

Branson and Table Rock Lake all in one shot is aboard a Duck. These WWII-era amphibious vehicles originally called DUKWs by the military have been modified to accommodate sightseers on an 80-minute land-and-lake adventure. From the time you leave the home base, next to Wal-Mart on The Strip, to the time you splash down in Table Rock, your U.S. Coast Guard-approved captain booms across the loudspeaker, pointing out interesting places and scenery along the way. He'll even throw in a joke or two and some fun facts about the history of Branson you may not hear anywhere else. The Duck route takes passengers along The Strip, down Mo. 165 past Table Rock Dam and the Shepherd of the Hills Fish Hatchery, and atop Baird Mountain, the area's highest peak, where you can get a magnificent view of Table Rock Lake. The captain will even treat you to a stop at the Ducks' own outdoor museum of vintage military vehicles.

From there it's splash-down time. The captain may let you try your hand at the wheel as you cruise by the *Showboat Branson Belle*. If you make it to the driver's seat, you'll get a nifty-looking honorary captain's license. Each passenger receives a free wacky quacker with each ticket purchase. These yellow, plastic duck-lip spit collectors make a rather obnoxious noise when you blow into them, sort of a whiney quack. If you have kids and want any peace at all during the trip home, you may want to pack the quackers in the trunk. Tickets (including tax) are $14.95 for adults and $7.45 for children ages 4 to 11. Toddlers not requiring their own seat ride for free. Ride the Ducks is open from March through December from 8 AM to 5 PM seven days a week. During the busy summer months the hours are extended. Tours depart every 15 minutes or so, and reservations are not required.

Showboat Branson Belle
4800 Mo. Hwy. 165 at
White River Landing
- **(417) 336-7400, (800) 775-BOAT**
- **www.silverdollarcity.com**

One of the Silver Dollar City-owned properties, the *Showboat Branson Belle* is a 1990's version of a turn-of-the-century paddle wheeler, sans the rats. At 278 feet long, 78 feet wide, and three stories tall, this 700-passenger vessel

INSIDERS' TIP

Many of our area attractions offer discounts off the listed ticket price for groups of 15 or more. If you know another family coming to town at the same time, why not save a few bucks by making reservations under one name?

ATTRACTIONS

Guests can have their photo taken for a small fee aboard the **Showboat Branson Belle.**

Photo: Branson/Lakes Area Chamber of Commerce

is an impressive sight on Table Rock Lake. When it was launched from White River Landing in 1994, bananas were used to grease down the path to the water in keeping with Silver Dollar City's environmentally correct modus operandi. You won't find any alcohol or gambling on this luxury ship, but you will find four live shows, four meals a day prepared on-board in the galley, and a breathtaking view of the lake during the day and a star-filled sky at night. In 1999

radio personality Paul Harvey was presented the official maritime captain's bell on board the Showboat making him an honorary captain.

The ship moves so slowly (an average of 6 mph) and quietly that once you're inside you hardly notice the movement at all. On deck, however, the cool breeze rising off the lake is the perfect prescription for unwinding at the end of a long day of sightseeing. The ship's interior spans three open stories with balconies on the second and third floors looking down on the stage. Fine draperies partially conceal the view from the dozens of windows overlooking the water. The tables are tastefully adorned with white tablecloths and attended to from the moment you arrive by a most courteous wait staff.

From April to October the first cruise of the day is the lunch cruise from 11 AM to 1 PM. The early escape dinner cruise departs at 4:30 PM and returns at 6:45 PM. The sunset dinner cruise is from 8 PM to 10:30 PM. From October through mid-December the Showboat offers a breakfast cruise from 8 AM to 9:30 AM.

The live entertainment lineup in 2000 includes the Steppin' Out show which has been named Branson's Best Dinner Show by the Branson All-American Music Awards. Hosted by Steve Grimm, who has toured the world with the New Christy Minstrels, the show highlights the kinds of music, singing, and variety acts that showboats are known for. Joining Grimm is the Russian adagio team of Andrei, from the Moscow Circus and Marina, from the Bolshoi Ballet. Their performance combines Andrei's acrobatic talents with Marina's ballet dance skills. Cast member and ventriloquist Todd Oliver involves the audience in his comedy routines along with his cast of characters, including a talking dog.

The summer lunch cruise features the Cirque Fantastique show, which is geared for families and children. In years past the show has included jugglers, acrobats, and other circus performers. The Showboat Follies show which runs during the spring, fall, and Christmas season aboard the lunch cruise features the ventriloquism of Todd Oliver and the Brett Family Singers. The Bretts, a Texas family of five, are known for their vocal harmonies and perform a wide variety of musical styles. A five-piece Dixieland and swing band backs the show.

The food aboard the showboat rivals any restaurant in town. The full-course meals served during the lunch cruise usually includes beef, orange-glazed chicken, rice, ginger carrots, green beans, salad, sourdough bread, and cheesecake. During the dinner cruises the meal includes prime rib, baked potato, ginger carrots, green beans, potatoes, salad, sourdough bread, and flaming baked Alaska for dessert. The breakfast cruise features standard breakfast fare served in true Silver Dollar City style. You'll be treated to pork chops, eggs, fruit, biscuits, orange juice, and coffee.

After the show and meal have ended, passengers have plenty of time to take a stroll on the upper decks and visit the pilot's house where the captain welcomes questions about the ship. Ticket prices for the cruises are as follows: breakfast is $29.65 for adults and $11.65 for children younger than 12; lunch is $34.95 for adults and $14.85 for children; the early escape dinner cruise and the sunset dinner cruises are $40.25 for adults and $16.95 for children. All prices include tax. Boarding begins 30 minutes before departure, and cruises always leave on time so don't be late. Before or after the cruise you might want to visit the gift shop at White River Landing. You'll find nautical-themed trinkets and other neat collectibles. To get to the *Showboat Branson Belle*, take Mo. 165 south of Branson. As soon as you cross the Table Rock Dam, look for the entrance sign to the parking lot on your right.

Spirit of America
380 State Park Marina Road
• **(417) 338-2145, (800) 867-2459**
• **www.boatbranson.com**

The *Spirit of America* catamaran is the one area attraction that will put you as close as you can get to Table Rock Lake without actually getting wet. This 49-passenger 48-foot long sightseeing vessel takes you on a 90-minute cruise. How far you go and how fast you get there is determined by the wind. On a calm day you won't need much hair spray, but on a windy afternoon you'd better bring along a scarf to hold it in place. Most people roll up their sleeves or don a swimsuit to soak up the rays and couldn't care less about letting their hair get messed up. The operators recommend that passengers wear rubber-soled shoes to prevent any close encounters with the fish. The catamaran docks at the Table Rock State Park Marina just off Mo. 165. Tours depart every day but Mondays from April through mid-October at noon, 2 PM, 4 PM, and dusk. Tickets are $16 for adults and $7 for children between the ages of 5 and 12. Kids 4 and younger ride for free. Private charters are available.

Table Rock Helicopters
3309 76 Country Blvd. • (417) 334-6102
•**www.tablerockhelicopters.com**

Right in the heart of The Strip across from Ripley's Believe It or Not! Museum, Table Rock Helicopters offers a variety of tours starting with the basic 5-mile flight to the edge of Table Rock Lake and back up to the 50-mile round trip to Eureka Springs, Arkansas. The 5-mile flight gives you about three minutes in the air. Along the way you'll see Mo. 165, the Welk Resort, Point

Royale golf course and, during the peak season, motorists patiently crawling along in traffic. The 10-mile flight lasts twice as long as the 5-mile flight and takes you on both sides of Table Rock Dam, past the Shepherd of the Hills Fish Hatchery, over Lake Taneycomo, and near Chateau on the Lake. The 15-mile flight takes you to Baird Mountain and out to Indian Point, where you can get a better idea of exactly how many resorts and marinas line the shoreline. This flight lasts approximately eight minutes. The 25-mile tour passes Shepherd of the Hills Homestead, Silver Dollar City, Table Rock Lake and Taneycomo. The 30-mile flight goes east to Powersite Dam, south of town to Table Rock Dam, and past the Chateau on the Lake. The 50-mile tour takes passengers over the historic town of Eureka Springs and near the Passion Play.

Both of Table Rock Helicopters' birds can seat up to six passengers and are operated by experienced pilots who offer a narration of the scenery on each trip that guests can listen to through headphones. Reservations are not necessary and prices are the same for adults and children. Expect to pay $17.95 for the 5-mile flight and there must be a minimum of 2 passengers. The 10-mile flight is $23.95 per person with a minimum of 2 passengers. The price for the 15-mile tour is $28.95 per person with a minimum of 2 passengers. The 25-mile flight is a flat rate of $225 for up to six passengers and the 30-mile flight is a flat rate of $270 for up to six passengers. The trip to Eureka is $95 per person with a minimum of four passengers. Toddlers aged 2 and younger ride for free on all flights. Table Rock Helicopters opens at 10 AM in the spring and fall, and closes each day when the crowds begin to thin out. During the summer they are open from 9 AM until 9 PM. No flights December through February.

Talking Rocks Cavern Park
Talking Rocks Rd.
- **(417) 272-3366, (800) 600-CAVE**
- **www.talkingrockscavern.com**

Talking Rocks Cavern, considered one of Missouri's most beautiful caves, is just a few miles west of one of the state's most famous caves, Marvel Cave at Silver Dollar City. To get to Talking Rocks, drive west on Mo. 76 out of Branson. Turn left on Mo. 13 at Branson West. Go 1 mile and turn left on Talking Rocks Road. Look for the signs leading you to the entrance.

The cave, on a 400-acre natural preserve, is said to have been discovered in 1883 by hunters when they chased a rabbit under a rock. In 1892

Truman Powell, the pioneer immortalized as the Old Shepherd in Harold Bell Wright's novel *The Shepherd of the Hills*, named the cavern Fairy Cave. Waldo Powell, Truman's son, opened the cave and the land surrounding it to the public in 1921. Today we know it as Talking Rocks Cavern and as one of the most unique geological sites in the area. The main chamber is 100 feet tall and extends over 600 feet. The wall formations are thick with stalactites and helictites that curl down from the ceiling like a candlemaker's creation. Colorful stalagmites dot the floor of the cave. Be sure to bring along your camera, as you'll want to capture these magnificent crystal creations on film. Although bats do not inhabit Talking Rocks cavern (be sure to ask your guide why bats do not reside there), it is a sanctuary for the Ozark blind cave salamander. This unique creature is on the rare and endangered species list, so be careful not to touch or otherwise disturb it should it make its presence known.

A well-trained guide leads each 50-minute walking tour. The cavern is open to the public from the end of January through the week before Christmas. The first tour of the day starts at 9:30 AM (12:30 PM on Sundays) with tours departing every 35 minutes until 5 PM. The cavern is open seven days a week from March through November. It is closed Wednesdays and Thursdays all other times of the year. Before or after a tour of the cave, you can enjoy a picnic or a hike along the nature trails at the Talking Rocks nature park. There's a gift shop and snack bar at the entrance to the park. Admission to the cave is $9.95 for adults and $4.95 for children aged 5 through 12. Children age 4 and younger get in free.

If the trek through Talking Rocks Cavern has left you wanting more, and you've got the guts for it, you can explore one of the other 8 caves on the Talking Rocks property. Ask for the Wild Cave Tour into Indian Creek Caverns. There's no electricity in this cave, which means no lights, no concrete paths, and no hand rails. This is real spelunking, by George! A pair of experienced cave guides will accompany you on the tour. You'll get a flashlight, a hard hat (you pay $10 to rent) and a real sense of what Truman and the rabbit hunters felt like on their first peeks into Talking Rocks Cavern. The cost for this adventure is $150 minimum for groups of 6 or less and $25 per person for groups of more than six. Groups are limited to 12 people. There's a $50 non-refundable deposit required to schedule a wild cave tour. The deposit will be refunded if the trip is cancelled due to wet weather. The guides are ultra-cautious when it comes to safety. Caves are not nice places to be during or following rain.

Shows and Presentations

Gotcha Laser Tag & Arcade
3107 76 Country Blvd. • (417) 332-2522
• **www.gotchatag.com**

Located just off The Strip behind the Riverboat Motel and the Starlite Theatre, Gotcha Laser Tag is like paint ball, target practice, cross-training, and star wars all rolled into one. Players, fitted with special laser sensing vests toting laser guns, enter the 4,000-square foot black-lit arena where they shoot it out for survival. The arena is set up like a maze, so players have plenty of places from which to launch an ambush or hide out to catch their breath. The goal is to make it to the end of the maze without getting "tagged" out. The attraction is open every day year round from 10 AM to midnight with some exceptions during the off season in January and February, when they close earlier. The cost for one round of laser tag is $7 per person. During the winter months they offer reduced rates for play. They'll be happy to host your birthday party or other special event. Call for group rates. One piece of advice—don't wear white. You'll be easier to spot under the black light.

IMAX Entertainment Complex
3562 Shepherd of the Hills Expy.
• **(417) 335-4832, (800) 419-4832**
• **www.bransonimax.com**

For the ultimate movie-going experience, you should definitely check out the IMAX Theater. With a six-story screen that projects an image 10 times larger than standard 35mm theaters, 44 speakers with a combined total of 22,000 watts of digital surround sound, and a seating arrangement that puts you right in the middle of the action, IMAX is a movie buff's dream. In 1997 the theater added a projector fitted with a special lens that made it possible to show 35mm feature-length motion pictures. What an idea that was! Since then, IMAX has shown first run movies like *Titanic, Star Wars Episode I–The Phantom Menace, Deep Blue Sea, The World Is Not Enough*, and others. The image area of the 35mm films fills more than half of the IMAX screen and takes full advantage of the surround-sound system. New feature films arrive every few weeks. Showtimes range from

7 to 9 PM depending on the season. Tickets are $7 for adults, $4 for children ages 4 through 12 and free for children younger than 4.

In 2000 IMAX plans to open a $1.5 million expansion to their entertainment complex which will include three 167-seat 35mm movie theaters. The theaters will have stadium style seating, digital surround sound, and will be designed to accommodate meetings, music shows, and other special events. The expansion will also make room for a fast-food court and arcade.

The documentary-style large format movies IMAX is known for are produced exclusively for the 100 IMAX theaters around the world. They usually average around 55 minutes in length and combine dramatic footage with an educational narrative. Some of the films shown in Branson recently include *Dolphins, Alaska, The Great American West, Speed, The Magic of Flight,* and *Grand Canyon.*

The signature film shown throughout the year exclusively at the Branson IMAX Theater is called *Ozarks Legacy & Legend.* Directed by Academy Award-winning director Keith Merrill and produced for a mere $3 million (cheap by today's titanic movie-making standards), the film tells the story of the fictional McFarlain family (after whom the complex's full-service restaurant is named), who inhabited the Ozarks between 1824 and 1950. They experience the triumphs and tragedies of pioneer life in the Ozarks with a touch of humor and a great deal of faith. The beauty of the untamed Ozarks is captured extremely well in a number of memorable scenes. The camera takes viewers on a ride with the vigilante Bald Knobbers, into the depths of an unexplored cave, aboard a flight on the first biplane in the Ozarks, and along for a chase involving a Revenuer and a moonshiner. The Civil War battle scenes are meticulously recreated right down to the last detail. (See the History chapter for more on the Civil War in the Ozarks.) All of this is underscored with original music and numerous realistic sound effects. *Ozarks Legacy & Legend* is presented a number of times each day.

Films are shown on the hour, every hour, beginning at 9 AM, seven days a week year round. Ticket prices for the large format IMAX films are $8 for adults and $4.95 for children ages 4 through 12. Children younger than 4 get in free.

Before or after the show you can pop into McFarlain's Restaurant. They serve up good old-fashioned home-style meals and some of the best pie in town. (See our Restaurants chapter for more information.) The specialty shops at the IMAX complex offer everything from costume jewelry to grandfather clocks. There's even a fudge shop that hands out free samples. (For more on the shops at IMAX, see our Shopping chapter.)

The Remember When Theatre

In 1998 the IMAX complex added a 210-seat live-performance theater for "Mike Radford's Remember When Show." The stage of the intimate venue is set to look like a typical grandmother's attic complete with more than 400 items, most of them donated by fans. You'll see old clothes, photographs, toys, military memorabilia, furniture, books, and Burma Shave signs. The lobby area looks like a 1940s main street. There's a barber shop, a toy store, and Mikey's 5 & Dime store, where you can buy Burma Shave items as well as Roy Rogers and Dale Evans memorabilia. Called one of the most talented communicators in America by Larry King, Mike Radford uses the props from the set to take audiences back to the days of live radio broadcasts, cap guns, cowboy heroes, and world wars. Mike Radford is Mr. Nostalgia. He combines comedy with vivid verbal images that bring a tear to the eye of many a guest. His patriotism is unmistakable and his show is an undeniable favorite among veterans. The show is presented at 10 AM Tuesdays through Saturdays mid-March through June, and September through mid December. Tickets are $15 for adults and free to children aged 12 and younger. When Mike's not performing in Branson, he's usually touring the country presenting his show or giving motivational speeches. Visit his website at www.mikeradford.com to learn more about this former Kansas City Royals shortstop player that turned Branson star.

Sharing the Remember When Theatre with Mike Radford is legendary songwriter Jimmie Rodgers. If you recall songs like "Honeycomb," "Kisses Sweeter Than Wine," "Oh-Oh," "Se-

Mike Radford performs at the Remember When Theatre inside the IMAX Entertainment Complex.

Photo: IMAX Entertainment Complex

cretly," "It's Over," and "Are You Really Mine?" then you'll enjoy Jimmie's up-close-and-personal nostalgic musical journey. With 38 top ten hits, Jimmie's song writing credits rival the most well known Branson stars. His shows are at 2:30 and 7 PM April through June and September through December. Call for exact days.

Stone Hill Winery
601 S. Mo. Hwy. 165.
• (417) 334-1897, (888) 926-WINE
• www.stonehillwinery.com

Like many of the businesses in Branson, Stone Hill Winery is family-owned and operated. Thomas Held, the son of Jim and Betty Held, who bought the original Stone Hill Winery in Hermann in 1965, runs it. At one time the Hermann winery, built in 1847 by settlers from the German Rhineland, was the third-largest winery in the world, until Prohibition shut it down. From 1933 until the Helds bought it, the winery's cellars were used to grow mushrooms. Today the Held family operates three

ATTRACTIONS

wineries in Hermann, Branson, and New Florence. Although no wine is actually made in Branson, an assortment of spumantes and fruit juices are bottled here. The 40-minute free tour of the winery include a tasting session where adults can sample dry and sweet wines while the kids sip grape juice. There is a short video presentation at the beginning of the tour that tells about the parent winery in Hermann. Along the tour you'll be treated to a winemaking course and a short history of winemaking in Missouri. The tours begin every 15 minutes from 8:30 AM until dusk Mondays through Saturdays year round. On Sundays tours are given from 11 AM to 6 PM. The gift shop stocks great gift packages that include meats, cheeses, and biscuit mix. You can pick out a bottle of wine and the staff will package it for you. They'll even throw in a glass or two. The winery is closed on Thanksgiving, Christmas, and New Year's Day.

The Butterfly Place
2400 Mo. Hwy. 165 • (417) 332-2231
• www.butterflyplace.com

The Butterfly Place is a live exhibit of approximately 2,000 butterflies representing 50 or more species from around the world. The 9,000-square foot enclosed greenhouse is kept at a constant 80 degrees to provide the butterflies with near ideal conditions. As you stroll through the lush flowerbeds in the aviary, you can watch the insects fly around freely from plant to plant. If you wear a bright yellow or red shirt, the colorful creatures may mistake you for lunch and try to land on you. The tour begins with a video presentation about the aviary and the lifecycle and habits of butterflies. Then you'll want to visit the emergence room, which contains chrysalids of hatching butterflies. There's a gift shop where you can buy what else—butterfly souvenirs, but you can also pick up books and other educational materials. The Butterfly Place is open from March through October from 10 AM to 5 PM and from 10 AM to 4 PM November through December. It is closed in January and February. Serious photographers may make reservations to bring in their tripods and other gear from 7:30 AM to 9:30 AM. Everyone else is invited to bring a camera or video recorder during regular business hours. Admission prices are $7.95 for adults and $5.95 for children aged 4 through 17. Children aged 3 and younger get in free. The family pass is $19.95 for two adults and two children.

Waltzing Waters Theatre
3617 76 Country Blvd.
• (417) 334-4144, (800) 276-7284

The folks at Waltzing Waters are so convinced that their attraction is one of the best you'll ever see that they will give you your money back if you disagree. This colorful 40,000-gallon water fountain display synchronized to music is certainly unique, you have to admit. With a ticket price of $6 for adults and children 12 and older, $3 for children ages 4 to 11, and free to kids 3 and younger, the 42-minute Fountains of Fire show is as good an entertainment value as you'll find. Continuously changing colored lights are aimed at the water fountains, which are manipulated to rise and fall with the rhythm of popular taped music. The term "liquid fireworks" appropriately describes the scene. Fountains of Fire is presented every hour on the hour each day except Monday from 9 AM to 10 PM, April through December. In January, February, and March the last show begins at 6 PM. Performer Frederick Antonio joins the liquid cast three times a day at 10 AM, 1 PM, and 6 PM for a little double-action piano playing. That's right, Frederick plays two grand pianos simultaneously while the fountains keep time to the rhythm of the music. The tickets to Frederick's shows are $12 for adults, $6 for children ages 3 to 11, and free to kids 2 and younger. During each show a child from the audience is allowed to participate in a demonstration of how the fountains work. You can save $2 off the admission price to Frederick's show and $1 off the Fountains of Fire show by bringing in a specially marked brochure, which can be found at any number of racks in town. Waltzing Waters is on The Strip next door to the Remington Theatre and behind the Carolina Mills Factory Outlet.

Spend the Day Outdoors

College of the Ozarks
Point Lookout
• (417) 334-6411, (800) 222-0525
• www.cofo.edu

Built on a bluff overlooking Lake Taneycomo is Point Lookout just 2 miles south of Branson on U.S. 65, College of the Ozarks is one of the area's more unusual attractions. The campus grounds, with their rose gardens and gently rolling hills, are immaculately maintained by students who work on campus in return for their tuition (see our Education and Child Care chapter for more information about the work program). The buildings include everything from an old-fashioned working gristmill to a neo-Gothic chapel to a modem greenhouse.

For a self-guided tour of the campus, all you have to do is follow the maroon line painted on the walkways. The "bobcat trail," as it is called, will lead you to the most popular sites on campus. The first stop on the tour is the Friendship House restaurant, which is at the entrance of the campus. Student workers serve breakfast, lunch, and dinner Mondays through Saturdays year round. There's also a gift shop that contains items made by the students, crafts, and other Branson souvenirs. Edwards Mill is an authentic working gristmill powered by a 12-foot water wheel, which is turned by runoff water from Lake Honor. You can watch as student workers grind whole grains into meal and flour. On the second floor of the mill, students use old-fashioned weaving machines to produce rugs, placemats, and shawls. All of the items produced at the mill are available for sale. The greenhouses at the college contain more than 7,000 plants, including orchids. Clint McDade, one of the school's first students, donated the bulk of the orchid collection. You can purchase orchids and other houseplants at the greenhouse.

The icon for the college is Williams Memorial Chapel, an impressive piece of architecture designed in the neo-Gothic style with an 80-foot vaulted ceiling and magnificent stained glass windows. The structure was dedicated in 1956 and is one of the area's most popular wedding sites. Ask locals and they'll tell you they've either been to a wedding there or were married there themselves. Attached to the chapel is Hyer Bell Tower, where carillon concerts are played at noon and 6 PM. Sunday services at the chapel are open to the public every week at 11 AM.

Students who work in the fruitcake and jelly kitchen produce more than 40,000 cakes a year, which are shipped all over the country for sale. Visitors can watch as students prepare apple butter and other jellies in the kitchen. And yes, you can buy any of their products on the spot. Other notable sites on the campus include M. Graham Clark Airport, (see the Getting Here, Getting Around Chapter), the Lake Honor Fountain, the Star Schoolhouse, Memorial Fieldhouse, and Ralph Foster Museum (see its listing in the Museums section of this chapter). The campus even has a working dairy farm where students arrive before their morning classes to tend to the livestock. If you're interested in getting some great photos of the campus, you can pick up one of the college's brochures that lists the best places to shoot. Smoking is prohibited in all campus buildings and is even discouraged outdoors.

Ozark Shooters Sports Complex
759 U.S. Hwy. 65 N., Walnut Shade
• (417) 443-3093
• www.ozarkshooters.com

This 45-acre gun-sport attraction 11 miles north of Branson offers everything from basic target ranges to competitive tournaments for the advanced shooter. The complex has sporting clay ranges with everything from bouncing bunnies, to snipe, to gobbling turkeys, to charging crows—10 forms in all. There's a rifle and pistol range where you can test your accuracy at 50, 100, 150, and 200 yards. You can bring your own gun or rent a Remington 1100 semi-automatic shotgun for around $2 a day. There's a metallic 22-rimfire silhouette range and five stand as well as trap and skeet fields. The rifle and pistol ranges are open to members only. The south ridge sporting clay course has 10 fields and 21 stations. For around $40 an hour you can enlist the services of an instructor who will teach you how to fire a handgun. If you're looking to buy a weapon, you can pick one out at the clubhouse where owner and gun dealer Peggy Siler will set you up.

The complex hosts a number of special events each month all year long including the Valentine Sweetheart Shoot in February, the Women on Target ladies event in May, the Bass Pro Fall Classic in August and the SCA Fun Shoot in October and many other cash prize tournaments. The entry fee for most of the competitions ranges from $4 to $50 per person. The cost for trap skeet, ball trap and wobble trap is $5 for 25. Sporting clays are $18 for 50 or $28 for 100. Ozark Shooters Sports Complex opens at 9 AM seven days a week year round. In the summertime the complex stays open until 7 PM, but during the winter it closes at dark.

Kidstuff

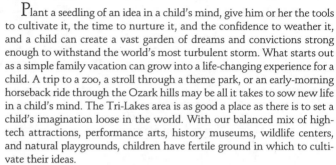

Plant a seedling of an idea in a child's mind, give him or her the tools to cultivate it, the time to nurture it, and the confidence to weather it, and a child can create a vast garden of dreams and convictions strong enough to withstand the world's most turbulent storm. What starts out as a simple family vacation can grow into a life-changing experience for a child. A trip to a zoo, a stroll through a theme park, or an early-morning horseback ride through the Ozark hills may be all it takes to sow new life in a child's mind. The Tri-Lakes area is as good a place as there is to set a child's imagination loose in the world. With our balanced mix of high-tech attractions, performance arts, history museums, wildlife centers, and natural playgrounds, children have fertile ground in which to cultivate their ideas.

The listings in this section by no means make a complete list of the interesting or appealing things available for children in the Branson area. We hope that you will consider flipping through the chapters on Lakes and Rivers as well as Recreation and the Outdoors as you begin your quest to find activities for children.

The attractions you'll find at Silver Dollar City combine the best of nature, history, technology, science, and art. The National Children's Festival, held each year during the summer months (see the Close-up in this chapter), showcases exhibits by Crayola, Hallmark, and the Smithsonian Institute Traveling Exhibition Service and the National Geographic Society. Even before the Children's Festival began in 1995, Silver Dollar City was a perennial favorite among children.

Many other outstanding activities for children are listed in our Attractions chapter. Ride the Ducks, IMAX Entertainment Complex, Ripley's Believe It or Not! Museum, the Hollywood Wax Museum, and the five area caves (including Fantastic Caverns) are hot spots for kids. There are also plenty of free and inexpensive things to do in Branson. With three lakes and a fish hatchery as well as a public playground on nearly every corner, kids have plenty of room to get out and explore the Ozarks. Many of the area music shows now admit children at no charge. Lodging facilities are also stepping up their efforts to attract families by letting children stay for free in a parent's room.

Nearby Springfield offers a number of interesting as well as educational kiddy attractions including Discovery Center, portions of the Bass Pro Shops and Dickerson Park Zoo. Our chapter on Daytrips contains other attractions such as Wilson's Creek National Battlefield and the Springfield Art Museum, which are popular destinations for school groups.

The list of activities in this chapter runs the gamut from arcades to zoos. You will undoubtedly find some treasures we left out. This listing is only meant to serve as fertile ground for your children's growing imaginations. Who knows what may come of their ideas? Maybe they'll decide to grow up to be country music stars or fishing guides. Or they'll do what a few native Ozarkers did and become both.

INSIDERS' TIP

If you arrive at Silver Dollar City after 3 PM, the next day is free.

World War II amphibious vehicles have been converted into land and lake sightseeing vessels.

Photo: Branson/Lakes Area Chamber of Commerce

Splash It

Bumper Boats Amusement Center
1715 76 Country Blvd. • (417) 335-2628

At Bumper Boats Amusement Center, pint-sized sea captains can board floating bumper vessels and set sail for nautical adventures on the mighty Atlantic. Okay, it's only a swimming pool, and the surf is none too mighty. Nevertheless, kids get a kick out of banging into each other in maneuverable inner tubes. Drying off after the big sea battle is great fun in the gyro-force orbiter as it whirls you head over heels. If that hasn't brought back memories of lunch, you can bounce around on the trampoline for a while. Bumper Boats Amusement Center is open seven days a week from mid-morning until midnight, April through October.

Cool Off Water Chute
2115 76 Country Blvd. • (417) 334-1919

This 560-foot water slide is built into the side of one of our famous Ozark mountains. It's got more twists and turns than a snake on hot asphalt. Kids with plenty of energy won't mind the long trek up the staircase to the top of the chute. They can slide 30 minutes for $6 or one hour for $8. The attraction is open daily from 10 AM to 10 PM, Memorial Day through Labor Day. It is the oldest water slide in Branson.

Sammy Lane Pirate Cruise
280 N. Lakefront Dr. • (417) 334-3015

Ahoy, little mates! If the 70-minute *Sammy Lane* guided sightseeing cruise is a bit too calm for those with underdeveloped attention spans and overactive imaginations, then pretend you're stranded on Waterworld with Kevin Costner. Never mind that you can see the banks of Lake Taneycomo on all sides. Just as the movie hero battled fierce water vigilantes, you may also get your chance to ward off a pirate attack. The 49-passenger cruise boat departs a number of times each day from April through October. Call for exact times. Kids younger than 3 board for free with an adult, and kids younger than 12 pay $6.50. Adult tickets are $9.75.

White Water
3505 76 Country Blvd.
• (417) 334-7487, (800) 417-7770
• www.silverdollarcity.com

One of Branson's premiere attractions for summertime kiddy fun is this 12-plus-acre tropical paradise. White Water boasts 14 water attractions including Paradise Plunge, a 207-foot, triple-drop slide. Surfquake Pool is a 500,000-

gallon wave pool, great for a little surf action or tubing. Fast-paced rides include Bermuda Triangle and Typhoon Tunnel, enclosed slides full of twists and turns; Hurricane Rapids, an inner tube ride down a fast slide; and Tropical Twister, a float trip with rafts large enough for the entire family. Paradise River offers rafters a slower ride down a gently moving river.

In 2000 the park will feature a new attraction called Monsoon Lagoon, a 20,000-square foot island with more than 60 different types of water elements including aqua shooters, water blasters, splash geysers, a 150-foot long slide and a tipping bucket that showers guests with 700 gallons of water. This expansion will provide space for an additional 800 guests per day. In 1998 the park added the Little Squirts' Waterworks area, which is full of colorful mazes of tunnels, slides, waterfalls, nozzles, and pools. The park also has a sand volleyball area, beach-gear shop and snack bar. Life jackets are free, and certified lifeguards are always on duty.

The park is open May through early September from 10 AM to 6 PM daily. Operating hours are extended during June, July, and August. Admission is around $24 for those aged 12 and older. Children aged 11 and younger get in for around $18. Kids younger than 4 are admitted for free. Season passes are available as well as combination tickets to other Silver Dollar City properties including Silver Dollar City, Showboat Branson Belle, Dixie Stampede, and the Radio City Christmas Spectacular. (See our chapters on Attractions and The Shows.)

Drive It, Putt It, Ride It, Just Don't Break It

Grand Country Resort
1917 76 Country Blvd. • (417) 334-3919
Formerly known as 76 Mall Complex, this newly renovated, 319-room resort features a 36-hole public indoor minigolf course (adults pay $5 and children younger than 12 are charged $2.50), a deluxe video arcade, and music shows. A new, interactive water-play area called Splash Country is reserved for overnight guests of Grand Country Inn only. It contains waterfalls, water slides, water guns, a floating river,

INSIDERS' TIP
The Dixie Stampede houses its show horses in outdoor pens from 10 AM until showtime. There's no charge to come by and look.

and a special area for toddlers. Children younger than 12 stay free with a parent at Grand Country Inn (see our Accommodations chapter).

Kids Kountry
2505 76 Country Blvd. • (417) 334-1618
Little tykes can step into their favorite fairy tale along the Mother Goose-themed miniature golf course or enter a house-size shoe to look for the Old Lady. Kids can also enjoy jungle gym equipment and electrical rides such as the train, carousel, bumper boats, and kiddy go-carts (the go-carts are only for kids weighing less than 40 pounds). Rides range from $1.75 to $3.50 a pop. Kids Kountry is open all year, except for January, from 10 AM to 8 PM daily. The attraction extends its hours to midnight during the busy summer months of June, July, and August. Mom and dad may want to stay next door at the Dutch Kountry Inn so they can keep an eye on the little ones. (See our chapter on Accommodations for more information.)

Pirate's Cove
2901 Green Mountain Dr.
• (417) 336-6606
If Tarzan played miniature golf, this is where you would expect to find him. He'd feel right at home amidst the tropical plants, palm trees, rock waterfalls, and mountain caves. Golfers have two 18-hole courses to choose from: Blackbeard's Challenge Course, for the experienced golfer, and Captain's Course, with its gradual slopes and numerous props. You can play daily from 9 AM until 11:30 PM, weather permitting. The indoor Fun Center is packed with video machines and games. If you're really into the jungle theme, you can spend the night across the street in the Safari suite at the Settle Inn Resort and Conference Center (see our chapter on Accommodations).

The Track Recreation Center
No. 1,1116 76 Country Blvd.
• (417) 334-1613
No.2, 1655 76 Country Blvd.
• (417) 334-1610
No.3, 2505 76 Country Blvd.
• (417) 334-1611
No.4, 3345 76 Country Blvd.
• (417) 334-1617

The Branson area has a number of miniature golf courses. Some are even indoors for rainy days!

Photo: Branson/Lakes Area Chamber of Commerce

No.5, 3525 76 Country Blvd.
• (417) 334-1619

One of the great debates among Insiders is which one of The Track's go-cart tracks is the best. If you've got little speed demons in your family, let them be the judge. Each of The Track's five locations has a different list of amenities. No. 3 has miniature golf, bumper boats, and an arcade room. No.4 also has a miniature golf course complete with statues of lurking alligators. Racers must be at least 54 inches tall; otherwise they'll have to stick to the bumper boats and golf. A few of The Track locations stay open year round, but most of them close in January and February. During the summer, they are open 7 days a week from 9 AM until 10 PM. Days and hours vary other times of the year.

Thunder Road
3235 76 Country Blvd.
• (417) 334-5905

At Thunder Road you'll find Major League Baseball players working on their swings in the batting cages; demolition derby drivers jockeying to keep their bumper cars in the game; PGA pros strolling along the two 18-hole miniature golf courses; Air Force fighter pilots defending the universe from alien attacks while tucked safely in the arcade room; and Indy car drivers zooming by on the outdoor racetrack hoping to quench their thirst for glory with a nice tall glass of milk. You probably won't recognize any of these superstars however, because they show up disguised as kids.

Smaller tots can enjoy a variety of mechanical games such as skeeball. The machines spit out tickets, which can be redeemed for treasures and trinkets. If you still have energy to burn, you can hop on the trampoline or check out the gyro-force orbiter. There is no admission to the facility but you must pay for individual activities. Thunder Road is open seven days a week March through November from 9 AM until 10 PM. Between May and September they stay open until midnight.

KIDSTUFF

Pick It, Sing It, Saddle It, Stay Over Night

Kamp Kanakuk and Kanakomo
1353 Lakeshore Dr. • (417) 334-0111
• www.kanakuk.com

One of the most popular attractions for kids in the Branson area is Kamp Kanakuk and Kanakomo. Kids have been spending their summers at these camps since the 1920s. Known for their Christian ideals and emphasis on physical activity, these camps offer seven-, 14- and 26-day terms May through August. Kids enjoy camping, boating, archery, climbing, basketball, and other sports. Parents of kids ages 7 to 18 must make reservations months in advance. The cost varies according to length of stay and the type of camp the child plans to attend.

Shirley M. Schaefer Boys and Girls Club
1460 Bee Creek Rd. • (417) 336-2420

Kids visiting the Branson area for a day, a week, or a month can find great fun at the Shirley M. Schaefer Boys and Girls Clubs in Branson, Forsyth, and Reeds Spring. This non-profit organization offers a supervised gathering place for kids to enjoy computers, basketball, racquetball, swimming, fitness equipment, games, crafts, and a library. The Branson facility can accommodate 250 children a day, but it is often packed in the summer. Call ahead for availability before dropping off your child. During the school year the facility is open from 3 PM to 8 PM and during the summer it is open from 7 AM to 7 PM. The annual membership fee was $10 in 1999 for children ages 5 through 18. Children ages 2 through 5 can stay in the licensed day care facility, Kim's Academy for an additional fee. (For more information on this organization, see our chapter on Education and Child Care.)

Persimmon Hill Farm
Lake Rd. 86-63, Lampe • (417) 779-5443
• www. branson.com/persimmonhill

Too many hours at the video arcade can turn your children into techno-zombies. Treat them to some fresh Ozark Mountain fruit at Persimmon Hill Farm. They'll experience the taste of blueberries, blackberries, raspberries, and gooseberries right off the vine. You pay for what you pick. The farm also grows Shiitake mushrooms, and employees make jams, jellies, and barbecue sauces while you watch. Their Blue-berry Barbecue Sauce took first place in the American Royal International Barbecue Contest in Kansas City in 1994, and their other products have received numerous awards each year since. You can have a gift pack sent to grandma filled with a variety of their top-selling products including their Thunder Muffins made with ripe blueberries that were picked just hours before. Call ahead to find out what's ripe for the pickin', and be sure to wear a hat on a hot summer's day and plenty of sun block if you plan to stay awhile. The farm is open from May through December. The hours vary according to the season. To get there from Branson, take U.S. Highway 65 south to Mo. Highway 86. Turn right on Mo. 86 and follow it to Lake Road 86-63. Go 1.5 miles, and the farm is on the left.

Saloon Photos
2817 W. 76 Country Blvd.
• (417) 334-4928

Need a publicity photo to go along with that demo tape from Singing Sensations (see the next listing)? It you're into the outlaw look, this is the place to go. Be sure to hold back on that smile if you want your photo to look authentic. At Moe's Old Time Photos, 3010 76 Country Boulevard, (417) 334-2004, which is owned by the same company as Saloon Photos, you can choose from Victorian-era costumes, Civil War-era costumes, Roaring '20s flapper dresses and more. Prices start at $12.95 for one person and $2 for each additional person you want in the shot. They are open March through December 7 days a week from 10 AM until 10 PM.

Singing Sensations
2800 W. 76 Country Blvd. at the Grand Village • (417) 335-4435

What did the Partridge family have that yours doesn't? A demo tape! At Singing Sensations they'll record your vocals against the music track of one of more than 400 popular songs. If you've been bitten by the showbiz bug of Branson, they'll even make duplications so you can send a copy to Starlite Kids Review or the Country Tonite show. Who knows? Maybe you'll even get your own theater or TV show someday. Walk-ins are welcome year round, and the whole process takes just a couple of hours. If you've got the moves to go along with the voice, you can even record a music video. Kids won't have to dip into their college savings for a demo from Singing Sensations either. Prices start at around $20.

Attractions in the Branson area position modern technology against a backdrop of natural beauty.

Photo: Branson/lakes Area Chamber of Commerce

Skateworld Family Amusement Center
100 Truman Dr. • (417) 334-1630

Want to become an Olympic ice skater some day? You can get started on 4 wheels at Skateworld. Little hopefuls can get in plenty of practice for around $4. The center has both in-line and speed skates. If you've got a special event coming up such as a birthday or graduation, call for rates on private parties. Skateworld is next door to Dixie Stampede. It's open daily year round from 7 to 10 PM. Ask about private skating lessons.

Uncle Ike's Trail Ride
W. Mo. Hwy. 76, Notch
• (417) 338-8449

The days of Tonto and Silver may have long passed, but kids of all ages can still enjoy a good game of Cowboys and Indians at Uncle Ike's Trail Ride, just a half-mile west of Silver Dollar City in the community of Notch. Ike has 40 horses available for the 2.5-mile rides, which last about 45 minutes each. Rides depart from 9 AM to 5 PM daily April through October. Children younger than 6 must ride with a small adult (less than 150 pounds). Each ride costs $12.50 per horse. Early risers can enjoy the breakfast ride that starts at 7 AM and lasts until 9 AM.

You must make reservations for this one, and the cost is $22.50 per horse. You get a hearty breakfast of eggs, hash browns, biscuits, and gravy. An experienced guide accompanies each tour.

Learn It

College of the Ozarks
Point Lookout
• (417) 334-6411, (800) 222-0525
Edwards Mill • (417) 334-6411 Ext. 3355
Ralph Foster Museum • (417) 334-6411 Ext. 3407

Two attractions on the campus of College of the Ozarks might be of interest to school-aged children: the Ralph Foster Museum and Edwards Mill. The mill is an old-fashioned, water-powered gristmill where college students grind flour and cornmeal while you watch. You can buy a bag to take home with you. On the second floor of the mill, students use weaving looms to make tablecloths and place mats. The Ralph Foster Museum houses three floors of antique trinkets and gadgets, including exhibits of nature and exhibits on Ozarks history. (For more information on the museum, see our Attractions chapter.) Both attractions are open

KIDSTUFF

Monday through Saturday. Admission is free to children younger than the age of 18.

Dewey Short Visitors Center
Mo. Hwy. 165 • (417) 334-4104

A trip to the Ozarks wouldn't be complete without a good dose of education about the area and its wildlife. The U.S. Army Corps of Engineers operates the Dewey Short Visitors Center just for that reason. Kids can look at the wildlife exhibits, learn about native flora along the nature trail, take in a film or lecture, pick up a book in the bookstore, and visit nearby Table Rock Dam and Powerhouse. There is no charge to the visitors' center, but there is a $2 fee to tour the dam. Children younger than 5 get in free. Dam tours are offered from 9 to 11 AM and 1 to 4 PM daily. The center is open seven days a week April through October from 9 AM to 5 PM. Both the dam and visitors center are open on Saturdays and Sundays November through March. (For more information on the visitors center, see our chapter on Recreation and the Great Outdoors.)

INSIDERS' TIP
The average daily temperature is 93 degrees in July, our hottest month and one of White Water's busiest.

Shepherd of the Hills Fish Hatchery
483 Hatchery Rd. • (417) 334-4865

If your kids spent all their money on video games at The Track (see earlier listing), they'll surely hit you up for more change to buy fish food at the Shepherd of the Hills Fish Hatchery. It's a real thrill to throw a handful of pellets into a tank filled with growing trout. They devour it so fast and furiously; it's almost comical. Try not to be disappointed if you show up about the time a school-bus load of kids pulls out—the fish may not be hungry anymore. In addition to the huge open-air holding tanks, the hatchery has educational exhibits, multimedia presentations, literature, and nature trails. You can always find a helpful conservation agent on hand to answer questions. (For more information on the hatchery, see our chapter on Recreation and the Great Outdoors.) Admission is free to the hatchery, which is just off Mo. Highway 165, 6 miles south of Branson.

Daytrip It

The listings in this section, although not in Branson, are well worth the trip if you can afford the time. We have focused primarily on the aspects of these attractions that appeal to children. You can find a more complete write-up of each one in the Daytrips chapter.

Springfield Area

Bass Pro Shops
1915 S. Campbell Ave., Springfield
• (417) 887-7334 • www.basspro.com

In his entire life Daniel Boone probably never saw as much wildlife as you can see in one hour at Bass Pro Shop. To say the place is as much of a museum as it is a retail store is an understatement. To get a truly concentrated dose of taxidermy you need to visit the Wildlife Museum, which is adjacent to the showroom. You have to pay to enter this part of the facility ($4 for adults and teenagers and $2 for children ages 5 through 12). They've got grizzly bears, moose, bobcats, caribou, birds, fish, and many other large predatory animals on display. You can see plenty for free at Bass Pro, however, including the 64,000-gallon freshwater aquarium. Kids can watch as divers feed the inhabitants by hand. There is also a 30,000-gallon saltwater aquarium filled with lobster, moray eels, and sharks. Experts offer free seminars from time to time in the 250-seat auditorium on everything from bass to water safety. Throughout the facility plaques encourage patrons to respect the environment and preserve wildlife.

Scheduled for a 2001 opening is a 92,000 square foot wildlife art and artifacts museum with a 30-foot waterfall and a live bobcat display. The 200,000-gallon saltwater aquarium will contain sharks and stingrays. (For more on this new addition to Bass Pro Shops see its listing in the Daytrips chapter.)

Dickerson Park Zoo
3043 N. Fort Ave., Springfield
• (417) 883-1570
• www.dickersonparkzoo.org

This 40-acre zoo includes a wide range of exhibits including gazelles, European white storks, East African crowned cranes, ostriches, giraffes, lions, cheetahs, and Asian elephants just to name a few. Throughout the year the zoo offers a number of special events. April's Teddy Bear Rally offers free admission to anyone carrying a teddy bear. In May there's Rep-

Little hillbillies and hounds find summertime fun in Branson.

Photo: Downtown Branson Main Street Association

tile Mania with educational activities throughout the zoo addressing the fear and fascination people have with reptiles. On Grandparents Day in September children get a 75-cent discount when accompanied by their grandparents. On October 31 of each year the zoo throws a Halloween party for children.

If you plan your vacation well in advance, you might want to call ahead to find out what special events may be coming up at the zoo. Admission is free for toddlers 2 and younger and $2.50 for ages 3 to 12. Adults are admitted for $4. Adults aged 65 and older get in for $3.25. The zoo is open from 9 AM to 5 PM daily, April through September and from 10 AM to 4 PM daily October through March, except during inclement weather and on major holidays.

Discovery Center of Springfield
438 E. St. Louis St., Springfield
- **(417) 862-9910**
- **www.communityconnection.org**

Inquiring minds will get plenty of neuron stimuli at Springfield's Discovery Center, a museum with dozens of interactive displays and exhibits on topics from archeology to TV technology. Plan to make a day out of this one. School-aged children as well as preschoolers find plenty to do at this state-of-the-art facility. You can even rent the entire facility for birthday parties and special events. Admission is $5 for adults, $4 for adults older than the age of 60 and $3 for children aged 3 through 12. Children younger than 2 get in free. The museum is open from 10 AM to 5 PM on Wednesday and Saturday, and from 1 PM to 5 PM on Thursday, Friday, and Sunday, and closed on Monday and Tuesday.

Exotic Animal Paradise
124 Jungle Drive, Strafford
- **(417) 859-2159**
- **www.enterit.net/Exotic3339**

You won't spot any singing purple dinosaurs at Exotic Animal Paradise, but you will see plenty of exotic animals as you drive through

KIDSTUFF

Kids Find More to do Than Ever at Silver Dollar City

Kids have been coming to Silver Dollar City since 1960, and never before have they had so many unique and exciting opportunities for fun. With 100 resident craftspeople, 17 rides, five world-class festivals, more than 50 live shows daily, and 60 shops and restaurants all nestled against a backdrop of natural Ozarks beauty, a trip to Silver Dollar City can enrich a child's imagination far beyond that which one might expect. That's the idea behind everything they do at SDC.

"We may entertain our kids at home with Nintendo, but here we encourage kids to use their imagination. We encourage them to entertain themselves, to explore the possibilities of make-believe," according to a Silver Dollar City spokeswoman.

And what possibilities there are! The National Children's Festival, held each year from mid-June through the end of August, is fast becoming one of the park's top draws. From 1996 to 1998 the festival featured the popular Nickelodeon U Pick Nick show. Set to debut in 2000 is the Nickelodeon production entitled Double Dare 2000. It's a new version of Nickelodeon's earlier obstacle course game show. Also coming in 2000 is Camp Nickelodeon, a children's activity center where kids can experience the Nickelodeon 3-D Scrapbook, meet Blue from Blues Clues, and participate in Big Help activities. In 1999 the festival included a creativity center presented by Hallmark and Crayola where kids got to unleash their ideas by making colorful works of art like birthday hats, masks, greeting cards, and giant murals. The Uncle Grumpy's Pork Chop Revue featured a troupe of trained singing pigs previously seen on The *Tonight Show* and *Entertainment Tonight* as they hammed it up in the Dockside Theatre.

Clogging kids from all over the country converged on Silver Dollar City for 1999's national clogging competitions June 16 through 19.

The LEGO fantasy land has been another popular mainstay of the festival, where a number of play areas are set up for kids to build LEGO creations of their own from thousands of LEGO bricks.

In 1998 the festival featured *Earth 2U, Exploring Geography*, an interactive geography adventure from the Smithsonian Institute Traveling Exhibition Service and the National Geographic Society. This multimedia display offered kids a unique way to explore geography facts and history with models, computer programs, videos, and clever text displays that posed questions and told stories and facts.

In 1999 Silver Dollar City unveiled a new permanent park attraction for adults and children alike called BuzzSaw Falls. The premise for this wet/dry rollercoaster is based on that of a logging operation in which guests float along in "john-boats" from an old logging camp to an abandoned Ozarks sawmill. The fun really starts when they're propelled toward a gigantic active buzzsaw. The "john-boat" then becomes a dry coaster and careens downhill at 50 mph, goes around sharp turns and up high into the treetops before plummeting down 6 stories into a reservoir. You have to be 42 inches tall to get on this ride. That pretty much excludes children under the age of 5.

In 1998 the festival debuted Splash Harbor, a three-story ship and four-level dockside tower loaded with hundreds of interactive elements including water cannons, aqua exploders, water blasters and other cool water toys. The ship, the *S.S. Tadpole*, is 45 feet long and topped by a smokestack that looms 32 feet above the deck. The kids can team up against the adults in an all-out water war with one group choosing the shipside and the other the dockside They can choose among the colorful devices to shoot water at each other. If you want to join in the fun but

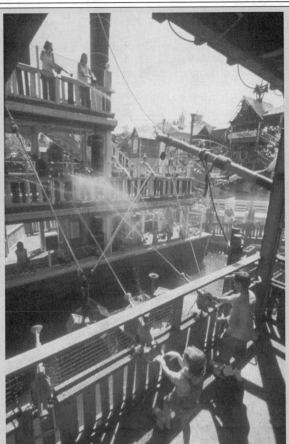

Water cannons are fun and popular during the summer at Silver Dollar City.

don't want to get wet, you can get a poncho as you enter the landing. This attraction is a park favorite all season long.

The creative concept of Splash Harbor plays off the tree-house story line of a once-dry village now driven into the trees by a geyser. That geyser, of course, is Geyser Gulch, another of Silver Dollar City's recent additions to their children's area. This treetop village has three main towers, three stories tall each, plus other smaller towers full of interactive gadgets for kids.

Smaller children may want to check out Tom Sawyer's Landing, where they're a lot less likely to get soaked by an older sibling. It has a bouncing-ball room, carousel, mini-roller coaster, and mazes of nets and rope walkways. There's also a petting zoo full of mighty friendly goats and other small animals.

Speed demons invariably head straight for Thunderation, one of the park's most intense thrill rides. This runaway mine railroad car is really a roller coaster that takes passengers on a speeding trip over the hills and through the trees. The Lost River of the Ozarks takes passengers down a not-so-calm river on huge rafts. Plan to get wet!

The opportunities for children to experience live musical entertainment are limitless at Silver Dollar City. During the Children's Festival, championship cloggers perform throughout the park a number of times each day. In 1999 the *Haygood Family: American Boys* music show played all year at the 1,000-seat Opera House as well as the hilarious *How The West Was Wed Show* at the Silver Dollar Saloon. After the park closes for the day, the 4,000-seat Echo Hollow Amphitheater hosts the *Harmonies From The Hollow* show featuring country, gospel and '50s rock.

In addition to more than 100 activities and games just for kids during the Children's Festival, Silver Dollar also presents craftspeople of every possible type including weavers, glass blowers, broom makers, blacksmiths, and candle makers showing off their art for kids to see.

The other four festivals held throughout the year at Silver Dollar City, including World-Fest, the Great American Music Festival, the Festival of America, and Old

(Continued on next page)

Time Christmas, offer other unique experiences for kids (see our Attractions and Annual Events chapters).

Silver Dollar City is open daily during the Children's Festival with a few exceptions from 9:30 AM to 7 PM. Tickets are $32.85 for adults, $22.25 for children ages 4 through 11 and free for children 3 and younger. Adults aged 55 and older get in for $30.75. All prices include tax.

For tickets or more information call (800) 952-6626.

this 40-acre park. They've got ostriches, long-horns, big cats, birds, monkeys, and more varieties of deer than you can count. These animals really love automobiles and think nothing of planting big slobbery kisses on your windshield. Kids can stretch their legs in the petting zoo where they'll find goats, geese, ducks, and llamas among other creatures. Admission prices are $5.99 for children aged 3 through 11 and $9.00 for adults. To get there from Springfield go east on Interstate 44. Look for the signs 3 miles east of Strafford.

General Sweeney's Museum of Civil War History
5228 S. Mo. Hwy. ZZ, Republic
• (417) 732-1224

Got a little history buff in the family? Or trying to create one? If you have a day to kill, head on up to Republic, which is north of Springfield, for a look at Gen. Sweeney's collection of unique Civil War artifacts including weapons, photographs, uniforms, and medical instruments. Adult admission is $3.50 and children younger than 12 get in for $2.50. The museum is open from 10 AM to 5 PM daily, except for November and February when it is open only on Saturday and Sunday from 10 AM to 5 PM. It is closed in December and January.

Eureka Springs, Arkansas

Turpentine Creek
239 Turpentine Creek Ln.,
Eureka Springs, Ark. • (501) 253-5841
•www.turpentinecreek.org

Turpentine Creek exotic wildlife refuge is a little out of the way but well worth the drive. With 450 acres inhabited by lions, tigers, cougars, leopards, bears, monkeys, exotic birds, and other wildlife, Turpentine Creek is a haven for previously neglected or unwanted animals. The facility is USDA licensed, and donations and guest admission fees ($7 for adults and $4 for kids ages 12 and younger and senior citizens aged 65 and older) support it. Guides offer up-close and personal information on each resident creature. The facilities allow you to get about as close as you dare to get to these animals. On one recent trip we even got to pet a litter of tiger cubs in the petting zoo. Turpentine Creek is 7 miles south of Eureka Springs on Arkansas Hwy. 23. Follow the signs out of town. The refuge is open to guests March through December from 10 AM until dusk.

Buy It

Since Branson is fast becoming known as one of the top shopping destinations in the country, kids can find a number of places to plunk down their savings on everything from comic books to school clothes. The three outlet malls offer a variety of clothing stores for kids and carry name brands such as OshKosh B'gosh, Eagle's Eye, Healthtex, and P.S. Originals. See our chapter on Shopping for information on Tanger Outlet Center, (417) 337-9328, Factory Stores of America, (417) 339-4812, and Factory Shoppes at Branson Meadows, (417) 339-2580.

Specialty stores abound in Branson, and we think your little shopper will have a blast at We're Entertainment, (417) 337-9327, in the Tanger Outlet Center, where they carry loads and loads of movie, music, and television memorabilia. Pick up some cool magic trick paraphernalia at Mark's Magic and Fun Shop, (417) 337-8353, located at 1105 76 Country Blvd. Show your kids what a real old-fashioned dime store is like at Dick's Old-time 5 & 10, (417) 334-

INSIDERS' TIP

Looking to save a buck? Area publications like *Travel Host* and *Best Read Guide* offer coupons for area restaurants and shows. Look for them in the entryways of restaurants, retail shops, and hotel lobbies.

KIDSTUFF

Branson USA Amusement Park offers kids a variety of rides like the ferris wheel.

Photo: Branson/Lakes Area Chamber of Commerce

2410, 103 W. Main Street in downtown Branson, where plastic knickknacks, candy and other treasures line the shelves. Kids on a budget looking for souvenir T-shirts are in luck in Branson. We've seen prices as low as three shirts for $5 at some stores.

Outdoor Fun

With three lakes, dozens of marinas, public swimming beaches, and plenty of on-call fishing guides, kids visiting the Branson area have lots of opportunities to enjoy the great outdoors. Moonshine Beach, just off Mo. Highway. 165 near Table Rock Dam, with its picnic area and playground equipment, is a favorite among local kids. For a list of swimming beaches on Table Rock Lake, see our chapter on Campgrounds and RV Parks. If you want to learn how to Jet Ski, scuba dive, or parasail, try State Park Marina, (417) 334-3069 on Mo. 165 just south of Moonshine Beach or Indian Point Marina on Indian Point Road, (417) 338-2891, for rental equipment. These places can even hook you up with fishing guides who enjoy working with kids. See our chapter on the Lakes and Rivers for more information on guides and marinas.

Totally Free

Kids can enjoy a variety of free things to do right in the city limits of Branson. We have a number of public parks with playground equipment, basketball courts, tennis courts, picnic tables, fishing docks, and softball fields. Two of our favorite public playgrounds are located at Stockstill Park on James F. Epps Road, just north of Roark Valley Road and at Mang Field, east of

BoxCar Willie Drive near downtown Branson on the Taneycomo lakefront. (For more information on these parks and others, see our chapter on Recreation and the Great Outdoors.) If you're heading down to the lakefront, take along some dried bread or crackers to feed the geese that meander up and down the shoreline. Be sure to bring along a camera so you can capture any Kodak moments that may arise.

Music Shows

Never before have kids had a better selection of live entertainment in Branson. Many of the theaters now routinely feature children in their shows and offer lower ticket prices or free tickets to children. Jim Stafford features his 7 year-old son, Schaefer, who is already wowing crowds on the drums and fiddle. The Country Tonite cast has a number of child performers who do everything from sing to dance to perform rope tricks. A pint-sized Kristina Marie steals the show in the Hughes Brothers morning show at the Hughes Brothers Celebrity Theatre. *The Promise* features a number of children in this musical on the life of Jesus. One show made up entirely of kids is the Starlite Kids Review show at the Starlite Theatre. These talented singers and dancers, between the ages of 5 and 17, come from all over the United States. The cast is constantly rotated so new performers get a chance to be on stage in Branson. Perhaps the best-known teenage performer in town is the daughter of Shoji Tabuchi. Christina

Tabuchi, is a highlight of her father's frequently sold-out show.

Three of the most popular shows for kids are the Kirby VanBurch Show, at the Kirby VanBurch Theatre, the Incredible Acrobats of China at the Wayne Newton Theatre and Waltzing Waters at the Waltzing Waters Theater. Illusionist Kirby VanBurch is known for using exotic animals in his show, and the Chinese Acrobats perform absolutely amazing physical feats. The Waltzing Waters show is a spectacular presentation of 40,000 gallons of choreographed vertical water streams that are colorfully lighted and synchronized to live piano music.

Kid-Friendly Accommodations & Restaurants

Many of the lodging facilities in the Branson area allow children younger than 18 to stay in a room with a parent for no additional charge, including Cascades Inn, 3226 Shepherd of the Hills Expressway, (417) 335-8424, (800) 588-8424; Barrington Hotel, 263 Shepherd of the Hills Expressway, (417) 334-8866, (800) 760-8866; and The Guest House Hotel, 165 Expressway Lane, (417) 336-3132, (800) 383-3132. A number of restaurants also offer kids menus with meals starting as low as $1.99. See our chapters on Accommodations and Restaurants for more information.

Annual Events

LOOK FOR:
• **Fishing Tournaments**
• **Auto Shows**
• **Craft Shows**
• **Music Festivals**
• **Summer Tent Theater**
• **Patriotic Celebrations**
• **Holiday Lights**

It seems like every little community in the Ozarks has an annual event designed to celebrate something or another, more of an excuse to have a get-together and renew acquaintances, make new ones, and blow off a bit of steam more than anything else. These celebrations are as Ozarkian as pie suppers, Saturday night fish frys and gospel sings. Whether it's Gainesville's Hootin an Hollerin, Houston's Emmett Kelly Clown Festival, Nixa's Sucker Day (not the kind that's born every minute, but an ugly but good-eatin' fish found in local streams) or Ava's Poke Salat Days (a salute to a wild greens plant), the affairs have contests, races, food, drawings, exhibits, and other events that can be interesting and fun for locals and visitors alike. Perhaps it's even more fun for the outsider, who can see the events with a fresh perspective.

Whatever it is we celebrate, major holidays like Christmas and Veterans Day or just the simple things like apple harvests or dogwood blossoms, we usually have done for ourselves and our communities. With the advent of tourism as a major industry, we've opened ourselves up and accepted those who want to join us, and recognizing that there might be a buck to be made at the same time while having our fun, we've actually begun to market some of the events. Some are even designed to attract outsiders of a certain type, like Eureka Springs's Corvette Weekend or the UFO convention there. It's a great way to meet folks (perhaps even some aliens!) who have similar interests.

We've put together a collection of the big and the small (and the bizarre) of our area's annual traditions. Use our list as a guide, keeping in mind that often the best experience of being a tourist and sightseer is taking the road less traveled. Doing so can result in a serendipitous experience of making a new friend, finding that just-right antique, or perfect crafts product that would never had happened if you stuck to the main roads.

If you're planning a trip to Branson, check out our list at the end of this chapter for sources that can help you in your travel plans. Or check the web address we give for an annual event; you may find some listed we didn't mention that will tickle your own special interest. Our own Branson/Lakes Area Chamber of Commerce, (417) 334-4136 is a great source for information about the area's annual events. Remember that the *Springfield News-Leader* has a calendar section in every Friday's paper that has a complete listing of area activities for the weekend.

Some of the towns for our Annual Events are listed in our Daytrips chapter, but not all. So pack a good Missouri road map because some of these small burgs won't be on your interstate highway map, but they'll all be within easy driving distance of Branson.

If the event is always a specific weekend or date, we've mentioned that fact, and we've arranged them in the approximate order of happening during each month. It's best to call ahead for costs, if any, and the exact dates.

January

Hot Winter Fun
Branson • (417) 334-4136, (800) 214-3661
• www.bransonchamber.com

January through March is the off-season in Branson, and many theater, restaurant, and shop owners take a rest to remodel, do some deep cleaning, or just relax and go on vacation themselves. However, we've found that some people like to visit Branson at that time, and there are entertainers who have decided that Branson needs a bit of hot winter fun to liven up the scene. Of course in 1999 and 2000, the Miss U.S.A. Pageant has been in Branson, and that certainly has livened up the normally slower winter scene with the visit by the Miss U.S.A. delegates, the various media events, and the live broadcast of the pageant from The Grand Palace. Bargain-hunting travelers will appreciate the reduced rates at hotels and restaurants during this off season. If you call the Branson/Lakes Area Chamber of Commerce, you can get a list of year-round entertainers and businesses, but don't expect to find the full-scale activity that you'd find the rest of the year.

February

Spring Fishing Classic
915 S. Campbell Ave., Springfield
• (417) 887-1915

Near the end of February or early March when thoughts lightly turn to fishing, Bass Pro Shops Outdoor World hosts this free show to provide everything you always wanted to know (or see) about fishing. There is all the latest gear and boats. There are professionals to offer tips and sign autographs as well as plug their latest lures and books. There are even special programs for the kids to lure them into becoming addicted anglers.

March

Branson Fest
an area theater
• (417) 334-4136, (800) 214-3661
• www.bransonchamber.com

The Branson Fest always takes place in late March or early April (call for dates) and is a four-day party and country spring celebration where you can sample the finest Branson en-

tertainment, cuisine, and craftsmanship. It's always hosted by one of the theaters (in '99 it was the Welk Champagne Theatre; in '00 it was at the Mel Tillis Theater) and is the season kickoff event that features a variety of talent from Branson's theaters previewing the season's shows. Tickets were $27 in 2000, with kids younger than 12 free. The events outside are free, and you can find live entertainment, and a celebrity autograph-signing booth. There's also food from various restaurants but you'll have to pay for that. You can get a jump start on the season and decide what shows you want to

Resources

We put together a list of names and phone numbers to help you plan your Branson visit.

Branson/Lakes Area Chamber of Commerce
269 Mo. Hwy. 248 W. at
U.S. Hwy. 65 N.
(417) 334-4136, (800) 214-3661
P.O. Box 1897 Branson, Mo. 65615
www.bransonchamber.com

Table Rock Lake/Kimberling City Area Chamber of Commerce
Mo. Hwy. 13 N. at Mo. Hwy. 00
(417) 739-2564, (800) 595-0393
P.O. Box 495
Kimberling City, Mo. 85686
www.tablerocklake.com/chamber

Springfield Convention & Visitors Bureau Tourist Information Center
(417) 881-5300, (800) 678-8767
3315 E. Battlefield Rd.
Springfield, Mo. 65804

Missouri Division of Tourism
(573) 751-4133
P.O. Box 1055
Jefferson City, Mo. 65102
For a free travel planning kit, call
(800) 877-1234
www. missouritourism.org

Arkansas Department of Tourism
(800) NATURAL
1 Capitol Mall
Little Rock, Ark. 72201
www.naturalstate.com

take in later in the year. You'll also know that your ticket cost went to a good cause: Profits from ticket sales go to local charities.

St. Patrick's Day Parade
Eureka Springs, Ark. • (501) 253-8737
• www.eurekasprings.org

Bring a float! March in the parade! Win a prize! Or just enjoy the fun, and frolic on the streets of Eureka. It's a nice time to enjoy the wearin' o' the green and do some early season shopping and dining in America's Victorian Village.

White Bass Round-Up
Upper end of Bull Shoals, Forsyth
• (417) 546-2741 • www.forsyth-mo.com

When the white bass are running (March through early May, depending on the weather, water temperature, the phase of the moon, and your luck), there is a fishing frenzy on Bull Shoals Lake and its tributaries such as Swan Creek and Beaver Creek. If you don't catch a mess, you can always come back in May for the Forsyth White Bass Fish Fry and have them ready-fixed.

Eureka Springs Annual Antique Show and Sale
Inn of the Ozarks Convention Center,
U.S. Hwy. 62 W. and Historic Loop,
Eureka Springs, Ark.
• (501) 253-7551, (501) 253-6025
• www.eurekasprings.org

For a decade during the third week-end in March (and again in the third weekend in November) vendors from more than 10 states converge at the Convention Center at the Inn of the Ozarks with a full range of quality antiques from small items (button hooks, coin purses, and snuff boxes) to furniture. It's a great place to perhaps find the bargain of a lifetime.

Eureka Springs Blues Festival
various locations, Eureka Springs, Ark.
• (501) 253-8737
• www.eurekasprings.org

Nationally known blues artists perform in clubs, hotels, and at the city auditorium the last weekend in May and the two days before.

This all-indoor event of world-class blues makes for a long weekend of great music in a unique setting. There are artists' parties and special events galore. Prices vary, but there are also free concerts at the Basin Park, and you can wander around on Spring Street and just soak up the blues and the atmosphere.

April

Ozark Mountain Country Dogwood Trail
Forsyth • (417) 546-2741 • www.forsyth-mo.com

This is a bloomin' good experience! Take a self-guided tour on the back roads and through the small towns into areas of the Mark Twain National Forest to find the dogwoods. Blossom time can vary a week or so from year to year, but mid-April is the usual time to take a peek at the peak season whites of the woods. You can pick up a map at the Forsyth Chamber of Commerce at 16075 U.S. Hwy. 160 or call the number above.

World-Fest
Silver Dollar City
• (417) 338-2611, (800) 952-6626
• www.bransonchamber.com or www.silverdollarcity.com

The World-Fest is the season kickoff event at Silver Dollar City, and it begins the second weekend in April, just as dogwoods are ready to bloom, and lasts a month, into May. The Ozarks area celebrates world diversity as more than 350 performers from 18 countries come to the theme park. You can hear dozens of languages and many varieties of English as you take in the art of national dancers, singers, and performers from an Israeli folk dance troupe to the a cappella boys choir from Zambia. You can find flag throwers, sword dancers, and bagpipe and tin-whistle maestros as well as old world glass blowing, armor construction, and egg decorating. The international flavor also involves food, and you can sample the culinary delights of the world in the confines of the park. Regular admission prices to the park apply.

Ozark-speak

Test this Ozarks weather predictor for its validity; when the grass is dry at morning light, look for rain before the night. When the dew is on the grass, rain will never come to pass.

You can get acquainted with citizens of the world at Silver Dollar City's World-Fest.

Photo: Silver Dollar City

Ozark UFO Convention

**Inn of the Ozarks Convention Center,
U.S. Hwy. 62 W. and Historic Loop,
Eureka Springs, Ark. • (501) 354-2558
• www.eurekasprings.org**

Calling all aliens and saucers seekers: The truth is out there! Uncover some of it during the second weekend in April at the Convention Center at the Inn of the Ozarks as lectures, audiovisual presentations, and panel discussions on all aspects of the UFO phenomena (abductions, crop circles, etc.) seek to answer some of life's most unusual questions. Authors, researchers, vendors, and those who have experienced phenomena will be on hand. This event gets bigger each year. The registration fee of $40 covers the weekend.

Kewpiesta
Branson • (417) 334-1548, (888)-322-2786
• www.bransonchamber.com

The International Rose O'Neill Club preserves the memory and work of one of Branson's best known and influential artists. The rebuilt home of Rose O'Neill at Bonniebrook, north of Branson, becomes a mecca for Kewpie collectors and Rose scholars from around the world, and the entire town commemorates our own Wild Irish Rose.

Forsyth Art Guild Spring China Show
Forsyth Art Guild building, Forsyth
• (417) 546-5439
• www.forsyth-mo.com

For about as many years as we can remember, local porcelain and china painters have showcased their work at the Forsyth Art Guild building on U.S. Hwy. 160 from mid-April to mid-May. It's the perfect place to get a Mother's Day present.

Easter Egg Hunt
Shell Knob
• (417) 858-3300
• www. shellknob.com

If you're in the Ozarks at Easter, you may want to drive around Table Rock Lake to Shell Knob and let the kids hunt for eggs at the old CCC Camp in the Mark Twain National Forest. It's good free fun!

Taste of Eureka
Eureka Springs, Ark. • (501) 253-8737
• www.eurekasprings.org

During the last Saturday of April, for a very nominal fee, you can taste the best selections from most of the fine restaurants of Eureka's unique culinary scene. They're all at one location next to the city auditorium. At 3 PM one local waiter will get a big tip as local wait staffers compete in a race to set tables for hundreds of dollars in prize money. Enjoy the Classical Music Festival and the All-Mustang Car Show this weekend too.

The Great Passion Play
Eureka Springs, Ark.
• (501) 253-9200, (800) 882-7529

This outdoor drama is, for many, the highlight of their trip to the Ozarks. See our Daytrips chapter for specifics.

May

War Eagle Mill Spring Antique and Crafts Show
11045 War Eagle Road, Rogers, Ark.
• (501) 789-5343, (501) 789-5398

Two times a year folks flock to War Eagle Mill, a working grist mill, which plays host to the biggest crafts and arts fair in Arkansas. The spring show has a focus on antiques and crafts, while the fall show features more arts and crafts. Serious collectors, dealers, and buyers as well as lots of lookers and gawkers come out in full force for this three-day show. Some people just go for the food and the flavor of the Ozarks found there. The old mill opens early for War Eagle Biscuits, made from flour ground at the mill, and gravy. You'll also find great barbecue, Indian tacos, cornbread and beans, and a host of other delectables and snacks. War Eagle Mill is 25 miles southwest of Eureka Springs, Arkansas and is in a secluded valley south of Ark. 12 and north of US 412. You can get to War Eagle on Benton County Road 98 from the north, but traffic is slow and is often backed up because of the one-lane bridge over the War Eagle River. We suggest you take Ark. Highway 303 from the south for easy access to free parking and the fairgrounds.

> ## INSIDERS' TIP
> The fox-trotting horse was developed in the rugged Ozark hills during the 19th century by settlers using stock from Tennessee and Kentucky. Ozarkers needed easy-to-ride but durable mounts that could travel long distances at a surefooted, ground-eating gait. They were the favorite mounts of sheriffs, country doctors, and cattlemen before improved roads appeared in the Ozarks. The Missouri Fox Trotting Horse Breed Association was founded in 1948 in Ava by those who wanted to preserve this rare breed.

Emmett Kelly Clown Festival
Emmett Kelly Park, Houston
• (417) 967-2220

This festival is now going into its second decade and honors clown Emmett Kelly, famous for the creation of Weary Willie. Kelly grew up east of Houston and always regarded Houston as his hometown. The festival is always the

Fire eaters, sword swallowers, and exotic artists of every ilk and nation can be found at Silver Dollar City's World-Fest.

Photo: Silver Dollar City

The Heritage Dancers celebrate at Springfield Frisco Days.

Photo: Collette

first Friday, Saturday, and Sunday in May and features Emmett Kelly, Jr. and clowns across the Midwest, more clowns than you're likely to see together at once anywhere else. All perform, and you can also amuse yourself on the midway or get your own face painted. There are arts and crafts and food booths too. Houston, in the state's biggest county which is appropriately named Texas, is east of Springfield about an hour and a half drive from Branson.

Artsfest on Walnut Street
Walnut Street, Springfield
• (417) 831-6200, (877) 900- ARTS
• www.saac.org

During the first weekend in May (10 AM to 6 PM both days), Springfield's historic Walnut Street district puts on a celebration at which more than150 local and regional artists display their work or perform. The Artsfest features food, dancing, art (paintings, sculpture, pottery, jewelry), crafts, and hands-on activities for children. Performers of all ages present ballet, theater, ethnic and folk music and dance, and choral and instrumental

music from several venues—the Show Wagon Stage, the bandstand, porches. Even the street itself becomes an arena for roving street performers. Admission is $2 for adults. Children 12 and younger get in free.

May Fine Arts Festival
Downtown Eureka Springs, Ark.
• (501) 253-8737
• www.eurekasprings.org

The arts are everywhere here. Eureka turns on the creativity all month, celebrating the arts with special events including an outrageous parade, kids' activities, performing arts, workshops, demonstrations, displays, weekend nighttime gallery walks, and receptions, a changing roster of featured artists and much more. Most events are free.

Sucker Day
Downtown Nixa
• (417) 725-1545
• www.nixa.com

That good-eatin' but ugly fish that spawns in the spring here in the Ozarks is the excuse for this celebration. During mid-April if you see people in trees along Ozark rivers

INSIDERS' TIP

You can get the best view of the lighting of the nativity scene after the annual Adoration Parade from the Main Street lakefront in downtown Branson to the top of the hill as you start up Mo. Hwy. 76 West.

and on bridges looking down into the water, they are probably trying to grab suckers. The third Saturday in May is Nixa's celebration of all things sucker, and thousands descend on the town to get their fill of fried suckers and a chowder they call sucker soup. There is a parade to kick off the day's events, and you can find craft booths, entertainment, and amusement rides that last into the night.

Nixa City-Wide Garage Sale
various locations, Nixa
• **(417) 725-5486**
• **www. nixa.com**

On the second Saturday in May, the Nixa Parks Department sponsors a city-wide garage sale. Every house in town seems to participate. People from Springfield and towns around Nixa flock to this small burg for the bargains, and Nixans get a lot of spring cleaning and clutter clearing done that day.

Forsyth City-Wide Garage Sale
various locations, Forsyth
• **(417) 546-2741 or (417) 546-4763**
• **www.forsyth-mo.com**

Hang around the area for another week after you visit the Nixa city-wide garage sale, and you can also take in Forsyth's. It's always the third Saturday in May, and it attracts people from near and far, as local folks, artists, and crafters reduce inventory and clean out the attic and garage. It's a city-wide party, arts and crafts event, and flea market!

Plumb Nellie Days
Downtown Branson
• **(417) 334-1548, (888)-322-2786**
• **www.branson.com/dbba**

This is when locals play the stereotypical hillbillies for ourselves and the tourists. This downtown Branson celebration gets us out in our bib overalls and calico and gingham dresses for the parade, the children's pet contest, and the contest for King and Queen of Plumb Nellie Days. We even have a beard-growing contest and an outhouse race. In fact, we have "plumb nellie everything" at this event, including more than 120 booths in large tents in the crafts festival and the merchants' sidewalk sale. Look for it the third weekend in May!

Annual White Bass Fish Fry
Shadow Rock Park, Forsyth
• **(417) 546-2741 • www.forsyth-mo.com**

Share all those white bass you caught earlier, or if you didn't catch any come anyway for a taste at the Forsyth Chamber of Commerce fish fry. Meet at Shadow Rock Park, but call the chamber for the exact date.

Eureka Springs Doll & Toy Show and Sale
Inn of the Ozarks Convention Center, Eureka Springs, Ark. • (501) 253-8737
• **www.eurekasprings.org**

Come as you are or get all dolled up. Antique, collectible, and artist dolls along with old toys, doll clothes, wigs, furniture, and anything doll related will fill the main level of the Inn of the Ozarks Convention Center the third Saturday in May. New, old and artist-made bears of all sizes also have a special place in the show. Appraisals are available for dolls that you may have, and door prizes, dealers from several states, and fellow hobbyists make this a fun weekend for children and collectors. Admission in 1999 was $3 for adults, $1 for children.

Great American Music Festival
Silver Dollar City
• **(417) 338-2611, (800) 952-6626**
• **www.bransonchamber.com and www.silverdollarcity.com**

Beginning the third weekend in May and lasting for three weeks you can celebrate American music with award-winning musicians as more than 200 musicians and groups across the nation and around the world (ever hear an Austrian bluegrass group?) perform bluegrass, country, gospel, and Dixieland throughout the park at Silver Dollar City. Regular admission prices apply to this special event.

Rods & Relics at Rockaway Beach
Mo. Hwy 176, Downtown Rockaway Beach
• **(417) 561-4280 (800) 798-0178**

Rods & Relics is a car club that has had its competition and meeting for several years at Rockaway, and they have been joined by several other car clubs to bring to this small town the best of antique cars and rebuilt, custom, and street rods. Come for the show, or come to flex that muscle car! Call for information.

June

Frisco Days
Commercial Street, Springfield
• **(417) 831-6200**

The first weekend in June features Frisco Days, a festival to commemorate the arrival of the first train to Springfield, the *Cuba*, which entered the city on April 21, 1870, only an hour after the last rail had been laid. It's a great way to learn a bit about the history of Springfield and its Commercial Street area. The festival encompasses six blocks of the old commercial area of Springfield. First, there is food: roasted peanuts, funnel cakes, homemade root beer, and other period eats and treats. There's also a costume parade, storytellers, living past speakers—William Jennings Bryan, Walt Whitman, Teddy Roosevelt—as well as ragtime piano players, a square dance, arts and crafts booths, silent movies, and antique tractors and steam engines. You'll get a chance to board a real steam train, and they just might let you pull the whistle cord! It's fun and it's all free.

SMSU Summer Tent Theater
Springfield
• **(417) 836-5979**
This summer theater under a tent is where Kathleen Turner, John Goodman, and Tess Harper got started in their careers, and it's on the Southwest Missouri State University campus outside Craig Hall. Productions are top quality, and during June and August it's a great way to spend an evening. In 1999 ticket prices were $8 for adults, $6 for students and seniors. See our Arts and Culture chapter for more information.

Oinklawn Downs Pig Races and Barbecue
Cape Fair • (417) 538-2222
Porker pride, we have it here. After all, the Ozarks is home to the Razorbacks down in Fayetteville, but in Cape Fair during the second weekend in June local businesses are thinking pigs, not pigskins, in competitive races run by porkers. You'd think that by mid-June the sap would have finished flowing, but Cape Fair is a slow, laid-back sort of place. It's all great fun—eating, wandering about, watching the races, and squealing for your favorite hog. We won't comment about all the informal wagers and bets placed on this competition; officially no betting is allowed. You can expect more than pig races. There are craft booths, entertainment of various types, and a barbecue. (Losers in the races aren't eaten; they are merely trained harder for next year's event!)

National Children's Festival at Silver Dollar City
Silver Dollar City
• **(417) 338-2611, (800) 952-6626**
• **www.bransonchamber.com** and **www.silverdollarcity.com**
This relative newcomer of events has grown up to become a favorite of ours because it keeps its kids outlook. It always starts the third weekend in June and runs through August. It is now recognized as one of the nation's largest children's festivals. There are games and activities galore, more than 100 of them, with interactive games from Nickelodeon—the only television network just for kids. Earth 2U: Exploring Geography is an interactive geography adventure from the Smithsonian Institution, and the traveling exhibit gives kids a new way to explore geography facts and history through models, computer programs, and videos. Adults will have fun too, and the events and activities are guaranteed to bring out the kid in you. Regular park admission prices apply. (See Kidstuff chapter.)

Dr. Mary Long Scholarship Ice Cream Social
Taney Center, Forsyth
• **(417) 546-2741 • www.forsyth-mo.com**
Who can resist homemade ice cream? Don't feel guilty about what you eat here because it's for a good cause: Proceeds from the event, which honors one of the area's pioneer doctors, provide medical scholarships for students. Bring your appetite to the Taney Center 2 miles south of Forsyth. Call for the exact date.

Poke Salat Days
Ava • (417) 683-4594
Ava's three-day festival honors the pokeberry plant, whose tender tops provide great greens and whose berries make a great magenta jelly. Events include craft booths, a 10K run, an antique car show, an old-fashioned melerdramer (known to some as a melodrama) at which you can boo and hiss the villain, and clogging demonstrations and contest.

Antique Tractor and Engine Show

Tapjac Home Center, Mo. Hwy. 39,
Shell Knob
• (417) 858-3300, (800) 658-0328
• www.shellknob.com

Whether you go for the tractors and steam engines or the country music and barbecue doesn't matter. You can get it all at this free show, usually held at Tapjac Home Center in Shell Knob. You'll see old Case steam engines, Molines, Fords and Deere "Johnnie Poppers," plus other antique farm machinery.

Ozark Village Days

Ozark Square, Downtown Ozark
• (417) 581-6139

The third weekend in June, Ozark has a festival that features arts and crafts, a Hillbilly Olympics, including an outhouse relay race, rolling pig toss, log chuck, and wheelbarrow race. There's also a petting zoo, games, and food. It all takes place on the Ozark Square, and it's free. If this isn't exciting enough for you, stroll down to the Finley River Park for the annual Missouri State High School Rodeo Finals, always held on the same date.

All Convertible Car Show and Parade

Downtown, Eureka Springs, Ark.
• (501) 253-8737
• www.eurekasprings.org

Go topless in Eureka Springs the third Saturday in June. This is the ultimate one-day convertible car show with 14 classes in competition for trophies and prizes. Convertibles from 1915 to the present will be on display and will parade through the historic district at 2 PM. Special classes include 4x4s, VWs, street machines, and more. Preregistration for cars was $12, $18 on day of show in '99. If you're just going to gawk, admission is free.

Inspiration Point Opera

Mo. Hwy. 65 W., Eureka Springs, Ark.
• (501) 253-8595
• www.eurekasprings.org

Opera in the Ozarks has a long tradition and a devoted following. Call for the summer schedule and ticket information, and see our Arts and Culture Chapter for more information.

Annual '50s-'60s Street Dance

Taneycomo lakefront
• (417) 334-1548, (888)-322-2786
• www.branson.com/dbba

The third Saturday in June is the date for this big event held along the Taneycomo lakefront. This is a late-night affair; it doesn't start until 9 PM and it goes until midnight. Many local entertainers provide live music for this nostalgic event for people of all ages. Bring lawn chairs, a blanket or cushion for sittin', and shoes for dancin'!

Rockaway Beach Hydroplane Races

Rockaway Beach
• (417) 561-4280, (800) 798-0178

Waves, wakes, and the roar of powerful engines! Always the last weekend of June, the races are exciting to watch from the safety of the beachfront, and there's always food and dance at the city park.

July

Firefall

5000 W. Kearney St. Springfield.
• (417) 864-1049, (800) 678-8767

Attend Firefall and you'll know why the Springfield Symphony Orchestra has such strong community support. This is some Fourth of July party—though it's not always held on the Fourth of July. Call to find out the exact date. It's an all-day-into-the-night affair, so pack a blanket and a picnic lunch, or buy lunch at the site. Entertainment is held throughout the day in the open fields near Springfield/Branson Regional Airport, and some of Branson's entertainers from shows on The Strip almost always participate. The climax of the evening is music by the Springfield Symphony with synchronized fireworks. There is always a large crowd (part of the fun) and parking is at a premium (not fun), but shuttle buses run from sites in Springfield to Firefall. The admission price is usually $5 per family or carload.

Other fireworks displays to celebrate Independence Day are held in Hollister, (417) 334-3050; Kimberling City, (417) 739-2564; Point Lookout, (417) 334-6411; Rockaway

"These roads is so damn crooked that a feller can't tell if he's goin' somewheres or comin' back home." A White River fishing guide speaking of Ozark roads in the 1920s. It still holds true today, especially if you get off the beaten track.

Ozark-speak

Beach, (417) 561 4280; and Shell Knob, (417) 858-3300.

Taney County Fair
Fairgrounds, Forsyth
• (417) 546-2741 • www.forsyth-mo.com

You'll like the livestock and agricultural exhibits, sheep dog trails, festival rides, games, and delicious smells that permeate the air on the banks of Bull Shoals Lake. Have some cotton candy, order a tasty Lion Burger (grilled by the local Lions Club) and visit the petting zoo. The summer may be hot, but the nights are always cool by the lakeside fairgrounds.

Annual Barbershoppers' Chorus and Quartets' Concert
Shell Knob • (417) 858-3300
• www.shellknob.com

For more than 25 years in mid-July, the folks at Shell Knob have been bringing their lawn chairs and blankets and sitting out under the stars (and the hot sun) listening to the harmonizing of groups that come from the tri-state area for this event. It's loads of fun, and it's free, but donations to benefit the area's First Responders are collected. Make certain you call for the specific date.

Ozark Empire Fair
Ozark Empire Fairgrounds, Springfield
• (417) 833-2660

This is the mother of all fairs in the Ozarks, second only to the Missouri State Fair at Sedalia. It always begins on the last Friday in July and extends through two weekends at the Ozark Empire Fairgrounds near Dickerson Park Zoo.

And what a fair! There's always a great midway and the usual fair fare of food, livestock and family-living exhibits, booths, and entertainment at the grandstand—usually a big-name star from rock or country music and sometimes both. Our fair favorites are the produce exhibits, the livestock shows (where you can see a calf born if you want to hang around long enough), the fish, snakes, and mammals at the Department of Conservation exhibit, and the Pineapple-Whip stand—not just for the cool, tasty delight but also for the amazing hoola-girl who dances atop the stand. Ad-

mission is usually $5 plus parking. Kids 12 and younger get in for free.

August

White River Valley Arts and Crafts Fair
Shadow Rock Park, Forsyth
• (417) 546-2741 • www.forsyth-mo.com

Exhibitors from across the country let you look for free at their art and wares, but be certain to bring your wallet because you're sure to find that perfect one-of-a-kind gift or that just-what-you-needed item. You'll find basket makers, knifesmiths, cornhusk doll artists, and other crafts.

Fall Hunting Classic
Springfield • (417) 867-1915

Prepare for hunting season and that trophy buck by getting information and tips from the nation's top hunters. Each year Bass Pro Shops Outdoor World sponsors this free event not only for area hunters but also for all those willing to make the trek to that mecca of sport in Springfield. You can see the latest and greatest in hunting and camping gear as well as learn how to keep hunting safe and enjoyable. Call for specific date.

Nike Greater Ozarks Open
Highland Springs Country Club, Springfield • (417) 887-3400

The Highland Springs Country Club is the field for up-and-coming PGA tour players. There are four levels of competition in the tournament that has a guaranteed purse of $125,000 and is traditionally held in mid-August, the hottest time of the year in the Ozarks. Lots of area golfers just go to watch the big dogs play and perhaps pick up a few pointers to improve their own games.

Cruisin' Branson Lights
Shepherd of the Hills Homestead
• (417) 847-3098, (800) 214-3661
• www.bransonchamber.com and www.oldmatt.com

Vintage cars, street rods, rebuilts—if you can imagine it, it's there, more than a thousand

INSIDERS' TIP

Branson has an annual rainfall of 43 inches a year. January is driest (1.79 inches) and coldest (31 degrees). June is the wettest (5.09 inches); and June, July, and August are the hottest months with an average of 78 degrees, but you can expect some days to be 90 to 100 degrees.

Veterans are honored during Branson's annual Veterans Day parade.

cars of every kind and color. The whole town gets involved. You can bop on over to the sock hop or check out the beach party, complete with sand and all. The registration fee in the past has been $35 for car show participants. Call for admission policies and prices.

Annual Old Time Fiddle Contest
Lake Taneycomo lakefront
• **(417) 334-1548, (888)-322-2786**
• **www.branson.com/dbba**

Held on the third Saturday in August on Branson's lakefront, this is always a great way to spend an evening by the air-cooling 55 degree waters of Lake Taneycomo after a hot August day. Amateur fiddlers from all over the United States compete for more than $2,000 in cash and prizes.

Crane Broiler Festival
Downtown Crane • (417) 723-5104

This small town is home to one of the biggest, oldest festivals in the Ozarks. For almost half a century, chicken has been cock of the walk the last Friday and Saturday of August, and you can smell it sizzling on the open charcoal pits for miles around. Perhaps that's what brings the 26,000 people who descend on this small Stone County town north of Galena on Mo. Hwy. 13. Or it could be the beauty pag-

eant (in which local lovelies vie for the title of Little Miss Chick and Miss Chick), craft booths, fireworks, country music entertainment, horseshoe pitching tournament, and carnival. Whatever the reason, it's a just an excuse to have some August fun in Crane.

Old Fiddlers Contest
Golden • (417) 271-3769, (417) 271-3532

August 2000 will mark the 50th year of this contest for amateur fiddlers, always the last Saturday in August. Folks come from miles around to eat the home-cooked food prepared by the Golden Circle Shores Association and listen as the best fiddlers from all over strut their stuff on strings. There are divisions for senior and junior fiddlers. Admission in 2000 was $2 for adults, $1 for those 5 years to 16, with children under 5 years admitted free.

September

Festival of America
Silver Dollar City
• **(417) 338-2611, (800) 952-6626**
• **www.bransonchamber.com or www.silverdollarcity.com**

The cream of the crop of American craftspeople is invited to display talents and arts at Silver Dollar City's big annual festival. Held in September and October when the Ozarks area is changing to its colorful fall wardrobe, this show has been ranked as one of the top tourism events in the nation. There are doll makers, wheat weavers, basket weavers, woodcarvers, potters, raku pottery firings, and glass blowers who do what they do best and answer questions from the curious. There is always a cornucopia of not only crafts and arts but also interesting and exciting foods. One nice thing about this big event is that regular park admission prices apply.

Missouri Fox Trotting Horse Breed Association Show and Celebration
Show Grounds, Ava • (417) 683-2468

This annual meeting (2000 marks the 42th) of the Missouri Fox Trotting Horse Breed Association, the group that promotes the Ozarkian's horse of choice, always starts on Labor Day and is a six-day event. Thousands of fox trotting breeders and horse lovers congregate at the Douglas County seat for one of the biggest shows in the nation. You don't have to own one to enjoy the show, and it's possible you might get caught by the fox trotting bug.

Banjo Rally International
Downtown, Eureka Springs, Ark.
• (501) 253-8737

Finger pickin' good could describe this event the first weekend in September and the two days before it. It's a gathering of top-rate banjo players replete with concerts, jam sessions, educational sessions on old-style techniques, workshops, and specialty vendors for banjo players or just those who love to hear a banjo. A concert on Saturday night is open to the public for a minimal fee (plan for about $5). Call for information about workshop fees.

State of the Ozarks Fiddlers Convention
Compton Ridge Campground,
Mo. Hwy. 265 • (417) 338-2911

Fine fiddling in the fall can be found at the Compton Ridge Campground. Fiddlers from around the country meet and perform day and night at various locations around the campground and at the Gathering Place, The Campgrounds Meeting Center. Awards are presented for oldest, youngest, most improved, and farthest traveled fiddlers. Come to play or just listen. Call for the exact date and details. (See our chapter on Campgrounds and RV Parks for information on Compton Ridge Campground.)

Annual Antique Automobile Festival
Pine Mountain Village, U.S. Hwy. 62 E.,
Eureka Springs, Ark. • (501) 253-8737
• www.eurekasprings.org

Vintage vroooom takes over the city as hundreds of antique cars gather at Pine Mountain Village in Eureka Springs for this event the second weekend in September. It's almost a 3-year tradition now. There are judging classes available for cars 25 years and older in both original and modified categories with trophies and prizes. The weekend also includes a reenactment of a 1922 bank robbery and much more, including the city's annual toy, doll, and train show. Admission for the Antique Automobile Festival is free, but if you have a car you want to enter, registration is $18.

Autumn Daze Craft Festival Downtown
Downtown Branson
• (417) 334-1548, (888)-322-2786
• www.branson.com/dbba

During the third weekend in September, Branson's downtown area is turned into a craft-lover's paradise. More than 150 crafters from all over the United States have displays and demonstrations, and the parking lots and sidewalks are filled with them and their work. This 27-year tradition is one of the best crafts shows in the nation.

Annual Eureka Springs Jazz Festival
various locations, Eureka Springs, Ark.
• (501) 253-8737
• www.eurekasprings.org

Enjoy one cool, long weekend of jazz and the beginnings of the fall color on historic Spring Street. The Jazz festival is always the third weekend in September. There's jazz around town indoors and out in clubs, bed and breakfast inns, restaurants, parks, and other venues. Renowned jazz headliners will appear in concert at the city auditorium on Saturday night. Prices vary at venues, and there are always free concerts of changing groups in the Basin Street Park.

Country Fair Days, Spaghetti Feast, and Octoberfest
Shell Knob • (417) 858-3300
• www. shellknob.com

You may be surprised what we do in small towns to have fun. This event is worth it just for the Ugly Dog Contest, but you can also find a car show, arts and crafts, and food (there is spaghetti for every taste), and fun. We like their

Veterans Are Welcome In Branson

In an attempt to establish Branson as the year-round, national home for all veterans, active duty military personnel, and their families, the non-profit Branson Veterans Task Force, Inc. has mobilized more than 150 businesses and countless volunteers to offer special events, conferences, music shows, parades, worship services, and traveling exhibitions throughout the year.

Of the dozen or so events that take place, the three centered around Memorial Day, the Fourth of July, and Veterans Day are the most popular.

By far, the largest celebration organized by the task force is Veterans Homecoming. The weeklong event has been touted as the largest Veterans Day celebration in America with more than 60 special events attracting upwards of 60,000 visitors. We've tried to outline a few of the more significant events you can expect to find in Branson during Veterans Homecoming, but for specific details call the Veterans Task Force at (417) 337-8387 or visit their website at www.bransonveterans.com.

The opening ceremony for Veterans Homecoming is usually held at one of the Branson theaters. In 1999 The Grand Palace hosted the event and featured the Elite Eagles Drill Team from Illinois and a performance by High Flight, the premier show group of the United States Air Force Band. Admission to the opening ceremonies is often free, but tickets always go fast.

Veterans may seek out old comrades through the reunion registry held each year at the 76 Mall Complex. Not only does the free computerized service allow veterans to obtain the home address of others who served in their units, but also to find out where old friends are staying while visiting Branson during Veterans Homecoming week. For example, many military units and organizations hold reunions in Branson during the week. For the past several years the popular Tuskeegee Airmen have reunited in Branson.

The 76 Mall Complex also plays host to the Veterans Patch Wall, which contains branch, division, and unit patches collected from veterans. The collection spans the Civil War through the Bosnian Conflict. By encouraging veterans and their families to donate to the Patch Wall, the sponsors hope to produce the largest veterans patch collection in the world.

Veterans and their families may also wish to visit the Welk Resort Center to see the traveling Vietnam Veterans Memorial, better known as "The Wall." This half-scale replica of the Vietnam Veterans Memorial in Washington, D.C. stretches nearly 240 feet. Like its big brother, it lists the names of the more than 58,000 servicemen and servicewomen who made the ultimate sacrifice in Vietnam. As is customary, the list of names inscribed on The Wall is read aloud continuously throughout the seven-day period.

Although the Vietnam Veterans Memorial in Washington, D.C. is the most-visited monument in our nation's capital, the appearance of the traveling Wall in Branson provides an opportunity for those in the Midwest to honor the memory of a fallen comrade or loved one. The location of a specific name can be determined with the aid of an on-site computer program.

In 1999 the Veterans Task Force announced the launch of a community-wide effort to raise money for the National World War II Memorial in Washington D.C. The task force and Table Rock Post 637 American Legion offered 9 holes of golf free during Veterans Homecoming '99 when you made a contribution to the WWII memorial fund. New fund-raising events like this one will be held each year.

Also in 1999 the Veterans Homecoming welcome center at the Factory Shoppes at Branson Meadows featured the National Flag Foundation Bicentennial Americana Art Collection free to the public.

The theaters roll out the red carpet for visitors during Veterans Homecoming week. Most of the shows include expanded patriotic segments, special guest performers and some of them even honor military personnel with on-stage recognition. In 1999 The Dutton family hosted a benefit show for the local Korean War Veterans Association, Harry S. Truman Chapter. Some shows offer complimentary or discounted admission to veterans, active duty military personnel, and their spouses. For a list of participating shows and businesses call the Veterans Task Force or the Branson/Lakes Area Chamber of Commerce at (417) 334-4136.

A few of the favorite shows among veterans and their families are the Lawrence Welk Show with the Lennon Sisters, The Bobby Vinton show with the Glenn Miller Orchestra, the Mike Radford Remember When Show, and the Jennifer Show starring Branson's only official worldwide USO spokesperson, Jennifer Wilson. For more information on these shows see The Shows Chapter. Local attractions like the IMAX Entertainment Complex even get in on the celebration. In 1999, the theater showed "Saving Private Ryan" on its 6-story movie screen.

In 1993 Tony Orlando began honoring veterans with a special 3-hour tribute performance. Today, his show is the standard for veterans shows in Branson. He has been honored by the American Legion and countless other groups for his continuing efforts to honor and entertain American veterans. In 1999 Tony presented his show at the Baldknobbers Theatre, and in 2000 Tony will be performing select dates at the Osmond Family Theatre. Your best bet is to call the task force for information on where you can catch Tony's show each year. It's always free to veterans, and tickets sell out quickly.

Chateau on the Lake Resort and Conference Center hosts the Armed Forces Banquet and Gala each year where guests are treated to fine dining in the Great Hall by the traditional call of the bugle, followed by patriotic musical entertainment and dancing.

The Paralyzed Veterans of America association holds a 10K race and 5K Run/

(Continued on next page)

The Country Tonite show honors veterans during Veterans Homecoming with a musical salute.

Photo: Branson/Lakes Area Chamber of Commerce

Visitors can watch the Veterans Day parade in downtown Branson.

Photo: Branson/Lakes Area Chamber of Commerce

Walk/Roll to raise funds for the Spinal Cord Research Foundation. Other similar fundraisers are scheduled each year.

For the past 65 years Branson has been honoring veterans with a special Veterans Day Parade. The parade is held each Veterans Day in downtown Branson at 11 AM and includes Branson celebrities, historical military vehicles, area high school bands, and veterans units from across the country. A traditional Veterans Day commemoration at Mang Field in downtown Branson follows the parade.

The Closing Ceremonies for the week-long event includes special performances by military bands and Branson entertainers, as well as a concluding opportunity for recognition of all veterans, living and dead. The event was held at the BoxCar Willie Theatre in 1999 as a special tribute to the late BoxCar Willie, who served in the Air Force before embarking on a career in country music. For more information on this event and the exact location of other events you may visit the Branson Veterans Task Force office located in the Falls Shopping Center on Mo. 165 just south of The Strip.

idea of getting the jump on everybody and having an Octoberfest in September! Call the Shell Knob Chamber of Commerce at the number above for the exact date.

Hometown Harvest Days
Webster County Fairgrounds, Marshfield • (417) 468-3943

The County Fairgrounds is the site of this arts, crafts, and entertainment show that attracts people near and far in Webster County. Marshfield is only minutes east of Springfield on Interstate 44.

Laura Ingalls Wilder Festival
Mansfield • (417) 468-3943

All of Mansfield turns out to celebrate its most famous citizen. The arts and crafts fair is at the homesite of author Laura Ingalls Wilder,

famous for her Little House books. There are all sorts of Laura-inspired activities: fiddle contests, pioneer children's games, and costume contests.

Hootin' N Hollerin'
Town Square, Gainesville • (417) 679-4913

Gainesville is the county seat of Ozark County, just east of Taney County. The drive on U.S. Hwy. 160 is slow and crooked, but going over there the third Thursday, Friday, and Saturday in September will give you some of the prettiest fall colors and scenery the area has to offer. The fall festival there celebrates everything hillbilly as the residents let down their hair and have fun in their local celebration with bed races, a quilt show, crafts and demonstrations (spinning, basket weaving, lye soap making, etc.), a turkey shoot, pet contest, costume parade, square dancing, and country music jam sessions on the courthouse lawn. Outsiders and flatlanders are welcome! Admission is free.

Moonlight Cruise
Table Rock Lake, Kimberling City
• **(417) 739-2564, (800) 595-0393**
• **www.tablerocklake.com/chamber**

You can see beautiful Table Rock Lake in the moonlight as you cruise aboard luxury houseboats and lake cruisers. You'll get on board, cruise to a local eatery for a fine meal, and enjoy the moonlight cruise back. Enjoy great entertainment and a delicious meal coupled with a romantic evening for only $25 per person (1999 price). They try to schedule this during the full moon so call the Kimberling City Chamber of Commerce at the above number for specific dates and times.

Apple Festival
Seymour Square, Seymour
• **(417) 935-2257**

All things apple fill the menu for this festival on the Seymour Square. Expect all kinds of apples, apple cider, apple pie, apple cobbler, apple butter, apple bobbing, and an apple-peeling contest, as well as Johnny Appleseed himself. Seymour is 20 minutes east of Springfield on U.S. Highway 60.

October

Homer Sloan Invitational Buddy Bass Tournament
Mo. Hwy. 39, Shell Knob
• **(417) 658-3300** • **www. shellknob.com**

Father and son, husband and wife, or just you and a friend get to spend all day catching bass on Table Rock Lake. Local fisherman Homer Sloan started the tournament years ago with proceeds to be used for community projects. If you're good (or just lucky), you might be able to walk away with some of the cash prize money and you'll have helped fund Shell Knob community projects. Don't let invitational in the name make you think you have to be a recognized bona fide fisher to be considered for this event. It's open to the public.

Corvette Weekend
Pine Mountain Village,
Eureka Springs, Ark • **(501) 253-8737**
• **www.eurekasprings.org**

More than 350 Corvettes will purr their way into Eureka Springs for this annual show and parade, now almost a decade old. See Vettes of all ages on display at Pine Mountain Village or out on a timed road rally. The sheer number of these classic cars all in one place is a sight to behold. Attendance is free, but it you want to enter your Vette, registration is $20-25. Call the above number for more specific information.

White River Gem and Mineral Club Show
Shadow Rock Park, Forsyth
• **(417) 546-2741** • **www.forsyth-mo.com**

Rock hounds, take note: the first weekend in October at Shadow Rock Park is this annual gathering of rock lovers, gemologists, and jewelry makers and dealers. You can look for free, but you may want to buy a rock, so bring your wallet. Many local stones polish up nicely, but you'll also find rocks from around the world—agates to zircons.

Festival of Quilts
Eureka Springs, Ark. • **(501) 253-8737**
• **www.eurekasprings.org**

Have a fun weekend that's high in fiber. From antique quilts to computer-generated patterns, this festival promises the ultimate experience for quilters and those who just appreciate quilts. Exhibits, open competitions with a $350 cash prize, demonstrations, silent auction, and a one-day workshop with a featured quilting artist are included in the admission fee (around $3). Certified appraisals on site are also available. The Festival is held the second weekend of October.

War Eagle Mill Arts and Crafts Fair
Rogers, Ark.
• **(501) 789-5398**

For almost 50 years now, crowds have flocked to the biggest crafts fair in the Ozarks. Last year an estimated 135,000 people came to the free four-day fair. You'll find more than 300 exhibitors from Arkansas, Missouri, Oklahoma, and Kansas. You'll see woodworkers, weavers, sculptors, and stained-glass artisans as well as basket makers, painters, and jewelry artisans. It's a great way to catch the fall color on the drive down, see the old mill there (and perhaps buy lunch or sample some exotic items from food vendors) and pick up one-of-a-kind items at the fair for Christmas presents.

The mill is 25 miles southwest of Eureka Springs, Arkansas. (See our May listing for specific directions.)

Ozark Native Arts & Crafts Festival Ozark City Park
Ozark • (417) 581-6139

Always the first full weekend in October, this event has grown to become one of the larger craft fairs in the Ozarks. Almost 400 vendors, crafters and artists pack in 10,000 people in the Ozark City Park. While there, you may want to take in some of the many flea markets and antique shops in Ozark.

Apple Butter Making Days
Town Square, Mount Vernon
• (417) 466-7654

Just the aroma is worth the trip to the Lawrence County seat, named after George Washington's home and host to one of the sweetest festivals in the Ozarks the second Thursday, Friday, and Saturday of October. It's free, but you'll want to pack some apple butter (made before your eyes in 60-gallon copper kettles) back with you so you can enjoy it at home. While there on the Mount Vernon square, admire the old courthouse, enjoy the parade, watch the terrapin race (or maybe bring your own entry), enter the tall-tale telling contest, take in the crafts and demonstrations—more than 370 booths last year—and listen to the live entertainment. Mount Vernon is west of Springfield but is only a bit over an hour's drive from Branson via the back roads of Mo. Hwys. 13 and 265.

Annual Fall Art Show
Forsyth Art Guild Building,
1600 U.S. Highway 160, Forsyth
• (417) 546-5439 • www.forsyth-mo.com

During the entire month of October, you're invited to stop by the Forsyth Art Guild building and see work of local artists and crafters. You'll find woodcarvings, watercolors, oils,

sculpture, and china paintings. Much of the work is for sale, so bring your wallet.

OctoberFest
Rockaway Beach
• (417) 561-4280, (800) 798-0178

Rockaway Beach celebrates the Germans with German food, German dancers, German music and entertainment, and German (and domestic) brews. You can expect exhibits and arts and crafts to be found at this free fall festival. You don't need to be German to join the fun. Call the Rockaway Beach Chamber of Commerce at the numbers above for more information.

Fine Arts and Crafts Festival
Reeds Spring • (417) 272-3283

The local arts village has a juried art show featuring the works of artists and craftspeople from a wide area. See the Arts and Culture or Daytrips chapter for more information.

Fall Festival of the Arts
Kimberling City Shopping Center,
Kimberling City
• (417) 739-2564 or (417) 739-5829
• www.tablerocklake.com/chamber

Sponsored by the Tablerock Art Guild, this arts and crafts show is a great way to get some of the Christmas shopping done. You'll find oil and watercolor paintings, sculptures, and a host of crafts and homemade items. Call the Guild at the number above for exact dates and details.

Ozark Mountain Country Fall Foliage Drive
Forsyth • (417) 546-2741
• www.forsyth-mo.com

See the Ozarks' "golden oldies": great hickory nut trees plus the reds and rusts of oaks and sweet gums as well as the scarlet of dogwood, sumac, and cinquefoil in this 75-mile drive. It's a great way to see the area, a world so different from that of The Strip, so pack up a picnic lunch and the camera and plan on taking the whole day. There are always fruit stands and antique stores as well as country stores to provide a change of pace. You can pick up a map at the Forsyth Chamber of Commerce at 16075 U.S. Hwy. 160.

INSIDERS' TIP

Woodcarver Peter Engler's work has been synonymous with Branson since the early 1960s when he and his carvings were featured on *The Beverly Hillbillies* and *Captain Kangaroo*.

Glade Top Trail Flaming Fall Revue
various locations, Ava • (417) 683-4594

Mother Nature gives a show of color in the Ozarks that rivals that of Ozark Mountain Christmas. You can catch the dogwoods, sumac, hickory, and various oaks at their finest in the Glade Top Trail Flaming Fall Revue when you drive the ridge roads in sections of the Mark Twain National Forest near Ava. The town has special events, and you can still catch the great farmers market on the town square Saturday morning.

November

Candlelight Christmas Open House
Downtown, Branson
- **(417) 334-1548, (888)-322-2786**
- **www.branson.com/dbba**

Although downtown Branson stores are open all year, the second weekend in December is a special time when merchants help everyone get in the Christmas spirit by dressing in Dickens-style costume. You'll hear carolers on the streets, get a chance to visit with Father Christmas, enjoy the fruits of the window decorating contest, and sample cookies and hot cider.

Annual Food & Wine Weekend
Various Restaurants, Eureka Springs, Ark.
- **(501) 253-8737**
- **www.eurekasprings.org**

Eureka's finest restaurants offer special multi-course menus for three days of epicurean delight in America's Victorian village during the second weekend in November. From exotic wines by the glass to a seven-course Renaissance feast, you can find a taste to suit your palate almost anywhere in town. Prices vary according to the restaurant, but you can find a feast to fit any size pocketbook.

Veterans Homecoming
Citywide locations, Branson
- **(417) 334-4136, (800) 214-3661, (417) 334-1548**
- **www.bransonveterans.com**

The week of Veterans Day has become a special event to many of us and our nation's veterans as Branson welcomes with open arms all those who have served their country. It's an opportunity to reflect on our nation's history, have an old-fashioned parade down the renamed Veterans Boulevard (U.S. Business 65) and give thanks to those who served. The parade tradition in Branson is 65 years old; it is always held on November 11 and begins at 11 AM. Many of

Andy Williams Christmas Show is one of the most popular tickets in town during Ozark Mountain Christmas.

Photo: Branson/Lakes Area Chamber of Commerce

Christmas is one of Branson's brightest seasons with millions of lights.

Photo: Silver Dollar City

the theaters have a veterans salute with special tributes and music that gives meaning to being an American.

Ozark Mountain Christmas
Branson-Lakes Area
• **(417) 334-4136, (800) 214-3661**
• **www.bransonchamber.com**

A decade ago this was part of the off-season in Branson. Not any more. More than 450,000 people come to see the lights, shop, and take in the special Christmas shows in November and December. It's no wonder that the American Bus Association has included Ozark Mountain Christmas in its list of "Top 100 Events in North America" for several years running. Radio City Music Hall puts a troupe on the road to perform a special high-kicking Christmas show at

The Grand Palace. Most of the theaters have special and spectacular Christmas shows, and Santa is certain to make an appearance at all of them. Silver Dollar City presents its Old Time Christmas, celebrating "Christmas Around the World" with the Christmas traditions of different nations and cultures from November 4 to December 30. The festival features a 5-story special-effects Christmas tree and a 17-foot talking Christmas tree that interacts with children, holiday shows, and more than 2 million lights. And everybody loves singing carols at the Wilderness Church and drinking mulled cider! You can take in the lights all around the area (see the next entry), do your Christmas shopping, and see some of the Christmas specials during a visit at that time of the year. The events vary from year to year, but you can get a complete list of holiday programs and events by calling the Branson/Lakes Area Chamber of Commerce at the numbers above.

Festival of Lights
Branson/Tri-Lake area
- **(417) 334-4136, (800) 214-3661**
- **www.bransonchamber.com**

Branson decks the streets and businesses with millions of lights, and folks come from all around to take in the multicolored lights and the animated light scenes. Kimberling City has its Port of Lights, a spectacular 1½ mile drive through an animated light display with the lake on three sides. (Admission was $5 per car in 1999). Silver Dollar City is like a fairyland at night with rides, buildings, fences, and trees covered in lights. The Shepherd of the Hills Homestead features millions of lights. And Branson has its own drive-through light spectacular at the Bee Creek exit north of town. (There's no fee, but you're expected to make a donation at the end of the drive.) Pack up the kids and a thermos and plan to make a night of oohing and aahing at what has become a major tourist attraction in itself.

Eureka Springs Annual Antique Show and Sale
Inn of the Ozarks Convention Center,
U.S. Hwy. 62 W, and Historic Loop,
Eureka Springs, Ark. • (501) 253-8131
- **www.eurekasprings.org**

A repeat of the spring show; see the entry under March.

December

Annual Adoration Parade and Lighting
Downtown Branson
- **(417) 334-4136, (800) 214-3661**
- **www.bransonchamber.com**

Mark the first Sunday in December for this event. Started in 1948, this noncommercial community parade has grown to include dozens of bands and bugle corps, floats, and antique cars. The event attracts thousands of people from the surrounding areas. The parade starts at 5:30 PM, and the event climaxes with the lighting of an adoration scene with 40-foot figures atop Mt. Branson. If you miss it, you can often catch it the next day on one of the local television stations.

Holiday Chocolate Extravaganza
Inn of the Ozarks Convention Center,
U.S. Hwy. 162 W, and Historic Loop,
Eureka Springs, Ark.
- **(501) 253-6767**
- **www.eurekasprings.org**

The Eureka Springs Association of Bed and Breakfasts, Cabins and Cottages goes all out for chocolate lovers as they try to outdo one another in all things chocolate in this fundraiser for the association which takes place the second weekend in September. There are chocolate and brownie entries, pies, cakes, and puddings. It's open to the public for a small admission price and you can eat until you OD on chocolate. What a way to go!

First Night
Downtown and SMSU areas, Springfield • (417) 831-6200

For almost a decade now, Springfield has thrown a big nonalcoholic New Year's Eve party that starts early in the afternoon and lasts until the new year. Events are scattered all about town but centered in the downtown and SMSU area. Activities include storytelling, rock, jazz, mimes and clowns, magic, ballet, drama, and stand-up comics. You can walk about, sampling various events and activities, and shuttle buses run between distant activities. A great way to usher in the New Year, this family affair has a single admission that gets you an admission button for all events.

INSIDERS' TIP

If you are going to make forays to Eureka Springs, Arkansas, from Branson, you might want to get a copy of the town's Four Seasons Visitor's Guide, which lists all the annual events at America's Victorian Village as well as other events and activities. Call the Eureka Springs Chamber of Commerce at (501) 253-8737. You can write them at P.O. Box 551, Eureka Springs, Ark. 72632. You can also visit their fantastic website at www.eurekasprings.org

Arts and Culture

Missouri has produced its fair share of our nation's artists and writers. Scott Joplin, George Caleb Bingham, T. S. Eliot, Langston Hughes, Kate Chopin, Robert Heinlein, Howard Nemerov, Maya Angelou and—oh, yes—Mark Twain. And many of them—Thomas Hart Benton, Vance Randolph, Laura Ingalls Wilder, Rose O'Neill, Harold Bell Wright, Zoe Akins, Janet Dailey—have had connections to that little area of our state known as the Ozarks. There is something about the Ozarks that has nourished the individual artist. Maybe it is the beauty of the hills, the many greens of trees in the spring, the riot of color of those same trees in the fall. Perhaps it is the strength and endurance of the hills themselves, or perhaps it was our great oral storytelling tradition. Others would say simply that it's because of "something in our pure spring water."

In any event, the Ozarks area has produced art and artists from an environment that did not have the best support system for the artist. There has always been an anti-art element in the Ozarks. Many schools did not allow school plays to be produced, even until fairly recently, and prohibited dancing (some still do). The fiddle itself was looked upon as "the devil's instrument." That was part of our early settlers' puritan heritage, and it still is strong as evidenced by the controversy over the Southwest Missouri State University production of *The Normal Heart* and the banning of a large photographic reproduction of the Venus de Milo in Springfield's Battlefield Mall several years ago. That heritage of an innate suspicion of the arts may explain why so often local public schools practice a benign neglect of the arts and humanities, and who without question will buy uniforms for sports programs but insist that the music program conduct fundraisers in order to buy new uniforms for the band. Or why the Branson school system has a football program that has a football field with fine grandstand seating and a practice field (supported by a football coaching staff of 12) while the speech and drama program, with only one teacher, makes use of a small, ill-equipped stage at one end of a gymnasium that is a practice basketball court.

Equally strong has been the faction that has pushed for arts education and encouraged development of the individual in the arts. As soon as crops were planted and a cabin built, some settlers organized amateur theatricals, Friday night literaries (declamations, debates, and readings), and "kitchen sweats" (in-home dances). A remnant of these gatherings can be found in "mountain jam sessions," gatherings in homes, old rural school houses, and community centers where Ozarkers gather to play "just for the fun of it." Music and storytelling are part of our folk culture. The traditional hardscrabble Ozark existence, a general independence, and the isolation from outside influences have developed a crafts tradition. The individual desire for perfection and decoration have produced utilitarian objects that border on fine art. Writers from Harold Bell Wright in the past and Janet Dailey and Jory Sherman today have found solace and seclusion in the hills around Branson.

As contact with outside influences increased with better roads and travel, there has been change in the arts as well as attitudes toward the arts. The music of old-time barn dances has evolved into a new country style "that built The Strip." Branson may not have fine examples of old architecture like Eureka Springs, Springfield, and Carthage, but we have some fine new buildings as a result of becoming a tourist town.

The development of the tourist industry has created a greater appreciation of art and design because theater owners, banks, and businesses recognize that architecture and decor are important for satisfying the aesthetic eye of visitors. For example, the bronze Freedom Horses Monument created by world famous artist Veryl Goodnight of Santa Fe, New Mexico greets visitors in the circle drive at The Grand Mansion. Sculptures by Frederick Remington can be viewed in the lobby of the Remington Theatre, and ceiling murals by Arthur Congero and wall murals by Antonio Arechega can be viewed at the Bobby Vinton Blue Velvet Theatre. Even plantings and landscaping are being used more artistically to catch the eye of the tourist. Many theaters and businesses have landscaping displays that are artistic delights. Blossoms of Branson is a program that encourages planting flowers to brighten up the scene and make Branson have more "eye appeal."

The old has not been abruptly replaced or obliterated by the new. Instead, there has been a melding, a flowing together that's incongruous but not infelicitous, rather like the unique blend of nectars that make Ozarks wildflower honey so tasty.

Today, Branson and the area is the center of well-known country and pop artists who lure hundreds of thousands to a small town that has more theater seats than New York City. What other town in the nation the size of Branson can claim the proximity of such artists and entertainment? In a sense, the area's performance art, as well as its history and natural beauty, is what brings people here. Increasingly, the local theaters are offering music that can hardly be called strictly country, and there is now more variety and theatrical entertainment than just three years ago. More people has meant changed entertainment; it has also meant more galleries and more artists—not just musicians, but also writers, dancers, and directors moving to the area. These artists find they feel welcome, comfortable, and inspired by the area. Consumers of the artists' products are finding quality, an exciting blend and evolution as well as an increasing variety in the artistic culture of the area. Branson is a great place for the artist and the art lover—and it's getting better all the time.

Art Galleries and Studios

Art galleries here in Branson tend to reflect the tastes of the buying public and probably the majority of the artists. The art tends toward pastoral, bucolic, wildlife, and western themes, sometimes of a super-realism nature. Functionalism is in, and galleries are frequently a mix of art and crafts. However, one can find "newfangled art" including cubist, impressionism, expressionism, and minimalism that sometimes reflects a regional quality. We've included some of the better-known galleries and studios in Branson and in the immediate vicinity. You may want to see our Daytrips chapter for information about Eureka Springs, as this small town has a number of shops, studios, and galleries that would entice the art lover.

Ace Jewelry Store
113 W. Main St.
• **(417) 335-3910**
This is not your mother's jewelry store! Australian Tony Harris fea-

tures one-of-a-kind jewelry designs—odd, interesting, unusual, and some would even say bizarre—and does custom designs for individuals. He also sells and incorporates into his work Australian opals and gems from around the world. Jewelry artist Jeanette Bair's work is also featured in the store. The store also stocks a wide variety of leatherwork and western buckles and bolas.

The Art of Glenda Turley
4354 Gretna Rd., Factory Shoppes at
Branson Meadows Mall
• **(417) 339-4197, (888) 445-9632**
• **www.glynda.com**
This shop is dedicated to the art of Glenda Turley, an Ozarks native from Heber Springs Arkansas, America's answer to Laura Ashley. She has made quite an inroad in the homes of those who like floral patterns and Victorian decor. The shop features numbered limited editions and canvas repli-

INSIDERS' TIP

The Springfield Area Arts Council publishes a calendar of arts events for Springfield area. Call (417) 869-8380 to get on the mailing list.

cas of Turley's work. It also carries licensed products of the artist, such as keepsake boxes, silk florals, table runners, and tapestry pillows. Turley's romantic art and designs have found their way into well-known stores and decorators' shops across the nation, but the Branson store is an outlet devoted to her products. She is at the store occasionally to meet customers, sign autographs and give advice on decorating.

Boger Gallery
Jones Learning Center,
College of the Ozarks, Point Lookout
• (417) 334-6411

This gallery frequently has visiting and traveling shows as well as student art shows. Exhibits are free. Call the college's art department at the number above or the Branson Arts Council, (417) 336-4255, for its current featured exhibit.

Burlington Store Annex
201 S. Commercial St. • (417) 335-4789

In this downtown Branson store, you'll find a full array of stained-glass work, as small as suncatchers and as large as windows, doors, and ceilings. It also carries an interesting variety of other quality gift items. Burlington artists do commissioned and custom stained-glass work. The Yellow Ribbon stained-glass window in the old Tony Orlando Yellow Ribbon Theater is an example of the work they do.

Hawthorn Gallery
1335 76 Country Blvd.
• (417) 335-2170, (800) 427-3128

Located in the Engler Block where you could easily wander about all day investigating the little arts and crafts crannies and nooks, the Hawthorn Gallery is a large shop that features a variety of fine art, from paintings and pottery to prints and engravings, bronzes and wood-carvings. More than 20 artists' work is represented in the gallery's bronzes, including mosaics by Ava's Juanita Herrell and sculpture by Branson's Tim Cherry and Michael Krone. The gallery also carries lead crystal pieces, the work of camouflage artist Beverly Doolitle, pots by raku artist Brent Skinner, the work of Springfield artist

Jesse Barnes, as well as art by 25 to 30 other artists with national and international reputations.

Hess Pottery and Baskets
Mo. Hwy. 13, Reeds Spring
• (417) 272-3283

Potter Tom Hess has a wide following locally for his beautiful, earthy clayware. He has a technique that seals the clay without using glassy glaze. The finished product is ovenproof, dishwasher safe, and microwave oven safe. A full range of functional and utilitarian work is in his shop, as well as the unique pine-needle baskets by Lory Brown. She uses 18-inch southern yellow pine needles and 10-inch ponderosa pine needles in her remarkably beautiful yet sturdy and durable baskets.

Huff Gallery
1335 76 Country Blvd. • (417) 335-4458

Ron Huff is a well-known scenic painter who sells his wares at his gallery in the Engler Block and also at Silver Dollar City. A curious combination of craft and folk art, his style is distinctive. Much of his material is a combination of artistic and utilitarian, such as mailboxes and signposts, and frequently has a place on which a person's name can be added. His works make great gifts to take back home to friends.

Mitch Yung Ceramic Studio
632 S. Emory Creek Ln. • (417) 337-9227

Mitch Yung is a ceramicist-potter whose Hot Fresco Pottery celebrates early Majolica wares of various Mediterranean cultures. His work is based on techniques of 15th-century Islamic artists who developed the white tin glaze onto which decoration was painted. The forms are classic and graceful with colors and designs that are sunny and bright, bold and simple. Yung was the subject of a *Design* article in the December/January 1988 issue. Yung pottery is represented by fine craft galleries and retailers across the country. He has an open stock policy, so if you break a bowl from a set, he can make a replacement. Yung's designs and work are timeless and (pardon the pun) forever Yung. All Hot Fresco Pot-

INSIDERS' TIP

Missouri has made an effort to promote its many writers, past and present. A 32-page booklet, Missouri's Literary Heritage, can be obtained from the Missouri Center for the Book, P.O. Box 387, Jefferson City, Missouri 65101. Enclose $1 for postage. Or call (573) 751-2680. You might want to request to be placed on the center's publications and news notices list.

Arts and crafts shows are a staple community activity in the Ozarks.

Photo: Branson/Lakes Area Chamber of Commerce

tery is food-safe (lead-, cadmium- and barium-free), dishwasher safe, and microwave-oven safe. If you don't have room to take back a full set of dinnerware, Yung Studios will ship it.

To find the studio-workshop, drive on U.S. 65 and take the Mo. Hwy. F exit. Turn right onto F, and after 50 yards, take the northeast outer road. Drive for about a mile, cross Emory Creek and start up the hill. After a bit, you'll see the sign and the studio on your left.

Mother Earth Pottery
Mo. Hwy. 248, Reeds Spring
• (417) 272-3669

Potters Doug and Christina Lorenzen's works are featured in a number of area shops in Branson, but you can check out their studio and shop, 10 miles northwest of the Mel Tillis Theater. They feature oil lamps, stress-relieving tabletop waterfalls, angels, and a variety of pottery that is both functional and artistic. Their works feature many glazes and techniques, but glaze colors tend toward the reds and burgundies with lots of earth tones. They are open year round, but closed Sundays.

The New Coast Gallery
10 Main St., Reeds Spring
• (417) 272-8386

Owner-artist Jeanette Bair features her own custom-designed jewelry in gold, silver and precious stones, but also includes lots more in art-work by local artists: Jim McCord, Lee Robertson, Denise Ryan, and Kate Nestler, an Arkansas botanical artist. You can find oils, pastels, watercolors, engravings, woodcuts and photography. The gallery has several special shows each year that highlight a local artist, and during the summer you can enjoy the art and plants in the nearby sculpture garden. New Coast is open all year, Monday through Friday, 10 AM-4 PM.

Omega Pottery Shop
Mo. Hwy. 248, Reeds Spring
• (417) 272-3369

Potter Mark Oehler features everything from bathroom sinks to lamp bases and from dinnerware to canister sets in his dishwasher-safe, ovenproof, and microwave-safe high-fired stoneware. In addition to the utilitarian, there are beautiful, unique, and exotic sculptural items. Oehler's palette of glazes leans toward the earth tones, but he also likes cobalt blue. Omega is open year round but is closed Wednesday.

Pete Engler's Design Shop
2800 76 Country Blvd. • (417) 335-6862

This small shop in the Grand Village features regional and folk art—mostly woodcarvings reflecting the major interest of owner and master woodcarver Pete Engler. The work of more than 40 Ozark woodcarvers is represented, including that of wood sculptor Bob Robertson from Hollister. The shop also carries work by Springfield resident Tom Cram, a well-known wildlife artist. The shop is open year round.

Tablerock Art Guild Gallery
Kimberling City Shopping Center
• (417) 739-5829

The Tablerock Art Guild is a local arts support group of area artists who operate a membership gallery. The eight members of a 1980 oilpainting class who decided to form an art guild didn't know that their efforts would turn into an organization with 200 members and its own art gallery. Formed "to promote the advancement of art in the local area and encourage members to further their talents," the guild has monthly meetings and offers educational programs, workshops, and art shows. The gallery displays and sells members' artwork The gallery is open Monday through Saturday.

If you are moving to the area or already live in the area and are interested in joining the guild, call the number above for membership information.

Tim Cherry Sculpture Designs
609 Parnell Dr. • (417) 335-3870

Sculptor Tim Cherry always has a few bronze pieces lying around the workshop of his home in the subdivision across from the Skaggs Community Health Center, but most of his work is cast in Colorado and sold in galleries across the nation and Canada. The blue heron fountain in Rocky's Italian Restaurant is a good example of his work. The years of experience as a professional guide in British Columbia show in his love of simple and graceful lines, a hallmark of his sculpture. Cherry says, "My sculptural approach involves the use of simplified shapes and lines to produce curvilinear forms. I enjoy orchestrating these elements into sculpture that is rhythmical, flowing and inviting to the touch."

Museums

Branson City Hall
110 W. Maddux St. • (417) 334-3345

Obviously the seat of our city government isn't a museum, but if you're in the vicinity, stop in and see some of the buildings and scenes of early Branson reflected in the fine watercolors of Eloise DeLaval. The City Hall also has a permanent collection of photographer-journalist Townsend Godsey's photographs of people, events and activities of the early days of Branson. Godsey chronicled Ozarks culture through photography in his book, *These Were the Last*.

Springfield Art Museum
1111 E. Brookside Dr., Springfield
• (417) 837-5700

Sculptures in this park setting immediately attract the eye. The lawn sculptures are by Jim Sterrit, Ernest Trova, and John Henry. Located on the edge of Phelps Grove Park, the original structure of the Springfield Art Museum is 40 years old, but the new Jeannette L. Musgrave Wing dates to 1995. It was built to house works from the museum's permanent collection of drawings, etchings, prints, and paintings. Thomas Hart Benton, George Burchfield, and Red Grooms are just a few of the artists represented, but there are also works by Durer, Rembrandt, and other masters. The museum is home of the Gertrude Vanderveer Spratlen Collection, an eclectic assortment of more than 450 paintings. The museum has an especially strong 20th century American collection, with a focus on watercolor. It has more than 20,000 square feet of exhibit space, a museum shop, 400-seat auditorium, classrooms, and studio space. Educational activities include sessions of studio classes open to the general public for preschool to adult groups.

Each summer the museum is home to Watercolor U.S.A., a nationally known juried show of watercolors. The show was started in 1961 by former museum director Ken Shuck and has grown to become one of the major watercolor shows in the nation. Last year the show drew more than 1,277 entries by 690 artists, with 101 works accepted.

Artists from nearly every state in the union were represented. The show usually consists of 100 to 115 pieces and is a summer highlight. Every two years the museum features the Moak (for Missouri, Oklahoma, Arkansas, and Kansas) Exhibition, an open, competitive, and juried all-media show.

Ralph Foster Museum
College of the Ozarks • (417) 334-6411

This museum is a veritable attic of interesting items and collections (see our Attractions chapter for more information). For the art lover, it houses an interesting collection of Rose O'Neill's kewpies and a small collection of paintings and drawings by O'Neill, Louis Freund, Thomas Hart Benton, M. E. Oliver (whose drawings for years graced the pages of *The Ozarks Mountaineer*), and others. For those in-

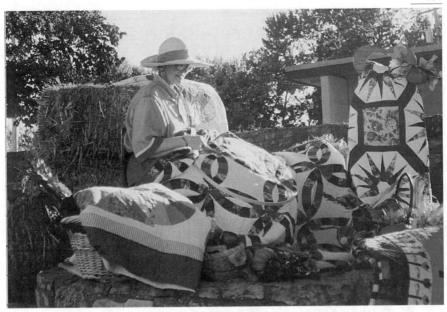

Quilting is a craft and an art, and quilt bargains abound in shops and shows.

Photo: Branson Downtown Main Street Association

terested in Native American art, the museum has a large collection of work by the artist Shipshee.

The museum also hosts the annual White River Painting Exhibit to showcase and encourage area artists. Many area businesses offer purchase awards, and you can see a fine collection of art as the result of the show in some area businesses, such at the local IGA grocery store.

While on the college campus, go over to the library and see the mural on the second floor by Steve Miller (friend of Benton) and local artist who was longtime curator of the Ralph Foster Museum.

Theater and Film

The evolution of The Strip has presented us with materials to make some interesting observations and predictions. Branson from its earliest days as a tourist destination has had theatrical attractions, whether stage and street shows at Silver Dollar City, the Shepherd of the Hills Outdoor Drama or, for many years, the

summer repertory productions at the Beacon Hill Theatre (1960-1989) of The School of the Ozarks (now College of the Ozarks). *The Promise* is only one of the current examples of theater in Branson (see our Shows chapter). In the last several years, other shows and dinner theaters have come and gone. Area residents and visitors can find student productions at College of the Ozarks and in Springfield at Southeast Missouri State University and Drury. More and more, The Strip diversifies its entertainment offerings to include something other than country music.

For the large number of people who come to Branson, we had surprisingly few choices in movie houses and cinemas, but that changed in March 2000 with the opening of the **Cinemas at Branson Meadows** in the Factory Shoppes at Factory Shoppes at Branson Meadows, 4562 Gretna Road. The mall now boasts a 30,000 square foot, 11-screen movie theater complex showing first run movies. The new cinema complex features stadium seating in a specially designed "stealth cinema" pie-shaped auditorium, digital "surround sound," the latest projection tech-

INSIDERS' TIP

The Branson area is not just country music country. Jazz guitarist Charlie Haden is from Forsyth. Check out his CDs, including *Under the Missouri Sky*, at music stores.

Brent Skinner—Raku Guru

Brent Skinner is a raku guru. Sitting at his wheel like a mud-smeared Buddha in a trance, he patiently and efficiently molds mud into objects d'art. He's one of a small number of Ozark potters who champions the ancient Japanese pottery art of raku. Raku is a low temperature firing process that originated in Japan during the sixteenth century. Fired to 1,700 degrees, the clay body remains porous, causing it to be unsuitable for holding liquids. Unlike most pottery, which is functional and utilitarian workhorse art that is meant to be used, raku is produced and admired purely for its aesthetic qualities.

That prized surface admired by Skinner and raku collectors is created by applying a colorful, metallic glaze to a bisque fired pot. The pot is then placed into a small preheated kiln. When the glazed pots reaches a temperature of 1700-1900 degrees, it is removed from the kiln with metal tongs and placed into a container of combustible materials (straw, leaves, newspaper).

The hot pot ignites the materials, and the potter smothers the fire to achieve a reduction atmosphere. It's a process that is dramatic, smoky, and which inspires awe and looks dangerous. "People watching may want to alert the fire department or call 911, but it's safer than driving on the highway in your car," says Skinner.

The process causes unpredictable glaze effects and blackens the clay where it is not covered by a glaze. "That's the beauty of the process. Unlike production pottery which strives for uniformity, every pot is unique and different, just like people."

When Skinner sold his first two raku pots within ten minutes at his first art show, Skinner knew raku was for him. Unlike many potters, who produce various kinds of pottery, Skinner specializes strictly in raku.

"Tons of clay went through my fingers before I became proficient, and even now with every ounce of mud, you learn something. Clay is natural. Playing in the mud is natural. There's something about the moldability quality of clay that brings out the creativity in a person," says Skinner, talking to a group of people at Silver Dollar City's annual crafts festival.

"The nice thing about this craft is that you're always learning. Every potter is a sage, a guru. You're always learning—and you're always sharing," Skinner says as he makes some canteen-shaped pieces that he has become famous for, "thrown and assembled" works. Some pots Skinner adorns with abstract "slip trailings," the liquid clay applied with a plastic squeeze bottle or with sculpted clay flowers and leaves.

Skinner has developed a unique glaze effect which he calls "slip and chip." He takes a bisque-fired pot, smears it with slip (liquid clay), and lets it dry. The slip cracks like the bottom of a dried mud puddle. The pot is again fired, smothered in paper or leaves, and the smoke infuses the cracks, staining the pot. When the pot cools, the slip is chipped and scraped off, leaving that part uncolored. The effect is a striking marble-like surface, not unlike that of the famous Carthage marble near Skinner's home near Diamond, Mo.

"You can get some neat surface effects, depending on the material you use when you bring out the hot pots. I've used horse hair and emu feathers before for some unusual effects."

Examples of Skinner's work can be found at Play With Clay and the Hawthorne Gallery at Engler Block in Branson, and he has been the featured raku potter on site at the Silver Dollar City Fall Crafts Festival for the last eight years. In 1998, he was "Craftsperson of the Year" in the SDC Festival.

Skinner numbers every pot, and he knows the name and address of all those who have bought his work, now up to number 11,538. He has works in galleries and private collections across the U.S., Canada, England, Germany, Ireland, Saudi Arabia, Scotland, and Japan. Skinner attends about six big shows a year. Between shows, he's busy making pots.

"It takes two months to get ready for the Silver Dollar City show, held from early September to the end of October. I'll take down over 700 pots I've already made, and I probably will use two tons of clay down there. I work and fire there all day, talking to people. Some will watch for hours. They're interested in the process. And they like to take home something they've seen being made. I make a lot of converts to the beauty of raku at that show."

Skinner isn't your stereotypical, quiet and morose artist. He's as garrulous as Mark Twain, and he talks while he works. Silver Dollar City master potter Todd Nelson says it is that "infectious talkativeness" that caused his peers to nominate him for "Crafts Demonstrator of the Year" in 1997. "Brent is outgoing, enthusiastic, and a good explainer. No question is dumb to him. He's a good teacher. but more than that, he's an up and coming potter-artist. We have people who come back each year just to get another one of his works. Because he's good, and such a crowd pleaser, is why he has the premier spot—just to the right as soon as you come into the park."

A 1900 degree pot gets smothered in a reduction firing in the raku process by Silver Dollar City potter Brent Skinner.

Photo: Silver Dollar City

Brent paused a moment from his work of making pots for the Silver Dollar City Festival and reflected about his craft. "The nice thing about this career is I can set my hours. If I need to take a break and mow the lawn, I can."

Brent wiped the sweat from his brow, leaving a streak of bright mud like a brave decorated with war paint. "And you know, it's as much fun as playing in the mud when you were a kid and making things with it. What person could ask more from life than that?"

It was a profound question and observation about life and art from Silver Dollar City's raku guru.

nology, and a special party room so you can plan special events, such as kids' birthday parties, at the cinema and mall. The cinema also features a large video arcade and game area. Call (417) 332-2884 for their latest cinema offering.

Branson Movies 4, (417) 334-4636, on The Strip next door to Applebee's, is a four-screen that also show current movies.

Branson has the big screen **IMAX Theatre** (417) 335-4832 on the Shepherd of the Hills Expressway that shows spectacular 70-millimeter movies on its 6-story-tall screen (see our Attractions chapter), and it recently installed a 35-millimeter projector and shows Hollywood productions using the theater's 22,000-watt Surround Sound system. (For a really awesome experience, you ought to see Titantic on this screen!)

A planned $1.7 million expansion project at Branson's IMAX is scheduled to open mid-summer of 2000. It will add three standard-size movie theater screens to the complex, all with state-of-the-art sound and seating. One theater will have a stage and can be used for conventions or other special events.

Branson Performing Arts Academy
590 W. Pacific St. • (417) 336-2223

The Branson Performing Arts Academy is an educational institution that offers instruction for area children and adults in various forms of dance and gymnastics, voice, musical theater, and acting. You'll find the entire range of age and talent, from preschool ballerinas to performers on The Strip who want to increase their range by taking acting or voice coaching.

Inspiration Point Fine Arts Colony
U.S. Hwy. 62 W., Eureka Springs
• (501) 253-8595

In the beauty of the Arkansas Ozarks, 7 miles west of Eureka Springs, is a summer opera treat. Top notch college/graduate level musicians and vocalists enroll for classes in this summer workshop conducted by well-known names in opera, and residents and tourists reap the benefit of nightly outdoor full-length orchestra accompanied opera performances. There are also orchestra concerts, opera scenes, and children's opera performances. In 1999,

IPFAC also did some painting classes, and some years they do a high school vocal jazz camp. You can enjoy a great sunset on the hills overlooking the White River 600 feet below and opera by some surprising and developing talent. For almost 50 years now, we've enjoyed our "opera in the Ozarks." Call for their summer schedule or if you are interested in participating.

SMSU Tent Theater
801 S. National Ave., Springfield
• (417) 836-5979

For more than 30 years, Tent Theater on the SMSU campus has provided summer repertory entertainment that presents the best of Broadway in an intimate, outdoor setting. Tent Theater alumni have gone on to become well known in professional theater and film, or active in area theater and education.

Recent productions included *Baby, Once Upon a Mattress, Damn Yankees,* and *Lend Me a Tenor* with a ticket price of $8. The season is late June, July, and early August. Give a call for shows, dates, and curtain time.

Springfield Little Theatre
311 E. Walnut St., Springfield
• (417) 869-1334

The historic Landers Theater is home to Springfield Little Theatre, one of the Midwest's finest community theater organizations. Built in 1909, the Landers is a fine example of Baroque Renaissance/Napoleon style decoration. Its audiences have seen touring artists and vaudeville stars ranging from Lillian Russell to John Philip Sousa and Fanny Brice on the Landers stage, and more recently, Tess Harper, Kathleen Turner, and John Goodman have performed there. Springfield Little Theatre, founded in 1934, bought the Landers in 1970 and began to restore it to its original elegance. In the newly restored showcase theater, SLT brings a main-stage season of seven plays and musicals. Recent productions were *Forever Plaid, Mame, Noises Off, Jesus Christ Superstar, Evita, Hello Dolly, Sweeney Todd,* and *The Belle of Amherst.*

SLT also offers a variety of entertainment activities in the adjacent 200-seat Vandivort Center Theatre including YES (for Young Entertainment Series), a

The Ozarks are alive with the sound of music during the Great American Music Festival.

Photo: Silver Dollar City

performance series geared for young audiences, and the Studio Series, offering nontraditional theater works in an intimate setting. Call for current shows, ticket prices and curtain time.

Springfield Regional Opera
109 Park Central Sq., Springfield
• (417) 863-1960

The stage of the historic Landers Theater is home to most of the productions of the Springfield Regional Opera. The opera began in 1979 and was the impetus of its first director, Dawin Emanuel. It has done much to further opera in the Ozarks and has performed much of the traditional operatic literature in some not-so-traditional performing spaces, including Fantastic Caverns (see our Daytrips chapter.) Past productions have included *La Traviata, Rigoletto,*

Richard Clark

Here in Branson, most everyone is an artist of sorts. It shouldn't surprise you if your coworker turns out to have a knack for woodcarving or is a talented banjo picker. Richard Clark fits somewhat into that category though his previous job as emcee of the $25,000 Wheel of Fortune Game Show here in Branson isn't exactly nondescript. However, his *American Highrise*, which began in 1977 as a simple doodle on the back of an airline napkin while his plane was circling the New York City skyline, shows that we all have talents that "just need a bit of time and development."

Clark threw away his napkin doodle, but the image kept haunting him, and he started it again—on the back of a poster for The Gong Road Show, which he was hosting and producing at the time and it grew.

Clark, who moved to Branson in 1993 to do the game show, has emceed more than 1,200 shows, including major Branson events such as fund-raisers and Branson Fest. His doodle evolved to a work that is an inspiring architectural, patriotic mural, with signed prints of the work on display at 191 U.S. military bases around the world, the Library of Congress, and the Statue of Liberty. The 8-foot original is on display at Branson's Ripley's Believe Or Not! Museum on 76 Country Boulevard. (see Attractions chapter).

Clark, a native Australian whose accent hasn't been influenced much yet by our Ozark twang and drawl, said that he used more than 4,000 ball-point pens and felt-tip markers and gallons of liquid paper in creating the architectural montage that features more than 50 buildings, about half of them actual structures found in cities across the United States and the other half his own architectural creations. He said he must have gotten his interest in architecture from his father, who was an engineer and architect.

The final work, much revised and drawn over, was reproduced by computer for the printing process. The public unveiling of the work occurred when

"American Highrise" by Richard Clark is part of Branson's Veterans Homecoming celebration.

Photo: Richard Clark

candidate George Bush used it and the image captured the imagination of viewers across the nation. Clark has received comments from former presidents, generals and world leaders from Bill Clinton and Ronald Reagan to Norman Schwarzkopf and Nelson Mandela. As of the end of 1999, more than 70 world leaders have accepted signed inaugural image copies of *American Highrise*. People have called *American Highrise* patriotic, inspiring, even geometric—"the vertical lines of the buildings superimposed on the horizontal lines of the flag like a Wall Street stock graph."

Viewers have said that it represents an image of America that is both stereotypical and at the same time basic. Tony Orlando said that it represents "the muscle of America," reminiscent of poet Carl Sandburg's "city of the big shoulders" line from Chicago. Orlando is also writing a song about the work of art.

When you are in Branson, you can see framed prints of *American Highrise* in the main lobby of the Branson post office and in the City Hall. The design was used for a U.S. Postal Service commemorative envelope for Veterans Day 1997. Branson Postmaster Alex Tipton Jr. got the ball rolling when it occurred to him that the drawing would look nice as a postal envelope or stamp. When Veterans Day 1997 rolled around, there was a special unveiling of the design attended by Branson Mayor Lou Schaefer, area entertainers, dozens of veterans and a crowd of the curious. Tony Orlando promised to use the envelope as a fund-raiser and match its sales with a donation to help raise money for a van to carry Branson-area veterans to hospitals.

Now the work is being considered by the U.S. Postal Service as a possible design for a postage stamp. Don't be surprised if you see American Highrise as a stamp on a letter you get in the future. If you do, remember that it all started with Richard Clark in Branson, who could give these words of wisdom to budding artists: Never throw away a doodle. You never know what it will grow up to be.

Interested in *American Highrise*? Contact Clark at: American Highrise Inc., P.O. Box 165 Branson, Mo. 65615, call (417) 335-4503. or check the internet: www.americanhighrise.com

---

Madame Butterfly, The Elixir of Love and operettas *H.M.S. Pinafore, Die Fledermaus,* and *The Merry Widow*.

Currently the SRO mounts two productions a year, with a fall and spring operatic offering. Casts are drawn from the extended area. The operatic chorus is volunteer but auditioned. Members come from communities as far flung as Gainesville, Marshfield, Branson and Ozark, and local church and college choirs actively participate. Principal roles are auditioned from the general community with some roles performed by imported stars.

In the works is a summer educational program, "Music, Words, Opera," at which students will study opera texts and literature, culminating in the writing and production of their own opera.

Stained Glass Theater
1700 N. Benton Ave., Springfield
• **(417) 869-9018**

For the past 18 years, Ron Boutwell, co-founder and executive director of the Stained Glass Theatre, has been bringing Christian drama to the Ozarks area. Productions are not "bathrobe drama" but high quality productions of quality plays at reasonable prices. (Tickets are $2.50 to $5.) The promise of entertainment with a moral message has drawn people who otherwise might not step into a theater. Stained Glass Theatre offers instruction in acting, directing and playwriting through its Christian Drama Institute and operates Stained Glass Theatre-West in Joplin. Like the traveling theater companies of yore, Stained Glass Theatre takes shows

INSIDERS' TIP

Rose O'Neill, best known for creating the kewpie doll, was also a sculptor. You can see two of her sculptures, *Embrace of the Tree,* and *The Fauness* on the grounds of the artist's rebuilt home, now operated as Bonniebrook Park, 9 miles north of Branson on Bear Creek.

into churches, stores, and communities in the Ozarks to audiences who might not ever get to see a live theater production otherwise. Call the above number for shows and information.

Tri-Lakes Community Theatre
P.O. Box 1301, Branson, Mo. 65615
• (417) 334-2581

Founded in 1983, the TLC Theatre draws from a wealth of area talent from the community and from shows on The Strip during the winter season when some of the shows are closed. The organization is run by a board of nine directors, and all the work from directing, acting, and building sets to box office and ushering are performed by TLC Theatre volunteers. It does two shows a year, and past productions have included *Neighborhood Watch, Little Shop of Horrors, 1776, You're a Good Man, Charlie Brown, Steel Magnolias, Oliver,* and *Fiddler on the Roof*. Productions usually take place in one of the local music theaters. Call the above number for current shows and ticket prices or if you want to become involved as a volunteer.

Dance and Music

Springfield Ballet
Vandivort Center, 305 E. Walnut St., Ste. 301, Springfield • (417) 862-1343

Incorporated in 1976, Springfield Ballet has been upgrading the quality of area ballet and bringing fine examples of dance art to area audiences. In 1986 the ballet moved to the Frances Vandivort Center next door to the Landers Theatre in downtown Springfield and began offering classes there and at satellite facilities. A community favorite for more than 13 years has been its annual production of *The Nutcracker*. Also important is the School Concert each May. Call the number above for a current schedule and ticket prices.

Mid-America Singers
P.O. Box 3239, Springfield
• (417) 863-7464

This group of talented amateurs with a healthy mix of professional singers directed by Charles Facer makes community appearances during the year with concerts and recitals.

Springfield Symphony Orchestra
1536 E. Division St., Springfield
• (417) 864-6643

Director Apo Hsu leads this orchestra, which has an established and still-growing reputation. The SSO features an eight-concert season that is a mix of pop and classical concerts. Recent guest artists and conductors have included Michael Miles, Bion Tsang, Nestor Torres, Brian Lewis, Yuri Rozum, Rosario Andino, Nai-Yuan Hu and Linda Hohenfeld. A number of special events concerts, including Independence Day celebration Firefall, are featured each year. Call for current concerts and ticket information.

INSIDERS' TIP

The 16-foot recycled stainless steel *Circle of Water* sculpture by Lee Robertson at the foot of Main Street in Lake Taneycomo was designed to camouflage the eyesore of the two remaining bridge pillars left of the bridge that used to cross the White River at that spot. The bridge was destroyed by the flood of 1927. The sculpture depicts rain as it falls into Table Rock Lake, travels over the dam into Lake Taneycomo and then rises into the clouds.

Support Organizations

No matter where you live, funding for the arts is meager to scarce. Although dance, music, and theater add much to what we call a civilized life, our orchestras, music schools, and dance companies frequently have a hand-to-mouth existence, especially at a time of declining federal support.

Most support organizations in the Ozarks have found creative ways to promote that which makes civilizations noble. If you visit the Ozarks, support the arts by attending a show or buying an art work. If you are new to the area as a resident, ask around: You can be sure there is some way you can get involved in the arts and culture of our area.

Branson Arts Council, Inc.
108 ½ S. Commercial St.
• (417) 336-4255

The BAC's mission is "to make available artistic, cultural, and education opportunities and support, strengthen and enhance these opportunities for all community citizens." It does that through membership and grants. The BAC has been active in purchasing arts educational materials for the local library as well as sponsoring plays, workshops, exhibits and concerts, including popular "milk and cookies" concerts for kids at the Taneyhills Library. It has established historical markers for Branson sites, sponsored art safety workshops for area artists and craft workers, developed a summer drama camp for children, and sponsored public murals and sculptures. The recently restored Old Stone Presbyterian Church at the corner of Fourth and Pacific Streets has become an intimate venue for BAC sponsored recitals, concerts and lectures. It publishes BAC Tracks for members. A call to the BAC can get you information about current shows and arts activities and information about becoming a member.

Ozarks Writers League
P.O. Box 1433, Branson, Mo. 65615
• (417) 334-5615

The Ozarks Writers League is open to writers of all stages of development, from rank beginner to published professional. It meets quarterly and features programs and workshops by members and outside experts for its 350 members, drawn from a 150-mile radius. It publishes a quarterly newsletter, *The OWLs Hoot*, and features writing contests for members. Call or write for membership information.

Writers within the Ozarks region network on an e-loop, the Ozarks Regional Writers Loop (ORWL) to share information about markets and writing. Membership in the e-loop is open to all writers in the Ozarks region and regisitration information can be found at http://www.onelist.com.

Springfield Writers' Guild
P.O. Box 6261, Springfield, Mo. 65801
• (417) 881-5691 or (417) 668-5977

This writers support group for Springfield

INSIDERS' TIP

Novelist and poet of the Native American experience John G. Neihardt lived for a number of years in Branson, writing much of his influential *Black Elk Speaks* in a little house that was located on a dirt road that later became Mo. Hwy. 76. You can read a plaque on a boulder in the Koi Garden Plaza near where the house stood at the junction of Mo. 76 East and U.S. 65.

---

and area writers is a chapter of the Missouri Writers' Guild and sponsors writing contests and workshops for members. The SWG hosts an annual October writing conference. The group has educational and scholarship programs for area students, and its members were instrumental in establishing the Missouri Writers Hall of Fame: It serves as a writers' networking organization and encourages smaller writing groups: Sleuth's Ink (a group of detective fiction authors), the Missouri Poets & Friends, and the Ozarks Romance Authors. The organization normally meets the fourth Saturday of the month and publishes a monthly newsletter, Free-Lancer. Call the number above for information.

Springfield Area Arts Council
Vandivort Center, 305 E. Walnut St.,
Ste. 312, Springfield, Mo. • (417) 869-8380

This nonprofit organization "fosters, promotes, and encourages the existing cultural and educational endeavors of Springfield and its environs." It sponsors the annual Arts Fest on Walnut Street the first weekend in May and First Night Springfield, a city-wide New Year's Eve gala (see our Annual Events chapter). It helps coordinate arts events in Springfield and publishes a calendar of events and arts directory.

Springfield Visual Arts Alliance
P.O. Box 11113 GS, Springfield, Mo. 65808
• (417) 885-9009

One of the enjoyable features of Springfield the last decade is finding an art display in an unexpected area, often by the SVAA. Founded in 1988, the nonprofit alliance seeks to create "a richer environment for the visual arts in the Springfield region." It offers professional exchange and exhibition for local and regional artists by displaying artwork in public locations.

Ozark-speak

An Ozark newspaper reporting a turn-of-the century "Friday night literary" on the debate, "Resolved: That life is not worth living," mentioned that the audience decided in favor of the affirmative and "made us feel so bad we wasn't able to eat but seven biscuits for breakfast."

Membership is open to artists within 180 miles of Springfield, working in any medium and at any stage of artistic development. The group publishes a quarterly newsletter, The Visual Voice.

Studio Fifty-Five Springfield
(417) 886-9953

This Springfield-based organization is for area artists 55 and older. It features juried shows for members and sponsors lectures and workshops for them. It especially focuses on the role of art for older citizens. Call the number above for membership and activities information.

Venues

Juanita K. Hammons Center for the Performing Arts
Cherry St. and John Q. Hammons Pkwy.
• (417) 836-6782

Performing arts in the area got a big boost with the opening of this fine facility in 1993. (You'll find the Hammons name on a lot of Springfield real estate.) It is the home of the Springfield Symphony, and the hall presents a concert and stage series that provides fare for every taste. Recent shows in the "Give Your Regards to Broadway" series included *Hello, Dolly*, *STOMP*, *Grease*, *West Side Story*, *Cirque Ingenieux*, *A Chorus Line*, and *Joseph and the Amazing Technicolor Dreamcoat*. The "Kids' Broadway" series included *Tom Sawyer*, *Cinderella*, and *Pocahontas*. Other recent appearances have been made by Hal Holbrook in *Mark Twain Tonight*, Bela Fleck, the Village People, The King's Singers, The Manhattan Transfer, Tom Jones, The Shirelles, the Trinity Irish Dance Company, the Preservation Hall Jazz Band, The Lettermen, clarinetist Todd Palmer, Gregory Peck, pianist Mikhail Yanovitsky, and the Queensland Ballet with the Kansas City Symphony Orchestra. If you don't find it on The Strip in Branson, you can find it "at the Hall!"

Call the box office for shows, curtain times and prices.

Recreation and the Outdoors

No matter how many shows you take in or how much shopping you do while here in Branson, take the time to try athletics and outdoors sports. Mix a little exercise into even your busiest trips, or at least take a look around. Even if you don't venture off The Strip, try walking it. It isn't all that long, and you may be surprised at how much you can see on foot while walking that you miss when in your car surrounded by traffic.

The great outdoors here in the Ozarks is so great that we actually have two chapters devoted to it. If you miss fishing, floating, boating, and water-skiing in this chapter, that's because our Lakes and Rivers chapter covers those outdoor activities. In this chapter we cover "the land activities" in the great outdoors and other types of recreation you'll find in the Branson area.

Most of the folks who live in the Ozarks are into the outdoors, and it's easy to see why the Ozarks would be home to Bass Pro Shops (see our Daytrips chapter). Lots of folks like to hunt, fish, boat, golf, or hike in what has been described as a sport lover's paradise. Our highways and roadsides are lined with wildflowers. People inside the Branson city limits put out salt for deer that nibble the shrubbery; sometimes you can see the deer even from motels on The Strip. We may have the neon glitz and glitter of The Strip and traffic so thick during the season you can't stir it with a stick, but we are also only a half-hour's drive from some of the best free-flowing floating streams in the nation and wilderness areas so untouched that you can hike for days and not see a soul.

Development in Branson has changed the nature of the hills, and we do have some raw-looking road cuts that have not yet had the softening weathering experience of rain, frost and lichens. But the nature that drew visitors here at the turn of the nineteenth century is still abundantly evident. As soon as high-pressure boilers allowed small steamboats to come up the White River in the 1850s, anglers and hunters came to the Ozarks. Often they'd have to spend a year because the river was only navigable in spring during high water. Sometimes they'd choose to leave via wagon or horseback later in the year rather than wait until the next spring to take a steamboat back down the White. With the coming of the railroad, the Ozarks became more accessible to sports enthusiasts. Game was plentiful. The scenery was breathtaking. The plow's touch was confined to the fertile bottomlands. That which attracted Harold Bell Wright into the Ozarks at the turn of the century can still be found. *The Shepherd of the Hills* has a cast of characters that are as big as the Ozarks' out-of-doors, and Young Matt, the hero, and Sammy Lane, the heroine, still cast a romantic shadow on our landscape.

Dams on the White River have changed forever the terrain and nature of the Ozarks (see our Lakes and Rivers and our History chapters), but the area continues to invite exploration. Our rivers and streams, lakes, woods, and balds are becoming more accessible than ever to today's

*Whether it's the White River or its many feeder streams, the Ozarks offers
canoeing opportunities both tranquil and exciting.*

Photo: A.C. Haralson/Arkansas Dept. of Parks & Tourism

hikers, bikers, campers, and nature lovers. Thanks to better roads, a better appreciation by locals of their own outdoor environment, and the development of private, city, state, and federal parks, and wilderness areas, more people than ever can appreciate the beauty that we who live here have so often taken for granted.

City Parks

"Parks give a community character," says Randy Warner, Branson's parks and recreation director. And Branson, that character of towns, is developing more character as it continues to provide adequate green space and parks as it grows. Currently within the city limits, Branson has more than 1,817 acres in its 16 public parks and wilderness areas. (The Ruth and Paul Henning State Conservation Area, a state park, is within the city limits.)

These parks provide green space and open space, and they also provide activity space for the city's parks and recreation programs. There are instructional programs in tennis and golf. A youth soccer program drew 630 participants in 1999. During that summer, a record 1260 children participated in the park's department's baseball and softball programs. Branson may be unusual in that it doesn't charge a fee for youngsters to play in Little League. The cost of the Little League program is subsidized by another park, the city-owned campground on Lake Taneycomo. Any child, regardless of economic background, can participate in the athletic events.

The programs aren't just for kids. Adult softball is big in Branson. In 1999 more than 1,110 participants came out for the summer and fall leagues of slow-pitch softball. There is a co-ed volleyball league, with 140 participants in 1999. And the adult basketball program is very popular, with 300 participants in 1999.

Recreation features of parks are balanced with environmental concerns. Many Branson parks take into consideration continuing change and wheelchair accessibility. Landscaping puts the emphasis on native materials to harmonize with the surroundings, and park trails are designed to minimize erosion.

With the realization that tourists list "trees, scenery, and environment" as the fourth most important reason for visiting the Branson area, according to a Branson/Lakes Area Chamber of Commerce survey, residents recognize the need to provide adequate green space and plantings that make the area attractive. A city ordinance that encourages builders and developers to save as many trees as possible on a building site has met with great success and unexpected cooperation. Developers increasingly use interior and exterior green space. Older businesses, which were exempt from the new requirement, are choosing to meet the code because it makes their locations more attractive. Whether you are a resident or a visitor to the Branson area, we invite you to pursue an activity that will get you out in our city's green space. More of our streets are now planned with sidewalks and with walkers in mind. We've listed our city parks below, large and small. Seek them out and enjoy them while you're here.

Alexander Park Sunset St.

Situated on the banks of Taneycomo Lake, this park can be seen on the east from the bridge as you cross the lake on U.S. 65. The facilities at the 5-plus acre park include a playground with a variety of equipment, two baseball fields, and tennis courts. The parks is a whirl of activity on summer evenings, for the light lasts longer on the east-west valley of Lake Taneycomo, and when it does get dark, electric lights continue league games until late. Neighbors and area residents use the perimeter streets for walking and biking.

Branson North Park
Lake St.

This is a 1-acre neighborhood pocket park with playground equipment in one of Branson's established residential areas, Branson North. It's largely a gathering place for neighborhood kids.

Cantwell Park
Oklahoma and Walnut Streets

This neighborhood park in the Cantwell Addition neighborhood features nearly 1½ acres of grassy slopes with huge old walnut trees, playground equipment, picnic tables,

INSIDERS' TIP

The Canada geese and the mallard ducks on the Taneycomo Lakefront are welfare birds and don't migrate. They are tourists who stayed—and they enjoy a handout.

and a basketball court. You'll often see area youngsters rolling down the green slopes in summer and sliding down theme whenever we get snow. It's a great place to take a picnic lunch.

City Campgrounds #1 and #2
Lake Dr.

On the shores of Lake Taneycomo, this 15-acre campground has rental sites, restrooms, shower facilities, and a public fishing area. Campground fees help fund activities sponsored by the Branson Parks Department. The banks that enclosed the old swimming area within Lake Taneycomo, before Table Rock Dam was built, are also a favorite fishing spot. The campgrounds can be seen from U.S. Business 65 as you cross the old Taneycomo Bridge. (See our Campgrounds and RV Parks and Retirement chapters.)

Eiserman Park
Compton Dr.

Eiserman Park, near the Branson Community Center, is 1 acre that includes a basketball court, playground, and covered pavilion. Adjacent to the park is the nine hole Don Gardner Pitch and Putt Public Golf Course, named after an early golfer who brought the sport to Branson with the development of the Holiday Hills Golf Course in 1939. Each hole is a par 3, and the course is great for sharpening short iron skills.

Jack Justus Park
Pat Nash Dr.

Currently in the initial stages of planning, this 5 acres of undeveloped park land is next to the Factory Merchants Mall on The Strip. Plans call for a walking path and picnic area for easy accessibility to Branson visitors.

Lakeside Forest Wilderness Area
Fall Creek Rd.

This 130-acre park opened in 1999, a gift of Dr. Lyle Owen, a retired college professor, who had bought the land in the early 1930s and built the 340 stones steps from the top of the bluff above Lake Taneycomo down to about 60 feet above the water's edge. It was no easy task carrying the stone and mixing the mortar at that time. Owen inscribed one step: "Let those who tread here not forget that these steps were not made of stone and mortar alone, but of sweat and blood and agony."

The area contains a trail to the steps, but if you go down the steps, you have to come back up them, and though it's only 340 steps down, it seems like 3,400 in the climb up! The trail and steps have a scenic view of the Lake Taneycomo valley and feature a natural waterfall and several caves, included one called "Old Soldiers Cave," which served as a hideout during the Civil War for a gunsmith. It takes about an hour to take the trail walk and the steps.

The Lakeside Forest Wilderness Area is open during daylight hours only in the fall and winter and from 7 AM to 7 PM during the spring and summer. Access to the area is from Fall Creek road, about .2 mile south of Mo. 76. Look for the sign on your left.

Mang Field
BoxCar Willie Dr.

Located near downtown on the Taneycomo lakefront, this just larger than 4-acre park is a center of activity on warm summer days. It has a ball field, playground, basketball court, and the city's public swimming pool. The stone bleachers and the lakefront's stone retaining walls and steps were a Depression-era WPA project. Only steps away to the north is North Beach Park.

Murphy Park
John G. Neihardt Dr.

This 5-acre park in the Murphy Addition has one of the city's two sand volleyball courts as well as a picnic area and playground. It's a centerpiece of neighborhood activity.

North Beach Park
Hawthorn and Sunset Streets

This scenic 9-acre park just north of the Main Street lakefront area and Mang Field is popular with visitors who discover it in their exploration of the downtown area. It's a favorite picnic area and spot to feed ducks and geese. It features a picnic pavilion with grills and eight picnic tables for general use. The pavilion can be reserved for special events, meetings, and family reunions by calling the Branson Parks Department, (417) 337-8510. There are also a number of open lakeside picnic tables, a large

RECREATION AND THE OUTDOORS

playground, walking trail, sand volleyball court, two lighted tennis courts, public bathrooms, and public fishing docks that are wheelchair accessible.

Old Branson School Park
Country Blvd.

Located on The Strip near the Dixie Stampede, this 1-acre park is a popular site for visitor picnics. There are picnic tables, a covered pavilion, and playground equipment. A new public restroom resembles the old one-room schoolhouse that was once at that site.

Parnell Park
Parnell Cir.

Located in the Parnell Neighborhood across from Skaggs Community Health Center, the 1-acre park features two tennis courts, picnic tables, and playground equipment. Close by is the Branson Community Center.

Stockstill Park
Melody Penner Ln.

The largest of Branson's public parks at 62 acres, Stockstill is on the north bank of Roark Creek west of the U.S. 65 Bridge that crosses the creek. It is accessed from James F. Epps Road. Amenities include restrooms, two adult softball fields, a large children's playground, two covered picnic pavilions, a 1/3-mile-walking path, and 6 tennis courts, two of which have lights. It is the center of activity of the Branson Parks and Recreation summer activity programs, and the shallow creek gets lots of little visitors who chase minnows and crawdads while parents, older brothers, or sisters are on the playing field.

Sunset Park
Sunset St.

This park is the large area of green space seen to the west as you cross Lake Taneycomo on U.S. 65. It is reached via Alexander Park by going under the U.S. 65 Bridge. The 10 acres of open space and trees contain a 0.6-mile walking path along Taneycomo where former president George Bush jogged during a 1992 campaign stop in Branson. The park, along with Alexander Park and nearby Branson Campground to the east, is a favorite cycling place since it is one of the few large, flat areas with little traffic.

Other Parks and Recreation Areas

Glades and Balds

Although hardwood forests cover much of the Branson area, one of the most notable and interesting features is the glades. Glades are frequently called "balds" by locals, and we noted their historic function as meeting spots for the vigilante justice gang in the 1880s called the Bald Knobbers in our History chapter.

Glades are islands of semidesert and prairie plants within the sea of oak and history that covers the Ozarks. Glades often occur on the south- and west-facing slopes of hills. The sunlight is intense and prolonged there, and the thin soil barely covers the dolomite bedrock, which breaks down slowly. Parts of the stone weather more quickly than others, resulting in fantastic, gargoyle-like shapes that resemble tiny gnarled totems. Decomposition of organic materials takes a long time, and there is little buildup of organic materials like you might find on northern and eastern slopes, which are largely forested. In early days fires started by lightning or set by Indians or early settlers enlarged these sites and kept them almost free of trees. With burning curtailed, many of the areas have become overgrown with the only trees that can survive in the semiarid environment—cedars. It was difficult to make a living from the hardscrabble land, so many of the glade areas were virtually wilderness regions. Many have come under the protection of the Missouri Department of Conservation. The fragile environment of the glades is easily damaged. In order to maintain the integrity of the land, the de-

> ## INSIDERS' TIP
> The Missouri Conservation Department publishes a number of good, inexpensive books that deal with the state's recreational activities: hiking, floating, bird watching, and nature study. They are available at bookstores and the state's four nature centers. If you are coming to Branson from the north, stop at the Springfield Nature Center at 4600 S. Chrismon Rd. on the south side of Springfield, just a mile off U.S. Hwy. 65 (see our Daytrips chapter).

The Buffalo National River south of Branson offers hiking and canoeing.

Photo: A.C. Haralson/Arkansas Dept. of Parks & Tourism

partment regularly sets prescribed, controlled burns of sections of the glades.

Though they seem barren, glades harbor a vast array of plants and wildlife. Spring rains produce a profusion of wild flowers, including the Missouri state flower, the yellow Missouri primrose, which thrives in the rocky, thin, dolomite soil. When you hike glades in the spring, look for some of the unusual wildflowers and specially adapted plants such as prickly pear cactus and the endangered glade bladderwort with its tiny yellow flowers. More common are May apples, pussy toes, serviceberry, Solomon's seal, and Indian paintbrush. Other seasons produce fewer and less showy but equally interesting flowers. Even the hot summer can provide an interesting and pleasurable hike.

Keep your eyes open for our largest spider, the tarantula, especially in the fall when they seem more noticeable as they search for a winter home. The tarantula, black or brown and very hairy, can be 5 inches across. Though they look scary and they can bite, they are generally harmless. Good advice is not to turn over rocks, which can uncover spiders, scorpions, and the black and orange giant centipede, which can be 10 inches long. Some of these have potentially fatal bites or stings, so you are better off leaving them alone—and so are the critters.

You may see our fastest snake, the slim coachwhip snake, which can reach lengths of 6 feet and slither faster than you can run. You'll also find other reptiles: skinks, fence lizards, garter snakes, three-toed box turtles, and eastern collared lizards. Locals call the 10-inch long critters that look like a miniature T. Rex, especially when they run so fast they rear up and run only on their hind legs, "mountain boomers." However, the lizard is voiceless, not at all like some of the spring tree frogs you may hear that "baa" like sheep. You may even see a roadrunner, which preys on the glade's reptiles and insects.

The glades an interesting, wonderful, and fragile ecosystem. We love to have visitors, and we want you to learn about our unusual areas. However, do respect them. Follow the old adage: "Take only pictures. Kill only time. Leave only footprints."

Buffalo National River
402 N. Walnut St. Ste. 136, Harrison, Ark.
• (870) 741-5443

The Buffalo River in the Boston Mountains is the last major undammed river in Arkansas, and it's going to stay that way. The 97,750 acres that make up the Buffalo National River and its tributaries became a national park in 1972. There had been plans all this century to build a dam on the river, and the Corps of Engineers had plans to build several dams on the Buffalo during the 1930s. World War II put those plans on hold. After the war when the dam projects were reconsidered, a coalition of locals and canoeists, who had discovered the whitewater experience of the Buffalo, made an outcry that called national attention to

Arkansas's scenic gem. The Buffalo National River Park was the result. When you are in Branson, you can glimpse the peaks of the Boston Mountains from the Inspiration Tower on The Shepherd of the Hills Homestead (see our Attractions chapter). It is worth a daytrip to hike the park or float a portion of the 148-mile Buffalo River. The bluffs, rising from the water's edge to a sheer rockface height of 400 to 500 feet and an additional 300 feet of outcroppings and trees, are best experienced from the river while dipping your paddle in its clear waters (see our Lakes and Rivers chapter), but a bird's eye view of the river from Big Bluff or Jim Bluff while hiking can be an equally thrilling experience. You can walk through thick forests, shallow-soiled glades and spring-filled hollows.

The Buffalo National River in Arkansas is a recent addition to the nation's park system, and development of walking and hiking trails is progressing as people recognize that the park offers interesting and challenging hiking and walking as well as floating. There are more than 100 miles of trails some maintained by the park, and others unmaintained (old logging roads, footpaths, etc.), with more planned. Some trails are for horse riders only. Eventually, the Buffalo River Trail will traverse the entire length of the park. Some trails are short walks that provide access to a particular bluff or interesting geological feature, but others offer miles of hiking along the 148-mile course of the river for those who want to experience the Ozarks before development. A hike along the river trails takes you up on the bluffs and provides spectacular views of the river, such as the one from Big Bluff, which at over 500 feet, is the highest bluff in the Ozarks. From some of the river's bluffs, you might catch a glimpse of the Park's elk herd. The aptly named Goat's Trail, 350 feet above the river along Big Bluff provides a heart-in-your-mouth hike. All park land is open to walkers and hikers, and you may to walk up the bed of a stream that enters the Buffalo.

The hike up Hemmed-In Hollow, a large box canyon, provides a glimpse of one of the highest waterfalls (200 feet) east of the Rockies, and it is always spectacular after a heavy rain. A hike into Lost Valley (just above Ponca) and back can take half a day. A walk into Hawksbill Crag (near Boxley) is shorter, and the view of the upper Buffalo River valley is spectacular. Standing on the crag, you can watch eagles and buzzards drifting in flight below you. Hiking is most popular in the fall after the first frost (when ticks and chiggers have been eliminated), and with the mild winters and the greater vis-

RECREATION AND
THE OUTDOORS

Hemmed in Hollow Buffalo in the Buffalo National River is a sight worth the hike.

Photo: A.C. Haralson/Arkansas Dept. of Parks & Tourism

ibility because the leaves have fallen, hikers can experience a facet of the Ozarks that is unavailable to summer-only hikers. Before venturing on the hiking paths of the Buffalo National River, know your limits and stamina and make certain you provide yourself with an up-to-date map of the areas you plan to hike.

Information about hiking trails can be found in *Buffalo River Hiking Trails* by Tim Ernst. The little book is dedicated to Neil Compton, "the man most responsible for saving the Buffalo River." Write Tim Ernst Photography, 411 Patricia Lane, Fayetteville, Ark. 72703. The park also publishes *Buffalo National River Currents* annually. This magazine is chock full of pictures and advice, and it has the latest information about the river and hiking trails. It is free at any park office. You can call the park headquarters at the number above for information about the river and the park and maps of the hiking trails. They'll be glad to send you an information packet about the Buffalo River.

The Buffalo River is just an hour and a half drive south of Branson. Park headquarters are in Harrison, Arkansas. Take U.S. 65 to Harrison. There are a number of Arkansas highways that enter the 148-mile long park, including Arkansas Highways 43, 7, 123, 374, and 14.

Busiek State Forest and Wildlife Area
U.S. Hwy. 65, 15 miles north of Branson
• (417) 895-6880

This rectangular 2,505-acre site has topography typical of the Ozark plateau, with steep, rocky hills and gravel-bottom creeks. Woods Fork of Bull Creek flows across 2½ miles of the area, and Camp Creek flows 2½ miles to its confluence with Woods Fork. More than 90 percent of the area is forested. It is open to camping, hiking, bird watching, hunting, outdoor photography, and picnicking (no tables are provided). There are self-guided nature trails. An unattended public shooting range is a quarter-mile west of Mo. 65 near the access road.

You can obtain information and a map of the Busiek Wildlife Area by writing the Mark Twain Forest district forester at 2630 N. Mayfair St., Springfield, Mo. 65803 or calling the number above.

To get to the Busiek Wildlife area, go 14 miles

north of Branson on U.S. 65 and make the first right (east) immediately after crossing Camp Creek. You'll see the sign on your right.

Dewey Short Visitors Center
Mo. Hwy. 165 • (417) 334-4101

Situated at the south end of Table Rock Dam, the center is a great place to learn about Ozark flora by hitting the short .8-mile wheelchair accessible nature trail that winds by the lake shore. The center itself has wildlife exhibits (they usually have raccoons, snakes, insects, and other local wildlife), films, wildlife art shows and photography exhibits, special lectures, and other educational programs offered by the U.S. Army Corps of Engineers. There's a 20-minute free film about the construction of the dam shown on request. You can take a guided tour ($2 per person) into the innards of Table Rock Dam for an interesting and eerie experience—a great way to spend an afternoon when it's too hot to hike. Named after the Missouri Congressman Dewey Short who had lobbied his colleagues for years to build flood control dams on the White River valley, the center is one of the 10 most-visited centers operated by the Corps. It's a great place—and a free one—to take the kids for the obligatory educational experience (see our Kidstuff chapter).

Dogwood Canyon Nature Park
Mo. Hwy. 86 W., Lampe, Mo.
• (417) 335-2777, (417) 770-5983

Dogwood Canyon is a 10,000-acre private wilderness refuge developed by John L. Morris, founder of the Bass Pro Shops. This incredible area is readily accessible to nature lovers. Crystal-clear Dogwood Creek flows through a high-bluffed, narrow canyon. The ridges on either side are forested with large trees. You can see herds of buffalo and elk—and Texas longhorns. You can learn about Fire Pit Cave and Great Spirit Rock Shelter where the oldest human remains in Missouri have been found.

Guest attractions include a Civil War museum, a long-abandoned lead mine worked by early settlers, the Dogwood Canyon General Store, and a handcrafted covered bridge built by the Amish. Hikers pay a fee of $7.50 per person, but you don't have to

INSIDERS' TIP
If you're in the Branson area during the slow month of February, venture out and see the vultures at the Shepherd of the Hills Fish Hatchery located below Table Rock Dam. It has become the winter gathering of hundreds of turkey vultures and black vultures, and the hatchery visitor center has a slide show about the birds. Call (417) 334-4865 for information.

be a fit mountaineer climber to experience the beauties of this Ozark area. You can take a guided tour of the canyon via a Jeep-pulled tram. In 1999 the 1-hour tour was $12.50 and the 2-hour tour was $17.50. To get to Dogwood Canyon from Branson, take U.S. 65 south to Mo. 86 and follow it west, going over the Long Creek Arm of Table Rock Lake toward Blue Eye. You'll see the turnoff to Dogwood Canyon a mile after you pass the Mo. 86 and Mo. 13 junction.

Drury-Mincy Conservation Area
Mo. Hwy. 76, 6 miles east of Branson
• (417) 334-4830

This 5,559-acre conservation area in southern Taney County is only minutes from downtown Branson. It is named for early landowner Frank Drury and the settlement of Mincy. It was the Missouri Conservation Department's first deer refuge. By the 1920s deer numbers had dwindled to the point that Missouri could claim only 14 herds. One of these lived in the Mincy area on the private Skaggs Game Preserve, and Frank Drury worked with the department to increase deer numbers. From 1939 to 1959 deer from the preserve were successfully used to restore populations statewide. Turkey from the preserve also provided the stock in the state-wide restoration projects during the 1960s. The Department leased the land in 1939 and purchased it in 1987. Fox, Bee, and Mincy creeks meander through stands of wild cane on their way to Bull Shoals Lake in this wilderness area, which is in the heart of the White River glade region. It is open for hunting, frogging, and stream fishing, hiking, bird watching, and nature study, picnicking, and outdoor photography. Camping is allowed on the Mincy portion only. The area has miles of foot trails for hiking. You can obtain information and a map of the Drury-Mincy Conservation Area by writing the Drury-Mincy Area Manager, HCR 2, Box 1040, Kirbyville, Mo. 65679 or by calling (417) 334-4830.

To get to the preserve, go 3 miles east of Branson on Mo. 76. As soon as you pass the Kirbyville School, turn south (right) on Mo. Highway J, which will take you right into the preserve. At Mincy you see the signs for the preserve.

Glade Top Trail
Mo. Hwy. 125, Bradleyville
• (417) 683-4428

The Glade Top Trail in the Mark Twain National Forest is Missouri's only National Scenic Byway. The 23-mile trail weaves along the narrow ridge tops and glades above the surrounding rolling countryside. The Glade Top Trail's historical significance is very important to many of the Douglas, Taney, and Ozark county residents who worked for the Civilian Conservation Corps in the late 1930s, and the trail has changed little since the CCC workers constructed the two-lane, all-weather gravel road. Now paved, the trail is a scenic nature getaway from Branson, and it provides an excuse to pack a picnic lunch and see the country. The drive is especially pretty in the spring when numerous dogwood, smoke, and red bud trees are in bloom. Fall has its own spectacular show and provides a flaming fall review (see our Annual Events chapter) and an excuse for another drive.

You can obtain more information about the Glade Top Trail and a map by writing the Mark Twain Forest Ava Ranger District, P.O. Box 186, Ava, Mo. 65608 or by calling the number above. The easiest way to access the Glade Top Trail from Branson is by taking Mo. 75 east past Bradleyville, turning south (right) on Mo. 125 and then crossing Beaver Creek. About 4 miles south of the junction of Mo. 125 and U.S. 160, you'll turn left on the Glade Top Trail (Forest Service Road 149).

Hercules Glades Wilderness Area
Eastern Taney County
• (417) 683-4428

Just 20 miles east of the glitter of The Strip in Branson is the Hercules Glades Wilderness. It's a varied and complex area of woods, glades, balds, springs, and creeks. This beautiful but hard-to-make-a-living area was so undisturbed that the glades were declared a Federal Wilderness in 1964 and are protected by federal law.

INSIDERS' TIP

Don't try to transplant wildflowers and native shrubs back home. Most don't transplant well when in full bloom (when you'll notice them) or they thrive in a very limited microenvironment with specific soil conditions. Besides, it's illegal to dig up native plants along Missouri highways. You can get many varieties of wildflower seeds and plants and learn if your planned home for them is suitable by calling Missouri Wildflowers Nursery at (573) 496-3492.

Meandering is evident beneath the ground in a cave cut by water in Ozark Karst topography.

Photo: Silver Dollar City

The Hercules area of 12,315 acres, more than 20 square miles, falls within the Ava District of the Mark Twain National Forest. If the neon lights of The Strip don't attract you—or if you want a diversion from them—the Hercules Glades is worth a trip for a day or longer. Hik-ing and horseback trails are the only way into the glades. Camping is available in areas of the surrounding Mark Twain National Forest and also just south of the glades at the U.S. Army Corps of Engineers campground at Beaver Creek access of Bull Shoals Lake. Primitive camping is available anywhere in the glades, as long as you are at least 100 feet off a trail. Don't bring electrical equipment such as radios or cell phones, as such items are forbidden and lessen the wilderness experience for you and spoil it for others. Campfires are permitted, but be certain to obliterate all traces of your campfire and site.

In the spring the glades have wet-weather springs and branches, and the hillsides are covered with a profusion of rare and beautiful flowers. Spring rains show off the cascading waterfalls, shoals, and splash pools that eons of time have cut into the limestone bedrock. The glades contain sculptured totems and gargoyles of limestone, weathered into fantastic shapes by time. Spring is the most comfortable time to hike in the area.

During the summer the shallow-soiled south-facing hillsides become almost semidesert, with a whole array of plants and animals. You'll see yucca, prickly pears, lizards, and roadrunners. Summer hikes can be hot so pack in plenty of water.

In the fall you can experience the vast array of colors contrasted with the greens of cedars and junipers as well as a totally different crop of late wildflowers. The fall season offers a more comfortable hike than in summer. Winter provides special attractions, and after a wet snow or an ice storm, the area is transformed into glittering beauty. Many people who like landscape photography find winter their favorite time to explore the glades.

The Hercules Glades lie between Mo. 125 and U.S. 160, with Mo. 76 forming the eastern border. Tower Trailhead is on Mo. 125, 8 miles south of Mo. 76. Coy Bald Trailhead is on Fairview Church Road, a gravel road 3 miles north of U.S. 160 and Mo. 125. For more information you can call the Ava Ranger District at the number above. You can also obtain information from the Mark Twain National Forest supervisor in Rolla, Missouri, by calling (573) 364-4621, and you can purchase U.S. Geological Survey maps for $4 each. Ask for the Hilda and Protem NE Quadrangle Maps.

Current and Jacks Fork Rivers
Ozark National Scenic Riverways,
P.O. Box 490, Van Buren, Mo. 63965
• (573) 323-4236

It's a long drive over to the Big Springs country, in a whole different watershed where the river flows east, but it's a pretty area—and pretty spectacular. It offers hiking and floating (see our Lakes and Rivers chapter). The area is 125 miles east of Springfield, but since U.S.

Highway 6 through Van Buren is a main conduit for folks coming to the Branson area from southern Illinois and Kentucky, you may want to make it a stop when you're coming (or going) that direction. A two-day float trip on the Jacks Fork or Current River could be your most memorable experience. The Current is fed by some of the largest springs in the world, and so it is floatable even in our dry summer months. The Jacks Fork, its major tributary, has less water but offers some excellent spring and early summer floating as it flows through a canyon in its upper reaches. The middle Jacks Fork valley is home to herds of wild horses, now protected by the National Park Service.

Like the Buffalo National River in Arkansas, the Current and Jacks Fork Rivers Ozark National Scenic Riverways is a recent addition to the national park system, and since most people come to float the river, development of walking and hiking trails has been slow and a feature not widely publicized. However, more and more, people are recognizing that the parkland along the river has interesting features not easily accessible to floaters, and so hiking is becoming more popular.

Currently there are 43 trails covering 48 miles, with more being developed, and existing trails are being upgraded. There are 14.2 miles of horse trails. Some hiking trails are merely short walks that provide access to a particular or interesting feature, but others offer miles of hiking for those who want to backpack in and camp and experience the Ozarks close-up and personal. Walking the Jacks Fork trails provides contact with the quiet environment of the Ozarks that author Sue Hubbell wrote about with such awe and admiration in *A Country Year*.

A hike along the river trails takes you up on the bluffs and provides spectacular views of the river and the valley below. You can look down on twisted junipers—scrawny, gnarled evergreens that rival California's redwood tree as the nation's oldest living plant. Frequently, they are draped with fisherman's beard (a plant much like Spanish moss) that provides an Old Southlike atmosphere. In the spring, bright flowers, including the intense yellow of wild coreopsis, dot the shallow soil of bluff tops. You might catch a view of the wild horses in the valley below. Along the trail, you may see whitetail deer, a reclusive bobcat or red fox, and hear the calls of crows or a pileated woodpecker. Since all land is open to walkers and hikers, you may want to leave the trail where a small stream enters the river and hike up the stream course where you can catch glimpses of ferns, wild orchids, and other shade loving plants. Such excursions often provide intimate glimpses of wildlife and serene sights of quiet pools or little waterfalls in a setting reminiscent of a Japanese garden. Hiking along the bluffs of the rivers often provides you glimpses of some of the state's many caves. Jam-Up Cave (see our History chapter) has an awe-inspiring entrance. Trails closer to the river are cooler and provide intimate contact with the many springs the feed the river. Before venturing on the hiking paths, make certain you provide yourself with an up-to-date map of the area you plan to hike.

Contact the National Park Service, Ozark National Scenic Riverways, P.O. Box 490, Van Buren, Mo. 63956, (573) 323-4236. They can send you an official map of the river with the hiking trails and recreation areas as well as a current list of canoe rental concessionaires.

Piney Creek Wilderness
Northeastern Stone County
• (417) 847-2144

Cut over for lumber and railroad ties in the late 1800s, this 8,142-acre preserve has reverted to its original primitive state. The area is the entire watershed for Piney Creek and a favorite haunt for local hikers, naturalists, and bird watchers who prize seclusion and solitude. The wilderness has 13 miles of primitive trail. Piney Creek is crystal clear and runs over gravel beds and solid rock. The holes at beds and beneath root wads harbor fish, turtles, frogs, and mink. Songbirds nest along the creek, while the ridges are favorite places for hawks, eagles, and buzzards.

You can obtain additional information on Piney Creek Wilderness Area by writing the Cassville Ranger District, P.O. Box 310, Cassville, Mo. 65625, or by calling them at the number above. A map of the wilderness with trails is available from the office for $3. U.S. Geological Survey maps of the area can be purchased for $4 each by calling the Mark Twain National Forest supervisor's office at (573) 364-4621, which is in Rolla, Missouri. Ask for the Shell Knob and Cape Fair Quadrangle maps.

Roaring River State Park
Mo. Hwy. 112 • (417) 873-2539

A river roars through this state park, just an hour's drive from Branson. A $5 million lodge overlooks it, and trout fishing in the cold, spring-fed waters is always good at this 3,354-acre park deep in the forested hollows of Barry County. Stonework laid by the hands of CCC

workers over 70 years ago still channel the fury of Roaring River Spring and hatchery. You can catch a nature program, enjoy the cool air at the spring (20.4 million gallons per day), fish, horseback ride (a one-hour trail, $12 per person), swim, dine, bike or hike the park's seven trails, including the Devil's Kitchen Trail, a challenging 1.5 mile trail that climbs 325 feet to the ridge top. The name is derived from an odd rock outcrop that forms a room-like enclosure. You may want to take a flashlight to explore some of the shallow trailside caves. If you're not too tired, you can take in the show about the Mountain Maid of Roaring River, (417) 847-4639, in the evening.

Nearby Cassville has some flea markets and antique shops you can check out, and the Pea Ridge National Military Park at Pea Ridge, Ark. on Ark.72 isn't far away. The park and some area attractions make a good daytrip (see our Daytrips chapter).

Ruth and Paul Henning State Conservation Area
Mo. Hwy. 76 W. • (417) 334-3324

One of the nicest aspects of Branson is that you are so close to two totally different worlds. Only a half-mile from where 76 Country Boulevard ends with the Country Tonite Theatre is the near-wilderness experience of the Ruth and Paul Henning Conservation Area, a 1,434-acre preserve of glades, hills, and valleys between the west end of The Strip and The Shepherd of the Hills Homestead—and it's within the Branson city limits! From the top of Dewey Bald, there is a lovely view of Mutton Hollow, Roark Creek Valley, and the lights of The Strip back east. Because the area is so close to activities on The Strip, it's easy to work in a half-day to get your exercise or to let the kids burn of extra energy.

Development further west of The Strip was effectively stopped when the land, owned by Paul and Ruth Henning, was donated to the Missouri Conservation Department. Paul Henning is known as the producer of "The Beverly Hillbillies" and "Petticoat Junction" TV series. Ruth is a native of Eldon, Missouri, near the Lake of the Ozarks.

Features of this conservation spot were immortalized in The Shepherd of the Hills: Dewey Bald, Boulder Bald, Sammy Lane's Lookout, Mutton Hollow, and Little Pete's Cave.

In the parking lot is a display that illustrates plants and animals you might see in the preserve and explains the ecology of glade areas. The Henning Conservation Area has several short hiking trails. Be sure to take your camera, not only for the great vistas but also for the unusual plants and animals you might encounter.

The 1.75-mile Streamside Trail may take you about an hour. The Glade Exploration Trail is a 1-mile loop of this trail that takes you around the top of an Ozarks glade where you can see first hand the grasses, cacti, and shrubs found on a glade. A half-mile section leads to the top of Dewey Bald where you can climb a fire tower for a panoramic view. There is a 1-mile section of the trail that takes you to an overlook deck of the area and back to the parking lot where you started.

A longer loop, the Henning Homesteads Trail, constructed primarily by Boy Scout Troop 2001, is 3.7 miles long. It is a moderately difficult trail and should take you about three hours to complete. You can pick up a brochure before you start that describes some of the features of the walk, which takes you by hand dug wells, fieldstone home foundations, log barns, springs, and other relics of some of the early homesteaders in the area.

During the season a naturalist is on duty to answer questions about flora and fauna and lead descriptive walks. This is a natural area, so smoking, fires, fireworks, or camping are not permitted.

Shepherd of the Hills Fish Hatchery
Mo. Hwy. 165 • (417) 334-4865

The Shepherd of the Hills Fish Hatchery is the largest trout-rearing facility in Missouri, producing more than 400,000 pounds of trout each year. Almost 80 percent of the production is released into nearby Lake Taneycomo. The hatchery complex includes a free visitors center where you can learn more about trout culture, aquatic life, fishing, and wildlife resource management. Fishing access areas and public boat launch on nearby Lake Taneycomo are available. Trails near the hatchery are appropriate for hiking and wildlife viewing, and many locals make the short drive just for a walk along the lake and amidst the wildlife. The area has become a winter roost for the hundreds of turkey and black vultures, sea gulls, red wing blackbirds, and robins. Missouri's state bird, the bluebird, is often seen around the hatchery, as are fish predators like the great blue heron, green heron, and belted kingfisher. The hatchery area is also home to a variety of other wildlife, including deer, turkey squirrel, raccoon, fox, mink, muskrat, and beaver.

The hatchery is a good place for the kids to get a close-up look at native Ozark fish in the large aquariums and feed the trout in the hatchery pools (see our Kidstuff chapter). Picnicking in allowed, and tables are located near Lake Taneycomo. The hatchery is 6 miles southwest of Branson on Mo. 165 just below Table Rock Dam.

Table Rock State Park
Off Mo. Hwy. 165 near Table Rock Dam
• (417) 334-4104

Table Rock State Park consists of 356 acres and is operated by the Missouri Department of Natural Resources. It's just south of the *Showboat Branson Belle*'s White River Landing on Mo. 165. For more information about the full-service marina, including scuba diving and sailboat rentals, see our Lakes and Rivers chapter; for more on the camping facilities, check our Campgrounds and RV Parks chapter.

The park has several miles of walking trails along the lake front and in the forest, a boat launch area (at which people frequently swim), and picnic tables, a covered pavilion with barbecue grills and tables, and playground equipment, including a volleyball court and softball field.

You can obtain information about Table Rock State Park and other parks operated by the Missouri Department of Natural Resources by calling (800) 334-6946 or writing P.O. Box 178, Jefferson City, Mo. 65102.

Wilderness Tours

Ozark Ecotours
Jasper, Ark. • (870) 446-5898

If you want to explore the countryside but don't know where to start or don't have any wilderness experience, Ozark Ecotours is for you. Funded by private and corporate grants, Ozark Ecotours is a project of the Newton County (Arkansas) Resource Council. Ecotours offers guided hiking and exploration tours, primarily in the Buffalo River region. You can take an easy 2-mile hike, a difficult 9-mile trek, or a guided canoe trip where you learn to read the water and handle a paddle. You can become a spelunker and explore a wild cave, learn camping and outdoor-cooking skills, hone map and compass skills, or learn to identify native trees, shrubs, and flowers. There are a variety of these outdoor, guided seminars, and they vary from season to season. The tours are limited to 12 participants, so every guest gets individual attention. The cost is around $50 per person, including a picnic lunch on a gravel bar or a buffet lunch on a bluff for the full-day tours. For a detailed brochure with descriptions of the latest outdoor offerings, write Ozark Ecotours, P.O. Box 513, Jasper, Ark. 72641, or call (870) 446-5898.

Biking

Because the topography and the traffic, Branson is not a very friendly place for bikers to enjoy their sport, pleasure biking isn't very popular here. Rides along Branson's Taneycomo lakefront from North Back Park to Sunset Park are level and pose few traffic problems. Although it's not a good idea to venture out on The Strip with a road bike, a number of the less traveled roads and highways can be a good deal of fun to ride, so we don't discourage you from bringing your road bike. Mountain biking is beginning to catch on in this area, as rugged individuals with their rugged bikes find that rides in our mountainous terrain are equal to those found in many other areas of the nation. If you are willing to drive a few miles, you'll find some pretty trails.

In the works is a proposal for lakeside bike trail along portions of Table Rock Lake. It will connect with the bike trail that is being constructed with the Ozark Highroad, which will loop around Branson. In the future when you come to Branson, you'll find that we cater to bikers better than we do now.

While in the area, you can always stop at DBA bike store (see listing) and talk to Craig Erickson, who is more than willing to provide maps and suggest rides for road bikers and share information about area trails for mountain bikers.

DBA: Downhill Bikes and Accessories
1200 Mo. Hwy. 248 W., Branson
• (417) 335-4455

Owner-manager Craig Erickson is one of the area's biggest fans of mountain biking, and he is spreading the word that this sport is fun and a great way to see the landscape. His store car-

ries a variety of bikes—Trek, Giant, and Raleigh—and biking accessories. If you find yourself in need of bike repair, DBA can take care of you. DBA also carries Dagger kayaks for those who may want to try the spring whitewater of Bull Creek or Swan Creek or the quiet coves and inlets of Table Rock Lake (see our Lakes and Rivers chapter).

Bowling

Dogwood Lanes
2126 Mo. Hwy. 76 E. • (417) 336-2695

Dogwood Lanes is a nice, clean 16-lane bowling alley and video arcade near the Holiday Hills Golf Course. The lanes host both day and night leagues and open bowling with glow-in-the-dark pins. The place is a favorite hangout for area teenagers on Saturday nights for Rock 'n' Bowl, when you bowl with black lights to rock and roll music. They have a snack shop and a small pro shop. In 1998 charges were $2.35 a game and $1.25 for shoe rental. Dogwood Lanes is located 1 mile east of the Lake Taneycomo bridge on Mo. 76.

INSIDERS' TIP

There are only four members of the pit viper family found in the Ozarks: the copperhead, timber rattlesnake, and the pygmy rattlesnake, all found usually in wooded or glade areas, and the cottonmouth, found along creeks and rivers. You're not likely to encounter any snakes at all, for they are shy and unobtrusive. If you do happen on a snake, don't bother it. Give it a wide berth and go on your way. You will have probably scared the snake more than it scared you.

Golf

We never thought that people would actually be coming to Branson just for the golf, but now that Branson has eight courses, we've begun to attract golf fanatics. If you are interested in golf, it's easy to work in some tee time during the day and the shows at night. Many of the new courses are part of resort complexes, so you could have a condo on the fairway for your stay. It was Missouri's Mark Twain who said, "golf was a good walk spoiled," but some of the newer courses are beautiful themselves. Coupled with the natural Ozark scenery, they make for a great walk even if you aren't a gung-ho golfer. If you're the competitive type, local courses give a wide range of challenges: tricky doglegs, narrow fairways, and shots over water that will test the best. We've listed clubs that are open to the public as well as to their guests

RECREATION AND THE OUTDOORS

(who often obtain reduced rates and priority on tee times). All courses accept credit cards. Information and fees are for 1999, but it's still best to call before you go.

Branson Creek Golf Club
144 Branson Creek Dr.
- **(417) 339-4653, (888) 772-9990**
- **www.bransoncreekgolf.com**

Branson Creek is Branson's newest golf course, and the last nine holes were opened in 1999 and received rave reviews. All 18 holes will be ready to play by the summer of 2000. The course was designed by noted course designer Tom Fazio, his first venture in a course in the Ozarks. He has designed such prestigious courses as Las Vegas' Shadow Creek, The Quarry in La Quinta, California, Champion Hills in North Carolina, and Hammock Dunes in Florida. Given virtually free rein as to cost and "as much land as needed," Fazio designed a course that he describes as a "top-notch world class course that is certain to be among America's top 100 courses." What he designed is a 7,000 yard, par 71, championship-level golf course that incorporates the natural terrain of the Ozark Mountains, creating exciting challenges for both low and high handicap players. Greens are bent grass with zoysia grass fairways. The 18th hole has been described by Fazio as "the Midwest version of the 18th hole at Pebble Beach—a tricky par 5 that doglegs left—but in place of water, there's a sea of trees."

The course is part of the network of more than 40 courses managed by Troon Golf worldwide. Facility Manager is Perry Leslie and Head Golf Professional is Tony J. Gill. The course is a spikeless course, and course rules require "appropriate golf attire." There is a driving range and practice facilities. Greens fees, which includes golf cart, vary from $65 to $110, depending on the season. Branson Creek is still under development, but the course currently has a pro shop and snack shop. Once constructed, the clubhouse with elevated patios and decks will sit high atop a hill, commanding a panoramic view that will overlook the golf course and offer a fabulous vista of Branson to the north. Branson Creek is located four miles south of Branson on the east side of U.S. 65, between Mo. 165 and 265.

INSIDERS' TIP

Want a cheap meal and some inexpensive fun? Pack a picnic lunch and go to one of our city parks, Shepherd of the Hills Fish Hatchery or Table Rock State Park by the Dam. Most have playground equipment for kids to work off excess energy.

Don Gardner Pitch and Putt Public Golf Course
201 Compton Dr.

Eiserman Park, near the Branson Community Center, is 1 acre that includes a basketball court, playground, and covered pavilion. Adjacent to Eiserman Park in Branson near the Branson Community Center is the nine-hole Don Gardner Pitch and Putt Public Golf Course. It's named after an early golfer who brought the sport to Branson when he built the Holiday Hills Golf Course in 1939. Each hole is a par 3, and lots of folks sharpen their short iron skills there. The course is open to the public and costs $5 for residents and $8 for non-residents to play the nine holes.

Holiday Hills Resort & Golf Club
630 E. Rockford Dr.
- **(417) 334-4838, (800) 225-2422**
- **www.holidayhillsgolf.com**

Holiday Hills is one place in Branson you can drive all day and never be stuck in traffic! On Mo. 76, 3 miles east of downtown Branson, the city's first gold course is now one of its newest. Chicago golf pro Don Gardner and his wife, Jill, moved to Branson and established the course in 1938, but a 1997 multi-million-dollar renovation has brought it up to PGA standards. In the old days Forrest Tucker and Charlton Heston flew in to the grass strip that was nearby and joined Don Gardner in a threesome, and now many of Branson's music stars who live here play the new course. It has bentgrass greens and hybrid bermuda grass fairways and tees. This 5771-yard public course is now par 68, with more than 50 large bunkers and water obstacles on 6 holes. The course meets the challenges of all levels of golfers, but hole No. 1, a par 4, might intimidate you with its long 432-yard drive with water on the left and sand on the right. However if you do well on this difficult hole, you may have your confidence boosted to meet lesser challenges!

The course has a restaurant and bar, the Grille on the Green, and a fully stocked golf shop that offers club repair and club rentals. Greens fees including a cart are $58 for 18 holes in the mornings ($48 after 11:00 AM) and $35 for nine holes. Holiday Hills is a spikeless course, and a collared shirt is required for play. Holiday

Hills also offers condo rentals and golf vacation packages. (See our Accommodations chapter.)

Kimberling Golf Course
1 Lakeshore Dr., Kimberling City
• (417) 739-4370

This is a great nine-hole golf course if you don't have much time or want to work on your short game, says resident PGA professional Vince Alfonso,Jr. The 2100-yard, par 34 course is in the midst of some grand mountainous terrain. The course has no par 5s, but hole No. 6 with a hard left dogleg is a very difficult par 4.

The course is open seven days a week and charges $11 per person plus a $6 per person cart fee, but carts are not required, so you can get the full exercise benefit of the game. Pull carts are available. It has a pro shop, putting green, the Memphis Café (specializing in Memphis-style barbecue) and banquet facilities.

To find the Kimberling Golf Course, turn south on Mo. 13 at the intersection of Mo. 76 and Mo. 13 in Branson West. As you're coming down the long hill into Kimberling City, you'll turn right at the first light.

Ledgestone Golf Course and Country Club
Intersection of Mo. Hwy. 76 W. and
Mo. Hwy. 365, StoneBridge Village
• (417) 336-1786, (800) 817-8663

This course is the heart of the Branson area's newest gated community of StoneBridge, which is near Silver Dollar City. The 18-hole, 6,800-yard, par 71 championship-style course was designed by the renowned golf course architectural firm of Ault, Clark and Associates. It was nominated as Best New Course in 1995 by Golf Digest. When you play this course, you never have to see other groups because there are no adjoining holes anywhere on the course. Much of the course meanders along the upper reaches of Roark Creek and incorporates its still pools, bluffs, and rock outcroppings in to the overall course design. Ledgestone, however, is more than just a pretty face; it is one of the Midwest's more demanding courses, with features like narrow, tree-lined fairways, sand bunkers and numerous water hazards. Hole No. 15 is a real challenge. It's a 177-yard, par 3 hole that has you teeing off from a 100-foot-high cliff.

Along with golf you can enjoy the large 20,000-square-foot clubhouse with pro shop, restaurant, activity rooms and exercise and fitness areas.

Greens fees are $80 during the week, $90 on the weekend and holidays, including cart fee.

The course's driving range is for use by people playing the course that day. There is also an 8,000-square-foot putting green. Ledgestone takes tee time reservations up to one week in advance.

Oakmont Community Golf Course
2722 Mo. Hwy. 86, Ridgedale
• (417) 334-1572

The Oakmont Course is located on Mo. 86 right across from the turnoff to Big Cedar Lodge. Established in 1987, this public course of 2,939 yards is par 36 for 9 holes and can provide a memorable short round. Oakmont's fairways are bermudagrass and mixed grass with bentgrass greens. Local golfers rate holes No. 2 and No. 4 as the most difficult. Oakmont's Martin Tate says No. 4 is a 395-yard, par 5 challenge that has a dogleg left requiring a 190-yard drive from the tee down a narrow fairway.

Greens fees at Oakmont are $12 for 9 holes and $17 for 18 holes. The cart rental fee (optional rental) is $12 for a 9-hole round and $17 for 18 holes. The course has a small pro shop and snack bar.

Pointe Royale Golf Course
142 Pointe Royale Dr.
• (417) 334-4477, (800) 962-4710
• www.pointroyalegolf.com

Pointe Royale advertises the course as "where the stars live and play." It's true that Branson's first gated community is home to a number of Branson's stars; and it's true that Andy Williams, Moe Bandy, and Mickey Gilley play regularly at the course, which was established on Lake Taneycomo just below Table Rock Dam in 1986. The course is right across from the Welk Champagne Theatre and Resort Complex on Mo. 165.

The 18-hole, 6,250-yard course is a par 70. It has bentgrass greens and bermudagrass fairways, with out-of-bounds stakes lining most holes. It offers one of the wettest courses in the Midwest-12 holes with water obstacles-plus a number with sand traps. Veteran golfers contend that you'll use every club in your bag if you play the course properly. One of the most challenging holes is the last one, a par 4, 411-yard uphill hole that requires a 200-yard drive to get to the top. Costs for playing at Pointe Royale are $65 for 18 holes and $35 for 9 holes. Prices include required cart.

The course has a complete pro shop and offers lessons and club rentals. Pro shop owner and golf pro Jeff Wallster says the course is challenging because it is hilly and has so many water hazards, but he is always available for advice. The Pointe Royale course has a restaurant and clubhouse with meeting rooms.

Pointe Royale offers weekly and nightly condo rentals or golf with condo packages. Call (800) 962-4710 for reservations and information.

Taneycomo Golf Club
379 Links Lane, Forsyth • (417) 546-5454

This 2819-yard, par 35, 9-hole regulation course is found in Forsyth, the county seat of Taney County, and is one of the older courses in the country, dating from the early '50s. It has bentgrass greens and bermudagrass fairways. If you are used to the spacious fairways and the long drives of newer courses, you'll find the shorter, narrow fairways and the small greens built on steeply sloped hills and real challenge. It's a good course to practice your short game.

Taneycomo Golf Club also has a driving range, where a bucket of balls will cost you $4.75. Greens fees are $13.50 for nine holes, $20 for 18 holes, with cart rental $11.50 per nine holes, though the course welcomes walkers. No tee time is necessary and soft spikes are required.

Thousand Hills Golf Club
245 S. Wildwood Dr.
• (417) 334-4553, (800) 864-4145
• www.thousandhills.com

This public course was inaugurated by Andy Williams in 1995, and it's just over the next ridge from his Moon River Theatre on one of Branson's newer roads, Wildwood Drive. It's one of two courses within the city limits.

The 18-hole course has a championship tee of 5111 yards and is par 64 with bentgrass greens and Zoysia fairways and tees. Wildwood Branch meanders through the course to nearby Cooper Creek and provides some special kinds of water hazards. Golf Pro Barry Storie says hole No. 3 has been described as "the hole from hell"—a 460-yard, par 4 that has a long 260-yard drive to the green. The green, carved out of a bluff, has a bluff in front of it and a bluff behind it. Miss it and you're up the creek by being in the creek or on the cliff. Hole No. 16 is the second hardest hole of the course with a hard dogleg to the right.

Greens fees in 1999 were $54 for 18 holes and $35 for 9 holes and that included cart expenses. Guest rates if you stay at the resort were $39 for 18 holes. Resident pro and pro shop manager Barry Storie will answer any of your questions (and rent you clubs if you forgot yours). The course has a club house with meeting and group facilities and a snack bar, full-service lounge, and grill. Thousand Hill offers nightly and weekly "stay and play" condo rentals. Call (417) 336-5873 or (800) 864-4145 for information.

Top of the Rock Golf Course
150 Top of the Rock Rd. • (417) 339-5225

Jack Nicklaus designed this 9-hole, par 27 course on one of Taney County's highest hills overlooking Table Rock Lake. Established in 1996 by John Morris of Bass Pro fame, the Top of the Rock features the first Jack Nicklaus signature course in the state and the first Nicklaus signature all-par 3 course ever built. The course is 47 acres, with more than 38 percent of the area kept in a natural state or planted with native grasses, wildflowers, or native trees. The water features of the course were created not only to add a challenge but also to enhance wildlife habitat. Giving new meaning to birdie, the course planners worked with the Audubon Society and incorporated interpretive tools into the landscaping, pro shop and clubhouse, so you can learn about our Ozark birds and wildlife as you play. The course is the only Audubon Society signature course in the state and the fourth in the nation.

The course has the flexibility to offer a challenge no matter what your skill level, whether you're a first timer, an avid golfer or just bringing the family there for an outing. Local golfers say hole No. 8 with its 186-yard drive is the most challenging. Greens fees are $30 for 9 holes and $45 for 18 holes, with a $12 cart fee per nine holes. Walkers, however, are encouraged and will be interested to know that the paths are made from recycled tires and have a soft, spongy feel.

Top of the Rock features a pro shop, clubhouse, and restaurant (see our Restaurants chapter).

Golf Equipment

Arnold Palmer Golf Company
300 Tanger Blvd. • (417) 337-5650

Located in the Tanger Outlet Mall, just off The Strip, Arnold Palmer golf carries signature golf equipment by the famous pro. You can get clubs, shoes—retail through pro lines—bags, shirts, and just about anything you need to start out on the course or add to your collection, For the ladies, there is a full line of Nancy

Lopez equipment. She joined the Company several years ago to market her line of golf equipment.

Gibson's Golfworks
876 Mo. Hwy. 76 E • (417) 334-8989

Wayne "Hoot" Gibson of Gibson's Golfworks likes to talk golf, and although he can fix or improve your golf gear, he leaves it up to you to improve your game. He can regrip, reshaft, refinish, or reweight your clubs. Hoot was nominated for Golf Club Maker of the Year of the Professional Club Makers Society in 1993. If your clubs are in need of professional repair, you can find Gibson's Golfworks two sharp curves before the Holiday Hills Golf Course, 1 mile east of the Lake Taneycomo bridge on Mo. 76.

Golf USA
4554 Gretna Rd.
• (417) 334-8079

Top-of-the-line clubs and golf sets, bags, balls, shoes, and golf apparel can be found at Golf USA in the Factory Shoppes of America Mall at Branson Meadows. They also have full line of golf accessories as well as golf gift and novelty items. If it relates to golf, Golf USA has it!

Horseback Riding

One of the best ways to take a break from the glitz and activity of The Strip and see the "real" Ozarks is to take a trail ride. Horses are able to get you back into hollows and recesses of the beautiful Ozarks that can't even be reached by 4-wheel drive vehicles. It's an easy, interesting, and fun outdoor activity. You can see the blush of red buds and the bloom of dogwood blossoms up close in the spring, and in the fall you can be right in the midst of the flaming fall review of oaks, sweetgums, sumac, and dogwoods. There are trail rides available at the Shepherd of the Hills Homestead. (See our Attractions chapter.) In addition, there are other local horseback riding opportunities.

Canyon Creek Ranch
700 Expressway Ln. • (417) 335-6003
• www: showtown.net/ccr

Canyon Creek Ranch takes you for rides up Roark Creek valley over a 430-acre area and is open, weather permitting, mid-March to mid-November, 7 days a week, from 9 AM-5PM. They have 35 horses, and the guided trail rides usu-

ally consist of about 15-20 horses and riders. Horses are described as being so gentle they can take the trail in their sleep! There are a number of riding options such as a one-hour scenic ride along the ridgetops over Roark Creek and creekside up the valley or a breakfast ride that is a two-hour adventure, complete with a breakfast cookout over an open fire: homemade biscuits, sausage gravy, scrambled eggs, hash browns, coffee, juice, and milk. For experienced riders, there's the "boss man ride," a ride that is not "all trail," but a free range riding experience, with a one-hour and a two-hour version, for experienced riders only.

The regular scenic ride is $15 per person (six and above), with children under six who can ride double with adults, $5. The breakfast ride is $25 person, with children under 6, $10. The "boss man ride" is $30 per person per hour.

To reach Canyon Creek Ranch, turn from Mo. 76 onto Gretna Road; turn left on Roark Valley Road at Mesquite Charlie's and cross over Shepherd of the Hills Expressway at the light. After that, take the first right and go one mile.

Uncle Ike's Trail Ride, Inc.
Mo. Hwy. 76, Notch
• (417) 338-8449

Uncle Ike's Trail Ride, the oldest in the area with 25 years in operation, is named after a character in *The Shepherd of the Hills* and is actually located at Notch where the prototype for Uncle Ike carried mail over some of the same trails you'll be riding.

There's a "daily ride" that is 2½ miles and take about 45 minutes. It's on a first come, first served basis, no reservations needed. The cost in 1999 was $12.50 per person. There's also a breakfast ride at 7 AM which is 4½ miles and takes just over 2 hours. Breakfast, cooked at about the halfway point, consists of sausage gravy, biscuits, scrambled eggs, hash browns, coffee, and juice—all you can eat, or at least all that the pack horses could pack in! Cost for the breakfast ride is $22.50, with children under 6 years, $8. Uncle Ike's Trail Ride is .5 miles past the entrance to Silver Dollar City on Mo. 76.

Hunting

At the turn of the twentieth century, hunters from St. Louis, Kansas City, and Chicago would come by train into the Ozarks to hunt. In fact, one of the early buildings on The School of the Ozarks campus at its new Point Lookout location was a log hunting lodge, the Maine Exhibition Hall at the St. Louis World's Fair, moved down here by a group of St. Louis sportsmen and reassembled for a "clubhouse." Hunting and float fishing were big business for locals who served as guides and who knew how and where to find game because it provided fare for their own dinner tables. They hunted deer, turkey, and small game: rabbits, squirrels, and raccoons.

Today our forests provide better hunting for white-tail deer than they did back then, but these pursuits are no longer the main reason tourists come to the Ozarks. Hunting is licensed and regulated by the Missouri Department of Conservation. We Ozarkers do share our forests with "come-here" hunters, and we know there is more than enough deer to go around. In fact, if you hunt in other counties in Missouri, you are probably hunting white-tails descended from Taney County stock. When the Conservation Department began its restocking of both white-tails and wild turkeys in the 1930's after much of the state had been depleted by overhunting, they came to the Branson area to the old Skaggs Game Preserve near Mincy to obtain the restocking animals.

Licenses and Seasons

In order to hunt in Missouri, you must have a permit. All hunters born on or after January 1, 1967, must have a certificate from an approved hunter education program. You must give evidence of this certificate before you can purchase a firearms hunting permit. Permit fees and season lengths vary from year to year for firearms, muzzle loading firearms, and archery, so it's best to contact the Missouri Department of Conservation for the latest information at (573) 751-4115.

Most permits for residents are fairly inexpensive ($15 in 1999) but more expensive for non-residents. In 1999 fees for non-residents were: firearms (includes muzzle loading fire arms) deer hunting permit, $125; archery deer hunting permit, $100; and fall firearms turkey hunting permit, $75.

More than 2,000 stores, bait, and tackle shops, resorts and other locations sell permits, but you can also contact a Missouri Conservation Department office or one of the four Missouri Department of Conservation Nature Centers in the state. You can also purchase a permit by phone by calling (800) 392-4115. The conservation department accepts major credit cards.

Dates vary each year for the season. In 1999 the rifle firearms deer season started on November 13 and ran through November 25. There was a second season January 8 through 11, 2000, for does and button bucks north of the Missouri River only. The muzzle-loading season was in December. The turkey season for firearms and archery was October 11 to 24, 1999, and spring 2000 was April 24 to May 15. Seasons are announced each year, so contact the Missouri Department of Conservation for the latest season information: (573) 751-4115.

During the firearms white-tailed deer season and both parts of the muzzle loading firearms white-tailed deer season, hunters must wear a cap or hat and a shirt, coat or vest of hunter orange that is plainly visible from all sides. The only exception to the hunter orange attire is for archers. The bright color will keep you from being mistaken for game, like Capt. Meriwether Lewis was by one of his hunters on the return leg of his famous expedition with William Clark. Fortunately, Lewis was only shot through the buttocks! Missouri wants its hunters to get game, not be game!

Migratory Waterfowl Hunting

The Ozarks is a fly-over zone for most migratory waterfowl, and so hunting of ducks and geese is not as prevalent or popular here as it is in the southeast and central portions of Missouri. A Migratory Bird Hunting Permit and a federal Water fowl Stamp are necessary if you want to hunt birds in Missouri. Costs were $6 in 1999 for the Missouri permit and $15 for the federal Waterfowl Stamp in 1999. These permits can be obtained at the U.S. Post Office or any Missouri Department of Conservation office. Penalties are stiff for violating state migratory bird regulations, so have the necessary permits before you pack your bird vest and shotgun.

Contact the Missouri Department of Conservation, P.O. Box 180, Jefferson City, Mo. 65102 for complete information on waterfowl seasons and hunting regulations.

Trap, Skeet, and Sporting Clay Shooting

There has been a decline in quail and dove hunting in the Ozarks in the last half of the century, largely because local farmers don't plant as much grain as they used to which served as cover and food for the birds. However, another reason is the recognition that increasing human population and habitat destruction has put a strain on bird species. The result has been the evolution of several fast-growing sports derived from bird hunting. One type of shooting, calling sporting clays shooting, is based on flying targets (sporting clays) designed to simulate an actual hunting situation. The targets fly in from all directions and heights. Sporting clays shooting differs from skeet shooting (in which the clay targets come from only two locations) since shots are fired from eight different stations in a 180-degree field.

Trap shooting has the target come from one spot, and shooters rotate through five positions. With both skeet and trap shooting, the slight angles and speeds of targets are constant. That isn't so with sporting clays, which mimics the actual field conditions of bird hunting and is thus more challenge. It provides the thrill of bird hunting without the kill.

INSIDERS' TIP

A paddlefish is the biggest fish ever caught in Missouri-134 pounds, 12 ounces at Lake of the Ozarks in 1992. This relic of prehistoric times has a long paddle-shaped bill, and the fish's roe is prized as caviar.

Ozark Shooters Sports Complex
759 U.S. Hwy. 65 • (417) 443-3093
• www.ozarkshooters.com

This complex at Chestnut Ridge, about 11 miles north of Branson, is the only shooting range in the area. Dale and Peggy Siler have an indoor handgun and rifle range and sponsor celebrity shoots at which you can join some of the stars from The Strip for a round or two to test your marksmanship.

Many of the country musicians are outdoors types (they either come by it naturally or think it's good for the image) and hunt or fish. Ozarks Shooters sponsors shooting competitions, often for some charitable cause, and Branson's stars are often involved. In 1995 Ozark Shooters Sports Complex was the site of the U.S. Open Sporting Clay Championship, the first time the event had been held in the Midwest. As the second-largest event of the National Sporting Clay Association, the five-day competition attracted shooters from across the nation and brought a good deal of local publicity to this rapidly growing sport. Ozark Shooters is open seven days a week, year-round, and you can participate in trap, skeet, and sporting clays shooting. The complex has a clubhouse, a gunsmith service, a small shooters' shop, and a gun rental service. It offers classes in handguns and shotguns for men, women, and kids, and often sponsors hunter safety classes.

Spectator Sports

Bransonites were as proud as anyone in the state when the St. Louis Rams won their first Super Bowl honors in 2000, and quarterback Kurt Warner and lineman Grant Wistrom (from nearby Webb City) are local heroes. However it's a four-hour drive from Branson to St. Louis or Kansas City, the nearest cities with professional teams, and you'd have to be a real, diehard fan to make it to all the games, so most folks are content to follow football and baseball via radio and TV. The nearest "high profile," professional team is a minor league team, the Ozark Mountain Ducks, a minor league baseball team who made the Ozarks their home in 1999 and whose home games are played at Price-Cutter Field, just north of Ozark, Missouri.

Bransonites, of course, root for the Cardinals and the Royals, but interest in the new Mountain Ducks has been high. Developer John Q. Hammons appears willing to step to the plate and build a baseball stadium in downtown Springfield, to be used by the Southwest Missouri State University Bears and, possibly, a Double-A minor league baseball team. It would be a $7-$9 million project, with seating for about 8,000. If the project develops, in conjunction with Springfield's Jordan Valley Park project, it will change not only the Springfield downtown area but spectator sports in the southwest Missouri area.

Right now, however, the focus is on local teams, and high school basketball is the big spectator sport. Though some of the area schools are quite small, they have won state championships over the years. Branson High School has had notable football teams, and the local high school football team has a big following. Folks in Branson are more likely to be in the stands at Alexander Park or Mang Field rooting for a Little League team or in the school gym backing the local basketball team than cheering on the Chiefs in Kansas City. They follow the Arkansas Razorbacks and the Missouri Tigers, but

RECREATION AND THE OUTDOORS

they tend to take more interest in the College of the Ozarks Bobcats or the Southwest Missouri State University Lady Bears ball teams—especially the Lady Bears. The SMSU women's basketball team could be said to be more popular locally than country mega-star Garth Brooks. The top attendance at Springfield's Hammons Student Center for the Lady Bears was 9,194 versus Brooks's 8,972.

In July of 1999 Springfield hosted the Amateur Athletic Union's girls' 12-and-under National Basketball Championship, an event that brought in 75 basketball teams from all across the United States. In March, 2000, Branson was deluged by basketball fans when The College of the Ozarks hosted the NAIA Division II men's basketball national championship. Folks who never had gone to a basketball game at the college found themselves caught up in the excitement when the unseeded underdog C of O team battled its way through the ranks, knocking off fetter-known and seeded teams to finally play for the championship, only to lose the final game. The NAIA tournament drew more than 30,000 fans, who also saw Branson, and the tournament will return to The College of the Ozarks next championship playoffs in March 2001.

Spectator sports are important to us in the Ozarks, but for most of us it is purely a local thing. However, recent events in the Ozarks have broadened the opportunities for being a sports spectator.

Swimming

Swimming here in the Ozarks is more of an excuse to get the family out to the river or lake during the heat of summer and have a picnic and cool off than it is a serious sport. It's more splash and play than swimming, and you'll see families on gravel bars at various holes on local creeks or at beaches or recreation areas on Table Rock or Bull Shoals Lake. Lake Taneycomo is too cold, even in 100 degree August weather, for swimming. Check out our Lakes and Rivers chapter for other water activities available in the area.

You can swim about any place in Table Rock

and Bull Shoals lakes, but use your common sense. Lots of folks swim at the boat launch area and the lakeshore at Table Rock State Park and at the lake front by Table Rock Dam at the Dewey Short Visitors Center. The water is refreshing and the beach rocky at both sites, and there are sudden and dramatic dropoffs at the underwater bluffs covered by the waters of Table Rock Lake. Since there are no lifeguards for such swimming areas, the play is always at your own risk.

Moonshine Beach, just north of Table Rock Dam, is a favorite public swimming area. This quiet cove faces west, so the afternoon sun is intense, and it is light until even after the sun has set. The swimming area is roped off so no boats can enter, and sand and pea gravel have been hauled in to make the beach easy on the feet. It's a great place to take a picnic lunch and spend the afternoon, and it's shallow enough for even toddlers, but there are no lifeguards, so you should be on your guard. To reach Moonshine Beach from Branson, take Mo. 165 south from Mo. 76. You'll see the turnoff to Moonshine Beach to the west just after you pass the entrance to Chateau on the Lake and before you start to cross Table Rock Dam.

INSIDERS' TIP
The best fall color in the Ozarks can be seen the last two weeks of October to the first week of November, but the time can vary from year to year.

Most hotels and motels have pools for their guests (see our Accommodations chapter) to cool off and play in. The Sammy Lane Resort has had such a pool since 1926, and at 60 feet by 155 feet, it is one of the biggest cement ponds in the Ozarks. There are several water slides and water chutes in the area, and White Water is a large water theme park on 76 Country Blvd. (see our Attractions and Kidstuff chapters).

There is a public swimming pool off BoxCar Willie Dr. on the Taneycomo Lakefront that is operated by the city of Branson, (417) 334-6998. It's close to Mang Field Park, the Sammy Lane Pirate Cruise, and the city tennis courts at North Beach Park. During the hot days of summer, you'll see locals and tourists cooling off there. A certified lifeguard is on duty during swimming hours. The facilities include a wading pool and picnic area. In 1999 an admission fee of $1 was charged. The pool hours are Monday through Saturday from noon to 7 PM; it's closed Sunday.

Lakes and Rivers

Long before the belch of the tour bus echoed off the highways, the purr of the motorboat reverberated across lakes and the whir of the fly-reel competed with the gurgle of streams. For those who know Branson only as the home of music shows, a production of an entirely different kind awaits in nature's own amphitheater, with a cast of thousands, a score that is truly surround-sound and lighting of the most spectacular subtlety and beauty. The prologue to the modern-day drama that is Branson tourism can be found in the lakes and rivers that wind in, around, and among the Ozark hills, valleys, and plateaus. Because of the dams and lakes created in the 20th-century, the White River in Missouri is no more, but its legacy is the advent of tourism in the Ozarks.

When the first railroads lumbered into the area around the turn of the twentieth century, they brought more than just the timber industry and commercial agriculture. They brought the angler, hunter, and outdoor lover who saw a bottomless pool of recreational natural resources in the crystal-clear waters of the lakes and streams. Waterfront resorts sprouted from the hillsides, and vacationers from all over came in ever-increasing droves to enjoy swimming, boating, fishing, hiking, and camping. Each new dam-made lake brought a new burst of pleasure boaters, who left economic growth and even more commercial development in their wake.

To provide the tourists with a little after-hours diversion, the first music show made its entrance some 30 years ago. Today, Branson is a glittering, internationally renowned entertainment city, with scores of performers who strut their stuff upon the stage nightly. From season to season they come and they go, followed into town today and out of town tomorrow by the fan clubs, the tour buses, and the whole neon hype of show business. Through it all, the lakes and the rivers remain, as popular today as yesterday, with no more advertisement needed than their very existence.

In the following sections we merely skip stones across the vast surface of the river of knowledge about Ozark lakes and rivers. Words alone cannot impart the thrill of hooking your first big trout on Lake Taneycomo; they cannot describe the serenity of a shady afternoon float down Swan Creek. The magnificence of the Ozark lakes and rivers can only be truly experienced in person. Once experienced, perhaps you will find yourself returning to the Ozarks again and again for an encore performance of what might turn out to be your favorite show of all, with yourself cast in the leading role and played out upon the scenic splendor of our beloved Ozarks waterways.

LOOK FOR:
- **Lake Taneycomo**
- **Table Rock Lake**
- **Water Recreation**
- **Fishing Guides**
- **Marinas**
- **Houseboat Rentals**
- **Swimming**

INSIDERS' TIP

To check on current water conditions, call these recorded messages: Table Rock/Beaver Lakes (417) 336-5083; Bull Shoals/Norfolk Lakes (870) 431-5311.

Locals and visitors alike enjoy feeding the ducks and geese that congregate on the shores of Lake Taneycomo in downtown Branson.

Photo: Branson/Lakes Area Chamber of Commerce

The Lakes

Lake Taneycomo

"Lake Taneycomo is one of the best, if not the very best, of all trout streams in the U.S." Harold D. Eastman, *Trout Fishing On Lake Taneycomo,* 1987.

Only in the Ozarks could you call a lake a stream—or call a stream a lake. Actually, Taneycomo is neither—and both. It was born in 1913 when the White River was impounded just south of Forsyth by Powersite Dam, creating the first major dam-made lake in Missouri. The name Taneycomo is derived from the abbreviation for Taney County, Missouri. At 2,080 acres of surface area, it's small by modern reservoir standards, but its impact on the area is big indeed. This early flooding of the White River Valley was the precursor to the flood of tourists to come. Hotels and summer resorts sprang up in Branson and Rockaway Beach, powered by electricity from the Empire District Electric Company's new dam. The accommodations offered fishing, boating, and, of course, swimming. For nearly a half century, the summertime flopping and splashing in the warm waters of Taneycomo was a familiar sight.

There's still plenty of flopping and splashing in Taneycomo these days, but now it's of the ichthyoid, not humanoid, variety. In 1958 the erection of Table Rock Dam, 22 miles up-stream from Powersite, had a chilling effect that would make Lake Taneycomo world famous for trout fishing. The water for Taneycomo is now drawn from the bottom of Table Rock Dam, some 140 feet below the surface of Table Rock Lake. The temperature never exceeds 58 degrees, which is cold enough to make insulated waders a really good idea. The resorts along Lake Taneycomo are still there, but now they cater more to anglers than swimmers.

Fishing Lake Taneycomo

Though the warm-water crappie and bass are gone, even first-timers should have no trouble reeling in the trout, thanks to the Missouri Department of Conservation. Each year the department stocks Lake Taneycomo with more than 750,000 rainbow trout and a smaller number of brown trout. They are raised at Shepherd of the Hills Fish Hatchery on Mo. Highway 165 (for more on the hatchery, see our Recreation and the Outdoors chapter) and lowered into the lake every month just below Table Rock Dam. The best spot to reel in these fish is usually not too far downstream from Table Rock Dam, where the water tends to be shallowest. But only fish until the siren blows! When you hear it go off, that means they're sending water through the hydro-electric generators just upstream from where you're standing, and it's time to move quickly back toward the bank. Those who do not heed the warning will find that peaceful Lake Taneycomo can be dam-dangerous.

When the water is running, of course, the fly-fishing is excellent on this well-stocked little lake. That's good, because state regulations require that only flies and artificial lures may be used on the upper portion of Taneycomo, defined as the area from the closed zone 760 feet below Table Rock Dam to the mouth of Fall Creek. Soft-plastic baits and natural and scented baits are prohibited in this area.

Drift fishing remains one of the most popular methods when the water is running. You simply motor up the lake to a particular starting point then drift back down with the current. Drag your bait or lure behind the boat. Watch your sinker placement so that the bait will float just above the bottom, perhaps bumping it occasionally. A miniature marshmallow threaded on the hook can help provide the right amount of buoyancy to keep it off the bottom.

In still water, baits of all types can be effective, and we've heard of success stories using everything from canned corn (whole-kernel only!) to salmon eggs. When fishing from shore the traditional carton of live nightcrawlers is still effective, and you can take it to the bank (so to speak). Despite the scores of fishing magazine articles and late night infomercials touting miracle lures, bait selection remains a highly personal decision. Go to any trout dock on Taneycomo, and we can almost guarantee that an old-timer hanging around will be happy to offer an opinion, even if you haven't asked for it.

The same goes for finding a favorite fishin' hole—everybody has an opinion and is willing to share it. Ask around, but keep in mind that Taneycomo is a dynamic living river, and last year's lucky lunker site may be too shallow, too deep, or too overgrown this year. Frankly, much of the fun of fishing a place like Taneycomo is the challenge of exploration and the thrill of discovery. So you might want to do what locals do: put in with a small johnboat someplace, and seek out the many nooks and eddies that finger off the lake all up and down the shoreline. Sooner or later you're bound to reel in something.

Table Rock Lake

What Lake Taneycomo is to trout, Table Rock Lake is to bass—and crappie, walleye, bluegill, and catfish. But if you think Table Rock is only about fishing, you'll miss the boat entirely.

INSIDERS' TIP

For swimming try the Table Rock Lake beach at the Mo. Highway 86 Recreation Area in eastern Stone County. It's small and cozy, with plenty of sand, shade trees, restrooms, and an outdoor shower for rinsing off afterwards. Its off-the-beaten-path location means it's usually not too crowded. Take U.S. Highway 65 south to Mo. Highway 86. Follow it to Mo. Highway UU and turn right. The beach is about a half-mile down at the end of the road.

Let's start with its size. At more than 43,100 acres (67.34 square miles) of surface area and with a shoreline of 800 miles, Table Rock seems as big, and as blue, as the Ozarks sky on a summer afternoon. Lined by cedar-covered bluffs and framed by rolling hills, it is an august sight indeed, which helps explain why skiers, boaters, swimmers, scuba divers, and Duck-riders are themselves such a common August sight. Table Rock seems tailor-made for summer fun, and in fact it was. In 1958 the U.S. Army Corps of Engineers completed Table Rock Dam and Powerhouse, which is 6,523-feet long and a spectacular 252-feet high. It signaled the end of the White River in Missouri, but also brought the beginning of a new era in watersports and outdoor sightseeing in the Ozarks.

Even if you're only coming to Branson for the music shows, set aside a few minutes to drive south on Mo. Highway 165 from The Strip. Almost without warning, you'll find yourself driving over the dam itself, with Table Rock Lake stretching away to your right. Now

Some of the biggest trout in Lake Taneycomo have been caught right from downtown Branson docks.

Photo: Branson/Lakes Area Chamber of Commerce

look to the left. It's amazing how very far below Lake Taneycomo seems to be. Keep going south on Mo. 165 as it loops to the east, and you'll come to a scenic overlook where you can pull off and get an unparalleled view of the dam to the west and Taneycomo below.

Along the way you'll pass the Dewey Short Visitors Center, which, among other things, offers an eerie guided tour down inside the dam itself (see the listing in Recreation and the Outdoors). Practically next door to the visitors center is Table Rock State Park, one of the nearly 25 public use areas on Table Rock Lake. It has a marina, boat launch ramp, camping and picnicking areas, as do many of the other public-use areas (see its listing in the Campgrounds and RV Parks chapter for more information). Other areas feature swimming beaches and playgrounds, and some have a marine gas facility, bait shop, or boat and motor rental. There are also a number of private marinas where you can rent Waverunners, ski boats, bass boats, and purchase fishing tackle.

You can also hire a fishing guide, but here are a few suggestions for the do-it-yourselfer: Start with a medium-weight casting rod, outfitted with jig-and-eel or jig-and-pork and 12-to 15-pound test line. Although with crappie and catfish you'll have the best luck at night, large-mouth and smallmouth bass can be caught during the day about 30 feet deep. They tend to cluster around the cedar flats or timber submerged when the lake was first flooded. When the water cools in the fall, try shallower areas in the many coves and feeder creeks that line the lake. For up to date fishing reports visit www.branson.com. or www.conservation.state.mo.us.html.

Table Rock Lake is about the only place where the indoor world of live entertainment and the outdoor world of fishing and recreation can share common ground or, in this case, common water. Many of the big music stars have homes overlooking the lake, so don't be surprised if you see a famous face trolling by on a bass boat. Around here performers like Shoji Tabuchi and Mel Tillis are almost as well-known for their fishing exploits as their music shows. Where else can you be a bass angler by day and a bass singer by night?

Although most people think of the theaters when they think of Branson nightlife, Insiders know that the lakeside is just as much the place to be as dusk falls. The roar of the powerboats has subsided to be replaced by the plaintive call of the solitary loon. The deep orange and violet of sunset is projected in 3-D beyond the far horizon of the lake, accompanied only by nature's own cricket-and-wave-ripple soundtrack. No wonder romance can spring into bloom at lakeside, even as the water flowers are folding their own blossoms for the night. Indeed, more than one transplanted city boy has been known to stroll down to water's edge in the fading light and slip a ring on the finger of his best girl, with only the rustling cedars to bear witness.

So whether you're young or just young-at-heart, don't think of Table Rock Lake only as a place for sports lovers and sunbathers. Have a quiet honeymoon dinner overlooking the cozy cove at Big Cedar Lodge, or celebrate your anniversary with an evening cruise on the Showboat Branson Belle (see our Attractions chapter). Once you've spent an evening at Table Rock, we think you'll view the lake in a whole new light. Even if it's dark.

Bull Shoals Lake

Most of Bull Shoals Lake is in Arkansas, a little farther from Branson than either Table Rock or Taneycomo. But for the serious angler, it's worth checking out. The northern end of the lake touches popular Shadow Rock Park near the mouth of Swan Creek in Forsyth, Missouri.

Bull Shoals is well known for white, large mouth, and spotted bass as well as channel catfish, bream, walleye, bluegill, and crappie. Even so, it has been overshadowed by the later arrival of its sister lake, Table Rock, and some say that has made Bull Shoals an underfished lake by comparison. But over the years Bull Shoals has yielded more than its share of trophy fish and state records.

The floodgates closed on Bull Shoals Dam in 1951, creating a 45,440-acre sports lover's paradise with 740 miles of shoreline. At flood-control stage, the size nearly doubles to 71,240 acres of surface area. With the surrounding steep bluffs and rock ledges, it almost seems like a highland mountain lake. Most of what little brush was on the original lake bottom has rotted away, leaving the chunk-rock banks and drop-offs to suffice as cover. The lake is deep, and it's not unusual to be in 50 feet of water when you're no more than 20 feet from the bank.

As with Table Rock, scuba divers and swimmers are attracted by the clear waters of Bull Shoals. The clarity also makes light tackle and light line the best choice for anglers. Both the depth and clarity of the water make night fishing the preference of many anglers. In the summer, night fishing is also a great way to beat the heat as well as prove that slower fishing in summer doesn't always have to be the case. Channel cat fishing is best in the spring, with September through December and March through May considered the preferred times for black bass.

Boat ramps, beaches, and campgrounds abound, with more than 20 local, state, and federal public-use areas. Still, Bull Shoals Lake somehow lacks the feeling of being overcrowded or overcommercialized, though there are plenty of motels and resorts scattered around it in Missouri and in the surrounding Arkansas towns such as Mountain Home and Lakeview.

The Rivers

Bull Creek

Bull Creek empties into Lake Taneycomo near the town of Rockaway Beach. It is one of the clearest streams in the Ozarks, which makes it a favorite of snorkelers and underwater photographers. The occasional deep pools are home to smallmouth and largemouth bass. For a leisurely float, put in at a low-water bridge off Mo. Highway 176, 3.5 miles north of Walnut Shade, and take out at the Mo. Highway F bridge, some 10 miles downstream.

Swan Creek

On the day following a heavy rain, this creek can be a great ride for the true whitewater canoeist. Normally in the summer, though, it is either not floatable or a low-water float at best with some walk-through required.

INSIDERS' TIP

The gnarled eastern red cedars you see on river bluffs are the state's oldest living things. One of them on the Current River is estimated to be 1,073 years old. At the turn of the century, many of the trees were cut down to make pencils at the pencil factory in Branson.

Lake Honor on the College of the Ozarks campus is a serene picnic spot.

Photo: College of the Ozarks

The total distance is only 21 miles, from the Mo. Highway 125 bridge at Garrison, Missouri, to the Shadow Rock Park campground at the town of Forsyth. For a shorter float, around 8 miles, you can put in at the bridge at Mo. Highway M and takeout at Shadow Rock Park.

Beaver Creek

Traditionally the realm of fly fishers, Beaver Creek is now a canoeist's favorite as well. Due to fluctuating water levels, both the fishing and floating are best after mid-June below Bradleyville, Missouri, where you can put in at the Mo. Highway 76 bridge and take out at the Mo. Highway 160 Kissee Mills Public Access, about 19 miles downstream. You can find black bass and white bass in a series of pools just before takeout. For canoe rentals call Beaver Canoe Rental & Sales at (417) 796-2336. For an all-day trip, put in instead at the Mo. 76 bridge 8 miles southwest of Ava, Missouri. For a shorter all-day trip, put in at the Mo. 76 bridge at Brownbranch and float to the Mo. 160 bridge or take out even earlier at the Mo. 76 bridge at Bradleyville.

The James River

A major tributary of the former White River, the James is best known for float fishing. Float fishing is popular in the Ozarks, and some say it was invented on the James River at the town of Galena. Using a johnboat, a long flat-bottomed boat squared off at both ends, the angler drifts down the river in ease and comfort. Before the advent of Table Rock Dam, johnboats could make a 25-mile float trip from Galena to Branson, but now most float fishing is done on a 22-mile stretch from Hootentown to Galena. Swimming on the James is not recommended on any portion below the city of Springfield due to wastewater runoff. The smallmouth bass fishing is good, but we recommend that you catch and release. The Department of Natural Resources has deemed 28 miles of the James River impaired by both urban point and non-point sources. The experienced ca-

INSIDERS' TIP

Harbor On Table Rock Lake, Indian Point Rd., (417) 338-2828, offers boat painting and repair and on-the-water storage.

noeist will enjoy the tremendous scenic variety of a winter float. The craggy bluffs, broad valleys, and the trunks of dark trees are quite majestic after snowfall. Canoeists can contact Hootentown Canoe Rental, Mo. Highway O, Crane, (417) 369-2266, or James River Canoe Rental, Mo. 13 and Mo. 176, Galena, (417) 357-6957, for floating gear and shuttle service as well as RV hookups and camp sites.

Buffalo National River

If there can be such a thing as a river that is too magnificent, this is it. Magnificence translates into popularity, and frankly the upper Buffalo is simply overrun by recreators on weekends in the summer. Why? Because the scenery simply takes your breath away for nearly 150 miles. From its source in the Boston Mountains to Lost Valley and Buffalo Point downstream, the Buffalo riverscape is unparalleled and virtually untouched. In the years following World War II, a coalition of outdoorsmen and environmentalists successfully opposed damming the Buffalo, and ultimately most of it was designated a National Scenic River under the supervision of the National Park Service. It remains the last major unimpounded river in Arkansas.

Floaters come from all over to revel in the Buffalo River's 500- to 1,000-foot wooded bluffs, clear green pools, and blue-and-white riffles. Fishing, swimming, canoeing, and camping all have their share of enthusiasts. You'll need a guidebook, and there are two in particular we recommend. For floating see *The Buffalo National River, Canoeing Guide* published by The Ozark Society, P.O. Box 2914, Little Rock, Ark. 72203. The landlubber will enjoy *Buffalo River Hiking Trails* by Tim Ernst, available from the author at 411 Patricia Lane, Fayetteville, Ark. 72703. (For hiking information see the Buffalo National River in our Recreation and the Great Outdoors chapter.) Both are also available at the listed park headquarters address, where you can also get maps and information on boating, canoeing, camping, commercial outfitters, and park facilities. The Buffalo is about a 1.5-hour drive from Branson but well worth the trip. For more information contact Park Headquarters, 402 N. Walnut St., Ste. 136, Harrison, Ark. (870) 741-5443.

Current and Jacks Fork Rivers

The Current River and its major tributary, the Jacks Fork, are located several hours drive east of Branson in a sparsely populated area of east central Missouri. Major portions of both rivers have been incorporated into Ozark National Scenic Riverways and thus receive federal protection and management under the National Park Service. Park headquarters is in Van Buren, Mo. Commercial development is minimal, yet you can still find sufficient lodging and commercial outfitting services.

Fed by big springs (hence the regional name Big Springs Country), the Current remains floatable even during the dry days of summer. The water is deeper than other Ozark streams, but it is a relatively safer float because there are fewer hazards. The scenery is remarkably diverse over the course of the two rivers' combined floatable length of 180 miles, with natural beauty that has remained virtually unchanged since it was first discovered. The Jacks Fork is unusual in that it flows between bluffs, canyon-like. Later it develops meandering qualities, with high bluffs on one side and broad valleys on the other. The float allows one to see huge caves, large springs, and perhaps catch a glimpse of the valley's herd of wild horses. Below Van Buren on the Current River be certain to check out Big Spring, one of the world's largest springs. (See our History chapter for more information.) The spring supplies the Current with 276 million gallons of water a day. Hiking and camping are favorite riverside activities. (For hiking information, see our Recreation and the Great Outdoors chapter).

The Jacks Fork joins the Current at a point known as Two Rivers. Jacks Fork is a much smaller stream than the Current, but it's well noted for the steep limestone bluffs that crowd the edge of the river canyon. For more information on the Current and Jacks Fork Rivers, con-

INSIDERS' TIP

The lobby at the Presley Jubilee Theatre is filled with photographs of Lloyd Presley, his wife, and their grandchildren holding their catches from the area's lakes. A few of Lloyd's prize catches have even been mounted. He'll be glad to chat with you after the show about his days as a fishing guide.

LAKES AND RIVERS

tact the Ozark National Scenic Riverways, 404 Watercress Dr., Van Buren, Mo. or P.O. Box 490, Van Buren, Mo. 63965. (573) 323-4236.

Activities and Gear

Canoeing and Kayaking

Ozark rivers offer something for both the whitewater canoeing or kayaking enthusiast and the pleasure floater. Some of the waterways offer a true thrill ride, especially in winter and spring or after a few days of heavy rain. But in the summer, water levels can be low enough on many area waterways as to make for a perfect daytrip or camping trip. It's an ideal outdoor activity for the family, with a leisurely pace, and spectacular landscapes full of varied and sometimes noteworthy flora and fauna.

Guides are available but probably unnecessary for an afternoon float trip, and for the shallower summer runs, no expertise or even equipment of your own is needed. Canoes, kayaks, and other gear can be rented by the day at any number of commercial outfitters throughout the Ozarks, even in the smallest of towns, as long as there is a popular put-in spot nearby. Typically, you park your car at rental headquarters (which are often a takeout point), and the outfitter shuttles both you and the canoes upstream, 7 to 15 miles for a daytrip, to put in. Many offer inner tubes or rafts as well as camping gear and supplies. It's a good idea to call the rental company in advance, especially if you are planning a float during a holiday.

The novice canoeist or kayaker should observe a few safety tips. Wear a life jacket in preparation for the unexpected because a flowing river can be as deep and treacherous in some spots as it is calm and shallow in others. Seal your wallet, fishing license, camera, and other valuables in waterproof bags or containers, and stow your gear low in the center of the craft. When selecting a scenic gravel bar as a campsite, keep in mind that river conditions can change without warning, and flash flooding from rains upstream is always a possibility.

Finally, know your river. The best way is to acquire a copy of *Missouri Ozark Waterways* by Oz Hawksley, available from the Missouri Department of Conservation, P.O. Box 180, Jefferson City, Mo. 65102 (573) 751-4115. This guidebook contains detailed maps of 37 major float streams in the Ozarks, together with distance information, difficulty ratings, and suggested put-in and takeout points. You should also talk to the rental company staff, who can alert you to any recent changes in the river and forecasted weather conditions.

Fishing Guides

Fishing is always more fun when you catch something, and hiring a guide goes a long way toward ensuring that you do. Of course, there's no guarantee, but an experienced guide will be familiar with the current hot spots and the best baits and lures to use.

Most marinas can refer you to a guide or make the arrangements for you. Some guides, like the ones listed here, can be telephoned directly. Usually they will meet you at a marina or other lakeside location, or they may pick you up at your waterfront lodging. Typically, the guide provides the boat, gas, bait and fishing gear (if you don't have your own). Some will also provide lunch on request. Most guide boats can carry two, or at most three, passengers. Half-day excursions start at around $75 and full day at $150, but it can depend on what is included, so make sure you always ask first. Advance reservations can help avoid disappointment. The prices we have listed here are starting prices for guides. More than 2 anglers in a party, snacks, meals, live bait, and transportation to and from your hotel may be extra. You must provide your own fishing license or trout tag prior to embarking on a trip.

As with any service of this nature, there may be those who hold themselves out as guides but may not have much experience; that's why a specific referral from a knowledgeable marina or resort is recommended. All of the guides listed here carry a current Coast Guard certification. In 1999 Coast Guard officials began stepping up their efforts to make sure fishing guides possessed current licensing and instated random drug tests to weed out unscrupulous guides.

The White River, a major travel route in the 19th century, is now a major floating and fishing river.

Photo: Arkansas Dept. of Parks & Tourism

Bob's Fishing Guide Service
Mo. Hwy. 76, Notch • (417) 338-2316

Full day or half, Bob Juneman provides the boat and all equipment for one or two persons to troll for bass on Table Rock or trout on Taneycomo. Rates start at $130 for 5 hours or $180 for 8 hours. Bob says 40 percent of his business is repeat customers. On a good day of fishing you can expect to reel in between 15 and 30 bass. You need to call 2 weeks in advance for summertime fishing excursions with Bob.

Hook's Table Rock Guide Service
Mo. Hwy. DD, Reeds Spring
• (417) 338-2277, (800) 603-4665

Your captain is Jim Van Hook, and he specializes in assisting the beginning angler. He's also a favorite among tournament participants. His rates start at $160 for 4 hours and $225 for 8 hours, all equipment included. Live bait is an extra charge as is picking you up at your hotel or resort. Jim only goes out on Table Rock Lake.

Mike's Professional Fishing Guide Service
121B Waterscape Rd., Ridgedale
• (417) 779-3010

Mike Sowders is known as the celebrity's fishing guide, and he counts Mel Tillis and Shoji Tabuchi among his regulars. He's been casting about in these parts for more than 20 years, and he is as active as ever in various competitive tournaments. Even so, Mike says that fishing is as much about the fun and camaraderie as anything, "and if you catch something, that's just a bonus."

Pete's Professional Guide Service
Rt. 3 P.O. Box 4955, Galena, Mo. 65656
• (417) 860-8163, (800) 882-1978

Pete Wenners is a 1999 qualifying participant in the K Mart Bassmaster 150 tournament. He's been a professional fishing guide for 9 years and specializes in helping to educate anglers on the ins and outs of fishing. He said he and his other two guides, Jerry Snieder and Bill Beck, try to help clients understand why fish bite when they do and what factors contribute to success. Rates begin at $160 for 4 to 5 hours and $210 for 8 hours for up to 2 people. Pete or one of his other guides will pick you up at your hotel for no extra charge and take you out on Table Rock Lake or Lake Taneycomo.

River Run Outfitters
212 S. Commercial St.
• (877) 699-3474
• www.branson.com/riverrun

River Run Outfitters is owned and operated by Stan and Carolyn Parker, each of whom have fished the area lakes and rivers for over 30 years. They offer wade guide trips starting at $80 for 4 hours for one person. Their instructional fly fishing trips are great for beginners and include nomenclature, basic casting, line tending, fly selection, and water reading. Rates start at $175 for one person for a full day. These rates include all equipment except for waders. You can pick up a pair at their shop which offers a good variety of fly fishing equipment such as wading wear, rain gear, fly tying materials, gifts, and many accessories for the fly fisher.

Fishing Licenses

The Wildlife Code of Missouri, which governs fishing, is what is known as a permissive code. The regulations tell you what you are permitted to do, in terms of what species you can take, when and how; everything else is off-limits.

Everyone who fishes must have a permit, except those 15 and younger and Missouri residents older than 65. In 1999 an annual fishing permit was $11 for residents and $35 for nonresidents. A daily permit is $5, but if you think you'll fish for more than 3 days, you're better off purchasing the annual permit. In addition, a trout permit of $7 is required to possess and transport trout. In some state parks a $2 daily trout tag is required. You can buy a permit at marinas, bait and tackle shops, and convenience stores, or get one directly from the Missouri Department of Conservation by calling (800) 392-4115 or visit their website for more information at www.conservation.state.mo.us.html. Always carry your permit while fishing or transporting your catch.

The daily aggregate limit for bass on Table Rock and Bull Shoals lakes is 15, with a minimum length of 15 inches (12 inches for spotted bass on Bull Shoals). In streams, the black bass daily limit is six, with a length minimum of 12 inches. The daily limit for crappie is 15 with a minimum length limit of 10 inches on Table Rock and Bull Shoals. On Lake Taneycomo there is a daily limit of five trout, only one of which may be a brown, and any between 12 and 20 inches must be released.

These are intended only as basic guidelines, of course, since it is always good practice to confirm the season and any limits in whatever particular lake or stream you intend to fish. Also, when fishing Table Rock or Bull Shoals lakes, which are each partly in Missouri and partly in Arkansas, ask locally about which, or if both, state permits might be required.

In Arkansas the fees and limits are similar. A nonresident annual fishing license is $30, and the nonresident trout permit is $7.50. Again, the licenses and a copy of the state regulations are available over the counter at sporting goods, fishing supply, and other stores. Or call the Arkansas Game and Fish Commission at (800) 364-GAME or visit their website at www.agfc.state.ar.us.

Both states are emphasizing catch-and-release (pleasure) fishing as a conservation measure that helps fish populations. And since you will probably be hooking some undersized fish anyway, it's a good idea to know the guidelines for survivable release. The fastest and best method is simply to cut the line without ever lifting the fish out of the water; the hook will usually fall off or be expelled by the fish. Or use barbless hooks, and always avoid excessive handling of the fish.

Fishing Tournaments

What would a spring or fall weekend be without a fishing tournament on an Ozarks lake?

The tradition is longstanding, and some tournaments often seem to grow in popularity year after year. Many tournaments are sponsored by area marinas, boat manufacturers, or tackle suppliers, with lucrative prizes of their brand-name goods as well as cash. Others are held to benefit charities, with thousands of dollars raised each year.

Earlier in this chapter we mentioned how catch-and-release fishing is catching on, and nowhere does it receive more prominence than in the tournaments. Boats are outfitted with live wells, which are small aerated water tanks to keep the fish alive and well until final weigh-in.

Tournaments can be either single competitor events or buddy tournaments, in which the catches of two anglers in a boat are weighed together. Most tournaments are open events, with the only prerequisite being payment of the entry fee ($70 to $500 a person for single events, $90 to $150 a boat for buddy tournaments). Same-day registration is usually available.

On Table Rock Lake many of the major tournaments originate at Port of Kimberling Marina (see the subsequent Marina and houseboat Rentals section) in Kimberling City. The Table Rock Lake/Kimberling City Area Chamber of Commerce helps keep track of these events; you can contact them at P.O. Box 495-98, Kimberling City, Mo. 66686, (417) 739-2564 or (800) 595-0393. Visit their website at www.tablerocklake.net for a yearly calendar of fishing tournaments. For more information on a tournament or a current schedule, contact the Missouri Bass Clubs Association, 1043 E. Mentor, Springfield, Mo. 65810, and (417) 887-3298. Also, check the bulletin board at marinas, bait and tackle shops, and convenience stores for postings.

Some of the prime events usually held each year at Port of Kimberling include: the Pro-Am Bass Tournament in early April; the Ronald McDonald, MOSTA and Make A Wish tournaments in early May; Operation Bass Advance, Guys & Gals and Operation Bass Redman tournaments in mid-May; Heartland Pro-Am Tournament in mid-June; Guys & Gals Tournament in mid-August; Tournament of Champions in mid-October; and Fall Pro-Am Tournament in early November.

Marinas and Houseboat Rentals

All three area lakes have a number of full-service marinas. Unless otherwise noted, the marinas listed subsequently sell bait and tackle, marine fuel, fishing licenses, and sodas and snacks. They also rent fishing boats or bass boats and pontoons. Rates range from $20 per hour to $200 a day. Fishing advice and tall tales are free. When you call, you might want to ask if the marina is affiliated with or adjacent to a campground or other services.

Many marinas also have houseboat rentals, and these are noted. Today's houseboats usually have the same modern conveniences you find in motor homes, such as TVs, microwaves, air conditioning, and electric generators. Most come fully outfitted with bed linens and table service for the kitchenette. Some even have VCRs, cellular phones, and gas grills. They sleep anywhere from 4 to 12 people or more. Make your reservations well in advance, and be prepared to pay a substantial deposit around $300 or more. Don't expect to be able to get any one-night or even two-night rentals during the summer; most rentals are by the week or for a minimum of three or four-night weekends or midweek periods. Houseboats are usually available March through late October.

In addition, most marinas can arrange a fishing guide for you or at least make recommendations and give you names and phone numbers. See the previous Fishing Guides section for a partial list of guides in the area.

Baxter Boat Dock
Mo. Hwy. H, Lampe • (417) 779-4301

Baxter is on the south side of Table Rock Lake, where it's a little quieter and less congested. The marina sells groceries and offers wet and dry boat storage. You can rent a fishing boat for $50 a day or get a pontoon for $75 for 4 hours or $135 for 8 hours. Ski boats go for $95 for 4 hours or $180 for 8 hours. You can rent a 4-person houseboat for $695 on a weekend or $1,095 for the week. The 8-person boats go for $1,095 on the weekend and $1,695 for an entire week. Owner since 1986, Sue Pollard will be glad to recommend a fishing guide if you need one. The marina is closed December through February.

Branson Highway K Marina
249 Marina Dr., Kirbyville
• (417) 334-2880, (800) 321-9465

On Bull Shoals Lake, the marina rents boat slips, ski boats, Waverunners, and houseboats.

Highway K Marina has three sizes of houseboats. The 40-foot houseboat sleeps up to four, the 45-foot up to six, and the 56-foot up to 10. They all come fully furnished with linens, TVs, VCRs, microwaves, and gas grills. The minimum rental period is four nights. Rates start at $650 for the smallest boat during the early spring and fall and go up to $1,750 for the largest boat in June, July, and August. If you rent a houseboat they will let you have a bass boat for $35 a day. (Regular price is $100 a day). They also offer discounts on jet skis, Waverunners, and pontoon boats as well if you rent a houseboat. Since the lake level falls in the late fall and winter, they do not rent houseboats between October 31 and the first of March. Other equipment may be rented year round.

Branson Trout Dock
305 BoxCar Willie Dr.
• (417) 334-3703

For the past 14 years anglers have been coming to the annual February trout tournament on Lake Taneycomo hosted by Branson Trout Dock. The entry fee is $60 per boat and all boats must have 2 anglers. The first place winner takes home around $1,000 or 35 percent of the total entry fee pot. The angler who reels in the biggest fish gets to take home $2 from every participant.

The dock has aluminum boats for rent at $30 for 5 hours and $50 for 8 hours. Bass boats go for $40 for 5 hours and $65 for 8 hours. If you want a bass boat with a trolling motor add $5 and $10 for half or full days respectively. Pontoon boats are $50 for 5 hours and $80 for 8 hours. Fishing guide Charlie Vincent charges a flat $75 a day for 1 to 2 people. In the spring of 2000 owners plan to open a small grocery story next to the existing tackle and bait shop.

Cape Fair Boat Dock & Marina
Shadrack Rd. (Lake Rd. 76-82,) Cape Fair
• (417) 538-4163

On the north edge of Table Rock Lake, Cape Fair Boat Dock & Marina is located next to the Cape Fair public campground and offers fishing boats for $39 for 4 hours, $50 for 8 hours or $65 overnight (pick up on day 1 and return by noon the next day). Pontoon boats rent for $100 for 4 hours, $150 for 8 hours or $200 overnight. Ski boats go for $125 for 4 hours or $190 for 8 hours. You can get ski equipment, tubes, boards, and other water devices for $7.50 per hour. Each September the marina hosts an adult/child fishing tournament. A portion of the $20 entry fees benefit St. Jude's Children's Hospital. During the summer there's a fishing tournament held each Saturday.

Fall Creek Marina & Trout Dock
1 Fall Creek Dr. • (417) 336-4937

On the Taneycomo lakefront behind Clarion at Fall Creek Resort, this marina added two brand new Landau pontoon boats to their fleet in 1998. Prices start at $20 per hour for a pontoon and $15 per hour for a fishing boat. Their rates stay the same year round. They'll be happy to set you up with a fishing guide for $190 per day. They provide the boat, tackle, and bait and you bring the snacks.

Gage's Long Creek Marina and Forever Resorts
1368 Long Creek Rd., Ridgedale
• (417) 334-4860

Known as the home of the Polynesian Princess excursion boat (see its listing in the Attractions chapter), Gage's also offers groceries, fishing guides, ski boats, Waverunners, and boat slips by the day or year. Forever Resorts offers houseboat rentals by the day or week. The boats come equipped with a variety of luxury features. If you're looking for something in particular, Forever Resorts probably has it. Call (417) 335-3042 or (800) 255-5561 in advance for reservations, especially in the summer.

Hitch-N-Post
Mo. Hwy. 165 • (417) 334-3395

Landlocked and not a marina, the Hitch-N-Post is still without peer as a place to load up on bait, marine fuel, camping supplies, life jackets, groceries, and anything else you might need. The shop also offers fishing guide referral and an up-to-the-minute daily fishing report. Hitch-N-Post is across from Table Rock State Park.

Indian Point Marina
Indian Point Rd. • (417) 338-2891

Located on the north side of Table Rock Lake near Silver Dollar City, Indian Point Marina rents 135-horse power ski boats for $95 for 4 hours and $175 for 8 hours. The 175-horsepower boats go for $127 for 4 hours and $220 for 8 hours. You can get a 24-foot pontoon boat for the same price as the 135-horse power ski boat. Ski equipment is extra. Their 40-foot house boats rent for $210 a night on weekends or $1,112 for the week for 4 people or for 8 people they go from $270 a night on weekends to $1,448 for a week. The deposit is $250. The marina is open year round but houseboats are only available April through December. Jet skis rent by the hour and start at $40 for a 1-seater and go up to $50 an hour for a 3-seater. Fuel is included in the Jet Ski rental price. Indian Point has 20 wet storage stalls, a snack shop, and tackle and live bait.

Lilley's Landing Resort & Marina
367 River Ln.
- **(417) 334-6380, (888) 545-5397**
- **www.branson.net/llresort or www.ozarkanglers.com**

Lilley's is a one-stop trout angler's dream. You can spend the night at the resort and then hook up with a fishing guide for a variety of different types of fishing adventures. All trips are on Lake Taneycomo with an experienced guide. Rates for 4-hour trips are $155 for up to 2 people and $230 for 8 hours up to 2 people. Fly fishing wading guides will schedule trips day or night for $100 for one person for 4 hours or $175 for 8 hours with one person. If you'd like to go out on your own in a boat they have johnboats starting at $40 for 4 hours, pontoons for $90 for four hours and aluminum boats with trolling motors for $30. There's always a boat mechanic on duty. The marina's specialty is selling artificial lures and flies, and it also provides hot shore lunches during some of the guide trips on Lake Taneycomo.

Main Street Marina
500 E. Main St • (417) 334-2263
- **www.branson.com/mainstreet/boat.html**

Main Street boasts a top-notch fishing guide service in addition to a full complement of bait and tackle and fishing boats for Lake Taneycomo. Owner Bob Klein emphasizes that his 4 fishing guides are all insured and will spend a little extra time with clients if the fish aren't a bitin'. Fishing guides go out for $130 for 4 hours and $220 for 8 hours on Lake Taneycomo and $165 for 4 hours and $220 for 8 hours on Table Rock Lake. Main Street Marina has been in business for more than 30 years and has a large selections of rental boats. Fishing boats go for $31 for a half day and $42 for a full day. Bass boats are $50 and $80 for half and full days. The 20-foot pontoon boats run $60 for half a day and $100 a full day. Twenty four-foot boats go for $10 more. The marina is open year round.

Ozarks Houseboat Adventures
Mo. Hwy. H, Lampe
- **(417) 739-4300, (800) 338-1126**

At Baxter Boat Dock on Table Rock Lake, Ozarks Houseboat Adventures offer Aqua Cha-

let fiberglass and aluminum pontoon houseboats, 30- and 40-foot sizes, outfitted with 90 hp outboard motors. The boats sleep six to eight, have all cookware and linen furnished, and include a sunning deck on top. The boats are available May through October.

Port of Kimberling Marina
Lake Rd. 13-50, Kimberling City
- **(417) 739-2315**

Touted as Table Rock Lake's largest marina, it also offers boat slips, dry storage, and a complete ski shop with sales, service, rental, and instruction. You may call Skiers Wharf directly at (417) 739-2628 .What's Up Dock rents speedboats and personal watercraft as well; call (417) 739-4511 Table Rock Lake Pontoon Rentals is also here at (417) 739-2732 or (417) 652-9884. For the campground, call (417) 739-5377. See the listing in Scuba Diving for the dive shop.

Riverlake Resort & Marina
146 Riverlake Cir., Hollister
- **(417) 334-2800**
- **www.branson.com/branson.rlake**

Bring the entire family to Riverlake on Lake Taneycomo for a summertime reunion and fishing trip. The 35-unit resort ranges from $49 per night to $155 per night. All units feature a kitchenette. They will be happy to cater a meal for your group and serve it outside on picnic tables. The marina features 16-foot aluminum fishing boats for $36 for a full day or $24 for a half day. One tank of fuel is included in the price. You can get a family-sized pontoon for $40 for 4 hours or $75 for 8 hours. The bass boats go for $35 for a half day and $60 for a full day. Fuel is extra. There's an annual trout fishing tournament held each year at the resort.

Scotty's Trout Dock
395 N. Lakefront Rd. • (417) 334-4288

Sometimes it's just as much fun to fish from the dock as from a boat, and Scotty's is located right on the Taneycomo lakefront next to a large public-access fishing dock. If you're not having much luck, you can get a fishing boat or a pontoon boat from Scotty's for around $34 an hour or $100 a day respectively. Scotty will set you up with a fishing guide for a half or full day starting at around $110 for two people.

State Park Marina
State Park Marina Rd., Mo. Hwy. 165
- **(417) 334-3069**

When the marina boasts everything on the water, it's not kidding. Besides the usual fishing watercraft, it also rents paddleboats, canoes, Waverunners, and ski boats. Or sign up for a little parasailing. It also has a general store and a dive shop, which is listed in the subsequent Scuba Diving section. This marina is at Table Rock State Park. The marina is closed December through March.

Tri-Lakes Houseboat Rentals
Lake Rd. 13-50, Kimberling City
• (417) 739-2370, (800) 982-2628
• www.tri-lakeshouseboat.com

One of the many marine services at Port of Kimberling, Tri-Lakes Houseboat Rentals features a full range of houseboats that sleep anywhere from 4 to 12 people. The 2-night minimum rate for a 4-person boat is $460 and $850 for up to 12 people. You can get boats by the week or month. Reservations are recommended and the deposit is $300.

What's Up Dock
Rock Lane Resort, Indian Point Rd.
• (417) 338-8424

This is a sister marina to the What's Up Dock at Port of Kimberling.

Where to Buy a Boat

Bass Pro Shops
1935 S. Campbell, Ave., Springfield
• (417) 887-7334, (888) 442-6337
• www.basspro.com

People come from around the world to visit Bass Pro Shops in Springfield and no doubt many of them come for the boats. Beginning when you drive by their huge outdoor showroom you are sure to be impressed by their overwhelming list of models, features, options, and prices. You can basically spend as much money on a boat as you so desire. You name the option and they'll customize the boat any way you like it. Want lime green stripes to match the ones on the RV? No problem. At Bass Pro you can find a full selection of Tracker boats including the popular Tracker, Sun Tracker, Tahoe, and Nitro models. The Nitro Savage 912 fiberglass boat with a single console lists for $25,695. If that's a little pricey, you can get the Tracker Party Deck 21 boat for around $14,595. If that's still too steep, there's an 11-foot aluminum boat for $599, but if you want a 6 horse-power motor to go with it, the price goes up to $1,759. The sales reps at Bass Pro will help you wade through the vast sea of options so that you've got enough left over for bait.

Hydrotech Marine
1806 Deffer Dr., Nixa • (417) 725-0600
• www. Hydrotechmarine.com

Serious boat shoppers can pick out a model at Hydrotech Marine and they'll even let you test drive it on Table Rock Lake. The emphasis is on "serious" here. In addition to their nice selection of Triton bass boats which top out at around $35,000 for a 22-footer with a Yamaha motor you can get Hurricane deck boats and basic Alumacraft aluminum boats for around $10,000. They are an official Yamaha service center, machine shop, and embroidery shop. Embroidery shop? That's right. Hydrotech's general manager Ron Crosswhite says his company does all the embroidery for the Triton and Yamaha pro clothing lines.

Scuba Diving

Snorkeling, scuba diving, spearfishing, and underwater photography are popular in the crystal-clear streams and lakes of the Ozarks. At Table Rock, Bull Shoals, Beaver, and Norfork (in Arkansas) lakes, visibility is often as much as 15 to 25 feet. The Ozarks has a surprising diversity of underwater wildlife, and its waters attract dive groups from as far away as Kansas City. Remember, safety first when diving; the following shops can help provide proper training and equipment maintenance.

INSIDERS' TIP
Two of Branson's oldest and best-known water attractions, the Lake Queen and Sammy Lane Pirate Cruise, launch from downtown Branson onto Lake Taneycomo. See their listings in the Attractions chapter.

Aquasports Scuba Center
5601 S. Campbell Ave., Springfield
• (417) 883-5151, (800) 743-8355

Aquasports provides instruction from snorkeling and basic open-water scuba to instructor-level classes as well as many specialty classes such as underwater photography, spearfishing, dry-suit diving, and ice diving. Before you buy or rent scuba gear, you can try it out in the center's heated indoor pool. Group excursions are available to Table Rock, Bull Shoals, and Beaver lakes.

Port of Kimberling Scuba
49-A Lake Rd., Kimberling City
• **(417) 739-5400**

This is a well-known, full-service dive shop, providing instruction at all levels, chartered dive trips, scuba supplies, and rental equipment.

State Park Dive Shop
State Park Marina Rd. and intersection of Mo. Hwy. 165
• **(417) 334-3069**

Full certification instruction is offered here, but before you jump in with both feet for extended lessons, you might try out what the shop calls a "scuba experience," a two-hour trial run. The shop also offers dive tours and group tours. It rents dive boats and scuba gear and provides sales and repair services.

Sailing and Parasailing

It's not uncommon to find a sailboat or three on Table Rock Lake during a windy summer day. Your best bet for rental equipment is the State Park Marina, at the Table Rock State Park, or the Port of Kimberling Marina in Kimberling City, (see previous listings). If sailing is what floats you, make the trip to Stockton, Missouri, home of the state's top sailing lake, Stockton Lake. For information call the Lake Stockton Association at (417) 276-5161. If the air on Table Rock Lake is a little too calm for sailboating, you might want to try parasailing instead. Many of the area marinas have rental gear and are willing to offer helpful tips for both the driver of the boat and the parasailer.

Swimming

Many of the public-use areas at Table Rock and Bull Shoals lakes have imported sandy beaches. The best known is probably Moonshine Beach on Table Rock, just north of the dam off Mo. Highway 165. The U.S. Army Corps of Engineers campgrounds also have public swimming beaches. Nominal day-use fees are charged at the rate of $1 a person age 13 and older, with a maximum of $3 a car. These rates are subject to change throughout the year. For a complete list of public access areas operated by the Corps, see our listing in the Campgrounds and RV Parks chapter or visit the Corps website

at www.swl.usace.army.mil/parks/tabrock/campsite-areas.html.

Resources

Missouri Department of Conservation
(573) 751-4115
• **www.conservation.state.mo.us**

The Fisheries Division publishes an annual fishing report called Fishing Prospects, which lists some of the more popular lakes and streams for fishing in Missouri as well as information on fish populations. It is available free by writing the department at P.O. Box 180, Jefferson City, Mo. 65102 or from any Fisheries office throughout the state.

Arkansas Game and Fish Commission
2 Natural Resources Dr.,
Little Rock, Ark. 72205
• **(501) 223-6300, (800) 364-GAME**
• **www.agfc.state.ar.us.html**

Call the toll-free number to order a fishing license or to get free brochures on fishing in Arkansas, boating regulations, and area wildlife.

U.S. Army Corps of Engineers
(417) 334-4101, (870) 425-2700 (for Bull Shoals and Norfork Lakes)

Dock permit information, a list of campgrounds and public use areas, Corps regulations, maps, and other information are available by contacting the Corps at the Table Rock Lake Office, 4600 Mo. Hwy. 165 Suite A, 65615 or Mountain Home Project Office, P.O. Box 369, Mountain Home, Ark. 72653. Visit the Corps website at www.swl.usace.army.mil/parks/tabrock.

Guys 'N Gals BASS Association
110 Cliborne, Republic • (417) 732-1566

Just like the name says, this association is for men and women who like to fish together. Owner, Ron Crosswhite says 85 percent of the club's 150 or so members are married couples. The yearly dues are just $30 per couple and tournament entry fees are just $90; a small price to pay for a chance to win a brand new 18-foot Triton bass boat. See, Ron is the general manager of Hydrotech Marine in Nixa, (see individual listing in this chapter) where Triton boats are sold. Through his nifty connection there he's able to award one lucky couple with the boat in a drawing at the Guys 'N Gals annual championship tournament which is held each

October. There are 7 regular season tournaments where couples can qualify for the annual prize.

Trout Fishing Organizations

Arkansas Chapter Trout Unlimited,
P.O. Box 4855, Fayetteville, Ark. 72702

Friends of Lake Taneycomo,
P.O. Box 1734, Branson, Mo. 65615

North Arkansas Fly Fishers,
P.O. Box 1213, Mountain Home,
Ark. 72653

Publications

Many of the libraries in the Tri-Lakes area have copies of the following guide books: *The Greatest Ozarks Guidebook* by Harry and Phyl Dark, published by Greatest Graphics, Inc., features plenty of information on the rivers, streams, and lakes as well as camping, state parks, and national recreation areas; *The Ozarks Outdoors* by Milton D. Rafferty, University of Oklahoma Press, is a well-researched and comprehensive resource about the Ozarks, with chapters on floating and fishing the lakes and rivers, hiking, and camping. There are also maps and addresses to write for more information on a region-by-region basis. *Ozark Trout Tales, A Fishing Guide for the White River System* by Steve Wright can be ordered from the White River Chronicle, P.O. Box 4653, Fayetteville, Ark. 72702-4653, (800) 418-7688, and is an excellent history and how-to of trout fishing in tailwaters below each of the following dams: Table Rock, Bull Shoals, Beaver, Norfolk, and Greer's Ferry. It is available in area bookstores or at the above address for $24.95. *Pro's Guide to Fishing Missouri Lakes* by Monte Burch, Outdoor World Press Inc., provides lake by lake descriptive information, maps, and fishing tips, including plenty of quotes from the pros who fish them. *Two Ozark Rivers* by Oliver Schuchard and Steve Kohler, University of Missouri Press, Columbia, has great photographs and a detailed historical and ecological perspective on the Current and Jacks Fork Rivers. Sign up to receive copies of the *Taneycomo Trout Times* by visiting the website http://www.branson.net/fishing/subscription.html.

Campgrounds and RV Parks

Long before the word tourism entered the vocabulary of native Ozarkians, people were coming to these parts to escape city life, fish in the rivers, hunt in the woods, and take in the clean, natural air of the Ozark Mountains. Some of them stayed with their country relatives, but most camped out along the White River, the James River and, after 1913, Lake Taneycomo. After Table Rock Lake Dam was completed in 1958, small commercial campgrounds began popping up around the newly impounded lake to meet the demand of outdoors lovers, who by now were making regular trips to the area. When the Mabe brothers began offering these campers a little weekend musical entertainment out of an old roller-skating rink, the word tourism became a common topic around here.

In a sense, not much has changed. The Mabe brothers are still entertaining, only now they have a fancy place on The Strip called the Baldknobbers Jamboree Theatre, and campers are still coming to enjoy the scenery and to hunt and fish. The major difference today is that their reason for coming has changed. They come for the entertainment, and while they're here they camp out.

Campgrounds and RV parks are big business in Branson. People aren't just coming to camp lakeside anymore. Many of the more than 5,000 campsites in the area are smack dab in the middle of town. The Pea Patch RV Park is just 100 yards off The Strip and KOA Campground is closer than that. The list of amenities at these places would make one of the earliest campers either jealous or offended. We've got campgrounds with swimming pools, laundry machines, grocery stores, car rentals, video arcades, full-service marinas, and more electricity than you can shake a stick at. Some of them are so popular they even host entire conventions.

Fortunately for those who prefer primitive camping, we still have plenty of places without cable television and phones. They are more the exception than the rule, however. If you're looking to really rough it, we suggest the nearby Mark Twain National Forest or the Hercules Glades wilderness area within the forest. (See our Recreation and the Outdooors chapter for more on these areas.) You can call the National Park Service at (417) 732-2662 for information.

LOOK FOR:
- **State Parks**
- **RV Sites**
- **Cabins**
- **Tent Sites**
- **Short-term Rentals**
- **Large Group Sites**
- **Rates**

When to Come and How Much to Pay

If you're bringing your own recreational vehicle to town, be sure to make a reservation before you leave home. Many of these places require a minimum stay and a deposit. If you're coming in peak season—June through August for camping—you could have trouble finding an available spot. The rates are also higher in the summer than in the spring and fall. The best times to come are early spring and late fall. You'll get the best rates and won't have any trouble finding space. Since Branson is quickly becoming a year-round destination, many of the parks are staying open all year, especially those in town. Rates are the absolute lowest in January and February, but you may get what you pay for as far as the weather is concerned. Our heaviest snowfalls don't last for more than a couple of days, but it's not uncommon to have several days in a row with temperatures in the low to mid 30s.

If your vacation is scheduled for August, never fear, most of the campgrounds and RV parks offer a number of discounts. They routinely offer Good Sam discounts, AAA and AARP discounts. They also offer fishing packages and extended stay packages, which can include show tickets and meals. Be sure to pick up brochures when you arrive because some of them have coupons attached. The average cost for a full RV hookup is around $20 a day (some places charge more if your party is larger than two people). Tent sites cost less, and cottages and cabins go for slightly more.

Policies

Many of the RV parks also have mobile homes, cabins, popup campers, and hotel units. Although they usually don't mind if you bring your pet along in your own rig, pets are generally not welcome in the rentals. The same goes for smoking. Be sure to ask these questions when you make your reservations. Some places prohibit alcoholic beverages so, again, ask if you're planning on bringing any.

If you're going to need phone service, you are generally out of luck. America's Best Campgrounds will hook up a private phone for a fee, but most of the others either have one or two pay phones or none at all. Again, don't wait until you check-in before you ask. Check-in time runs around 3 PM and checkout is generally 10 AM or before. A few of the places have offices that stay open 24 hours a day but most do not. However, owners tend to stick nearby and often live on the properties year round.

Many of the listings in this section are located within a few blocks of The Strip. The ones a little further out generally offer shuttle service into town either for free or a small charge. Or you can arrange to have a rental car delivered to your campsite before you arrive. (See our Getting Here, Getting Around chapter for a list of rental car companies.)

Location

The commercial campgrounds and RV parks in this section have been listed according to location. The Branson City Campgrounds, listed in the Public Campgrounds section, are on Lake Taneycomo. All the Indian Point Road commercial campgrounds are on or near Table Rock Lake. Since many of the places do not have numbered addresses, be sure to call for specific driving directions. We have given our directions based on the assumption that you will be leaving from The Strip; however, if you are coming from out of town, there may be a better route than the one we have described.

Public Campgrounds

Branson City Campground No.1 and No.2
200 S. BoxCar Willie Dr.
• No.1, (417) 334-2915;
No.2, (417) 334-8857

It's not uncommon to find the same faces year after year at the Branson City Campgrounds. More than 36,000 campers rent space each year. Retirees have long enjoyed the superb location and the camaraderie with the other

residents. (See our listing for Branson City Campgrounds in the Retirement chapter as well.) With a combined 350 sites, the campgrounds are located on Lake Taneycomo in downtown Branson. The folks in the campgrounds enjoy feeding the geese that gather along the riverbanks, fishing for trout from one of six fishing docks or shoving off from one of three boat ramps. There are three large picnic shelters plus a number of tables. The showers and restrooms have recently been renovated and now in-

INSIDERS' TIP

Pizza Chef in Branson West, (417) 336-5232, makes deliveries to Indian Point Road until 8 PM. There is no delivery charge, but drivers do appreciate tips.

clude central heating and air conditioning. Swimmers and tennis players will find their fun at nearby North Beach Park, which is located just north of the campgrounds.

The rates are $15 per day for a full hookup. Just water and electricity are $14. Campground No. 2 closes during the winter, but No. 1 stays open all year.

Table Rock State Park
U.S. Hwy. 165 • (417) 334-4704
• www.boatbranson.com

This 35-acre park, located just south of the Table Rock Dam, near the Showboat Branson Belle, is run by the Missouri Department of Natural Resources. Its 165 campsites come with basic and full hookups available only on a first-come, first-served basis. You can use the concrete boat launch for free. The park has a full-service marina with rental boats and scuba-diving equipment. The marina can be reached by calling (417) 334-2628, or you can write to the Missouri Department of Natural Resources at P.O. Box 176, Jefferson City, Mo. 65102. Call them at (800) 334-6946 for more information about the Table Rock State Park and other state-run parks.

U.S. Army Corps of Engineers Campgrounds
Main Office, Mo. Hwy. 165 adjacent to Table Rock Dam • (417) 334-4101
Aunt's Creek, Reeds Spring
• (417) 739-2792
Baxter, Lampe • (417) 779-5370
Big M, Cassville • (417) 271-3190
Campbell Point, Shell Knob
• (417) 858-3903
Cape Fair, Galena • (417) 538-2220
Cow Creek, Blue Eye • (417) 779-5377
Cricket Creek, Omaha, Arkansas
• (870) 426-3331
Eagle Rock, Eagle Rock • (417) 271-3215
Indian Point, Branson • (417) 338-2121
Joe Bald, Kimberling City • (417) 739-2787
Long Creek, Ridgedale • (417) 334-8427
Mill Creek, Lampe • (417) 779-5376
Old Highway 86, Blue Eye
• (417) 779-5376
Port of Kimberling, Kimberling City
• (417) 779-5377
Viney Creek, Golden • (417) 271-3860
Viola, Shell Knob • (417) 858-3904

The U.S. Army Corps of Engineers operates 16 public recreation areas on Table Rock Lake. All come outfitted with toilets, showers, drinking water, fire rings, picnic tables, swimming beaches, boat-launching ramps, and parking spaces. The campgrounds have electric hook-ups and dump stations for your travel trailer. The Corps of Engineers campgrounds open between April 1 and May 15. A few close after Labor Day, but some of them stay open until the end of October.

The Corps allows up to 70 percent of the campsites in any given park to be reserved in advance. The remainder are available on a first-come, first-served basis. The fees vary according to what type of site you request but generally run between $10 and $15 per night, plus an additional $3 administrative fee. You can make reservations by mail with a check or money order, or reserve by phone with a credit card. Day use fees for the swimming beaches and picnic areas are $1 per person with a maximum of $3 per car. The boat launch fee is $2.

Visitors over the age of 62 can request a Golden Age Passport that entitles the holder to a 50 percent discount off camping and day-use fees at any Corps-operated facility on any of the area's lakes. The lifetime pass costs $10 and is available at any park attendant booth or at the Corps of Engineers Visitors Center on Mo. Highway 165 adjacent to Table Rock Dam.

Campers can get a guidebook at the visitors center, which lists each campground's location and amenities. For driving directions you may call the campgrounds individually.

Commercial Campgrounds In and Around Branson

Acorn Acres RV Park & Campground
W. Mo. Hwy. 76
• (417) 338-2500, (800) 338-2504
• acornacresrv@juno.com

To get to Acorn Acres from Branson, follow The Strip west out of town. After you pass the Indian Point/Silver Dollar City turnoff, go 1 mile and look for the signs on your left. The park has 55 full-hookup RV sites with 20 pull through sites, and 9 tent sites. You can get 30- or 50-amp electrical service and cable TV with your hookup. The park features a swimming pool, private showers, laundry facility, covered pavilion, concrete patios, game room, playground, horseshoe pit, and plenty of shaded picnic tables. Rates range from around $16 a day for a tent site to $24 a day for a full hookup. The manager will be happy to make your show ticket reservations and put together a complete vacation package with meals and all. They will

Bull Shoals Lake is less crowded than Table Rock or Taneycomo in the summer.

Credit A.C. Haralson/Arkansas Dept. of Parks & Tourism

also arrange for your transportation into town. Acorn Acres is open year round.

America's Best Campground
499 Buena Vista Rd.
• **(417) 336-4399, (800) 671-4399**
• **abcbransonnow.com**

This large campground is well off the beaten path, but only a half-mile north of the Mel Tillis Theater on Mo. Highway 248. You can't see it from the highway so look for the red, white, and blue sign on Mo. 248 directing you west to Buena Vista Road.

There are 150 pull throughs with full hookups, concrete patio, picnic table, and grill. Sites have 30-, 50-, and 100-amps of electricity. Satellite TV is available at every site. Six well-kept cabins come with air conditioning, heat, and TV, but no restrooms or linens. There are a few tent sites with water and electricity.

The amenities at ABC include a swimming pool with a hot tub, phone hookups, picnic tables, barbecue grills, laundry facilities, a gift shop, and convenience store, basketball courts, horseshoe pits, playground, air-conditioned recreation room, and closed-circuit camera for security. They also have a 1,200-square foot pavilion, which can be reserved for large group events. Sites run between $18 and $29 a day

depending on what type of services you choose. The cabins run close to $30 and can sleep up to four. The campground is open all year. Be sure to take advantage of their valet parking.

Branson Musicland Campground
116 N. Gretna Rd. • (417) 334-0848

Just one block off The Strip, Musicland Campground caters to RVs only, but does have five four-person cabins with no plumbing. Huge trees provide great shade in the summertime, and guests can cool off in the swimming pool or step inside the recreation room. With 120 sites in a prime location, guests are usually advised to make reservations well in advance.

Rates range from $22.50 for a basic hookup to $29.50 for a bus-chassis vehicle. The cabins go for around $30 a night. Amenities include a laundry facility, cable television, restrooms, and a small gift shop. Alcohol is not allowed on the grounds. The campground is closed November through March.

Branson Shenanigans RV Park
3675 Keeter St.
• **(417) 334-1920, (800) 338-7275**
• **www.branson.com/bsrvpark**

Branson Shenanigans boasts the most private bathrooms of any RV park in the area.

Each bathroom has a private entrance, sink, toilet, and shower. You'll also find a luxurious clubhouse with plenty of comfortable furniture, a fireplace, and a deck overlooking a shaded creek. The park has 30 sites with 25 pull throughs and sits just off The Strip near the Dutton Family Theatre. The hookups have 30- and 50-amp electrical service, free cable TV, and barbecue grills. Shenanigans also has a laundry room, picnic areas, and a public phone. They offer valet parking and shuttle service in town.

The park is open from March through November and rates run between $18 and $25 a night.

Branson Stagecoach RV Park
5751 Mo. Hwy. 165
• (417) 335-8185, (800) 446-7110

Located just 1 mile south of Table Rock Dam, Branson Stagecoach RV Park is far enough out of town to be well-secluded but less than 15 minutes from The Strip. The park has 40 full-hookup sites that come with 30- or 50-amp electrical service and average $19 per day. The park has large, level sites and can accommodate the largest of RVs. On the grounds you will find a swimming pool, spa, picnic tables, recreation room with video games, library, 24-hour laundry facility, playground, dump station, public telephone, private showers, and a meeting room for up to 36 people. There is also a restaurant adjacent to the park. They will cater your next group gathering, shuttle you around town, or set you up with a rental car if you need your own wheels. The office is open 24 hours a day and the park is open year round.

Chastain's of Branson
397 Animal Safari Rd.
• (417) 334-4414, (800) 467-7611
• chastainsrv@tri-lakes.net

To get to Chastain's from The Strip take Mo. Highway 165 south past the Ain't Misbehavin' Supper Club. Turn right onto Animal Safari Rd. Look for the signs on the left leading you to the entrance road. At Chastain's, you'll find a variety of accommodations including cabins, mobile homes, tent sites, and RV hookups. There is a shaded swimming pool, (children under the age of 12 are not allowed to swim without an adult present), grocery store, laundry facility, pavilion, exercise room, restrooms, playground, and picnic tables. The RV sites are paved and come with 30- and 50-amp electric service, satellite TV, and propane. They offer shuttle service to The Strip and will arrange to have your show tickets delivered before you arrive. The air-conditioned conference building accommodates 600 people. They'll be happy to help you find catering services for your next event.

The rates at Chastain's range from $21.50 for a basic tent site with water and electricity. RV sites are from $17.50 to $26.50 and the cabins go for around $30 per night. The fully equipped mobile homes are $60 a night and can sleep eight.

Compton Ridge Campground
Mo. Hwy. 265 • (417) 338-2911, (800) 233-8648; Lodge, (417) 338-2949; North Park, (417) 338-2747

Fiddlers from across the country gather each May and September at the 85-acre Compton Ridge Campground for the State of the Ozarks Fiddlers Convention (see our Annual Events chapter). Spectators are welcome to drop by the 650-seat convention building and listen to these musicians play their fiddles, which is one of the area's most popular instruments.

The campground is divided into three sections. The main campground is reserved for tents and pop-up campers. You can rent a furnished pop-up, just bring your own linens. The Lodge has large guest rooms with kitchenettes. The North Park has full-hookup sites, barbecue grills, and picnic tables. All guests can take advantage of their three swimming pools (one of them is indoors), the kiddie wadding pool, tennis court, playground, laundry facility, and hiking trail. They also have an 80-square-foot covered kitchen shelter with each site. Rates vary according to the type of site you request but average around $30 a night. If you need assistance with your show ticket reservations, they will make the calls for you. They also have rental cars available.

Compton Ridge is 1 mile south of Silver

> ## INSIDERS' TIP
> Many of the theaters and restaurants have special parking places for RVs. But if you're taking your rig into downtown Branson, better think twice. You can't park along the streets and some of the parking lots do not accommodate long vehicles. Call the Downtown Branson Main Street Association at (417) 334-1548 for information on RV parking.

Dollar City and 5 miles north of Table Rock Dam. To get there from The Strip go west to Mo. 265, then turn south and look for the signs.

Pea Patch RV Park
3330 W. Harvey Harvey Ln.
• (417) 335-3958, (800) 810-9333

Located right in the heart of the action, Pea Patch RV Park sits behind Ripley's Believe It or Not! Museum just off The Strip on Harvey Lane. They have 83 full hookups, a swimming pool, laundry facilities, restrooms, a dump station, picnic tables, and free morning coffee. The property sits high on a hill, and from the pool you can see clear across town. Their rates are $22 for back-in sites and $24 for pull-throughs. You can also arrange for a rental car at Pea Patch through A-1 (417) 335-3932 or Dollar (417) 335-8588. Pea Patch is open year round.

Silver Dollar City Campground
Mo. Hwy. 265
• (417) 338-8189, (800) 477-5164
• www.silverdollarcity.com

Since this 185-unit campground is owned by Silver Dollar City Properties, guests who purchase a Camper Club membership receive discounts at all the SDC properties in Branson as well as free admission to Dollywood in Pigeon Forge, Tennessee, and White Water and American Adventures, both in Atlanta.

Club members also get 10 percent off their campsite rates. You can choose from tent sites, full-hookup sites, or one-room cabins. The campground has a swimming pool, playground, video arcade, grocery store, laundry facility, and restroom. They offer free shuttle service to Silver Dollar City. The rates range from $11 for a tent site to around $35 for a 50-amp hookup. This campground is open from March to December.

Indian Point Road

To get to Indian Point Road from Branson, go west on The Strip past the Shepherd of The Hills Homestead. Go 5 miles and look for the signs leading to Silver Dollar City. When you come to the second stoplight, turn left onto Indian Point Road, just as if you were going to Silver Dollar City. You will come to the SDC parking lots on your right and left, but go right past them and within 200 yards or so you will begin to see signs directing you to the resorts and marinas on Indian Point. Indian Point Road is quite narrow in places and can be treacher-

ous in bad weather. There are very few places to turn around or pull off.

Antlers Resort and Campground
Indian Point Rd. • (417) 338-2331

Antlers Resort and Campground has one-, two-, and three-bedroom cabins, mobile and RV hookups. Some of their cabins can hold up to 12 people. They come fully furnished with kitchens and decks. The campground has tent spaces with prices starting at $14 a day. A full hookup runs about $18 a day. These rates are for two people. Each additional person is $2. The campground is located right on Table Rock Lake just 1 mile south of Silver Dollar City. From Indian Point Road, turn left on White Wing Road, then go 3/4-mile and Antlers will be on your left.

Antlers has a variety of rental boats available, including pontoon boats, ski boats, bass boats, and boats with trolling motors as well as water-ski equipment. The 20-foot Bass Buggy pontoon boat goes for $120 a day plus gas, and the basic boat without a motor is just $10 a day. The campground has a launch ramp and a 22-slip covered dock. The campground's general store sells tackle, worms, groceries, and fishing licenses, too. If you need a fishing guide, the staff will schedule one for an additional fee.

The campground also has a swimming pool, picnic tables, barbecue grills, and recreation room with pinball, pool table, and video games. The RV and tent sites sit back from the shoreline, but the cabins and mobile homes are right next to the water. Antlers is open year round.

Deer Run Campground
Indian Point Rd.
• (417) 338-2222, (800) 901-3337

At Deer Run Campground you don't get a view of Table Rock Lake, but you do get to be just 200 yards from Silver Dollar City's front door. For those of you who don't want to make the trip on foot, you can get a ride from your campsite. Deer Run has 140 shaded RV sites, plenty of tent sites, and cabins. The cabins are little more than four walls and a roof; they are not sheet-rocked or painted. You do, however, get a ceiling fan and a window in each one. They come with three twin beds and that's all, folks. The cabins are $22.00 per night for two people. Add $2 per person per night.

If you're looking for a little more comfort, you can rent a 23-foot travel trailer with a full bathroom, kitchen, and two double beds. The RV sites come with 50-amp electrical service, water, and sewer. Rates range from $15 to $30 a night. The campground also has a swimming pool, play area, game room and private showers. For a small fee, the staff will shuttle you into town. The ride to SDC is free. If you want all the comforts of home, right next door is the 90-room Deer Run Motel. They have modern, spacious rooms, units with kitchenettes, and cable TV. Standard room rates run around $65 a night. You can reach the motel at (417) 338-2223.

Trail's End Resort and RV Park
Indian Point Rd.
- **(417) 338-2633, (800) 888-1891**
- **www.indianpoint.com**

The lodging possibilities at Trail's End Resort and RV Park range from RV hookups to cottages to log cabins to two- and three-bedroom mobile homes. The park has 12 RV sites and each one comes with 20-, 30-, or 50-amp electrical service, water and sewer, picnic table, and barbecue grill. You can also rent RVs from the park. Each RV comes fully furnished with a queen bed, full bath, kitchen, cable TV, air conditioning, picnic table, and barbecue grill. The mobile homes also come fully furnished. The resort's grounds feature a swimming pool, volleyball net, horseshoes, tetherball, shuffle board, playground, hiking trail, and boat dock with rental boats. The full hookup sites run around $16 a day and the three-bedroom mobile homes go for up to $89 in peak season. There is no charge for children younger than the age of 4.

Lake Taneycomo

Branson KOA Campground
1025 Headwaters Rd.
- **(417) 334-7450, (800) 562-4177**
- **bransonkoa@aol.com**

This new camping facility, located five miles west of Mo. Highway 65 on Mo. Highway 165 near Table Rock Dam, sits right on the shore of Lake Taneycomo. With 170 full hook-up RV sites, 10 cabins and 10 tent sites, this is one of the area's larger camping establishments. RV hookups come with 30- and 50-amp electrical service and run about $25.95 per night. The cabins, which average $35.95 per night, have beds, electricity, and outdoor picnic tables and fire rings. The campground has a laundry facility, general store and gift ship, swimming pool, basketball goals, a playground, and horseshoes. They offer free shuttle into town and will make all your show reservations for you. The campground is closed December through February.

Cooper Creek Resort & Campground
471 Cooper Creek Rd.
- **(417) 334-4871, (800) 261-8398**
- **wwwbranson.com/coopercreek**

To get to Cooper Creek from The Strip take Fall Creek Road south approximately 1 mile. Look for the signs on your left. Cooper Creek offers 91 RV sites, and 19 one-, two-, and three-bedroom cabins that come with decks, fully equipped kitchens, ceiling fans, air conditioning, and cable TVs. Most of the sites have a view of Lake Taneycomo, depending on how thick the leaves are. The roads are paved at Cooper Creek so you don't have to worry about getting your rig stuck in the mud on a wet day. The hookups come with 30-or 50-amp electrical service and run about $24 a day. The cabins are slightly more.

The campground caters to anglers at Cooper Creek and offers bait and licenses, two lighted fishing docks, boat and motor rental, and a concrete launch ramp. Other amenities at the park include two swimming pools, laundry facilities, a grocery store, picnic tables, video arcade, and playground. The staff also offers shuttle service into Branson. Trout fishing enthusiasts are catered to at this resort. Ask for room service, and you'll get it. The park is open year round.

> **INSIDERS' TIP**
>
> If you're staying in a furnished cabin or mobile home at one of the area's campgrounds, you are still required to bring your own towel to the pool.

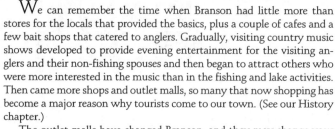

Shopping

We can remember the time when Branson had little more than stores for the locals that provided the basics, plus a couple of cafes and a few bait shops that catered to anglers. Gradually, visiting country music shows developed to provide evening entertainment for the visiting anglers and their non-fishing spouses and then began to attract others who were more interested in the music than in the fishing and lake activities. Then came more shops and outlet malls, so many that now shopping has become a major reason why tourists come to our town. (See our History chapter.)

The outlet malls have changed Branson, and they may change your idea of shopping. Savings of 40 to 60 percent might change any shopper! Many manufacturers have shops in the outlet malls, and you'll have to check each mall for your particular quarry or just browse around and see what interests you. We've divided the Branson area into several different types of shopping according to our logic, and we hope it serves as a general guide.

Branson and its environs are home to scores of talented artists and craftspeople. Some of your best buys in crafts can be had at the many area crafts shows (see our Annual Events chapter). If you're in the market for handcrafted treasures, check the shops at Silver Dollar City, the Engler Block, and The Grand Village, which we've listed in this chapter. We don't want to imply that our list is a comprehensive directory of all the shopping places in Branson. Far from it! It seems like every time we go out we discover another neat store tucked away somewhere. However, our list should get you started. We've included phone numbers for the stores. If a store doesn't have a number, that's because it's in a mall with a central phone number or because it is written up more fully in another section of shopping or another chapter (see our Index).

Unless we mention it, all stores willingly accept your plastic as well as cash, and many accept checks, but ask before writing one. Lots of the little retail shops, especially those in the theaters, may be closed during the slower months of January and February, but the bigger shopping centers and major stores are open year round.

Malls and Shopping Districts

Downtown Branson

Since the turn of the century, locals have made the trek from the outlying areas for their store-bought staples, hardware, and tools as well as Levi's and Big Smiths. Downtown hasn't changed much. It's a bit bigger, but the whole area is only about four square blocks, and it caters a bit more to the outsiders and tourists than it used to. There are more ice cream and crafts stores and several flea markets (see our Antiques, Crafts, and Flea Markets section later in this chapter). Main and Commercial streets could easily be a movie set for Middle Town, America. Whether you get off a tour bus or leave your car with the out-of-state plates, you'll feel at home with locals, and they'll go out of their way to show you a good time.

Exploring the couple dozen shops by foot is an adventure in itself, and you'll find yourself wanting to poke in just about every store. About half are open six days a week (closed Sundays), and many are open seven days a week, with reduced hours during the off season of January and February.

Check out some of our favorites in the downtown area. Dick's Oldtime 5 & 10 is worth poking in just for the vintage music on the jukebox. Its creative clutter of 50,000 plus items gives rise to the local saying, "If Dick's doesn't have it, you don't need it." (See our Specialty Shops section in this chapter for more on Dick's.) Branson Mercantile & Co., (417) 334-3634, is an old-fashioned dry goods store that has a great selection of jeans and overalls. Reish Shoe Store, (417) 334-3635, has been fitting Bransonites' feet for more than 60 years; it has a great bargain basement. Marlea's, (417) 334-5445, offers glitz and glitter for Branson's show girls and the woman who just wants to stand out from the crowd (see our Specialty Shops section in this chapter). Brier Rose Quilts and Gifts, (417) 336-3436, is Branson's quilt headquarters (650 of them ranging in price from $40 to $4,000), with quilting supplies and country gift items.

Downtown Branson also has a large array of restaurants, eateries, and snack shops for you to stop for a respite from the rigors of shopping. (See our Restaurants chapter for details.)

Outlet Shopping

Since the first settlers made their way into the remote Ozarks, we hillfolk always had to look beyond the hills for our store-bought necessities. Going to Springfield to do some shopping was a big deal for some of us, and for a real adventure, St. Louis and Kansas City beckoned. After becoming accustomed to leaving the hills for our "serious shopping," never in our wildest dreams could we have imagined that folks would be coming to Branson for the shopping. But that is exactly what has happened. Now fishing and country music aren't the only things that'll make you feel good when you come to Branson.

Outlet shopping is now a major reason for folks to make Branson their destination. Our first outlet store was the Carolina Mills Factory Outlet way back in 1975, and its dry goods products were of great practical value to residents and visitors alike. Then in 1988 the Factory Merchants of Branson, or Red Roof Mall as we locals call it, opened. The first year there were so few customers it was like shopping in a ghost mall. But like a field of dreams (build it and they will come!), the mall was soon crowded, and it even expanded to include more shops. When the Factory Shoppes of America (referred to as the Branson Meadows Mall by locals) opened in 1995 in Branson Meadows, Branson became one of the nation's major outlet shopping destinations.

Outlet shopping has changed Branson, and it may change you because few things make you feel better than saving money. Savings of 50 to 60 percent off the regular retail price is nothing to sneer at, so you may want to spend a few hours in each, checking out what is tempting and finding that special something that you just can't live without.

Branson has become a destination for shoppers.

Carolina Mills Factory Outlet
3615 76 Country Blvd. • (417) 334-2291
If you think only of sheets and towels when

you think of this outlet, think again. Yes, you can get lace, upholstery fabric, pillow cases, and sheets and towels, but this 5,000-square-foot, barn-like store also has a host of other items: gift closeouts from major stores and men's and women's ready-to-wear clothing, with an emphasis on Western wear. (It's a great favorite for square dance clubs to buy costumes!) Lots of entertainers from The Strip check in every so often to see what's new, and area Elvis impersonators buy scarves by the gross to throw to audiences after a sweaty encore of "Love Me Tender." There is also a large selection ladies' denims. A great favorite is the $5 room, where every item is $5 or less or two for $5.

Factory Merchants of Branson
1000 Pat Nash Dr. • (417) 335-6686

Located just off The Strip by White Water, this two-story red-roofed complex has nearly a hundred factory outlets, making it one of the largest outlet malls in the state. Locals refer to it as the "Red Roof Mall." It's large, and since it's on two levels, we suggest that you stop by the mall office so that you can pick up a guide and map. Shoppers will find children's and maternity fashions, home furnishings, jewelry and cosmetics, luggage and leather goods, shoes, women's and men's clothing (including full-size fashions), and accessories in a host of stores with internationally recognized brands: Samsonite, Eddie Bauer, Pfalzgraff, Lenox, Oneida, Corning, Bugle Boy, London Fog, Florsheim, Izod, Hush Puppies, and others.

Kids (and grownups) will like the clothing at Buster Brown Kids' Clothing and the Baby Guess and the huge selection of toys and games at Toys Unlimited. The do-it-yourselfer can find the latest tools and gadgets at two tools shops, Tools & More and Black & Decker. The Chicago Cutlery and Case Pocket Knives outlets have blades for both hunting camps and finest home kitchens. If you need sustenance for a renewed bout of shopping, there are five restaurants and snack places, including Apple Annie's Deli, Noodles Pizza & Pub, Auntie Anne's Pretzels, and the Rocky Mountain Chocolate Factory.

Stores are open most of the year from 9 AM to 9 PM except Thanksgiving and Christmas,

but with reduced hours of 10 AM to 6 PM during January and February.

Factory Shoppes at Branson Meadows
4562 Gretna Rd.
• (417) 339-2580, (800) SHOP-USA
• www.factorystores.com

This Victorian-themed outlet mall is Branson's newest, opening in 1995. It has handsome buildings in a nicely landscaped arena. An added attraction is the new Cinemas of Branson Meadows, an 11-screen movie theater complex showing first run movies which opened in March 2000. There is a large Spiegel outlet and a 30,000-square-foot VF Factory Outlet. For those not in the know, VF is the world's largest publicly held apparel manufacturer, encompassing brands like JanSport, Vanity Fair, Lee, Wrangler, Jantzen, and Healthtex. Around these two large anchor stores are more than 40 other outlets that include men's, women's, and children's apparel, footwear, jewelry, cosmetics, and home accessories. There's a Big & Tall store for men and a Dress Barn for women. Here's our list of favorites: the spacious atmosphere and inexpensive books at Foozles, the "food from around the world" at Vasken's International Market, and the nuts, dried fruit, exotic food items, and candy at Mountain Man Nut & Fruit Company. If you need a rest from shopping, Vasken's International Market offers great deli food.

And while you're waiting for your order, you can browse the foods from near and far, including locally produced raw Ozark wildflower honey.

The mall at Branson Meadows is open all year, usually from 9 AM to 9 PM, with reduced hours in January and February. It's closed Easter, Thanksgiving, and Christmas days.

Tanger Factory Outlet Center of Branson
300 Tanger Blvd.
• (417) 337-9328, (800) 407-2762
• www.tangeroutlet.com

Carved right out of a hillside and not visible from the highway, this outlet mall with 90+ shops is behind the Peppercorn Restaurant just before you reach Andy Williams' Moon River

> **INSIDERS' TIP**
> If you can't wait until you get back home to get those pictures developed, Branson Photo, (417) 337-5747, conveniently located at the junction of Mo. Highway 76 and U.S. Highway 65 in the Koi Garden Plaza, has one-hour developing. Also, both Wal-Mart and the Walgreen Drug Store have one-hour photo labs.

Outlet shoppers delight in finding name-brand clothing at rock-bottom prices.

Theatre on The Strip. Watch for the sign that tells you when to turn off on Tanger Boulevard. Brand name merchandise is featured at cut rate prices, including Ralph Lauren, Coach, Tommy Hilfiger, Van Heusen, Levi's, J. Crew, Haggar, Guess, Ann Taylor, SAS, Reebok, and others. Appealing to the younger set are Tommy Girl, Gap, Polo Jeans, and Disney outlets. You can find hosiery and intimates, housewares, home furnishings, accessories, books, CDs, and men's, women's and children's apparel and footwear. The sporting arms enthusiast will like the new Smith & Wesson outlet (order only) and their line of clothing. One of our favorites is We're Entertainment, a store which features music, movies, and nostalgia and collectible items connected with the entertainment industry. If you feel faint from shopping, The Fudgery can provide sustenance. Lots of folks do their Christmas shopping in July, outfit the kids for school, or load up for the year's birthday and wedding presents at Tanger. Whether you call it smart shopping or guilt-free shopping, Tanger advertises that if you find any item you buy advertised for less than you paid for it within 30 days of your purchase, bring in a copy of the ad and the Tanger merchant receipt to any of the 26 Tanger Outlets in the nation, and they'll refund the difference in cash.

Tanger is open from 9 AM to 9 PM every day of the week most of the year, with reduced hours January, February, and March. It's closed for Easter, Thanksgiving, and Christmas days.

Strips on The Strip

When you drive down The Strip, you'd think that it is one gigantic strip mall interspersed between live music theaters. Closer inspection proves that it is an adventure for the exploring shopper, jammed as it is with quaint shops and stores, shopping centers, and mini malls. Lots of the shops offer the same souvenirs and T-shirts, but some are unique, and we've mentioned some of the best in the Specialty Shops section of this chapter.

We've mentioned some of the malls on The Strip for your convenience with a few highlights, but it's up to you to explore and plunder all the stores in each one. Happy shopping!

Branson Heights Shopping Center
1557 76 Country Blvd. • no central phone

This was Branson's first shopping center, built way out in the country when there was nothing but barren roadside to the west and woods between it and downtown Branson. It has the usual mix of professional offices and shops. It has the Koin-O-Matic Laundromat in case you need some clean duds during your Branson visit. Gary's Coiffure's, (417) 334-2184, takes walk-ins, and you may see some of the stars from The Strip getting a trim there. Worth checking out are Hank's 20th Century Farm Power, a veritable museum of more than 800 precision made-to-scale replicas of classic farm machinery (see our Specialty Shops), and Quilts & Quilts Country Store, (417) 334-3243, one of the largest quilt shops in the tri-state area. Hollyhocks, (417) 334-1743, has an outstanding collection of country collectibles for the home, including a number of golf accents for the den. The center is also home to the Branson Heights Flea Market (see our Antiques, Crafts, and Flea Markets section later in this chapter).

Branson Mall
2206 76 Country Blvd. • (417) 334-5412

The 20-something shops and kiosks are packed in like books between the bookends of Wal-Mart and Nowell's Market, the two big stores in this shopping center. Every-one knows about Wal-Mart, and Nowell's is one of the largest grocery stores in the area. If you stay here from three days to a week, you'll find yourself taking advantage of the necessities of the two bookend stores, but don't neglect the shops between them. The Branson Mall is home to Happy Days Steak and Seafood (see our Restaurants chapter) and the 50s At the Hop Show (check our Shows chapter). There's an arcade where the kids can park while you investigate the place. While wandering around in the mall area, you can find our favorite place for corny, funny, and downright tacky hillbilly gifts—hillbilly toilet tissue (corncobs) and such stuff—at Hicks from the Sticks, (417) 334-2017, but you can also find nostalgia items and memorabilia and absolutely fabulous posters there. Owner Carol Hicks makes shopping for souvenirs and gag gifts fun. Once In A Blue Moon, (417) 336-6463, has lots of 99-cent items and others not much more expensive, as well as wind chimes, collectibles, and figurines. Melody's, (417) 335-6044, is a smart boutique that offers a touch of

Beverly Hills in Ozark Country. Maurices, (417) 335-6964, also offers fashions for those in the market for clothes. Southwest Accents, (417) 335-8916, has all sorts of items—jewelry, pottery, dolls, sand paintings—to give your home the flavor and the look of the Southwestern United States. The Ernest Tubb Record Shop has one of the best country-western music selections in the area, and the vintage albums always attract interested browsers (see our Music and Instruments section in this chapter). There are kiosks that cater to odd and interesting items as well as lots of comfortable chairs and benches so you can take a load off your feet and watch the tourists and locals pass by as you enjoy a cone filled with one (or more) of the 16 flavors from the nearby Hard Rock Ice Cream & Deli, (417) 334-3911. Locals say, "You can do it all at the Branson Mall!"

The Grand Village
2800 76 Country Blvd. • (417) 336-SHOP

You could easily miss The Grand Village, but you shouldn't. It's tucked away next to The Grand Palace. It's not exactly a strip mall, but a small shopping center, tastefully decorated and landscaped, conducive to wandering about in specialty shops and sitting on park benches in the mini-parks on the streets. If you've been to Silver Dollar City, you'll recognize the comfortable and casual style, fitting like an old pair of jeans and just as down-home. Owned and operated by SDC, The Grand village gives you shopping in style—no barns or warehouses. There's a central clock tower, a fountain and cobblestone streets, all slightly reminiscent of Old Charleston.

If you're shopping for the home, The Grand Village has a wide assortment of perfectly quaint shops. One of our faves is Remember When, Branson's best nostalgic shopping store. Where else can you get Three Stooges ties and Grapette soda signs? Peter Engler Designs, a shop that features unique work by Branson's most renowned woodcarver, has carvings and one-of-a-kind gifts and items (see our Arts and Culture chapter). Pretty Victorian accents can be found at Abbey Rose (417) 336-7229, angel collectors

INSIDERS' TIP

If they're in season, taste some famous Ozark tomatoes. You'll know why we swear that it takes rocky Ozark soil to raise tasty tomatoes. You can pick them up along with other fresh vegetables, flowers, and farm produce at the seasonal farmers market on the Branson lakefront. Look for signs at the end of Main Street, or call the Downtown Branson Main Street Association at (417) 334-1548 for market dates and times.

Downtown Branson is a shoppers paradise especially during the Christmas season when the stores stay open late to accommodate larger crowds.

Photo: Branson/Lakes Area Chamber of Commerce

will love the Angels Amongst Us store (417) 336-7235, and if you're into Coca-Cola collectibles, stop in at Classic Collectibles (417) 336-7253 where you can find anything connected with old Coca-Cola advertising—and even get a Coke! Storybook Treasures, (417) 336-7212 features a memorable children's shop with dolls and stuffed animals, toys, books, games, and puzzles. Reigning Cats & Dogs (417) 336-7247 features everything for pets and their owners. Browse the spacious bookshelves of T. Charleston & Son Books (417) 336-7233, Branson's largest family bookstore. The Grand Glitz (417) 336-7251 carries flashy fashions and is not for the conscious conservative. Even if you don't buy, it's fun to check it out! Kringle's (417) 336-7246 is Missouri's largest Christmas store—three spacious rooms of Christmas decorations, including Department 56 collectibles. Check our Specialty Shops and the Unusual section in this chapter for more details on some of our favorites. If you tire of shopping, and it's snack time, The Village Café has pastries and cappuccino, and the Hard Luck Diner (417) 336-7217 features treats and meals.

Even if you're not a shopper, The Grand Village is a great place to spend some time before catching a show at The Grand Place or other nearby theaters. No motor traffic is permitted on the village streets and you can wander, shop, or just relax. The Grand Village is open seven days a week from May through December, with shorter hours January through March. Call the number above for hours of operation.

Strips Off the Strip

You'll have to venture off The Strip to find these places, but with more of our visitors learning about and using the alternative routes now (see our Getting Here and Getting Around chapter), you may just find yourself right in front of some of these shopping centers. Stop and check them out.

Cedar Ridge Plaza
1447 Mo. Hwy. 248 at Epps Rd.
• **no central phone**

The local Kmart is found here, plus Country Mart, a very large grocery store. Country Mart has the usual groceries and features a large fresh fruit and vegetable section, an in-store bakery, and a spectacular deli. It's a great place to hit if you plan a picnic or an in-room dinner. They have smoked fish and meats, pickled herring, barbecue, an array of cheeses and deli meats, and the bakery is a wonderful source of a variety of rolls, breads, and desserts to go with your meal. The Wine Company next door has a big selection of vintages (see our Specialty Shops section in this chapter) to round out any al fresco dining.

The center is also home to the usual array of stores and Luigi's Pizza Kitchen, (417) 339-4544, which offers both dine-in and takeout and is a favorite for some quick pizza or pasta.

The Falls Center
3265 Falls Pkwy. • (417) 343-3400

Less than a mile south of the Mo. 165 junction at The Strip, this shopping center has more than a dozen shops, restaurants, and businesses.

If you're inclined to take a rest from the live shows and have a movie in the room, The Movie Shop, (417) 445-8914, features the biggest collection of classic movies in town. Elegant Illusions, (417) 336-4882, has replicas of fine jewelry—the look of the real thing without the stiff price. Dressin' Gaudy, (417) 336-3465, is a favorite place of college students who want to make a splash in fashion without the cost. They have stylish imports, hip fashions and swanky costume jewelry at rock-bottom prices. Another inexpensive place to find clothes is the nearby Second Love of Branson, (417) 336-6144, which features quality collectibles and gifts, including Fiestaware. Golf USA has it all for the golfer—clothes and clubs, balls and bags—even shoes and socks (see our Recreation and the Outdoors chapter). The Falls Center is a great place to spend a few hours just looking before you catch the next show.

The Marketplace
1972 Mo. Hwy. 165 • (417) 881-0600

The Marketplace is a small collection of shops adjacent to the Welk Resort Center, a great place to stop before a Welk matinee. It includes the Old West Art Gallery, (417) 339-4101, which carries Western-theme art: paintings, sculpture, blankets, cow skulls, and buffalo and longhorn cattle horns. The spicy, western-style barbecue nearby might just inspire you to buy that 6-foot set of longhorns for the fireplace mantle!

INSIDERS' TIP

Dueling fruitcakes! Locals swear the two best fruitcakes in the world are made in the Ozarks. College of the Ozarks makes tons of fruitcakes a year. You can place an order by calling the college at (417) 334-6411, Ext. 3395. The other cake offering is made by Assumption Abbey on Bryant Creek 14 miles east of Ava. You can fax an order to (417) 683-5658 or write Route 5 Box 1056, Ava, Mo. 65608. Order from both, and you be the judge in the duel of our area fruitcakes!

IMAX Entertainment Complex
3562 Shepherd of the Hills Expy.
• (417) 335-4832

When you think IMAX, you think big movies, and that's the big draw here (see our Attractions chapter). It's also home for the "Remember When" show with Mike Radford. However, the 21 shops and kiosks in the center provide some interesting diversion while waiting for the shows as well as some excellent buys. Shadow Box Gifts, (417) 335-7822, provides home appointments and decorations. It's Unique, (417) 334-5008, offers odd and interesting gifts and items "for kids 1 to 90." Fabulous Fakes, (417) 336-2983, allows you to buy that ostentatious diamond without being a millionaire—and some great fragrances that smell like the real thing but at a lower cost. Father Time Clock & Collectibles, (417) 336-8777, offers clocks from grandfather to mantle and miniatures as well as a variety of time-theme collectibles. If you get hungry, you'll find help at The Fudgery (always a show there!) and at McFarlain's Restaurant.

Victorian Village Shops
3044 Shepherd of the Hills Expy.
• (417) 334-6625, (800) 789-7001

Just east of Shoji's theater, the Victorian Village Shops advertises itself as "where we take shopping ... personally." Certainly the shops have personality, and certainly the Village contains the biggest collection of unique shops under one roof in Missouri. Designed to look like a rambling Victorian house, it is a veritable attic of treasures and unique and odd items. Gingerbread Kids, (417) 335-7900, specializes in quality children's clothing, gifts, and educational toys. Mulberry Mill, (417) 336-4300, is the place for floral favorites, natural gifts, and specialized knickknacks. Pretty Lady Jewelry & Gifts, (417) 335-3779, has a selection of jewelry, clothing, gifts, and accessories at fantastic prices. Heirloom Lace, (417) 334-7048, features lace curtains, doilies, and other lace items, many in easy-care polyester, at amazingly low prices. Everything related to the circus and clowns can be found at the 3 Ring Circus Gallery & Gifts

(417) 336-5090, Leather Etc., (417) 336-4333, is where Glenn Haworth makes and sells belts, wallets, purses, and just about all things leather. Cappuccino Country, (417) 335-6887, features much more than coffee and tea, and Nancy Apprill will be glad to let you taste and browse to your heart's content. Sweet Dreams has fudge and the area's largest selection of sugar-free candies (see our Snacks and Treats section in our Restaurants chapter). There is a regular cornucopia of shops under the roof of the Victorian Village. See our Specialty Shops and the Unusual section in this chapter for more information on some of them.

Antiques, Crafts, and Flea Markets

Branson has just a small number of antiques shops that deal only with antiques, but you're not likely to find the fine-quality antiques that you find in shops in the eastern half of the nation. You will find, however, a wide selection of primitives including furniture and tools—frequently handmade and other objects that were part of the early settlers' lives, at reasonable prices. You'll find lots of crafts stores and outlets. The major theme parks of Silver Dollar City and Shepherd of the Hills (see our Attractions chapter) have practicing artisans who make and sell their works in the parks. The Engler Block on 76 Country Boulevard is a mall devoted to crafts with crafters and virtually every area festival celebration in the Ozarks will have its share of crafts booths (see our Annual Events chapter). Though the dividing line between crafts and arts is often not finely drawn, especially in the Ozarks, we've put those shops and galleries specializing more in the fine arts in our Arts and Culture chapter, but they also tend to have crafts items.

As for flea markets, the area has more of them than a dog in August has fleas, and you can find some amazing treasures if you are willing to spend the time exploring. Ozark, between Springfield and Branson, has recently developed as a major stopping point for those interested in antiques, flea market items, and collectibles. There are no fewer than five large stores within yards of each other at Finley River Park at the junction of Mo. Highway 14 and U.S. Highway 65 in Ozark. If you come into Branson from the north, you'll notice them on your right (west side) just before you cross the Finley River. If you go east on Mo. 14, you'll find another half-dozen antiques stores and flea markets. If such treasure hunting is on your agenda, you can see why it is worth stopping in Ozark or making it a whole daytrip. If you're up to the rigors of such overload looking and shopping.

We've not begun to list all of the stores but we've featured the cream of the crop. We've put antiques, crafts, and flea markets together because many of the stores in the Ozarks are a strange but interesting conglomeration of all three. Most places will accept your plastic; some will not accept out-of-state checks or any checks; all will accept the green stuff. A caveat: we found that most places keep pretty standard 8 AM to 5 PM business hours, but some tend to keep what's known locally as banker's hours, 9 AM to 3 PM, and when the white bass are running or deer or turkey season opens, don't count on some shops being open at all.

Antique Emporium
U.S. Hwy. 65 and Mo. Hwy. CC, Ozark
• (417) 581-8544

Just north of the Tracker Boat Factory in Ozark on U.S. 65, take the CC exit, and right behind Lambert's Cafe (home of the "throwed rolls," see our Restaurants chapter) you'll find the Antique Emporium. The two together would make an afternoon and evening, with dinner down-home style at the cafe after you've tuckered yourself out shopping. With more than 100 booths, the Antique Emporium is a place you'll find more than the usual assortment of old tools and small farm machinery, fishing tackle and gear, boat motors, old advertising items (we wondered if Lambert's had done some shopping for their decor there!) and sporting antiques such as old golf and billiard gear. They also offer a variety of antique housewares, china, glass, and clothing.

The Apple Tree Mall
1830 76 Country Blvd., Branson
• (417) 335-2133

An old supermarket building has been converted into one of the largest crafts malls in the area, though some booths feature antiques and flea-market type items. The mall has more than 400 different booths, and you can find everything from local honey and homemade jams and jellies to handpainted crosscut saws and mailboxes, dried flowers, and woodland wonders, fossils, and rock paintings as well as handmade quilts, afghans, and doilies. It's a great place to wander about and explore and big enough to almost get lost.

Branson Heights Flea Market
113976 Country Blvd.,
Branson Heights
Shopping Center
• (417) 335-3165

Jack Wallace has converted the old grocery store of the shopping center into one of the biggest flea markets in the Branson area. You can find it all. Books, records, collectibles, crafts, antiques—just a bit of about everything. One of our prize purchases was a first edition of Ernest Hemingway's *In Our Time* for a dollar.

Cadwell's Flea Market
116 E. Main St., Branson
• (417) 334-5051

This large flea market is just downhill from The Flea Bag and across from The Card Shop. For the last 16 years it has attracted Branson visitors and locals with its large selection of the old and new. We know of a local girl who financed a semester of college with a 1930s Mickey Mouse toothbrush holder and cup that she bought for $25 and resold.

Coffelt Country Flea Market
& Craft Village
675 Mo. Hwy. 165 ••(417) 339-5373

Once part of the old Coffelt family farm, this is an interesting and crazy place, deliberately designed and built to look like a ramshackle Ozark Mountain town. That's part of the old-fashioned fun as you wander in the 35 shops

and stores. You can find quilts at the Quilt Connection, (417) 334-6523, homemade lye soap and herbs at The Backward Seed, (417) 339-1700, and have a custom-made house sign in red cedar made while you watch at Jake's Cedar Signs. Whether it's candles, airbrush artistry, copper jewelry, handcrafted dolls, woodcarvings, rag rugs, or antiques and collectibles in the old red barn, you'll find it all at Coffelt Country.

It's a half-mile south of the stoplight at the junction of Missouri Highways 76 and 165, right next to Ain't Misbehavin' Supper Club.

There's plenty of room for bus and RV parking.

Crossroads Antique Mall
2004 W. Evangel St., Ozark
• (417) 458-0428

Crossroads prides itself in strictly dealing with antiques with no crafts, a fact they include in their advertising. One of the half-dozen stores catering to antiquers, collectors, and flea market bargain-hunters in the Finley River Park, Crossroads has more than 60 dealers who take antiques seriously and provide the best of their selections at this mall. You can find furniture and household antiques and items. We were especially awed by a large collection of carved briar and meerschaum pipes, most from the 19th century, during a recent visit.

Engler Block
1335 76 Country Blvd. • (417) 335-2200

What does a person do with a vacant factory warehouse? If you are woodcarver Peter Engler, you convert it into a crafts mall and call it the Engler Block, a one-stop shopping experience for crafts, supplies, instruction, and entertainment. Here you'll find woodcarvers, potters, basket makers, candle makers, leather workers, glass blowers, and candy makers, plus more than a dozen shops that feature odd and unusual crafts products. You can stand in awe in front of woodcarver Jesse Kuh's Santa's Workshop, a 14-foot carving that shows Santa as a woodcarver, tools in hand. It's possibly the largest carving ever from a single basswood log, just less than 44 feet through at the base. Watch

INSIDERS' TIP

With the new improved roads in the Branson area, traffic gridlock is seldom the problem it used to be. The one exception seems to be the Friday after Thanksgiving. Tourists and locals descend on the outlet malls and stores for bargains. If you plan on shopping the two days after Thanksgiving, be certain you check out and know the off-the-Strip routes. (See our Getting Here, Getting Around chapter.)

the woodcarvers make short work of a long piece of wood; they'll take time to give advice and tips for a beginner. You can buy patterns and tools but not accident insurance. You can also buy finished carvings from the massive to the miniature. Fascinating are the staffs, canes, pig pokes, and cattle sorters—just the thing to give you that extra hand or leg and provide you with a great pointer. While there, check out the huge mural on the back wall!

John and Pamela Hagen in Play in Clay Pottery, (417) 239-1127, can hook you with not only the beauty of their thrown and hand-built pottery, but also their insights on the Ozarks and tips on how to make mud into objects of beauty and utility. They also carry pottery by well-known Ozark potters.

Greg Vidito of Sunrise Leatherworks, (417) 335-5311, produces leather purses, wallets, and hats. He'll have a belt just your size and style.

Hawthorn Gallery, (417) 335-2170 has imaginative and beautiful paintings and sculpture (see our Arts and Culture chapter). Morning Glory Glassworks, (417) 334-0564, features ready made stained glass windows and suncatchers, or they'll build to your own designs or design for you. You'll see their work in local businesses and theaters. Mastercraft Puppets, (417) 337-5100, is a great source for clowns, storytellers, librarians, ventriloquists, and magicians. Unique Impressions, (417) 335-4817, describes itself as a rubber stamp, stencil, and scrapbooking superstore, and they have stamps ranging from the whimsical, hilarious, and beautiful to the cynical—something for anyone's character. Regional history and local color books are in a branch of the Ozark Mountaineer Book Shop, (417) 335-4195, and you can browse to your heart's content! (See our Bookstores section of this chapter.) If you're in need of a snack or sustenance while wandering this maze of art, artisans, and crafts, the Cobbler & Sandwich Shoppe, (417) 335-2611 can provide fare that will cause your taste buds to stand up and dance! The Engler Block gets our vote as the best place in the area to spend a rainy afternoon.

Finley River Heirlooms
105 N. 20th St., Ozark ••(417) 581-3253

This Ozark enterprise into the old (with a bit of just the old-looking) is operated by Mace Gallery. It has 300 dealers from more than eight states, so you get a generous mix of collectibles and antiques. We noticed that it seemed to have more glassware and furniture than the other malls in the Finley River Park complex. This antiques mall has a 60-seat cafe that features

quiches, soups, salads, and gourmet sandwiches made from fresh-baked bread plus a wide range of desserts. Maybe the dealers figure if they feed you, you'll have strength for more shopping!

The Flea Bag Flea Market
106 E. Main St., Branson • (417) 334-5242

The attractive river limestone cobbles of this store was a style popular in the Ozarks from about 1913 to about 1930, and this building once housed the local Catholic church. Now it is one of the area's more interesting flea markets, housing the selected merchandise of 65 dealers from a five-state area. The market has been at this location since 1989 and was added on to in 1990, keeping the stained-glass windows from the church as part of the decor. This is a favorite place to browse, not only for the quality and variety but also for the attractive displays and friendly atmosphere. The Flea Bag is right up the hill from Cadwell's Flea Market, so you can hit two major markets easily.

The Flea Collar
1 Downing St., Hollister • (417) 335-4056

At the south end of Downing Street in downtown Hollister, The Flea Collar has the largest and most unusual collection of items in the area. The Flea Collar has the largest inventory of very old items in the area. Each first and third Saturday evening of the month at 6:30 PM The Flea Collar hosts an auction of estates, antiques, and antique reproductions. It makes a great show, equal to anything on The Strip, and the local color and the chance at a real bargain makes it worth a visit if you are nearby. This spring we saw a 1930s phonograph, built as a miniature grand piano get knocked down for $1,500, and the new owner was sure he could more than triple his money.

Green Lantern Antiques
15 Downing St., Hollister • (417) 334-7441

This is the other major antique/flea-market shop in Hollister, just a half-block north of The Flea Collar. This small shop is crammed with a lifetime of antiques and collectibles buying, and the crowded, cluttered atmosphere invites long and loving looking. It's a rare person who doesn't find something to add to a personal collection.

Maine Street Antique Mall
1994 Evangel St., Ozark • (417) 581-2575

The first of the antiques and flea markets at the Finley River Park in Ozark, this store opened in 1988, and locals thought Carl Miller, an out-of-the-area developer, was an out-of-his-mind entrepreneur. A decade later the 27,000-square-foot mall has 130 dealers from eight states, and business is better than ever because of nearby competing malls. You can find all sorts of collectibles and antique items. Last spring we saw a booth that had the biggest collection of cookie jars we had ever seen, including a rare Casper the Ghost jar. Each Labor Day and Memorial Day, the Maine Street Mall and the antiques malls in the Finley River Park have an outdoor flea fest that brings dealers with booths outside plus all the things inside. The Maine Street Mall also has The Eatery, which features great sandwiches made with homemade bread and, for your sweet tooth, out-of-this-world fudge.

Midtown Mall Arts & Crafts
3027 76 Country Blvd., Branson
• (417) 339-2406

Right across from John Wayne is the way some people give directions to this large crafts store. It's opposite the Hollywood Wax Museum (see our Attractions chapter) with the huge sculptures of Wayne and other Hollywood personalities a la Mount Rushmore, and this 32,000-square-foot shop is becoming one of the area's premier one-stops for arts, crafts, antiques, and collectibles. Owner Jack Wallace believes that you'll find home décor items, quilts, stained glass, jewelry, pottery, dolls, and enough interesting knickknacks and bric-a-brac to furnish your entire home state. There are lots of craft vendors in a huge space, giving you about as much variety as you will find anywhere.

The Old Barn
Mo. Hwy. 13, Reeds Spring
• (417) 272-3605

You'll see The Old Barn on your right as you come down the hill into Reeds Spring from the south, and you'll see that there's just enough paint on it to be red. You can find books and baskets, quilts (old and new), and a collection of antiques and crafts. In this 100+ year old barn they have a large collection of shot glasses, depression glass, handcrafted furniture, cedar chests, boxes, and antique dolls.

The Old Spring Flea Market
Main St., Reeds Spring • (417) 272-3173

Right on the curve in Reeds Spring and almost within spittin' distance of the town's namesake, this recycled grocery store is a veritable maze of booths, with more than 50 dealers. Though crafts and new items are represented, the bulk of the merchandise is antiques. Mo. 13 becomes Main Street, and The Old Spring Flea Market is just past the sharp curve in town. You'll find antique tools, housewares, depression and carved glass, china, cabinets, and furniture to store your treasures.

Ozark Antique Mall
200 S. 20th St., Ozark • (417) 581-5233

In the Finley River Park complex of antique shops in Ozark, this 17,000-square-foot store has a mix of old and new. The atmosphere is friendly, and the store encourages browsers and talkers. We liked the fact that you can pick up cards to keep notes about potential buys as you do your browsing. You can actually learn about items here. If you don't know what it is, Dan and Kathy Walter do, and they say they spend as much time "talkin' and educatin' as sellin'." But they admit they wouldn't have it any other way. The store seems to carry lots of collectibles from WWII and from the 1930s and '40s era.

Riverview Antique Center
909 W. Jackson St., Ozark
• (417) 381-4226

Turn east on Mo. Highway 14 (Jackson Street) in Ozark when you exit U.S. 65 and you'll be going towards downtown Ozark. There are several small antiques shops and flea markets in the Riverview Plaza with the Finley River so close you can spit out the back door and hit it. Continue on Jackson Street, and you'll encounter at least a half-dozen more antiques shops and flea markets within a mile. What we liked about the Riverview is that if you don't have any idea what the gizmo you're interested in is worth, they have a large library of books and price guides so you can do some checking. There is a nice mixture of tools and collectibles, with lots of stuff from the 1920s through the '60s.

The Wild Goose
2673 Mo. Hwy. 176, Rockaway Beach
• (417) 561-4812

Come by land or water! The Wild Goose, right on the waterfront and owned and operated by Florence and K. J. Hall, has a dock so you can come via Lake Taneycomo. They have a remarkable collection of the old and new, and if you don't find what you like at The Wild Goose, you can feed the not-so-wild Canada geese who have taken up permanent residence on the lake at Rockaway Beach.

Music and Instruments

Branson has become known as the "live music capital of the universe" and with so much music and so many musicians, you'd expect to find more than just a few shops that cater to music lovers. For professional songwriters and musicians, there are music publishers and professional recording studios. A number of shops (including area pawnshops) carry musical instruments, records, and music-related items from T-shirts to guitar picks. We've highlighted the notables for you.

Ernest Tubb Record Shop
2206 76 Country Blvd., Branson Mall
• **(417) 336-5605**

Of course you'll find Ernest Tubb selections here, but you'll also find Branson's biggest selection of other country-western music artists. The "Tubb" has cassette tapes, CDs, and vintage vinyl. Most are for sale, though some are for display only. These old C&W albums always attract the browsers and are certain to initiate a conversation—and manager Bonnie Feuerborn is always willing to jaw about music. Whether you're buying or browsing, the Ernest Tubb Record Shop is one of the Branson Mall's obligatory stops.

Guitar Shop
704 S. Commercial St.
• **(417) 334-3030**

The Guitar Shop has all kinds of new string musical instruments but they specialize in vintage and used string instruments: fiddles, banjos, steel guitars, mandolins, dulcimers—you name it, they have it. The Guitar Shop is the repair shop of choice for entertainers on The Strip, and employees have repaired overworked instruments by overwrought stars from Roy Clark to Jim Stafford. They also repair amplifiers and give guitar lessons. When it comes to guitars, the staff sells them, repairs them, plays them—and can teach you to play them too!

Mountain Music Shop
4562 Gretna Rd. Factory Shoppes at Branson Meadows • (417) 334-0515

If you're dying for a dulcimer or just want to fiddle around, the Mountain Music Shop is the place to come. You can be fitted with a fiddle, dulcimer (string or hammer), banjo, guitar, mandolin, or harmonica. They carry factory seconds, and a blemish that is not discernible to the average person can save you up to 70 percent They have a large selection of handmade mountain dulcimers. If you can't play a thing, they'll give you free lessons for 10 minutes so you can at least play something when you take it home. They may even brag on you and say that with a little practice, you too can have your own theater on The Strip.

The Music Stand
3004 Shepherd of the Hills Expy., Branson Victorian Village Shopping Mall
• **(417) 335-5457**

The Music Stand is the best shop in Branson for the serious collector of vintage vinyl—rock, pop, jazz, country, and bluegrass, whether 45s or LPs. The upper level of the Victorian Village is a mecca for collectors. Fanatics have been known to spend hours just in the record collection. The store also offers music memorabilia, '50s and '60s stuff, poodle skirts, and vintage clothing, Route 66 items, party favors, neon signs, posters, and the strangest assortment of phones we've ever seen: phones disguised as a VW bug, a Harley Davidson motorcycle, train engines, and other neat decorator items that you'd never believe could hide a phone. Owners Mark and Brenda Alyea are willing to give you history and insights into not only the things they sell but that whole nostalgic '50s and '60s rock period. Boomers will love this place!

Music 4 Less
1000 Pat Nash Dr., Factory Merchants Mall
• **(417) 335-3690**

Music 4 Less is Branson's most complete music store. It has music videos, CDs, and cassettes, and it carries all types: classical, jazz, rock, rap, and country. If they don't have it they'll order it for you, with arrival usually within three days. Music 4 Less has a special section devoted just to Branson entertainment and entertainers. The store also has T-shirts for bands, musical groups, and performers as well as professional wrestling T-shirts plus other gift items related to the music industry.

Ozark-speak

Thriftiness is a great virtue in the Ozarks, but an overly thrifty person is described as "tight as the bark on a tree" or "so tight he skins fleas for their hides and the tallow."

Singing Sensations Recording Studio
**2800 76 Country Blvd., Branson,
The Grand Village • (417) 335-4435**

You can be an instant star with the help of a bit of coaching and prerecorded background music. For less than $15 you can record your favorite song (from about 500 titles), and additional cuts are only $8 each (1999 prices). It's great fun, and the cassettes make tremendous gifts, if only gag gifts. This instant-recording studio caters to groups and motor-coach tours, so the entire group can get in the act. You can even make your own music video, with appropriate backdrops for the song. This is a great place to bring out the talent in your kids and provide gifts for grandma back home (see our Kidstuff chapter). The store also carries karaoke systems and machines, recording equipment, microphones, and accessories. Singing Sensations Recording Studio lets you be the music star in the town of stars.

Specialty Shops and the Unusual

Aloha Nonie Lani's Tattoo Art Studio
**1931 S. U.S. Bus. Hwy. 65, Hollister
• (417) 336-8535**

If you're looking for a souvenir to take home that will never get lost or broken, we suggest a trip to Nonie Lani's, the local tattoo studio. The studio has thousands of designs to choose from or the tattoo artist will customize something new just for you. (How about a permanent Branson bracelet?) A basic tattoo starts at around $30, but the average cost ranges from $50 to $200. Some of the more popular designs include dragons, flowers, hearts, and military-style tattoos. The studio is open everyday until 9 PM and three licensed artists wait to make their mark on you. They even do body piercing (only from the neck up). Ask about their permanent cosmetics.

Ben's Decorative Lighting
**500 N. Gretna Rd., Branson
• (417) 334-8304**

If you're looking for the odd and unusual, check out this place. Do you need, or just want, an outdoor clock? Ben's has an 11-foot Compton Clock, which is double-faced, electric, and all aluminum, that can grace your front yard and a 13-foot Boston Twin clock that really makes a statement. The store has patio furniture, including a popular bear bench, decorative lights

of every kind, fountains, carousel horses, and yard ornaments galore, including a 7.5-foot Statue of Liberty replica with a glass torch that really lights. You can be the first in your town to have one and get written up in your local paper! You can see some of their furniture and yard ornaments as part of the lobby decor at the Mel Tillis Theater. If you can't carry it back with you, Ben's will ship anywhere in the United States.

Cappuccino Country
**3044 Shepherd of the Hills Expy., Branson,
Victorian Village • (417) 335-6887
1335 76 Country Blvd., Branson,
Engler Block • •(417) 334-6333**

Cappuccino Country is more than just cappuccino. It's a gourmet market of coffees, teas, honey, pickles, jams, and condiments. They serve lunch (rich soups, heavenly fresh-baked breads, and desserts) and have a full espresso bar with a wide range of teas and coffees (our favorites are the Branson Blend and Sticky Buns, a roast that has overtones of classic iced cinnamon rolls). The shop also has the mugs and china for tea and coffee, classic designer Fitz and Floyd collector tea pots, tea sets, tea cozies, and high-quality imported and domestic gift items, including Sorrento inlaid wood boxes. There's a smaller version of the store in the Engler Block crafts mall, but the full array of products is at the Victorian Village.

The Card Shop
1213 E. Main St. • (417) 335-4330

This shop at the corner of Main and Sycamore, in one of the few old buildings that survived the town fires early in the century, specializes in all kinds of collectible cards, especially sports—baseball, football, basketball, and soccer. The Card Shop has a number of other old cards featuring old-time baseball greats that could find a new home with you. The Card Shop also carries Disney and fantasy cards.

Coca Cola Store
**2800 76 Country Blvd., Branson, The
Grand Village • (417) 336-7253**

Who'd have thought it? An entire store devoted to classic Coca-Cola collectibles! If you're looking for reproduction Coke glasses, serving trays, signs, soda-fountain tables, restored Coke vending machines, T-shirts, key rings, antique Coke bottles, and other Coke memorabilia and paraphernalia, you'll think you've died and gone to Coca-Cola heaven. You can even sip a Coke while gawking at this remarkable collection.

Dickens Gift Shoppe
3630 76 Country Blvd., Branson
• (417) 334-2992

This shop is a bit like Charles Dickens' Old Curiosity Shop—it has a bit of everything. You'll find everything from upper-end collectibles like Department 56, Boyd's Bears, Cherished Teddies, Precious Moments, Emmett Kelly clowns, and Norman Rockwell to Branson souvenir key rings and T-shirts, birdbaths, lawn ornaments, and concrete deer, frogs, and gorillas. (Now you know where McGuffey's Restaurants got their gorillas!) Dickens is a great place to spend some time between shows.

Dick's Oldtime 5 & 10
103 W. Main St., Branson • (417) 334-2410

Here's a store where you can easily spend several hours strolling the narrow aisles, gawking at the more than 50,000 different items in stock, and listening to the old-time tunes on the authentic jukebox. Not only the items for sale but also the museum-type displays will bring back memories of the old five and dime. It's been a landmark store since 1929. You can find what you need and lots that you don't, but we bet you won't leave the store without buying something! Blue Waltz perfume, fragrant rose pod sachets, paper dolls, soap-on-a-rope, Necco candy, pant creasers, marbles, mothballs, Clark's Teaberry gum: you'll see why Dick's says, "We've got what you forgot!"

The Doll Depot & Gift Box
112 S. Commercial St., Branson
• (417) 335-4438

For your little child or the little child in you, The Doll Depot is the largest doll dealer in the area: kewpies, beanie babies, handmade vinyl and porcelain heads. The store has many dolls that are creations of Ozark dollcrafters. It also features miniatures for your dolls, and it has a large selection of music boxes, Victorian collectibles (especially frames and shoes), and Victorian lamps.

Father Time Clocks & Collectibles
3562 Shepherd of the Hills Expy.,
IMAX Entertainment Complex
• (417) 336-8777
1335 76 Country Blvd., Engler Block
• (417) 339-4320

Want some fun? Step into the shop right on the hour and listen to all the clocks go off! (The kids will think it's just the greatest!) It seems like there are a kajillion chimes, clangs, and rings. Father Time has two tick-tock shops in Branson

to serve you and ships worldwide. A real eye-catcher at the Engler Block shop is the handcarved German cuckoo clock, one of the world's largest at 10 feet, 3 inches. Now that's a clock to look up to! You can find grandfathers, grandmothers (clocks, that is), mantle clocks, and novelty timepieces at Father Time.

The Flagstore
1318 76 Country Blvd. • (417) 334-1776

With the International Festival at Silver Dollar City and the Veterans Day and Independence Day celebrations (see our Annual Events chapter), Branson is frequently awash in flags and color, and the place to get it is from Betsy Ross (honest!) at The Flagstore. For flags from every nation and every occasion and for historical flags, people seek out one of Branson's most unusual stores. The store also has flagpoles from 12 feet to 120 feet, windsocks, religious flags, seasonal flags, patriotic bunting and decorations, decals, bumper stickers, and pens. If you don't find the flag that you want, they'll make it to order. The Flagstore is located on the south side of the highway just a ways west of the Branson Heights Shopping Center.

*Downtown Branson shopping
provides variety in a small area.*

Photo: Downtown Branson Main Street Association

Hank's 20th Century Farm Power
1141 76 Country Blvd., Branson Heights Shopping Center • (417) 337-9222

You don't have to have been a farm boy or girl or be a current farmer for this shop to interest you. You can see how tractors and other farm implements have evolved through the decades in these scale models, from early steam-powered threshers to the latest quad-tracks that currently till the fields. Replica aficionados can expand their collections with hard-to-find models or use Hank's finder service. If you get back home and want to kick yourself for not getting that special tractor, don't worry: Hank's also does mail orders!

Kringles
2800 76 County Blvd., Branson, The Grand Village • (417) 336-7213

Christmas in July and August? Yes! Believe it or not, next to December, that's the busiest time at Missouri's largest Christmas store. There are three large rooms devoted to Christmas decorations, ornaments, and wrapping paper. One caters to a Victorian theme, one to the comical and whimsical, and the third to Christmas collectibles, including Department 56 collectibles. During the hot summer, stepping into Kringles may just be the way to cool off!

Lefty Lane & Gifts
104 N. Commercial St., Branson • (417) 336-3920

Lefties of the world, unite! This store caters to you, though the language doesn't. (*Gauche* and *sinister*, French and Latin for left, have pejorative meanings in English, but *dexter*, Latin for right, produces words with good connotations: dexterous, ambidextrous.) This lefty store has "left pride" T-shirts and bumper stickers: "I may be lefthanded, but I'm always right!"

They also have practical items for that minority of the world: can openers, measuring cups, rulers, mugs, notebooks, knives and corkscrews. You'll enjoy reading their Left Hand Hall of Fame, a list of famous lefties.

Marlea's
114 W. Main St., Branson • (417) 334-5445

Where do Branson's lovely show girls get their fancy duds? Some of them shop at Marlea's in downtown Branson. Marlea's carries a wide assortment of evening gowns, costume jewelry, and other accessories that are sure to show up on stage. If you haven't gotten that big break

yet, but still want to stand out in the crowd, Marlea's has an assortment of street wear complete with sequins, beads, and fringe. They carry misses and women's sizes and offer the same kind of personal attention ladies got in dress shops of long ago.

Mountain Man Nut & Fruit Co.
4210 Gretna Rd., Factory Shoppes at Branson Meadows Mall • (417) 336-6200, (800) 336-6203

The Mountain Man says "Nuts to you!" and this store provides all kinds of nuts for you, imported as well as the king of nutmeats, the Ozark black walnut. The stores also have a wide array of dried fruits, jams, jellies (our favorite is the muscadine jelly), more than a dozen different types of trail mixes, honey, regular and sugar-free candies, gourmet coffees (ever try Fuzzy Navel coffee?), and exotic and unusual foods. It's fun to taste the free samples and wander around the gift-filled nooks and crannies of the store. It's a great place to shop for a special snack to take back with you.

Remember When
2800 76 County Blvd., Branson The Grand Village • (417) 336-7240

Remember When is a store that proves there's a great future in the past. It has everything that will bring back fond memories of yesteryear for the oldsters and the latest campy objects newly discovered by the younger generation, featuring Elvis, James Dean, and the Rat Pack. Popular items include hysterical greeting cards from old-timey photos, period advertising signs, toys (a great collection of toy tractors and farm machinery), and video "time capsules" (what did happen the year you were born?). Be careful, not so much of the three large rooms at different levels, but because you can easily wile away an entire afternoon, lost in remembering when.

Storybook Treasures
2800 76 Country Blvd., Branson, The Grand Village • (417) 336-7212

Storybook Treasures is a great place to shop for Christmas and birthday presents for all those little people in your life. The store has old-fashioned wooden toys, puzzles for all ages, educational toys (ones that are really fun!), modern action toys, stuffed animals, and books. You may want to stop at the nearby Kringles Christmas store for your Christmas wrapping paper for those presents!

Stone Hill Winery
610 S. Mo. Hwy. 165 at Green Mt. Dr., Branson • (417) 334-1897
• **www.stonehillwinery.com**

Early in this century, Missouri was one of the major wine-producing states, and the Stone Hill Winery at Hermann, Missouri, which dates back to 1847, was the third-largest winery in the world and the second-largest in the nation. This thriving industry became illegal with Prohibition in 1920, and it is now just beginning to recover its former glory. At this outlet you can taste various vintages and take a tour of the wine room to learn how grapes are processed into vino and bottled. There are tours every 15 minutes, and large groups are welcome. It's a great place to taste the grape, discover some new varieties, and pick up some vintages to take back home for yourself or for gifts. Stone Hill is open all year, from 8:30 AM to dusk except Sundays, when hours are 11 AM to 6 PM. (Also see our Attractions chapter.)

Toys Unlimited
1000 Pat Nash Dr., Factory Merchants Mall • (417) 335-8047

For newborns to great-grandparents, Toys Unlimited really has an almost unlimited number of toys, games, puzzles, and books in the largest toy store in the area. The latest action figures or old standards (Old Maid, Authors, Monopoly) can be found in one of our favorite browsing stores.

3 Ring Circus Gallery & Gifts
3044 Shepherd of the Hills Expy., Branson, Victorian Village • (417) 336-5090, (800) 654-4725

In the upper level of the Victorian Village, 3 Ring Circus attracts people like honey attracts bees because it seems as if nobody can resist the call of a circus calliope. (No, the store doesn't have a calliope, but it does have calliope tapes and plays them constantly.) It's all part of the circus atmosphere: posters, toys, and down collectibles, including Emmett Kelly figures. (See our Annual Events chapter for information on the Clown Festival at Houston, Missouri, where

Kelly grew up.) The 3 Ring Circus has Red Skelton collectibles, including original paintings and lithographs. Another attraction is a Children's Corner. With life-size carousel horses and model circus wagons, you have "The Greatest Show on Earth." If you miss the popcorn and peanuts, you can find them at some of the other shops in the Victorian Village complex.

The Wine Company
1447 Mo. Hwy. 248, Cedar Ridge Plaza • (417) 334-4551

The Wine Company has a large selection of domestic wines, including Arkansas and Missouri vintages (Stone Hill, St. James, Les Bourgeois, and Wiederkehr) as well as imported wines and microbrewery and specialty beers—over 130 and still growing. They have some great wines and great labels. A bottle of Toad Hollow is worth the price just for the label. The store advertises itself as having "Taney County's largest wine selection," and it seems an undisputed fact. They also feature premium cigars and imported cigarettes. They have wine gift packages, and gift wrapping is available for other purchases.

Bookstores

Book Warehouse
1000 Pat Nash Dr., Factory Merchants Mall • (417) 334-6820

When they say warehouse, that's what they mean! Books are everywhere, yet arranged for browsing. This large bookstore features discount books (up to 75 percent off), remainders, seconds, publishers' overstocks, a large collection of audio books, current bestsellers, and a selection of local and regional books. It also carries stationery and gift items.

Foozles
4540 Gretna Rd., Factory Shoppes at Branson Meadows • (417) 339-2424

Foozles is large, well-lit, and made for wandering. They have the area's greatest selection of children's books and travel guides, but they

---

INSIDERS' TIP

Crime is not a big concern in Branson, but do watch your purse. Remember to lock your car, and keep packages and valuables out of sight in the trunk. The Branson Police Department reports that the most common crime is shoplifting. Don't get your name in the local paper In the Court Report section by forgetting to pay for an item you've picked up.

also have a good selection of books, guides, and self-help for the computer user. Though discounted books are their specialty (up to 75 percent off) they also carry the latest bestsellers and a large selection of local and regional books. It's a favorite gathering place for quick readers, and readers are encouraged, but it is a rare person who can resist the book bargains found there and walk out without a book in hand.

Gethsamane Gifts & Books
116 W. Main St., Branson • (417) 334-7262

Just down the street from the Branson Cafe, this store features Christian gifts and books. In the book line, all kinds of Bibles are available as well as a large selection of Christian fiction and nonfiction, including faith books and devotionals.

Half Price Used Books
1819-C 76 Country Blvd., Branson
• (417) 334-7970

Heidi Sampson has a large selection of all sorts of used books, paperbacks, and hard-cover, that run the range from romance to science fiction to local history to biography in this crowded but comfortable book outlet. In eight short years the store has become a local fixture, and it also features antique books, maps and collectibles. It's a great place to browse on a rainy day. When you stop in, be certain to give Calvin the cat a pat.

The Ozarks Mountaineer Book Shop
4168 E. St., Mo. Hwy. 76, Kirbyville
• (417) 336-2665
1335 76 Country Blvd., Engler Block
• (417) 335-4195

If you have an interest in things Ozarkian, the Mountaineer bookshop is for you. Barbara Wehrman, owner and publisher of *The Ozarks Mountaineer*, stocks books of local and regional interest as well as general interest Missouri books. Local history (Native American, Civil War, the Bald Knobbers), folklore, regional fiction, children's nature, and the out-of-doors, fishing and hunting, arts and crafts including

woodworking and woodcarving, cookbooks, and guide books make up a stock that you can browse through for hours. The help will be glad to answer any questions, and if they don't have what you need in stock, they can order it for you and ship it.

Paperback Exchange/
The Comic Corner
114 E. Main St., Branson • (417) 334-8735

For almost 27 years locals have been going into the Paperback Exchange to trade in and stock up on a variety of genres: romance, mystery, Western, and science fiction. They have a large selection of used paperbacks, and for every two you bring in, you get your pick of one they have in stock. They also sell and trade comic books.

Publishers Warehouse
300 Tanger Blvd., Tanger Factory
Outlet Center • (417) 336-8532

This bookstore has a large selection of remainders and publishers' overstocks, all at tremendous savings. They have a big selection of audio books and large-print books. Cookbooks and gardening books are a strong feature, and if you are willing to wait until bestsellers have peaked, you can save up to 90 percent on former *New York Times* list bestsellers.

Publishers Warehouse also carries a large selection of CDs and tapes, great music at discount savings.

T. Charleston & Son
2800 76 Country Blvd., Branson,
The Grand Village • (417) 336-7230

T. Charleston is one of the several shops in The Grand Village where you can wile away an entire afternoon. It's Branson's largest family bookstore, and it certainly looks booky—with browsing sections, tall shelves, ladders, and ready and knowledgeable service. Tourists like the wide variety of selections, especially those on local history and subjects, and locals like the "if we don't have it, we can get it for you" order service.

Daytrips

Branson may be the reason and the focus of your visit to the Ozarks, and we'd be the first to admit that there are more than two weeks' worth of exciting things to do in just Branson. We've lived here for years and haven't seen it all, and with the way the area is growing, we probably never will. However, there are only so many shows you can take in before becoming satiated. (Still, we know of folks who have seen two and three shows a day for a week and still not seen them all and not gotten tired!)

Branson is an ideal center for exploring Ozark Mountain Country, that area roughly within a 100-mile radius of Branson. We stress that that's not all of the Ozarks, and we encourage you to trek beyond and discover what the rest of the Ozarks have to offer—country lanes, meandering creeks, small-town general stores—the best of the bucolic that rural America offers. We had to limit ourselves. If we didn't, this book would get out of hand and become a travelogue encyclopedia! Our daytrips are just that: a trip that will fill your day, often from daylight to past dark. Some areas you might want to spend the night or even longer, as you'll find that towns that do not have Branson's fame offer their own uniqueness for the adventuresome traveler.

Better roads in the area have made travel faster and exploring easier in the local environs, but remember that once you get off the main arteries, the roads are much more meandering and thus slower. That's often their beauty and charm, a virtue high on the list of some visitors but low on a highway engineer's. We've organized such trips according to the name of the surrounding communities, and we provide you with a bit of history and background to some of our near neighbors. For some areas, we've listed area attractions and you can pick and choose as your time allows. On others we've provided a suggested itinerary.

LOOK FOR:
- **Springfield, Mo.**
- **Civil War Sites**
- **Museums and Attractions**
- **Crafts**
- **Shopping**
- **Art Galleries**

Springfield and Immediate Environs

The "Queen City of the Ozarks" has had her royal nose tweaked by upstart Branson in the last decade as millions have passed by Springfield, or seen the city only as a stopping point, on their way to the tourist playground of the Midwest. Now that Branson has become a shopping Mecca as well as "the live music capital of the universe," there has been mild concern in Springfield at the competition and the loss of sales tax revenue. And when its airport changed its name from Springfield Regional Airport to Springfield-Branson Regional Airport a couple of years ago in order to better designate the destination for so much of its passenger traffic, Her Royal Highness was a bit miffed. The name change came on the heels of a change in nearby Lakeview, which now calls itself Branson West, and prompted Branson wags, braggarts, and boosters to label Springfield as "Branson North."

In spite of beneath-the-surface rivalry and competition, there is a sense of shared community and cooperation. We Bransonites respect and appreciate Missouri's third-largest city (140,760 population) and fastest growing of our state's "Big Three" for the services, cultural activities, and amenities that a larger city offers—and for its citizens who come down to shop and take in our music shows. The "big city" nearby merely makes Branson a better place to live. That close relationship will undoubtedly get closer as Springfield expands south and Branson expands north along the U.S. Hwy. 65 corridor, especially as more of U.S. 65 is four-laned, making travel time between the two cities quicker. We'll share more of what each has to offer if regional planners are correct in their speculation that the Springfield-Branson megalopolis will soon have a population of a million as we're into the next millennium.

There will be much more to share in the future. Springfield's downtown area is undergoing a huge, multi-million dollar "green space addition," with the 260- acre Jordan Valley Park, scheduled to open in sections over the next decade. The first phase, over 35 acres and scheduled to open in the fall of 2001, will include a recreational ice skating facility. Springfield had a $100 million burst of construction activity in 1999, including the opening of the 83,000-square-foot state-of-the-art Library Center. A new hotel-motel tax earmarked for developing a $40 million-plus, 92,000-square foot Fish and Wildlife Museum scheduled to open in 2001 and the 260-acre downtown Jordan Valley Park project, with its twin ice rinks and a proposed convention center/sports arena with hockey, indoor football and basketball, will be much appreciated by Branson residents.

Springfield is the 133rd-largest city in the nation. It's where we go for "serious doctorin'." Its "medical mile" (National Avenue) on the south side makes it convenient for Bransonites. It's where we go for our "high culture" including Broadway plays and concerts and the Springfield Symphony at the Juanita K. Hammons Center and the Springfield Little Theater at the downtown historic Landers Theater. It is still the major mercantile center, and if we can't find it here at Wal-Mart or Dick's Five and Dime and still think we need it, we drive up to see the Queen. Its Battlefield Mall, with 150 stores and a six-plex theater, is the only large climate controlled mall short of the four hour drive to Kansas City or St. Louis.

With its major university (Southwest Missouri State University, enrollment just short of 17,000) and two private liberal arts colleges (Drury and Evangel), we consider it a major education center and send our grown youngsters there for a liberal arts education—far enough for them to be independent and close enough for us not to worry too much. The city has 13 parks, with activities frequently scheduled in them (Springfield's parks are used!). It has a nationally recognized zoo and an art museum that hosts one of the best watercolor shows in the nation every summer.

There's enough in Springfield alone to make a week's worth of daytrips, so pick and choose from the smorgasbord! Springfield is also, we've been told, the place that has more restaurants and fast food places per capita than any city in the nation (cashew chicken was invented there!). You won't starve in Springfield!

Attractions

Bass Pro Shops and American National Fish and Wildlife Museum
1915 S. Campbell Ave., Springfield
• (417) 887-7334 • www.basspro.com

We feel obligated to put a store in Attractions because "the world's largest sporting goods store" has become Missouri's premier tourist attraction, pulling in more than 4 million visitors a year. You'll see in the parking lot license plates from every state and Canada, and tour buses with Japanese and European visitors have a special "bus lot." You'll not only find sporting goods, acres of fishing tackle, guns, camping gear, and boats, but you'll also find aisle upon aisle of sport and casual wear for women and children as well as men.

If you tire out, there is always space to sit and listen to the roar of the four-story waterfall and watch native fish and the lifelike stuffed animals that serve as the theme decor. Half the fun is wandering about the store, gawking at the mini-exhibits of wildlife in near-real settings. Especially good picture points are marked, so be sure to bring your camera.

Hemingway's Blue Water Cafe on the third floor is a great place for lunch, as you could make this an all-day experience. Or you can rest at its smoke-free marble and mahogany bar and sip a drink and watch the bartender work in front of a floor-to-ceiling 30,000-gallon saltwater aquarium that serves as the backbar.

If it has to do with sports, golf, canoeing, basketball, cricket, soccer, you-name-it, Bass Pro will have it. There's an indoor shooting range—both archery and gun. Wildlife experts hold seminars in a 250-seat auditorium on the lowest level. There's an art gallery, devoted to wildlife art, of course. You can even get a hair cut at the Tall Tales Barber Shop on the balcony overlooking the main showroom—a great place to people watch. And if you are so inclined, you can take a lock of your hair to the fly department and have it incorporated into a custom-made fishing fly!

There's even a Wildlife Museum, in a temporary home. Entrance is opposite the grand entrance to Bass Pro, at the top of the steps. You can wander amongst moose and grizzly bears safely and marvel not only at their size but also at the art of the taxidermist.

But scheduled to open in the fall of 2001 is a $40 million-plus, 92,000-square foot building to house the collection of wildlife art and artifacts and stuffed animals—and also live ones—as big as all outdoors. A boardwalk will snake through treetops with wild turkeys and waterfowl below. A 30-foot waterfall will plunge into a 150,000-gallon pool of fresh water. It's the Wonders of Wildlife, part of planned "total outdoors experience." There will be galleries displaying a community pond, sinkholes, and mounted animals in dioramas. Behind a waterfall there will be a gallery where live bobcats prowl. A 200,000-gallon saltwater aquarium will display varieties of ocean life, including sharks and stingrays. There will be a cavewalk with live bats, salamanders, and cave fish, all behind Plexiglas. Gary Ellison, museum public relations director, calls it "the Smithsonian of the outdoors."

Admission for the museum, unlike the store, costs. (However, it may be cheaper than the shopping spree in the store!) For the current museum, adults are $5.50, $4.50 for seniors, and $2 for children ages 5 through 17. There are special rates for scheduled bus and school groups. To get to this indoors marvel devoted to the out-of-doors, take the Sunshine Street Exit as you come up north on U.S. 65. Turn left (east) on Sunshine and continue 4 miles until you come to the Sunshine and Campbell intersection. Turn left on Campbell. If you don't see it, you're not looking!

Crystal Cave
7225 N. Crystal Cave Ln., Springfield
• (417) 833-9599

Crystal Cave was one of the area's first tourist attractions, opened for tours by Alfred Mann back in 1893. The cave remained in the family until the 1960s. Now operated by Loyd and Edith Richardson, the cave offers a guided 80-minute tour. Wear your Nike's for the trip that takes you down into the limestone that was

the seabed in the Ozarks millions of years ago. You can actually see the fossils! You'll also see evidence of native American inhabitants, marvel at the Upside Down Well and see the Rainbow Falls and The Cathedral. Crystal Cave is a "living cave" (one that is growing), so note the spelotherms in many unusual shapes and forms.

To get to the cave, take Exit 80-B off I-44 on Springfield's north side. It continues out of the city and becomes Mo. Hwy. H and weather permitting, the cave is open year round. Admission in 1999 was $5 for adults and $3 for ages 4 through 8.

Fantastic Caverns
U.S. Hwy. 20, Springfield • (417) 833-2010
• www.fantastic-caverns.com

If you want to see the Ozarks underground without having to walk, this is the place! Propane-powered Jeep trains take you right through the cave, billed as "America's Only Ride-Thru Cave." (We have BIG caves in Missouri! Beat that, Texas!) This also is probably the only cave in the nation that is wheelchair accessible.

On hot summer days, there can be a line, and if you have to wait, a good side trip to hike off the kids' excess energy is Canyon Trail, a mile walk through the woods to the Sac River.

The Caverns operates a research program that tracks, by the use of dyes, the flow of underground water. The program has discovered through tracing rainwater and sink hole drainage that the cavern has a watershed of about 15 square miles. The program helps educate groups and school children about our Ozarks underground by demonstrating this drainage and by taking them into parts of the cave not normally toured.

To get to Fantastic Caverns, take Mo. 13, exit off I-44 on Springfield's north side. Go 1.5 miles north on Mo. 13, turn west on Fantastic Caverns Road and follow the signs. As we say in the Ozarks, you can't miss it! Admission in 1999 was $12.50 for adults, $6.25 for ages 6 through 12.

Exotic Animal Paradise
124 Jungle Dr. at Mo. Hwy. 00, Strafford
• (417) 859-2159
• www.enterit.net/Exotic3339

Don't let the Strafford address worry you! It's only 8 miles east of Springfield on I-44. Open to the public since 1971, this 400-acre park is home to more than 3,000 wild animals and birds. It's a great hot day activity, as you can drive in air-conditioned comfort in your car through a landscape dotted with lakes and

"The Smithsonian of the Outdoors": architect's rendering of American National Fish and Wildlife Museum, to open fall of 2001.

Photo: Bass Pro Shops

ponds. The animals roam free in the wilderness park except for the dangerous big cats and bears, which are kept in a large fenced area. The animals are curious and expect treats. When you buy your ticket, you can buy a supply of Range Cubes to feed them, but it's not a good idea to let them take their treat from your hand.

Halfway through your trek, you can stop at the Safari Outpost, an outback compound with two gift shops: one with basic curios and souvenirs, and the other, the Kenya Connection, with authentic items from not only Kenya but also countries all over the world. There is also the inevitable (but appreciated) snack bar, and what is even more attractive to the kids, a baby animal nursery and petting zoo. You can wander among (and feed) pot belly pigs, goats, deer, geese, ducks, and llamas.

You get to the Exotic Animal Paradise by taking I-44 east 8 miles to Exit 88. Signs along the south outer road will direct you. Admission is for $9 adults and $5.99 for ages 3 through 11.

Dickerson Park Zoo
3043 N. Fort Ave., Springfield
• **(417) 833-1570**
• **www.dickersonparkzoo.org**

The zoo owns 175 acres, much of it undeveloped, but it's home to a variety of species.

The land for the zoo was purchased in 1922 and was developed during the late 1920s and the '30s. Dickerson Park has continued over the years to grow and has become an attraction worthy of a half-day's time.

The zoo has developed an international reputation for its work in breeding elephants, and in the past has invoked area school children in contests to name newly arrived pachyderms. A 1995 addition, now a thriving pachyderm toddler, was christened Asha, Hindu for hope. The newest arrival was November 28, 1999: a bouncing 378-pound baby named Haji after a pregnancy of 674 days and a 34-hour labor, the first Asian elephant in the world born as the result of artificial insemination.

During its annual Teddy Bear Rally in April, free admission to anyone carrying a teddy bear packs the zoo. Of course, the spring weather and the trees and shrubs in bloom are a big draw, too. Other events during the year include Mother's Day and Father's Day activities, a Reptile Mania Day in May with educational activities throughout the zoo addressing the fear and fascination people have with reptiles, and an Ice Cream Safari in July. On Grandparents Day in September children get a 75 cent discount when accompanied by their grandparents. And on October 31 of each year the zoo throws a

Halloween party for children! The Zoo hosts Zoofari, an early fall outdoor fund-raiser dinner to which many come in costume. It's the one time people are more exotic than the animals! There is a gift shop at which you can purchase animal-related items and books. You can even take home a bag of "zoo-doo" for your flower bed!

To get to the zoo, take the Mo. 13 exit off I-44, and immediately turn right at the light on Norton Street. You'll see the zoo on your left in a few blocks. The zoo is open from 9 AM to 5 PM daily, April through September and from 10 AM to 4 PM daily October through March, except during inclement weather and on major holidays. Admission: $4 adults, $2.50 ages 3 to 12, toddlers and babies are free.

Missouri Sports Hall of Fame
5051 Highland Spring Blvd., Springfield
• **(417) 889-3100, (800) 498-5678**
• **www.mosportshalloffame.com**

Whether it's the late golf great Payne Stewart or former pitcher "Preacher" Roe that draws you, you can find the entire gallery of Missouri's sports legends memorialized here. The Hall of Fame and the nearby Highland Springs Development, one of Springfield's most exclusive, was developed by John Q. Hammons. (You'll see his name plastered on a number of SMSU campus buildings and community developments.) The Hall of Fame is right next to the Highland Springs Country Club on Springfield's south side. The spectacular homes are also worth the short drive through the park setting.

To get to the Hall of Fame, as soon as you cross Lake Springfield on U.S. 65, turn east on U.S. 60. After a quarter-mile drive to the top of the hill, you'll turn right. Admission is $5 for adults, $3 for students and $4 for senior citizens.

Springfield Conservation Nature Center
4600 S. Chrismon Rd., Springfield
• **(417) 888-4237**

The 80 acres of woods and park are Springfield's urban homage to the natural world that exists beyond the city's sprawl. There are 3 miles of wood-chipped hiking trails. (No pets are allowed; they'll disturb the natural critters!) During your hike you can observe birds from the trail and from blinds, and you can hear more than you can see—your walk is accompanied by a symphony of bird songs. There are boardwalks over the marshy parts of Lake Springfield (James River). If you're lucky, and quiet,

you might catch a glimpse of the many deer that make the Center their home.

The Center's complex, near the entrance, is a wood and rock building that seems to be part of the ground it emerges from. Inside are exhibits, both permanent and traveling, and a small auditorium that often features programs and speakers.

It's a challenge getting to the Nature Center, but don't despair if you first miss it. As you come up U.S. 65, take the second exit on the right (west U.S. 60) after you cross Lake Springfield. After a mile, take the Glenstone Avenue Exit. Turn left (south), cross the James River Expressway, go through the traffic light, keeping a lookout for the next left, the outer road, which takes you back east to the Nature Center. It's a bit tricky, even if you know the way, but the Center is well worth it.

Museums and Historic Attractions

Air & Military Museum of the Ozarks
2305 E. Kearney St., Springfield
• **(417) 864-7997**

World War II buffs and vets will find this 3,600-square-foot museum a treasure trove of artifacts, mostly from WWII to the present. There are airplane models and uniforms from the various military branches. There's even a PX where you can get military memorabilia and that inevitable vacation T-shirt! Admission is free, but call first to check hours of operation. The best way to get to the museum is to take the Kearney Street Exit from U.S. 65 and head west.

Discovery Center of Springfield
483 E. St. Louis, Springfield
• **(417) 862-9910**
• **www.communityconnection.org**

This hands-on, interactive museum is fun for children and adults. It features science, architecture, archeology, energy, and health exhibits at one of Springfield's newest attractions. Don't expect your typical museum with behind-the-glass-displays. You get down and "get dirty" and learn and have fun as you explore a variety of interest areas, including the Exploratory Lab.

A special display is "Discovery Town," which features a miniature supermarket, bank, newspaper, TV station, doctor's office, and various other town features. Kids can write their own news story about themselves, take their picture, and print the paper right there, appearing on page one! In the TV studio, they can operate the camera, see themselves on the monitor, and do a newscast as a TV news anchor. You can marvel at the giant 8-foot eyeball model or learn about different cultures in a rotating multicultural exhibit. There's a special area called Wonderland for preschoolers. EnergyWorks has a life-size statue of Benjamin Franklin flying a kite, and the museum store features educational toys, games, puzzles, and puppets. The Discovery Center has group tours for area school children and special classes during the school year for area youngsters to explore and discover in an interactive way. It has become an important educational asset to schools.

The Center was helped on its way by donations from Springfield citizens. Former Springfieldian Brad Pitt pitched in with a $120,000 donation to help fund what will become one of the state's most kid-friendly museums.

To discover the Discovery Center, take the Chestnut Expressway Exit from U.S. 65. Turn left (west) on Chestnut and travel until you come to Glenstone Avenue. Turn left (south) on Glenstone, and just after passing over the railroad tracks, turn right on St. Louis Street. The Discovery Center is on your left, about a mile and a half, just after you pass the Shrine Mosque and before you reach Park Central in downtown Springfield. Any construction you see is part of the planned 260-acre Jordan Creek Valley Civic Park, a renovation of Springfield's downtown area.

Admission is $5 for adults, $4 for adults older than the age of 60, and $3 for children aged 3 through 12. Children younger than 2 get in free. The museum is open from 10 AM to 5 PM on Wednesday and Saturday, and from 1 PM to 5 PM on Thursday, Friday and Sunday, and closed on Monday and Tuesday.

Frisco Railroad Museum
843 E. Commercial St., Springfield
• (417) 866-7573

The Frisco logo, a stretched coon skin with Frisco emblazoned on it, was a familiar sight in the Ozarks during the railroad's heyday. Railroad buffs will delight in this small but growing museum. It houses more than 5,000 artifacts, of which 2,000 are on display. The oldest item is a hand-drawn book of survey maps and notes, dated 1854. If you are a Frisco fanatic, you may be interested in membership in Frisco Folks. The organization has more than 900 members in all 50 states and six foreign countries. Membership includes *All Aboard*, a quarterly magazine, an annual calendar, and free admission to the museum. Admission is $2 for adults and $1 for children 12 and younger.

General Sweeny's Museum of Civil War History
5228 S. Mo. Hwy. ZZ, Republic
• (417) 732-1224

Near the Wilson's Creek National Battlefield at Republic, a few miles south of Springfield, this museum is the result of a hobby gone wild. Dr. Tom Sweeney, who started collecting Civil War artifacts at the tender age of 12, is owner and curator of this privately owned museum. His collection now fills more than 50 display cases. The interest comes naturally. An ancestor of his, Gen. Thomas William Sweeny, lost his right arm while serving in the Mexican-American War. His handicap didn't hold him back in his chosen career. He made the rank of general and fought with Gen. Nathaniel Lyon's Union forces at Wilson's Creek. It's in honor of him that Tom Sweeney (the final e" cropped up after the war" in the family name) named General Sweeny's Museum of Civil War History, opened in 1992.

The collection is housed in a specially designed and custom-built museum that is the envy of many museum curators. Dr. Tom, as he's known to area residents, takes an interest in the most minute details from the past, and the focus of the museum and its displays and collections feature aspects of the Civil War not found in typical history books. The museum has several gems in the large collection, including the only known Confederate Indian flag in a private collection, carried by Gen. Stand Watie, the only Native American fighting for the Con-

INSIDERS' TIP

If you know you're going to be exploring some areas of Missouri before you come to Branson or after you leave our town, you can get a Missouri Travel Guide that provides information about our state and its areas of Interest with a state highway map. To request a copy (do so several months before you travel) write: Missouri Division of Tourism, P.O. Box 1055, Jefferson City, Mo. 65102, or call (888) 925-3875, Ext. 124.

federacy and the Confederate general to never surrender.

The museum is open from March through October, Wednesdays through Sundays, 10 AM to 5 PM In November and February it's open only on Saturday and Sunday from 10 AM to 5 PM. It is closed in December and January. Group tours are available on request. It is best to call before coming. Follow directions for Wilson's Creek National Battlefield. The museum is on the east side of Hwy. ZZ, just north of the Battlefield. Admission is $3.50 for adults, $2.50 for kids 5 through 11, and $3 for seniors.

History Museum of Springfield-Greene County
830 Boonville Ave., Springfield
• (417) 864-1976

If you want an overview of the area's history, this is the place—from Ozark cave dwellers to today's condo dwellers. A favorite feature of the museum is the Native American Room. There is a 10-minute video that provides a history of Native American life in the Ozarks. There, the kids can grind Indian corn using a mano, a hand-held stone for grinding grains on a metate. In the main gallery they can dress up in uniforms from the Civil War period and clamber on a real, honest-to-goodness Springfield Wagon.

In addition to its many public displays and hands-on activities, the museum is home to the Fulbright Family Archives, which contains more than 30,000 books and documents and 20,000 historical photographs that relate to Springfield's past, making it a major research source for local historians. The three-story building itself is something of a museum piece. The handsome dressed limestone structure dates to 1894 when it was the U.S. Customs and Post Office building. From 1938 to 1992 it served as Springfield's city hall, and many people even today refer to it as "the old city hall building." The building dons gay Christmas apparel for the holidays when the museum hosts its annual gingerbread house contest. Organizations, businesses, and individual bakers offer their best in the tasty culinary architecture contest.

The museum is on the third floor, but is handicapped-accessible by elevator. It's open Tuesday through Saturday from 10:30 AM to 4:30 PM and by appointment. Group tours can be arranged. You can reach the museum by taking the Chestnut Expressway Exit from U.S. 65 and turning west (left). The museum is on the corner of Chestnut Expressway and Boonville Avenue. Admission is free, but a donation of $3 for adults and $2.50 for students and seniors is suggested.

Springfield National Cemetery
1702 E. Seminole St., Springfield
• (417) 881-9499

The large, parklike area is ablaze in fall color with red maples and sweet gums, and in spring with redbud, dogwood, and crab apple and pear blossoms. This 130-year-old cemetery is the final rest for both Confederate and Union soldiers and a lone Revolutionary War veteran who made it this far west. It is also the cemetery for veterans from conflicts after the Civil War, including five Medal of Honor recipients, whose headstones are engraved in gold.

The cemetery is decorated with small flags on Memorial Day, and many area families make the annual trek there to honor their nation's soldiers.

Springfield Art Museum
1111 E. Brookside Dr., Springfield
• (417) 866-2716

Springfield Art Museum has a small, but fine, collection and hosts each summer Watercolor U.S.A., a nationally known watercolor exhibition. (See our Arts and Culture chapter.)

Wilson's Creek National Battlefield
U.S. Hwy. 182 and Mo. Hwy. ZZ, Republic
• (417) 732-2662

You can enjoy the park any time, but August 10 is a great day to do so because it's then that the annual commemoration of the Battle of Wilson's Creek takes place with an army of Civil War enactors. That date, in 1861, marked the serious beginnings of the Civil War in Missouri.

The Battlefield, just south of Springfield, is a park operated by the National Park Service. The visitors center features a film about Missouri's biggest Civil War battle, a battle map and a museum. In 1999, on the 138th anniversary of the battle, it was announced that funding had been secured to double the size of the visitors center. The center is visited by 250,000 tourists each year. The enlarged center will house the nation's largest Civil War library collection, a multi-purpose educational room and offices. The project is expected to be completed in time for the summer 2000 re-enactment activities.

During the summer, there are weekend events, living history events, demonstrations of 19th-century medical treatments, and Civil War firearms demonstrations. There are hiking and biking paths that wander through the park, or you can drive along a road tour on which you see battle sites such as Bloody Hill and the Ray farmhouse, used during the battle as a field hospital by the Confederates.

To get to the park, if you are already in Springfield, just follow Sunshine Street (U.S. 60) west out of town to Mo. Road M. Turn left on M and then right on Mo ZZ. The park is 2 miles south on this road if you're coming up from Branson and want to avoid the Springfield traffic, take the Mo. 14 Exit at Ozark. Turn left (west) on 14. You'll go through Nixa and cross U.S. 160. The rest of the way is a pretty drive on 14 to ZZ, where you'll turn right (north).

Carthage

Carthage is a right smart piece from Branson, but it's a right smart town that can easily fill your day. This county seat of Jasper County, with a population of 11,000, is about 100 miles northwest of Branson, and the quickest way to get there is to take U.S. 65 north to I-44 and drive west toward Joplin. Carthage is 6 miles north of I-44 on U.S. Hwy. 71A.

Carthage was a handsome town when Branson was just a group of log homes on the White River. It gained its prosperity from lead and zinc mining after the Civil War. At the end of the 19th century, Carthage had more millionaires per capita than anywhere in the United States. It was "their town," a good place to raise a family while the rough and ready mining camps just a little bit south made the money. Area granite and the famous Carthage marble made beautiful and durable building materials. You can see some of the old homes, restored to their original splendor, and even stay in some that operate as bed and breakfasts.

It wasn't always so splendid. Founded in 1842, the village had a rough childhood. You can compare the Old Cabin Shop, which was used as the first county courthouse, with the present beautiful white marble courthouse built in 1894. Early growth came to a halt when the Civil War started. Carthage was the site of the first major battle of the Civil War, July 5, 1861, preceding the first Battle of Bull Run by 16 days and Missouri's biggest battle at Wilson's Creek by more than a month. The town was occupied several times by both Union and Confederate forces, and most of the buildings in the town were torched. Bands of guerrillas and bushwhackers terrorized the surrounding countryside.

The 1860 census counted 6,883 residents in Jasper County, but by the end of the war only 30 were left. After the war, farmers and settlers returned and began rebuilding. Then the miners came. Mineral wealth had been discovered and was exploited, and when the railroad came in 1872, Carthage was on its way to becoming a major cultural and architectural center. Today, it's a quiet, thriving town, proud of its Victorian beauty and past.

The Chamber of Commerce will be glad to send you information if you call (417) 358-2373, or you can pick up brochures and information in the office at 107 E. Third Street. Here are some things you'll want to see in Carthage.

Battle of Carthage Civil War Museum
205 E. Grant Ave., Carthage
• (417) 358-6643

Start here on your study of Carthage and the Civil War. The museum provides artifacts and information about the Battle of Carthage. Its focal point is an elaborate 7 x 5 foot mural by local artist Andy Thomas. Admission is free, and the museum is open all year, seven days a week.

Battle of Carthage State Historic Site
E. Carter St., Carthage
• No phone

Events of this first major battle of the Civil War are highlighted in a kiosk of text and graphic illustration at the park located next to Carter Park on East Chestnut Street.

Jasper County Courthouse and Downtown Carthage Square
Grand Ave., Carthage • (417) 358-0421

The turrets, towers, and arches of this Romanesque Revival masterpiece evoke the feel of a medieval castle. Designed by M.A. Orlopp, Jr. of New Orleans, the courthouse, which has been called "one of the handsomest in the coun-

INSIDERS' TIP

Don't take RVs on the streets of Eureka Springs. Plan on parking and walking, or use the trolleys to get around town. Bring your most comfortable shoes because there are lots of steps, the streets are steep and, besides, walking is by far the best way to take in this town's charming ambiance.

try," dominates the town square. The building is on the National Register of Historic Buildings. Inside is a wrought iron cage elevator, an array of military artifacts, and local mining and mineral specimens. A prominent feature is artist Lowell Davis's "Forged in Fir" mural that vividly portray the county's history.

The downtown Carthage square is lined with specialty shops: a 1950s-style deli, tea room, espresso bar, antique and collectible shops, and craft and gift shops.

Kendrick Place
Mo. Hwy. 571 and Mo. Rd. V, Carthage
• (417) 358-0636

A mile north of Carthage is Kendrick Place, one of the few structures in the county to escape the Civil War unscathed. Built in 1849 and used as a command post by both Union and Confederate forces during the conflict, it has now been restored to its pre-Civil War appearance. Call for tour or group meal information.

Old Cabin Shop
W. Mound Street Rd., Carthage
• (417) 358-6720

This cabin from the 1830s served as the county's first courthouse. You can browse through the retail shop and check out the large collection of Native American artifacts. There's also a large collection of guns of the types used by Jasper Countians on both sides of the law.

Phelps House
1146 Grand Ave., Carthage
• (417) 358-1776

The late-Victorian Phelps family mansion recalls the opulence and elegance of old Carthage. Constructed in the 1890s of huge blocks of gray Carthage limestone, it conveys the image of solid strength so important to the wealthy of that era. The interior displays elaborate and unique features: hand-painted wallpaper, beautiful tile mosaics, gold-trimmed woodwork, a Shakespeare stained-glass library window, and a hand-operated rope pulley elevator that serves the four floors. The home has 10 fireplaces, all with different color tile.

Phelps House is open for tours and can be rented for special occasions. A step-on-tour-guide for touring buses is available with advance request. Admission is $2 for adults, $1 for children ages 6 to 12.

Powers Museum
1617 W. Oak St.,
Carthage
• (417) 358-2667

The museum displays a variety of textiles (quilts and fashions), furnishings, decorative arts, archival resources, and Powers family memorabilia that highlight

Getting there can be more than half of the fun on an Ozark daytrip.

DAYTRIPS

Carthage's history from the late 19th and early 20th centuries. If you have an interest in the Victorian era as reflected in Midwest culture, this is the place for you. The museum was a gift to the community by Marian Powers Winchester in honor of her parents, Dr. Everett Power and Marian Wright Powers. The museum and gift shop are open February Through December, Tuesdays through Sundays. Admission is free.

Precious Moments Chapel Complex
480 Chapel Rd., Carthage
• (417) 358-7599, (800) 543-7975

More than a mere chapel, Precious Moments chapel is a theme park based on characters and ideas of Sam Butcher. Artist Sam Butcher's waif-like ceramic figurines and drawings have a following around the world. Butcher fell in love with rolling hills near Carthage when he pulled off the interstate in 1984. So he bought land along Center Creek, a parcel big enough to take in its broad meanderings and large enough for his grand plan, and created a chapel that has become one of Missouri's most popular attractions, drawing more than a million visitors a year. You're likely to encounter tourists from around the world at the Spanish Mission-style chapel, which features more then 50 spectacular murals and 24 stained-glass windows. It's a quiet place of beauty and inspiration in a park-like setting. Sam Butcher's vision is a growing one. There's the new inspirational Fountain of Angels, featuring 120 one-of-a-kind Precious Moments sculptures cast in bronze, and a sound and light show. Near the Chapel is the Precious Moments Gallery that houses Butcher's original art, out-of-production figurines, and mementos and gifts he has received over the years.

A three-story Victorian home has been moved from Carthage to Dusty's Honeymoon Island (like all of the islands and greenlands, Dusty is named for one of Butcher's grandchildren) that's smack-dab in the middle of a 40-acre lake. It's available for honeymooners, and if you're planning on getting married, there's even a wedding chapel nearby to accommodate you. Tiffany's is a restaurant on the grounds that provides tasty fare for the many visitors, and Royal Delights provides deli items and desserts for those who need only a snack. You can even tour Butcher's home (there's an admission charge for that) and see how an artist decorates a house! The complex is even competing with Branson's music shows with its own gospel music shows by Al Brumley, Jr. (son of the famous gospel songwriter) and a group called the Chapelaires.

This amazing complex is cared for by a friendly staff of more than 300 who answer questions from curious visitors and keep the flowers fresh and watered and the grounds groomed. If you need a place to stay, there's a 90-unit RV park and the Best Western Precious Moments Hotel, (417) 359-5900 or (800) 511-7676.

Precious Moments is easy to find. After you exit off I-44 onto U.S. going to Carthage, you'll turn at State Route HH. Just follow the signs. Admission is free, but a donation is requested. There are small admission charges for the house tour and the Fountain of Angels show.

Victorian Homes Driving Tour
Various sites, Carthage • (417) 358-2373

The Victorian Homes Driving Tour is a leisurely drive-by tour of Carthage's most beautiful and architecturally significant mansions built between 1870 and 1910. Stop by the Carthage Chamber of Commerce at 107 E. Third Street, or call them at the number above for a map and descriptive brochure. It's an especially nice drive during the height of the fall leaf color. Several of the mansions have been converted into bed and breakfast inns, including the Grand Avenue Inn, (417) 358-7265, at 1615 Grand Avenue and the Leggett House, (417) 358-0683, at 1106 Grand Avenue.

Joplin

Though larger, Joplin isn't as well-known to tourists as Carthage, but as the state's fourth largest metro area and with its colorful lead-mining past, it's worth the short 8-mile drive from Carthage for a bit of exploration.

Worth the excursion alone is the Thomas Hart Benton Mural, *Joplin at the Turn of the Century, 1886-1906* in the Joplin Municipal Building at 303 East 3rd St. The building is open Mondays through Fridays, 8 AM to 5 PM, and

Ozark-speak

Someone who is unduly thrifty is described as "tight as the bark on a burr oak" or "so tight he squeezes a nickel until the buffalo burps" or "so tight he'd skin a flea for its hide and tallow."

admission is free. Benton began his artistic career in Joplin and visually celebrates his memories of the rough-and-tumble town of his youth in his only autobiographical mural. This is the last mural completed by artist, the only one on panels and only one he ever signed. Support exhibits show the models Benton created for the piece.

Of course with the town's rich mining past, there are many antique stores located in and around the Joplin area, rumored that they slowly sell off antiques of the town's old families who are down on their luck. Our personal favs—**The Antique Mansion** and **The Gingerbread House**—the latter still particularly good for astounding "finds." The Antique Mansion, (417) 781-0300, is at 4830 East 32nd St. at I-44 crossover. The Gingerbread House, (417) 623-6690, is located at 4060 Coyote Drive.

The **Joplin Convention and Visitors Bureau** at 222 W. 3rd St. offers shopping and tourist information. Call (417) 625-4789 or (800) 657-2534 or on the web connect to www.joplincvb.com for updates of events in and around Joplin.

Joplin Museum Complex
P.O. Box 555, Joplin, Mo. 64802
• 417-623-1180.

The Joplin Museum Complex, located in historic Schifferdecker Park, consists of the Dorothea B. Hoover Historical Museum and the Everett J. Ritchie Tri-State Mineral Museum. The Mineral Museum focuses on the what is historically known as "the Joplin District"—the lead and zinc mining camps that peppered southwestern Missouri, southeastern Kansas, and Northeastern Oklahoma and which

poured wealth into the town near the end of the nineteenth century. Mineral specimens on display showing the amazing purity of the lead and zinc deposits of the area, as well as other minerals found locally. The Historical Museum focuses on the history of Joplin, especially the effect of "instant wealth" on the homes and businesses in the area. Other highlights are the Merle Evans Circus Tent #24, Circus Room, and a fine collection of porcelain and bisque dolls.

The Museums and their gift shops are open Tuesday through Saturday 9 AM to 4 PM and Sunday 1 PM to 4 PM. Admission is free.

The easiest way to reach the museum complex is to take the Schifferdecker Street exit (Exit 4) north from I-44 to Old Route 66 (7th Street). You'll see the museum buildings on your left.

George Washington Carver National Monument
Diamond, Mo. • (417) 325-4151

Administered by the National Park Service, this park includes the birthplace site and area in which the famous agronomist, botanist and "stove-top chemist" George Washington Carver (1864-1943) grew up. Carver, born a slave, is best known for his development of many uses for the peanut and soybean. The park includes the Carver family cemetery, a museum, and a self-guided nature trail. Picnic facilities are available, and the park often sponsors special afternoon and weekend programs. Hours are 9 AM to 5 PM daily. The park is closed Thanksgiving and Christmas. Admission is free.

To reach the Carver National Monument, take U.S. 71 to Diamond, Mo. Go west 2 miles on Mo. Hwy. V and then south about 1 mile. Watch for the signs.

> ## INSIDERS' TIP
> Missouri has more than 5,000 reasons to be known as "the cave state," and a dozen new ones are discovered every year. Caves are a great way to beat the summer heat. Remember that although it may be 90 degrees outside, a cave will be a constant 60 degrees. When it's hot outside, the cave will seem cool; in winter when it's cold outside, the cave will seem warm. Wear a sweater and your comfy walking shoes.

Eureka Springs, Arkansas

It would be nice to spend several days in Eureka, but it is close enough that you can get a good taste in a single day. It's a pretty drive through the winding wilderness of Arkansas to this "Little Switzerland of the Ozarks," and you'll love the meandering streets, quaint shops, and Victorian-era homes.

There is no single attraction that makes this town remarkable; the attraction is the entire town. People were coming as tourists to Eureka Springs when Branson was only a couple of log

Many Ozark towns have Farmers' Markets selling baked goods,
produce and plants, and craft items.

Photo: A.C. Harlson/Arkansas Dept. of Parks & Tourism

cabins in the White River wilderness. Eureka Springs developed as a spa town when people traveled from all over the country to bathe in the town's many mineral springs, hoping to find cures to everything from blindness and rheumatism to "the vapors," the then-popular term for female depression.

American Indians had known about the many springs in the area and shared the secret of their cures with settlers. Soon people began coming to the "Indian Healing Spring," also known as Basin Spring because the water flowed into a natural stone basin. During the Civil war, Dr. Alvah Jackson established a hospital in the "Rock House," a cave near the spring, treating the wounded of both sides. He must have done some good. After the war news of the springs' cures spread, and people came from miles to camp nearby and "take the waters."

By July 4, 1879, more than 400 people were camped nearby, and it was decided to form and name a community. Trees on the hillsides furnished lumber for permanent homes, and the sawmills quickly stripped the area of trees. The hills were so steep and the houses so close that they were stacked in layers upon layers up the sides of the steep slopes. In fact, according to local history, the first lawsuit in Eureka Springs resulted when a woman carelessly threw dishwater out the back door and down the chimney of her neighbor, damaging the furniture.

Basin Spring water was bottled and sold nationwide, and the face of the "Ozarka Girl" became a familiar trademark and spread the town's growing fame.

The railroad came to the town in 1883, and connections with the Frisco line at Seligman, Missouri, assured the success of Eureka Springs as a health spa. Six trains a day came into the town, and its population of 5,000 full-time residents made it the fourth largest city in Arkansas.

By 1885 the gas-lighted streets were graded and paved or sprinkled daily during the summer to keep down the dust. In 1910 streetlights were electric, and the town had a new Carnegie library. Hotels were built, and by the 1890s it had become one of the most fashionable spa towns in the United States, rivaled only by Hot Springs in central Arkansas. Bathhouses and hotels that featured hydrotherapy attracted the rich and famous, along with those who preyed on them and provided services for them.

The town whose fame was founded on water attracted people who wanted something stronger than water, and area moonshine found a ready market. Interestingly, temperance crusader Carrie Nation spent her last years in Eureka. She died there in 1911 after a stroke following one of her famous fire-and-brimstone temperance speeches at Basin Park.

The town, which grew like wildfire, paid the price, suffering four major fires in the years 1883-93, which destroyed large sections of the town but which resulted in building codes and general rebuilding in stone rather than wood. But the rebuilding, plus expensive civic luxuries that saddled the city with debt and a general decline in the public's belief in the curative powers of spring waters, put the city in a depression that began in 1907. By the time the Great Depression came upon the nation in 1929, Eureka Springs was still struggling. The town dwindled from its former glory. Of the 30 hotels during its heyday, only three were still in business in the 1930s, and by the 1950s, the town's population had shrunk to fewer than 200.

The impounding of the waters of the White River behind Beaver Dam in the 1960s, and the attraction of the Ozarks in general as well as the development of Branson in particular, have brought new life and prosperity to this quaint town. It has grown to almost 2,000 residents now. Today you can enjoy its colorful and ornate Victorian architecture in newly restored stores and homes. You can shop the variety of specialty shops and galleries, more than 150 of them, along meandering Spring Street, mentioned by Ripley's Believe It or Not! museums as the street that contains more S curves than any street in the nation.

We suggest you obtain a map of the town when you get there, as the winding streets make it easy to become disoriented. You can get information ahead of time by calling the **Arkansas Chamber of Commerce** at (501) 253-8737 or **Eureka Springs Tourism** at (800) 643-3546, or visit the **Chamber of Commerce** on Ark. Highway 62 W.

Start your adventure at the base of the valley along Main Street, then walk up Spring Street, stopping at sites and stores that interest you. Walk until you get to the top (or get tired), and come back down the other side. On the way enjoy the 12 spring sites, of more than 63 in the town, that have become miniature parks.

The Eureka Springs Preservation Society publishes a series of six self-guided walking tours. At $1.25 they are worth their weight in gold, not only for the historical information, but also to keep you from getting lost. If

INSIDERS' TIP

Missouri has a connection to the stars, and we don't mean those in Branson. Marshfield was the birthplace of Edwin Hubble (1889-1953), known as the Columbus of the Cosmos. You can see a one-quarter size replica of the telescope that bears his name now in space sending back pictures. And astronaut Tom Akers is from the small town of Eminence, east of here.

you do get lost, don't worry. The town is small enough that you can't wander far before you'll be back in familiar territory; besides, getting lost can be the most interesting way to discover the town!

Another way to become oriented is to buy an all-day trolley pass and ride the loop once just to scope out the situation. The pass is only $3, and by the end of the day your feet will think it was money well spent. The trolleys stop in front of virtually every hotel and motel and have regular stops downtown. Tickets can be purchased at many shops and at the downtown trolley depot on Spring Street.

There are lots of restaurants, delis, and dessert shops in the town, so there is no danger of not finding a good place to eat. No matter how eclectic or discriminating your taste, Eureka Springs has a restaurant that will tease your palette. The town is a mecca for chefs, many of whom have established their own restaurants. You can eat out every meal for weeks in Eureka Springs and never tire of the variety—continental to Asian, barbecue to baklava. An Annual Food and Wine Weekend has become one of the most popular events in Eureka Springs and one our favorites. (We love our food!) Chefs around town showcase their talent, matching food and wine at different meals throughout the day. Brunch, lunch, and dinner along with simple "splash in the glass" tastings are available.

As you walk the town, you'll pick up a New Orleans atmosphere without the flat ground. It's a quality that is just emanated by the wrought-iron work on some of the buildings and perhaps by the large number of musicians, artists, and general character types that have come to live in the town. In fact, the town owes much of its revival to the fact that large numbers of the "hippie element" of the '60s were attracted to the town, liked it, and stayed to become more staid town elders now.

If you happen to be in town in September, you can catch the **Eureka Springs Jazz Festival**, and in June there is an annual **Blues Festival** (see our Annual Events chapter).

It's about a 45-minute drive to Eureka Springs. The simplest way to get there is to take U.S. 65 south to Harrison and pick up U.S. 62 west just after Bear Creek Springs. The other option, a more scenic route, is to take U.S. 65 south to Mo. Hwy. 86 west, then Ark. Hwy. 23 south. We suggest, just for variety and to see more of our beautiful Ozark country, you take the scenic route down and the other route back.

Spring Street
Eureka Springs Tourism
• (501) 253-8737,
(800) 643-3546

Eureka Springs is an artsy town. This street alone boasts almost two dozen studios and galleries, many of them on Spring Street. You'll like the Spring Creek Pottery Shop where you can buy the practical as well as artistic and even fantastic sculptures in clay. Quicksilver Nature Gallery at 99 Spring Street sells art with a natural theme. You marvel how everyday items and natural objects are transformed into art. Happy Things at 55 Spring Street specializes in furniture, figurines and anything you might want for dollhouses and collector boxes.

Gazebo Books
86 Spring St. • (501) 253-9556

This bookstore carries everything from bestsellers to odd, interesting, and off-the-wall

INSIDERS' TIP

For a town of 5,000, Branson uses a lot of water! The record of 5.8 million gallons was set August 1, 1999. Peak usage is the "5 o'clock flush," that hour when thousands of visitors return from daytime activities to their motel to get ready for dinner and an evening show.

selections. The store advertises its self as "the bookstore with the world view," and you can increase your view of the world with art books, exotic geography, travel, and cookbooks and books on religion and history. Gazebo Books also stocks local interest books, children's books, and a fine selection of "how to" books.

Quigley's Castle
Quigley Castle Rd. • (501) 253-8311

Rightly known as "the Ozarks' strangest dwelling," this curiously designed home (built in 1943) includes suspended rooms, secret passage ways, floor-to-ceiling windows, and inside planting areas. The eccentric Mrs. Quigley loved collecting and incorporated in the walls of home, and even on the furniture, her rock, arrowhead, and butterfly collections. The castle has been open to the public for over 40 years. Hours are 8:30 AM to 5:30 AM during April 1-October 31, but the Castle is closed Sundays and Thursdays. Admission is free for children 15 and younger, $3 for adults.

Rosalie House
282 Spring St. • (501) 253-7377

In the middle section of Spring Street where it levels out (yes, it runs sideways along the hillside at times!), you may want to tour the colorful Rosalie House. The burgundy brick house has ivory, gray, and green ornate gingerbread. It's open daily for tours and weddings. Admission is free for children 12 and younger and $5 for adults.

Queen Anne Mansion
115 W. Van Buren
• (501) 253-8825, (800) 626-7426

This magnificent home has been featured in *Southern Living* and *Victorian Homes* magazines, and it is often scheduled for "Victorian weddings." There are two historic homes at the site (the other is The Wings) but don't miss the Queen Anne. It's a lavish three-story, 12,000-square-foot Victorian home that was originally built in Carthage, Mo. (See "Carthage" in this chapter.) In 1984, it was moved piece by piece to Eureka Springs at a cost of over half a million dollars. Rebuilt, it has been decorated in fine, Victorian fashion with period antiques. Notable is the woodwork, best exemplified in the seven hand-carved fireplace mantels and five pocket doors.

Admission is $10 for both homes or $6 for the Queen Anne.

Turpentine Creek
239 Turpentine Creek Ln.
• (501) 253-5841
• www.turpentinecreek.org

With 450 acres inhabited by lions, tigers, cougars, leopards, bears, monkeys, exotic birds, and other wildlife, Turpentine Creek is a haven for neglected or unwanted exotic animals. The facility is USDA licensed, and it's supported by donations and guest admission fees. The facilities allow you to get about as close as you dare to get to these animals, and in the petting zoo you can even pet tiger and lion cubs. Turpen-

tine Creek is 7 miles south of Eureka Springs on Ark. Hwy. 23. Follow the signs out of town. The refuge is open to guests March through December from 10 AM until dusk. Admission is $7 for adults and $4 for kids ages 12 and younger and senior citizens aged 65 and older.

The Great Passion Play
Passion Play Rd.
• (501) 253-9200, (800) 882-PLAY

The play usually runs from April through October. It's a spiritual and theatrical extravaganza done in pantomime (with professionally recorded voices) with more than 200 actors, sheep, donkeys, and camels that recreate the life, death, and resurrection of Jesus Christ in a two-hour show. There are also two pre-play performances: gospel concerts and Parables of the Potter presentations. These are free to the public on the nights the play is performed.

In 1999 Passion Play tickets cost $14.25 to $15.25 for ages 12 and older and $7 to $7.50 for ages 4 to 11. All seats must be reserved, so call ahead for tickets at the number above. The drama is performed nightly, except Mondays and Thursdays, with curtain time at 8:30 PM. After Labor Day, the show begins an hour earlier.

On the grounds are other attractions, including a 10-foot section of the Berlin Wall on which an East Berliner inscribed a line from the 23rd Psalm. There is a Bible Museum with more than 6,000 bibles in 625 languages and a lifesize reproduction of DaVinci's *Last Supper*. The museum features an interesting video about the history of the Bible. At the end of Passion Play Road, you can't help but see the 67-foot Christ of the Ozarks, used as a landmark by aviators. It weighs more than a million pounds and is the product of Emmit Sullivan, one of the sculptors of Mount Rushmore. Some say that the statue looks like Willie Nelson. Other say it looks like a milk carton with outstretched arms. Others say that its eyes follow you. Many of the attractions on the grounds are free.

Thorncrown Chapel
U.S. Hwy. 62 • (501) 253-7401

The chapel is just west of the Eureka Springs

The 67-foot Christ of the Ozarks is visible from the historic Crescent Hotel in Eureka Springs, Ark.

Photo: Craig Ogilvie/Arkansas Dept. of Parks & Tourism

on U.S. 62. Designed by world-renowned Arkansas architect E. Fay Jones, the chapel seems a jewel of light in its Ozark mountainside setting and has been called one of the finest examples of religious space in modern times. It rises to the sky like the forest that surrounds it. The chapel, majestic in its simplicity, has 425 panes of glass divided by a lattice of native pine. The chapel was honored as Building of the Decade in 1991 by the American Association of Architects and has been featured in numerous magazines. It's closed during January, February, and March but open the rest of the year. Hours vary with the seasons so call the number above if you plan to visit.

Eureka Springs & North Arkansas Railway
North Main Street • (501) 523-9623

The depot is on North Main Street (you may want to check out some of the flea markets on that street) as you come into town via Ark. Hwy. 23 N. You'll enjoy the historic station, gift shop with train memorabilia, and the vintage railroad car and steam engines display— all free. The ride itself lasts about an hour. You'll be pulled in vintage steam locomotive comfort and enjoy lunch in a restored dining car while a panorama of scenery passes by your window. Check the depot for the schedule and prices.

Mountain View, Arkansas

Everywhere you go in Mountain View, you'll hear the sound of authentic mountain music. Banjos, dulcimers, guitars, harmonicas, and other unplugged instruments play century-old folk songs. The music gathers thousands of visitors to the area each year to hear music on the square. The town is the proclaimed "Folk Music Capital of the World" and so the tradition of impromptu music by pickers and singers on the town square was born. The Mountain View square has been for decades the site of a spring music festival, and purists insist that the amateurs who jam on the courthouse lawn are as good or better than the folk artists at the nearby Ozark Folk Center. One of the first and most obvious factors that attracts people to Mountain View to live or just to visit is its location. The town is nestled into the hills and valleys of the beautiful Ozark Mountains. Touched by the White River and several year-round creeks, streams, and springs, the area around Mountain View is truly majestic. You'll enjoy the drive down to Mountain View, though it is 150 miles over roads that would not qualify as even moderately straight for more than a mile stretch.

Because it's a rather long (and slow) drive, you may want to make this out-of-Branson excursion an overnighter. Mountain View has a number of motels and bed and breakfast inns, and overnight accommodations at the Ozark Folk Center are available at the Dry Creek Lodge, (870) 269-8871. Baxter and Stone Counties of Arkansas have been two of the state's fastest growing counties, and there is a world of natural beauty and several attractions to tempt the tourist. For more on attractions in this area, contact the Arkansas Chamber of Commerce, P.O. Box 133, Mountain View, Ark. 72560, (870) 269-8068.

The quickest way to get to Mountain View and the Ozark Folk Center from Branson is to take the scenic drive down U.S. 65 south to Harrison, Arkansas, and then to the town of Leslie, Arkansas. There you'll turn east on Ark. Hwy. 66, which will take you into Mountain View. Just so you can have an equally scenic and different drive back, take Ark. Hwy. 5 to Mountain Home, and come back to the Branson area via Gainesville. As we mentioned, this is our longest day trip, and we suggest you make this an overnighter. There's just too much to cram into a single day when you have to travel our slow roads.

Ozark Folk Center

P.O. Box 500, Mt. View, Ark. 72560;
Ark. Spur 382 off Ark. Hwy. 9
• (870) 269-3851, (800) 264-3655
• www.ozarkfolkcenter.com

The center is an expansive park with restaurants and shops, demonstrations of folk arts and crafts, a conference center with classrooms, landscaped grounds, and even overnight accommodations. The center's intent is to give the visitor an insight into Ozark history, crafts, and arts in a frozen-in-time re-creation. It contrasts with Branson, which represents the eclectic and evolving Ozarks, with electric guitars and music influenced by rock elements, neon, bright lights, and glitz. They're two different versions of the Ozarks: one past, the other present.

The Ozark Folk Center, an Arkansas State Park that opened in 1973, is dedicated to preserving the music, crafts, art, and history of our mountain way of life from about 1850 to 1930. You can see Ozark craftspeople at work weaving baskets, throwing pots, shoeing horses, and forging tools and knives. You can listen to unplugged country music and sample Ozark cuisine or get some quick lessons in jam and jelly making and some home canning. If you want to spend more time, you can learn some of these old skills at sessions from sorghum making to herb gardening. The conference center is the setting for the classes, elderhostel programs, workshops and seminars, and if you're planning your trip well in advance, you may want to write the Center for information. It has three large meeting rooms, a small (160-seat) auditorium, and an impressive Ozark Folklore Research Library.

Admission prices vary a good deal because you can purchase tickets just for the music performances, and there are one- and three-day combination tickets or season passes. It is best to call for prices, but a family pass costs $32.50 for a day's visit to everything the center has to offer. The regular season is mid-April through October, and the center is closed from December through March. Call for more information.

Blanchard Springs and Blanchard Springs Cavern
Blanchard Springs Cavern Rd.,
Blanchard Springs, Ark. • (870) 757-2211

Only 14 miles from the Ozark Folk Center is a natural wonder. More than a dozen new caves are discovered each year in the Ozarks, but nothing has been as spectacular as this 1963 discovery. Blanchard Springs Cavern's lower level had been known for years. In fact, the explorers who found the "new cave" were on their 27th trip into the cave when they noticed the telltale red clay at the top of a large room. Red clay is normally found only on cave floors, and some caves are entirely filled with the clay, waiting to be washed out and reveal a new cave. Recognizing that an upper cave might exist, they poked around and found the cave discovery of the century. The cave has many awe-inspiring rooms and passages including a beautiful Dripstone Tour, and is impressive because it is totally uncorrupted and not vandalized. In order to keep it that way and so as not to disturb humidity and cave life, visitors enter through specially constructed "air locks." Nearby Blanchard Springs is impressive, as is

Ozark-speak

When someone obtains something more by luck or chance than skill or intelligence, an Ozarker is likely to remark, "Even a blind hog gets a good acorn once in awhile."

the river that emerges from the cavern. The walk up the trail to the source is especially pretty in the spring when the dogwood and redbud are in bloom.

The cavern is in the Ozark National Forest and is operated by the U.S. Forest Service. There is an excellent movie presentation about the cave, its past and formation and its discovery in the Cavern Visitors Center. The center also carries books about caves and the flora and fauna of the area. The cavern is on Highway 14 west of Mountain View. Call for information or directions.

Calico Rock, Ark.
Hwy. 9 • (870) 297-4129

Calico Rock is a tiny town whose main street is on the National Historic Register. Calico Rock is named for the colorfully splotched 200-foot bluffs of the White River, the same White River that flows through Branson. Calico Rock was at one time an important river town when steamboats were the only method of transportation into the White River country. Later it became an equally important rail town after the railroad snaked its way up the White River valley. It is worth the drive to check out the several craft stores and the best old-time hardware store we've ever found.

You can catch an excursion up the White River valley on the White River Railway. Call (800) 305-6527 for times and ticket information. If you need an overnight stop because you've worn yourself out, our favorite place is the old 1923 Riverview Hotel, (870) 297-8208, right in the town near the bridge, now a quaint bed and breakfast operation overlooking the valley below.

Hollister

We've come to think of Branson's "sister city" across the lake as if we were Siamese twins. The two towns, with separate but cooperating city governments, are looked upon by natives as extensions of each other. To get to Hollister, take U.S. Business 65 (or Veterans Blvd.) in downtown Branson east. As soon as you cross the Taneycomo Bridge, turn right.

Before Branson, there was Hollister, which developed as the area's first tourist attraction after the coming of the St. Louis Iron Mountain & Southern Railroad. It had the area's first iron bridge, which still spans Turkey Creek, the first paved street, electric lights, movie house, and steam-heated hotel. Named after a Hollister

in California, the town developed as the result of nearby vineyards, orchards, and truck farms. J. W. Blankenship started the development of an English style village to attract tourists, and the Tudor Revival architecture along Hollister's Downing Street was placed on the National Register of Historical Sites in 1978.

In pre-dam days, Turkey Creek and the White River frequently flooded the town. Vintage photographs show trains plowing through water that reached up and covered the tracks in the town and johnboats floating in the dining room of Ye English Inn. You can inspect the old Ye English Inn, built in 1912, without danger of being flooded. Ask to see the fossilized fish built into its cobblestone walls, which are made from rock from nearby Turkey Creek. It was a popular stopover for the area's early travelers, and though it can't claim George Washington slept there, it can claim that Clark Gable slept there. The inn contains a popular local pub. (See our Restaurants chapter). While strolling down Downing Street, stop at No. 10 and have your picture taken. One of the most picturesque train stations in the nation is now Hollister's chamber of commerce.

Green Lantern Antiques and the Flea Collar are shopping stops. (See our Shopping chapter). If you want to inspect a real old-time country feed mill, stop at the Mule Barn under the U.S. Business 65 bridge over the railroad tracks. Reading the local bulletin board and talking with the proprietor about his jumping mules is worth the short walk to it. A good place to eat on Downing Street is the Ye Olde Iron Kettle, a quaint little place that serves hamburgers, sandwiches, and soups, as well as complete meals.

Information and a map of the town are available from the Hollister Chamber of Commerce. It's housed in Hollister's old train depot. Call (417) 334-3050.

Ozark/Mansfield/Seymour

Here's a way you can work in a number of sights and activities in a single day if you've had an overload of shows in Branson—and have a pleasant drive in the process. You can take in some antique shops, visit a shade garden and the Laura Ingalls Wilder house museum, and inspect "Amish country" at Seymour.

Start early—by 8 AM—and drive north on U.S. 65 to Ozark. After you cross the Finley River, you'll take the Mo. 14 east through Ozark. You might want to stop and take in some of the antique shops and flea markets in

DAYTRIPS

Ozark, but don't dawdle too long. Continue east on Hwy. 14 toward the towns of Sparta and Ava. Your first stop will be the Garden of Dreams. **The Garden of Dreams**, (417) 683-3733, is a gardener's delight and is only 1 mile south of Mo. 14 between Sparta and Ava. Look for the signs. You'll enjoy the shade garden on a hot day. Though there are lots of sun-loving plants and gardens, Dr. Bill Roston, the owner, is known for his "hosta hobby." There are more than 10,000 hosta plants encompassing some 600 varieties in the garden, plus dozens of different types of ferns, impatiens, and other shade-loving plants. You may want to buy some plants for your own shady area.

After you leave the Garden of Dreams, continue east on Hwy. 14 and enjoy the scenery on the way to the small community of Dogwood. When you get to Mo. Hwy. 5 in Ava, turn left (north) and drive toward Mansfield. Watch for the signs directing you to the Laura Ingalls Wilder Historic Home and Museum, located a mile east of the Mansfield town.

Laura Ingalls Wilder Historic Home and Museum
3068 Mo. Hwy. A • (417) 924-3626
• www.bestoftheozarks.com/wilderhome

Wilder's *Little House* books are classics of children's literature, and because of the TV series (still aired in Europe and Japan) you're likely to see a bus of Japanese tourists there. Laura lived most of her life on the farm she named

Rocky Top. She moved to the Ozarks in 1894 but never wrote a Little House in the Ozarks. When she settled down, she stayed. The home was listed on the National Register of Historic Places in 1957, the year that Laura died at age 90. She and her husband, Almanzo, and daughter, Rose, are all buried in the Mansfield Cemetery. You can see the writing desk where she penned her Little House books and some of her handwritten manuscripts. You may feel a bit like Gulliver in the land of the Lilliputians because Almanzo custom built counters and much of the furniture to accommodate the diminutive 4-foot 11-inch Laura. Next door is the Laura Ingalls Wilder-Rose Wilder Lane Museum, which has Laura's earliest needlepoint sample, Pa's famous fiddle, collections of household and farm implements, and memorabilia from Rose, a celebrated author in her own right. You'll also like the Little House Bookstore where you can purchase books in the Little House series, as well as books by Rose, dolls, posters, T-shirts, puzzles, and games.

If you come in late August, you might want to take in the community production of Little House Memories at the Mansfield City Park in the evening. Call for information about times. The house and museum are usually open daily during the season, March 1 to October 31. During the month of November the museum and house are closed, but during December there is a special Christmas open house. You may want to call for dates. Tickets to the house and museum are $3 for ages 6 to 18, $5 for seniors and $6 for everybody else except kids under 6 who get in free. Signs will direct you to the Home and Museum, which is only a mile east of the Mansfield town square on Mo. Hwy. A.

After leaving the Laura Ingalls Wilder House and Museum, continue north on Hwy. 5. At the junction of U.S. Hwy. 60, you'll turn left (west) toward Springfield. Your next stop is Seymour.

Dance scene from "Little House Memories" at Mansfield.

Photo: Mansfield Mirror

Seymour, in Webster County, is a typical small Missouri town built around a square. Just north of the town, in Wright County, is the headwaters of Bryant Creek, which flows south to the White River. Though you would never know it from your view from the highway, the incline at Cedar Gap, north of town, is one of the longest and steepest in the state.

Marshfield, the county seat, can boast being the highest county seat in the state at an elevation of 1,490 feet. In fact, of all the towns along I-44, Marshfield is the highest town on the route east of the Rocky Mountains. The county was named after Massachusetts Senator and orator Daniel Webster and the county seat was named after Webster's hometown, Marshfield, where he had died October 24, 1852, three years before the county was formed from Greene County.

Because Webster County has such a high elevation in comparison to surrounding counties, it is also the "mother of rivers." Five noteworthy streams originate in Webster County, flowing to various points of the compass. The James and Finley rivers flow west and southwest. The Pomme de Terre River takes off to the northwest. The Niangua River flows to the north toward the Lake of the Ozarks. The Osage Fork of the Gasconade River meanders to the northeast.

In Seymour, you may want to investigate the town square and poke in at some of the antique shops. **Murphy Orchards**, (417) 935-2270, right on Hwy. 160, is worth stopping, especially during apple season, and Seymour hosts an annual apple festival (see our Annual Events chapter).

There is a sizable Amish community in the vicinity, and you may want to check out the **J & A Country Amish Store**. The market features arts, crafts, and items made by the local Amish community. The Amish themselves run a store—no phone number, of course! Just turn right off Hwy 160 on Mo. Hwy. C and drive 5 miles. If you want to see more of these efficient and unique farmers and their community, call **Amish Country Tours**, (417) 935-2910, ahead of time for prices and directions. You can take a 45-minute horse and carriage tour of the Amish community there.

You may find that you don't want to make it back to Branson that night! If that's the case, try the B and B experience at **Amish Country Inn**, (417) 935 9345, www. welcome.to/amishinn. This barn, built in 1915, serves as the comfortable inn and has a gift shop with lots of Amish-made items. Turn left of U.S. 160 onto Mo. Hwy. K. After the first sharp bend to the right, you'll see the B and B on your left.

With this day trip, you'll have had a full day and will have seen a lot of country. On your way back to Branson, you'll continue on U.S. 60 west to Springfield, then take U.S. 65 south to Branson. If you haven't dawdled around too long, you may even be able to take in a show that night!

Reeds Spring

To get to Reeds Spring, go west on Mo. 76 to Branson West. Turn right on the Mo. 13. It's just a short mosey down the road. According to newspaper editor Truman Powell, Reeds Spring in 1883 consisted of only a log cabin, which was used for a school. Named for two brothers who settled there in the 1870s and gave their name to the spring (still flowing), the town came to life with the building of the railroad. Just east of the town is the 2,000 foot long tunnel, 18 feet high and 24 feet wide, that was drilled through the solid rock of an Ozark mountain. Italians, Austrians, and African-Americans, some 250 of them, working on each end with steam drills and dynamite, removed 10 feet of rock a day. When they met in the middle four years later, they were only a fraction of an inch off from each other. The payroll of $700 a day brought prosperity to the developing town.

In the early 1900s, Reeds Spring was the tie capital of the United States. Before the railroad reached the area, ties were hacked and rafted down the James River. Later they were loaded on the new railhead in the town and shipped all over the country. By 1915 most of the big timber had been logged off, and the tomato industry developed to replace it. Hundreds of acres of tomatoes were grown on farms in the area for the two canneries in the vicinity of Reeds Spring, but that too declined with depleted land and changing markets.

When Table Rock Dam was completed in 1959, tourism became an important part of the economy. The town changed little until recently. The 1930 and 1950 census both list the town with a population of 313. The Branson Boom changed all that. Reeds Spring now has a population of more than 500 and Stone County has been one of the fastest growing counties in the state the last decade.

Now Reeds Spring calls itself "The City of Art." You'll see why when you stroll the rustic Main Street, Mo. 13, of this artsy, laid-back burg. There aren't many side streets, as the town is built in two very steep, narrow valleys, and you won't get lost in Reeds Spring. There are fine art galleries, silversmiths and coppersmiths, jewelers, and stained-glass artisans. As you come into town on Mo. 13, you can't help but notice The Castle. It turns heads. The black, wrought-iron fence at the valley floor contains a 10-acre private estate that climbs the ledges and bluffs of the steep hillside on your right. From Mo. 13 you can see a large waterfall, a giant bronze eagle with a 12-foot wingspread, and endless native rock retaining walls in a landscape of pools surrounded by natural and sculptured shrubs.

If you like antiques and flea markets, there's the **Old Barn**, the **Time Tunnel**, and the **Old Spring Flea Market**, veritable museums of interesting and odd items. If it is "fine art" you're interested in, drop in at the **New Coast Gallery**. You'll like the little sculpture garden beside the shop at 10 Main Street. Check out the spring that gave the town its name, newly refurbished with a gazebo made by the shop students at the local high school. The **Sawdust Doll** is also certainly worth a stop. Turning right on Mo. 248 and going under the road trestle on the leg home, you'll find the **Omega Pottery Shop**. They sell finely crafted products the world over.

We suggest you go back to Branson via Mo. 248, perhaps stopping for a Greek lunch at **Papouli's**, on the left just past the Omega Pottery Shop. (See our Restaurants chapter.) When you drive up the other narrow valley, notice the ruins of several old canneries. Turn right when you get to the stop sign at the top of the hill, and you'll have a meandering, picturesque drive back to Branson, experiencing what it was like to drive "old Highway 65." On the way back you may want to make a short detour and stop at the **Sycamore Log Church**. Turn right on Sycamore Log Church Road and make the short drive down hill to sample what early churches were like in the Ozarks: small, sincere, and serene. Several miles before you come back into Branson you'll cross over the Ozark Highroad, being constructed as a giant loop around Branson with exits for its major attractions. Come back in 10 years and you'll be able to drive on it.

Rockaway Beach and Forsyth

Only nine miles from Branson, Rockaway Beach, like Hollister, is a town with a past. Just a mile or so upstream from Powersite Dam, the first dam on the White River, Rockaway Beach was the first resort on Lake Taneycomo. To get to Rockaway Beach, go 4 miles north on U.S. 65 and take the Mo. Hwy. F exit. After crossing Bull Creek and going up the hill, F meets Mo. 176. Turn right on Mo. 176, and in a few hundred yards you'll see signs to Rockaway Beach. Bear right, and after you pass Merriam Woods, the road turns and drops sharply downhill, makes several hairpin curves and becomes Beach Boulevard. You're in Rockaway! (Don't be confused. Natives almost always drop the "Beach" from the name.)

Willard and Anna Merriam (Merriam Woods was named after her) had the little town, originally called Taneycomo, renamed after the famous New York resort. They had big visions. They adapted the Adirondacks architectural style—knotty pine interiors, native stone rockwork, and bent-limb furniture—to the Ozarks and attracted the developing tourist trade including famous defense lawyer Clarence Darrow and writer Sherwood Anderson, who came down to enjoy the serenity and the then-warm waters of Lake Taneycomo. Several large hotels sprang up, and some of them were run by former vaudeville stars who settled in Rockaway after the developing movie industry killed old-time vaudeville.

Business boomed during the 1920s, '30s, '40s, and '50s. Vacationers took the train to Hollister and boarded a boat to cruise down to Rockaway for several weeks of serenity and swimming. They hiked, fished, water-skied, participated in archery, badminton, and golf, and listened to hot jazz in the cool evenings. All this came to an end when the lake turned cold because of the release of water from the base of Table Rock Dam. Gone are the grand hotels and the activity, but Rockaway is in a revival because of some gung-ho newcomers and as tourists discover its past and seek some solitude, knowing they are only minutes away from the bright lights of Branson's shows.

The cabins and kitchenettes are reasonably priced, and the quiet family atmosphere with the lakefront park make it a good place to hold family reunions. You can fish off the town pier and keep an eye on the kids as they feed the geese and ducks. If you need gear and tackle, they can be had at the Taneycomo Market.

Check out one of the area's most interesting flea markets, the **Wild Goose** for bric-a-brac and treasures. (See our Shopping chapter.) The **Hillside Cafe** and the **Pizza Cellar** are good local eateries. (See our Restaurants chapter.)

An interesting day's excursion to Rockaway Beach would be to skip the drive and rent a boat at Branson's Main Street Marina or the Branson Trout Dock. That's the way folks used to get there before roads, disembarking at the Hollister or Branson depot, and completing the journey by boat. You can fish for trout on the 6-mile cruise down the lake and watch great blue herons, ducks, geese, and the landscape. On the right, about a mile below Branson, you'll see a white Southern-style mansion with grounds that slope to the water's edge. That's **Belle Rive**, the former home of world renowned romance writer Janet Dailey and her husband Bill until they decided "something smaller" would be easier to take care of. She is a bestselling writer, and they both have been active in local affairs for years. You can tie up in Rockaway, spend the day browsing the shops and take your boat back that evening. Not a bad way to spend the day, even if you don't catch any fish!

During the year, the town has a number of "special events." For information on Rockaway Beach and a special event schedule, call the Rockaway Chamber of Commerce, (417) 561-4289 or (800) 798-0178.

Forsyth

If you drive to Rockaway Beach, you may want to come back to Branson through Forsyth, the county seat of Taney County. When in Rockaway, just take Beach Boulevard (Mo. 176) east to U.S. 160. Turn right at the junction with U.S. 160, and the highway will take you right through Forsyth.

Forsyth sits safe, comfortable, and sleepy atop a bluff overlooking Swan Creek's confluence with the White River (now the upper part of Lake Bull Shoals). When it was founded in 1837 as the county seat, with high hopes that steamboat traffic would eventually make it that far up the White River, it was down at the present day Shadow Rock Park, where Swan Creek flows into the lake. When the lake is low, you can see the old steamboat tie-ups, though it wasn't until 1852 that a steamboat was able to make it as far as Forsyth. (See our History chapter.)

The Civil War saw Forsyth changing hands several times between the North and the South. By 1863, nothing was left of the town except the burned out brick walls of the courthouse. After the war, the area was plagued by bushwhackers and the later Baldknobber problems, but gradually rebuilt itself—only to be forced to higher ground as the result of the 1947 decision by the U.S. Army Corps of Engineers to build Bull Shoals Dam. By 1950, the entire town was relocated atop the bluff. Today, Forsyth tenaciously keeps its old-fashion small-town charm.

The town doesn't have any major tourist attractions, but there are several antique shops and **The Gingerbread House**, (417) 546-3996 or toll-free (877)-GBDolls, specializing in porcelain dolls, bisque kits, greenware, supplies, and instruction. The **Forsyth Art Guild Gallery**, (417) 546-5439, is another interesting "poke-in," a place where you can find some interesting and inexpensive art. If you would like to see Forsyth's quaint old business district, turn left (east) at the junction of Mo. 160 and Mo. Hwy. Y. If you decide to eat in Forsyth, we recommend **The Fox and Turtle**, 16229 U.S. 160, (417) 546-6335, for good food as well as local atmosphere. It's the local eatery for merchants and those who have come to town to do business, but they welcome tourists too. Old fashioned burgers, hot dogs, and an amazing variety of shakes and sundaes can be found at the **Forsyth Drive-In**, U.S. 160 & Mo. Hwy. Y, (417) 546-5271, located just west of the Hwy. Y intersection.

To check out Powersite Dam, go west on Hwy. Y. After following the ridge top, the road will head downhill and lead you to Empire Electric Park—a great area for a picnic lunch, fishing, and

Ozark-speak

Someone who is mean or just plain lowdown is described as being "lower'n a mole's navel on diggin' day" or "so low he could walk underneath a rattlesnake standing up."

Shepherd of the Hills Homestead is the home of award winning Clydesdale horses. Wagon tours depart a number of times each day at the park.

Photo: Shepherd of the Hills Homestead

camping. Bull Shoals Lake begins at the low side of the dam, and Lake Taneycomo ends on the high side. When the Table Rock Dam generators are producing electricity and releasing water from Table Rock Lake, or during high water, Lake Taneycomo spills over the dam.

By today's standards, the dam isn't very impressive (546 feet long and 70 feet high), but when it was finished in 1912, it was one of the nation's largest privately owned dams, and it was important in bringing electricity to the area, as well as helping start the Branson-area tourist industry.

When you leave the dam, continue following Hwy. Y along the lowlands. (Just don't take any road that forks off to the left.) You'll come to the old bridge that crosses Swan Creek; turn left after crossing Swan Creek bridge and follow the road heading that heads under the higher steel bridge across the creek.

You are now in Shadow Rock Park. The park gets its name from the high bluff on the north side of Swan Creek. The area that is now the park was an important Indian trading post in the early nineteenth century and later was Old Forsyth. It now has playground equipment and a reconstructed old log home. Two commemorative plaques to the right of the cabin will give you some of Forsyth's historic highlights. The park is host to a number of outdoor events (White River Valley Arts and Crafts Fair in August and the White River Gem and Mineral Club Show in October) and the August Taney County Fair (see our Annual Events chapter).

When you leave the park, follow the main road uphill and turn right. Turn right again at the stop sign at Mo. 160/76, and immediately turn left at the light and go over the Mo. 76 bridge over Bull Shoals Lake. The next 12 miles is up and down and around, but you wind up on the Hollister side of the Taneycomo bridge in Branson. After you go over the bridge, you're in downtown Branson.

Roaring River State Park and Cassville

Roaring River State Park features the rugged and scenic terrain of the southwest Ozarks, and a daytrip over that direction gives a respite from the the glitz of The Strip and allows you to see what folks came to the Ozarks for in the early part of the twentieth century.

The best way is to make a loop. Take Mo. 76 west early in the morning to Branson West, Reeds Spring, Cape Fair, and then to Cassville. You'll be passing through part of Piney Creek Wilderness area. (See our Recreation and the Outdoors chapter.) Cassville has some flea markets and antique shops you can check out (Cassville Chamber of Commerce: (417) 847-2814 or e-mail Cassville@mo-net.com).

If you are so inclined, **Crystal Springs Trout Farm**, (417) 847-2174, just north of Cassville is open year-round for family trout fishing. There's no license or fee required, no limit, and you pay only for what you catch: $3.75 a pound. Trout are cleaned and iced free. Your bait is free, and even your tackle is free if you don't bring your own. Take Mo. 37 north out of Cassville, turn right on Barry County Rd. Y, right on Partridge Drive, and go a quarter mile. Watch for the signs.

If you have your tackle and don't mind the cost of a fishing license and trout stamp (See our Lakes and Rivers chapter for details), you might want to try your luck at **Roaring River State Park**. Take the scenic route Mo. 112 south out of Cassville to the park. A river roars through this 3,354-acre state park and a $5 million lodge overlooks it. Stonework by CCC workers over 70 years ago channels the fury of Roaring River Spring, gushing out more than 20 millions gallons a day to form the headwaters of Roaring River. In the spring, a waterfall pours from the mountainside into the river. The stream is stocked daily during the March 1-Oct. 31 trout season and provides excellent fishing for rainbow trout.

If you're not the fishing type, you can catch a nature program, enjoy the cool air at the spring, horseback ride (a one-hour trail, $12 per person), swim, dine, bike, or hike the park's seven trails, including the Devil's Kitchen Trail, a challenging 1.5 mile trail that climbs 325 feet to the ridge top. The name comes from the odd rock outcrop that forms a room-like enclosure, once used as a hideout by bushwhackers. Take along a flashlight to explore some of the shallow trailside caves. There are 20 caves within the park and 15 alongside the hiking trails. Lunch can be a picnic, packed before you start for the day, or at the **Tree Top Grille** (from $3.50 to $7) in the park. Don't forget to take in the park's nature center, which has changing exhibits and programs.

If you're not too tired, you can take in the show about the **Mountain Maid of Roaring River**, (417) 847-4639 for admission prices and information, in the evening before driving back.

If you're not the hiking type but still want to see some scenery, take the Mo. 76 further south toward Seligman. There's a free observation tower about 3.5 miles from the park. Turn on Forest Road 197 and follow along 8 miles to Mo. 86. This is the Sugar Camp National Scenic Byway of the Mark Twain National Forest, noted for its local scenic quality. Leave in time to take dinner at the **Devil's Pool Restaurant** on the way back to Branson (see our Restaurants chapter) via Mo. 86. You may wish to make reservations before you take this daytrip.

Coming back to Branson from the south will complete your loop. You'll take Mo. 86 east through Blue Eye coming back. The turnoff to Big Cedar Lodge, a mile before Mo. 86 joins U.S. 65 will take you down to Devil's Pool Restaurant. After dinner, continue on Mo. 86, turn north on U.S. 65, and drive the 10 miles back to Branson. You'll have had a full day!

Real Estate

"Aint' nothin' to a flat country nohow. A man jest naturally wears hisself out a walkin' on a level 'thout ary hill t'spell him. An' then look how much more there is of hit! Take forty acres o' flat now an' hit's lest a forty, but you take forty acres o' this here Ozark country an' God 'lmighty only know how much 'twould be if hit war rolled out flat. Tain't no wonder 'tall, God rested when he made these here hills; he jest naturally had t'quit, for he'd done his beatenest an' war plumb gin out."—Harold Bell Wright, *The Shepherd of the Hills*, chapter 1

There's something about the Ozarks that has always attracted people. Whether it's something in the water or the air, or the sight from a hill top of fog in a valley, or the sound of a stream falling over itself on its wandering way to something larger, the ineffable result is love that can only be felt and never explained. We admit that it never was easy to eke out a living on this hardscrabble land, but it's a lot easier now with tourism and related industries. It sure beats tie-hacking, stave-bolt cutting, and growing tomatoes for the canneries! Early settlers in the area used wood from the abundant forests for cabins, but these rude dwellings have largely rotted away after being abandoned for better sawmill lumber homes. However, some older homes have remnants of old log cabins. Many older homes were built of native field stone, creek rocks, or quarried stone, and those with a keen eye and a knowledge of the area can tell you precisely where the stone came from. Such stone construction is less prevalent now, except in more expensive construction, because it's labor intensive and therefore costly.

Movin' to Missouri has a nice ring to it, and moving to the Ozarks is more attractive than ever. The Branson area has become a desired place to live for lots of reasons: clean air and water, low property taxes, quiet towns, and good neighbors. It's secluded but not desolate, with a rural atmosphere yet close to big-city services and plenty of entertainment and activities. Many come for lakeside living. Table Rock Lake covers 52,000 acres to create nearly 750 miles of shoreline. The lake has been proclaimed as one of the three cleanest in the United States. Fishing for bass, crappy, catfish, and a host of other game fish is a year-round sport. Water sports are abundant also (see our Lakes and Rivers chapter). With a usually mild climate, Table Rock Lake is used 12 months every year.

The lake never freezes, and you can leave your boat at the dock. Close by, just below Table Rock Dam, you will find Lake Taneycomo, which is famous for trout fishing. Below Taneycomo's Powersite Dam begins Bull Shoals Lake, known for years as one of the best striped bass lakes in the nation, with much of its waters in Arkansas. Above Table Rock Lake, the newest dam (and the one highest up on the White River) backs up the waters of Beaver Lake in Arkansas. Check our Lakes and Rivers chapter for detailed information on these areas. You'll understand why lots of people find the laid-back lake living here in the Ozarks appealing.

Rental Housing

If you're moving to Branson, you might want to try it on for size first by renting and living in the area for a short time to see if you really like it. Use the rental time to do some homework and find your dream home or acreage. If you plan on renting, we suggest two things: contact a property management agency to see what is available and get a local paper for the housing rental section. Branson has at least four properly management firms: **A-1 Property Management**, (417) 881-7859; **Apple Real Estate**, (417) 334-7888; **Residential Marketing Network**, (417) 335-2448; and **Rivermonte Realty**, (417) 336-6400. Other real estate companies may also manage rentals; check with them if you call around. We can tell you that good, clean, fair-priced rentals are not abundant in Branson, especially during the season of March to December, in spite of the building boom several years ago. If you plan on renting, January and February are your best months to sign a lease. You can expect to pay $370 to $500 a month for a two-bedroom apartment. Some rentals may include water and trash service in their price, but others may expect you to pay all utilities. A two-bedroom house may rent from $475 to $675 a month and a three-bedroom house, $550 to $850 a month. Another rental alternative is a condo. The Branson area is as well-stocked with condos as Lake Taneycomo is with trout. Many offer nightly and weekly rentals (see our Accommodations chapter). Here's a selection of condos that offer nightly, weekly, and long-term rentals: **Treehouse on the Lake** on Table Rock Lake's Indian Point, (417) 338-5199; **The Village**, also on Indian Point, (417) 338-5800; **Foxpointe**, just north of Branson, (417) 334-1990, (800) 334-6590; **Thousand Hills**, just south of The Strip in Branson, (417) 336-5873, (800) 864-4145; **Plantation at Fall Creek** (417) 334-6404, (800) 562-6636 on Mo. Highway 165; and **Pointe Royale**, on Mo. Highway 165 just north of Table Rock Dam, (417) 334-5614, (800) 962-4710. A condo rental is a good way to "try out Branson" as you investigate longer term commitments. The price of a condo varies a good deal depending on location, quality, amenities, and whether it is furnished or unfurnished. Rates for a one-bedroom are between $375 and $425 and a two-bedroom can cost $475 to$600 a month. A three-bedroom condo in a desirable location with fireplace, Jacuzzi, and other amenities can run $1,000 to $1,400 a month. With any rental you can expect to pay first and last months' rent or a security deposit, but again, that varies a good deal. Renting is a good way to become acclimated to the area, and it is also a good way to get your foot in the door to home ownership.

Buying a Home

Branson has changed more in the last decade than in the previous century, and that includes size and area, as well as economically and culturally. At the last census, Branson's population was under 4,000; now it is over 5,000. During 1999 the city limits of Branson grew by more than four square miles to 16 square miles, due to voluntary annexations of Pointe Royale and other areas on the southwest side of the city. The city limits now touch Table Rock Lake. Construction values in 1999 in Branson were $65.7 million, $22 million more than 1998, and the highest value since 1994 when the city recorded $87 million in new construction. More than 10 percent of 1999's projects were new condominiums built for time share rentals. That increase was not lost on businesses that provide for the construction industry. Lowe's, a hardware/lumber yard that caters to the building and home improvement urge, will open a $15 million mega-store late in 2000 in the South Towne Center in Hollister. The new 115,000-square-foot store will satisfy demand for the growing condominium and home construction business in the Branson area and northwest Arkansas. Lowe's, which had opened a store in Springfield in 1985 and another one on the city's northside in 1999, said that its demographic studies indicated that the Branson location was prime and that it would not siphon business from its two Springfield locations. With the planned Branson Creek 7,500-acre development south of Hollister, the tendency of area homeowners to improve or expand their existing homes, and the desire to build and "up-grade" better than a home they may have bought during the Branson Boom in the last decade, it seems as if the boom period is being extended. The Branson Boom of the early 1990s resulted in lots of speculation and a good deal of building—not just theaters, motels, and condominiums—so that right now, according to our observations and from talking to real estate agents, we can report it's definitely a buyer's market. Lots of builders built homes on speculation; lots of buyers bought at artificially inflated prices during the go-go period of the boom. Now if the builders or owners want to sell, they'll have to expect to sell at what the market is today, not what it was six years ago. Then you could take the lot, acreage, or house you bought one week ago and sell it at a nice profit the next. Sellers have seen property sit and sit and sit.

Even Springfield was affected by the Branson building boom and had its own round of overbuilding. Springfield Realtor Carol Jones in 1998 called the housing market there "glutted," with bargains abounding. At the same time, however, according to the National Association of Realtors, in 1999 Springfield saw the median price of an existing home rise from $82,200 to $88,000, and the typical homeowner saw the home's value increase by 3.9 percent.

Those interested in moving or retiring to Branson and area will find they can pick and choose, and there are bargains to be found. Statistics and averages are misleading for this area because prices can vary widely, depending on zoning and location. There is high-priced commercially zoned property on The Strip that has sold for more than $16 a square foot, which is $696,960 an acre, but then there are acreages in the eastern part of Taney County that can be had for less than $900 an acre.

Price depends not only on what others are willing to pay, but also on what you're looking for and how badly you want it. Housing in the Kimberling City, Branson, and Table Rock Lake areas include small lake cabins for vacations and weekend getaways, condos, and full-time residences. Permanent residences range from the moderate price of modulars, to more elaborate two- and three-bedroom abodes for the retiree, to upper bracket four- and five-bedroom homes for larger families You can live way back in the woods with complete privacy or you may wish for a lakefront or lakeview location. For some the hustle and bustle of Branson is more important. If that's the case you can find a home right in the middle of town. Houses are available for $50,000 to $500,000, with an average price of approximately $75,000. Building lot prices generally start from a low of about $5,000. Homes, lots, and acreages with a lake view or lake access are, of course, more expensive. Lakeview lots range from $15,000 to $31,000. Very special lakefront lots are priced in the $80,000 range. Weekend cabins will usually range from the low $40,000s to wherever you may want to stop.

Although Branson's population in the city proper is just over 5,000, an additional 15,000 people live within a 4-mile radius. There are homes on acreages, tiny subdivisions with three or four homes, and large developments with hundreds of homes. You can find new subdivision homes in the $75,000 to $110,000 range, but you can also find homes between $300,000 and $600,000. There have been quite a number of expensive, custom-built homes on hills, in hollows, and on lake coves.

INSIDERS' TIP

We all know that trees clean the air and add beauty to any community. Most developers take pains to preserve existing trees, and Branson itself has a tree ordinance that encourages builders and developers to preserve existing trees and to plant replacements for those destroyed during construction. According to a poll of tourists, the fifth ranked reason for visiting the Branson area was "nature and the beauty of the environment."

In general, the four-county area of Taney, Stone, Christian, and Greene has seen the average price of a home rise over the last decade. The booming economy has prompted people to build bigger and more expensive houses there. The average cost of a home rose from about $60,000 in 1990 to about $95,000 in 1999 for the four-county area. In the immediate Branson area, the figure is lower. The average home price sold in the fourth quarter of 1999 was approximately $75,000. Figures we offer are ballpark averages, and anything we present has two caveats: do your homework and ask questions. If you're coming from either of the coastal areas, you may consider the real estate here cheap. On Commercial Street and Main Street you may see tourists and potential retirees gawking at the pictures with prices of homes posted on the windows of real estate offices. We still hear, "Wow, that's really cheap!" and "What I'd give to have that house on my lot back home!" In fact, the complaint by locals is that people retiring from Chicago, New York, or California can buy twice the house they had there for half as much—and in so doing, drive up the price of real estate for local homebuyers. However, others from small towns in the Midwest wonder why the prices are so high. It all depends of where you come from and what you're willing to do and pay to move to the Ozarks.

If you're city folk and not used to buying rural property, get advice from your Realtor. Learn to ask questions, the more the better. How deep is the well? How many gallons per minute does it produce? Where's the septic field? When was it built? Does it meet the current standards and code? We recommend that you hire a property inspector. When you move to a rural area, don't assume that you'll have full-time paid police and fire departments. Sometimes there are only a sheriff and a few deputies to cover an entire county. As for fire protection, often you are the fire department if you want to serve with your neighbors as one of several volunteer firefighters. Your local real estate agent can give you the lowdown on such issues, but you have to know the questions to ask.

Home sales in 1999 set a record nationwide, in spite of increasing interest rates. In the Branson area sales in 1999 could be called very good. The annual home sales reached record highs, with 1,118 homes sold in the Tri-Lakes area, well over 1998's previous record of 1,005. In addition, the supply of homes available dropped well below the five year low. The "over supply" situation associated with 1995 and 1996 has reduced significantly as the number of homes available dropped below 1,500, according to Cooper Appraisal, a local firm that keeps tabs on the Branson area real estate scene.

Layne Morrill is a descendant of Harold Bell Wright's "Uncle Ike" of **The Shepherd of the Hills.**

Photo: Shepherd of the Hill Realty

Homes priced toward the lower range (less than $90,000) generally have marketing times of less than six months. More expensive homes may be on the market for a year and sometimes longer. Some sellers have had to lower their list prices in order to remain competitive. However, exclusively priced homes (more than $250,000) have shown no decrease in the number of sales, in spite of the rising interest rates.

With the booming national and local economy, home sales have been strong. Some people who were renting are now making the decision to buy; some are moving up to bigger and better houses. It seems that people are in a buying mood. But the drop in the market after the boom in the early 90s was a long one, and the professional mortality rate amongst real estate agents was high. Only the best survived, and they did so by cutting back and tightening their belts. The number of companies declined, with quite a few going out of business, and there have been lots of mergers and buyouts in the 1990s. The job of an appraiser has not been easy one the last several years, and it seems as if the depressed real estate market has reached the nadir of the depression, property values have stabilized and started back up. In any event, the local real estate market has, over the years, gone through a number of such cycles as the market slacked off, only to rise again on the next wave.

The local tourist economy drives the real estate market. Several long-term development projects indicate that some people with big bucks are bullish about the area's development. One is a more than 8,500-acre project south of Hollister by developer Glenn E. Patch. Plans are for a $12 million, 200-acre golf course, single-family and multi-family housing, a multipurpose center with seating for up to 12,000, and a railroad theme town near the tracks that border the property. The past four years has seen the building of basic infrastructure for the development. Now the actual development is beginning, including the Fazio-designed golf course, which opened in 2000.

Another major project is a luxury marina development by Rex Maughan of Forever Living Products International, the billion-dollar-a-year aloe vera empire. Located on the Long Creek arm of Table Rock Lake, the marina facility will rent luxury houseboats to upscale area visitors. Springfield in 1999 had a $100 million burst of construction activity, with the opening of the 83,000-square-foot state-of-the-art Library Center, among various other projects. In early 1999 residents approved a hotel-motel tax that is earmarked for developing a $40 million-plus, 92,000-square foot Fish and Wildlife Museum (See Bass Pro Shop in our Daytrips chapter) scheduled to open in 2001; and the 260-acre downtown Jordan Valley Park project, with its twin ice rinks and a proposed convention center/sports arena with hockey, indoor football and basketball. The convention center/arena is estimated to cost between $19 and $24 million. Through these facilities, Springfield can be expected to attract a larger share of the current tourist trade as well as attract some new varieties of visitors, many of whom will also visit Branson attractions. What is good for Springfield is also good for Branson and future growth.

Concerning the Branson Boom of the early '90s, Taney County planner Chris Hall notes, "the building part of it never has really slowed down. It's simply happening at more of a stable pace." Since any future development and growth depends on getting more people into the area, the city has undertaken a massive road building program. With the widening of U.S. Hwy. 65 between Springfield and Branson (and continuing south of Branson to Harrison), the initial phases of the Highroad loop around Branson and the almost completed Mo. Hwy. 13 Bypass around Reeds Springs, more tourists will find that the road to Branson is paved and increasingly straight.

The Branson/Lakes Area Chamber of Commerce marketing budget is at an all-time high and is aimed at increasing Branson tourist counts to record levels. The future of tourism in Branson looks good, and that means the long-term real estate market will likely be bright. Look in the Yellow Pages of the local phone directory and you'll see several pages of real estate companies, all of them eager to sell you a piece of the Branson action, that retirement home or an Ozarks summer home. Most of the companies we have listed belong to the multiple listing service (MLS) of the Tri-Lakes Board of Realtors, but you might want to ask the individual company if it has all local listings available. Even though the Ozark Mountain Country area encompasses many towns we've only listed, in alphabetical order, the major companies in Branson and the immediate surrounding communities.

Neighborhood Areas and Developments

Though Branson is known as a neighborly town and prides itself on that reputation, only about 17 percent of the area within the city limits was actually zoned residential. With the annexing of the Branson North subdivision and the Pointe Royale development, that figure has gone up to about 28 percent.

Most of the people here have lived, and continue to do so today, outside the city proper. Like the Ozarks—which has a myriad of micro-environments, depending on the elevation, slope, and geology—neighborhoods as such cover a wide range. There are subdivisions of up to a dozen homes, large subdivisions of more than a hundred homes, neighborhood areas of several blocks in town, and gated golf communities that are out in the country but have all the amenities of a big city. A home in Omaha, Arkansas, Forsyth, or Branson West still puts you close to Branson's activities and entertainment as well as its shopping. You can find a wide variety of options, so if you're looking for a particular kind of lifestyle, community, or environment, it's best to let your Realtor know.

A local wag remarked that "Branson has been growing so quickly, we could have a subdivision of the month club." There is truth to his remark. In fact, a computer survey of subdivisions and developments in Taney and Stone counties turns up a total of 738. We have River Bluff Estates, Country Bluff Estates, Friendly Hills, Savannah Hills, Cougar Trails, Skyline Drive, Blue Meadows, Woodridge Estates, Notch Estates, The Woodlands, the Patterson Duck Club, and other names designed to attract the ear and give one "the right address." We've listed only some of the larger, better-known developments, both old and recent, and areas that we locals consider a neighborhood or area by name, even though it may actually consist technically of a number of old adjacent developments.

Such neighborhoods may not be for you; you may find the home of your dreams on a small acreage or tucked away in some hollow or atop a hill with virtually no neighbors. Or you may like the quiet of some of the tiny subdivisions that consist of no more than a half a dozen homes. Look around, the variety will surprise you!

Inside the City Limits of Branson and Hollister

Branson North

Developed in the 1960s before U.S. Hwy. 65 bypassed downtown Branson, the town has developed to enclose this large, wooded area. It has James F. Epps Road as a border on the west and Mo. Hwy. 248 on the north, with entrance to the development from Mo. Hwy. 248. Pioneer developer Dwayne Henss promoted the area as "Branson's best address," and in spite of many newer developments, it still is one of the best. Moving to Branson North almost symbolizes to the community that you've made it. Most streets are curbed and guttered. The modern and upscale construction, with many of the original forest's trees remaining and established plantings that have matured, present a cultivated but woodsy environment. Skaggs Community Health Center and downtown shopping are close, and it's easy to get to The Strip too. Homes start at about $150,000 and top out at $450,000.

Cantwell Addition Area

The Cantwell Addition Area takes in several subdivisions that grew over the years in the area around Cantwell Park. It is bounded by Mo. 76 on the south, U.S. 65 on the east, Roark Valley Road on the west, and Roark Creek and the railroad tracks on the north. Because the area has developed over many years, some homes date from the late '50s while other homes were built within the past year. The neighborhood is quiet, with large trees and established home landscaping. It has easy access to downtown, Cedar Ridge Shopping Center, and The Strip. Stockstill Park is close by, on the north side of Roark Creek. Homes are neat and well-kept and range from $60,000 to $190,000.

Country Bluff Estates

Located off Fall Creek Road on approximately 50 acres, this is an upscale subdivision with paved and guttered streets, central sewer and water. It is only minutes from the east side of The Strip and Mo. Highway 165 to the west. Homes are new and modern, mostly of brick construction and are on large lots. It is obvious that great effort has been made to preserve large, existing native oaks and walnuts. There are approximately 106 restricted lots. Homes range from $150,000 to more than $300,000.

Cozy Cove Condominium Community
341 Loganberry Rd. • (417) 335-2644

On the banks of Bee Creek at its confluence with Lake Taneycomo is the gated condominium community of Cozy Cove. Cozily situ-

> **INSIDERS' TIP**
>
> If you're looking at property around the area, a good map that has all the roads less traveled on it is the Taney County 911 map. You can obtain a copy at the Branson/Lakes Area Chamber of Commerce office on Mo. 248 for $2.80.

ated on 35 acres in the Bee Creek valley beneath Oak Bluff, the development consists of 58 two- and three-bedroom units. It's north of Branson's city limits just off U.S. 65 and is only minutes from Branson High School, downtown Branson, and Mo. 248. The development has county water and its own community sewage system. Streets are paved and curbed. Amenities include a boat dock with access to Lake Taneycomo, swimming pool, and a 12-acre private park at the mouth of the creek. Units range from $75,000 to $100,000. Access to Cozy Cove is the first right (Loganberry Road) on Bee Creek Road before you cross the creek.

Hiawatha Heights Neighborhood

Once considered out in the country, this area is now in the heart of the town. This area has U.S. 65 as a border to the east, 76 Country Music Boulevard to the north and west, and Cliff Drive to the south. The homes on Cliff Drive have a spectacular view of Lake Taneycomo, and the Cliff Drive address was considered the place to live when Branson was very tiny. Most of the streets are curbed as part of Branson's efforts to curb and gutter all the city streets. The area still has some forest, and giant established trees in many of the yards of older homes make for a feeling of being in the woods.

The neighborhood offers insulation from the commercial development on The Strip, yet residents are only minutes from downtown Branson, the hustle and bustle on The Strip, and access to any point north or south of Branson via U.S. 65. The neighborhood is close to Alexander Park on the Taneycomo lakefront and the jogging track at adjacent Sunset Park (see our Recreation and the Outdoors chapter). Homes range from $70,000 to $300,000.

Lakewood Estates
700 Parnell Dr. • (417) 334-4170

One of Branson's earlier high-quality developments, this neighborhood of 53 duplex condos (106 units) has a private entrance and maintains its own streets. Right on the banks of Lake Taneycomo, only two blocks from Skaggs Community Health Center and a block from the Branson Community Center, this neighborhood has been the choice of retirees and professionals who don't want to bother with home maintenance. The neighborhood is totally managed by the homeowners. The assessment fee includes trash pickup, home maintenance, insurance, and ground maintenance. The development is on the city sewer system. Amenities include a pool clubhouse, small fishing dock, and workshop for hobbies and crafts. Parnell Park, with its tennis courts, is only a block away. The development is unusual in Branson: it is one of few totally flat areas in the city. Units in Lakewood Estates sell from $75,000 to $133,000.

McGee Addition, Hollister

This old, established neighborhood is nestled between Lake Taneycomo on the north and a steep hill and bluff on the south. Its eastern boundary is the railroad and trestle over Lake Taneycomo and its western line is U.S. 65. Entrance to the area is via Railroad Avenue from U.S. Business 65 in Hollister. The neighborhood evolved and developed during a period of 40 years or more. It has homes that range from trailers and modest summer cabins to older expensive homes with enviable boat docks and slips on Lake Taneycomo. It is right across the lake from the homes that border Alexander Park and Sunset Park in Branson. The new neighborhood's location makes for easy access to downtown Branson or Hollister, yet its only minutes from The Strip and its activities. More recent development west of U.S. 65 is accessed through the subdivision's Wilshire Drive, which goes under the highway. The newer area includes Taneycomo Terraces, condominiums for those 55 and older. Homes in the McGee Addition can range from a low of $30,000 to a high of $170,000.

Murphy Addition

Developed largely during the '70s, this area is near the heart of Branson's entertainment activity on 76 Country Boulevard, which forms its southern boundary. Roark Valley Road provides its northern boundary. Dr. Good Drive,

INSIDERS' TIP

Rural properties must have a septic tank system. Soils vary in the Ozarks as to their ability to provide an adequate absorption field. Ask your real estate agent about whether or not your dream lot will pass what's called a "perk test" for a septic tank. You may even request passage of a perk test of the owner before buying.

REAL ESTATE

named for a respected president of College of the Ozarks, forms its western edge. Murphy Park, with its 5 acres of playground, picnic area, and sand volleyball courts, serves as the neighborhood's center. It has easy access to The Strip and downtown Branson. The Branson Heights Shopping Center is nearby. Homes range from $75,000 to $150,000.

Oak Bluff

Located on the bluff point formed by the cut Bee Creek makes to enter Lake Taneycomo, the development boasts a spectacular east view of Lake Taneycomo 350 feet below and the valley across the lake. It is one of Branson's most exclusive home sites. Streets are paved but not curbed. Homes are on community water and private septic systems. Homes in Oak Bluff start at $235,000 plus. Access to Oak Bluff is via Fagan Drive off Bee Creek Road near Branson High School and then turning on Oak Bluff Road.

INSIDERS' TIP

Branson usually has several snowfalls each winter, with the deepest ones in February or early March, but they usually don't last more than several days. Average annual snowfall is 15.9 inches. Usually school districts build five snow days into the schedules for adverse weather conditions.

Rockwood Hills

Rockwood Hills, located north of Branson just off Mo. 248, is a subdivision that offers quick access to the west end of The Strip via the Shepherd of the Hills Expressway and is only 2 miles from downtown Branson. The subdivision is on the north side of Branson, just outside the city limits. Rockwood Hills is accessed from Mo. 248 via Eagle Rock Road. The neighborhood surrounds a 5-acre lake, which is a favorite playground and fishing hole for neighborhood kids. Roads are paved, community water is available, and sewage service is via individual septic tank. Homes in Rockwood Hills are priced between $70,000 and $190,000.

Pointe Royale Village and Country Club
Mo. Hwy. 165 • (417) 334-0634

People stopping at the scenic view on Mo. 165 south of Hollister see a bucolic community spread out beneath them in the White River valley. That's Pointe Royale Village and Country Club on Mo. 165 opposite the Welk Theatre and Resort. Pointe Royale sets the Branson standard for the country-club style of living and

gated community security. It is the home or second home for 961 families. Developed on 290 acres along upper Lake Taneycomo, Pointe Royale is only 3 miles from Table Rock Lake and 2 miles from Branson's 76 Country Boulevard. Clearing of land began in the spring of 1985, and construction started on condominium units and the 18-hole championship golf course that fall. The course opened in October 1986. Nearly 200,000 square yards of sod were used in building the challenging 6175 yard, par 70 course. There are 12 holes with water.

Created by a master plan to achieve harmony with the environment, Pointe Royale condominiums, patio homes, custom-built homes, golf-front, and lakeside-site homes make for an idyllic living area. Golfers like the pro shop. A clubhouse, swimming pool, and tennis courts complement the heart of Point Royale. The development features the Pzazz Restaurant and Lounge (see our Restaurants chapter.) The golf course weaves ingeniously through the entire development. Pointe Royale currently has 249 single-family residences and patio homes as well as almost 600 condominiums. It is home for both year-round residents and seasonal visitors, and building construction and real estate sales continue at a high growth rate. Pointe Royale offers nightly condo rentals too. Pointe Royale Realty handles the listings, call (417) 334-0079.

Neighborhoods Outside the City Limits of Branson and Hollister

Emerald Pointe
Mo. Hwy. 265
• (417) 336-8700, (800) 872-7889

Emerald Pointe, developed by Branson businessman and theme park owner Gary Snadon, is the area's newest planned community of more than 600 acres. It is just 4 miles south of Hollister on County Road 265-20, just off Mo. 265. All lots have views of Table Rock Lake, and the development includes single-family homes as well as townhouses and condominiums. The architectural restrictions ensure strong property values. It has underground utilities, sewer, and water service, and curbed and guttered streets. The development includes a spacious marina, security-gated entry, and a clubhouse with complete amenities, including tennis courts and swimming pool. Big Cedar Lodge and the Jack Nicklaus signature golf course are close by. Its location gives views, privacy, and seclusion yet easy access to all that Branson offers.

Oakmont Community
2308 Mo. Hwy. 86, Ridgedale
• (417) 334-2106

One of the first really big developments around Table Rock Lake, Oakmont is south of Hollister near the Arkansas line. It is between U.S. 65 and the Long Creek Arm of Table Rock Lake. It consists of a variety of pocket developments and communities, from mobile home clusters to large exclusive lakeview and lakefront lots with homes as expensive as you'll find in the area. Amenities include the Oakmont Community Golf Course (see our Recreation and the Outdoors chapter) and a community recreation center.

The development is near the Big Cedar Lodge and Top of the Rock restaurant and golf course (see our Restaurants and Accommodations chapters). Most of the streets and roads are paved. Water is by individual or community wells. Sewage is by individual septic systems. Prices of homes depend on the restrictions, lot sizes, and lakeview/lake access.

Riverside Estates, Hollister

Nestled on the low-water side of a bend in Lake Taneycomo, Riverside Estates provides a great view of a bluff across the lake and easy access to the lake with a community launch ramp. Pointe Royale development is just around the bend on the opposite side of the lake. Short Creek forms the eastern boundary of the neighborhood, and Lake Taneycomo completes the western and northern boundaries. Streets are paved and some are guttered; it has community water and a community sewer system. Both homes and condominiums are in the development, with homes ranging from $90,000 to $400,000 plus, depending on view and lake access.

The neighborhood is neat and clean, with lots of large trees along the lakefront and in the yards of homes. The area offers seclusion but is only five minutes from Branson and Hollister. Riverside Estates can be reached via Acacia Club

Road from Mo. Highway V south of Hollister and Point Lookout or by Iowa Colony Road from Mo. 165.

Spring Meadows, Hollister

Spring Meadows is another popular subdivision that is conveniently located 1 mile east of Branson just off Mo. 76. It overlooks a small wet-weather creek valley and is accessed from Mo. 76 via Meadow Parkway. Holiday Hills Golf Course is only a quarter mile away, and Forsyth is only 12 miles further east. Downtown Branson is only a three-minute drive to the west. Streets are paved and curbed, and community water is available. Sewer is handled by a community sewage plant. Homes are priced between $60,000 and $180,000.

StoneBridge Village
1600 Ledgestone Way, Reeds Spring
• (417) 336-1700

A 3,200-acre development just east of Silver Dollar City at the intersection of Mo. 76 and Mo. 265, StoneBridge Village is Branson's newest gated community. Developed by Cooper Communities, this still-growing neighborhood has the 18-hole Ledgestone Championship Golf Course at its heart (see our Recreation and the Outdoors chapter). Cooper Communities has been building master-planned communities since 1954, and property owners enjoy access to four other private recreational communities in Arkansas, Tennessee, and South Carolina. StoneBridge offers homesites, town homes, and condominiums. For vacation, StoneBridge has vacation exchanges with RCI in more than 2,900 locations around the world. For those owners and StoneBridge's permanent residents, it offers amenities of a 20,000-square-foot golf clubhouse, lighted tennis courts, swimming pool, exercise room, and nature trail. The carefully planned community is only minutes from Silver Dollar City and Branson's famed entertainment on The Strip, and it's 20 minutes from the three major lakes (Bull Shoals, Table Rock, and Taneycomo) with more than 90,000 acres of combined water surface area.

Table Rock Heights, Hollister

Table Rock Heights is aptly named. This hillside community has a panoramic view of Table Rock Lake and Dam and the Taneycomo valley. The development is about 300 feet higher than the scenic view overlook on Mo. 165 south of Hollister. Entrance to the neighborhood is

REAL ESTATE

via Table Rook Heights Road from Mo. 165 and Mo. 265. The neighborhood is only an eight-minute drive to Branson and Hollister. Lots are large, and the steep hillsides are thickly wooded. Community water is available; sewage is by individual septic systems. Homes range from $100,000 to $200,000.

Taneycomo Acres, Branson

Just down the lake and across from Point Lookout, Taneycomo Acres is on the ridge between Cooper Creek and Lake Taneycomo and is about as near to the city of Branson as can be without being in it. The neighborhood offers seclusion but is only four minutes from downtown Branson and the east end of The Strip. Nearby is the Thousand Hills Golf Course, and there is easy access to Mo. 165 and Table Rock Lake via Fall Creek Road. Access to the area is by several streets off Fall Creek Road. The development has paved streets and community water and sewer. Lots are large, and there are large areas with forest. Since this is a fairly recent development, homes are modern and range from $100,000 to $270,000.

Real Estate Companies

Aux Arcs Real Estate
Mo. Hwy. 13 N., Kimberling City
• **(417) 739-5487, (800) 296-LAKE**
• **www.aux-arcs.com**
Pronounced simply "Ozarks," this firm was founded 8 years ago by seasoned area Realtors to provide comprehensive, professional real estate services to Ozark Mountain Country. Aux Arcs specializes in sales of residential and commercial properties on Table Rock Lake, in Branson and Kimberling City. The Aux Arcs office is equipped with an up-to-date computer system. Every agent has a personal computer, which is linked to the local multiple listing service so that the agent is able to find property in the area that fits your needs, instantly. All office computers are networked so that each agent is able to access the others' files in order to offer service to another agent's customers and clients when necessary.

Apple Real Estate
157 Chad Ln., Hollister
• **(417) 334-7888**
Suzy Samsel's business card says she "specializes in honesty," and this area native has a long track record of selling commercial and residential properties in Arkansas and Missouri. Apple Real Estate is especially active with property listings south of Hollister and in the Missouri-Arkansas border area. She and her husband also handle rentals management and nightly condo rentals.

Branson Hometown Realty
2105 Mo. Hwy. 248
• **(417) 337-8118**
Rex Asselin got off the water and into land. This third-generation Branson resident and his parents created the Sammy Lane Pirate Cruise, and Asselin was Capt. Rex for a number of years. His grandparents and Don Gardner helped bring golf to the Ozarks in the development of the Holiday Hills Golf Course in 1938. Vintage photographs of his ancestors and interesting things they did or witnessed decorate the office walls. Co-owner of Branson Hometown Reality with Rex is Pamela Ledbetter, who is a fifth-generation native. Thus the agency's motto is "Our hometown heritage is your advantage." The company, founded in 1989, handles both commercial and residential listings. Branson Hometown Realty is active in developing Meadow Brooke Ranches, just northeast of Branson near Walnut Shade, which has 10- to 20-acre parcels of close-in, rural land.

Branson Realty, Inc.
1440 Mo. Hwy. 248
• **(417) 334-3466, (800) 766-0922**
Ron Jones is new owner of Branson Realty. Branson Realty is the oldest real estate company in Branson, having been in business since 1948. Jones and his staff of four deal in both residential and commercial property, with the bulk of their listings being commercial.

Carol Jones Realtors: An Amerus Co.
3265 Falls Pky., Ste. 1 • **(417) 335-5950**
Mo. Hwy. 76 and Mo. Hwy. 13 in Morris Plaza, Branson West • **(417) 272-8417**

> **INSIDERS' TIP**
> Some rural properties have community water but most do not. If your dream lot doesn't, you should know that drilling a well to the necessary 400 to 600 feet, casing it and buying a pump will add $4,000 to $6,000 to the cost of constructing your home.

REAL ESTATE

Condominium resorts can be found along the shores of Lake Taneycomo

Photo: Branson/Lakes Area Chamber of Commerce

158 Pointe Royale Dr., Ste. B
• **(417) 334-0079**

Carol Jones which has its headquarters in Springfield, also has offices in Branson, Pointe Royale, and Branson West. It is one of the older established companies in the area, specializing in both residential and commercial properties. More than 30 brokers work out of the Branson area offices. Carol Jones has had great success because of a multimedia approach to advertising including newspaper, direct mail, distinctive signs, magazine advertising, the Internet, and a TV program, *Homebuyer's Guide*. The company even makes copies of the program to mail to potential customers moving into the area.

Coldwell Banker First Choice
16205 U.S. Hwy. 160, Forsyth
• **(417) 546-4766, (800) 873-4486**
• **www.realtor.com/branson/cbfc**

Owner Dave Oliphant and his team of eight brokers cover the area, but they specialize in properties in the Forsyth, Rockaway Beach, eastern Taney County, and Lake Bull Shoals areas. The company prides itself on its personal service and in six years has established a reputation for reliability.

Century 21 Gerken & Associates
1157 W. Mo. Hwy. 76 • **(417) 334-1892**

Owner-broker Duane Gerken served as presi-

dent of the Tri-Lakes Board of Realtors in 1985, and in 1998 he was installed to serve at the Missouri Association of Realtors as that association's president. He's been active in the real estate scene for more than 23 years, and he helped start the Tri-Lakes Board's multiple listing service. He and his wife, Kay, manage the firm, whose staff of eight brokers have a solid community reputation. Century 21 Gerken & Associates deals with all facets of local property, residential, and commercial.

Clemenson Realty
400 W. Pacific St. • **(417) 334-4694**

Clemenson Realty was established in 1991 by David Clemenson, who has been in the real estate business since 1972 and is licensed in Missouri and Arkansas. Clemenson Realty is a MLS member company, and Dave wears two hats as he also owns and operates H & R Block Income Tax Service at his office on Pacific Street. Clemenson Realty handles all types of properties except for rental and rental management.

ERA Table Rock Realty
1294-A Mo. Hwy. 248 • **(417) 334-3138**
• **www. era.com**

The original Table Rock Realty was formed in 1950 when the U.S. Corps of Engineers needed to purchase land for the new Table Rock Lake. The office was in downtown Branson until 1996, when the firm moved to its present location on the newly five-laned Mo. 248. ERA Table Rock Realty has three broker owners: Jim Asbury, Donna Moon, and Nelda Lies, with an additional seven sales associates. The half-century-old firm mostly services Stone and Taney Counties, but it is also licensed to serve outside of its home area.

Foggy River Realty
122 Symington Pl., Hollister
• **(417) 334-5433, (888) 934-5433**
• **www.foggyriver.com**

Broker-owner Anne Symington has established, in just six years, a reputation for finding the just-right property or house for her clients. She and Booker Cox III take the time to ask the right questions so they know what you're looking for and won't waste time showing you something that doesn't fit your needs. Symington was a top seller for other area firms and finally took out on her own with great success. From her office on Turkey Creek on the east side of the one-lane bridge in Hollister, she has built a reputation that ranks high among locals.

Kimberling Hills Real Estate
Mo. Hwy. 13 S., Kimberling City
• **(417) 739-4367, (800) 659-4687**
• **www.realator.com/branson/boboitker**

Just south of the Kimberling Golf Course, Kimberling Hills Real Estate can boast of being one of the longest standing companies in the Table Rock Lake area. It was founded in 1976. John Emmons, Larry Curnes, and Veronica Oitker and are the current owners, and John and his wife, Connie, are managers of this established-but-still-growing firm. They have a high degree of customer loyalty because Kimberling Hills Real Estate knows its people are what sells real estate.

RE/MAX Associated Brokers
109 N. Sixth St.
• **(417) 334-1374, (800) 220-2302**

Since its inception in 1988, owners-brokers Kelly Grisham and Jan James, with their staff of eleven brokers, have consistently ranked number one in Branson in the number of transactions and dollar volume sold. RE/MAX lists and sells not only residential property, but also lots, acreages, condominiums, commercial development, motel/resort and business properties.

Round the Clock Realty, Inc.
107 E. Main St.
• **(417) 334-1980, (800) 842-1980**
2740 Mo. Hwy. 176, Rockaway Beach
• **(417) 561-4030**

From its office on Main Street, Round the Clock has lived up to its name by working around the clock for its clients. Its unusual name and sign have been associated with Branson's downtown area for more than 20 years. Owner Nancy Chevalier and broker Glenda McCormick and the staff of 10 sales people have earned a reputation for success, honesty, integrity, and hard work. Round the Clock deals in both residential and commercial property. The Rockaway Beach office specializes with listings in the Rockaway Beach, Forsyth, and upper Bull Shoals Lake areas.

Shepherd of the Hills Realtors
Kimberling City Shopping Center,
Kimberling City
• **(417) 338-8400, (800) 748-8163**
Mo. Hwy. 76 W. • **(417) 338-8400**

Shepherd of the Hills Realtors first hung out a shingle in Kimberling City in 1963, anticipating great development as the result of the recently impounded Table Rock Lake. Owned by fourth generation Ozarks native Layne Morrill, Shepherd of the Hills Realtors is one of the oldest companies in the area, specializing in both residential and commercial properties. The Branson office, just west of Silver Dollar City, was opened in 1992. Broker-owner Morrill is past president of the National Association of Realtors.

StoneBridge Village Realty
1600 Ledgestone Way, Reeds Spring
• **(417) 332-1300, (888) 918-4653**

This agency exclusively sells homesites, condominiums, and town homes in the 3,200-acre StoneBridge development just east of Silver Dollar City at the intersection of Mo. 76 and Mo. 165. LaNora Kay and three other agents deal with properties around the new Ledgestone Golf Course. (See our Recreation and Outdoors chapter and Neighborhoods section of this chapter.)

Tri-Lakes Realtors, Inc.
1940 Mo. Hwy. 165, Ste. 111
• **(417) 335-5253**
Mo. Hwy. 39, Shell Knob • **(417) 858-3344**

Tri-Lakes Realtors specializes in selling residential, land, and commercial properties. The company is bullish on the area's growth and expects increased volume of sales due to the increased interest in Branson as a major retirement region. Owner-broker Rick Witeka, who started the firm in 1995 (making it one of the newer ones in the area), has impressed the community with his firm's rapid growth.

Real Estate Publications

A handsome, glossy publication about the area that contains relocation and demographic information is **Slip Away**, published by the Branson/Lakes Area Chamber of Commerce. If you are moving to the area, call them for a copy at (417) 334-4136 or fax (417) 334-4139. You should also request a relocation packet and visitor packet. The materials will give you a broad perspective on the area. It will also get you on the list of the Tri-Lakes Board of Realtors, with more than 500 members, and you'll start receiving brochures and information from area real estate companies.

Discover Real Estate Magazine, (417) 334-3161, (800) 280-3210. This monthly real estate magazine, with information about the area and lists of properties and real estate companies is published by the *Branson Tri-Lakes Daily News*. A subscription to the newspaper includes the *Discover Real Estate Magazine*.

Parade of Homes, (417) 334-6671. *Parade of Homes* is a monthly publication that's available free in local real estate offices and racks in restaurants, malls, and local grocery stores. It contains area demographic information and other facts and figures of interest to people who might be moving to the area or buying property. It also contains a number of local companies' real estate ads and listings. Parade of Homes is distributed nationally by subscription, $10 per year, by calling the number above.

Retirement

The National Tour Association and the American Bus Association have consistently rated Branson among their top tour destinations. Since most motorcoach travelers are over the age of 55, it is clear that people in this age bracket consider Branson one of their favorite places to visit.

Not only is it one of their favorite places to visit, it is fast becoming one of their favorite places to live. In the last few years Branson has been rated by publications such as *Money* and *Retirement Places Rated* as one of the best retirement cities in the United States. Recent population figures reflect the growing interest in the Tri-Lakes area. Population in Stone and Taney counties has risen from approximately 45,700 in 1990 to more than 60,000 in 1996. The percentage of people older than the age of 60 in Stone County is estimated more than 65 percent, and the average age in Taney County is 45. Big name stars and endless rows of outlet malls may lure visitors here, but it's the scenery, climate, fishing, availability of health care, and good, old-fashioned Ozark Mountain hospitality that lures retirees.

Local county governments have done their share to attract older residents. The Stone County Senior Services Fund is a 5-cent-per-$100 assessed valuation tax on real estate, which was passed in 1992 for the sole purpose of providing services to citizens older than 60. Richard Meyerkord, president of the service fund board of directors, says the goal is to help people stay at home and out of nursing homes. In 1997 the board's budget was $125,000 with 85 percent of the money going to the Stone County Council on Aging, the agency responsible for delivering meals to homebound seniors and providing them with housekeeping services. In addition to providing money to the Stone County Council on Aging, the service fund helps support the Ozarks Lake Country Senior Center in Kimberling City and the Crane Senior Citizens Center.

The list of natural amenities in Ozark Mountain Country rivals those of other major retirement areas across the United States. We have four distinct seasons here, unlike Florida and Texas, and the winters are much milder than in the New England states. From your retirement condo overlooking one of the area's three lakes, you can watch the leaves turn in mid-October, the snowfall in January, the flowers bloom in late April and the grandkids water-ski in July. Trout fishing on Lake Taneycomo outdoes any in the Midwest. With a golf course practically on every corner, retired golfers can spend their days tearing up the greens and their nights taking in free music shows. That's right, free shows. Each year when the theaters open in March and April some of them offer what are called area-appreciation shows. Residents of Stone and Taney counties get in for free. A donation is sometimes requested and seats are usually based on availability. The entertainers like local residents to see their shows so they can make recommendations to tourists during the year. Some of the theaters even offer area appreciation shows at the beginning of the Christmas season as well.

The undeniable hubs of activity for seniors are the community centers in Branson, Forsyth, and Kimberling City. These centers are partially funded by the Southwest Missouri Office on Aging and serve lunch each weekday for a donation of $1.50. Homebound seniors can have their lunch delivered. The centers offer a variety of activities ranging from bridge games to tennis matches. Many of the area fraternal organizations and clubs meet at the centers.

One thing the Tri-Lakes area is not short on is clubs. Each week the Branson *Tri-Lakes Daily News* publishes a listing of club meetings and reports. We have a club for just about every interest imaginable, from amateur ham radio operators to Rose O'Neill fans.

Condominium developments, time shares, apartments, and housing developments all seem to attract retirees. Many retirees choose to live near Kimberling City, Forsyth, or Reeds Spring instead of inside the Branson city limits due to the shortage of housing in Branson as well as the shortage of available residentially zoned property. Besides, only a few neighborhoods in Branson can boast a view of the lake.

Many part-time residents enjoy campground living during the summer and fall. Branson has a number of campgrounds, RV parks, and mobile home parks that attract retirees. (For more information see our chapter on Campgrounds and RV Parks.)

After you've seen all the shows and visited all the antique shops, you may be looking for something a little more meaningful to do with your time. Consider volunteering at one of the many area libraries, senior centers, home health agencies, charities, or adult basic education centers. If you need help finding your niche, call RSVP in Springfield at (417) 862-3595. (For more information, see the listing later in this chapter.) They should be able to put you to work right away.

Whether you choose to spend your time enjoying the quiet beauty of the Ozark hills from your assisted-living facility or volunteering to work on the Christmas parade, the Tri-Lakes area is a retiree friendly place. After all, almost 7 million people a year come here and many of them choose to stay.

Senior Services

Southwest Missouri Office on Aging
1735 S. Fort, Springfield
• **(417) 862-0762, (800) 497-0822**
• **www.swmoa.com**

The Southwest Missouri Office on Aging (SMOA) provides funding, training, and support for senior centers in 17 counties in southwest Missouri. SMOA sponsors the Daily Bread program at the senior centers in Stone and Taney counties. SMOA also provides help with housekeeping, shopping, and meals for a nominal donation. If you would like to volunteer or need assistance, call SMOA or one of the senior centers listed in this section.

Taney County Council on Aging
13879 U.S. Hwy. 160, Forsyth
• **(417) 546-6100**

The Taney County Council on Aging is based at the Forsyth Senior Friendship Center. The council provides ill or needy residents in the Branson and Forsyth areas with housekeeping workers. If you cannot afford to hire a housekeeper or home health aide, call the Council on Aging to arrange for help. Those in need of area transportation can ask about their free Good Neighbor Transportation program.

Taney County Health Department
1440 Mo. Hwy. 248 Ste. J
• **(417) 334-4544**
15479 U.S. Hwy. 160, Forsyth
• **(417) 546-4725**

The Taney County Health Department provides free blood pressure clinics a number of times each month at various locations in Branson. Check the local *Branson Tri-Lakes Daily News* for dates and times. If you are planning a trip to Forsyth, you can drop by for a blood pressure check without an appointment. The Taney County Health Department's breast and cervical cancer control program provides examinations for seniors 55 and older who meet income guidelines. For more information on the health department's immunization and family planning services, see its listing in our Healthcare chapter.

Senior Centers

Residents in Branson, Forsyth, Kimberling City, Branson West, Hollister, Rockaway Beach,

INSIDERS' TIP

Be sure to give your age when you make your ticket reservations for shows. Many of the theaters offer senior discounts, and restaurants and motels also give as much as 15 percent off.

RETIREMENT

Kirbyville, Taneyville, and Reeds Spring are served by three senior centers, each of which offers a variety of social and health programs. All of the centers serve lunch each weekday to people older than 60 for $1.50 or they will deliver the meal to your home hot or frozen. If you need transportation to or from the senior center in your area, you may call OATS Transportation Service at (800) 770-6287 or the senior center. For more information on OATS, see our listing later in this chapter.

Branson Community Center
201 Compton Dr. • (417) 337-8510
• www.cityofbranson.org

The Branson Community Center is the place to go if you want to rub elbows with the natives. Located just off U.S. Highway 65, and near the banks of Lake Taneycomo, the community center is where seniors gather for duplicate bridge, china painting classes, ceramics classes, exercise classes, and square dance classes. If you're into something a little more adventurous, you can join the mixed doubles tennis club, which meets at Stockstill Park. The Don Gardner Pitch-n-Put Golf Course is a nine-hole course located next to the community building. The Branson Parks and Recreation Department oversees the course, as well as all the city sports programs. You can reach them at (417) 335-4801 for more information or they'll be happy to send you a brochure.

Forsyth Senior Friendship Center
13879 U.S. Hwy. 160, Forsyth
• (417) 546-6100

Located 2.5 miles north of Forsyth, the Forsyth Senior Friendship Center offers just what the name implies. Friends gather here for activities ranging from billiards to cards to exercise classes. Not only does the center provide a hot lunch each weekday for a suggested donation of $1.50, you also may have it delivered to your home hot or frozen. Call the center to find out more about their health screening workshops and tax counseling sessions. If you'd like to volunteer, the center always needs people to help community members with transportation or housekeeping chores.

Ozarks Lake Country Senior Center
63 Kimberling Hills Blvd., Kimberling City
• (417) 739-5242

The seniors at the Ozarks Lake Country Se-

nior Center rarely sit still. While you will find some playing cards, carving wood, and making hand crafts, more often than not they're line dancing, exercising, or off seeing the shows in Branson. The 16-passenger OATS bus (see the listing in this chapter for more details) comes by each Thursday to take passengers around town for errands and doctors appointments. Lunch is served at the center each weekday for $1.50 or you can call and ask that it be delivered to your home hot or frozen. In the spring the center offers income tax consulting. In early 2000 the new Ozarks Lake Country Senior Center building, located just off Missouri 13, next to the Shepherd of the Hills Lutheran Church, was completed. With 10,000-square feet of space the new center includes an exercise room, a billiards room, and plenty of elbow room.

Home Health Services

A number of home healthcare services have sprung up in the Tri-Lakes area in the last few years. Licensed healthcare workers staff each of the companies listed here. A few of the companies use the services of trained volunteers. The average daily rate for a visit from a home healthcare worker is $100. Most companies accept Medicare and Medicaid. It may be a good idea to call the Better Business Bureau, 2101 Mo. Hwy. 248, (417) 335-4222, for a reference when deciding which home healthcare company to use.

Community Hospices of America–Tri-Lakes
1756 Bee Creek Rd., Ste. G
• (417) 335-2004

Serving Taney, Stone, and Barry counties, this hospice chapter cares for terminally ill patients with a staff of 22 medically trained personnel including nurses and certified nursing assistants. Forty-eight volunteers assist with errands and other housekeeping chores. A full-time chaplain is on staff to counsel patients and family members. The social worker provides assistance to patients as well as their family members.

Ozark Mountain Hospice and HospiHelp
118 N. 3rd St. • (417) 334-1222

Run by trained volunteers, this hospice group provides services to patients with tem-

---

INSIDERS' TIP

Money magazine ranked Branson as one if its 20 top retirement towns in the December 6, 1996 issue.

---

porary medical problems as well as terminally ill patients. Funded by area organizations such as the Lions Club and private donations, Ozark Mountain Hospice and HospiHelp makes referrals to local home health agencies.

Skaggs Professional Home Care
N. Bus. 65 & Cahill Rd. • (417) 335-7203

A service of Skaggs Community Health Center, this organization serves the Branson, Forsyth, and Kimberling City areas with 60 employees. It provides services in physical therapy, speech therapy, occupational therapy, and skilled nursing. A nurse is on call 24 hours a day.

Visiting Nurse Association
260 Terrace Rd. • (417) 334-1821

Affiliated with St. John's Regional Health Center, the Visiting Nurse Association provides medical assistance to approximately 100 residents in the Tri-Lakes area. Their staff includes registered nurses, occupational therapists, and medical social workers. They make nursing home referrals, and can assist patients in securing financial aid. You may call them directly or have your doctor arrange for a visit.

Housing

The availability of low-income senior citizen housing in Branson is rather limited due to the lack of facilities, and both Oak Manor and Branson Manor have long waiting lists. However, other low-income apartment housing in Branson, not specifically for seniors, is available. (See our chapter on Real Estate for more information.) Many seniors enjoy campground life and find the city-owned campgrounds as good as any in town.

Branson City Campground #1 and #2
200 S. BoxCar Willie Dr. • (417) 334-2915

Many seniors enjoy full- and part-time residence in the Branson City Campgrounds right on the shores of Lake Taneycomo in downtown Branson. Nestled on 15 acres, the 350-site campgrounds feature restrooms, showers, 6 fishing docks, 3 boat ramps, and good old-fashioned camaraderie with campers. You can hook up for $15 a day. Campground #1 is open year-round. (See also our Campgrounds and RV Parks chapter). Campground #2 is open April through November.

Branson Manor
218 Old County Rd. • (417) 334-3800

Don't let the address fool you. This low-income senior housing development is located in the heart of Branson just south of The Strip. The five-floor high-rise often has a waiting list of more than 20. Residents here enjoy potluck meals, church services, and regular bingo. The OATS bus makes two stops here each week.

Lakewood Estates
700 Parnell Dr. • (417) 334-4170

One of the oldest developments in Branson, Lakewood Estates is located just off U.S. 65 across from Skaggs Community Health Center. The homes range in price from the low $90,000 to $130,000. The Lakewood Estates Condominium Association oversees the operation of a clubhouse, swimming pool, and fishing dock on Lake Taneycomo. Although the association does not have any age requirements for home ownership, most of the residents are at least 55 years old.

Oak Manor
320 W. Main St. • (417) 334-4236

This 40-unit apartment complex consistently has a waiting list of more than 20 with an average move-in time of approximately 6 months. Applicants must meet income guidelines. All units are unfurnished. Each year the complex hosts a Thanksgiving and a Christmas dinner as well as monthly birthday parties for residents. The OATS bus stops at Oak Manor once a week. A Social Security representative from Springfield stops at Oak Manor twice each month to accept Social Security applications from area residents. Call for specific days and times.

Residential Housing

Residential care centers are great alternatives to nursing homes provided you're fairly self-mobile. The residential care centers in the Tri-Lakes area cater to affluent seniors who can afford to pay anywhere from $400 to $1,000 per month in rent. All the facilities in this section welcome drop-in visits by prospective tenants and family members.

Foster's Forsyth Residential Care Center
2803 Mo. Hwy. Y, Forsyth
• (417) 546-3081

Overlooking Lake Taneycomo, Foster's Forsyth Residential Care Center provides assisted living services to seniors who need a little help with their medical and other day-to-day needs. The center is licensed for 60 occupants and features private rooms and baths. The center serves three meals a day plus snacks and takes care of the laundry and housekeeping chores. Twenty-four-hour medical care is available. Residents enjoy many activities at the center, including bingo and regular church services. For a little adventure, the residents head to shows and shopping in Branson.

Tablerock Retirement Village
HCR 3, Box 116, Joe Bald Rd.,
Kimberling City • (417) 739-2481

Country living at its best is at the Tablerock Retirement Village. Seniors at this 120-bed skilled-nursing facility live in one- and two-bedroom apartments with decks overlooking the beautiful Ozark Mountains. Each unit has a kitchenette, but when you're not in the mood to cook, you can enjoy a meal planned by the full-time dietician. The facility features a variety of medical services including physical therapy, occupational therapy, speech therapy, psychotherapy, dental care, and ophthalmology. In addition to the 150 staff members, the facility welcomes volunteers. The Pink Ladies is a group of volunteers who are always on hand to assist residents with their various needs. One of the most interesting features of the facility is its employee-housing complex. Twenty duplexes located in what the staff calls the upper village are reserved for employees and their families.

INSIDERS' TIP

Much of the theater work force is made up of retired residents. They hold jobs such as ushers, ticket takers, gift shop clerks, and concessions clerks. Many retirees say one of the benefits of working at a theater is getting to know the stars who perform there.

Wedgewood Gardens
17996 Mo. Hwy. 13 65737
HC 6 Box 4475, Reeds Spring
• (417) 272-6666

Located on Mo. Highway 13 in Branson West, Wedgewood Gardens is a family-owned and operated assisted-living facility. It is state licensed for 46 residents. The facility opened in 1996 and features one- and two-bedroom living areas. All meals are provided along with laundry and housekeeping services. Bird watchers can spend their day enjoying the aviary or reading a book on the birds of Missouri from the facility's library. In addition to the 150-gallon aquarium, the facility boasts a central living room with a fireplace. The husband and wife owners, Marty and Bill Kenny, a registered nurse and a licensed administrator respectively, are both on hand to answer questions and provide information.

Transportation

OATS Transportation Service
3259 E. Sunshine St. Ste. L, Springfield
• (417) 887-9272, (800) 770-6287

OATS Transportation Service provides daily bus service to folks in the Tri-Lakes area. You may call the Springfield number to arrange a ride. Please give at least two days advance notice. Each Monday the OATS bus makes a trip from Branson to Springfield and back. The cost is $6 round trip, and you may ask to be picked up at your home. If you are traveling to Springfield for a doctor's appointment they ask for a donation of $4. A round trip in Taney County is $2, and a round trip in Branson is $1.50.

Educational Opportunities

Gibson Technical Center
Mo. Hwy. 13 S., Reeds Spring
• (417) 272-3410

Gibson Technical Center offers a number of Community Education Classes of interest to senior citizens. These classes are not part of the center's regular degree program. (For more information on the degree program, see our chapter on Education and Child Care.) The community classes, which average less than $100, are offered in the spring, summer, and fall and last from 1 to 8 weeks. You can take classes on Windows 98, Internet, Microsoft Office, cake decorating, sign language, floral arranging, accounting, welding, and auto body repair. If you are interested in learning about a particular subject, or would be interested in teaching a class, call the center and let them know. They try to tailor their course offerings according to demand.

Employment

Job Council of the Ozarks
1514 5. Glenstone Ave., Springfield
• (417) 887-4343, (800) 562-7284

Each year the Job Council of the Ozarks sponsors two four-week training sessions for people older than 55 who are interested in learning customer service skills. The Hospitality Host

Calm weather makes for peaceful jaunts on the lake.

Photo: Donna L. Perrin/Arkansas Dept. of Parks & Tourism

Program is free to seniors who meet income guidelines and are seeking employment in the Ozarks. The spring training session is held in Branson at the Missouri Division of Employment Security, 1756 Bee Creek Road Suite 13, (417) 334-4156 and the fall session is held at the Job Council office in Springfield. The training sessions teach interpersonal communications, stress management, and job searching skills. After you receive your certificate of completion, the Job Council will assist you with your job hunt. Call the Job Council for specific information and dates of the training sessions.

Recreation

Dogwood Lanes
2126 Mo. Hwy. 76 E.
• (417) 336-2695
Dogwood Lanes bowling alley offers a senior citizens mixed bowling league for those interested in competing in ABC and WIBC tournaments. The league travels throughout Missouri, Illinois, and Iowa. If no openings currently exist for the league, you may

still sign up to be an alternate. (For more information on bowling alleys, see our chapter on Recreation and the Outdoors.)

Special Interest Activities

Branson TOPS 468
St. Paul's Lutheran Church, 221 Malone St.
• (417) 336-4662
The Branson TOPS (Take Off Pounds Sensibly) group meets each Friday at 8 AM at St. Paul's Lutheran Church just across from Skaggs Community Health Center. The group's philosophy is based on a combination of moral support and sound nutrition practices. The dues are $20 per year plus $2 per month. Guest speakers from area healthcare facilities drop in from time to time.

International Rose O'Neill Club
P.O. Box 668, Branson, 65615 • (417) 334-3689
The world headquarters for the International Rose O'Neill Club is lo-

INSIDERS' TIP

If you need a prescription filled after hours in Branson, go to Walgreen Drug Store, 210 S. Mo. 165 (on the corner of Mo. 165 and The Strip, next to the Osmond Family Theater) or call them at (417) 339-3996. Their hours are 8 AM to 10 PM Monday through Friday, 8 AM to 6 PM Saturday, and 10 AM to 6 PM Sunday.

RETIREMENT

cated where else but in Branson, where Rose O'Neill, creator of the famous Kewpie doll, once lived. The club has affiliate chapters in many states and Japan. Each year members gather for Kewpiesta, one of the area's most extravagant festivals (see our section on Annual Events). Many of the club's members also belong to the Bonniebrook Historical Society, P.O. Box 263, Branson, Missouri 65615. While the International Rose O'Neill Club is primarily concerned with the study of O'Neill's various works of art, the historical society helps raise money for Bonniebrook Park (485 Rose O'Neill Road, Walnut Shade). For information on the historical society, call (417) 334-3273.

Kimberling Amateur Radio Club
American Legion Table Rock Post 637, 52 Lake Rd., Kimberling City
• (417) 739-2888

With more than 200 members from across the globe, the Kimberling Amateur Radio Club does its duty to spread the word about Ozark Mountain Country. Ham radio buffs know it by its call letters, KOEI. The first Saturday of each month, the club gives FCC license exams at its regular meeting spot, the American Legion building next to Harter House. The cost to take the exam is $6.35. If you want to enjoy their breakfast buffet beforehand, bring another $4. Members range in age from 8 to 90. (More are closer to 90 than 8.) Not only do these people like to talk, they like to pitch in to help their community. Each year the Kimberling Amateur Radio Club helps organize the Kimberling City Christmas parade. Occasionally they put on a garage sale to help pay for repeater equipment.

Taney Talents
Taney Talents Gift Shop, 16069 U.S. Hwy. 160, Forsyth
• (417) 546-4141

The Taney Talents craft club owns and operates the Taney Talents Gift Shop located next door to the Forsyth Chamber of Commerce. Seniors 55 and older sell their creations on consignment. You'll find ceramics, decorated sweatshirts, wood crafts, knitted items, and other unique treasures for anywhere from 50 cents to $450. Club members operate the shop Monday through Saturday. Each club member must put in half a day at the shop each month and pay $5 a year in dues. On Friday afternoons you'll find club members in the back room sharing their craft ideas or playing a game of bridge.

Libraries

Forsyth Library
162 Main St., Forsyth • (417) 546-5257

With the exception of one librarian, the Forsyth Library is run entirely by volunteers. From time to time the library hosts guest speakers and special workshops for seniors. The Friends of the Library club operates the Markdown Thriftshop, which is located next to the library just across from the courthouse.

Kimberling Area Library
52 Lake Rd., Kimberling City
• (417) 739-2525

With just 20,000 volumes, the Kimberling Area Library may not have as many books as some of the other libraries in the area, but it has much to offer in the way of services. If you want to learn more about computers or the Internet, the library can set you up with a facilitator for $1 an hour. A special tax consulting workshop is held each year for seniors, and the Investment Club meets at the library to discuss stocks, bonds, and other money making opportunities. Literacy tutors offer free help to area adults so they too can enjoy the escapades of the Play Readers Club, which gathers regularly at the library. The volunteer staff is available to help you find information and phone numbers for area senior citizen services. The Friends of the Library club raises money to help buy new books and brings in guest speakers each month.

Lyons Memorial Library
College of the Ozarks, Point Lookout
• (417) 334-6411 Ext. 3411
• www.cofo.edu

Just southwest of the chapel on the campus

INSIDERS' TIP

Home Bound Medical, located at 208 E. College St., (417) 336-3228, rents medical equipment and supplies ranging from walkers to wheel chairs to hospital beds and oxygen systems. They offer short and long term rentals and have a 24-hour answering service in case of emergencies. They are open from 8 AM to 4:30 PM Monday through Friday.

RETIREMENT

Relax aboard the Showboat Branson Belle and take in the sights of Table Rock Lake on the open air deck.

Photo: Silver Dollar City

of College of the Ozarks, the library features a variety of books on religion, history, and education. Missouri and Boone County Arkansas residents may obtain a library card by showing proof of residency or a driver's license.

Stone County Library
106 E. 5th St., Galena • (417) 357-6410

The Stone County Library, which sits on the south side of the square in Galena, is a great resource for local history and books on Missouri. Funded by county tax revenue, the library has 55,000 books and a large selection of books on tape as well as access to the Internet.

Taneyhills
Community Library
200 S. 4th St.
• (417) 334-1418

This privately funded library is home to nearly 36,000 books, and with the help of the Taneyhills Library Club that number is climbing. The Taneyhills Thrift Shop is located in the lower level of the library and contains clothing,

housewares, and other used merchandise. Volunteers from the Taneyhills Library Club operate the shop and help out upstairs as well. You can find a good selection of reference books at this library as well as books on tape.

Volunteer Opportunities

Christian Associates
Greenwald Professional Building, Suite 5,
Mo. Hwy. 13, Reeds Spring
• (417) 272-8004

Christian Associates is a comprehensive, private social services organization that provides assistance with cash, food, clothing, transportation, domestic violence counseling, holiday help, and support to area residents in times of crisis. Of their more than 200 volunteers, 95 percent are senior citizens. Funded by state grants and local donations, Christian Associates helps place domestic violence victims in shelters and offers a number of programs

INSIDERS' TIP

Retired residents should be leery of potential scam artists. If someone calls you on the phone and asks for a credit card number or bank account number, don't give it out. Call the local police department if you suspect you may have been the target of a crime.

for teens and children. Senior citizens in the area greatly benefit from the services of Christian Associates as well as contribute to the organization's efforts to help others.

RSVP
627 N. Glenstone Ave., Springfield
• (417) 862-3595

The Retired Senior Volunteer Program (RSVP) coordinates the efforts of some 800 seniors 55 and older in a variety of programs throughout the Ozarks. In Taney County volunteers oversee the Source Water Mentor Program to make sure homes and businesses have clean well water. In Springfield seniors help students in the public schools, assist with functions at the Juanita K. Hammons Center for the Performing Arts, assist the staff at area hospitals and help run many of the area's visitor information centers. Volunteers also give lectures to area clubs and organizations. If you have extra time on your hands and want to find out more about RSVP, request a copy of their newsletter.

Skaggs Community Health Center
N Bus. 65 & Skaggs Rd. • (417) 335-7140
• www.skaggs.net

The Skaggs Community Health Center Aux-

iliary provides more than 180 volunteers known as Pink Ladies (some of the volunteers are men). The volunteers staff the hospital's six information desks, operate the Forget-Me-Not Gift Shop and the Pink Door Thrift Shop in Hollister, and help out at the various community wellness events. In one recent year, the auxiliary gave 33,837 volunteer hours to the hospital. If you would like to get involved, call the Community Relations Department at the number above.

Fraternal Organizations

Each Wednesday the Branson *Tri-Lakes Daily News* prints an area clubs page that lists the meeting dates and times for the following organizations. You may also request a copy of the Branson/Lakes Area Chamber of Commerce's Community Guide by calling (417) 334-4136. The guide lists information about group such as the Branson-Hollister Rotary Club, Daughters of the American Revolution, Forsyth Masonic Lodge, Knights of Columbus Council #6470, Lake Taneycomo Elks Lodge #2597, Masonic Lodge #587, Sertoma Club and the Salvation Army.

Healthcare

Branson has consistently been rated in surveys and publications as a good area for retirees (see our Retirement chapter). Its clean environment, fresh air, and clean water as well as entertainment options rate high with those looking for a place to settle in for their golden years and those who consider these factors important in a good environ in which to raise a family. These individuals are also interested in healthcare facilities and hospitals, and their continued growth. In fact, the two large area hospitals, Cox Health Systems and St. John's Health System, with 7,600 and 6,900 employees, are the top two Springfield-area employers. Such growth will continue, as it is expected the population of Taney and Stone counties will grow 20 percent by the year 2002.

Branson has its own nonprofit hospital, Skaggs Community Heath Center, and Branson is only minutes from the large hospital facilities in Springfield. Because Branson is also a tourist area, we have some special healthcare issues and problems.

With its 105 beds, Skaggs Community Health Center and its newly opened $23 million five-story outpatient medical facility, is a hospital unusual in size and quality for a community with Branson's deceptively small population. Each year some 25,000 people find themselves in the Skaggs emergency room, a number that is average for a hospital three times its size. The 7 million tourists who visit Branson each year bring with them their heart conditions. They are involved in fender-benders, or worse. They fall and break bones or catch themselves on their own fishing hooks. They get their backs out of whack playing too hard. Children get into poison ivy or end up with scrapes and cuts or broken bones in their pursuit of fun on the family vacation. In fact, about 40 percent of the ER patients in our local hospital are tourists.

Branson's emergency room care received good marks in the Missouri Department of Health's report in the *Show Me Buyer's Guide: Hospital Emergency Services*, a statewide survey of 128 hospitals in 1997. The Skaggs emergency facilities were praised because among the hospital's emergency service personnel 80 percent of the full-time physicians are board certified. All of the registered nurses had completed Advanced Cardiac Life Support training. Specialized medical practitioners are on call. The medical director and all of the nursing staff have specialized pediatric training. Because of the large number of retirees in the area who demand high quality medical services, Branson has a higher than average number of specialized medical practitioners for a town its size.

In October of 1999, an Iowa tourist became the first Branson visitor saved by the Branson Fire Department's new automatic external heart defibrillator. Branson, as a tourism magnet, is a natural location for such equipment because of its high resident population of retirees and because it gets a lot of older visitors. In fact, of 147 people who died of cardiac arrest in Taney County the year before, 48 were tourists. So Branson has become "heart-friendly." The Branson school district bought five defibrillators, one for each building and one for the football facility. And Ozark Mountain Bank offered interest-free loans for the first 100 businesses who buy the defibrillators, which cost $1,500-$3,000 each.

A growing number of patients and a long waiting list have pushed

LOOK FOR:
- Hospitals
- Urgent Care
- Mental Health
- Hospice
- Pet Health Care
- Emergency Numbers

Ozarks hospitals to add magnetic resonance imagine machines to their facilities. Skaggs Community Health Center, as well as Cox Health Systems and St. John's Health System, will add the MRIs to their facilities in 2000. The million dollar machines use a magnet and radio frequency to get a picture of the body's tissue that wouldn't show up on an X-ray machine.

If you are on vacation, Branson is as good an area to get sick or have a medical emergency as any. We don't encourage you to do so, and we hope our visitors have a safe and healthful vacation. But if you don't, we have the facilities to take care of you.

We've included information about the general state of healthcare in the Branson area, what to do in case you're involved in an accident and a list of emergency numbers. We've even provided medical information for your pets.

Community Health Resources

Taney County Health Department
15479 U.S Hwy 160, Forsyth
• (417) 546-4725
1440 Mo. Hwy. 248, Ste. J, Branson
• (417) 334-4544

The Taney County Health Department, in cooperation with the Division of Health of Missouri, has both a Branson and Forsyth office and plays a vital role in promoting the general health of the people of Taney County. Its services are offered on a sliding fee scale or are free of charge. It provides a general immunization clinic and annual flu clinics; offers family planning (annual physical and pap test and a year's supply of birth control); a breast and cervical cancer control project; women's wellness program; WIC (Women, Infants, and Children) program for supplemental nutrition and education for pregnant/postpartum women and for children up to the age of 5; prenatal services (including pregnancy testing); blood pressure screenings; communicable disease program (tests for HIV, STDs, and TB); preventative hepatitis A program; and rabies control program (with annual rabies vaccination clinics). Some of its programs and offerings are specifically for seniors, but all of its programs are open to senior citizens (see our Retirement chapter). You may obtain a list of the department's programs and a descriptive brochure by writing the Taney County Health Department, P.O. Box 369, Forsyth, MO 65653 or calling either

INSIDERS' TIP

A great booklet listing area emergency services and health services is *Community Resources for Stone and Taney Counties and the City of Branson*, published by the Community Health Improvement Board. You can obtain a free copy from the county health departments in Stone or Taney counties, or you can write the Taney County Health Department, 15479 U.S. Hwy. 160, Forsyth, Mo. 65653 or call (417) 546-4725.

the Branson or Forsyth office at the numbers listed above.

Hospitals and Institutes

Skaggs Community Health Center
251 Skaggs Rd. • (417) 335-7000
• www.skaggs.net

Skaggs is a 105-bed community-owned and supported healthcare facility recognized by Medicare as a Sole Community Provider. Close to 100 medical doctors are on staff with specialties in cardiology, gynecology, internal medicine, nephrology, neurology, oncology, ophthalmology, orthopedic surgery, pathology, pediatrics, plastic and reconstructive surgery, pulmonary medicine, and urology, among others. Skaggs provides 24-hour emergency care at its Level III Trauma Center with a physician always on duty.

Skaggs offers other services to meet the health needs of the Branson community. Skaggs Professional Home Care offers skilled home healthcare services to residents of Taney and Stone counties. The Skilled Nursing Unit cares for people who need continued recuperative care after the acute phase of hospitalization.

Skaggs operates 11 satellite clinics in Stone and Taney counties that are staffed by physicians specializing in family medicine, infectious disease, internal medicine, obstetrics/gynecology, pediatrics, and urology. They are Branson Family Medicine Clinic, Branson Neurology and Pain Center, Skaggs Family Health Clinic, Skaggs Internal Medicine Clinic, Skaggs OB/GYN Care, Skaggs Pediatric Care, and Tri-Lakes

Urology, all located in Branson; Branson West Medical Care and Rehab Services in Branson West; Crane Medical Care in Crane; Forsyth Medical Care in Forsyth; and Skaggs Medical West in Kimberling City.

Skaggs Health Center has been adding services since its opening in 1950 to meet the growing and diverse medical needs of the tri-lakes area residents and visitors. Construction began in 1998 on a $23 million, five-story outpatient medical facility and opened in 2000. The new 112,000-square-foot building houses a lab, radiology service, cardiac rehabilitation services, and other testing facilities. At the same time, because of the growth of permanent population and tourism, approval was gained to increase the number of beds in the critical care unit from 8 to 14.

The hospital's helicopter service can airlift patients to Springfield and other facilities when necessary. Free transportation to and from the hospital is available to the elderly and handicapped. Call (417) 335-RIDE.

Columbia Hospital South, Springfield
3535 S. National Ave., Springfield
• (417) 882-4700
Columbia Hospital North, Springfield
2828 N. National Ave., Springfield
• (417) 837-4000

Columbia Hospital South is a JCAHO and ADA accredited facility serving as a community hospital that, coupled with the Springfield north facility, has about a 15 percent share of the Springfield market. Columbia's Springfield south and north facilities are able to provide approximately 88 percent of all healthcare service needs, and they refer the reminder of patients requiring more extensive treatment to facilities that deliver specialty care. The Springfield south facility has a 24-hour emergency room, an obstetrics unit and ward, an intensive care unit, and other general hospital services.

Columbia's north Springfield facility features a women's care facility, outpatient/ambulatory facility, an Occupational Health Center and an extended hours clinic.

Cox Medical Center North
1423 N. Jefferson Ave., Springfield
• (417) 269-3000

Cox Medical Center South
3801 S. National Ave., Springfield
• (417) 269-3000

Cox Health Systems is a three-hospital system in southwest Missouri, with the two Springfield hospitals of most interest to those living in the Branson area. Cox North is a 274-bed community hospital in north Springfield; Cox South is a 562-bed tertiary care facility in south Springfield. The third, Cox-Monett Hospital, is a 78-bed hospital in Monett. The Springfield south facility is the newest of the three. Other Cox facilities include 50 regional clinics throughout the Ozarks; Primrose Place Health Care Center; Oxford HealthCare, a home health agency; Home Parenteral Services, a home infusion-therapy agency; and Burrell Behavioral Health, which offers behavioral health services in 19 locations in southwest Missouri.

The Cox System evolved from the Burge Deaconess Hospital, which opened in Springfield on Thanksgiving Day in 1906 in a modest frame duplex. Cox has provided medical care for Springfield and area residents for more than 90 years. Today Cox Systems provides medical care for an 18-county primary service area in southwest Missouri. To get an information packet about Cox Health Systems, call Cox public relations at (417) 269-8161.

St. John's Regional Health Center
1235 E. Cherokee St.,
• (417) 685-2000

Founded in 1891 by three members of the Sisters of Mercy, St. John's became Springfield's first hospital to serve the growing town of 22,000. Housed in a small brick home, the new hospital had four patient rooms. Its stretcher was an old door. Today the hospital includes a 1,016-bed medical facility, 375 physicians and home-care services for southwest Missouri and northern Arkansas. St. John's provides expertise in 40 medical specialties as well as services in general areas such as pediatrics, mental health, nutrition, pregnancy, intensive care, heart disease, and many others. The hospital is active in education programs and offers support groups and outpatient services. St. John's will provide a services and information packet if you call the number above.

INSIDERS' TIP

Ozark granny women believed that an empty hornets' nest hanging in a room eased the pain of childbirth as did an axe put under the birthing bed. "It has to be razor sharp though," said one granny woman. "A dull axe may do more harm than good."

HEALTHCARE

Special Needs and Services, Support Groups, Substance Abuse, and Counseling

Alcoholics Anonymous, 145 Major St., Hollister; Branson (417) 334-0263; Forsyth: (417) 546-4556; Hollister: (417) 336-3721

Center for Addictions, Cox Medical Center North, 1423 N. Jefferson Ave., Springfield, (417) 269-3269, (417) 269-2273

Lakes Country Rehabilitation Center, 2626 W. College St., Springfield, (417) 869-1779

Ozarks National Council on Alcoholism and Drugs, 25 St. Louis St., Springfield, (417) 831-4167

Tri-Lakes Sigma House, 360 Rhinehart Rd., (417) 335-5946

Crisis Intervention

Christian Associates of Table Rock Lake, (417) 739-2118, (800) 831-6863 (24-hour crisis intervention)

Family Violence Center, (417) 837-7700 (office) 837-7777 (hot line)

Missouri Victim Center, 943 Boonville Ave., Springfield, (417) 863-7273 (office); (417) 889-4357 (emergency hot line)

Women's Crisis Center of Taney County, 213 W. Atlantic St., Branson, (417) 335-5181 (office); (417) 335-3197 (24-hour crisis hot line)

Family Planning Services

LAPS (Living Alternatives Pregnancy Services), 833 Lakeshore Dr., Branson, (417) 336-5483

Planned Parenthood, 1412 5. Glenstone Ave., Springfield, (417) 883-3800

Springfield Healthcare Center, 1837 E. Cherry St., Springfield, (800) 666-7298

Other Assistance and Organizations

AIDS Project of the Ozarks, 1901 E. Bennett St., Ste. D, Springfield, (417) 881-1900, (800) 743-5767

Taney County Chapter of the American Red Cross (417) 335-3100

The Shealy Institute
1328 E. Evergreen. Springfield
• (417) 865-5940

Dr. C. Norman Shealy is internationally recognized for his pioneering work in the treatment of pain and stress-related problems. Among his innovations are transcutaneous electrical nerve stimulation (TENS), now used worldwide for pain relief, and biogenics, a system for retraining the nervous system. With more than two decades of experience, the institute and its staff of doctors have a distinguished record for innovative pain and stress management and research, following a holistic philosophy and avoiding, if possible, invasive surgery. The institute continues to do research in pain therapy and management, backache, headache, and other types of pain. Connected with the institute is the Prevention and Wellness Center of the Ozarks, dedicated to the philosophy that 75 percent of illness is preventable by following an optimal lifestyle.

Quick Medical, Dental, Chiropractic, and Eye-Care Help

If you need some general medical attention and are a tourist or newcomer, it is rather difficult to obtain an appointment unless you have a personal physician in the area. It's expensive to go to the local hospital emergency room for a problem that is not major or life-threatening, and it ties up facilities for someone who may need help more desperately. The area has some

HEALTHCARE

clinics at which you can obtain general, on-the-spot attention for non-medical emergencies or fill a prescription.

Visitors may experience various types of medical emergencies: a tooth chipped or knocked out in a fall, glasses broken in a fender-bender accident, a dislocated shoulder from too much casting for Taneycomo trout, or a crown that comes loose in some irresistible taffy. Whatever the problem is that can't wait until you get back home, Branson has some medical professionals who are willing to go the extra mile and work you in so your vacation won't be spoiled. Last year a visitor who had a crown pop loose at breakfast got it fixed by 9 AM—and picked up two free tickets to a local music show the dentist couldn't make that evening because of a suddenly called meeting. Happenings like that maintain Branson's reputation for hospitality and provide the best type of public relations there is: word-of-mouth publicity.

> ## INSIDERS' TIP
>
> Sassafras tea, made from sassafras roots in the spring, is supposed to thin or purify the blood. Whether it does or not is debatable, but it does have a fine flavor, especially when sweetened with honey.

practic problems during his regular business hours, Monday through Saturday at his practice in downtown Branson, Just west of U.S. Business Highway 65.

Branson Chiropractic Center
120 E. Price St., Branson
• (417) 334-4441

Dr. James Thress's practice, located at the corner of Price and Sycamore Streets in Branson, only blocks from the Branson City Campgrounds No. 1 and No. 2, treats emergency chiropractic patients. Clinic hours are Monday through Friday, 8 AM to 12 and from 1 PM to 5 PM.

Extra Care Chiropractic
Corner of Fall Creek Rd. and Spring Creek Rd., Branson
• (417) 334-5330

Dr. A. Russell Markin provides chiropractic care for walk-in patients at his practice just off Fall Creek Road in Branson.

Dental Care

Keith Wall, D.D.S.
221 College St., Branson • (417) 334-5000

Dr. Keith Wall advertises, "When you don't know who to call, call us!" If you"re in the area and have an emergency dental problem, it could be some very good advice. As you turn west off U.S. Business 65 in downtown Branson, Dr. Wall's practice is one block west on College Street.

Nickolas C. Yiannios, D.D.S., P.C.
1151 Country Blve.,
Branson Heights Shopping Center, Branson
• (417) 334-2131

Dr. Nickolar C. Yiannios, D.D.S., P.C., accepts emergency dental patients at his practice on the east end of The Strip in the Branson Heights Shopping Center. Dr. Yiannios is open Saturday and evenings for appointments.

Chiropractic Care

Arnold Chiropractic Center
118½ N. Third St., Branson
• (417) 334-8828

Dr, Frank Arnold treats emergency chiro-

Walk-in Clinics

Branson Mediquick Walk-in Medical Clinic
1940 Mo. Hwy. 165, Ste. 10, Branson
• (417) 337-5000

Quick medical help is available from this walk-in clinic in Corporate View near Pointe Royale and the Lawrence Welk Champagne Theatre. The clinic is open from 9 AM to 7 PM seven days a week.

Bridges Walk-In Clinic
256 Mo. Hwy. Y, Forsyth
• (417) 546-4200, (888) 925 5462

Here's family medical practice taken to new dimensions. Husband and wife doctors Leonard and Rachelle Bridges provide medical care in this extended-hours clinic in Forsyth. Hours are from 9 AM to 7 PM Monday through Friday and 1 to 5 PM Sundays.

Skaggs Medical West
Kimberling City Shopping Center,
Kimberling City • (417) 739-2520

Located in the shopping center near the Mo. Highway 13 bridge, Skaggs Medical West sees walk-in patients from 4:30 to 7 PM Monday through Friday and Saturdays from 9 AM to noon.

HEALTHCARE

Eye Care

Ozarks Family Vision Centre
530 U.S. Bus. Hwy. 65 N., Branson
• (417) 334-7291
15688 U.S. Hwy. 160, Forsyth
• (417) 546-4464

Sore eyes, pollen reactions, eye injuries, broken glasses or frames, and lost contact lenses are eye emergencies that can be handled by Ozarks Family Vision Centre opposite Skaggs Community Health Center in Branson. They can mend frames, usually provide a temporary contact lens or just reassure you with an eye examination after an eye accident so that your vacation can be worry-free.

Pharmacies

The Yellow Pages of the phone book will direct you to any number of local pharmacies that can handle your medical prescriptions dur-

> ## INSIDERS' TIP
> Mix a clove of cooked garlic with a spoonful of sulfur and enough molasses to make It edible, then consume two spoonfuls a day for three days before picking blackberries and it's supposed to keep the ticks and chiggers off you.

ing their regular hours. Currently there is no 24-hour pharmacy in the immediate Branson area. A pharmacy at Walgreens in Springfield, at Campbell Avenue and Battlefield Road south, is open 24 hours. The Walgreens in Branson at 210 Mo. Highway 65 S. near its junction with 76 Country Boulevard has the longest opening hours: Monday through Friday, 8 AM to 10 PM; Saturdays, 8 AM to 6 PM; and Sundays 10 AM to 6 PM. You can call them at (417) 339-3996.

Mental Health Services

The organizations listed below provide services to help individuals achieve, maintain, and improve their emotional well being. These services include psychological evaluation and testing, sexual and substance abuse counseling, divorce mediation, bereavement counseling, referral assistance, and educational programs and workshops. They also have counseling for vet-

What to do in case of an accident

Accidents do happen, and in an area in which you have lots of people not familiar with the roads and gawking at the various sights, straining to read road signs and trying to ignore the fighting children in the backseat, you have more than usual. If you're involved in a traffic accident while in Branson, here is what the Branson Police Department suggests you do.

If it is a minor accident in which no one is hurt and the road is blocked, first move the vehicles so traffic is not blocked. Dial the local police department, (417) 334-3300 (not 911) and report the accident to the authorities. While waiting for an officer, exchange driver information: name, address, phone, insurance company and vehicle information and identification. Since insurance companies rely on the officer's report, it is important that such a report is filed with basic information about the accident.

If there are witnesses to the accident, ask them if they are willing to stay at the scene until the investigating officer arrives. If they can't, get their names, addresses, and phone numbers so that they can be called by your insurance company for accident verification.

If someone is injured in the accident, dial 911 for emergency services. Do not move the vehicles until the investigating officer arrives and directs their removal. Obtain all the information as above in a non-injury accident.

If the accident occurs on private property—such as the parking lot of a theater or restaurant—call 911 and have the officer deliver a private property accident report in which the parties involved exchange basic information: name address, phone, vehicle information, insurance company, etc.

HEALTHCARE

erans, individuals, families, groups, and married couples. For assistance get in touch with Burrell Behavioral Health, 1756 Bee Creek Rd., Ste. F, Branson, (417) 334-7575; Center for Self Control at Skaggs Community Health Center, U.S. Bus. Hwy. 65 N. and Cahill Rd., Branson, (417) 882-9734; Family Life Center, 714 5. National Ave., Springfield, (417) 864-6088; Family Therapy of the Ozarks, Inc., 200 E. College in Branson Town Center, Branson, (417) 335-3633, (888) 449-2229; and Forest Counseling Center, 2323 U.S. Bus. Hwy. 65 S., Hollister, (417) 334-2502.

Hospice Services

Branson is blessed with several facilities offering alternatives in case of life-limiting illness. Counseling services for the patient and family in bereavement are helpful. Some points you may want to consider when selecting a hospice: Ask if the institution is Medicare/Medicaid certified and if it accepts private insurance. Check to see if it has a 24-hour emergency service line. Inquire as to whether the hospice has membership in national certifying organizations and what types of licenses it holds.

INSIDERS' TIP

Snake doctor is a local term for dragonfly that comes from the erroneous folk belief that the insect ministers or cures sick snakes. Other names for this insect are snake feeder, mosquito hawk, or skeeter hawk.

Community Hospices of America
1756 Bee Creek Rd., Ste. G, Branson
• **(417) 335-2004**

Community Hospices of America is a Medicare- and Medicaid-certified hospice facility that serves the counties of Stone, Taney, Barry, and Ozark. It focuses on special needs of the patient and those of the family, helping meet physical, emotional, and spiritual needs to those who are diagnosed with a terminal illness and have a life expectancy of six months or less.

It has a staff of 22 medically trained personnel as well as 48 volunteers who assist with errands and other housekeeping chores. A full-time chaplain is on staff to counsel patients and family members. It offers hospice care free of charge. Additional services are provided for those who use private insurance or Medicare/Medicaid Hospice Benefit.

Ozark Mountain Hospice and HospiHelp, Inc.
118 N. Third St., Branson
• **(417) 334-1222, (417) 334-5591, (417) 334-1751**

Run by trained volunteers, this hospice group provides services to terminally ill patients in Taney and Stone counties as well as those who are not ter-

Emergency Numbers

For emergency service (fire, police, etc.) in Taney County you can simply dial 911. For non-emergencies, dial the number listed below. In Stone County dial the number listed below for both emergencies and non-emergencies.

911 Emergency Service in Taney County only	911
Branson Police Department	(417) 334-3300
Branson Fire Department	(417) 334-2600
Branson Ambulance Service	(417) 334-1441
Hollister Police Department	(417) 334-6565
Hollister Fire Department	(417) 334-3000
Kimberling City Police Department (Stone County)	(417) 739-2131
Kimberling City Fire Department (Stone County)	(417) 739-4343
Kimberling City Ambulance Department (Stone County)	(417) 739-4600
Forsyth Police Department	(417) 546-3731
Forsyth Fire Department	(417) 546-3473
Reeds Spring Police Department (Stone County)	(417) 272-3309
Reeds Spring Fire Department (Stone County)	(417) 272-8834
Rockaway Beach Police Department	(417) 561-4424
Rockaway Beach Fire Department	(417) 561-4200
Civil Defense	(417) 334-3952

minally ill. Funded by area organizations such as the Lions Club and private donations, Ozark Mountain Hospice and HospiHelp, the area's first hospice, makes referrals to local home-health agencies. Staff is available for patients 24-hours, every day. The agency provides patient transport and sickroom equipment and will run errands pertaining to medical needs. Care of the family extends through the bereavement period.

INSIDERS' TIP

A common Ozark superstition is that a male visitor should always leave a house by the same door he entered. If he fails to do this, it may mean that there'll be an increase in the host's family.

Skaggs Professional Hospice
Skaggs Community Health Center
251 Skaggs Rd. • (417) 335-8818

A team of healthcare professionals, social workers, chaplains, and trained volunteers provides ongoing support for the terminally ill patient and the family in the home setting. A complete range of hospice services is available to the patient on a 24-hour basis. A service of Skaggs Community Health Center, it is the only not-for-profit hospice organization operating locally and is Medicare and Medicaid certified.

Veterinary Services

Bransonites love their animals, and it does seem like we have a high animal population, both wild and domestic. Area farmers often need the services of veterinarians for cattle and horses and other farm animals. Many retirees keep pets. Tourists who travel with pets sometimes need a doctor for their dog or cat. There are several area veterinarians at the service of Fido when he's on vacation, and you'll find services for pet grooming and pet boarding in the Yellow Pages of the local phone directory.

Branson Veterinary Hospital
208 E. College St., Branson
• (417) 337-9777

Dr. Ray Reynolds at his practice in the Branson Town Center east of Branson's Commercial Street takes veterinary emergencies during his regular hours, 8 AM to 5 PM Mondays through Fridays and 8 AM to noon on Saturdays.

Countryside Animal Hospital
1405 U.S. Bus. Hwy. 65, Hollister
• (417) 334-8980

Located just east of the Turkey Creek bridge in Hollister, the Countryside Animal Hospital will see your Fido or Fifi on a walk-in basis.

Education
and Childcare

Travel in the Ozarks prior to graded roads and paved highways was difficult and slow even in the best of weather but area residents and the United States Mail took it in stride. How is this for service that neither rain nor sleet nor gloom of night (and we could add bad roads) affects? Teacher Lizzie Johnson, who lived at Forsyth, and taught school at Reuter, a distance of 14 miles, wrote home on a one-cent postcard, postmarked November 12,1908: I would like to come home Saturday, but don't think I can get a horse. I thought if papa would send old Prince by the mail carrier Friday, I could come home Saturday and return Sunday, then he could lead the horse back home on Monday.—from p.261 of *Elmo Ingentron's The Land of Taney*, The Ozarks Mountaineer Press, Branson, Mo., 1974.

LOOK FOR:
- **History**
- **Recent Growth**
- **Enrollment Requirements**
- **Public and Private Schools**
- **Home Schooling**
- **Higher Education**
- **Childcare**

Education

Settlers arriving in the Ozarks did their best early on to establish schools for the widely scattered homesteads. Students would often walk miles through the woods to attend "subscription school" financed by the parents of a community, who paid $1 or $2 a month per child to the teacher. Prior to the Civil War, these schools provided the only means of education, other than home schooling. Not until the decade after the war were feeble attempts made to establish public schools, as the White River valley and Missouri-Arkansas border area was virtually a no man's land because of marauding bands of guerrillas and bushwhackers. Whether subscription or public, these rural schools, with a single teacher whose education frequently was only a few grades above the oldest students', provided the basics and usually encompassed grades 1 through 8, with students ranging in age from 5 to 20. The master provided readin', 'ritin', and 'rithmetic, taught to the tune of the hickory stick. These early pedagogues knew how to make quill pens from feathers and ink from oak galls or pokeberries with the necessary preservatives to deter fermentation. Paper was scarce, and some students shared a common slate whose surface could be spit on and rubbed clean with the sleeve. Probably the new knowledge of pathogenic organisms and how they were transmitted caused the slate, as well as the common dipper and drinking cup used by everyone in school, to disappear shortly after the turn of the century.

Books were as rare as paper and usually were donated or loaned. Later schools made use of *McGuffey's Eclectic Spelling Books* and *Readers* (now used as a theme for a local restaurant's menus) and *Barnes' Brief History of the United States*, as well as *Steel's Hygienic Physiology*. As school districts were formed by act of state legislature under the direction of an elected county superintendent of schools, they were often named for the locale or community nearby. Some had picturesque names (sometimes a nick-

The College of the Ozarks mill is an attraction, a museum, and a student work station.

Photo: College of the Ozarks

name) such as Three Johns, Box, Iron Sides (because the building was sheeted with tin to prevent it from burning when fires were set in the woods to kill ticks and chiggers), Brown Branch, Hogdanger (in Ozark County, so named for the free range hogs that slept under the school), Possom Trot, Gobler's Knob, Lone Pilgrim, Loafer's Glory, and in Douglas County the school whose name every scholar aspired to: Neverfail. In 1890, 26 districts operated schools in the county, and by 1914 the number grew to 75. Most schoolhouses were made of logs, but the county already had two frame schoolhouses in 1892. In 1869, there were 1,145 pupils enumerated, but the enrollment was only 300. A growth in school-age population and an increased interest in schooling caused enrollment to rise, and the county schools reached their maximum enrollment of 3,687 students in 1904. Social and economic conditions pushed many rural families to migrate to larger cities and other states. As the rural population declined, especially during the Depression and the years following, and as school districts with their one-room schools were consolidated, the county superintendents went by the wayside. Taney County's last one was elected in 1967. Today, just Kirbyville, Taneyville, and Mark Twain School near Protem retain systems that encompass only grades kindergarten through 8. Because students frequently were called upon for work at home, especially during planting and harvesting times, education was often haphazard and sporadic. Organized high schools simply didn't exist or were too far for students to attend. Distances were often great, but even if not far, transportation over trails and roads wasn't easy. Little is known about the first schoolhouse in Branson, but the April 1907 school election saw voters approving bonds in the amount of $1,000 by a vote of 14 to 5 to construct a new school building. The town grew rapidly after the coming of the railroad, and by the school term of 1925-26, Branson was maintaining a first-class high school. There was a general interest in education at the turn of the twentieth century, and the Presbyterian Church formed The School of the Ozarks in 1908 as a private boarding school in Forsyth to provide an education for poor but deserving students, grades 1 through high school. The school was unique in that its students worked to pay for their room, board, and tuition.

As better roads developed, public high schools began providing free public education to many area students, but The School of the Ozarks existed as a private high school until 1967 and capitalized on the growing need for higher education by adding a junior college in 1958, then a college (1965), but still keeping to the philosophy and practice of having students work to pay for the expense of their education.

Now the Taney County area has three major public school districts—Branson, Hollister, and Forsyth—and two smaller ones—Bradleyville and Blue Eye—plus three districts that have grade schools only. Branson and Hollister public schools are only across the river from each other, a carry-over from the days when the White River would get so high there would be no crossings. It was practical to have schools on each side of the river, but with bridges across the river and the building of Table Rock Dam to control flooding, it made sense to consolidate the two schools. Town rivalries, however, persisted and prevented consolidation. The rapid growth of both communities provided equally rapid growth for the schools, and the area's population can easily support two high schools in such close proximity.

Branson has always been the wealthier of the two school districts. Hollister patrons have frequently had to vote themselves higher taxes than Branson because so much of the district's land was not taxable as it is owned by The College of the Ozarks. Bradleyville, likewise, has had higher school taxes because much of the district falls within the federal Mark Twain Forest.

The public school districts in our neck of the woods generally have as high or higher standards than the state sets. District scores on assessment tests overall meet and often exceed state averages. School board elections in Taney County are often hot contests and result in voter turnout as high as Presidential campaigns. The Branson Boom in the 1990s resulted in a large influx of school age children, and area schools were caught unaware. The result was a shortage of classrooms and frequently crowded classes. Citizens rose to the occasion, however, and voted to tax themselves to build new schools. Even outlying schools, such as Omaha, Ark., Taneyville, Spokane, Reeds Spring, and Blue Eye, experienced rapid and unexpected enrollment. In the past decade, there have been several private schools founded.

Another phenomenon schools have experienced as the result of the interest in Branson is student mobility. A student may be in school for only several months and then move, but another moves in as a replacement. For example, Taneyville school district lost 38 students in a semester but gained 40 new ones. In the quiet pre-boom days, it was likely that those children who entered the 1st grade would be in the graduating class 12 years later, with no or few new faces added along the way. The influx of people who work in Branson's service industry are likely to move on to greener, or at least different, pastures, which causes a certain student instability in schools.

Because of the large number of people who work in the service industry jobs on The Strip, which are often seasonal, many of the area's school's students meet standards for free or reduced-cost school lunches. At some schools, as much as 60 percent of the students are on free or reduced-cost lunches.

The start of school varies a little, depending upon how many snow days each district builds in, but most schools start early in September before Labor Day, and some start as early as August 20. The school year is usually over by June 1. Though the area doesn't get that much snow, when it does snow or we experience an ice storm, school is often canceled. Buses simply can't navigate the area's hilly and twisting back roads. Such weather frequently results in no spring or Easter vacation (those days being used as snow days), an extended school year or Saturday classes—and sometimes all three.

In Missouri, children must turn 5 by July 31 to enroll in kindergarten that fall. Registration and testing/screening begin in the spring for most schools. The Missouri Department of Health and Family Services requires students enrolling in public school to be current with vaccinations for diphtheria, tetanus, polio, whooping cough, measles, mumps, rubella, and hepatitis. Kindergarten screening includes ear, eye, and speech exams. At the screening, the student's social security number and state birth certificate must be presented.

The Missouri Safe Schools Act of 1996 requires of all enrolling students, including transfer students, a nota-

INSIDERS' TIP

The Ozarks has made its contribution to the world of theater. John Goodman and Kathleen Turner are SMSU alums. Actors Brad Pitt, Robert Cummings, Don Johnson, and Tess Harper are from the area as is Pulitzer Prize winning playwright Lanford Wilson and opera singer Meredith Mizell.

rized form that provides a variety of information, including proof of residency and a list of the enrolling student's law enforcement record. Parents planning to enroll children in school should contact the school superintendent's office in the district where they'll be living or the headmaster of the private school. Each district decides what credits to accept from transfer students. Parents or guardians will need to request that records or transcripts be forwarded to a student's new school.

Public Schools

Blue Eye R-V Public School
Mo. Hwy. EE, Blue Eye • (417) 779-5331
• www.blueeye.k12.mo.us
The Blue Eye School District, home of the Bulldogs, takes in 98 square miles in southeastern Stone County on the Missouri-Arkansas border. It has an enrollment of just under 700. It consists of three schools: an elementary school, middle school, and high school. The elementary school has 322 students (grades kindergarten through 5) and 23 certified teachers including specialists in special education, art, music, library, and remedial reading. The middle school has 148 students (grades 6 through 8) and 11 certified teachers. The high school has 207 students (grades 9 through 12) and 17 certified teachers. The school is fully accredited by the Department of Elementary and Secondary Education. The assessed valuation of the district is $51.1 million with a tax levy of $3 55. The school, like many in the area, has had growth due to the Branson Boom, mostly confined to the elementary level, but not as much as Branson and Hollister. Growth is steady and is expected to continue.

Bradleyville Public School
16472 Mo. Hwy. 125 • (417) 796-2288
Bradleyville R-I School in the eastern part of Taney County encompasses a district of 137 square miles. Much of the district is in the Mark Twain National Forest. Total enrollment is 233 students, with 82 students in grades kindergarten through 6 and 151 in grades 7 through 12. Assessed valuation is about $5.3 million with a levy of $3.70. The district has not been affected much by the Branson Boom except that it pro-

vided employment for a large number of people already living in the district. The school suffered a major disaster several years ago when a building collapsed, but generous support from district patrons and fund-raising by Branson theaters, along with federal monies, helped build a new building in 1996. The school received a technology grant two years ago and added several networked computers with access to the internet. All the classrooms and offices are connected through the networks, and the library has a computer lab for students to conduct online research.

Branson Public School
400 Cedar Ridge Dr. • (417) 334-6541
The Branson School District, home of the Buccaneers, is the largest in the area with 111.47 square miles and an enrollment of 2,889. It has an assessed valuation of $429.3 million and a levy of $3.24 per $100 assessed valuation. Current facilities include four campuses. Thirteen kindergarten classrooms are housed in the Kindergarten Center, (417) 336-1887, at the corner of Sixth and College streets. Grades 1 and 2 are housed in the Primary Campus, (417) 334-5137, located nearby at 611 South Sixth Street. Grades 3 through 6 are housed at the Cedar Ridge Elementary campus, (417) 334-5135, located on Cedar Ridge Drive, just off Mo. Highway 248. The Junior High School (7 and 8 grades), (417) 334-3087, is in a separate building adjacent to the Cedar Ridge campus. The Branson High School campus, (417) 334-6511, is located at 263 Buccaneer Boulevard just off the Bee Creek interchange on U.S. Highway 65 north. District offices are located at the Cedar Ridge campus.

Many of the buildings of the school system are new, but even the old ones are well-maintained and clean. The high school makes an attractive impression with the large, colorful, and appropriate theme wall murals done by the art department teachers and students. A nice touch in the junior high is framed picture portraits of teachers at their classroom door created by students. The Branson School District has 206 certified instructors as well as seven counselors, two speech therapists, three librarians, and a testing coordinator. The school is accredited by the Missouri State Department of Education under the Missouri School Im-

INSIDERS' TIP
State law requires all childhood vaccinations of any child in a daycare facility with 10 or more children.

provement Program Standards, the highest accreditation awarded by the department. The primary elementary was named one of eight "Blue Ribbon" elementary schools in the state. Exact percentages vary from year to year, but 60 percent to 70 percent of the high school's graduates seek post-high school education, and students on all levels score consistently above the norms on standardized achievement tests.

The Branson School District was probably more prepared for the Branson Boom than other districts, but not quite enough. Voters approved a bond issue in 1992 that provided the new junior high and elementary facilities. Located on a 110-acre tract, the two newest schools have adequate room for future expansion, and expansion is already needed as students currently occupy six mobile classrooms.

A $36.7 million bond issue was approved by voters in 1998. The issue provides funding for a new elementary school, additions to the current junior high school, and a new high school. The new K-2 building is currently under construction and is being built on the Cedar Ridge Elementary campus. Classroom additions to the current junior high school are complete and in use. Construction is underway on the new high school, located one mile north of the present high school. The elementary school is expected to be completed by the fall of 2000, with a completion date of 2001 set for the new high school.

Forsyth Public School
178 Panther Rd., Forsyth • (417) 546-4561

Forsyth Public School, home of the Panthers, is located in the county seat of Taney County and draws students from a 132-square-mile district. It has a central campus but separate building for elementary, middle, and high school. It has an enrollment of 1,030 plus 81 tuition-paying students from Taneyville and Mark Twain schools. Its assessed valuation is $51.1 million with a levy of $3.35 per $100 assessed valuation. The high school offers a dual diploma education (general track and college prep) and requires 25 credits for graduation but 28 credits for the college prep diploma. It offers more than 100 classes for credit. The school also offers adult education classes from time to time in response

to community survey needs, and it has a GED program and an early school program for preschoolers. All classrooms and the library have internet access, and all teachers and student have e-mail access. The school also has a U.S. Marine Corps ROTC program. It has 91 teachers, one-third with advanced degrees. The school prides itself on its student/teacher ratio with an average of 20 to 1. More than 90 percent of the classes have the state's desirable teacher to student ratio, and all classes meet the required ratio average. The school experienced a great jump in enrollment during the Branson Boom, increasing from 800 to 1,000 students in two years, but enrollment has been stable at 1,100 for the last several years. The student mobility rate is high with about a 33 percent turnover each year. There is a Boys & Girls Club housed on campus (a new Boys & Girls Club building is on the drawing board), which provides activities after school and serves the community as a latch key program.

Gibson Technical Center
21030 Main Street, Reeds Spring
• (417) 272-3410
• www. wolves.k12.mo.us

Gibson Technical Center, in Stone County, provides education in technology to area high school and adult students. High school students attend from 11 schools: Blue Eye, Bradleyville, Branson, Chadwick, Forsyth, Galena, Hollister, Hurley, Reeds Spring, Sparta, and Spokane. Tuition is paid by their home district. Adult students are expected to pay their own tuition; however, financial aid programs are available for assistance. The center offers programs in auto collision technology, automotive technology, building maintenance, business technology, construction technology, creative arts, culinary arts, computer technology, health technology careers, practical nursing, printing technology, small engines and marine technology, and welding technology. In addition, the center offers a variety of short-term classes and seminars to serve the needs of the community; such class offerings are of interest to the large number of retirees in the area. Classes are offered in the fall, spring, and summer.

The center is accredited by the Missouri

Ozark-speak

Something with a smooth surface is often described as being smooth as a school marm's leg or smooth as a baby's bottom.

State Board of Education, and the practical nursing program is accredited by the Missouri State Board of Nursing.

Hollister R-V Public Schools
1798 Mo. Hwy. BB, Hollister
• (417) 334-6119

The 1,086 students who attend the Hollister Schools, home of the Tigers, live in a 71-square-mile area within Taney County. The assessed valuation of the district is more than $73.1 million, and the school tax levy is $3.92 per $100 assessed valuation. The school is fully accredited under the new Missouri School Improvement Program Standards, the highest classification standards established by the Department of Elementary and Secondary Education. The school tries to maintain a teacher-pupil ratio that allows for maximum individualized instruction. Approximately one-third of the faculty have advanced degrees. The elementary facility houses 606 students, including 70 preschoolers. A latch key program is offered at the elementary school immediately after school for students who have working parents; call (417) 334-5112 for details. The middle school (grades 6 through 8) has 243 students. Students are exposed to the traditional subjects of math, science, language arts, reading, health, social studies, and physical education but can also take word study, keyboarding, art, and music.

Extracurricular activities include art club, basketball, environmental club, chess club, Model UN, and quiz bowls. The high school has 307 students. More than 90 units of credit are offered from which a student must select 24 for graduation. The Hollister District has obtained three technology grants. As a result, networked computers have been placed in the middle school core-subjects classrooms, the high school computer labs and most of the elementary classrooms. The district is participating in MOREnet, a state-sponsored program that allows access to the internet and e-mail services for teachers.

Kirbyville Public School
4278 E. Mo. Hwy. 76 • (417) 334-2757

Kirbyville School, located 2 miles east of Branson, encompasses grades kindergarten

through 8. Students grade 9 through 12 in the district may elect to attend high school in Branson or Hollister. The school has an enrollment of 440, an increase of almost 150 since 1994. Growth has been so great, a new middle school (grades 6-8) was built in 2000, and there are plans to add a high school by 2002. Grades K-5 will occupy the existing school building. A pre-school program was added in 1999. In spite of the student increase as a result of the Branson Boom, the school has an impressive student-teacher ratio of 12 to 1. More than 90 percent of district patrons attend parent-teacher conferences. The assessed valuation is $17.1 million and the tax levy is $4.06 per $100 assessed valuation. The district is classified as accredited, the highest classification given by the Missouri State Department of Elementary and Secondary Education.

Mark Twain School
377707 U.S. Hwy. 160, Reuter
• (417) 785-4323

Mark Twain School, located in the extreme southeastern corner of Taney County, is a small school, kindergarten through 8, that retains some of the best characteristics of the area's old one-room schools. The area seems isolated because it has not had the road improvements that other parts of the county have experienced. This is because so much of the district is in the Mark Twain National Forest and there is no bridge over Lake Bull Shoals to the south. The school even takes in some Arkansas students on the north side of Lake Bull Shoals. The Branson Boom has had little effect on its enrollment, nor is student mobility a problem. In fact, its enrollment of 54 is down slightly from the year before. The school is fully accredited, and with five full-time and five part-time teachers, it has one of the lowest student to teacher ratios in the county, eight to one. The district has an assessed valuation $4.1 million and a tax levy of $2.75 per $100 assessed valuation. The school recently received a computer grant and has a computer lab with internet access. High school students in the district may elect to attend Forsyth, Bradleyville, or Lutie School in Ozark County.

INSIDERS' TIP

If you need a list of day care providers, you can call (800) 743-8497, the Child Care Resource and Referral Project of the Council of Churches of the Ozarks. They will take into account your needs and requests, then provide you with some options and a list of various daycare providers. But be warned: Most providers will put you on a waiting list.

Reeds Spring Public School
Mo. Hwy. 13 • (417) 272-8171
• www.wolves.k12.mo.us

The Reeds Spring School in Stone County, home of the Wolves, has been one of the area's schools most impacted by the Branson Boom. The growth of Silver Dollar City with the development of immediate area motels and restaurants in Branson West and Kimberling City resulted in a population explosion for the district. For many people who work at the theme park or on the west side of Branson, Reeds Spring became the logical place to live. The school's district is 188 square miles with a total enrollment of 1,969 in grades kindergarten through 12, an increase of 125 from the year before or a five classroom equivalent. There are 446 students in primary school, 470 in the intermediate, 455 in the middle school, and 698 in the high school. From 1990-1997, Reeds Spring was the fastest growing school district in the state. The growth mandated construction of a new high school, which opened in 1997. Existing buildings were renovated for the intermediate and middle school populations. Through the mid-90s Branson Boom has tapered off, the school district is still playing catchup. The district has a property valuation of $175.5 million and a levy of $2.75 per $100 assessed valuation. The district is classified as accredited, the highest classification given by the Missouri State Department of Elementary and Secondary Education. A unique feature of the Reeds Spring district is the Tri-Lakes Telecommunications Community Resource Center (TCRC), a partnership between Reeds Spring and Skaggs Community Health Center of Branson and the University of Missouri Extension Service. The center provides programming, professional training, and economic development training for the surrounding four-county area. It is a long distance learning center, with an interactive video classroom, a multipurpose computer lab classroom, a training classroom, a multimedia production suite, and a public access area for local residents to get on the internet.

The center offers both credit and non-credit classes from the University of Missouri and other institutions as well as continuing education in a variety of fields. It also provides special training for area businesses as needed or requested.

INSIDERS' TIP

You can sit at a student desk in a one-room rural Ozark school at College of the Ozarks. Star School was moved from Flat Creek in Barry County and restored in the late 1970s. It serves as an excellent example of turn of the century school architecture.

Spokane R-VII Public School
1123 Spokane Rd., Spokane
• (417) 443-3502

Spokane is a small school in Christian County north of Branson. Like most of the communities in the immediate Branson area, it has had some fallout from the Branson Boom. There has been movement into the community, as it is about halfway between Branson and Springfield. Many of its residents work in one town or the other. In 2000 Spokane had an enrollment of 766 with a student to teacher ratio of 17 to 1. But like many schools, it has been hard pressed to keep up with the unexpected growth. The school has had to build additions to both the middle school and the elementary school. In 2000 the district had an assessed valuation of $19.1 million and a tax levy of $4.60. In 1999, it received a grant to work for Missouri's A plus rating, a three year process. Undoubtedly the district will continue to grow as more people perceive it as an ideal location in which to live, a short commute to either Branson or Springfield.

Taneyville R-II Public School
302 Myrtle St., Taneyville
• (417) 546-5803

Taneyville, named after U.S. Supreme Court Justice Roger Brooke Taney (as was the county), is a small village 18 miles east of Branson on Mo. Highway 76. This largely farming community has been justly proud of its small kindergarten through 8 school. Graduates attend either Forsyth or Bradleyville high schools. Agriculture is the largest industry in the district, but many parents commute daily to jobs in Forsyth, Branson, and even Springfield. Like many communities in the eastern part of the county, it has not enjoyed the wealth of the Branson Boom, but it has had to contend with some of the fallout problems. The district has experienced an average growth of 4.6 percent a year since 1991. More than 60 percent of its students qualify for free or reduced-price school meals. It has had a high mobility rate, with some students living in the district only a few months then moving, but enrollment stays constant because of new students moving in. In 2000 its enrollment was 198, with 22 teachers and a student-teacher ratio of 14 to 1. Its assessed valuation was just over $6.2 million, and the tax levy was $3.53. Teacher turnover rate is low, and parental involvement in school activities is good. About 90 percent of the parents attend parent-teacher conferences with the other 10 percent contacted by phone. The area will continue to attract residents and grow since the cost of land and housing is considerably less than in Branson.

Private Schools

New Life Academy
347 Mo. Hwy. V., Hollister
• **(417) 334-7084**
• **www.newlifeacademy.net**

Dr. Neil Smith is headmaster of this 9-year-old private school located across from College of the Ozarks. It advertises a biblically integrated college prep program within a Christ-centered environment. It has a kindergarten through 12 curriculum and a preschool enrichment program for 2 to 5 year olds. It prides itself on an intensive kindergarten through 6 phonics program as well as computer and foreign language (Spanish) instruction for grades 1 through 12. Sports include basketball, volleyball, track, and golf. New Life is a member of the Association of Christian Schools International and is accredited by the Missouri Christian Schools Accreditation Council. In 2000 it had an enrollment of 153 with a 9 to 1 student-teacher ratio. Tuition is $2230 per year, payable monthly.

Rising Star Academy
2066 E. Hwy. 76 • (417) 336-4345

Rising Star Academy and its headmaster Kevin Miller provide creative, specialized learning on an individual basis for a small number of students. The school is, in a sense, an alternative school, and it uses alternative methods such as self-paced work and computer assisted learning to succeed where mainstream learning techniques have failed. It provides a solid basis in reading, writing, mathematics, and the sciences, for grades 8 through 12. The school is often the choice for students who are involved in the Branson entertainment industry because it is willing to work around their show schedules and provide private tutoring. Tuition is $275 a month.

The enrollment is 15 students, and students receive plenty of one-on-one teaching. There are three computers for that small number, and students often receive computerized, individualized instruction. The school requires 25 credits for graduation.

Riverview Bible Baptist Christian School
13901 U.S. Hwy. 160, Forsyth
• **(417) 546-4580 • mkfish@tri-lakes.net.**

Founded in 1982, Riverview Bible Baptist Christian School offers a program for grades kindergarten through 12. It uses the Accelerated Christian Education (A.C.E.) curriculum. Sports programs include basketball (boys) and volleyball (girls). Riverview is a member of the American Association of Christian Schools and the Missouri Association of Christian Schools. In 2000 it had an enrollment of 60. Tuition is $130 monthly.

Home Schooling

Newcomers to Branson and Missouri should be aware that Missouri has one of the most liberal home schooling laws in the nation. According to Missouri law, any parent may educate a child at home. The parent does not have to have a teaching certificate or meet any education requirements. The parent must provide 1,000 hours of instruction during the school year, with at least 600 hours in the basics (reading, language arts, mathematics, social studies, and science). At least 400 of the 600 hours must be taught in the home location. There is no registering of home schooling intentions. The statute says the parent may notify the superintendent of schools or the recorder of county deeds in the county where the parents reside, but it is not mandatory. Parents who home school a child must maintain certain records: a plan book or diary indicating the subjects taught and the activities engaged in, a portfolio with examples of the student's work, and a record of

If something is a time saver, it is described as handy as a hog with handles. Hogs are notorious for being stubborn. Free range hogs, fattened on fallen acorns, could only be driven to market or a railhead easily when they had their eye lids stitched together—except for the single lead hog.

Ozark-speak

evaluation. An information packet and guide about Missouri's home schooling law can be obtained from Families for Home Education, 400 E. High Point, Columbia, Mo. 65203.

Higher Education

Only in the past three or four decades has there been a great need for higher education in the immediate Branson area, and it has only been recently that enough people have lived here to support a college. Those who were inclined went to the University of Missouri or some other college out of the area. Only Springfield's Southwest Missouri State was within easy distance. As the need increased, College of the Ozarks filled the gap somewhat by becoming first a junior college, then a four-year college in 1965. However, with its mission

of accepting only those who couldn't easily pay for a college education and by not broadening its mission to include a growing multitude of part-time, working, married, and continuing-education students, a need developed for higher education alternatives. Several colleges opened branches in the area after the Branson Boom, Ozarks Technical College was established to provide for the area's growing need for technical education. And, of course, Springfield's colleges have expanded rapidly to meet the needs of a changing, growing area. Springfield has always been far enough away so that students from the area felt they were getting away and close enough so that parents weren't unduly concerned about their offspring. Most students who attend Springfield colleges become residents of the town, but with the improvements on U.S. Highway 65 between Branson and Springfield, a growing number elect to work and live in Branson and attend class in Springfield.

College of the Ozarks
Point Lookout
• **(417) 334-6411, (800) 222-0525**
• **www.cofo.edu**

College of the Ozarks is the only college in the immediate Branson area. Founded in 1906 at Forsyth as The School of the Ozarks by Reverend James Forsythe, a Presbyterian minister, the college evolved from the original Forsyth boarding grade school and high school. Now located 2 miles south of Branson on U.S. Highway 65 at Point Lookout on a high bluff overlooking Lake Taneycomo, the beautiful 1,000-acre campus with its manicured grounds makes an impression on visitors. Its president, Dr. Jerry Davis, has said "image is everything," and the campus and the fact that students work

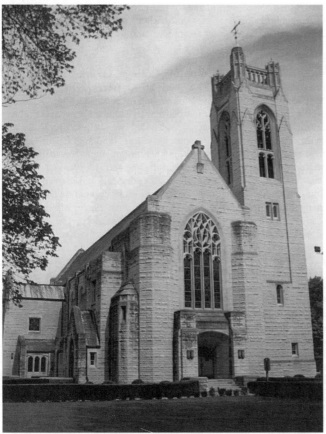

One of the area's most beautiful churches is Williams Chapel at College of the Ozarks.

Photo: College of the Ozarks

to pay for their tuition makes the college attractive to donors. Recent speakers on the campus—Oliver North, Ralph Reed, William Bennett, Gerald Ford, Dan Quayle, Margaret Thatcher, and Elizabeth Dole—indicate the intent, bent, and balance of its philosophy. Enrollment is capped at 1,500, and the college's endowment of more than $240.1 million divided per student, makes it one of the wealthiest colleges in the nation. It has 90 full-time faculty, and more than 50 percent hold terminal degrees. Fifty percent of entering freshmen have an ACT score of 21 or above. The college offers both bachelor of arts and bachelor of sciences degrees. Because students pay as they learn with their work, the college has been listed several times in national publications as a best value school and a college at which students have low debt loads upon graduation. After the epithet Hard Work U was used in a *Wall Street Journal* article about the college, the college adopted it as an unofficial motto. Notable alumni include ABC news reporter Erin Hayes, Missouri State Senator Doyle Childers, actor and director Jerry Tracy, and opera singer Meredith Mizell.

A special commitment of College of the Ozarks is to serve the youth of the Ozarks region. The founding charter commits the college to serving "especially those found worthy but who are without sufficient means to procure such training." This commitment is reflected in the policy that 90 percent of each entering class is limited to students whose families would have a difficult time financing a college education. The remaining 10 percent are primarily children of alumni or employees, athletic scholarship recipients, and a few international students. The college guarantees to meet the cost of education for the full-time students; that is, all costs of the educational program (instruction, operating cost, etc.), a figure estimated at about $10,000. The college requires that all students apply for any state and federal grants using Free Application for Federal Student Aid (FAFSA). The student's combined state and federal grant money plus wages from work at an assigned campus job pay for tuition. Students work 15 hours a week during the academic year plus two 40-hour weeks when the school is not in session. Jobs include everything from A to Z: the college's airport to zoology. In between are positions at the dairy, greenhouse, and academic offices. Room and board and incidental fees ($2,650 per year) as well as book costs (about $500 per year) are generally paid by the student, but a limited number of room-and-board scholarships allow students to meet that cost by working 12-40-hour weeks during the summer.

Although primarily a residential college, College of the Ozarks admits a limited number of commuting students from the surrounding area. Part-time commuters (11 hours or less) pay $125 per credit hour toward the cost of education charge with the remaining costs met by various grants and the institutional scholarship. The college does not allow students to obtain principal-delayed federal loans, however, private educational loans are available to creditworthy students at approximately 8.5 percent interest. The minimum loan is $1,000, the maximum is $7,500 and repayment begins immediately after the loan is obtained. The 1,500 students, most of whom work a second job on The Strip in addition to their campus work assignment, are an important addition to the area's employment scene. The bright-eyed and eager young man or woman who serves you your dinner, takes your ticket, parks your car, or dips your ice cream for your after-show snack might very well be a local college student.

Columbia College, Ozark Branch
753 N. 20th St., Ozark
• (417) 581-0367, (800) 928-8843

Located in the Diamond Center at U.S. Highway 65 and Mo. Hwy. 14 junction in Ozark, this extended studies branch of Columbia College offers an array of night classes for those who work full time and still want to work toward that college degree. The branch opened in 1997 to serve the area's population that needed a degree program with classes offered during evenings and in short sessions. The main campus, located in Columbia, dates to 1851 as the Christian Female College, the first four-year women's college chartered by a state legislature west of the Mississippi River. In 1970 the college changed both its name and student population, becoming Columbia College, a coeducational, four-year liberal arts institution.

Although it retains a covenant with The Christian Church (Disciples of Christ), Columbia College is a nonsectarian institution. Columbia College awards more than $14 million annually in federal, state, and institutional funds for need-based and merit-based scholarships, grants, and loans. The Extended Studies Division at Ozark offers relevant degree programs, convenient scheduling, and affordable tuition at $115 per credit hour in 2000. Classes are offered in eight-week sessions in the evenings and on weekends. Class size at the Ozark

College students enjoy Table Rock Lake in the summertime.

Photo: Branson/Lakes Area Chamber of Commerce

branch is small, often fewer than 10, so students get lots of individual attention.

Springfield Colleges

The state's third largest city spills over from Greene County into Christian County to the south, and the city's south side is the area that has shown most of the growth. When Ozark, Nixa, and surrounding towns are included, this metropolis has a population of almost 250,000. Springfield is home to nine institutions of higher learning, including three bible colleges (Evangel University of the Assemblies of God, Baptist Bible College, and Central Bible College) and two for-profit technical/career colleges (Springfield College and Vatterott College). The high ratio of students to general population makes for a city with a plethora of fast food restaurants as well as an active and interesting nightlife scene, mostly centered in the downtown area. The increasingly easy access between Branson and Springfield makes for mobile students who partake of the advantages of both a major metropolitan area and a national tourist playground.

Drury College
900 N. Benton Ave.
• **(417) 873-7205, (800) 922-2274**
• **www. drury.edu**

The oldest of Springfield's colleges, Drury was founded in 1873. Its 60-acre campus is situated in the elegant, old part of the city. The college has an enrollment of 1,600 and offers both bachelor's and master's degrees. President John Moore has done much to reaffirm the college's excellent academic reputation after a decade and a half during which the college lived on its past reputation. It has an undergraduate faculty of 108, of which 97 percent have terminal degrees. Drury has an endowment of just over $100 million, and students paid tuition and fees of $10,459 plus room and board of $4,000 in 2000. The college has one of the highest academic standards in the state and no student who has an ACT score of under 25 is accepted. Notable alumni of Drury include John Morris, founder and president of Bass Pro Outdoor World; Tom Whitlock, Academy Award winner; and Betty Dukert, producer of *Meet the Press*. The college often features nationally known guest speakers, poets, and writers, and the campus hosts the area's PBS station, KOZK.

Evangel University
1111 N. Glenstone Ave.
• **(417) 865-2811, (800) 382-6435**
• **www.evangel.edu**

Evangel University is the four-year arts and sciences college of the Assemblies of God, whose international headquarters is in Springfield. Founded in 1955, it is situated on Springfield's north side on a 60-acre campus. It offers both bachelor of arts and bachelor of science degrees, with masters degree programs in education, psychology and guidance and couseling. The college has an enrollment of 1,500. Its students come from 49 states and territories and 12 other countries. Students pay annual tuition and room and board fees of $13,604. Faculty consists of 90 full-time and 50 part-time instructors. Evangel has recently been on a building binge, and since it is a relatively young campus to begin with, its campus structures present a clean, modern appearance.

Ozark Technical College
933 East Central.
• **(417) 895-7000** • **www.otc.cc.mo.us**

Founded only in 1990 to provide technical education for area students, the OTC district encompasses eight counties in the immediate

A student at "Hard Work U" earns her tuition.

Photo: College of the Ozarks

Springfield area, including Stone and Christian counties. It provides high school technical programs, customized training, continuing education, adult basic education, and college credit courses leading to an associate degree. The college, with its motto of "Learn a Living," has met with enthusiastic success and growth. Its enrollment has quintupled from 1,198 in 1991, its first semester, to 5,922 in 1999. That growth has made it the third largest community college in Missouri and the second largest higher education institution in Springfield. Its main campus is at the corner of Chestnut Expressway and National Avenue. Plans are on the drawing board to bring all the functions and classes into one central location. The college offers an Associate of Applied Science Degree, one-year certificates in a variety of technical programs and a two-year associate of arts degree. It has a full-time faculty of 140, with an additional 400 continuing-education instructors and part-time faculty. Tuition is $49 per credit hour for in-district residents, $69 for out-of-district residents and $99 for out-of-state students. Financial aid by Federal Pell Grants and Guaranteed Student Loans are available as well as other scholarship and financial aid packages.

Southwest Missouri State University
901 S. National Ave.
• **(417) 836-5000** • **www. smsu.edu**

SMSU, founded in 1905, is the state's second largest university, and though it offers both the bachelor's and master's degrees, its focus is on undergraduate education. It is a public, coed university supported by the state, but it has an endowment of $28 million. The university has been the fastest growing campus in the last decade, and it has an enrollment of 17,500, with an additional 1,397 at the West Plains campus. Since it has a large number of applicants, SMSU has been able to raise the standards for admission, and 75 percent of the last freshman class had ACT scores of 21 or above, with an ACT average of 23.4. It has a faculty of 816 (528 full-time, of which 74 percent have terminal degrees). State resident tuition in fall of 2000 was $106 per credit hour. Notable alumni include David Glass, retired CEO of Wal-Mart; actors John Goodman, Tess Harper, and Kathleen

Turner; and developer John Q. Hammons. The university figures prominently in the area's cultural events. The Juanita K. Hammons Center, the home of the Springfield Symphony Orchestra, frequently features cultural events and touring Broadway productions. Individual academic departments often host speakers or programs.

The university's summer Tent Theater offers a repertory bill each year that has become famous. The campus is also home to KSMU, the area's NPR station, with satellite rebroadcast towers in Branson, Joplin, Mountain Grove, and West Plains.

Webster University
321 W. Battlefield Ave., Springfield
• **(417) 883-0200**
• **www.webster-springfield.com**

From its home campus in St. Louis, Webster University reaches out to encompass a network of more than 70 campuses through the United States, Europe, Bermuda, and Asia. It is accredited by the North Central Association of Colleges and Schools, including all of its undergraduate and graduates levels at all locations where the University offers programs. Webster University opened its Springfield campus in 1998 to offer the greater Springfield area seven Master's Degree programs in convenient one-night-a-week formats with a 9-week term. Webster was welcomed with twice the number of anticipated enrollment, and enrollment has grown by 500% in two years. The graduate degrees offered are: Master's of Business Administration, M.A. Human Resources Management, M.A. Human Resources Development, M.A. Health Services Management, M.A. Management, M.A. Computer Resources Information Management, and M.A. Business.

Childcare

Beyond the beautiful scenery, the shows and attractions, and the lights of The Strip, Branson is known for being a boom town. The tremendous influx of people during the Branson Boom resulted in an increased demand for childcare. Since so many of the jobs in the area are seasonal and often pay minimum wage or slightly

If you need a list of daycare providers, you can call (800) 743-8497, the Child Care Resource and Referral Project of the Council of Churches of the Ozarks. They will take into account your needs and requests, then provide you with some options and a list of various daycare providers. But be warned: most providers will put you on a waiting list.

higher, many families depend on two paychecks. Such families need childcare. So how does southwest Missouri rate in terms of childcare? An article in the November 1997 edition of *Ladies Home Journal* ranked Springfield 197 out of 200 for education and childcare, but their study missed several accredited day care centers. Still, the statement on Springfield's seven accredited centers of 15 in all of southwest Missouri doesn't speak well for an area where so many parents work outside the home. Branson probably isn't any better.

For an area as kid-friendly as Branson (see our Kidstuff chapter), surprisingly few alternatives to traditional childcare exist. Traditionally, couples didn't need childcare. They had relatives and older siblings to take care of children in emergency situations. And children in the Ozarks were expected to take care of themselves after they got a bit older. Women didn't usually work outside the home, and if they did, they were frowned upon. Times have changed. Now most women in the area work outside the home, and the need for childcare has increased but alternatives haven't. And attitudes have been slow to change. Several years ago, just down the road from Branson in Berryville, Arkansas, a pastor of a Baptist church closed the church's daycare center, saying that it "only encouraged women to work outside the home merely to be able to buy microwaves and bigger TVs." It was a controversial (and not a very popular) decision.

Working women and dual-income families in the area worry about finding adequate childcare. Most can't afford a full-time nanny or an au pair, and if they can, they probably won't be able to find one here. Most can't depend on relatives, either. People moving into the area don't have relatives here, nor do they have contacts. Newcomers should immediately establish a network by asking their employer and fellow workers for recommendations. Another source is churches. Many churches, recognizing the need for child and daycare, have built childcare facilities, and operate daycare centers, so check your church or call churches in the community. Be warned, many church facilities have waiting lists. Also be aware of Missouri's standards when it comes to childcare. Applications for being a daycare provider are available to anyone. An array of types of facilities exist: daycare homes, unlicensed (with four children or fewer); daycare homes, licensed (up to 10 children); group homes, licensed (10 to 20 children); and daycare centers, licensed (21 or more kids). Related children, even second and third cousins of the provider, are not included in this count. Then there is a category of church-operated daycare centers, which are license exempt but many make the extra effort to become licensed. Private schools also can be unlicensed childcare providers. Licensed facilities have annual visits and must meet

INSIDERS' TIP

Daycare costs per child, per week will run from a low of $60 to a high of $120. The average would be about $70.

certain safety and sanitation standards, and their enrollment numbers are controlled. Unlicensed facilities have no monitoring. The lack of adequate care results in thousands of providers that each care for a single child. What we call babysitting is probably the biggest underground institution in the area. You can find excellent single-child providers, but it is up to you to do any checking of facilities and evaluating of competence. It is probably best that any daycare provider you choose be licensed. The facility will meet certain minimum standards, and it will be checked and inspected every so often by officials.

Media

Since the Tri-Lakes area is not exactly a major population center, the news on any given day might include a report from a city council meeting, the score from last night's high school football game, or a story about a local charity fund-raiser. Since life is pretty laid back in the Ozarks, so is the news. If you want to find out what is going on in the national or international scene, you can tune in to CNN on one of the local cable stations, or you can pick up a copy of the *Kansas City Star* newspaper, which is sold in stands at area motels and gas stations. The *Springfield News-Leader* also runs Associated Press articles of national and international significance. The three major area television stations, KYTV, KOLR, and KSPR in Springfield, focus on events primarily in southwest Missouri and north central Arkansas.

Those in the business of providing information to Tri-Lakes area visitors know that when you come here to relax you're probably less concerned about foreign trade policies than you are with finding the best new restaurant or the hottest new music show. The *Branson Tri-Lakes Daily News* usually contains one or two pages of entertainment stories each day including interviews with the stars, announcements for new shows, and show reviews. There are a number of other publications too numerous to list here, which are printed weekly or monthly that give more specific information on the shows, restaurants, lodging facilities, and special events. Most of these free publications can be found at any one of the area visitor information centers.

As you drive into Ozark Mountain Country you can begin to pick up many of the radio stations listed here starting about 100 miles away. Expect when you get into the hills to have FM stations fade out at times and as you go into a valley you can expect the same from mobile phones. Surprisingly enough, the music mix for an area of this size is quite varied. Most locals prefer country music, but since radio stations want to attract visitor listeners too, everyone gets a nice variety of formats from which to choose.

LOOK FOR:
• **Tourist Publications**
• **Radio**
• **TV Channels**
• **Newspapers**

Publications

Though the Tri-Lakes area offers only two daily newspapers, the *Branson Tri-Lakes Daily News* and the *Springfield News-Leader*, you can find a number of good tourist magazines at any tourist information center namely the Branson/Lakes Area Chamber of Commerce (located on Mo. Highway. 248 at U.S. Highway 65). Each year the Chamber publishes *Slip Away*, a comprehensive guide to area music shows, attractions, lodging, restaurants, and the lakes. You can request a free copy of *Slip Away* by calling (417) 334-4136 or stop by their visitors' center and pick up a copy for a small charge.

All Roads Lead to Branson
P.O. Box 10504, Springfield
• (417) 889-9115
    One of the area's most complete entertainment-oriented publications, *All Roads Lead to Branson* contains information on music shows, restaurants, and lodging facilities.

VISIT US TODAY!
www.insiders.com

MEDIA

Each issue has three or four feature stories on some aspect of Branson entertainment and many shorter clips on individual music shows. It also contains a handy grid of shows and their phone numbers, stars, and curtain times. The magazine is printed four times a year and can be picked up at retail shops and theaters.

Branson Tri-Lakes Daily News
200 Industrial Park Dr., Hollister
• (417) 334-3161

Only in the last few years has Branson had its own daily newspaper. In the early '90s the weekly *Branson Beacon* became the *Branson Tri-Lakes Daily News* and went to a Tuesday through Saturday publication schedule. The weekend edition comes out on Saturday. There is no paper on Sunday or Monday. Branson Take-1, the local television guide, is inserted in the Friday edition. The guide lists a complete television schedule according to all cable TV channels in the Tri-Lakes area.

Each Wednesday the newspaper prints a local calendar of events covering area organizations and their meeting dates and times. The newspaper's primary focus is on local topics including government, the courts, schools, and of course entertainment. Each issue features a section on religion, business, education, and lifestyles that rotates throughout the week. Local columnists generally steer away from controversial topics, and editorials rarely take unpopular positions on community issues.

In addition to the newspaper, Tri-Lakes Newspapers, Inc. publishes the monthly *Ozark Mountain Visitor* tabloid, which is distributed locally in racks. The free publication includes feature stories on the music shows, restaurants, and attractions. The *Branson Tri-Lakes Daily News* office is located 2 miles south of Branson in the Hollister Industrial Park. The average Sunday circulation for the paper is around 12,500. The paper is distributed in racks and to subscribers through the mail.

The New Branson's Review Magazine
670 N. U.S. Bus. Hwy. 65 Suite 6, Branson
• (417) 334-6627

This magazine focuses on the entertainment scene in Branson. Printed six times a year, the publication has a loyal subscriber base and is geared toward letting folks who live out of the area know the inside scoop on changes in the music show business. Each issue's cover story profiles an area entertainer or special event. There's also a calendar of events and a section on fun and exciting things for children to do in Branson. You can pick up a copy of the magazine at many of the area's retail stores.

Best Read Guide
139 Industrial Park Dr. Building 1 Suite A, Branson • (417) 336-7323
• www.bestreadguide.com

If you're looking for a detailed show schedule or coupons for motels, restaurants, attractions, or shows, you might want to grab a free copy of *Best Read Guide*. This pocket-sized guide prints four times a year and contains feature stories on the music shows, shopping locations, and special events in Branson. Call the *Best Read Guide* B-line and listen to a recorded message about each of their advertisers at (417) 335-5463.

Music Country News
P.O. Box 6492, Branson 65615
• (417) 334-1445

This monthly tabloid publication includes lengthy feature stories on area entertainers. Owners Brian and Valerie Seitz do all of the work themselves—they sell the advertising, write the stories, and even take the photographs. Brian makes sure his advertisers get plenty of coverage and in return they routinely give him the backstage scoop on their shows and lives. You can get a free copy of *Music Country News* at almost any retail store, restaurant, or theater.

Shepherd of the Hills Gazette
5586 W. Mo. Hwy. 76 • (417) 334-4191

This free tourist guide is published six times each year and features timely articles on entertainment in Branson. It also contains a show listing, an area map, and feature stories on outdoor activities in the Ozarks. You can find the *Shepherd of the Hills Gazette* in racks or you may subscribe for just $6 per year.

INSIDERS' TIP
If you're thinking about relocating or starting a business in Branson, you might want to request a copy of the annual *Progress* magazine, published by Tri-Lakes Newspapers, Inc. It contains highlights from the previous year's news plus information on what's coming up next year. Call (417) 334-3161.

Springfield News-Leader
651 Boonville, Springfield
• (417) 836-1100
• www.springfieldnewsleader.com

This daily newspaper, owned by Gannett River States Publishing Corp., is the area's largest source for local, national, and international news. The Friday edition contains a special tabloid insert called *Weekend* that includes information on area entertainment and cultural events, including the music show scene in Branson. While the *Springfield News-Leader* does devote most of its coverage to hard news, it focuses primarily on the Springfield area but also covers events in Branson. The Sunday edition with a circulation of approximately 102,000 features a section called *Life and Times*, where feature articles on interesting people, or events, or unusual places are highlighted. The newspaper offers home delivery to subscribers in the Branson area and can be picked up in local racks.

Taney County Times
253 Main St., Forsyth
• (417) 546-3305 (home office)
220 W. N. Commercial, Branson
• (417) 334-2285 (branch office)

Published each Wednesday, the *Taney County Times* focuses on county government, schools, churches, family news, and what's happening in the Taney County communities of Bradleyville, Kirbyville, and Taneyville, just to name a few. Assistant managing editor, Linda Morgan likes to profile interesting people in Taney County and her feature articles cut right to the heart of what life around here past and present is really like. You can pick up a copy of this newspaper in racks, or you may subscribe.

The Ozarks Mountaineer
4168 E. Hwy. 76, Kirbyville
• (417) 336-2665
• www.runningriver.com

If you really want to learn about the lifestyle of the Ozarker, get a copy of *The Ozarks Mountaineer* magazine. Published every other month since 1952, this publication focuses on significant topics past and present. A pool of local freelance writers provides colorful stories on early life in the Ozarks, the land, and arts, and cultural events. The magazine has music and book reviews and a calendar of events that cov-

ers both Missouri and Arkansas. You can find a copy in retail shops throughout the Tri-Lakes area, or you may subscribe.

Radio Stations

Locals have their favorite picks, and KRZK 106.3 FM, Branson's Hometown Radio, usually comes out on top in surveys. The "Steve and Janet Show" with Steve Willoughby and Janet Ellis will wake you up and have you asking, "What did she say?" Not because of anything off color, but together Steve and Janet make a wacky comedy duo. Another favorite station is KHOZ 102.9 FM. Based in Harrison, Ark., the station broadcasts the "Bob Mitchell Show" live from the Mel Tillis Theater in Branson each weekday afternoon except for Monday. Bob brings in Branson entertainers and other country music personalities for anything-goes live interviews. KTTS 94.7 FM, out of Springfield, is the area's largest country station, with regular news and weather reports. If you are looking for National Public Radio affiliates dial into 90.5 FM or 91.1FM in Springfield.

INSIDERS' TIP
If you're looking for coupons for show tickets or restaurants, stop by a visitor information center. Many shows print coupons and place them on the counters.

Adult Standard
KOMC 100.1 FM • (417) 334-6003

Big Band
KTOZ 1060 AM • (417) 831-1060

Christian
KADI 99.5 FM • (417) 831-5234
(Contemporary Christian)
KLFC 88.1 FM • (417) 334-5332
KLFJ 1550 AM • (417) 831-5535
(Christian, Easy Listening)
KWFC 89.1 FM • (417) 869-0891
(Southern Gospel)

College Radio
KCOZ 91.7 FM • (417) 331-8111
ext. 4279 (Jazz, Blues, New Age, Soft Rock; College of Ozarks)
KSMU 91.1 FM • (417) 836-5878
(National Public Radio, Classical, Variety; Southwest Missouri State University, Springfield)
KSMS 90.5 FM • (417) 836-5878
(National Public Radio, Southwest Missouri State University, Springfield)

Contemporary

KGBX 105.9 FM • (417) 866-1069
(Adult Contemporary)
KHTO 106.7 FM • (417) 577-7458
(Contemporary Hits)
KKLH 104.7 FM • (417) 880-5677
('70s,'80s Hits)
KOMO 104.1 FM • (417) 732-1993
('80s Hits)

Country

KCTG 92.9 FM • (417) 335-2261
(Country Classics)
KGMY 100.5 FM • (417) 866-0050
(Country Hits)
KHOZ 102.9 FM • (417) 334-6750
KLTO 96.5 FM • (417) 862-9965
KRZK 106.3 FM • (417) 334-6003
KTTS 94.7 FM • (417) 577-7000
KTTS 1260 AM • (417) 577-7070

Easy Listening

KOMC 1220 AM • (417) 334-6003
KTXR 101.3 FM • (417) 862-3751

News

KWTO 560 AM • (417) 862-5800
(News, Talk Shows)

Oldies

KOSP 106.1 FM • (417) 886-5677

Rock

KT0Z 95.5 FM • (417) 869-9550
(Alternative/ '80s-90's Rock)
KWTO 98.7 FM • (417) 852-5600
(Classic Rock)
KXUS 97.3 FM • (417) 831-9700 (AOR)

Television Stations

The two major network affiliate stations covering Ozark Mountain Country are KYTV Channel 3 and KOLR Channel 10, both based in nearby Springfield. These stations primarily focus on events in Springfield but occasionally cover significant events in the Branson area. Branson is served by Rapid Cable, which carries each station listed in this section. As of the printing of this book, the only newscast originating from Branson is produced by The Vacation Channel. "Ozark Mountain Country Update" is taped weekly and

INSIDERS' TIP

Wondering what to wear? The Vacation Channel airs the local weather forecast a number of times each day. Check it out before you leave your hotel room.

features news about area events and entertainment.

Channel 27, KDEB

3000 Cherry, Springfield • (417) 862-2727
Home of "Ally McBeal" and other Fox programming, this independent station carries a variety of cartoon action shows for children each weekday beginning at 2 PM. KDEB is broadcast on Rapid Cable channel 7.

Channel 10, KOLR

2650 E. Division, Springfield
• (417) 862-1010 • www.kolr.com
KOLR, the area's CBS affiliate, up until 1999 had an office in Branson staffed by full-time reporter. Of the three major network affiliates, KOLR still provides the most complete news and information on Branson. KOLR is broadcast on Rapid Cable channel 10.

Channel 21, KOZK

821 N. Washington, Springfield
• (417) 865-2100
This station broadcasts local and national programming provided by PBS. KOZK is broadcast on Rapid Cable channel 13.

Channel 33, KSPR

1359 E. St. Louis, Springfield
• (417) 831-1333
ABC affiliate KSPR airs daily local newscasts as well as standard ABC programming. KSPR is broadcast on Rapid Cable channel 8.

Channel 3, KYTV

999 W. Sunshine, Springfield
• (417) 266-3000 • www.ky3.com
The area's NBC affiliate, KYTV broadcasts local news programs at least four times each day. KYTV is broadcast on Rapid Cable channel 3.

The Vacation Channel

282 Wintergreen Rd. • (417) 334-1200
The Vacation Channel is an excellent source of information for the new visitor. Locally produced programming is designed to familiarize you with the roads, music shows, restaurants, lodging, and special events. You can tune in to their local news program, which runs a number of times each day or the local weather reports. The Va-

cation Channel is broadcast on Rapid Cable channel 6.

UPN
100 Fall Creek Dr., Suite A
• **(417) 336-5545**

This United Paramount Network Affiliate station broadcasts paid programming, programs for children and afternoon talk shows. UPN is broadcast on Rapid Cable channel 5.

Cable Television

Cablevision
115 Industrial Dr., Excelsior Springs
• **(800) 234-2157, (502) 527-3211**

Cablevision services Forsyth and Kimberling

City in Missouri and other cities outside Ozark Mountain Country.

INSIDERS' TIP

The visitor center at the Branson Lakes Area Chamber of Commerce gives away Springfield/Branson area phone books free for the asking.

Friendship Cable
5A Fire Station Rd., Kimberling City
• **(417) 739-1265**

This is the primary cable provider for the Kimberling City, Blue Eye, Reeds Spring, Branson West, Kissee Mills, Lampe, Galena, Taneyville, Powersite, and McCord Bend areas.

Rapid Cable
106 Wintergreen Dr., Branson 65615
• **(417) 339-2200, (800) 972-0962**

Rapid Cable serves the Branson, Indian Point, Venice on the Lake, and F Highway areas along with Compton Ridge, Rockaway Beach, and Merriam Woods.

MEDIA

Worship

Long before the area surrounding Branson was called Ozark Mountain Country, it was known as Shepherd of the Hills Country. Many tourists who visited these parts in the early 1900s came here as a result of the writings of a young preacher named Harold Bell Wright, who, with publication of his enormously famous novel, *The Shepherd of the Hills,* some say single-handedly started the tourist trade here.

When Wright came to these parts in 1896 he did not come to preach, or even to write, but to restore his health. Yet he became both a preacher and a writer. The God-fearing people he befriended and the peaceful inspiration of the hills led to the writing of his tale.

Today Branson and Ozark Mountain Country are still influenced by Wright's story and by the same kind of religious climate he encountered a century ago.

In the days of schoolhouse services and traveling preachers, the church often served as the center of social activity in any given community. It was more the rule than the exception for people of varied denominational beliefs to all worship under one roof.

While the Sunday service was the tie that bound them together, parishioners could turn any wedding, funeral, pie supper, birthday, or holiday into a religious gathering. In the absence of a religious leader, the elders would gather up the younger folks to sing hymns and tell Bible stories.

In Dr. Robert Gilmore's book, *Ozark Baptizings, Hangings and Other Diversions,* he tells of the struggle many smaller area churches encountered in their quest for regular visits from traveling preachers. Many of the preachers did not request or expect payment for their services since they routinely held other jobs; however, they were more apt to show up if the promise of a hearty meal was part of the deal.

One of the highlights of religious life was the camp meeting, a weeklong, sometimes even month-long, revival full of all the spectacle of a Branson music show. Folks from miles around would gather in a tent, a shed, a brush arbor, or even outside to sing, sermonize, repent, and convert lost souls. Today some of the local theaters offer special musical services reminiscent of old-fashioned revivals.

While the method of worship has changed in the Tri-Lakes area over the decades, the makeup of denominational faiths really hasn't. Protestant churches, primarily Baptist, Methodist, Assembly of God, Pentecostal, and Church of Christ denominations, encompass the majority of faiths. However, Branson has one Roman Catholic Church, one Mormon Church, and Rogersville is home to the nearest Jewish Synagogue. A number of non-denominational churches can also be found in the area.

Each Saturday the *Branson Tri-Lakes Daily News* publishes a devotional page that lists phone numbers for Tri-Lakes area churches according to town and denomination. Most area churches welcome out-of-town visitors, but you might want to call first to confirm the worship times. The Branson/Lakes Area Chamber of Commerce, (417) 334-4136.prints an annual community guide with a listing of area churches including their phone numbers.

The area's only Christian conference center, Stonecroft Conference Center, (417) 334-2404, 590 Windmill Road, Hollister, hosts 14 weeks of Bible conferences each year. Each week you can hear a different speaker and musical guest. Stonecroft has 72 rooms, a 240-seat dining room, and an auditorium that seats up to 450 people. In addition to programs for adults, teens, can attend Bible study programs during the summer.

INSIDERS' TIP

In Eureka Springs, Arkansas, you'll want to see Thorncrown Chapel, an architectural masterpiece made entirely of glass and pine. The chapel welcomes visitors to stop in and look around. (See Daytrips for more information.)

Twice each year the Revival Fires Ministries based in Branson West, (417) 338-2444, holds gatherings at The Grand Palace and packs in more than 20,000 people over the course of the 4-day events. Dozens of speakers, performers, and religious leaders come to the gatherings. For more information on Revival Fires Ministries call the above number or visit www.revivalfires.org.

Musical Worship Services

In the last few years, a number of Branson theaters have begun offering free Sunday morning worship services. Since many of the music shows are closed on Sundays, theater owners decided to bring in ministers and special musical guests to provide a unique service to visitors. Most of the services go heavy on the music and light on the preaching, with some exceptions. All of the following services are free. A donation may be requested.

The Barbara Fairchild Sunday Morning Worship Service at the Welk Champagne Theatre, 1984 Mo. Hwy. 165, (417) 334-6400, begins at 10 AM each Sunday and features two hours of music and preaching. For more information log on to Barbara's website at www.barbarafairchild.com. The Grand Old Gospel Hour at the Braschler Music Theatre, 3044 Shepherd of the Hills Expwy., (417) 337-8888, is hosted by Sam Stauffer, who delivers a 45-minute sermon preceded by 30 minutes of music performed by a different area entertainer each week. Services begin at 10 AM. For more information, log on to their website at www.showtown.net/gospelhour.

Sunday Praise Gathering at the Jim Stafford Theatre, 3444 76 Country Blvd., (417) 335-3519 or (417) 337-5424, is held each Sunday at 9:30 AM and is presented by Day Star Ministries of Branson. A new musical guest is featured each week. Rev. Dave Hamner, Branson's resident magician-preacher and his wife and magic partner, Denise, present Sunday Happening at 10 AM each Sunday at the Remington Theatre, 3701 W. 76 Country Blvd., (417) 336-6220. The service is a non-denomination hour of music, inspirational messages, and fellowship.

Associations

The non-profit Branson Gospel Music Association, 3044 Shepherd of the Hills Expwy., Suite 536, (417) 332-2119, with its nearly 200 members, welcomes fans of gospel music to attend the free "Jammin' for Jesus" concerts held on the first Sunday of each month at the Braschler Music Theatre. The concerts showcase aspiring gospel musicians and singers as well as professionals who are eligible to receive the annual Sonrise Award that is voted on by the BGMA membership. Annual dues for the BGMA are $75 for professional gospel music artists and $50 for everyone else. For more information you can visit their website at www.bgma.com.

INSIDERS' TIP

Springfield is home of the world headquarters for the Assemblies of God, 1445 Boonville Ave., Springfield, MO. 65802-1894, (417) 862-2781.

WORSHIP

Index of Advertisers

Index